784.18

ILLUSTRATED COMPENDIUM OF MUSICAL TECHNOLOGY

Illustrated Compendium of Musical Technology

TRISTRAM CARY

faber and faber

LONDON · BOSTON

First published in 1992
by Faber and Faber Limited
3 Queen Square London WCIN 3AU

Photoset by Intype, London SW19 8DR
Printed in Great Britain by Clays Ltd, St Ives Plc

The following figures appear by permission: fig. 56, from
Moorer and Grey, *Lexicon of Analysed Tones*, Pt. 2, Vol.
1, No. 3, by permission of The MIT Press, Cambridge,
Massachusetts; fig. 91, from M. Levinson and W. A.
Sentance, *Introduction to Computer Science*, New York,
Gordon and Breach, 1969, by permission of Gordon and
Breach Science Publishers Inc; fig. 119, from Alec Nisbett,
Use of Microphones, London, Focal Press, 1983, by
permission of Focal Press; fig. 164, reproduced by kind
permission of John Chowning.

A CIP record for this book is
available from the British Library

ISBN 0-571-15251-1

Contents

Preface

There are whole libraries of books, from elementary to expert level, on both musical and audio technology, and a similarly large international spread of magazines and journals, of varying repute and usefulness. When one is faced with such a huge mass of literature, getting reliable and immediate information about a particular problem can be a daunting task. This book does not claim to be exhaustive, but it does bring together a large body of information on music technology in one volume, and in an easy-to-look-up format.

Achieving that obviously involved both compression and omission. In many years of professional music-making and teaching I have observed the kinds of musical problems that puzzle technicians, and the technical processes that musicians find hard to grasp, and I aimed to make my choice of material on this basis. Increasingly, the musician works in a high-tech environment, grappling with the paraphernalia of a recording studio, or, more elaborately, the inclusion in scores of complex electronic instruments and treatments. To produce such scores, or purely electronic music, composers must be able to talk to computers and technicians in a meaningful way. Nearly all the entries which follow are the result of someone asking 'Could you tell me about this equipment (or this principle)? I've never understood how it works.'

There are many acknowledged quotations from expert sources, but otherwise the text of this book is one person's work. Some articles inevitably reflect personal viewpoints, and it would be surprising, and not really desirable, if everyone agreed with all the views expressed. I have included quite a lot of historical background, and I hope that the book may be interesting on several levels: as a quick guide, as something to dip into at random, and as general background reading for students and music lovers.

In order to keep it to sensible proportions, decisions had to be made about what *not* to include. For example, there is little biography – no entry exists simply to give someone's career details. Plenty of names do appear, of course, though mainly when a person's innovation or other

important contribution should be noted. Some organizations and manufacturers are mentioned, but only when relevant to an explanation. Some
products are also mentioned; but no attempt is made to provide complete
or 'best buy' lists of commercially available equipment, partly because
such lists are almost immediately obsolete, and also because recommendations vary with local conditions. What I have tried to do is provide
enough explanation of fundamental principles to enable readers to make
wise choices for themselves. I originally intended to include audio-visual
media (film, TV etc.), but it was simply not possible except where they
were strongly associated with a musical topic.

Another deliberate exclusion is short-lived or local jargon. Often a
phrase will be current for a year or so in some part of the world and
then disappear. Styles of music-making generate their own vocabularies,
and I have tried to judge the permanence of such terms and decide
whether to include them or not. The main emphasis is on musical
electronics, but I have also given musical terms specific to one instrument
or class of instruments, because I know from experience that musicians
are often fairly ill-informed about instruments they do not play themselves, and also because technicians need to converse knowledgeably
with musicians about their instruments. This type of entry is selective:
for example the break of a clarinet is explained, but ordinary musical
terms like 'mezzo forte' will not be found; in fact basic musical knowledge and the ability to read music are assumed.

In technical explanations my aim has been to avoid mathematical
analysis (although a few simple formulae are unavoidable, and useful),
since I have found that, tackled in the right way, fairly complex principles
can be understood without it. However, the Bibliography will enable an
interested reader to continue study at a greater depth. A number of key
texts are included whose own references lead further still.

Articles covering important specialist areas (e.g. **digital synthesis techniques**) are necessarily quite large, but they are subdivided into sections,
and there are plentiful cross-references (in **bold**) to other relevant entries.

Any selection of topics is bound to reflect a personal choice. All the
same, I shall be glad to hear from readers who fail to find something
they think ought to be here. Possibly it was not included for one of the
reasons given above, or it may be there but hard to find because my
look-up word is unhelpful. Or it may be, simply, that I overlooked it.
Whatever the reason, it will be good to know of such cases so that they
can be assessed for future inclusion.

T. O. C.
Adelaide, 1989–90

Acknowledgements

Of the many people who have been marvellously generous with their time and expertise during the preparation of this book, two deserve very special thanks: Jane Delin read the whole book several times at different stages and gave me invaluable advice on grammar and style. Jane made the perfect 'average reader', enabling me to assess the clarity of explanations etc. Robbie Squire, studio technician at the electronic music studio, Elder Conservatorium, Adelaide University, and an audio engineer of wide experience, read the entire text for technical mistakes and obscurities, and I am extremely grateful for the many hours he gave to this laborious task. The Conservatorium office staff, particularly Helen Simpson, were unfailingly helpful when my photocopying demands were added to their already heavy workload.

Many thanks also to the following musical colleagues, friends and audio specialists for their cheerful response to notes, phone calls and other cries for help: Gordon Abbott, Music Librarian, the Barr Smith Library, Adelaide University, who sought out many books and papers for me; Jim Barbour (SAFM, Adelaide); Chris Barter, Chairman of Computer Science, Adelaide University; Peter Brown (Allans Music, Adelaide); Warren Burt, composer; my son John Cary; Joel Chadabe (SUNY, Albany) and John Chowning (Stanford University); Neville Clark (Adelaide Tape Duplicators); David Dunn, composer; William Harrison (SATE Recording Pty Ltd., Adelaide); Brian Hodgson and Mark Wilson (BBC Radiophonic Workshop, London); Don Krahenbuhl (Don's Records, Adelaide); Bruce Manser (Syntec International, Adelaide); Peter Messer (Entertainment Audio, Adelaide); Bill Moran (Professor of Pure Maths, Adelaide University); Curtis Roads, composer and writer (MIT); George Stephens (Organ Builder, Lonsdale, South Australia); David Swale (Organist, St Peter's Cathedral, Adelaide); James Thacker (Assistant Organist, St Peter's, also computer expert); Bert Turetsky (Bassist, UCSD, California); Martin Wesley-Smith, composer (NSW State Conservatorium, Sydney).

Introduction

The intention of the main part of this book is to give information in as straightforward and concise a way as possible, and not to obtrude my own views unless it is unavoidable. In slight compensation for this self-effacement, therefore, I am here allowing myself the indulgence of some personal reminiscences, and the expression of some of my own opinions. Since these appear outside the main alphabetical listings, no one will be plunged into them unwittingly while searching for something else. This introduction is also a good place to look at some of the earlier history of science in music, because in the body of the book the discussion is mostly about what is happening now. I will begin, then, by taking a look at some of the antecedents of today's music technologies.

Music has always been linked to science in at least two ways. From the time when Pythagoras, over 2500 years ago, showed the relationship between pitch intervals and number ratios, musical sense has always appeared to be mathematical sense as well, and this is even clearer today when computers enable us to capture sound, as it were on the point of a pin, and study it in greater detail than ever before. Without being mathematicians themselves, composers tend to order their work in ways that mathematicians find interesting. So one link with science is mainly theoretical and speculative.

The other is severely practical. A musical instrument is a piece of mechanical engineering that must work with complete reliability, often under adverse conditions. For an orchestra to be possible at all, a very large number of wires, strings, pegs, levers, reeds, pistons, rods, pads, skins, pedals, ratchets, hammers, joints and so on, have to work perfectly and most of them silently, for hundreds of thousands of operations. The reliability of all this machinery is remarkable, and in many cases design patterns were set by ancient, anonymous craftsmen whose ingenuity has not been bettered even in our high-tech age. Music technology is thus nothing new; it is part of the essential fabric of the art.

More links have been added in the last century or so. Musical **acoustics** as a scientific study hardly existed before Helmholtz produced his great work *On the Sensations of Tone* (Helmholtz, 1862), but has burgeoned into a respectable and well-studied branch of physics. Its cousin, **psychoacoustics**, is opening up knowledge about how the mind deals with sound, and how the composer composes.

Even before Helmholtz there was another new input to musical technology, which in the end had more influence for change than any other – electricity. An early instance is a wonderful description by Berlioz in his *A Treatise on Modern Instrumentation and Orchestration*, of a device to give the beat to off-stage musicians in an opera house (now done by closed-circuit TV). A key on the conductor's desk dips a contact ('protuberance') into a cup of mercury, and at the other end a rod like the finger of a metronome is deflected. Berlioz muses that the conductor 'could, were it needful, conduct, from the middle of the opera orchestra in Paris, a piece of music performed at Versailles' (Berlioz, 1843). And this was the early 1840s.

Electricity spawned an irrepressible offspring: electronics, and between them they hatched a new kind of performance instrument, innocent of bow or breath. And in due course there also arose a new kind of composition – of music without performers. Unlike the new electric instruments, which worked in a different way but essentially imitated their acoustic relatives, the new compositions proposed new criteria as well. Instead of writing a score for others to play, the composer would personally manipulate the sounds.

Though we think of this as a twentieth-century innovation, there were people of imagination who dreamed of manipulating sound in ways ordinary instruments could not, many years before there were any means of doing such things. The following, now very famous passage from Francis Bacon's *New Atlantis* appears in almost every book and major article on electronic music, but it is such a stunningly acute piece of prophecy that it is quite proper to quote it yet again:

We have also sound-houses, where we practice and demonstrate all sounds, and their generation. We have harmonies which you have not, of quarter-sounds, and lesser slides of sounds. Divers instruments of music likewise to you unknown, some sweeter than any you have; together with bells and rings that are dainty and sweet. We represent small sounds as great and deep; likewise great sounds extenuate and sharp; we make divers tremblings and warblings of sounds, which in their original are entire. We represent and imitate all articulate sounds and letters, and the voices and notes of beasts and birds. We have

certain helps which set to the ear do further the hearing greatly. We
have also divers strange and artificial echoes, reflecting the voice many
times, and as it were tossing it, and some that give back the voice
louder than it came; some shriller, and some deeper; yea, some rendering the voice differing in the letters or articulate sound from that they
receive. We have also means to convey sounds in trunks and pipes,
in strange lines and distances. (Bacon, 1622)

From nearly 400 years ago, this passage foreshadows microtones, non-
instrumental music, speed changing, artificial **vibrato** and **tremolo**, truncated sounds, speech synthesis, **headphones, echo** and **reverberation,
amplifiers, filters** and long distance transmission.

Maybe it is not so surprising that a century and a half after Bacon,
in an eighteenth century which not only produced magnificent art and
architecture, but delighted in every kind of ingenious artifact, composers
like Mozart tried their hands at pieces for clockwork instruments, and
generally explored, at the trivial level such devices offered, the possibilities of non-human performance of human musical ideas.

For composers of an exploratory turn of mind, the most frustrating
limitation of normal instruments is their inability to play more than a
few selected pitches within each octave. Even in oriental systems with
small subdivisions (e.g. the Indian *sruti*) the main intervals of the scale
are no smaller than in Western music, and sometimes larger. Of course
there are some instruments, like the violin, the trombone and above all
the voice, which can sound any pitch at all within their compass, but
microtonal intervals are hard to notate and harder still to play in tune.
Composers wanted to see what would happen if they could sound such
intervals with guaranteed accuracy. Various theorics were advanced over
the centuries, and a number of ingenious mechanical contrivances built.
The real breakthrough in pitch control, however, was electrical, and
non-instrumental tone generation began about a century ago.

Thaddeus Cahill's 'Dynamophone' of 1906 (for a description see **analogue synthesis techniques** 1) was not very successful in itself, but made
a great impression on Ferruccio Busoni, not only an important pianist
and composer but a prophetic voice. His influence on the young Edgard
Varèse started a train of thought that became an obsession. For years
Varèse experimented with instrumental microtones, and waited
impatiently for electronic music to happen. Almost though fortunately
not in fact too late for him, it did, and in the 1950s he at last made
some electronic pieces – the most celebrated being 'Poème électronique',
for the Brussels EXPO of 1958.

In his small book *Sketch for a New Aesthetic of Music* Ferruccio Busoni takes the view that 'what we now call our tonal system is nothing more than a set of "signs"; an ingenious device to grasp somewhat of the eternal harmony; a meagre pocket-edition of the encyclopaedic work; artificial light instead of the sun' (Busoni, 1911). No wonder he found the invention of a calibrated variable-pitch machine exciting: '[Cahill] has constructed a comprehensive apparatus which makes it possible to transform an electric current into a fixed and mathematically exact number of vibrations. As pitch depends on the number of vibrations, and the apparatus may be set on any number desired, the infinite gradation of the octave may be accomplished by merely moving a lever corresponding to the pointer of a quadrant.'

Continuous pitch control is only one aspect of the new musical attitudes implied by machines such as Cahill's. Once the idea germinated, it quickly led to the prospect of musical generators capable of encompassing the whole orchestral panorama – it seemed merely a matter of size. It is worth noticing that in terms of philosophical position and historical development, there is a striking parallel between electronic music and the pipe organ. Instruments such as organs and carillons, even ordinary church bells, have always depended on mechanical assistance to help them work, just as any machine above a certain size exceeds the strength of human muscle to control it unaided, and must invoke levers, pulleys, winches, and later steam, electric or oil engines to do the heavy work.

Organs, and to a much lesser extent keyboard strings like harpsichords, were the only pre-electronic instruments that attempted to be solo orchestras. With someone pumping away at the back to provide the energy input, the organist could become a melting oboe, a silvery flute or a dignified, expansive bass, or call on a number of sounds special to the organ, such as choruses of open flues and pungent mixtures of odd harmonics not heard in orchestras. Extra manuals and pedal boards, swell boxes and combinations all had the same goal – the concentration of the maximum expressive power in one person. If that person were also the composer (as very often), the total production from brain to audience was wholly in the control of one individual creative mind. This is also true of a piano or violin composer/virtuoso, but not to anything like the same extent, because the organ is deliberately designed to be a chameleon of music, a magic colour box. Pianos and violins, however expressive, are single instruments with observable timbral limits.

Enthusiastically applied engineering skills from the Middle Ages onwards continually added to the size and complexity of organs, but the increase in musical expressiveness was not in direct proportion to the greater dimensions of the instruments: each mechanical or pneumatic 'improvement' tended to move the player's fingers (and feet) further from positive contact with the sound. The introduction of electric power caused a veritable explosion, because the already ingenious **servo** mechanisms embodied in pneumatic motors and the like could now be further mechanized by electricity. Electricity could also do the job of the manual air pump, and force unheard-of pressures into ever louder, more grandiosely named stops. In the general expansiveness of the time both the orchestra and the organ became unduly inflated. However, whereas in the orchestra's case composers like Wagner and Mahler could handle it, the number of organ compositions that really benefited from the largest contemporary instruments is quite small – most of the celebrated repertoire of the late nineteenth century sounds better on smaller, lighter organs, with less sheer power but more subtlety.

Discerning organ makers began to realize this and apply corrections, and it is interesting to observe that for the last fifty or sixty years, in the face of a rising tide of gadgetry and clever technology, the organ has been getting simpler, the link between the player and the sound more direct. The rediscovery of baroque and earlier organ music was one important factor; the new revival of Bach, and the austerity of scholars like Schweitzer, was another; and by the late twentieth century we find that the very newest instruments often use the same direct tracker action as the organs of the seventeenth and eighteenth centuries (see **organs** *pipe*).

The history of electronic music-making has been bedevilled by the 'organ syndrome': it has been tempting to build huge complexes of equipment which supposedly do everything the composer wants, but are too often engulfed by their own ingenuity. That has been a continuing danger in the forty years that electronic music has been an active medium, and its best corrective is to promote dialogue between technologists and musicians that makes sense to both groups. This book is intended, in a modest way, to help that dialogue. The following section describes how I became involved in the discourse myself, and my final paragraphs look at the present position in computer music, venturing a few speculations on its possible future.

The notion of realizing music as a recording rather than as a performance seems to have grown almost simultaneously in the minds of a number of individuals, myself included, during the Second World War. In retrospect it seems a fairly simple idea, but it nevertheless involved the mental jump from considering a recording as merely a means of reproducing a performance with as much fidelity as possible, to the revolutionary idea that the recording itself would be the primary, indeed the only, medium of performance.

In my own case, I was later to hear of experimental pre-war work by the young John Cage, the theories of Varèse and Harry Partch, and the ingenuities and prophecies of other pioneers; but when I had my first thoughts about the new music I was in the Navy and knew nothing of all this. I had no access to specialist books, and no understanding ears to tell my ideas to. Though I had been playing music from about the age of five, and started composing at fourteen or so, I had not yet studied music as an intending professional. I went in for radar because I had a boyhood background of building short wave radio sets, and enough theory to get me started. Radar being top secret, I didn't know very much about it till I was among the privileged few thousand to be taught those secrets, and the technology was even more fascinating to a lad of nineteen than I could have dreamed. A key device of the time was the cavity magnetron, now in every home microwave, but then a very secret power oscillator/transmitter for centimetre-wave radar. We also had magnetic wire recorders of poor quality but great technical interest to me, and somewhere along the line it struck me that a recorded sound could be a creative statement in itself.

The trigger that set all this going was the knowledge that a means of recording on continuous magnetic material had been brought to a much higher technical level than the crude wire machine could offer. Unfortunately the main developments had taken place in Germany, so the war had to be over before those of us on the other side could verify it; but we imagined the new ribbon or 'tape' was a scratch-free, editable, very high quality recording medium. It was obviously essential for the quality to be good if the idea was to work, because in the new music the recording would be the listener's only criterion. (Allowances can be made for a bad instrumental recording because one knows what the real instruments sound like.) In the event the early tape recorders did not fully come up to these heady expectations. But it was not long before they almost did, and by the mid-1950s even four-track working was possible. There have been many improvements since, but I have tapes recorded in 1952 that still sound quite good, though the tape itself has by now become very brittle, the oxide coating flaky and unstable.

So in the imagination a new idea was launched, and long before one could achieve any practical result – certainly in my case since I went straight from being a poorly-paid Naval officer to being an even poorer

student – the new aesthetic established itself in the mind. Salient features
of my own thinking were:

1. By means of recording, any sound at all was available to the
    composer. The act of composing was what you did with the
    sound. You immediately crossed the frontier between 'legit-
    imately musical' sounds such as trumpets and triangles, and
    'non-musical' sounds, because anything that could be heard and
    recorded was valid material. For example, you could substitute
    a recording of thunder for a drum roll; you could record and
    manipulate the songs of birds.

2. By means of oscillators, you should be able to create quite new
    sounds and actually extend the aural experience. In practice, and
    for technical reasons discussed elsewhere (see **analogue synthesis
    techniques** and **digital synthesis techniques**) this proved to be
    very difficult.

3. One would not be confined to standard tuning. If conventional
    harmony was required, it could be perfectly in tune, not cor-
    rupted by the strictures of equal **temperament**. As well as glis-
    sandi of unlimited range, any system of fixed pitches could be
    used.

4. By editing, and by speed and direction changing, it would be
    possible to use parts of sounds, and to cut together quite dispar-
    ate sound sources. This turned out later to be one of the most
    powerful tools in **musique concrète**.

5. By **montaging**, an 'orchestra' of any desired size would be poss-
    ible.

6. Because one would not be working in real time, elaborate cross-
    rhythms, extremely fast tempi, etc., could be used, since the
    limits of dexterity or fatigue in a human performer would be
    absent.

7. In a timbral context, one would not be confined by the practical
    ranges of real instruments. A timbre could be moved freely up
    and down, without set pitch restrictions and, of course, most of
    these timbres would be new and non-instrumental in any case.

In fact nearly all of these were, as I later found, more difficult than I
naively supposed. But that didn't prevent me from dreaming. I determined to spend the first money I could get hold of on some kind of
recording machine, and when I was released from the Navy in 1946, I
spent my gratuity of £50 (say £1000 in today's money) on the cheapest
disc lathe available (78 rpm only). I built the electronics by cannibalizing

war surplus equipment, which was plentiful, cheap, and usually brand new. In 1948 I expounded my ideas to my composition teacher, the late George Oldroyd. He utterly failed to grasp what I was talking about, and we both fell in each other's estimations, I fear. After that, I got on with my counterpoint and never again mentioned my outlandish experiments. About a decade later I was trying to get the same ideas across to the Performing Right Society, who at first would not recognize tape compositions as music, on the grounds that you often could not represent them as dots on paper.

I made a keyed oscillator with adjustable tuning by fitting the keyboard of an old harmonium with contacts and using pencil lines of varying density as tuning resistors. I think it must be the only oscillator ever built that you could tune with an indiarubber. Ruari Maclean, later of publishing and typographical fame, made this drawing of me in 1947, my Naval officer's cap still in evidence.

With my disc equipment I could make ordinary recordings, of course, and I made a little money out of this, because the days of cheap tape recorders of reasonable quality were far in the future, and many of my friends and fellow students wanted to hear themselves perform: one of my clients was my school friend and university contemporary, Donald

Swann. I also experimented with the rather limited sound treatments that are possible with disc recording (see **disc manipulation techniques**), but the pressures of ordinary life kept my work in the field trivial and miniature for some time. As soon became clear, the penalty to the composer of transferring the actual production of the music from platform to workshop was that the financial onus was also transferred. The new medium, if it was to come up with a professionally usable product, was expensive.

When tape recorders did arrive, they were, for the most part, enormous pieces of engineering with great flywheels and enough motor power to propel a truck. Housed in suitably massive frames and cabinets, they were hand-crafted and, of course, as inaccessible to me as a Rolls-Royce.

Before long, though, a few companies were making semi-professional decks, sold without electronics but with recommendations on what circuits to build yourself, and in 1952 I bought an excellent deck by Bradmatic of Birmingham, which transformed my life. It worked well for twenty years, and was incorporated in a complex of gear known to my family as The Machine. In this photograph of 1956 the Bradmatic can be seen behind the papers, and the 78 rpm disc lathe is on the right.

I am showing off my newest and proudest possession – an EMI TR51 full-track mono semi-portable, which I used for mastering radio and film tracks (all mono in those days).

During this period I was quite detached from the mainstream of serious contemporary music, and though I did achieve a few perform-ances of instrumental chamber works (some piano pieces, some songs, a cello sonata), my main thrust was simply towards making a living from composing. I now regret the rather stubborn attitude I took: instead of trying to interest people who might have helped financially to forward my own musical projects – arts funding bodies, the BBC, universities, audio and radio manufacturers – I took the view that a composer should be a viable, earning member of the society he inhabits, a workman in something of an eighteenth-century sense, except that private employ-ment in the service of some great household was now out of the question. I also had a family to feed and educate, so I became a working composer, living by commissions from films, theatre, TV and radio. The BBC was my most constant employer, and although they paid poorly they paid promptly, and in the 1950s the Third Programme was a marvellous vehicle for musical adventure. I worked with magnificent writer/pro-ducers like Louis Macneice, Douglas Cleverdon, Laurence Gilliam, Francis Dillon, Frederick Bradnum, and other leading figures in that Golden Age of radio.

It was in this field that I made my first major electronic pieces, for example *The Children of Lir* (1959), a version of the Irish legend – Shakespeare's *Lear* is a distant relation – written by the late H. A. L. Craig and produced by Douglas Cleverdon. *Lir* was developed as a close collaboration between writer and composer which would have been impossible in a normal instrumental context. Harry Craig would sketch out a major scene, for which I would do rough tracks in my Earls Court studio and play them to him. That might trigger amendments to the text because the sounds I made suggested words. The new words would spur me to develop new sounds, and so on. I wrote songs for and pre-recorded that splendid actor/singer Marjory Westbury, then added treatments to the songs. I faked a group of swans taking off by bashing my arm with rolled-up newspaper and mixing in water sounds and a real recording of swans. In the end we had, under Douglas Cleverdon's expert and sensitive direction, a completely integrated work with a character uniquely of its medium.

The result of choosing to plough my own furrow, neither trying for grants, hard to get anyway at that time, nor joining the teaching com-munity, was that I never became involved in the rich variety of new musical experiments going on in Europe and the USA. I never went to Darmstadt. I didn't visit the Paris or Cologne studios in those early days. I didn't meet Stockhausen till 1968, Henze till 1970, or Berio till 1975. I knew none of the prominent US composers mentioned in the body of this book until after my first trip to the USA in 1969.

There was some correspondence, however. I seemed to have made a small name for myself, and letters would arrive. I remember one from Bell Telephone Labs in 1960 or so, enclosing a tape of early computer music, which I still have, and asking for comments. I was not terribly impressed, and said so, but the experiments represented by that tape were in fact of great importance (see **computer music composition techniques**). My worst mistake, perhaps, was not realizing the importance of putting together a corpus of concert music in my twenties and thirties. There never seemed to be time: constant financial pressures combined with a steady flow of work kept me composing for money rather than glory. All the same, there were great compensations in being independent, and sometimes a real sense of creative adventure, in both the instrumental and electronic fields. There were some concert pieces in the late 1950s and early 1960s (a Sonata for solo guitar, a Decet for mixed ensemble), but my personal milestones were in radio and film, with scores such as *The Rhyme of the Flying Bomb*, to a poem by Mervyn Peake, written for two actors, mixed quintet and tape, produced for the BBC by Laurence Gilliam. Another important piece was the radio version, adapted by Christopher Holme, of Muriel Spark's *The Ballad of Peckham Rye*, which won the Prix Italia in 1962, and was later done, with additional material, as a stage musical at the Salzburg Festival in 1965. *The Ha-Ha* (Jennifer Dawson) was for me an important piece of experimental radio music – Michael Bakewell was the producer – and my skills were fully extended by *The Little Island* (1958), an animated film without dialogue by Richard Williams, which won prizes in Venice, London and elsewhere, and was shown at the Brussels EXPO, a few pavilions away from where Varèse's piece was running. The sketch overleaf by Dick Williams during the making of the film illustrates a common problem of communication between composer and producer.

I gradually built up my stock of equipment, and in 1962 moved it from London to Suffolk. But without any outside support the studio obviously lacked the (to me) splendid facilities of the growing number of radio and university studios around the world. On the other hand, I did not have to share my studio with anyone, and its modest contents included items that no one else had because I had designed and built them. In fact it seemed normal in those days to spend a day or so building

something so that a particular sound treatment would be possible. I sometimes surprise myself when I play an early track to realize how much could be done with so little. And over the years the studio did grow to quite a sizeable complex, probably the best private studio in England in the late 1960s.

In giving all this personal reminiscence I am trying to convey the flavour of the time. There was a limited choice of possibilities, but an exciting sense of discovery, of actually hewing away at a new musical rock face. Scoffers were quick to point out the obvious drawbacks, such as the total determinism of a performance that consisted merely of playing a tape, and the lack of visual interest and interpretative subtlety. There were some who felt that this kind of music should be confined to radio, because it is the normal expectation for radio music to come from a loudspeaker and have no visual element. But composers had good reasons for wishing to play their tape pieces under concert conditions:

1. playback levels and the quality of the sound system were under the composer's control, and the reproduction – of great importance in a tape piece – much better than that of an ordinary radio set;
2. one of the great freedoms of electronic music in two or more tracks is that spatial movement, not possible with real instruments, can be dramatically exploited. In those days radios were monophonic, but tape music was capable of using up to four tracks quite early, e.g. Stockhausen's *Kontakte* (1959).

As time went on, the basic compositional ideas were understood more generally, and 'schools' developed, with their advocates and opponents. Studios started to be more methodically equipped, though there was an increasing tendency to talk not about composing but about machinery. Leaping forward thirty years, I was pleased at a recent Paris conference when, after I had delivered my paper, someone congratulated me on a talk that was actually about music and not about (his word) 'plumbing'.

Simple automation appeared, and then keyboards. It became easier to do quite elaborate things. But the effect of greater complexity was that the studio began to control the composer. Keyboards are a good example – I listed earlier some of the dreams I dreamed in 1945, and among them was freedom from standard tuning: I only discovered later what Busoni had written many years before. The arrival of keyboards, and later complete keyboard synthesizers, immediately confined the pitch scope to a twelve-note octave. Because composers are on the whole not technicians, much of the development work was done by engineers whose musical ideas were simple, and the devices they produced were aimed at a compositionally traditional market. I naturally bought some of these devices if I thought they would be useful in my studio, but very often I had to rebuild them to suit my purpose, or else I used them in ways not intended by their designers.

In the 1950s we astonished with the exciting newness of the medium (how on earth did you do *that*?). In the 1960s electronic music became firmly established; but as studios became more expensively equipped they also became more bureaucratic and unadventurous. Many good composers who had worked in the medium in its first decade – Ligeti is a good example – abandoned it as not fulfilling its promise. I remained, and remain, convinced that the way to succeed with electronic composition is to use it for music that can only be electronic, i.e. to exploit the special advantages of the medium which I mentioned above when describing my early thoughts. With the new techniques and equipment this could be done better than ever, but too many pieces were poor imitations of music much more effectively done with normal instruments. As always, some of the most successful works were mixtures of live performance and tape, usually pre-recorded but sometimes, as in my piece *Narcissus* for flute and tape (Cary, 1969), recorded and manipulated during the performance.

By the middle 1960s many instrumental composers felt that they should at least know something about electronic music, and through the Composers' Guild I ran a surprisingly successful composers' course at my Suffolk studio. An interesting cross-section came, including among others Alan Rawsthorne, Francis Chagrin and Ernest Tomlinson, and my library still contains the rather strange creative exercise that the group collectively realized in my studio. In the same year, an important new adventure was a commission to do all the sound for the Industrial Section of the British Pavilion at EXPO '67, Montreal (designed by Crosby, Fletcher, Forbes, now part of the international design team Pentagram). This not only gave me my first opportunity to cross the Atlantic, but opened up new compositional horizons. The problem of entertaining a continuously through-moving audience is quite different from playing music to a captive, seated one. The showpiece was a three-screen film *Sources of Power*, directed by the Australian Don Levy, past whose enormous pictures the crowd slowly shuffled. I later made these complicated tracks into a concert piece (*Birth is Life is Power is Death is God is . . .*).

About this time two things happened which brought me out of the private world of my personal studio. One was that Keith Falkner, then Director of the Royal College of Music, asked me if I would found a teaching studio. It forced me to organize my thoughts, theories and experience into a teachable format. The other was joining with Peter Zinovieff and David Cockerell to form Electronic Music Studios (London) Ltd. This made me face the problems, not just of making something for my own studio and in order to realize my personal ideas, but trying to think up approaches that might be attractive to many people, i.e. that would sell. Robert Moog had already introduced the voltage-controlled synthesizer, and he is undoubtedly the founder and progenitor of the voltage-controlled period in electronic music (Moog, 1965). But his machines were expensive, and we set out to make a more compact, easier to use and cheaper package.

In fact our aim at the start was to make a synthesizer that would sell for under £100 – achieved for a very short time only. The late Don Banks, later a great friend in Australia, got us thinking by offering a challenge: build me the most useful and versatile composer's package you can manage for £50. We put our heads together, David went to work, and the result was a personal machine for Don – the VCS1, still extant in the memorial collection of Don's things in Canberra. VCS1 was limited in several ways and had only one channel. The upgraded version in stereo became the VCS3, sold as The Putney on the US market, which we were advised prefers names to numbers. It became EMS's most successful product. In the photo, which shows a corner of my studio at Fressingfield, Suffolk, in 1972, I am using two EMS VCS3 synthesizers with a special one-off keyboard console unique to my studio. In the background is the prototype VCS3, now in my collection of electronic archaeology, and still functioning.

In London, in the Zinovieffs' charming riverside house at Putney, EMS had a splendid studio which I could also use, but rarely did. The picture below shows it in 1972 (Zinovieff seated on right). The racks on the left contained the computers (some DEC PDP8s and some designed and built in our workshops). Behind me is the Synthi 100, an advanced hybrid synthesizer and EMS's top product at the time. These machines are still giving good service all over the world. The Putney studio attracted composers such as Henze and Birtwistle to work there, and we also ran a series of important concerts beginning in 1968 at the Queen Elizabeth Hall, with a programme that contained the first live computer piece ever heard in London, Zinovieff's *Partita for Unattended Computer*. From this time I began to compose concert pieces much more regularly. But they had to be fitted in to my busy schedule of film and TV work.

The compactness of solid-state, voltage-controlled machines also opened up new possibilities for live performance electronics, up to then very cumbersome in any other form than the simplest – performer plus tape. From the 'serious' music field there was also a spill over into rock and pop groups, with the most adventurous, like Pink Floyd, beginning to use electronics in imaginative ways. Also, the more successful of

these groups were wealthy enough to commission special equipment and experiment with it, and this brought benefits to everyone. The rapid advance of digital technology in the 1970s, and the increasing use of electronics in pop, rock and jazz (apart from simple amplification, which had been there since the 1930s) changed the whole emphasis of electronic music. I comment on these changes in **computer music composition techniques**.

It is a strange paradox that several centuries on from Bacon's fantasy we have machines that would have been considered a mad scientist's dream even thirty years ago, which are capable of doing all that Bacon, Busoni and Varèse dreamed of – and more – and yet, somehow, they are not doing these things at all. The technical advances have not brought with them the artistic miracles we hoped for. It is naive, of course, to think that they should – making a better paint does not make a better painter, and the statistical occurrence of creative genius in the world community is probably about the same as it always was. It is worth pondering, though, that most of this talent never surfaces at all. There are vast numbers of brilliant minds in China, India, Africa, South America who do not have the chance to achieve even literacy, let alone to develop creative paths outside their traditional folk idioms. If electronic devices, through being cheap and accessible, can serve as mouthpieces for some of these unknown musical poets, they are worthwhile for this alone.

In 1968 I attended an Electronic Music Convention in Florence, and was pleased to find that my tapes held up well against the products of the large European and American studios. At last I began visiting studios in Europe and the USA, and made friends and contacts I should have made years before – Milton Babbitt, Max Mathews, Michael Koenig among many others. I wrote articles for *Electronic Music Review*, a now defunct publication linked with Robert Moog's synthesizer operation in Trumansburg, NY. By 1970 I had become much more involved in the concert world than before. I presented tape, or tape and live concerts in Cheltenham, London, Dublin (the first) and elsewhere. I wrote most of a book on electronic music, but failed to finish it because of the usual time and money pressures. These activities, plus EMS and the RCM teaching studio, also brought me into regular contact with many more of my British contemporaries. Galliard (Stainer and Bell) published a couple of my electronic pieces. I did some TV programmes for the infant Open University, and some scores for the Old Vic, the new National Theatre and other stage companies.

Much of this activity, however, was either unpaid or absurdly unlucrative; my weekly class at the RCM made a net loss. My older children were beginning to emerge from the educational pipeline, but a steady flow of commissions, mostly TV by now, was absolutely necessary to keep things going. Having retreated to Suffolk in the early 1960s to compose in rural quietude and be able to play loud electronic music at 3 a.m. if I wanted, I seemed to spend increasing amounts of time tearing up and down the 100 miles between London and Fressingfield, and was not happy either with my life or my composing.

There was a dichotomy between the instrumental and the electronic sides of my work that had always been there from the earliest days and which I tried to resolve in my instrumental/tape pieces, though never quite satisfactorily. Since I had thought it out from fundamentals my electronic work was confident and sure, but my instrumental music seemed to get stuck in conventions that I didn't particularly respect but couldn't shake off. I wrote my biggest piece to date (text as well), *Peccata Mundi*, for chorus, orchestra, four tracks of tape and speaking voice, and came the nearest yet to producing a coherent whole from the two halves of my musical creativity. The piece was given at Cheltenham in 1972, with Brian Priestman conducting the Northern Sinfonia and the Schola Cantorum of Oxford. The audience reaction was enthusiastic, but the notices cool. *Peccata Mundi* is a political statement as well, because around 1969 it became clear to me that the human race was heading for inevitable mass suicide, and the cantata looks back at our final years from a far future when we are all long dead. Nothing has happened since to change my mind, and with environmental disaster very much in people's minds today, the piece now seems prophetic. I later revised and improved the script, score and tapes for a performance in Adelaide in 1976, in which the speaking part was taken by Don Dunstan, then Premier of South Australia. The conductor was Malcolm Fox, now well known for his children's operas, and at one time in my RCM class.

My early intention, to be self-supporting by composing, had long been achieved, and as well as possessing a well-equipped personal studio I had access to several others, including the BBC's Radiophonic Workshop, whose facilities I rarely called on but could if I wished when doing BBC work. However, I was now past forty-five, and felt I needed new goals to aim at. The opportunity for total change came when the late George Loughlin, then Ormond Professor of Music at Melbourne University, called on my RCM class one day in 1973 and invited me to visit his Department, which had ordered a Synthi 100 (shown in the Putney photo). 'Come and show us how to drive it' was the way he put it. I had never really thought of visiting Australia, but if someone was paying my fare and a splendid fee, why not? Also, the visit was to be in August, and I would lose little work by going at a time when most of one's potential European employers are sitting on a beach somewhere.

I found that George had fixed me up with lecture dates all over Australia and I was captivated by the immensity and variety of the country and the freshness and enthusiasm of the people I met. I returned the following year as Visiting Composer to Adelaide University, they offered me a permanent senior post which I accepted, and I became, for the first time, a salaried person. I shipped out the Fressingfield studio and incorporated some of it with the small amount of equipment they already had, as the foundation of a new teaching/composing studio. In 1978 I ordered a computer synthesizer from America, and in 1983 we were the first studio in South Australia to offer digital recording.

Since coming to Australia I have several times toured the USA and often revisited Europe, watching the progress of studios and meeting the composers who work in them (see **computer music composition techniques**). I have made many new friends, in music and out of it, both near contemporaries and among the younger groups of artists, to whom the technologies which are the subject of this book come not as untilled fields, as they did to me in 1945, but at least partly cultivated. During these years I have written a number of pieces, instrumental, electronic and mixed, and had time to ponder my composing philosophies without the constant economic pressures of earlier years. I'm not saying that I've solved any problems, but at least I have faced and thought about them.

In 1985 (at sixty) I left my academic position and returned to self-employment (a condition more natural to me, in fact, than being an organizational cog), and a major task in this re-discovery of living by my wits has been the putting together of the book you now hold. Some kind of cycle seems to have completed itself, at least for the time being.

I have already noted that in the 1960s, with greater automation, there was a tendency for the studio to control the composer in ways that had not been a danger in the early years (which were by then being called the period of the 'classical studio'). A parallel but different position arose as computer music moved from being the province of expensive and exclusive research projects to an everyday facility affordable by almost any composer who wants to use it – a process that has been gradually taking place over the last twenty-five years.

If we make computer music languages that are easy to use and require little or no knowledge of programming, the penalty is rigidity of compositional outlook. The only way to make software simple for the user is to reduce the options. We are used to limitations, of course: in instrumental composition, for example, some things are very free, but others, like the way instruments are built and played, are subject to strict limits. We learn to live with this, and for the most part can move about freely in the creative space without hitting too many boundaries.

In electronic and computer music, however, the more open the approach sought by the composer, the more necessary it is for him to learn programming and write his own software. In 'The composer seduced into programming', Gareth Loy, a composer who has faced these problems head on, writes:

> One frequent result of the involvement of musicians with computers is that the mastery of the required technology is so foreign that, even if eventually successful, the musician emerges from the experience drained of the will to pursue it further ... it takes a long time to acquire the detailed knowledge of computer technology that allows one to make interesting music on computers. (Loy, 1980–81)

Dr Loy writes from a fairly privileged position – working with a large system one can at least find out if one has the necessary patience to surmount such obstacles. But most composers neither are expert programmers nor intend to be, and hope, reasonably enough, to get interesting results from the packages you can buy at the music store. Many of these systems are ingenious and easy to use, yet make assumptions about your compositional style, taking it for granted, for example, that you wish to write music on five-line staves with key and time signatures, and use instruments which play twelve notes to the octave and make sounds in the same timbral area as familiar acoustic instruments.

This is a far cry from the creative adventures of the early days, and such problems are in fact now being actively addressed (see again **computer music composition techniques**). But if composers can articulate their needs clearly, solutions can nearly always be found, and one aim of this book is to make musicians aware of what lines of development may be possible. Computers have already invaded every aspect of our lives, sometimes to an irritating extent, but much time and energy is wasted in blaming the machine, instead of the people who talk to it. Musical discovery will continue, and no one can tell where it will lead. The music machines of the future must allow for progress in any musical direction, however unexpected.

The pace of development is such that we are already seeing systems where the rigidity and coldness of the electronically drawn empty stave are replaced by a wide choice of input gestures (including, of course, the empty stave as one option). The computer itself is already reaching a very complex condition. All the same, as with our own miraculous body systems, the complexity will eventually be hidden from the user; the interface with the machine will be simple and direct. To respond to the fountain pen that I see on the table by moving a hand and grasping it, is an elaborate process, followed by an even more elaborate one – moving the pen in such a way that thoughts generated in my brain are converted into a commonly understood code, readable by other people and capable of being stored in *their* brains. These actions are in no sense robotic; they are controlled by a complicated program that can be drastically changed at any instant, by the phone ringing, the appearance of coffee, or the pen running out. It is a matter of using the technology for what it is good at. The computers we currently have are good at doing, accurately and tirelessly, the kind of tasks that human beings find tedious and unnatural, such as churning through long lists to find some desired feature, remembering and efficiently filing masses of boring but necessary information, and working out complex sums at amazing speeds. The ability to organize, list and choose has alone opened up new strategies in composition that could not be contemplated before (again see **computer music composition techniques**).

At any period the avant-garde is quite small: most artists are content with the conventional methods of their time. Because the demand is insignificant, adventurous composition is getting a raw deal from the designers of budget-priced mass market machines, and this is particularly to be regretted in places where the seeds of new ideas are sown – in schools and universities, and in the workshops of composers of modest means. But this is easy to put right. There is every sign that the power so far available only at privileged places like IRCAM, Stanford and MIT may well sit on our desktops at home or at school sooner than we think. The technology is there already; it is merely a matter of implementation, which means motivation and money.

There is no doubt at all that the future of music lies largely with electronics, even though acoustic musical intruments will always be made and exist alongside electronic ones. Many people still cling to an illusion that things are as they were. But the revolution has already happened. In 'The futures of music' F. Richard Moore notes:

Music is no longer limited to the immediate surroundings of its generation, to a travelling minstrel's roadshow, or to a demure court of well-behaved aristocrats. Music permeates our lives, thanks to audio technology, and the music of our time is consequently different, for the true instrument of our age is not the lute or guitar or piano or drum or organ or even the electronic synthesizer – it is the loud-speaker. (Moore, 1980–81)

Nearly all the music we listen to comes from loudspeakers, and has done for some years. Recordings have been getting ever better, and concerts more and more expensive; it now requires some ingenuity to juggle concession prices so that students can afford to go to opera at all. Computer musical instruments are merely adding another factor to the Loudspeaker Age, but it will be an increasingly important one as the machines get more subtle, and high quality conventional instruments become collector's items for the very rich.

What follows the loudspeaker age? Possibly a means of getting straight through to the aural mechanisms of the brain, by direct access. I did offer myself, years ago, to some medical students at Oxford, for an experiment to look for evidence of the 'mind's ear'. My idea was to redesign an electroencephalograph so that it would respond to audio instead of sub-audio frequencies, and see if we could find any sound in the brain. I was told, firmly, that my idea was naive, impractical and possibly dangerous (though I have recently found out that work was in fact done on this as early as 1934, see **bio-music**). But there is a slow progress towards greater understanding of these mechanisms, and it is still possible that, before I have to leave this earth, someone will find a way of allowing a composer to sing his inner thoughts straight on to tape. Beethoven in his final years would have found it very useful.

As a corrective to these high-tech speculations, it is worth reflecting that in an art form only forty years old it is much too soon to say that any technique is out of date. One can still make pieces by cutting up tape, and even with all the latest equipment to hand, there is no other way to make some pieces.

One of the fascinations of art is that nothing dies. Everything gets richer all the time, because old experience underlies and enriches new techniques. In the history of instrumental music there are many cases of an instrument being apparently superseded by a 'better' one, until it is discovered that 'better' should have read 'different'. Consider the number of sackbuts, crumhorns, harpsichords, fortepianos, recorders, simple system woodwinds and natural horns being made today.

We have today an astonishing array of sound sources at our disposal: most of the main music-making devices from a spread of six centuries are readily available, and actually used. The musical technology of the future can only add more richness to this already rich treasure. It certainly can't take anything away from it.

THE COMPENDIUM

A

A The note traditionally used to check the tuning of instruments, and for which a **frequency** is specified when setting a **pitch** standard. In an orchestra of mixed types of instrument, the oboe gives the tune-up A because being conical (see **woodwind instruments**) its range of adjustment is very small (a millimetre or two by sliding out the reed assembly). In piano concertos, naturally, the piano takes this role because its tuning cannot be adjusted at all at the time of performance.

The international standard for the musical middle A (A_4) is at present 440 Hz (**hertz**), which in equal **temperament** gives a middle C of 261.6 Hz. For various reasons pitch tends to creep up, one of them being the desire by conductors to enhance the 'brilliance' of their orchestral sound. Today, with so many reproduction baroque instruments being made, 415 Hz (slightly more than a semitone lower than 440) is usually given as seventeenth- to eighteenth-century pitch (though in those days all sorts of local and empirical standards were used), and one of Handel's surviving tuning forks gives 422. During the nineteenth century orchestral pitch moved up alarmingly, one reason being the introduction of valved brass, which were tonally less brilliant than their natural counterparts, and tended to be tuned high in an attempt to compensate.

In 1859 the French introduced a standard 'diapason normal' with A at 435 Hz. English pitch in the late nineteenth century rose as high as 461. The coming of recording, broadcasting and a new mobility among the musical fraternity made it essential to have some kind of international standard, and in 1939 the western world agreed on 440 (just before it disagreed about everything else).

To the dismay of some, there is again a tendency to push the pitch up – some orchestras are tuning as high as 443. The effect of this is to make nonsense of the careful choice of pitches by composers. Singers complain about punishingly high notes in earlier scores, and with reason, because the notes they have to sing are higher than those intended by the composer. See also **absolute pitch**.

Absolute pitch   The ability to name single, isolated notes (as opposed to a sense of relative pitch or interval recognition). Also called 'perfect pitch'. Possessed fully by only a few people, not necessarily musicians, it seems to have some hereditary continuity. Though the gift of instant and correct identification of any note is rare, some people can learn one pitch and estimate the interval to the note heard; others use even less precise signposts, for example the lowest or highest note they can sing. An obvious problem is the changing pitch standard (see A above) – Handel's Bb is not ours – so the possessor of perfect pitch must still learn the accepted contemporary standard. It is very useful to singers and string players for example, but it can be disconcerting. One singer of my acquaintance who certainly has perfect pitch is severely put out by recordings etc. played at slightly the wrong speed. See Taylor (1965), Wood (1962), Roederer (1979) and Deutsch (1982, chapter 14) for a summary of some research.

AC   See **alternating current**

Acceptor   1. See **tuned circuit** 2. See **semiconductors**

Acetate   1. A catch-all term for a group of compounds used as lacquers (on aluminium) for disc recording blanks (e.g. cellulose nitrate), and as 'base' material for earlier magnetic tapes (e.g. cellulose triacetate), later replaced by PVC, Mylar (polyester) etc. 2. The test recording made at the same time as the 'master lacquer' (which will be plated and cannot be played) to assess the quality of the disc before going ahead. Acetates wear out quickly but yield excellent, noise-free quality for a few playings. Before tape was used in radio studios, two duplicate acetates of a music recording were made, one to wear out at rehearsal, one kept in virgin condition for transmission. See **sound recording techniques**.

Acoustics   From the Greek *akouein* meaning 'to hear'. 1. The study of sound as a branch of physics, in theory confined to vibratory phenomena within the **frequency** range sensible by human ears (say 20 **hertz** (Hz)–20 kHz). In practice a much wider frequency range than that described as 'sonic' or 'audio' must be considered. Sound vibrations reach our ears through a medium which is usually air but may be a liquid, a solid body, or a succession of several materials. Many vibrations at frequencies above and below the normal musical range are felt rather than heard, but they must be included in acoustic studies because they modify the sounds we hear in the conventional sense. 2. The behaviour of an environment to which sound is introduced (e.g. the acoustics of a hall). This branch of acoustics, which includes control of industrial noise and vibration, is largely outside the scope of this book, though a number of articles touch on aspects of it (see **acoustic treatments**). 3. Used as a description of instruments, for example acoustic guitar, piano, when an electrical version is common. Incorrect because the word refers to input, i.e. hearing, not output, but a general usage nevertheless.

In sense 1 acoustics studies such questions as how sound is propagated, how objects respond to various excitations, speech (acoustic phonetics) – in fact any aspect of sound that can be measured and analysed. As soon as sound is heard and interpreted by people, exact measurement has to give way to subjective observation, and we enter the field of **psychoacoustics**. Because music is essentially a human activity, much of musical acoustics properly falls into that area; for example where acoustics measures the **frequency** of something vibrating, psychoacoustics investigates a person's sense of **pitch**.

The most important field of purely acoustic study in music is the design and development of musical instruments. Although today every scientific aid is used, including computers, to improve design, it is worth noting that the almost miraculous development of musical instruments to the high state of refinement they had reached by the end of the nineteenth century, was achieved almost entirely without the benefit of scientific study except for some very basic rules propounded by Pythagoras almost three millenniums ago.

The first scientist to gi serious attention to the acoustics of musical sound was Hermann von Helmholtz, whose book *On the Sensations of Tone* appeared in 1862 (Helmholtz, 1862). It is still fascinating reading and contains many original theories and ingenious experiments, though we now know that some of his conclusions were wrong.

Helmholtz's problem was to make recording devices that could capture the dynamic changes in a sound, and he was forced to do much of his work using models or analogies of the real thing (e.g. recording a much slower vibration of a similar type by scratching a line on smoked glass). If he had anticipated Edison, who invented the phonograph only a few years later in 1877, his methodology might have been transformed. Because of such experimental limitations, Helmholtz often assumed steady state conditions which we now know do not obtain – on the contrary nothing in sound is steady for even a few milliseconds.

Some of the modern methods of analysing these phenomena are discussed in **digital synthesis techniques** 1–3. There is no shortage of texts describing the basic behaviour of sound waves, though recent research in this fast-moving field means some of the older ones are not always reliable. Recommended books which concentrate particularly on musical acoustics are Taylor (1965), Wood (1962), Olson (1967), Roederer (1979), and the early chapters of Ballou (1987). Hutchins (1978) is a collection of articles on vocal and instrumental acoustics. Another useful study is chapter 2 by Wayne Slawson in Appleton (1975), which looks at the topic from the electronic music composer's point of view. Some of these studies are partly in the area of psychoacoustics (where further reading is listed), but as mentioned above the physical and psychological aspects are not really separable in a musical context – Roederer (1979) makes a parallel exploration of the two.

See also **bowed string instruments, brass instruments, coloration, combination tones, control room, decibel, difference frequency, dissonance, formant, fundamental, harmonic series, Helmholtz resonator, logarithm, organs, partial, phon, pianos, reverberation, standing wave, stereo, studio design, sub/-, super/sonic, temperament, timbre** and **woodwind instruments.**

Acoustic treatments   Modifications to the construction, dimensions, and/or surface finishes of a room or studio to achieve specific sound characteristics. Everything in an interior space, including people (even the clothes they wear), contributes to the complex patterns of **echo** and **reverberation** unique to that space. Exterior locations are similarly affected by the placing, size and nature of buildings, etc. but are obviously much harder to control deliberately.

Laboratories may include anechoic, or totally absorbent, chambers, to test (among other things) microphones and loudspeakers under controlled conditions. Such rooms are lined on all six sides (including the back of the door) with long wedges of cloth-covered absorbent material (e.g. glass wool or foam rubber). Equipment to be tested stands on a false floor of open wire mesh fixed above the wedges on the floor, and all tests are done by remote control because anybody in the room affects its deadness. Many people can only stay inside a dead room for a minute or two without panicking, because the quietness is such that all you can hear is your own body systems.

Rooms approaching this degree of deadness are used in drama studios to simulate echoless open air conditions such as deserts and arctic plains, which come as near to total absence of echo as can be achieved in the real world. Musicians dislike playing in such an environment, because their instruments sound as if they were packed in cotton wool, and the problem is to make a studio 'live' enough to produce a pleasant performing ambience without bringing out the undesirable acoustic qualities which lurk in most rooms, given a chance to show. Among the pitfalls are rumbles and roars from air-conditioning systems, **flutter echoes** from parallel walls, sharp **resonances** at certain **frequencies**, and focusing effects due to concave surfaces. Apart from treatments to the studio itself, correct **microphone placement** can help to minimize bad effects.

Because music and musicians vary a great deal in their requirements, any working studio must be capable of some acoustic adjustment. A simple course is to make a number of moveable screens with hard panels on one side and absorbent material on the other, and a step up from this is to make hinged sections of the walls similarly equipped. Sometimes a particular artist (e.g. percussionist, singer) may be placed in a special isolating box or behind portable screens. The most elaborately variable room to date is at IRCAM, Paris. For details of this room, L'Espace de Projection, see **studio design**.

Recent advances in the design of **reverberators** now enable the sound engineer to create at will a large variety of quasi-natural spaces, from small, bright 'bathroom' acoustics to imaginary halls of enormous proportions, plus a number of completely artificial environments in which composers can create new **timbres**. Consequently the tendency now is to build studios on the dead side, and leave the addition of liveliness, i.e. reverberation, to the recording producer in a separate **control room** (which should itself be as acoustically neutral as possible). The musicians need not feel the 'cotton wool' effect, because **foldback** is used to feed reverberant ambience back to them. A similar process, but more complicated because it involves time delays, is used in some concert halls to liven up an unduly dead auditorium (see **public address**).

See also **Helmholtz resonator**. Studio design and layout problems are also discussed in Nisbett (1970), Olson (1967), Runstein (1989) and Nisbett (1983). The early chapters of Ballou (1987) have detailed studies of various aspects of architectural acoustics in concert halls, cinemas etc., as well as studios. For **psychoacoustic** aspects of room conditions, see Deutsch (1982), chapter 5.

Active device   One that contains an **amplifier** to compensate for **loss** or add **gain** and therefore needs a power supply as well as **signal** input/output. See also **passive device** and **unity gain**.

ADC   See **analogue-to-digital converter**

Additive synthesis   The production of a complex wave by adding together simple ones, usually **sine waves**. In theory the 'purest' method, because a controlled combination of known ingredients is used. The opposite process is **subtractive synthesis**, in which a deliberately over-rich sound is refined by **filtering**.

Adding sines was one of the first methods used in taped electronic music, but often resulted in rather dull sounds, because not enough individual wave sources were added to achieve richness and variety. Stockhausen, in his trail-blazing *Study II* (1954), used a non-standard pitch division to produce a new, non-instrumental additive timbre. Instead of a pitch ratio per step of $^{12}\sqrt{2}$ or $^{24}\sqrt{4}$ (i.e. 1.059463), which gives standard equally tempered semitones (see **temperament**), he used $^{25}\sqrt{5}$ (i.e. 1.066495), which is not only a slightly wider step, but does not repeat at octaves at all. Sine tones in clusters and chords based on this pitch division were then treated with a lot of **reverberation**, in order to apply random time delays and produce timbral masses instead of chords. (For further details, see Stockhausen, 1957, p. 50.)

Pure additive synthesis is hard to achieve successfully with analogue electronics, because it is difficult to generate sine waves of sufficient purity. **Oscillators** tend to **drift**, and to control all the **parameters** of all the **partials** of a complex sound is an elaborate and time-consuming process. More successful results are obtained with digital techniques, see **analogue synthesis techniques** 4, and **digital synthesis techniques** 4. Because two or more sources are combined, the word additive is some-times applied also to essentially multiplicative processes like **frequency** or **ring modulation**.

ADSR   The commonest type of 'instrumental' **envelope shaper**, consist-ing of four separately controllable 'segments' Attack, Decay, Sustain and Release. See also **analogue synthesis techniques** 4.

AF   See **audio frequency**

AI   See **artificial intelligence**

Aleator/ic, -y   See **random and chance procedures**

Algorithm   An old word (based on an Arabic name) for arithmetic. A procedure for problem solving which involves clearly defined steps and rules. Some musical problems are capable of algorithmic treatment, for example, 1. generating notes in a digital **synthesizer**, 2. working out how many different permutations of a given set of notes there are.

Computers are ideally suited for such tasks. For creative and compositional problems, which are often impossible to state in clear-cut terms and where it is normal to have open and loose ends, a **heuristic** approach is often more suitable. See also **artificial intelligence, computer languages** and **computer music composition techniques**.

Alias/ing Also 'foldover'. The production of spurious data in a digital sound system, when the **frequency** of the input or the generated signal is higher than half the **sampling rate**. The frequency of the alias is found by subtracting the input frequency from the SR. See **digital synthesis techniques**.

Alphanumeric Describes a set of **characters** which contains both letters and numbers, plus other necessary signs such as punctuation marks, accents, spaces etc. (Alpha[betic]+numeric) See **ASCII**.

Alternating current (AC) An electric current which **periodically** changes direction at a certain **frequency**, unlike **direct current**, which always flows in the same direction. It is normally thought of as a single **sine wave**, but may not be, for example, the electrical **analogue** of music is made up of many sinusoids at different frequencies and **phases** summed to make a single complex wave. For the behaviour and measurement of AC under various conditions, see **capacitance, inductance, impedance** and **root-mean-square**.

ALU See **central processing unit**

AM See **amplitude modulation**

Amp/ère Named after André Marie Ampère (1775–1836). An SI unit of **current**, related to the flow of charge: one amp = one **coulomb** per second. One **volt** can send one amp through one **ohm** (see **Ohm's law**). Symbol for amps is A. Currents in electronic applications are normally small, hence expressed in mA or μA (see **SI units**). The symbol for current as an abstract concept is I (C being reserved for **capacitance**).

Amplifiers Devices that cause an input **signal** to interact with a power source so as to output a larger copy of itself. Unqualified, the word implies a **linear** transfer of the signal, the amplifier contributing only **gain** and not **distortion, noise** etc. In modern audio amplifiers, these requirements are generally met very well, most distortion occurring in input/output **transducers**. For general background on circuit behaviour, see **capacitance, impedance, inductance, Ohm's law** and **watt**. Electronic technology as such is outside the scope of this book, but amplifiers are so essential to all music work that some explanation of the basic principles is relevant.

Amplifiers for radio **frequencies** do not concern us here. The range of frequencies relevant to musical applications extends outside the audio **band** itself (*c.* 20 **hertz**–20 kHz), downwards to **DC** (0 Hz) and upwards to *c.* 200 kHz (for bias/erase circuitry in tape recorders, see **sound recording techniques**). The amplifier is the key device around which the whole science of electronics came into being.

Instead of processing current flowing in wires, electronic devices work by operating on free electrons, either in a near vacuum (the vacuum tube or valve), in a gas, or in specially treated crystalline substances (**semiconductor**). For nearly all applications the transistor (and its derivative, the **integrated circuit**, IC), has replaced the earlier valve, but not entirely (see Power Amplifiers, below). The main disadvantages of valves, which made the transistor such a revolutionary and welcome arrival, are 1. their large size for the function performed; 2. their thermionic operation, involving a hot electron source, which generates unnecessary heat and needs special power supplies; 3. their high, sometimes dangerous operating voltages, as against the few volts needed to drive a transistor.

Valves
The point at which an electron stream leaves a wire to enter the freer environment, or vice versa, is an 'electrode', and two-electrode devices (the minimum for a through current) are **diodes**. These are truly 'valves' in the sense that they are one-way streets for current, and have many applications. But to achieve gain, a three-electrode or triode device is needed. A DC power supply (the necessary energy input) sends a steady current between two of the electrodes, electrons being drawn from the negative end (electron source) to the positive. In the path of this current is a third, control electrode.

Fig. 1a shows that in a valve a wire fence or 'grid' is placed in the stream of electrons flowing between the heated cathode (−) and the anode (+). Unconnected, the grid simply allows the electrons to flow through, but if a negative voltage is applied, the grid will repel (like charges) some of the electrons crossing it, reducing the anode current. If increasing the negative charge proportionally reduces anode current the relationship is linear, and the essence of the amplifying action is that a small change of grid voltage has a relatively large effect on anode

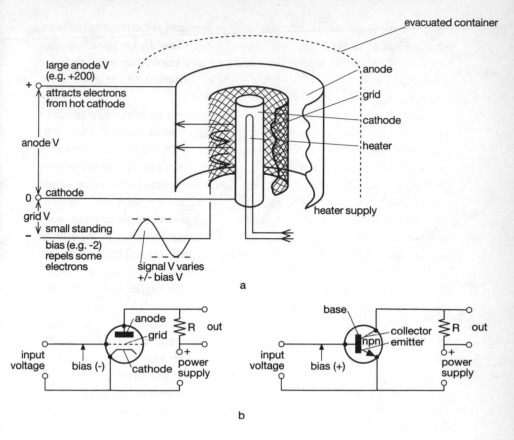

Fig. 1

current. With an alternating input, however, there will be positive swings as well, but these must not be allowed to send the grid positive or the control action is destroyed – the grid becomes like an anode, attracting electrons and itself passing a current. To prevent this, a standing negative voltage (bias) is applied, ensuring that the grid remains negative even on positive swings of the signal (see again fig. 1a). Outside the valve the anode current is passed through a load **resistor** to provide a voltage output (see **Ohm's law**).

Transistors

In a transistor (*trans*[fer res]*istor*), cathode–grid–anode becomes emitter–base–collector. A stable, electrically neutral crystalline material, usually silicon, is 'doped' with charged foreign atoms (see **lattice** and **semiconductor**). One treatment gives the material a permanent surplus of electrons (N-type or negative), and the other a permanent lack of them (P-type – the empty spaces are called holes and amount to positive charges). A transistor is a sandwich with two junctions, the middle section, or base, being of opposite type from the two ends (and with one such junction, we have the semiconductor **diode**). There are thus two main types of transistor, PNP and NPN, and the important action takes place at the junctions.

If a voltage is applied in the 'forward' direction, i.e. encouraging the natural tendency for electrons from N to move over and fill holes in P, current flows easily and the **resistance** is low. In the other, 'reverse' direction, resistance is very high, so little or no current flows. In the valve amplifier described above the cathode is common to both grid and anode circuits. To take the equivalent transistor configuration called the 'common emitter' mode the emitter/base junction is forward-biased and the base/collector junction reverse-biased. Under these conditions a small current change in the low-resistance emitter/base circuit causes a large current change in the high-resistance emitter/collector circuit. In essence, a valve is a voltage amplifier, and a transistor is a current amplifier. Either device can be biased or driven so that it cuts off completely, and used as a switch, i.e. output simply switches on or off as input varies, or to perform a logic function (see **Boolean algebra**). Fig. 1b shows valve and transistor amplifiers reduced to basics for comparison. Practical amplifiers, with biasing arrangements, power supply lines and input/output circuitry are outside our scope here – there are many good studies of elementary electronics, circuit books etc. (See Capel, 1988, and Grob, 1987, for example.)

Gain (the size of the output compared to the input) may be expressed in voltage, current or power terms, depending on application, and is measured in **decibels**. A single stage of amplification may not provide enough gain, in which case several stages follow each other, each output feeding the next input. In **block diagrams** any amplifier can be represented by the triangular block shown in fig. 2a.

Pre-amplifiers
The familiar domestic hi-fi amplifier divides into two parts with different

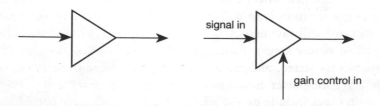

signal in

gain control in

a   Fig. 2   b

functions, whether or not it is actually in two units or 'integrated' (not to be confused with the use of the word in **integrated circuit**) i.e. in a single box, possibly with a radio tuner as well. The input section is the pre-amplifier, almost invariably two identical chains for stereo, and it has several well-defined jobs: 1. Accepting a range of different inputs, from very low (e.g. **microphones**, magnetic **pick-ups**) to quite large (e.g. CD player, tuner), and providing fixed **equalization** where necessary. In most cases inputs are selected by one or more switches. 2. Volume and tone controls of varying complexity, and possibly some switched **filters** for different purposes. 3. Balance control, deciding the proportions of L and R signal at the output. 4. Line amplifier, delivering a corrected, balanced and strong signal (frequently at 'line level', see **decibel**) at the output for connection to a power amplifier. There may be several 'extras', the commonest being a 'loudness' switch, which lifts levels at both ends of the frequency range to give a better aural balance at low volumes (see **phon** and fig. 155). The processing of every aspect of the signal, except its final magnitude, is done in the pre-amplifier. For professional work switched inputs do not give enough flexibility, and in recording or composing studios all the functions of a pre-amp are incorporated into the **mixing desk**, where each input channel contains at least all the facilities mentioned above, often many more, and all inputs can feed to the outputs simultaneously.

Power amplifiers
Alternatively 'main amp' or just 'amplifier'. Pre-amplifier stages are as nearly as possible 'wattless' – they amplify only signal voltage while drawing the minimum supply current. The final stage in a music system, however, must deliver enough energy to drive the **loudspeakers** – anything from a few milli**watts** for a pocket radio to thousands of watts for an open air rock concert. Power transistors therefore need to pass high currents and are mounted on finned 'heat sinks' to keep them cool. There are various approaches designed to maximize power output and fidelity while keeping operating power demands as low as possible. For high power work **field effect transistors** have a better thermal perform-ance than the junction type described above, and some engineers and rock musicians still favour valve or hybrid amplifiers (transistor early stages, valve power stage). Amplifiers, except the largest, are usually built in pairs for stereo, and sometimes both amplifiers can be linked to provide a double-power mono unit (a process called bridging). High power mono uses include **public address** systems. Some amplifiers have volume controls, others have no controls except a power switch. Some are fitted with fully calibrated wattmeters, others have **LED** level indi-

cators, simple overload lamps, or no indicators at all. They vary, also, in the degree of safety protection, for example fuses in case of overload in output circuits. For further aspects of power circuits see **impedance matching, public address, harmonic distortion**, Capel (1988), Capel (1981) and Grob (1987). There is also plenty of informative manufacturers' literature, magazine reviews etc.

Because amplifiers are central and ubiquitous in so many different electronic applications, there are literally hundreds of types. A few of particular relevance in music work are:

D.C. (Direct Coupled) amplifiers   Amplifiers capable of dealing with steady voltages or very slow changes. Essential in some electronic music applications where frequencies may be well into the sub-audio region, and **DC** control voltages may need amplification (see **analogue synthesis techniques** 4 ff). There are certain design problems, for example, **capacitors** cannot be used for signal coupling, but some audio amplifiers will operate with DC signals in any case.

Distorting amplifiers   An amplifier deliberately designed to change the **waveform** of the input, for example it may be overdriven into heavy **clipping**, which results in a **square wave** output from a **sine wave** input. The resulting square wave is then **filtered** to produce a desired sound. See **digital synthesis techniques** 7, on transfer functions.

Guitar amplifiers   Because an amplifier in combination with loudspeakers is really part of the instrument, **electric guitar** performers do not choose amplifiers by the normal hi-fi criteria, but to give the sound they prefer, which may well include some distortion and an uneven frequency response. Smaller units are self-contained with carrying handles and built-in speakers, and may feature **mixer** inputs, **reverberation** and variable **harmonic distortion** as well as the normal volume and response controls. Larger kits have 'heads' (amp and effects electronics) standing on 'bottoms' containing the speakers. Both solid-state and valve models are available (see also **loudspeakers** 3).

Operational amplifiers (op amps)   As their name suggests, these were originally designed to perform arithmetic operations in analogue computers. They are integrated circuit direct coupled amplifiers with two inputs (inverting and non-inverting) and one output, configured in many ways by changing the external circuitry so that they form the basis for different circuits with very different functions. Wide application in audio devices.

Voltage controlled amplifiers (VCA)   In normal amplifiers, each stage has a fixed gain, and output level is controlled by reducing the level at some point between stages, thus reducing the overall gain of the whole chain. In a VCA the gain of the actual amplifying device is dynamically controlled by an applied (control) voltage which changes the effective gain of a transistor. In block form an extra input is added for this control voltage (fig. 2b). The control signal and the input and output audio signals are completely separate and many different types of control signal can be applied, from steady DC to a **noise** signal. If the VCA is made as a DC amplifier this adds to its versatility. Together with the voltage controlled **oscillator** (VCO) it is one of the key devices in analogue music synthesis (see **analogue synthesis techniques** 4ff). The VCA has found many applications including **amplitude modulation** and automated level control in, for example, computerized **mixing desks**. Loudness levels are perceived **logarithmically** (see **phon**), so the most 'natural' approach to voltage control of output levels in audio applications is a linear voltage/log gain relationship (for example, 12 dB per volt, a conventional control slope giving 60 dB of gain variation for a five volt control range). In a typical composing studio VCAs are used as component parts of complete synthesizers, but others may be available as standalone units that can be **patched** in (i.e. connected in a line) to automate or modulate amplitudes where necessary. In **live performance electronic music**, VCAs can be arranged as automatic **panners**, and they are also the basis of voltage controlled **filters**.

For further study of all aspects of amplifiers see, for example, Bernard Grob's *Basic Electronics* (Grob, 1987) and relevant sections of Ballou (1987).

Amplitude   Of **alternating current**, the maximum departure of a wave in either direction from the central position (regarded as 0) to the positive or negative peak. It is sometimes given as a peak-to-peak value, which is twice the above quantity. It can also refer to an instantaneous amplitude at any point in the **cycle**. See **amplitude modulation** and **root-mean-square**.

Amplitude modulation (AM)   Probably most familiar in the expression 'AM radio', this is the method of transmitting sound used from the earliest days, but now sharing the air waves with **frequency modulation** (FM). In AM, the **amplitude** of one wave (the 'carrier') is changed at the **frequency** of another (the 'modulator'). AM is a multiplicative rather than an additive process, and its main applications fall into

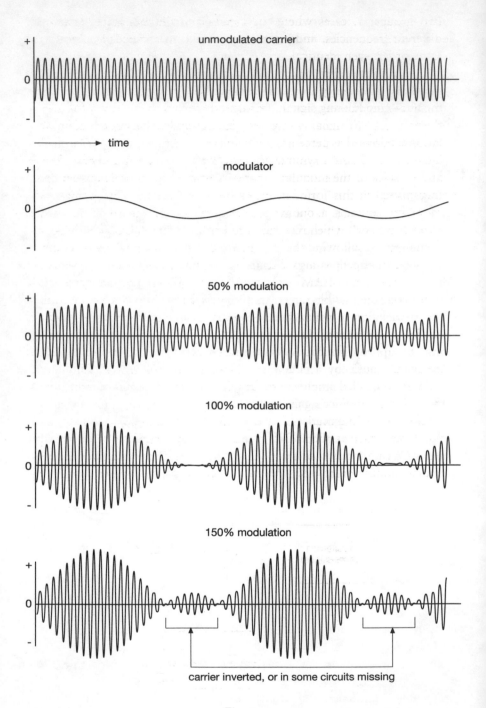

Fig. 3

two groups: 1. cases where the carrier and the modulator have very different frequencies, and 2. cases where the two frequencies are of the same order, even identical.

Typical of the first kind is AM radio, where a medium wave carrier may have a frequency around 1 megahertz (MHz), 1000 times faster than the audio modulating signal (average around 1 kHz). The appearance of this kind of AM signal is shown in fig. 3, with various depths of modulation (expressed as percentages of carrier amplitude). Because the modulated carrier forms a symmetrical **envelope** about its centre zero, the + and − sides of the modulator cancel out, and the modulated carrier is transmitted in this form. In order for us to hear the programme, the radio set contains a one-way circuit called a demodulator (in older usage 'detector') which removes half of the carrier and makes the signal asymmetrical, allowing the modulator to be heard (the high frequency carrier component is also **filtered** out by the audio circuitry). Another case of this kind of AM is the musical **tremolo**, where the carrier (the note) is in the audible range and the modulator in the sub-audio range (i.e. a variation in volume of a sound as distinct from **vibrato** which is an FM phenomenon). In conventional instruments it is applied by varying the appropriate loudness controls − bow, air stream etc., and in electronic music by a circuit such as fig. 4. The control input of the voltage controlled amplifier (see **amplifiers**) causes the modulating signal to vary the amplifier's **gain**.

The same configuration is used where the modulating frequency is of the same order as that of the carrier, giving a quite different audible result. Assuming two **sine wave** input signals, a carrier at frequency A, and a modulator at frequency B, the multiplicative process results in

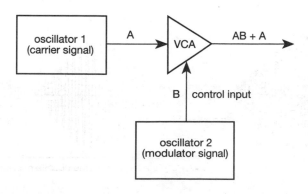

Fig. 4

two new tones, frequencies A+B and A−B, and the original carrier signal (A) is also present in the output. For instance if we modulate a carrier of 600 Hz with a modulator of 500 Hz (interval of a minor third), the output will contain 600 Hz and two new 'side' frequencies at the same distance (that of the modulator frequency) below and above the carrier − 100 (i.e. 600−500) and 1100 (i.e. 600+500) Hz. If the modulator is not sinusoidal but a richer **waveform**, the output will contain sums and differences of all its **partials**, and the resultant groups will not be single frequencies but **sidebands**. This is a powerful method of **timbre** modification, since it enriches the input by adding new tones to it. In the above case, the inputs are in a simple integral relationship (6:5), and the modulation products are all in a **harmonic series** based on a **fundamental** of 100 Hz. In the special case where A=B, the result of modulating is only the octave, since the sum tone is 2A, difference tone 0. Non-integral ratios will give **inharmonic** products.

For 'suppressed carrier' modulation, a type of AM which produces an output of AB only, see **ring modulation** and **analogue synthesis techniques 5**.

Analogue (US: **Analog**)   The English spelling is used throughout this book, but 'analog' is now common worldwide in technological usage. It refers to different systems that can be expressed in each other's terms − for example the mechanical qualities of mass and **compliance** are analogous to the electrical ones of **inductance** and **capacitance**, and equivalent circuits can be used to study their mechanical behaviour. In analogue devices adjustments are made along a continuous scale (by sliders, knobs etc.) unlike the discrete numbers, frames, steps etc. of **digital** devices.

Analogue synthesis techniques   This entry deals mainly with generating and manipulating sounds rather than organizing them into musical compositions, though in electronic music the boundary is not always clear cut. For other perspectives see **live performance electronic music**, **musique concrète** and **tape composition techniques**. Almost all manufactured electronic music equipment is now digital, but this does not make a study of analogue methods irrelevant. The 'wavy line' concept of music is intuitively more natural than the 'list of numbers' one, and although digital technology is (for very good reasons) steadily becoming the norm, the tactile directness of analogue and tape editing methods has never lost its appeal for many composers. It is interesting to note that the composer's need for the freedom to extemporize was well catered for by the analogue equipment of the 1960s, hardly at all by the 'severe' early computer music programs, but is increasingly met, in the new generation of digital synthesizers and computer software, by the inclusion of quasi-analogue interfaces like knobs and sliders, foot pedals, wheels, freehand drawing options, etc.

Among other reasons why analogue techniques are very unlikely to disappear are: 1. Many analogue modules can be built with limited skills and modest budgets, and in many applications work just as well and are simpler to use than their digital equivalents. 2. There are many good live performance pieces which cannot be mounted properly without the analogue equipment specified for them, and in some cases equipment once discarded has been revived.

1. Early history

Mechanical substitutes for human performers go far back into musical history, but until fairly recently the sounds themselves were always acoustic. By the end of the nineteenth century telephones and acoustic (purely mechanical) recording existed, and a patent for a magnetic wire recorder (the 'Telegraphone') was granted to the Danish inventor Valdemar Poulsen as early as 1899, but progress was limited because there was no way of enlarging the weak signals from a microphone to provide adequate driving power for a recording machine, or to make the development of **loudspeakers** possible.

The enormous (200 ton) Dynamophone or Telharmonium, introduced by Thaddeus Cahill in 1906, produced sound from rotating electromagnetic toothed wheels, and was an amazingly advanced project for its time, not only generating live polyphonic music played from keyboards, but piping the output to paying customers – a precursor of muzak. This was all accomplished without amplifiers; the sound was heard through modified telephone earpieces. The history of Cahill's prolonged and in the end tragic efforts has recently been researched by Reynold Weidenaar, Weidenaar (1988), Rhea (1988). At the same time as Cahill was developing the Dynamophone, Lee de Forest, another American pioneer, was working on a new device, a vacuum tube with three **electrodes** (see **amplifiers**). The valve (UK) or tube (US) was the key invention (1904–6) from which the new science of electronics was to grow, and it enabled alternating signals of a wide range of **frequencies** to be enlarged while retaining their original internal proportions. The vital component, the amplifier, had arrived. Given the amplifier, developing **oscillators** was only a matter of time, and de Forest had produced a practical design by 1915. Although the main thrust in early electronics was towards improving radio, electronic musical instruments began to appear soon after the end of the war in 1918.

The arrival of a new kind of music, without the restrictions imposed by traditional performing instruments, was predicted by Busoni and Varèse (see introduction) and some other original spirits long before it happened, but a suitable recording medium (tape) had to be invented before these advanced ideas could be implemented. Most of the early electronic instruments, on the contrary, were completely conventional from the musical point of view and most were aimed at the conventional organs market. With few ways of generating complex tones or interesting **envelopes**, acceptable organ quality was easier to achieve than any other because the basic sounds of the 'real thing' are reasonably invariant and the envelope is simple. The first market was smaller religious establishments, who wanted something more versatile and powerful than a reed organ (harmonium), but for whom a pipe instrument was out of the question. The fashion for electronic sound then spread to popular music, and compact organs, under various patent names, appeared in clubs and dance halls during the 1930s.

An organ must be fully polyphonic, of course, and the largest electronic instruments, with the bulky components of the time, were almost as big and expensive as their pipe equivalents, with a separate oscillator for every note, several manuals, many stops, full pedal board, etc. Smaller organs used **frequency dividers** to derive all their notes from one octave of oscillators, and simpler still were monophonic 'melody' keyboards (e.g. **Solovox**), needing only one oscillator and designed to clip on below the treble end of a piano keyboard, allowing 'instrumental' melody lines (right hand) to be accompanied by chords etc. in the left hand.

With electrical oscillators as tone sources stability of tuning was a continual problem, and some designers avoided them altogether. Electro-acoustic instruments are in essence amplified acoustic sources such as strings (see **electric guitar**) or metal bars (see **pianos** *electric*). Another way round the problem was used for one of the most successful organs, the Hammond, from 1935. In direct line of descent from Cahill's leviathan, this had 'tone wheels' on a common shaft as basic generators (see section 4 below). A good historical survey of organ-type instruments is Alan Douglas's *Manual* (Douglas, 1976). For comment on today's digital organs, see **organs** *electronic*.

There remains the category of non-keyboard electronic instruments, the most noteworthy for electronic music composers because, instead of being primarily imitative, they were aiming at new sounds and new types of performance, particularly by escaping from the rigidity of twelve-notes-to-the-octave keyboards. In 1920 a new instrument was announced by the Russian inventor Lev Termen (b. 1896), and became known (in a gallicized form of his name) as the **Theremin**. Based on the beat-frequency oscillator (see **oscillators**), it was played without being touched, which must have seemed miraculous at the time. Termen improved on the original idea and made several models including one with two antennae, one vertical and one horizontal, for pitch and loudness control. The (monophonic) output was a continuous tone but, by careful manipulation of the level, separate notes could be articulated. The instrument was not easy to play, but inspired at least one virtuoso, Clara Rockmore, whose work has been issued in a recording, with notes by Shirleigh and Robert Moog,* reviewed (with photographs) in Rhea (1989). Nowadays, 'Theremin' is often used loosely to describe any proximity-controlled **transducer**.

A few years after the first Theremin, two more continuously tunable electronic instruments appeared, the **Ondes Martenot** (1928), designed by Maurice Martenot, and the Trautonium (1930), by Friedrich Trautwein. Both resemble normal keyboard instruments in general appearance, but their pitch scales are in fact continuous. The Trautonium was given music by Strauss, Hindemith and others. The Ondes Martenot has an assured permanence because of the quality of the literature written for it by a long list of composers including Honegger, Milhaud, Varèse, and particularly Messiaen. These three instruments were the most notable, but many similar experiments were made, see Sadie (1984).

By 1939 electronic instruments were well established, with some quite advanced and reliable techniques already developed. Poulsen's magnetic recording idea was coming to fruition as the modern tape recorder (see **sound recording techniques**), and the scene was set for the development of a new art form. If the war had not intervened, taped electronic music would probably have been well established by the mid-1940s. For supplementary reading on the pre-history of electronic music, see Appleton (1975), chapters 1 and 6, Ernst (1977), Russcol (1972), Manning (1987) and Griffiths (1979).

2. Comparing acoustic and electronic systems

Nearly all the standard acoustic musical instruments have been in existence for centuries, and the composer/performer using one begins with a

*Rockmore, Clara, *The Art of the Theremin*, Compact Disc, produced by Shirleigh and Robert Moog, D/CD1014. Delos International, 2210 Wilshire Boulevard, Suite 664, Santa Monica, CA 90403, USA.

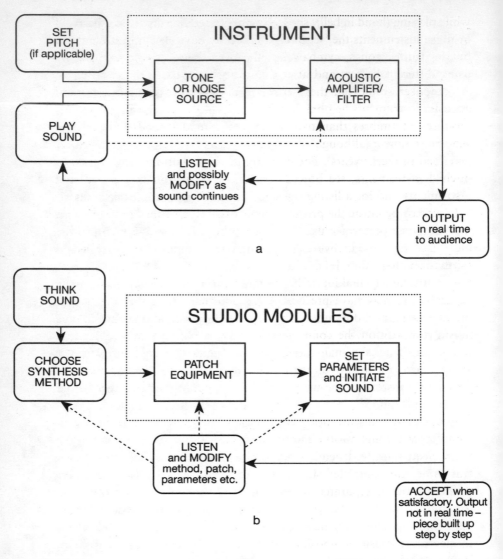

Fig. 5

known set of fixed and variable features. The action of playing an acoustic instrument is illustrated in fig. 5a.

With some instruments (e.g. bowed strings, wind), the performer is in a real time **feedback** loop because the note is controllable throughout. But (with few exceptions) percussion instruments (e.g. piano, xylophone) give no opportunity for modifying the sound after it has started unless a rapid repetition mode is used (e.g. drum roll). In some instruments (e.g. French horn) the player can also modify the resonating system while playing (hand in bell), shown by the dotted line input. In unpitched or **noise** instruments the 'set pitch' input may have no application at all, but in drums, gongs, cymbals etc. the pitch **band** can be changed by using different beaters and attacking different parts of the instrument. A composer studies all these effects, but when working with normal acoustic instruments he obtains innovative sounds more from ingenious mixtures of timbres than from trying to extend the possibilities of a single instrument (although all instrumental techniques have been greatly extended in recent years). For working principles of the main classes of pitched instruments, see **bowed strings, brass instruments, woodwind instruments** and for a listing by type, see **musical instruments, types of**.

In electronic music the process begins one stage further back, because the composer/performer usually creates the instrument as well as the piece (see fig. 5b). In live electronic music performed on a **keyboard synthesizer**, for example, the performance part will again look like 5a, but an instrument-making stage (to make the synthesizer perform in the desired way) may have preceded the performance. Composing (rather than performance) does not normally take place in **real time,** but in tape music composition the composer can stay in the feedback loop at all times, and this is a main distinction between tape and instrumental composing – the music can be heard and controlled at every step in the production instead of the whole work being committed to paper before a note is played.

Acoustic systems are not only complex in behaviour but change in complexity throughout the duration of a note, and success in imitating them electronically depends partly on the way the original instrument was built and controlled. Instruments which are pre-tuned and where the performer is separated from the sound generator by a mechanism (e.g. harpsichord) can be synthesized much more convincingly than those (e.g. violin) where every nuance is continuously moulded by the player. In electronic music composition the approach can be completely non-instrumental, the composer looking, not for imitations, but new sounds that exploit the advantages of the medium rather than emphasizing what it does not do particularly well. Examples are many-layered textures that change character slowly, accurately tuned microtonal intervals, rhythms of a speed and/or complexity impossible in live performance, large pitch ranges and long glissandi without timbral breaks, percussive attacks that become long sounds, reversed attacks, sounds that transform from one timbre to another, etc. Some of these can be done orchestrally, and it has been interesting to note the influence of electronic textures on instrumental scoring, but in the main the most successful analogue tape pieces have been those that could only exist in that medium.

The need to understand more about how acoustic instruments behave is not eliminated by the above, however, because the acoustic model can be the starting point for new sounds. From Helmholtz (1862) onwards different ways of making an accurate analysis were tried, but real progress was not made until computer analysis began in the 1960s (see **digital synthesis techniques** 3ff). The best reconstructions of acoustic instrumental sounds are undoubtedly digital, because only computers can handle the mass of data with enough precision to follow the subtle changes involved. The strength of analogue systems (or quasi-analogue systems with suitable digital equipment) is the ease with which rich and varied sounds can be generated and gesturally manipulated.

3. Patches, block diagrams etc.

The analogue studio can be considered as a number of separate items with different functions, and this section looks at how the various components are identified and connected together.

To make an electronic sound we must connect at least three things together (generator, amplifier, loudspeaker), but in most cases much more than this is needed. Some connections need not change (e.g. power amplifier to speaker), but others are made for a specific job, then uncoupled and **patched** differently for the next one. A device, however complicated, can be represented as one of five basic types of box or block according to general function, a connected group of which forms a **block diagram**.

Fig. 6 shows the five types. Inputs and outputs refer to signals, i.e. 'work' currents, rather than power and other 'services'. The first type (A) represents signal sources, i.e. there is an output but no electrical input. Devices like **oscillators** and **noise generators** need no input except power, but sources also include **microphones, pick-ups** and other kinds of **transducer**. These do have inputs, but in a different form of energy, so they are not shown in a purely electrical block diagram. Type B blocks are intermediate devices with an output corresponding to each input, such as a single channel **filter** (one in, one out), or a stereo amplifier (two in, two out). Type C comprises modules which assemble or reduce signals, such as **mixing desks** (more inputs than outputs). Type D devices have more outputs than inputs, i.e. they split or distribute signals. A **panpot** (one in, two out) is an example. Type E shows modules at the end of the chain – the opposite of sources. It includes transducers like **loudspeakers** (acoustic output), but also measuring devices such as meters and **oscilloscopes** (visual outputs).

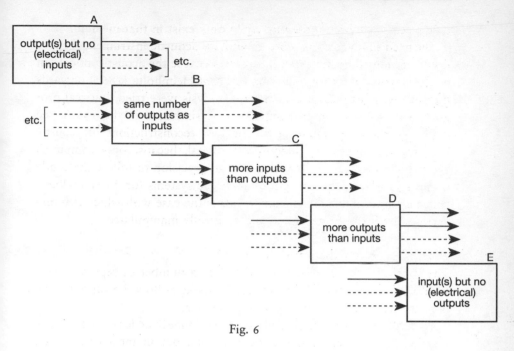

Fig. 6

Some modules change their box type depending on how they are being used. A tape recorder while in record mode (with no playback) is type E. In playback it is type A, but becomes B if you are recording and monitoring off tape as well. In most cases also, there are 'boxes within boxes' (see fig. 23). A multi-purpose device like a synthesizer has comprehensive internal patching, and its block type as a whole unit depends on how this is set up. Some boxes have control as well as audio input/output signals, and voltage control is discussed below (section 4ff). Audio signals may also be used for control, but to distinguish the two functions, controls are usually shown entering a box at right angles to the audio flow. Some devices are given special shapes so that they are easily picked out, for example, amplifiers are shown as triangular.

Fig. 7a shows a voltage controlled oscillator (VCO, see **oscillators**) in which the frequency control is unspecified. In 7b, VCO1 is controlled manually, and its output is both an audio signal and a control for VCO2. In 7c a power amplifier is connected to a speaker, and 7d shows a voltage controlled amplifier (**VCA**, see **amplifiers**), whose control input will affect the **gain**.

For small arrays of equipment needing only a few configurations (e.g. a home hi-fi system) patching can be done by switches, but the only completely versatile solution for complex studios is to bring the inputs and outputs of everything to a convenient central position. The

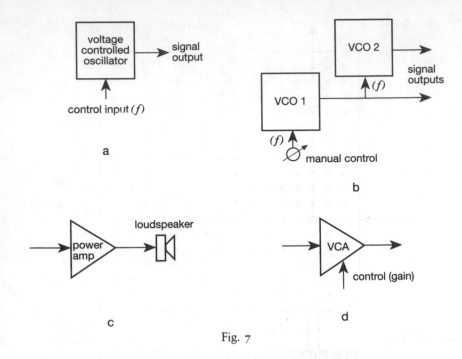

Fig. 7

commonest system is the 'post office' patch, with rows of sockets which can be connected by 'patch cords' – short lengths of wire with a **jack** at each end. Connections may be made by removing as well as inserting patch cords ('normalling', see **patch**). Any patch must be able to route a signal to several places by **paralleling**, and groups of paralleled sockets, not connected to any particular device, are called 'multis'. A different approach is the pin matrix patch, which avoids both loose cords and multis.

Fig. 8a shows a matrix with 256 (16×16) pin locations. Beneath the non-conducting top plate are contact strips aligned below each row (left to right) of holes. Under this plane another set of strips lies under each column (top to bottom). Inserting one pin into a hole makes a unique connection – one row to one column. Using a plain pin simply shorts the two strips, but in most cases pins are like tiny **jacks** (8b) with two insulated parts, so a resistor or other modifying component can be inserted.

Parallels are made by putting more than one pin in a particular row or column. In modern studios, matrix patching can be completely automated, pins being replaced by electronic switches controlled by a computer (see **patch**). A matrix is limited by its construction to a certain number of inputs/outputs, and expansion is achieved by using some lines

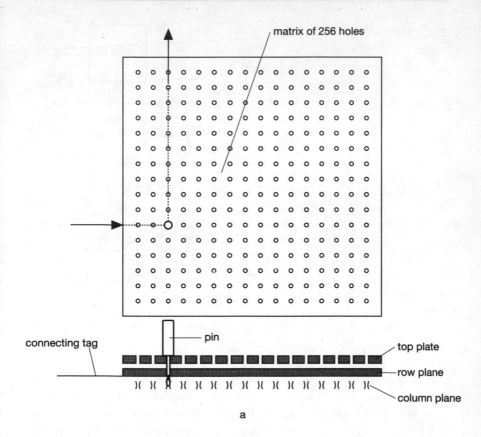

matrix of 256 holes

connecting tag

pin

top plate

row plane

column plane

a

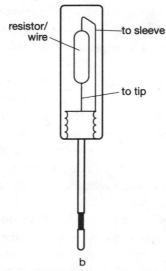

resistor/
wire

to sleeve

to tip

b

Fig. 8

to connect further matrixes. Jack and socket patches are less structured, and easily adaptable to changing circumstances.

Sketches of patches, showing blocks and connections, and possibly notes about settings, timings, changes etc. are basic paperwork in a composing studio, and a series of patch diagrams can amount to the working score of a composition. Let's now consider how the various devices are used.

4. Generators, shapers, filters, etc.

The chain of synthesis begins with a generator, or source, of which there are two basic kinds. **Oscillators** have periodic outputs and are discussed in a separate entry. **Noise generators** are sources of aperiodic or unpitched sound, which is also essential material, and discussed later in this section.

What follows assumes knowledge of the relationship between 'time domain' **waveform** and 'frequency domain' **spectrum** described in **digital synthesis techniques** 3, and for general information about instrumental **timbre** – see **formant, harmonic series** and **partial**. As we noted in section 2, the timbre of real instrumental sounds is never constant (i.e. it changes during a note), but at any instant it can be described by identifying the partials present and the energy in each. The fundamental, determining the pitch of the note, may not be the strongest, and can even be missing – an example is that we tolerate, even enjoy, music played on a pocket radio with a tiny speaker. Any pitch below the middle-to-high range is simply not there, but we can still imagine we are listening to bass voices, trombones and cellos (see **fundamental**).

Methods of synthesizing complex pitched sounds divide into two main classes: those that combine simple sources (additive), and those that refine already rich sources (subtractive). Additive synthesis involves using a separate **sine wave** (single frequency) generator for each **harmonic**, tuning each oscillator to the correct frequency, adjusting its output level to the correct proportion of the total and mixing all the outputs together. It is not difficult to see that this is cumbersome and time-consuming to set up. With eight oscillators, each having a frequency and a level control, a minimum of sixteen fine adjustments must be made for every note.

There are other problems as well: 1. Drift. For such a group of sines to sound like one timbre rather than a chord of sine waves, their frequencies must be in accurate ratios and very stable. The tuning of most oscillators drifts slightly, however carefully set up. 2. Sine purity. For additive synthesis to work, the waveforms of the partials must not themselves contain partials because some of them will be **inharmonic** to the main series and ruin the effect. So not only do we need many oscillators to make one note, but they must generate adequately pure sines.

These problems were tackled in an ingenious way in the design of the Hammond organ. Harmonics are generated by shaped tone wheels turning past **electromagnetic** pick-ups and mounted on a common shaft, so their frequency ratios cannot change even if the basic tuning pitch (speed of the shaft) does. The performer uses drawbars to select harmonics, and drawbars are still fitted to some modern digital organs (see **organs** *electronic*). Both these methods, however, produce an invariant sound – each partial has a fixed level throughout the note. To imitate a real instrument, different **envelopes** (see below) must be applied to each partial (see again **digital synthesis techniques** 3), and this makes the process very complex indeed. In general, the sine additive method can be used empirically to create new timbres (see **additive synthesis**), but as a basic controllable technique is more feasible in a digital environment. (See the next section, however, for modulation, a variant of additive with different results.)

Subtractive synthesis involves generating a tone which is already rich in harmonics, and tailoring it with **envelope shapers** and **filters** to produce the desired dynamic and harmonic proportions. The source may be the result of some previous additive process, or a generated **waveform** with a known **spectrum**.

Fig. 9 shows a sine and four easily generated straight-line waveshapes with their associated spectra. The energy in each harmonic is shown as a fraction of that in the fundamental, though this assumes a perfection of waveshape that is never achieved in practice. The ramp, or sawtooth, and the pulse are asymmetrical waves (the ramp's two half-cycles are mirror images), and contain complete harmonic series. Symmetrical waveforms contain odd-numbered harmonics only, and are useful for creating certain kinds of timbre (e.g. square for clarinet-like sounds, see **woodwind instruments**). The triangle wave, which has a rapidly decreasing series of odd harmonics, is the nearest of the straight-line shapes to sine tone, and produces a sound not unlike a flute in quality. The ramp is the most used of the group, since it contains a complete series of strongly represented harmonics, and has been for many years the source waveform for most electronic organs. In raw form (i.e. before filtering), all except sine and triangle sound harsh.

The most versatile tone source for electronic music is the voltage controlled **oscillator** (VCO), whose block diagram we noted above, with

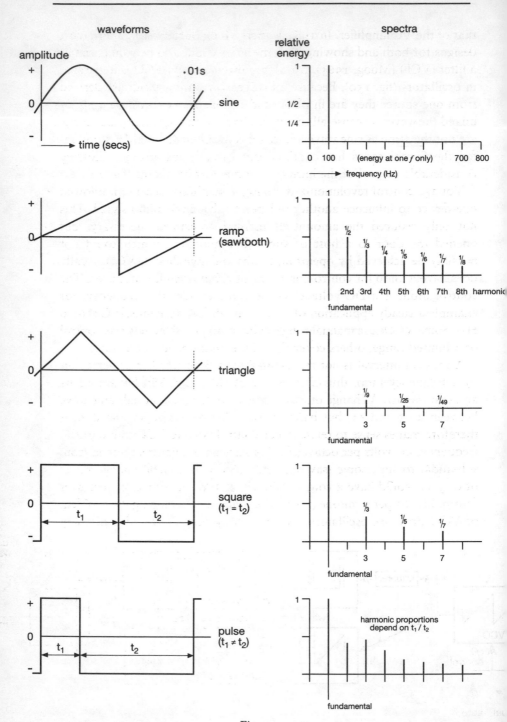

Fig. 9

that of the VC amplifier. In 1964 Robert Moog published a paper giving designs for both and showing how the VCA could also be configured as a filter (VCF) (Moog, 1965). Moog's multi-waveform VCO is illustrated in **oscillators** (fig. 150). Because all waveforms in its output are derived from one source they are in **phase** and can be used either separately or mixed (however, because all the waves have complex spectra the results are not the same as sine wave additive). A VCO made by EMS (London) for the Synthi series has continuously variable waveforms, allowing considerable control of the harmonic content of its output (fig. 10).

Voltage control revolutionized analogue synthesis, because it allowed one device to influence another independently of the audio signal. This not only reduced the amount of manual adjustment necessary, but opened the door to a host of subtle manipulations which could not possibly be achieved by operating knobs and switches. A VCO usually does have a knob for controlling frequency, but often it is not used. The control input is a **DC** voltage whose value decides the frequency, for example a steady application of +1.5 V might produce middle C (261.6 Hz). Some VCOs use manual range switches to give relatively fine control of a limited range, others cover the whole audio band in one range.

A musical interval is not represented by a fixed number of hertz, but by a frequency ratio, thus 27.5, 55, 110, 220, 440, 880 Hz are all As an octave apart. A change of, say, 12 Hz would be about half an octave between 27.5 and 55, but barely perceptible between 440 and 880. It therefore makes sense to relate linear control volts to logarithmic (ratio) frequency, i.e. volts per octave; for instance an oscillator sweeping from sub-audio to supersonic (say ten octaves) with a control voltage range of 0–5 V, would have a control 'slope' of .5 V per octave, or just over four millivolts per semitone (for further comment, including the problem of VCO drift, see **oscillators**). An unvarying voltage will give a steady

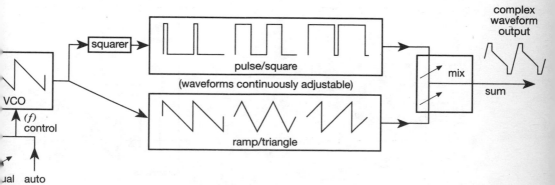

Fig. 10

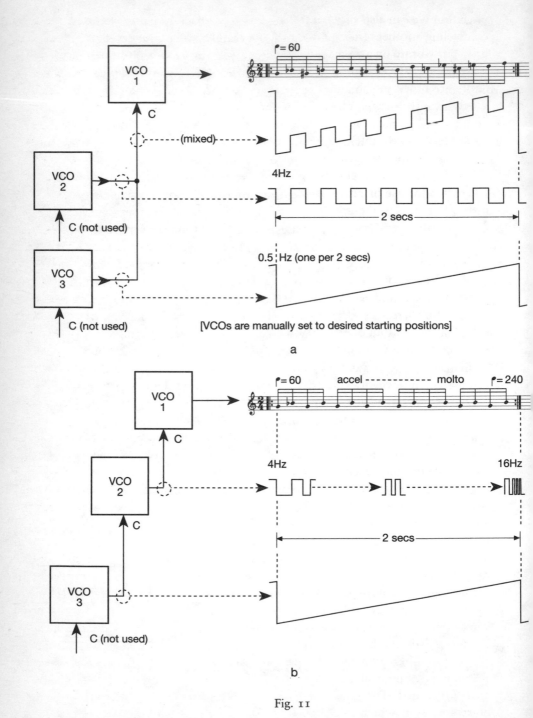

Fig. 11

pitch, but we can also vary control voltages continuously. One oscillator controlling another results in **frequency modulation**. A simple case would be to put **vibrato** on a pitch, but more complex effects are easily achieved.

In fig. 11, VCO1 is producing the audio output. The other two oscillators are tuned to sub-audio frequencies and applied as shown. In 11a the two control waveforms are summed to produce a 'castellated' ramp, and a possible musical result is shown (there will be a slight upward glissando on each note). In this patch VCOs 2 and 3 are manually set. In 11b everything is much the same except that VCO3 is now controlling VCO2, which in turn controls the audio oscillator. The tremolo figure will not now rise in pitch, because the ramp is not applied to VCO1. Instead, it affects the *speed* of the tremolo. These effects would be impossible to carry out manually, although knobs would be used to set the various levels and starting frequencies. The example also shows that for some controls we need oscillators reaching well below the audio range. It is easier to refer to very slow oscillations by the reciprocal **period** rather than frequency, for example, 40 seconds per cycle is more meaningful than .025 Hz. Sometimes slow oscillators are made specifically for control, but often the same device (which must be DC coupled, see **amplifiers**) covers both sub-audio and audio.

If a wave is made progressively more complex and many inharmonic components added, it will begin to sound 'noisy'. We need noise for many sounds, but a better way of making it than adding periodic sources is to use a random or **noise generator**.

Fig. 12a shows a sine wave compared to a typical noise waveform. The corresponding spectra (fig. 12b) show that whereas the sine has all its energy concentrated at one frequency only, that of the noise is distributed over a continuous band of frequencies. The 'white' noise shown contains an equal amount of energy at all frequencies (i.e. the same amount of energy between 10 and 20 Hz as between 1010 and 1020 Hz). In practice the generated noise is 'band-limited' to the range we are interested in, extending from around 20 kHz into the sub-audio range at the low end (for control purposes as with oscillators).

Environmental noise sources (for example, sea surf, a gas jet) tend to contain more power in the lower than the upper frequencies, and noise whose energy is inversely proportional to frequency is called 'pink' or 1/f noise. This can be produced from white noise by passing it through a low pass **filter** with the very gentle slope of −3 dB per octave. Fig. 12c illustrates pink noise attenuated by 50% (−3 dB) per octave from 50 Hz upwards. The final sketch shows a typical filtered or 'coloured' noise spectrum which might be useful in composition. If we continue

waveform types

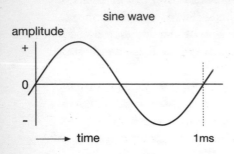

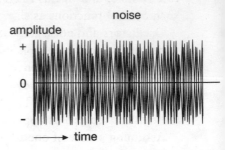

a

spectrum types

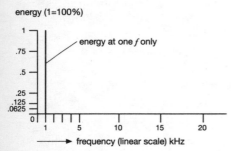

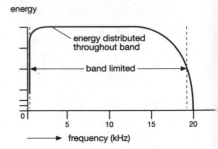

b

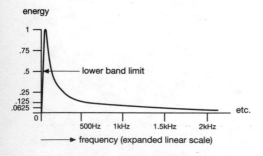

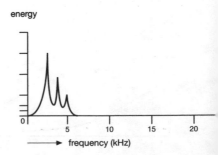

c

Fig. 12

this process of losing the top, 'hissy' end, noise eventually becomes a low rumble, and in this range (or even inaudibly low) can be used for such control functions as slightly randomizing ('humanizing') a vibrato.

Oscillators and noise generators provide us with the raw material, but to turn these continuous phenomena into useful musical events we must apply a time/amplitude **envelope** to shape the dynamics of the sound, and treat the deliberately over-rich source sounds with filters to provide the final timbre we want. These can come in either order, and sometimes the dynamic control is applied directly to the source oscillator.

Assuming a note of one second's duration, fig. 13 shows a number of

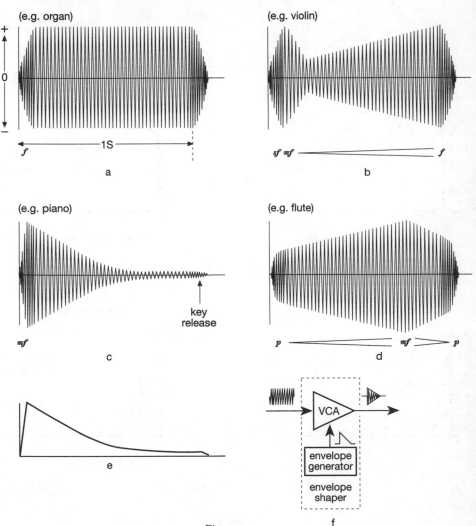

Fig. 13

typical envelopes, which are in effect **amplitude modulation** of the signal. Because the shape is symmetrical, one side only need be shown (13e). In a practical **envelope shaper**, the signal is sent through a voltage controlled amplifier (VCA) whose gain is controlled to give the desired amplitude contour. The varying voltage to do this is supplied by an envelope generator (fig. 13f), a special purpose sub-audio oscillator whose waveform, a series of jointed straight-line segments, is adjustable by the user. The more segments it has the more flexible its shape. In

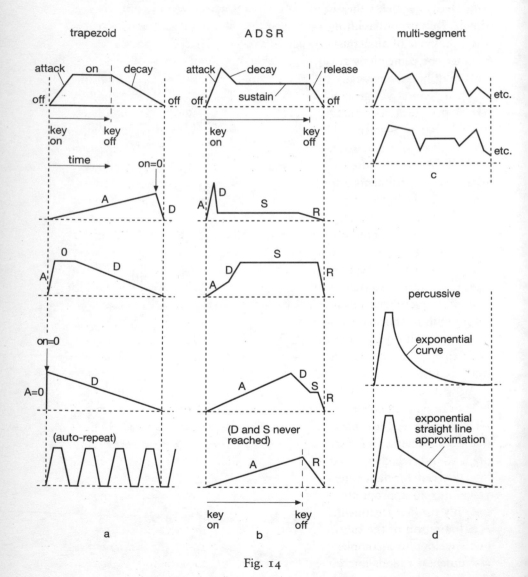

Fig. 14

nearly all cases the note will begin from silence and decay to silence, and the simplest useful shape has three segments in trapezium form, with each segment separately adjustable (fig. 14a). The commonest envelope for keyboard synthesizers is the 'ADSR', shown in fig. 14b.

Unless set to 'free run', a shaper is a 'one-shot oscillator', going through one cycle and stopping at OFF. In a keyboard synthesizer with ADSR shaper, pressing a key sends a starting **trigger**, but only part of the cycle is automatic, because after going through the pre-set Attack and Decay segments the shaper waits on Sustain as long as the key is down. Release (after lifting the finger) is the final decay, modelled on the behaviour of an acoustic instrument when input is stopped.

Once the principle is grasped, the variations are endless. Trigger signals may be automatically sent by timing devices. In a **gated** 'free run' mode a shaper will generate groups of repeated notes. Several shapers can be used in series or parallel, with cross-triggering patches. Increasing the number of segments (fig. 14c) can change a short envelope into a long term dynamic contour. Keyboard actuated shapers may respond to key velocity and/or after-touch (pressing on an already depressed key). In acoustic instruments a loud note has a different attack shape from a soft one, and a higher key velocity may be made to shorten and sharpen, as well as increase the amplitude of the attack segment (see section 6).

One of the commonest envelopes is the percussive (fig. 14d), with a very short attack time going immediately into a decay which in natural percussive sounds is **exponential**. Exponential shapers are not difficult to make, but the straight-line compromise shown is aurally acceptable (compare 'piece-wise linear', **digital synthesis techniques** 3), and can be set up with the normal straight segments. Envelopes may be deliberately unnatural, with decay segments going upwards, for example. Before or after enveloping, the source sound (unless it is already the wanted one) must be filtered.

As with envelope shaping, there is a great variety of ways in which filters can be used either separately or in groups, see **filters**. Apart from a filter's action (e.g. low pass, band pass etc.) the most important practical question is whether it is fixed or variable, and, in the context of synthesizing a sound, whether it is dynamically variable. In instrumental modelling, a fixed **formant** filter may be the main component in shaping a wave into an appropriate timbre, and in some electronic organs this is the only timbral treatment.

A limitation of the subtractive method is that because we apply only one envelope to a complex wave, internal timbre changes (which make instrumental sounds interesting) do not occur – all harmonics are given the same contour. A way to overcome this is to change the filtering during the course of an envelope, using, for example, a sharp attack with many upper harmonics, followed by a diminuendo during which nearly everything but the fundamental dies away. This sound, unique to electronic music, was one of the first to become familiar. It is made by a voltage controlled filter (illustrated in **filters**) which has been set up to pass more upper harmonics when its controlling voltage is high (see fig. 15). Numerous other configurations are possible.

Filters set for processing pitched sounds usually have broad-band, fairly gentle **responses**, and may have **resonant** peaks (if several peaks are needed, a number of filters will be used). In noise shaping, on the other hand, the filter is the only pitch controller, and is likely to be more sharply tuned. For example a procedure to make a high 'chink' sound would start with a noise generator/band pass filter/shaper patch, possibly with some **reverberation** at the output end. A very short, sharp envelope would be set, and a very narrow pass band moved up the range until the most convincing sound is found. If the envelope voltage is fed to the filter as well as the VCA the short sound will also change pitch during its course (see again **filters** for more on noise controlling). Noise and tone sources are often combined in parallel; thus we might aim to produce a flute- or organ-type note most of which is periodic but whose attack has a characteristic 'breath' or 'chuff' sound, an effect built in to many organ designs. The noise is only needed for a few milliseconds, but calls for different filtering and envelope from that applied to the tone (see fig. 16).

For further comment on subtractive synthesis see **digital synthesis techniques** 5, Strange (1983), and Wells (1981). Strange gives many

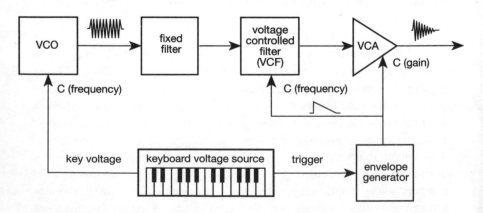

Fig. 15

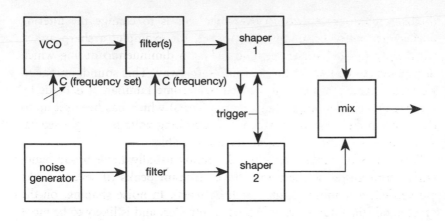

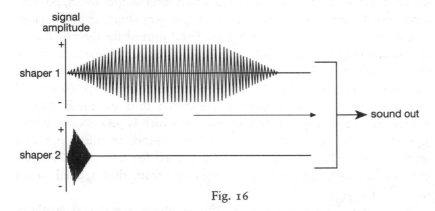

Fig. 16

examples of synthesis patches, Wells concentrates more on how devices work, with a section on filters, for which see also Chamberlin (1985).

5. Mixing, montage and modulation etc.

In all but very simple studios the **mixer** or **mixing desk** is the central unit through which all work is processed, closely associated with the patchbay, and the link between the generators and treatments and the recording machines. Its essential function is to accept a number of inputs, adjust their mutual levels, and route them to chosen destinations. Overall handling capacity is described by inputs and outputs, thus sixteen into four means that any of sixteen inputs can be sent to any or all of four output **buses** (or **groups, masters** – nomenclature varies). In most cases **panpots** allow continuous movement between two selected outputs. Groups may be further split into sub-groups (e.g. 24–8–4), and in a large desk several independent processes can go on simultaneously.

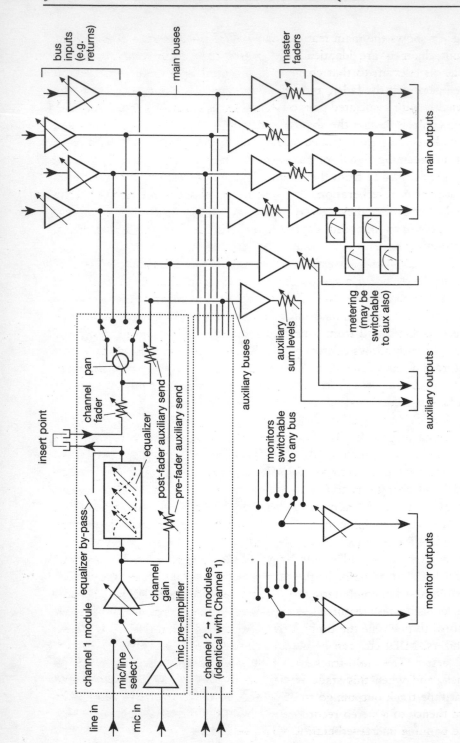

Fig. 17

Fig. 17 shows the main features of a typical small mixing desk. All the input channels are identical, and consist of a 'strip' carrying all the controls relevant to that channel. In a typical strip the control nearest the operator is the **fader,** and behind this a minimum of channel routing switches with associated panpot(s), input select switches associated with gain controls so that the channel can accept a wide variety of levels and **impedances,** a parametric **equalizer,** and auxiliary 'sends'. A send takes off an incoming signal, or part of it, at some point in the input chain, and sends it away from the mixing desk for processing. The most used treatment is **reverberation,** so on some desks sends are marked 'echo send', but in fact they can be used to access any 'outboard' treatment (as opposed to 'onboard' devices actually in the desk), such as a **digital multi-effect unit.**

The 'send' signal is treated and afterwards brought back to a 'return' on the desk – either a special input, a spare main channel or directly to an output bus. In the case of treatments such as reverberation, most of the signal is wanted in its direct form, which simulates a normal interior space (direct sound from source to ear is the earliest and loudest), and the split path allows control of the direct/treated ratio. Sends taken off before the main fader (pre-fader send) will be made even if the main fader is closed. Post-fader sends are linked with the main level, so the direct/send ratio remains constant at all fader settings.

Monitor outputs allow listening levels to be controlled independently of output line levels. Oscillators for **lining up** and many other facilities may be included, such as **MIDI** or computer control (see again **mixers**). It is impossible to give typical procedures because the desk is central to nearly all operations and using it depends not only on its own features (from primitive and fully manual to elaborate and fully automated) but on the other equipment in the studio (e.g. whether multi-track tape recorders are installed). A simple case in composing a tape piece might be: a group of sound events has been set up, and a multi-track tape recorder is to be used. In the first pass through the mixer the sounds are rehearsed in combination and sent to separate output buses and tape tracks, using desk features (e.g. equalizers) and external filters (via send/return) to fine tune the timbral balance. If **sequencers, time code** synchronizers, MIDI etc. can be used to control timing and levels, so much the better. The multi-track recording might then be built up track by track, and when this stage is satisfactory, the studio is re-patched so that tape track outputs go to mixer inputs routed to two outputs only, and thence to a stereo recording machine. On this pass, end processing like panning and reverberation might be added.

Mixers can be used in series, sub-mixers feeding the main desk, for example a small unit for microphones only could feed a pre-mix to one input of the main desk. See also **sound recording techniques** and **tape composition techniques**.

One use for a mixer would be to implement the sine additive synthesis described in section 4, but, as we saw, it is a cumbersome way to generate complex tones. Another combining process that needs only two, not eight or more sources is **amplitude modulation (AM)**, whose multiplicative (rather than additive) action is outlined under that heading. A distinction is made between AM with an audio **carrier** and a slow modulator (an example of which we saw in envelope shaping), and that with two audio inputs, which generates new tones and is therefore a potential timbre enricher.

Normal amplitude modulation retains the carrier frequency in its output, but the most musically useful type of AM is the 'suppressed-carrier' modulator (SCM), also known as **ring modulator**. An SCM can completely transform a sound, because neither input appears at the output. In the case of two sine inputs, the output consists only of the sum and difference frequencies of the two (called side frequencies). Thus if we input two sines at the consonant interval of a perfect fifth (3:2) apart, say 300 and 200 Hz, the output will contain neither 300 nor 200, but 300−200 (= 100) and 300+200 (= 500). To show this in musical notation, call 200 Hz the G below middle C (actually 196 Hz). Fig. 18a

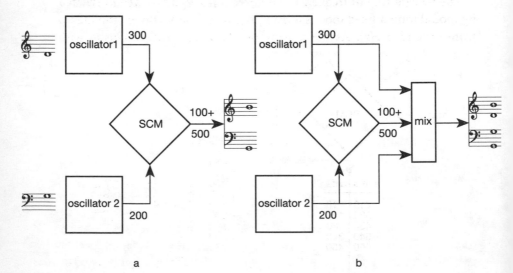

a   b

Fig. 18

shows the patch and the output pitches, and 18b shows the major chord which results if we add back the original inputs. The diamond shape is commonly used to represent an SCM, and since it is a multiplier it produces no output unless two inputs are present. For a waveform illustration of the action, see **difference frequency** and fig. 46.

If one of the inputs is not a sinusoid, the output becomes very much richer, because each partial of the complex waveform produces a pair of sidebands in the output. If both inputs are non-sinusoidal, the result is usually too noisy to be useful, but may be suitable material for subtractive treatment.

A common use for this type of modulator is the production of bell- and gong-like sounds, which contain varying amounts of **inharmonic** partials. If we take the example above (two sinusoids in a 3/2 relation-ship), and change the frequency of one of the inputs by even a small amount, the partial ratios become complex instead of simple.

Fig. 19 shows a sinusoid of 100 Hz and another tone with five components, a fundamental of 110 Hz and its first four harmonics. The modulation products are shown as a list and in chord form; none of the pitches can be accurately represented on the stave, but arrows show whether pitches are sharp or flat of the written note. Sounds like this, given a percussive envelope, are reminiscent of chimes or bells, which have several fundamentals, each with their own partials. The pitches will also vary greatly in loudness, but I have not attempted to show this.

The relationship of frequency ratio and harmonicity is well illustrated by modulating a fixed tone (say 100 Hz), with a sliding one (moving up from around 0 Hz). As the moving oscillator approaches unison with

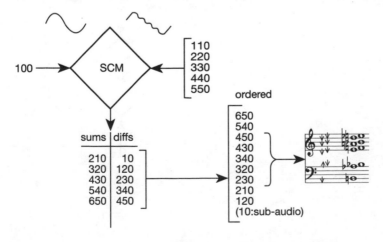

Fig. 19

the fixed, the difference frequency falls towards 0 and the sum rises towards 200 Hz. The texture varies continuously in richness, and points of consonance occur when the instantaneous ratio is simple. At the precise unison the device acts as a frequency doubler (sum=2f, diff.=0). The sidebands will always appear above and below the carrier frequency at the distance (in Hz) of the modulator on each side of it. The reason for the strange-sounding effects is that a linear shift is being applied in a naturally logarithmic system, and the spectrum reflects this distortion of normal harmonic ratios. Modulation of live instruments has been much used as a transforming technique, and it is also possible to design a single-sideband modulator (see **frequency shifter**).

When looking at VCOs in section 4 we noted the **frequency modulation** of one oscillator by another. Those examples (like AM and the shaper) involved sub-audio modulators acting on an audio carrier, producing vibrato, scales, glissandi etc. (see also next section). The products of FM with two audio inputs are, as with AM, a set of sidebands, but the results are more complex, and are discussed in **digital synthesis techniques** 6. The effect is easy to set up with analogue equipment, but very hard to control reliably, and as a basic synthesis technique it is, like additive synthesis, more effective in the digital domain. Both AM and FM can of course be literally played by ear and used freely as empirical sources of interesting sound.

The term modulation (apart from its musical usage meaning a move to another key) is used to describe several other phenomena, see **cross modulation, phase modulation** and **spatial modulation**. AM and FM as timbre modifiers are both spectral modulators, see Chamberlin (1985), Wells (1981) and Strange (1983).

So far we have regarded the equipment as a collection of separate items: stand-alone modules, patched in as needed, always have been and still are part of any studio. But even in the 1950s studios were already becoming complicated and untidy to patch and work in. It seemed to some designers a good idea to package compatible devices in a rational way, and the word 'synthesizer' entered the musical vocabulary.

6. VC synthesizers and computer hybrids etc.

As observed in the entry on **synthesizers**, the idea of the universal music machine never quite works, but two notable early attempts were the Siemens Synthesizer in Munich and the RCA Synthesizer in New York. These very expensive one-off machines were built in the late 1950s; the latter is still extant at the Columbia–Princeton Electronic Music Center in Manhattan. Though well thought out and beautifully crafted, it was never a great success, being difficult to use and only mastered by a few composers, notably Milton Babbitt. It is fully automated (very difficult at the time), and is input from wide punched paper tape not unlike pianola rolls. For further details see Harry F. Olson's *Music, Physics and Engineering*, chapter 10.4 (Olson, 1967). Olson was one of the designers of the machine. There are also several articles on the subject by Milton Babbitt, e.g. Babbitt (1964).

The voltage controlled synthesizer, pioneered by Moog in the mid-1960s, was a different concept. Though also intended to be a versatile sound-making kit, it used VC to obtain a wide range of sounds from a much smaller array of modules, and it was manufactured, available and reasonably portable. In a short time there were a number of makers using different approaches. Some units were switch-patched and compact but not very flexible, others were modular, 'open' and expandable as budgets and demands allowed. Some (e.g. Moog) used open jack patching, others (e.g. the EMS [London] Synthi machines) used pin matrices. The device line-up for a medium-sized synthesizer might be two or three VCOs, a noise generator, envelope shapers and VCAs, a selection of filters, a ring modulator, reverberator, some internal mixing, various types of manual controller, and possibly provision for audio inputs (e.g. microphones), and built-in speakers etc. Fig. 20 is a typical block diagram of such a synthesizer.

Apart from offering convenience and compactness, the new synthesizers brought keyboards into studios. A VCO can be controlled by a 'ladder' of voltages selected by a keyboard, and we have discussed the principle of triggering an envelope each time a key is pressed, as well as the possibility of a dynamic (velocity-dependent) output. The keyboard's output is a **staircase**, and an additional feature may be a portamento or glissando option, the **slew rate** of the voltage steps being adjustable by the player. The limitation of the simple ladder is that it can only send one value of voltage at a time (i.e. it is monophonic), but the synthesizer itself could often only produce one or two voices simultaneously in any case. Keyboards made conventional music easier to realize electronically, and brought the creation of the first big selling electronic albums, for example, Carlos's *Switched On Bach*, realized on a Moog synthesizer. VCOs are prone to frequency drift, however (see **oscillators**), and holding tuning with acoustic instruments was always a problem, especially in live concerts.

As well as a keyboard giving discrete voltage steps, one needs continuously adjustable voltage inputs to vary filters, loudness levels and other parameters that do not respond well to steps. Two ways of doing this

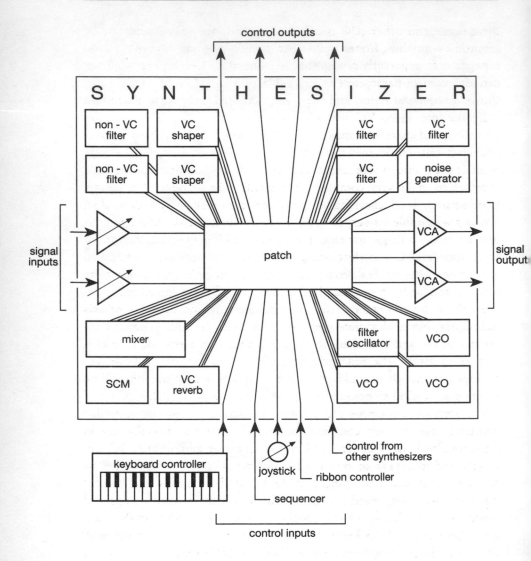

Fig. 20

are: 1. a 'ribbon controller' (Moog's device) – a length of spring steel stretched over a resistive strip. A finger can press it down anywhere along its length, and perform slides and vibrati much as on a violin string; 2. a **joystick** geared to two variable resistors, giving two outputs in an XY configuration (see fig. 104). Trigger inputs can be provided in various ways, by push buttons for example, or (in the ribbon device) a slot which can be bridged anywhere by a finger.

Because keyboards and continuous controllers are fully patchable, and their range and offset (DC mean level) adjustable, scales need not be semitonic – anything from a microtonal pseudo-glissando to wide-spaced arpeggios, to apparently random successions of pitches, is possible. They can also control parameters other than pitch, e.g. filtering. Fig. 20 also shows a **sequencer** input, and these are discussed under that heading.

By the late 1960s VC synthesizers were becoming larger and more powerful, and apart from making possible a new kind of tapeless, performed electronic music, they took their place with the free-standing equipment in the studio, where several complete synthesizers might be patched together to make very complex instruments. The amount of patching, knob-setting, level checking etc. became formidable, and even then nothing was stable for very long because the smallest change in temperature or mains voltage, for example, would upset something. But at the same time as VC was developing, the first mini-computers were also appearing, offering real computing power (though very modest by today's standards) in reasonably compact and affordable packages.

Synthesis by computer is discussed in the entry on **digital synthesis techniques**, but at that time could only be done on large expensive-to-use machines, and even then not in a real time interactive mode, which was years away. The practical, accessible studio of the day was VC analogue, although it could be seen that it was only a matter of time before pure digital techniques would take over (as indeed they have).

The early mini-computers had neither the speed nor the **resolution** for synthesis, but in 1967 computer control of analogue equipment was pioneered by James Gabura and Gustave Ciamaga in Toronto (Gabura, 1964), and in a year or two it had become apparent to a number of designers that small computers could be used to handle the control side with precision, speed and repeatability (since complete set-ups and sequences could be stored in memory). Among the leaders in this field were Zinovieff and Cockerell of EMS (London), who made a range of VC synthesizers using both commercially available mini-computers and specially designed digital sequencers to control a number of parameters simultaneously. To indicate the size of analogue patch that digital control made possible, fig. 21 shows the patch for my piece *Romantic Interiors*, for violin, cello and tape, as sketched at the time.*

This work was written in 1973 for realization on the Synthi 100, the largest standard EMS machine. Its sequencer is digital, fully editable and outputs 6 × 256-step staircases, with triggering (keys) in pairs, plus an

*Cary, Tristram, *Romantic Interiors for 4-track tape, violin and cello*, first performance Queen Elizabeth Hall, London, 1973.

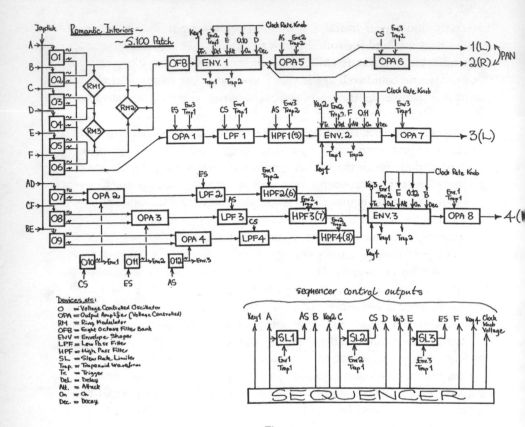

Fig. 21

independent key track and a time control voltage (labelled CLOCK KNOB VOLTAGE) which is voltage control of a clock oscillator. At the bottom of the sketch are the sequencer outputs, letter and number coded to the control inputs of the audio patch at the top. Note that the description ring modulator is used, not SCM, and the slew limiter is, in effect, a variable portamento control.

Hybrid techniques of this kind are still an option, and most electronic music studios are a mixture of older analogue and modern digital gear with some **keyboard synthesizers**. Although nearly all synthesizers on sale now are digital, analogue and hybrid working is common in live performance set-ups, which may use, for instance, MIDI control of an analogue mixer.

7. Conclusion

The analogue methods outlined include powerful ways of making interesting sounds, but textures of any complexity are hard to control precisely and repeat exactly; a useful working motto in an analogue studio is: if you find the sound you want, get it on to tape before it goes away. Hybrid techniques can overcome this problem to some extent, but today one could well argue that if you are going to use a computer at all it is simpler to stay in the digital domain. There is a naturalness about analogue synthesis that appeals strongly, and we noted that much effort goes into designing digital machines that have an analogue 'feel'. There is an important place in music for the uncalibrated, extempore gesture, and alongside the high-tech electronic equivalents of elaborately organized instrumental scores there will always be simple but effective pieces needing little equipment and no automation at all. Modern electronic devices last for a long time, and even if no new research is done on analogue synthesis, most of the thousands of machines now existing will still be playing for many years to come.

To summarize the relevant references, Wells (1981), Chamberlin (1985) and Strange (1983) are recommended for theory and studio methods. References mentioned at the end of section 1 as having useful historical comment, i.e. Appleton (1975), Ernst (1977), Russcol (1972), Manning (1987) and Griffiths (1979) also refer to technical aspects of analogue studio development, and some have analyses of pieces. Two further relevant books are Adams (1986) and Keane (1980). An interesting study of one person's search for new methods of synthesis is Daphne Oram's *An Individual Note* (Oram, 1972).

Analogue-to-digital converter (ADC) An input device for a digital system, which converts steady voltages (**DC**) or continuous functions into lists of discrete numbers. In digital processing of sound, the ADC is fed by a microphone or audio line, and its accuracy and that of the complementary **digital-to-analogue converter** (**DAC**) are limiting factors in the fidelity of the whole system.

The principles of sampling are explained in **digital synthesis techniques** 1. Designing ADCs for high quality audio work proved difficult for many years, because of the high speeds and **resolutions** called for. The basic problem is that the digital system cannot predict what the sound will do next, and must examine and evaluate each voltage sample separately. Because conversion takes time, the continuously varying input is processed by a **sample-and-hold** circuit, giving a series of discrete voltages that remain constant long enough for the converter to operate.

There are several methods, but for music applications the most popular is the 'successive approximation register' (SAR), which works by using a DAC within the ADC. Each incoming voltage sample is compared with the voltage generated by the DAC, in turn generated by an equivalent **binary** number. With the most significant (lefthand) bit set to 1, and the other bits to 0, the DAC will output half its maximum voltage (e.g. the maximum for six bits (111111) is 63; 100000 = 32). Comparing this voltage with the input, the associated logic either leaves the 1 in place or sets it to 0, depending on whether it finds the sample above or below .5 maximum value. Continuing through the number to the least significant end, all the bits are set with increasing precision until the whole word is as near as possible to the digital equivalent of the analogue voltage.

High quality music conversion requires at least fourteen bits of accuracy and sampling rates of 40 kHz or above (see again **digital synthesis techniques**), a combination which involves the SAR in over half a million approximations per second per audio channel. Numerous problems with stability, the production of spurious data, etc., have largely been overcome in today's converters, which meet high standards of quality but are in general more complex and hence more costly than DACs of comparable performance. For more details and descriptions of other types see Pohlmann (1989), Barbeau and Corinthios (1984), Chamberlin (1985) and Watkinson (1988).

Anechoic   Having no **echo** or **reverberation**. Anechoic chambers are used for tests requiring a totally lifeless acoustic. See also **acoustic treatments**.

Antinode   In a **standing wave** system, the point of maximum amplitude, and the opposite of **node**. See also **bowed strings, brass instruments** and **woodwind instruments**.

Antiphase   See **phase**

Aperiodic   Having no discernible cycle of repetition, so no tendency to **resonance**, e.g. **noise**. See **period/ic**.

Arithmetic and logic unit (ALU)   See **central processing unit**

Artificial intelligence (AI)   The early computers were enormous, slow, temperamental and difficult to use, but a common popular description was 'electronic brain', largely because, unlike simple calculators, they could perform logical operations and had memories. The expression 'artificial intelligence' was also coined some time ago, and many people thought that it would not be long before computers really could be made to work like human intelligences.

The progress of computers and of research into the brain have run side by side for some years, but there is little sign of the gap closing. It is unlikely that even the operating principles are similar, and the mysteries of emotion, intuition and other qualities we take for granted have not begun to be solved. An interesting look at this dichotomy can be found in 'Artificial Intelligence: Prospects', chapter 19 of Douglas R. Hofstadter's *Gödel, Escher, Bach* – indeed the whole book is recommended reading (Hofstadter, 1980). In essence AI is an approach to programming designed to reflect the way a person goes about learning and decision-making, and it has wide applications in music software.

Computer programs divide into two main classes. In **algorithmic** programs a definite solution is sought, and an appropriate procedure (algorithm) is designed for the purpose. A musicological research program might say: 'Sort through these 500 Byzantine chants and list those that have as their second interval a rising minor third.' Precisely devised music can also be generated in this way – 'I want the following pitches at the following starting times, durations and loudnesses, and here is the **timbre** specification.'

The other approach is **heuristic**, or 'finding', which needs a different kind of program allowing trial and error methods to be used. It works by user interaction, and leaves room for uncertainties and missing input data that would cause a rigidly precise program to crash. A composer may wish to build a piece from all sorts of starting points, not necessarily from pitch or time information. AI programs can be designed which learn the composer's preferences and methods of work.

The commonest application of the AI type of program is in games like chess. The machine appears to respond 'intelligently', but only because of the human ingenuity that went into writing the software. Making art can certainly resemble a game, with a protocol of rules, structures that must be built in certain ways, legal and illegal moves, and provision for chance occurrences by controllable degrees of randomness, like games with dice. The most rewarding results happen when both person and machine are doing what each does best – the composer providing the ideas, intuition and emotion – in fact the brain power, and the computer its tirelessness, speed, accuracy and almost faultless memory.

There are new approaches to AI which were inconceivable in the days of small resident memories and slow-access bulk storage. One of these is industrial robotics, where machines have to make a large number of decisions, some of them based on visual inputs. Another is an 'expert' system, in which a data base is stocked with a mass of information relevant to a particular set of problems. A whole library of medical data can thus be stored, with details of drugs, diagnostics, case histories etc., and be accessible to many users. When relevant details of a case are input, the machine searches for matching data and suggests a course to follow. If it needs more data it will ask for it, and its answers can certainly include 'can't do it' and 'I'm not sure but try X'. The problem with such systems is that human beings must constantly check and update them because the machine cannot distinguish useful data from garbage (though it can of course query something it considers abnormal, for instance, in a sequence of numbers expected to fall within a certain range).

Expert systems for music might be personalized to the needs of one composer, or hold a general fund of data, perhaps for interactive teaching. A system that is gradually absorbing a composer's work and methods could respond to: 'Give me the retrograde version of the note series I used in last year's quartet', or 'For this passage use texture no. 104'. In a modest way, reference library facilities can be incorporated into quite small systems.

AI is a very large subject, occupying whole university departments. For more reading on AI in music, **psychoacoustics** and musicology, a good starting point is two special issues of *Computer Music Journal* (Roads, 1980), with articles by Curtis Roads, Marvin Minsky and others, under the general title 'Artificial Intelligence and Music'. See also other references to AI in Hofstadter (1980) chapters 10, 18 and 19.

ASCII   American Standard Code for Information Interchange. Worldwide standard communication code, using seven **bits** of a **byte** to give a possible 128 characters. The eighth ('parity') bit may be either 0 or 1.

Assembly code   See **computer languages**

Asymmetrical waveform   See **symmetrical waveform**

Attack   The onset of a musical note, very often the part that best reveals the character of the instrument making it. Some attacks are not at all aggressive, but the term still applies. In **envelope shapers**, the attack is the first segment.

Attenuat/ion, -or   The opposite of **amplifier**, this is a device designed to reduce a signal's **amplitude** by a known amount. May be complex, but often a simple **pássive, resistive** device.

Audio frequency (AF)   A **frequency** (measured in **hertz**) within the audible range. Frequencies outside it may also have an audible effect, such as **sub/-** and **super/sonic** tones, which can interact with and change audible ones, and must therefore be considered. For young human ears, a range of *c.* 20 Hz–16 kHz or higher is normal, but older people must expect a progressive loss of range, particularly at the high end (see Taylor (1965), Wood (1962), Olson (1967) and Roederer (1979)). AF **amplifiers** should be substantially **linear** well outside the actual limits of hearing, and may have a **response** from 0 Hz (DC) to 50 kHz or higher.

Azimuth   The angle between the head gap(s) and the tape path in a tape recorder (it should be exactly 90°). See **lining up, tape recorder design** and fig. 206.

B

Background noise An ingredient (usually unwanted) in nearly all environments. In analogue systems it may be generated internally (e.g. **thermal noise,** tape noise) or acoustically collected with a wanted input. In digital systems it may cause errors. Also generally applied to any unwanted material – thus TV commercials are noise *vis-à-vis* the film they interrupt. Noise is very much part of our lives, and it can be alarming to remove it altogether (see **acoustic treatments**). In some cases steps can be taken to reduce it (see **noise reduction**), and it is important to distinguish between noise as a nuisance and noise as a creative tool (see **analogue synthesis techniques 4**).

Background processing Non-urgent jobs (e.g. lengthy calculations) to which a computer can revert when not occupied with high priority tasks such as running **real-time** music.

Balance 1. (verb) To achieve the best results in a recording session by adjusting **microphone placement,** recording levels at the **mixing desk,** etc. 2. (noun) In **stereo,** the left/right proportion of a signal.

Balanced line A signal transmission system with two **phase**-opposed lines. For details and illustration see **unbalanced.**

Band/pass, /reject See **filters**

Band/width An inclusive range of **frequencies,** used typically to describe the output of an **aperiodic** device like a **noise generator,** or the **response** of e.g. an **amplifier** or **filter.** It is described by stating the lower and upper frequency limits, but since these points are rarely sharply defined the band is by convention measured from the points at which the level drops below −3 **decibels** of the average level within the band (fig. 22). See also **formant** and **resonance.** In digital systems bandwidth is related to **baud rate.**

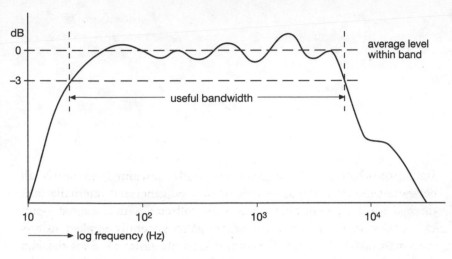

Fig. 22

Basic   See **computer languages**

Baud rate   Named after Emile Baudot, this was originally a telegraphy word, but now refers to **bits** per second (also BPS), a measure of a system's **bandwidth** or speed at which it can handle a serial bit stream. Edmunds (1985) suggests that BPS should be used, and the meaning of baud changed to transitions per second, a better measure of bandwidth since in codes like EFM (see **compact disc**) one transition can represent several bits. See also **sound recording techniques** 3.

Beats   A periodic rise and fall in the loudness of a sound produced when two notes of slightly different **frequency** are sounded together. The beat frequency is equal to the difference in the two frequencies. See **difference frequency** and **dissonance**.

Beat frequency oscillator (BFO)   See **oscillators**

Bel   See **decibel**

Bias/ing   A constant voltage or current applied to ensure that a device operates in the way intended for a particular purpose. For biasing of transistors and valves, see **amplifiers**. To maximize **linearity** of perform-ance, tape recording heads are biased with a supersonic AC, typically 100 kHz or higher (see **sound recording techniques**). Also a verb, 'to bias' something.

Bi-directional   Describes a microphone responsive on both faces, but not to sounds from the sides. Also called figure-of-eight response. See **microphones**.

Binary code   The two-digit (0 and 1) arithmetic system universally used in computers (some early machines were decimal, but ten-state circuitry is cumbersome). The basic device in a binary machine is a simple two-way switching circuit whose output is either high or low voltage, representing the switch states on/off, the logic states yes/no or the logic digits 1/0. Huge numbers of switching circuits are needed, but both size and cost are tiny and they can operate at very high speeds – several million of them may reside on one **chip**.

Binary code (radix = 2) represents numbers in the same way as decimal (radix = 10), with the most significant **Bit** (BInary digiT) on the left, but the carry is at powers of 2 instead of powers of 10 (i.e. each shift to the left is a doubling). The lower place value has the effect that numbers (**words**) are longer than their decimal equivalents – 10000 (binary), for example, is only 16 (decimal). One way in which computers are rated is by the number of bits that can be processed simultaneously in parallel, and bits are usually processed in groups or multiples of 8, an 8 bit word being called a **byte**. Memory capacity is rated in kilobytes and megabytes.

It is rare for a user to have to deal directly with binary code, but on occasions when working with music software it may be necessary to convert numbers, and it is useful to know how to do so. Apart from decimal, there are two commonly used shorthand notations for binary which are much easier for human beings to memorize than long strings of 0s and 1s, see **hexadecimal, octal**.

Take the number 785, for example. To convert to binary, we first find the nearest power of 2 below it – in this case 512 (i.e. 2^9). Each column of digits in the binary system represents a value of a power of 2 as illustrated below. Put down a 1, and 512 beneath it. Subtracting 512 from 785 gives 273, and we look for the next power of 2 below this – 256. Put another 1 to the right of the first in the 256 column. 273 − 256 = 17, so the nearest power of 2 is 16, and just 1 is left over. Note the three powers between 256 and 16, and put a 0 for each, then a 1 for 16, three 0s for 8, 4 and 2, and finally the odd 1 at the least significant end. The conversion should look like this:

1	1	0	0	0	1	0	0	0	1
512	256	(128)	(64)	(32)	16	(8)	(4)	(2)	1

After converting you also know that a minimum of ten bits are needed to represent 785 in binary. To convert the other way, run to the left along the word noting the value for each position, pick out the 1s and add their values together. See also **Boolean algebra**.

Binaural   The binaural effect is our ability to identify the location of a sound source, mainly by detecting the **phase** (or time) difference between the arrival of a pressure wave at the two ears. For further discussion see **stereo**, which aims to construct the effect artificially. See also **cocktail party effect** and **psychoacoustics**.

Bio-music   Sometimes used of any 'natural' acoustic occurrence given musical significance (e.g. some **environmental music**), but usually music in which the feedback loop (see **analogue synthesis techniques** 2) includes input from the body itself (e.g. brain or muscle activity). The audio possibilities of electroencephalograms were looked at as early as 1934, and David Rosenboom, one of the pioneer workers in the field, summarizes the history in 'The Performing Brain' (Rosenboom, 1990). One of the first pieces using brain current (the alpha rhythm) was Alvin Lucier's 1965 *Music for Solo Performer* (see Strange, 1983). Another early experimenter was Manfred Eaton, who describes work at the University of Missouri in the early 1970s in Eaton (1970). Dancer-controlled music using sensitive floors or radio transmitters has been designed by Greg Schiemer in Australia, and many other examples can be found (an early body-controlled instrument was the **Theremin**). The arrival of **MIDI** in the 1980s has opened up new possibilities, and one of the most elaborate bio-control systems to date is Stelarc,* which features control by brainwaves, heartbeats, muscles, blood flow and voice, and has laser beams which follow eye movement. Two other bio-music artists of particular note are Michel Waisvisz and Jeanette Yanikan. See also **live performance electronic music**, Cope (1977) chapter 25 and Ernst (1977) chapter 8.

Bistable   Describes a switching circuit having two states (typically 'set' = 1, 'reset' = 0), both of them stable until triggered into the other state. See **flip-flop** and **Schmitt trigger**.

Bit   BI(nary digi)T. See **binary code**.

---

*Stelarc, *Beyond the Body* NMA 6, pp. 27–30. NMA Publications, PO Box 185, Brunswick, VIC 3056, Australia.

Bit stream   See **baud rate**

Black box   A catch-all term for any device or complex which can be regarded as performing a particular function but whose internal workings are not specified. In designing a new system, for example, there may be several unspecified black boxes in the sketches, for devices that are foreshadowed as necessary but not yet thought out. See **block diagram**.

Block   A group of similar units regarded as an entity for processing purposes, thus a block of sound samples is a large number of **words** of the same length representing one sound (see **digital synthesis techniques** 1–3). In programming, a group of instructions may be regarded as a block. In storage media, usable space is divided into blocks of equal size.

Block diagram   A simplified hardware plan, showing functions rather than physical characteristics, and usually omitting necessary but ancillary services such as power supplies. Like maps, such diagrams can be drawn on a wide range of scales. Fig. 23 shows the equipment of a small studio in four degrees of detail.

     Blocks can be classified into five different types (see **analogue synthesis techniques** 3). The same general principles are used for digital as for analogue block diagrams, but in some cases 'ribbons' or 'roads' are drawn instead of single connecting lines, the width of which indicate the number of parallel **bits** carried by the link. Diagrams of this type, but for software, are called **flowcharts**. See also **patch**.

Boolean algebra   Named after the English mathematician George Boole (1815–64), this is a system of symbolic logic, with little resemblance to conventional algebra. Typical Boolean operators are *and* and *or* and a typical logical instruction to a computer could be: *if* (the equation) a = b (is true), *and* [if] x > y (is true), *then* z = 10. The computer tests both equations for truth, and does nothing if either is false. The practical form of the conditional depends on the **computer language** being used. It is the ability to use logic that makes computers more than mere number machines, and arithmetical and logical operations work well together since both are binary (having only two states). See **binary code** for the relationship between binary and decimal notations.

     The logical *and* gate is like two switches in series: no current flows

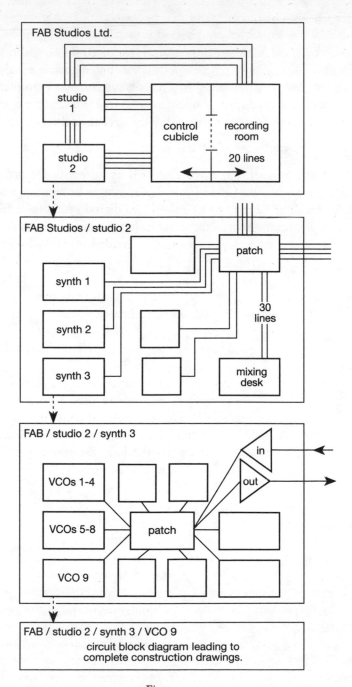

Fig. 23

unless both are closed; *or* resembles two switches in parallel: current flows if either is closed. It also flows if both are closed, so this is called the 'inclusive' *or* ('You can have eggs or steak for lunch' allows the possibility of having both). A third operator is the 'exclusive' *or* – *xor*, which means 'either but not both' ('That person is either dead or alive'). The behaviour of each type of operator can be summarized in a 'truth table'. In the following diagrams, 1 stands for true, o for false:

A	B	A *and* B
o	o	o
1	o	o
o	1	o
1	1	1

A	B	A *or* B
o	o	o
1	o	1
o	1	1
1	1	1

A	B	A *xor* B
o	o	o
1	o	1
o	1	1
1	1	o

A *not* gate reverses logic states, i.e. input 1 gives output o, and vice versa. Thus groups of different logic 'gates' can be used to perform various complex functions. In a Boolean operation on a group of digits, each vertical pair is tested separately – there is no carry as in normal arithmetic, though one can choose to read a group of logical outputs as a number (i.e. with place significance). For comparison, here are two arithmetic and three logical operations on the same binary groups, with decimal equivalents in brackets:

add	*subtract*	*and*	*or*	*xor*
1001 (9)	1001	1001	1001	1001
0101 (5)	0101	0101	0101	0101
1110 (14)	0100 (4)	0001 (1)	1101 (13)	1100 (12)

It may seem that all this has little to do with music, but some knowledge of logical manipulation is useful in compositional programming (see **computer music composition techniques**). There is an extensive literature on symbolic logic, some of it in the realm of philosophy. A clear, readable exposition is Allan Lytel's *ABC's of Boolean Algebra* (Lytel, 1969). See also **mask**.

Boom   1. Unwanted low frequency **resonance** in an environment. 2. The moveable arm of a **microphone** stand, varying from small ones like those used to suspend a microphone over a table, to the very large booms used in film and TV studios.

Bowed strings   All pitched acoustic instruments except **idiophones** are 'coupled systems', in which a tone generator is linked with some kind

of amplifier or **resonator**. Loudness depends on the amount of air disturbed by a sound source: a string by itself, having no surface to speak
of, moves very little air and makes a thin, ineffectual sound. In all string
instruments the vibrating string is therefore invariably coupled to a
resonating system or acoustic amplifier. This may be a large flat surface
(piano soundboard) or two surfaces enclosing a body of air (guitar,
violin etc.).

The most obvious differences between the portable plucked strings
(guitar, banjo etc.) and the bowed strings are in the height of the strings
above the body and the curvature of the top of the **bridge** (see fig. 27).
These features enable the player to change the angle of the bow freely
and play each string separately. Fig. 24 shows the main parts of a violin.

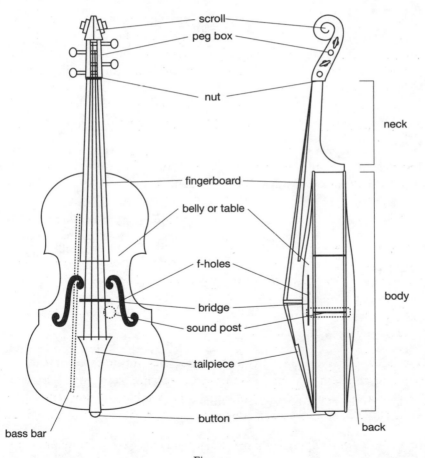

scroll
peg box
nut
neck
fingerboard
belly or table
f-holes
bridge
sound post
tailpiece
body
button
back
bass bar

Fig. 24

Strings

A vibrating string or wire sets up **standing waves** (see fig. 191) in a series of modes which form a **harmonic series**. Since the ends are fixed, they must be points of no activity (**nodes**), and in the **fundamental** mode the whole of the string moves in a body, the centre being the point of maximum displacement (antinode). This mode produces the lowest note possible, and its **frequency** is determined by the length of string free to vibrate, its mass per unit length, and its tension. Its length is clearly fixed in any one case, and for ease of control and tonal coherence its tension should be kept as similar as possible for all strings. This leaves its mass as the only convenient variable, which is why heavier gauges are used for lower strings, and they are often artificially weighted by winding with metal wire (covering).

All notes apart from the fundamental are produced 1. by 'stopping' the string against the fingerboard, which inactivates the portion between the finger and the nut, or 2. by causing the string to vibrate in a higher mode by inducing more nodes than just those at the ends. In this technique a finger is held lightly against the string at one node point, forcing the other nodes to appear since the string can only divide into precisely equal segments. This gives a harmonic appropriate to the number of segments (so, for instance, four segments will give the double octave of the fundamental), and when playing any of these 'natural harmonics' the whole string is active (the principle is shown in fig. 26b). Both pitch-changing methods can be combined as 'artificial harmonics', where the string is firmly stopped by one finger and lightly touched further up by another.

Whichever way the basic pitch of the note is determined, the string never vibrates at that pitch only. Different proportions of many higher harmonics ('overtones') are always present (and probably some **inharmonic** tones as well), and this complex wave is passed down to the body of the instrument, contributing to its **timbre**. The richness of this timbre depends partly on the way the string is made to vibrate.

Bow

The bow consists of a bundle of horse hair under adjustable tension, and the modern concave ('incurved') shape was introduced in the later eighteenth century. Rosin (solidified distilled gum of turpentine) is applied to the bow to increase friction, its action usually being described as 'stick-slip'. The bow grips the string, which increases its restoring force as the bow displaces it, until it overcomes the friction and springs back to beyond its position of rest. On its return it is gripped again, and so on. The resulting **waveform** approaches the harmonically rich **ramp** or sawtooth (see fig. 55 in **digital synthesis techniques**), but the actual vibration pattern of the string depends on factors like the bow's pressure, speed and position within the string's length – the nearer to the bridge (sul ponticello) the bow is used, the more upper harmonic generation will be encouraged.

Body
The table or belly of a violin is made of spruce, which carries sound much faster down the grain than across. The back is maple, which is harder and denser. The bridge is held in place solely by string pressure, and can be adjusted to fine-tune the tone. The sound post, adjacent to the top-string foot of the bridge, carries high frequencies through to the stiff back of the instrument, while the bass bar, glued under the table from near the 'bass' foot of the bridge, helps to distribute the lower frequencies through the more flexible belly. With the air inside (vented by the two 'ʃ' holes), the whole forms an elaborate acoustic system. Its proportions are traditionally based on the **golden section**, and although the acoustic significance of this method has never been clearly established, it has certainly worked well for nearly four centuries.

We have only looked at a few of the many features and techniques of this richly endowed family of instruments; others include the plucking mode (pizzicato), the use of mutes, multiple stopping, glissando etc. See Hutchins (1978) and Leipp (1969), both of whom have interesting analyses of violin construction and acoustic action, while Turetsky (1989) gives extensive information about contemporary string techniques (in this case the double bass). For general background Taylor (1965), Wood (1962), Olson (1967), Hutchins (1978) and Roederer (1979) are useful books on musical acoustics. See also **analogue synthesis techniques 2, brass instruments, partial** and **woodwind instruments**.

Brass instruments   The material from which it is made has little bearing on whether an instrument is classed as brass or woodwind. 'Brass' instruments can be made of wood (cornetto, serpent), and 'woodwinds' are often of metal (most flutes, all saxophones). The main distinguishing features are: 1. Woodwinds use reeds (real or air 'reeds') to generate sound; brass instruments use the lips of the player. 2. Woodwind instruments are pierced, changing the length of the tube by opening holes, whereas the brass are airtight systems with no holes (pierced, cup mouthpiece instruments like serpent, key bugle, ophicleide are now obsolete as orchestral instruments). 3. Woodwinds use only the first few harmonics (see **harmonic series, woodwind instruments**), but the brass play at least up to the eighth, sometimes to the sixteenth. The two parts of the coupled system can be looked at separately.

Generators

Unlike a string (see **bowed strings**), a lip generator by itself has poor frequency definition. The lips are stretched across a cup-like opening, making an 'embouchure'. The size and shape of the cup help to define the pitch area (larger for low instruments) and the 'bite' or upper harmonic content of the final output. For less 'brassy' instruments like the French horn the cup is more gently conical and the edges of the opening to the main tube less sharp. Fig. 25 shows typical sections of mouthpieces for horn (25a and b) and trumpet (25c).

The **frequency** at which the player's lips vibrate depends on the wind pressure applied and the tightness of the lips. The aim is to match the initial lip vibration as closely as possible to the pitch expected, so that the pipe coupled to the mouthpiece at once sounds the correct harmonic. If this target is missed, or only reached after the note has begun, wrong or 'cracked' notes result.

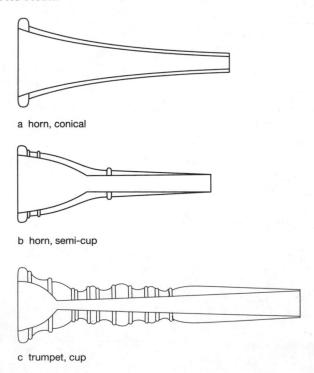

a horn, conical

b horn, semi-cup

c trumpet, cup

Fig. 25

Resonators

Again in contrast to the strings, it is the resonator that determines the exact pitch of the note, not the generator. The **resonance** in the pipe causes **standing waves** (see fig. 191) to form in the air column. These waves must have antinodes (areas of maximum air activity) at the open ends of the pipe, but the number of antinodes and nodes (points of no activity) within the pipe is variable, giving a number of notes which ascend as a harmonic series. Instruments in which the length of the pipe cannot be changed (bugle, hunting horn) can only sound the notes of one harmonic series typically in such instruments the third, fourth, fifth and sixth (the notes of nearly all bugle calls), but occasionally the second, seventh and eighth. Hence the **fundamental** mode has one node at the centre of the pipe and an antinode at each end. Fig. 26 shows the nodal pattern for fundamental (first) and third harmonics for a cylindrical open pipe (26a) and a string (26b) (for comment on stopped and conical pipes see **woodwind instruments**).

For some instruments (e.g. trumpet, trombone) the normal working compass ends at the eighth harmonic, but others (e.g. French horn) are

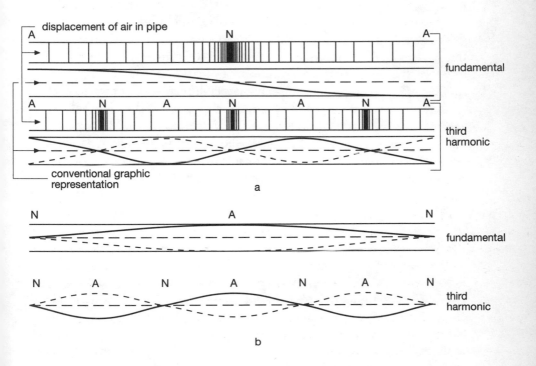

Fig. 26

designed to exploit the close harmonic spacing between the eighth and sixteenth harmonics, allowing conjunct melodic music to be played. Since non-variable instruments can only play broken chords (and only one chord at that) below the eighth harmonic, some means had to be found to adjust the length of the tube and hence the pitch of the entire harmonic series.

The simple and elegant slide of the trombone (earlier the sackbut) has been in use for centuries. The more complicated valve mechanism gradually took over on trumpets, horns and other instruments during the nineteenth century. Most brass instruments are designed to play melodic music only as far down as the second harmonic, not the fundamental, and the principle is to provide enough pitch variation – by means of additional series – to cover one semitone short of the widest gap, which is the perfect fifth between the second and third harmonics (see fig. 99). The gap to be covered is seven semitones. In slide instruments there are seven 'stopping places', but of course everything in between is possible as well. In valved instruments, pistons or rotary mechanisms switch in extra lengths of tube while keeping the whole system airtight. Three valves lower the pitch by a half tone, a whole tone and one and a half tones respectively, and combinations of no valves to all three together give the necessary seven pitches. Further up the series there are many overlaps, and notes can be played as, for example, the fourth harmonic of one series or the fifth of another. For the few instruments (e.g. tuba) that play conjunct music down to the fundamental, a fourth valve lowers the pitch by two and a half tones.

Much has been omitted from this brief description, mutes, 'crooks' of different lengths to change key, tuning slides, combination and 'double' instruments. A good survey of the whole subject is Anthony Baines's *Brass Instruments, Their History and Development* (Baines, 1976). For acoustic analysis of pipes see Hutchins (1978), Taylor (1965) and Olson (1967).

Breadboard/, -ing The rough hook-up of a circuit, for prototype test purposes.

Break 1. A term used particularly of the clarinet family of **woodwind instruments**. The place in an instrument's compass where the first **overblown** series begins, and the area of weakest notes. Clarinets overblow at the twelfth (third **harmonic**), not the octave (second harmonic) and in the case of the Bb size (lowest note E below middle C), the break is at B above middle C. 2. A similar phenomenon with voices, when changing over to a different part of the range. 3. In jazz, a short, often florid solo passage. 4. In music notation a short pause usually indicated by a comma-like sign.

Bridge 1. In a string instrument, the link between the string(s) and the resonator. May be a long, curved bar with pins to guide the strings (piano), a shaped wooden piece held in place by string tension (violin), or a bar glued to the body of the instrument (guitar). Fig. 27 compares violin and guitar bridges. See **bowed strings** and **piano** *acoustic*. 2. Type of circuit **network**.

Buffer 1. In computers, a temporary store to hold data during processing. 2. In analogue circuits, an isolating device, interposed to prevent one circuit influencing another.

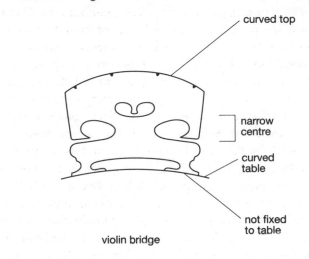

curved top

narrow
centre

curved
table

not fixed
to table

violin bridge

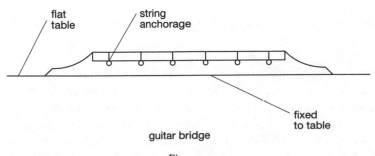

flat
table

string
anchorage

fixed
to table

guitar bridge

Fig. 27

Bus (sometimes **buss**) As with the motor variety, this is short for omnibus. A common line to which a number of branches are connected, taking from, adding to, or merely looking at the contents of the bus. Bus architecture looks like a main road with side roads connected to modules of different kinds. Alternative architectures are rings, where modules are arranged in continuous succession, or stars, where all peripheral modules are referred to a central one. In analogue equipment, the output of a bus will be the sum of all the signals feeding it. See **analogue synthesis techniques** and **mixers and mixing desks**.

Buzz track Tape or magnetic film that has been run in record mode but carries no **signal** (can also be used of optical track). For cutting in if 'silence' is required, because any change in the normal noise levels for that particular system or batch of stock will be evident. Completely silent stock, such as **leader,** can sound like an accidental switch-off.

By-pass A direct connection across a whole circuit or device, inactivating it. By-pass switches are useful to check 'before and after' conditions when setting a **treatment,** or to allow devices to be active or not without re-**patching**.

Byte A group (**word**) of **bits,** normally eight. See **binary code** and **nibble**.

C

Cancellation The result of adding two identical waves in certain special circumstances. Waves involve positive and negative variations. If one wave's positive portion exactly mirrors the other's negative portion then cancellation occurs. This may happen in electrical circuits through, for example, **phase** inversion. It is rarely complete in acoustic waves because the complexity of their reflections destroys precise symmetries. See also **node** and **standing wave**.

Cannon The brand name of the latching plug and socket system universally used for connecting **microphones** and other equipment in studios, concert halls etc. Also known as XLR. See also **din** and **jack**.

Capacitance, -ive, -or Symbol C. The ability of a conductor or a system of conductors to store a **charge**. A practical capacitor (in older usage, 'condenser'), i.e. a device with capacitance, consists of two conducting surfaces separated by an insulator **dielectric**. The greater the area of conductor and the thinner the dielectric the greater the capacitance, measured in farads (named after Michael Faraday). Practical capacitors have sizes more conveniently expressed in μF or pF (see **SI units**). Capacitance (like **resistance** and **inductance**) is a property of all electrical circuits, thus an ordinary two-core cable has capacitance between the conductors.

To a standing (**DC**) voltage, a capacitor is like an open switch, and passes no current, but under changing conditions (**AC**) it responds by charging up and discharging, allowing current to flow in proportion to the capacitance even though there is no continuous conducting path. The amount of current depends also on the **frequency** of the AC, the effective resistance of the capacitor reducing as the frequency increases. The capacitor's effect in controlling the size of an alternating current is called capacitive reactance (X_c), and (like resistance) is measured in **ohms**.

There are many uses, but two common ones are shown below. In

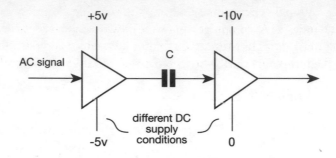

a coupling & isolating with C

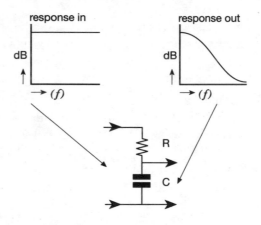

b simple top-cut filter

Fig. 28

fig. 28a capacitance is used for coupling parts of a system together, when DC voltages (e.g. power supplies) must be isolated from AC signals (compare a similar use for **transformers**). In 28b it is used in a **filter**, where the capacitive reactance's dependence on frequency is exploited to change the **response** of a circuit.

Combined with inductance (L), C forms an LC or **tuned circuit**. See also **loudspeakers**, **microphones** and **oscillators**.

Capacitor microphone   See **microphones**

Capstan   See **tape recorder design**

Capsule   The **transducer** part of a **microphone**, sometimes removable.

Card 1. A single circuit board (usually removable) forming part of a complete unit. 2. A computer (punched) card, once widely used for handling mass data. In Music V (see **computer music composition techniques**) the term 'note card' is still used even though the card itself is not.

Cardboard tube effect See **reverberation**

Cardioid A heart-shaped response pattern (see **microphones**).

Carl Computer Acoustic Research Laboratory. Part of the Center for Music Experiment, University of California, San Diego, CA 92093, USA. Tel: (619) 534 4383.

Carrier In **amplitude** and **frequency modulation**, the wave acted upon by the modulating wave. In radio technology the carrier used for transmission is at a much higher frequency than the modulator which contains the information, but in musical applications the waves may be of similar, even the same, frequency, so the notion of one wave 'carrying' the other on its back does not have the same force. The term is convenient, though, to indicate which wave is modulating the other. See also **analogue synthesis techniques** 5, **digital synthesis techniques** 6, **ring modulation** and **sidebands**.

Cartridge 1. A type of cassette used mainly in radio studios (see next entry). 2. The active end of a gramophone **pick-up**, containing the stylus and **transducer**, and usually removable. Compare **capsule**.

Cartridge player A tape machine that takes cassettes loaded with loops of ¼ in tape running from *c.*35 secs to 6 mins or longer. Widely used by radio stations, which broadcast many often-repeated short items (commercials, trailers) between the normal programme segments. As well as audio tracks, a 'cart' tape has a pulse track which automatically positions the loop for the next use, and can also start another cart player. A typical rock station using mainly short items can pre-load and completely automate whole sections of programming.

Cassette duplication Unlike vinyl and compact discs, which are physically manufactured, every pre-recorded cassette must be electrically copied. There are currently three main techniques for mass cassette duplication:

1. Real-time This is best for quality, but slow. Tapes are copied at the normal speed (1⅞ in/sec) from 'master' cassettes or from quarter-inch tape. To speed the process, banks of 'slave' machines record simultaneously.

2. High speed in-cassette In this, master and slaves are run at up to sixteen times normal speed, which is obviously much faster, but the whole musical spectrum is shifted up four octaves during copying, requiring an excellent supersonic frequency response to maintain quality. At these high speeds, any mechanical defects in the cassettes themselves are also more of a problem.

3. High speed bin-loop This is the fastest of all. The quarter-inch master is looped, and a special signal recorded on it to mark the end/beginning of the programmes (A and B sides run together, one of them backwards). The looped material (running from a bin, not spools) is repeatedly copied to open-reel machines carrying cassette (3.81 mm) tape, at up to 64 times the normal speed. A cassette loader then loads the tapes into pre-leadered 'shells', cutting and automatically joining them to leader when it detects the code signal. Large numbers of cassettes can be produced by this method.

For illustrated details of duplicating equipment see Runstein and Huber (1989).

Cassette recorders (audio) When the 'compact cassette', using 3.81 mm tape and running at 1⅞ in (4.76 cm)/sec, was developed by Philips in the 1950s, it was thought of as a low-quality convenience format, unlikely to be a serious contender in the hi-fi market. But as we have seen, the cassette went on to rival the vinyl disc as a domestic pre-recorded medium, and it has the positive advantage over disc of working well in mechanically unstable conditions (cars, boats), where turntables (unless elaborately stabilized) are useless. Capstans, pinch rollers and other mechanical parts referred to below are discussed in **tape recorder design**.

Quality in tape recording depends on **frequency** and **dynamic ranges** captured, the level of tape noise (i.e. **signal-to-noise ratio**), and on the mechanical side tape speed accuracy and stability. Good figures for any of these are much harder to achieve with the narrow tracks, low speed and miniature tape transports of cassette machines than with open reel tape, but market demand and intensive development have produced remarkably good results. **Bandwidths** have improved from 3 kHz in the early days to 20 kHz or more, and dynamic range from 40 to over 80 **decibels** (dB).

Frequency range   The bass end is not a serious problem. High frequency response depends mainly on tape speed (the higher the better), head gap (the narrower the better) and the **resolution** (particle size) of the magnetic coating of the tape (see **sound recording techniques**). Domestic cassette recorders run four or eight times slower than professional quality open reel tapes, and their speed cannot be changed, so design has concentrated on making head gaps smaller and producing better tape stock. In most domestic quality machines (two heads, including erase), one head has to serve for both record and playback, and the gap is a compromise. In three-head machines (allowing off-tape monitoring and essential for serious applications), the record head has (correctly) a wider gap than the playback head, whose gap has in some cases been reduced to less than 1 **micron** (metre$\times 10^{-6}$). As well, new magnetic materials for the heads themselves give greatly improved outputs, and new tape stocks have been introduced (chromium dioxide, metal) which are of much finer grain than the older types. Denser packing of smaller particles not only gives less background hiss from the tape, but means that higher signal levels can be recorded before the tape **saturates**. **Bias** and **equalization** settings must also be correct for the tape being used, and in the best machines fine control of bias is provided, either by a manual control or automatic bias setting in which the machine runs the tape and optimizes the bias for it.

Dynamic range and noise   These are limited by magnetic saturation of the tape and/or the head at the upper end, and by tape noise at the lower. Both have been extended by better tapes and heads, as mentioned above, and noise figures can be further improved by the use of various **noise reduction** systems.

Speed stability   In cassette machines (unlike open reel tape decks) important parts of the tape transport mechanism (pressure pad, tape rollers, spools) are in the cassette itself, and outside the deck manufacturer's control. For one's own recordings it is obviously possible to avoid faulty cassettes, but pre-recorded cassettes are another matter. Apart from performing better generally, a well-designed deck is more likely to play a bad cassette successfully.

In most decks a single capstan pulls the tape across the heads, and the sprung pressure pad within the cassette is relied on to maintain adequate head contact. This works well provided everything is perfectly aligned and in good condition, but does not give good control over the heads. One well known high precision transport is that produced by the leading maker Nakamichi, which uses two capstans of slightly different diameter, giving firm control of tape tension between them (see closed loop transports in **tape recorder design.**)* In this system the cassette's pressure pad is disabled, leaving tape-to-head contact entirely in the hands of correct tape tension and tape path geometry, as in professional open reel machines.

Cassettes are so convenient and versatile that they are found in numerous applications and configurations. Examples are: 1. Data storage for small home computers. Slow, but cheaper than **floppy disk** drives. 2. Multi-track 'studios', sold under various names, e.g. Porta-studio, Mini-studio, MultiTracker. Some of these run the cassette at the faster speed of 3¾ in (9.525 cm)/sec, for higher quality, and all use noise reduction. Instead of four tracks configured as two in each direction, all four run together in the same direction. A **mixer** is also included, and these machines are in effect tiny versions of a professional multi-track studio, enabling a complete recording session and **mixdown** to be done in home conditions, and at surprisingly good quality. They are often used for demo tapes and musical experimentation at a fraction of the cost of buying time in a full studio. 3. Loop cassettes, for short messages, etc. **Cartridge** machines are, however, a better format for loops. 4. Self-reversing cassette machines in which the user only has to insert the tape once to play both sides of it. Some detect the beginning of the blank **leader**, reducing the amount of silence (or the break in a recording) to a fraction of a second. 5. Mini-cassettes, about a quarter the size of standard cassettes, which find their main application in dictating and telephone answering machines.

It might have been expected that the pre-recorded cassette would have ousted the vinyl disc from home entertainment, particularly as cassette machines can record as well as play, but this has not happened, probably because the quality of the disc version of a recording is nearly always much better than a tape produced by high-speed **cassette duplication**. And just as vinyl is rapidly giving ground to **compact disc**, so the analogue cassette is sure to be progressively replaced by **digital audio tape**.

Cathode ray oscilloscope (CRO)   See oscilloscope

Cathode ray tube (CRT)   A funnel-shaped vacuum tube with viewing screen at the wide end. A cathode (negatively charged) 'gun' emits free electrons which are accelerated towards and through a hollow anode

*Nakamichi Corporation, Shinjuku Daiichi Seimei Building, 2–7–1 Nishishinjuku, Shinju-ku-ku, Tokyo, Japan.

(positively charged), focused and deflected as required, and 'fired' at a phosphor-treated screen which the beam causes to glow, producing a spot on the screen. For TV the deflection of the beam is **electromagnetic**, using coils on the neck of the tube. **Oscilloscopes** use **electrostatic** deflection by means of plates within the tube. Brightness is controlled by a negative 'grid' placed in the path of the beam. A CRT can be seen as a special purpose thermionic valve (see **amplifiers**).

CCIR Consultative Committee for International Radio. Standardization body. CCIR **equalization** curves for recording/playback are the European standard. See **NAB** and **sound recording techniques**.

CCRMA Center for Computer Research in Music and Acoustics, Department of Music, Stanford University, Stanford, CA 94305, USA.

CD See **compact disc**

CD–ROM **Compact Disc Read-Only Memory**, i.e. the use of the CD format for mass data storage such as encyclopaedias, reference works and 'expert' systems (see **artificial intelligence**). CD players are becoming available that will interface both with a hi-fi system for music and with a computer for CD–ROM purposes.

CEC Canadian Electroacoustic Community/Communauté Electroacoustique Canadienne, Case Postale 845, Succursale Place d'Armes, Montreal, Quebec, Canada H2Y 3V2.

Cent A logarithmic unit of relative pitch. 100 cents = 1 equally-tempered semitone (see **temperament**), or 1 octave = 1200 cents.

Central processing unit Usually referred to as CPU or CP (Central Processor), this is the essential computer, stripped of **peripheral** devices. In order to work at all, a computer must have at least three things in appropriate communication with each other. These are 1. A **memory** of adequate size and as fast and accessible as possible. Nothing can happen unless all relevant data is immediately available. Some of this data is the material to be manipulated, and some of it is instructions – how to deal with the material. 2. An Arithmetic and Logic Unit (ALU), to do the necessary calculations and logical manipulations. 3. A control unit which oversees and clocks the operation, and communicates with the outside world (input/output). This complex of units is known as the CPU.

Ceramics   A class of materials with many applications in music technology, such as **dielectrics** in **capacitors**. Some have **piezo-electric** properties, and are used in **microphones** and **pick-ups**. See also **ferrites**.

Chance   See **random and chance procedures**

Character   A group of **bits** (often a **byte**), recognized by a computer as having a specific symbolic meaning. A 'set' of characters specific to, say, a music language, typically contains both normal **alphanumeric** characters and non-printing characters like 'ring bell'. See **ASCII**.

Character recognition   The automatic 'reading' by a computer of symbols or codes, usually specially designed for the purpose, for example, magnetic ink on cheques, bar-codes used in supermarkets. Recognition of handwritten words or music is being actively researched, but there are many problems to be solved before a handwritten score can be read by a machine.

Charge   A fundamental electrical property possessed by electrons (negative) and protons (positive). The **SI unit** is **coulomb**, symbol C. On the large scale a charged object is one which has gained or lost electrons making it overall negative or positive. The normal state of materials is electrically neutral.

Chip   A fragment of silicon (typically quarter of an inch square) on which one or many components are formed, such as transistors, **resistors**, **capacitors**, conducting paths and everything necessary for a complete miniature circuit. In manufacture the circuit is often formed many times over in dividable sections like a chocolate bar, then sliced up to make individual chips. Too small to be handled directly, chips are packaged in relatively large containers to facilitate wiring, commonly into a **printed circuit** board (PCB). See also **integrated circuit**.

Chorus effect   This occurs when a group of similar instruments or voices is playing (or singing) in unison, adding random elements not present in a solo performance, particularly the combined effect of different speeds and depths of **vibrato**. This produces complex interference patterns of cancellation and reinforcement. Apart from sounding different from a solo, the net effect is a reduction in combined energy output – a single soloist can easily be balanced against a sizeable group playing the same instrument (or singing) in unison.

Chorus effect is one of the things which distinguishes a 'chamber' from an 'orchestral' sound. In electronic music, chorusing is imitated by multiple time delays modulated at varying low frequencies, and 'string synthesizers' use techniques of this sort. Massed strings are very hard to imitate, but 'vocal' chorusing, when well done, can sound quite convincing. See **reverberation**.

CIME   See **ICEM**

Ciné spool   See **spool**

Circuit   A continuous electrical path (including the part through the energy source, e.g. battery, generator, if any), containing any number of **active** or **passive** elements interconnected in **series, parallel** or complex **networks**. If a circuit is broken at any point by a switch or a fault, for example, it is an 'open' circuit.

Classical studio   See Introduction and **tape composition techniques**

Click track   See **time codes**

Clipping   A type of **distortion** caused by overdriving an **amplifier** stage, i.e. using such a large input signal that it enters the limit regions of **saturation** and/or **cut-off** (fig. 29). The peaks of the signal are clipped off at the output.

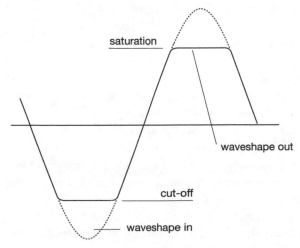

Fig. 29

Clipping is usually undesirable, but in rock music clipping amplifiers ('fuzz boxes') are used to produce deliberate distortion effects. One reason why some musicians prefer valve (tube) amplifiers to transistor amplifiers is that valve clipping has a gentler onset and is richer in even harmonics (see **harmonic series**), giving a 'rounder' sound than the odd-harmonic distortion typical of transistor clipping. See also **harmonic distortion**.

CMA See **International Computer Music Association**

Coaxial cable Designed for high frequency work, a precisely-dimensioned two-conductor cable in which one conductor is a tube surrounding the other, and is separated from it by a layer of non-conductor, e.g. polythene. Usually of flexible copper braid, and **earthed** (grounded), the outer conductor shields the live inner from interference. For audio frequencies, shielded cables made in the same way but to lower standards of accuracy are adequate. See **unbalanced**.

Coaxial loudspeaker See **loudspeakers**

Cocktail party effect Our ability to select one input of interest from a mixed jumble of sounds at more or less the same level. Probably in part due to the **binaural** effect in hearing, but also to complex tone discrimination, i.e. we can 'home in' on a particular **timbre**. An effect of wearing a hearing aid is often that the ability is lost. See also **psychoacoustics** and Roederer (1979).

Coil See **inductance**

Coloration A modification of the 'natural' tone quality expected from a given instrument or voice, typically by non-linear processing in **transducers** (e.g. **microphones** or **loudspeakers**) or by the peculiarities of an acoustic environment. It is the result of mild **distortion** of a **formant** nature (i.e. affecting a particular frequency area whatever the type of excitation). Sometimes a good characteristic ('this hall adds warmth in the middle bass'), but usually undesirable (a 'tubby' or 'shrieky' speaker system).

Coloured noise See **analogue synthesis techniques** 4

Comb filter A filter with a **response** consisting of alternating peaks and nulls, resulting in frequency-selective distortion of the **spectrum**. It may consist of a **series**-connected bank of tuned filters, or a delay line configuration. See **filters** and fig. 89.

Combination tones   An acoustic phenomenon giving similar results to **amplitude modulation**. Apparently caused by the non-linear response of the ear (see Taylor, 1965, Wood, 1962 and Roederer, 1979). Two tones heard together, particularly loud ones, tend to produce in the ear/ brain system additional difference and sum tones. See also **difference frequency** and **dissonance**.

Comma   See **temperament**

Compact disc (**CD**)   A digital/optical storage medium, with a sampling rate of 44.1 kHz and a **resolution** of sixteen **bits**. For the general principles of digitally encoding sound, see **digital synthesis techniques**. Introduced to a limited market in 1982, '900,000 players and 17 million discs were sold in 1984, making the CD the most successful electronic product ever introduced.' (Pohlmann, *Principles of Digital Audio*, 1989). Its popularity shows no sign of waning, lists of new and 're-mastered' recordings on CD get longer, prices of both players and discs are falling, and the uses of the medium are being extended by **CD–ROM**. Many market experts think that the demise of the vinyl disc is much closer than anyone would have predicted in 1982.

Recordable CDs (some types erasable, some 'write once', see **WORM**) are being actively researched and developed, but at the time of writing no system has been publicly released. As well as technical and cost problems there are legal difficulties similar to those which delayed the introduction of **digital audio tape**. This entry is confined to the CD as a reproducing medium.

A type of **read-only memory** (**ROM**), a CD stores data as a series of sausage-shaped pits impressed into a smooth 'substrate', coated with aluminium to make the surface reflective, and covered with a further layer of protective transparent plastic, making the finished disc a very durable object. CDs are single-sided, and 'played' from underneath, so that to the laser pick-up the pits are actually the high parts and the lands (untreated surface between the pits) the lower. To the naked eye the spiral of pits is invisible (sixty of them would fit into one groove of a vinyl LP), but they can nonetheless be reproduced (like LPs) by a mechanical pressing process, whereas magnetic media like cassette tapes must be individually copied (see **cassette duplication**).

Philips (in the Netherlands) proposed an optical disc in 1974, and with Sony (in Japan) were the primary developers, though many individuals and companies co-operated to ensure uniform and reliable standards for a commercially feasible system. The CD itself, and the linked optical, electrical and mechanical systems of the player, are complex in design and manufacture, and the wonder is that they are so cheap and work so reliably. The disc, though only 120 mm in diameter, could hold a great deal more data than it does (for one thing it could be double-sided). The maximum playing time of 74 mins was largely a marketing decision.

Taking the main components of the system separately:

The disc
The tape master for a CD is in **video cassette PCM** format (though the music recording may have started life as an analogue tape), and when suitably re-coded (see below) is copied to the glass master (glass coated with photo-resist) by a laser cutter. The photo-resist layer is then developed, the laser-cut areas (pits) being etched away to the level of the glass, and from this point on a series of plating processes produce metal master (negative), metal mother (positive) and finally son or stamper (negative), from which the final disc is made, layered as already described. To retain the tiny pits through all these processes requires elaborate quality control and surgically clean conditions.

Digital coding
For basic information see **binary code** and **pulse code modulation**. The unit of data is the 'frame', containing music, error correction and other codes in a standard protocol recognized by all CD players. In the error

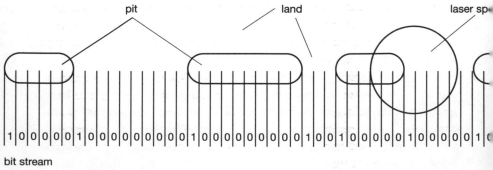

Fig. 30

correction process (Cross-Interleave Reed–Solomon Code or Circ), data is deliberately de-localized so that possible errors (e.g. caused by damage) will affect it slightly in a number of places rather than massively in one place, which might stop performance altogether. The lands and pits on the disc do not in themselves denote os and 1s. Instead, every change of level (land/pit or pit/land) indicates a 1, and flat surfaces (pit or land) represent strings of os proportional to their length (see fig. 30). This is an efficient data packing arrangement, but requires data to be presented in a special code with certain rules: 1. 1s must be separated by at least two os. 2. Strings of os are limited to a maximum of 10. In conversion, eight bit half-words (two to a sixteen bit 'music' word) are translated to a fourteen bit code obeying the above rules, by a process called Eight-to-Fourteen Modulation (EFM). In this form, frames of 588 'channel bits' are recorded on the CD, and later decoded by the player (see **sound recording techniques** 3).

Optics
Reading the disc's pit spiral poses some formidable engineering problems: 1. Focusing a beam of laser light to a spot no more than two **microns** across (turns of the spiral are 1.6 microns apart). 2. Detecting the change in level between pits and lands, and outputting these changes. 3. Tracking the spiral correctly without any mechanical connection, even if the disc is slightly eccentric, and the machine subjected to shocks and vibration of the kind likely in an average entertainment environment.

The light generator is a special form of LED (**light emitting diode**) called a semiconductor laser, which produces coherent (in **phase**) light of one wavelength only. The beam may be split into a main and subsidiary side beams (for tracking, see below), and is passed through an ingenious polarizing and prism system which separates the transmitted beam from that reflected from the surface of the disc. Final focusing is done by the transparent coating of the disc itself, and is automatically adjusted to allow for small variations.

The mirror surface of a land reflects the whole beam (maximum output). When over a pit, part of the beam is still striking the land beside it, and pit depth is chosen so that the 'long' and 'short' paths cancel each other, resulting in very little or no reflected light. On return, the now modulated beam is directed onto a photodiode which converts it into an electrical signal.

Tracking of the pit spiral is sometimes done by the main beam itself (through a **servo** control). If the spot wanders to the left or right it picks up too much land and not enough pit, increasing the pit signal. In a three-beam system the direction and amount of tracking error are determined by the polarity and size of the imbalance of the two side beam signals (equal when tracking is correct). For illustrations of CD optical systems see references below.

Mechanical

Unlike an LP, in which the groove velocity slows as the pick-up approaches the centre, a CD player reads the pit spiral at a constant velocity of 1.25 metres/sec (and in fact reads the disc from inside to out). The motor speed therefore depends on where the pick-up is, and a servo system adjusts it continuously as the disc plays, making major speed changes when the pick-up is moved suddenly (as in track selection). The pick-up has its own motor, which is servo controlled by the tracking system.

Fig. 31 shows the main interconnections of the complete system. The electronics include microcomputers and are very complex compared with those for analogue LPs, since all the EFM and Circ coding (see above) must be unravelled, the original music code restored, all musically irrelevant data removed, left and right channels separated, and **digital-to-analogue** conversion (DAC) and **filtering** applied, before the output signal can be sent to amplifiers and speakers.

The compact disc format described so far is already becoming an obsolete technology, but the massive investment in manufacture, selling,

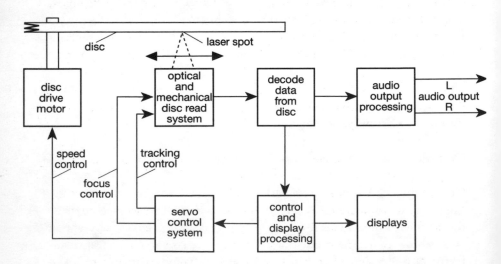

Fig. 31

disc catalogues etc. will ensure that it remains a standard in the hi-fi market for some years at least, and future formats will probably be arranged so that current CDs can be played on the new machines. Sampling rate will certainly be much higher, which will avoid filtering problems at the DAC – many manufacturers raise the rate artificially at this stage by **oversampling** to improve performance.

As well as references given, see also **digital audio tape**, and, for arguments for and against digital recording, Fellgett (1983). For an assessment of CD players see Greenspun and Stromeyer (1986). Pohlmann (1989) and Watkinson (1988) both have full descriptions of electronic and optical systems, and a useful booklet, *Principles of Compact Disc*, is published by Thorn EMI (1986). For photos of CD manufacture, see Runstein and Huber (1989).

Compander   A portmanteau word for COMPressor-expANDER, used of a device that performs both complementary functions. Typical use is in **noise reduction** systems. See also **compressor**.

Comparator   A device that compares an input with a reference – typically a known voltage. Output can be arranged in various ways, such as no output if inputs equal, output only if equal etc. Often used to switch or **gate** a signal, control a motor, etc. (see **tape recorder design**).

Compensation   One term for a fixed correction curve applied in, for example, a **pick-up** playback circuit, and of opposite slope to that applied when recording (see **sound recording techniques**). Sometimes synonymous with **equalization**, but only when that term is used to describe a fixed (though possibly switchable) **filter** circuit. See also **pre-emphasis**.

Compiler   The software that translates a program written in a 'human interface' high level language into 'machine code', for execution by the computer. See **computer languages**.

Complex wave   A wave consisting of two or more **sine waves**.

Compliance   A property of mechanical systems, related to mass in the same way as **capacitance** is related to **inductance**. Compliance refers to the **frequency**-dependent resilience or stiffness of, for example, a spring or a rubber joint. The behaviour of compliant materials is an important factor in the design of electro-mechanical **transducers** such as **pick-ups** and **loudspeakers**. See also **filters** and **resonance**.

Compress/ion, -or   The process of reducing the dynamic range of a signal while retaining its internal proportions. Recording and broadcasting systems are limited in the range they can handle by a number of factors, but most obviously by the necessity for the quietest sounds to be above the background noise levels of the system, and the loudest below limits like tape **saturation**, amplifier **distortion**, speaker capacity, and (in the case of broadcasting) **overmodulation**. Of the familiar media, AM radio has the most restricted range (about forty **decibels**). Good analogue recordings and FM radio are better at about 50–70 dB, and digital recording can reach 90 dB, but a live orchestral performance may span as much as 120 dB between the quietest and the loudest sounds.

A degree of manual compression is used in recording by studio engineers, who 'ride the pots', easing levels up on quiet passages, and pulling back to soften the blow of a coming climax. But automatic compression and its relative, 'limiting', ensure that signals are kept within bounds at all times. Fig. 32a shows (using musical dynamics) the characteristics of a pure compressor. All the dynamics within the music are brought proportionally closer together, and the compression is set so that the loudest sounds (*fff*) just reach but do not exceed the maximum allowable. In practice, though, we need all the level possible for the quieter sounds, and it is more effective to leave them uncompressed and set a threshold (fig. 32b) at which compression begins.

Compression is defined as a ratio: 5:1 means that a 5 dB increase in input level will cause only 1 dB increase in output. The highest practical ratio is about 20:1, and this degree of compression is called 'limiting', because all levels trying to rise above the threshold are virtually clamped down to it (fig. 32c). Limiting produces an unnatural, held-back effect, but is useful in noisy and unpredictable situations like outside broadcast interviewing, because even though the gain is changing continuously, and the background surges up and down like surf, speech is always intelligible and unexpected loud sounds do not ruin the recording and the interview. Some devices such as wireless microphones (see **microphones** 4), would be impossible to use without some kind of automatic gain control – the need for manual adjustment would destroy their usefulness.

Most compressor/limiters have an indicator (a meter or **LED** display) to show the amount of gain reduction currently being applied, which helps the operator to set a suitable threshold for the material in hand. A popular compromise is the 'over-easy' curve (fig. 32d), in which the compression ratio is progressively and automatically increased as input level rises.

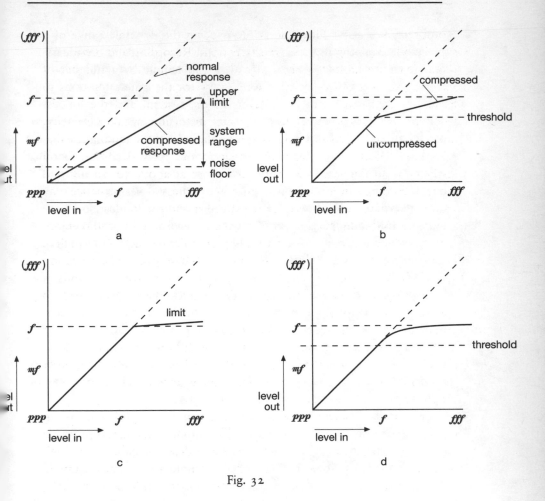

Fig. 32

If music always proceeded by gradual crescendos and diminuendos, compression would be almost unnoticeable, but in reality it is full of sudden loud chords and just as sudden empty pauses. Naturally a compressor circuit must detect a peak very quickly or it may have passed before it is detected, and in some compressors the signal can be delayed very slightly, allowing compression to be applied *before* the peak is heard. But if the gain reduction is made fully effective immediately the peak is detected, and return to full gain happens as soon as the level goes below the threshold, the result is a kind of dynamic strangulation, accompanied by the 'pumping' and 'breathing' of noise levels. So at least two variable delays are necessary (there are often several additional controls): an 'attack' time which decides how long it will take for the gain reduction to be fully active, and a 'release' time which controls the rate at which normal gain is restored. Setting these two times is a matter of trial and error, but as a general rule the more contrast and sforzando a piece contains, the harder it is to find musically satisfactory delay times.

In studio conditions, the most natural recordings are achieved by a combination of careful dynamic control by the conductor, and optimum level setting by the engineer – compression is avoided if possible. But when the unexpected may easily happen – in jazz for example – a compressor/limiter with a fairly high threshold will retain most of the natural dynamics but prevent a whole take being ruined by one or two over-the-top sounds. The complementary device is an expander (see **noise reduction**). For further reading see Nisbett (1970), Wells (1981), Runstein (1989) and Ballou (1987).

Computer *analogue*　A calculating machine based on modelling some event or sequence by mechanical or electrical analogy, and able to manipulate continuous functions. Instead of dealing with numbers, it adds movements, rotations etc., using cams, differentials etc., or voltages, using, for example, operational **amplifiers**. Typically designed for one particular type of job (such as monitoring an environment, where inputs from various sensors are assessed), analogue computers usually operate in real time, and their 'memories' are recorded data like plots, not general purpose number stores as in digital computers. In music some **sequencers** are in effect analogue computers.

For most applications analogue computers have now been replaced by digital machines, and the analogue component reduced to input/output devices like **analogue-to-digital** and **digital-to-analogue converters**.

Computer *digital*　A device invariably referred to by the single word 'computer' in today's usage. A machine that manipulates all types of data as numbers. The word connotes more than 'calculator', and implies the ability to: 1. perform logical as well as arithmetic operations, i.e. to make choices based on logical conclusions; 2. store, retrieve and process data under the control of a program (software); 3. communicate with people and other machines through suitable **interfaces**.

Historically, digital and analogue computers had separate areas of application, but the great advantage of digital machines is versatility – one computer can perform many different functions, whereas analogue computers tend to be designed for one or a very few. Even the theoretical analogue advantage of dealing with continuous phenomena has largely disappeared with the increased speeds of calculation and very high numerical **resolutions** of digital machines.

See the many entries on different aspects of computers relevant in music, e.g. **algorithm, artificial intelligence, binary code, Boolean algebra, central processing unit, computer languages, computer music composition techniques** and **digital synthesis techniques.** The specialized literature is vast, and we have listed only Edmunds (1985), a useful guide to hundreds of computer terms and methodologies.

Computer languages (programming languages)   The means of communication between the person and the machine, languages are sets of logically connected syntactical conventions, often designed to do one kind of job particularly well. Some languages are designed specially for algebraic problems, some for **artificial intelligence** problems, etc. None are anything like so generalized and versatile as human languages, because a computer needs unequivocal input. A 'high-level' (see below) language steers a middle course between being so cryptic that it bears no resemblance to ordinary human language at all, and being so 'human' and conversational that it involves both sides of the **interface** in unnecessary work (more typing for the person, more time- and space-occupying operations for the machine). Programming is an enormous subject which occupies whole sections in libraries and bookshops, and this article only attempts enough description and definition to provide back-up for other entries. For detailed study of particular languages see the specialist literature.

The computer deals with two sorts of input: data (information to be processed) and instructions (on how to process it). Both types of data must ultimately be presented to the machine as **binary code.** In the early days computers were loaded, very slowly, by banks of switches representing the state (0 or 1) of groups of **bits.** A group of eight switches might be set 01110110, and this **word** would be loaded as the minimum computer-comprehensible unit of 'machine code'. The programmer had to know exactly what the computer would do with each item, and there was no question of 'language' in any normal sense. As better, faster machines with more memory came along, ways were found to use coded **mnemonics** as shorthands that the computer could convert into machine code for itself. Such a 'low-level' language is assembly code (no. 3 in fig. 33), which is not at all 'linguistic' in the conventional sense, but easier to use than raw machine code. An associated assembler (no. 6) automatically translates the assembly code into machine code.

The next step was a group of languages that have now been in use

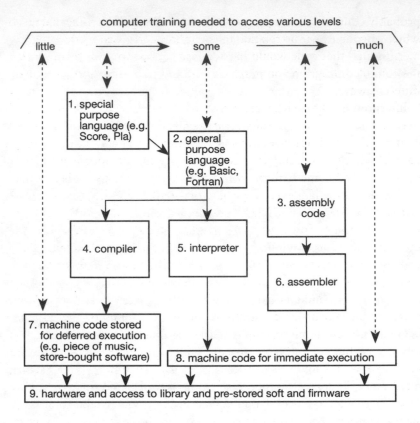

Fig. 33

for many years, and modified to suit various machines and conditions. These were the first efficient 'high-level' languages, in which instructions are grouped as statements, and 'normal' (human) words and symbols appear (e.g. BEGIN, ELSE, +, DO). Between assembly and machine code there is a one-to-one instruction relationship, but a high-level statement may result in many machine code instructions, thus the one command SQRT (number) could cause the computer to look for and implement a complete built-in routine for finding square roots. The job of breaking the statement down and organizing the data for execution is done by a compiler (no. 4 in fig. 33) or an interpreter (no. 5). Compilers translate the entire program (source code) into machine (object) code, and either hold it until further orders from the user (no. 7) or execute it automatically. This means a wait while compilation goes on, but efficient execution of the program thereafter. Software bought in a computer shop is already in compiled form – you simply run it. This user software probably contains all sorts of greetings and messages in ordinary English, which of course bear no relation to the source code used by the programmer (though that code would include instructions to print them). In fact the compiled program you purchase could have been arrived at in many different ways.

Interpreters take each program statement and execute it at once, which may or may not be as satisfactory as compiling, depending on the context. Like assemblers, compilers and interpreters are out of the direct control of the programmer (though they were of course written by someone), and come with the machine as part of the **operating system**.

Well known high-level languages originating in the 1950s include Fortran (FORmula TRANslator), Algol (ALGOrithmic Language), and Cobol (COmmon Business Oriented Language). The mid-1960s saw the birth of Basic (Beginner's All-purpose Symbolic Instruction Code), originating at Dartmouth College, USA, and the most widely known of all languages for the past twenty years because it is available on almost all business and home microcomputers, is easy to learn, and by now has many enhancements and variations which lift it out of the complete beginner's level. In microcomputers Basic is mainly executed through an interpreter, but compilers are also available. Another early language, not nearly so well known as the above, but of great interest to artificial intelligence and music programmers, is Lisp (LISt Processing). More recent arrivals have been Pascal (not an acronym, but named after the seventeenth-century mathematician), APL (A Programming Language), C (better than A or B), and Forth (also not an acronym). There are numerous 'house' languages developed and mainly used by particular laboratories or universities, such as Sail (Stanford Artificial Intelligence Language). Many readers will have some acquaintance with Basic. Good introductions to Lisp, Pascal and Forth are Touretzky (1984), Conway (1976) and Brodie (1981).

All the above belong in box no. 2 of fig. 33. Box no. 1 is for special languages which are 'subsets' of a general language, with a specialist vocabulary. Some musical examples are Music v (Fortran), C-sound (C), Pla (Sail), MPL (APL). The list of languages based on the main programming languages is endless, and new ones turn up every month in the literature. An excellent introduction to language theory and programming problems as they relate to music is contained in the series *Machine Tongues* (I to XI [XI is mis-numbered as a second X]) published over several years in *Computer Music Journal*, and listed under Abbott, Curtis *et al*. See also Hofstadter (1980) chapter 10 for a historical analysis of the development of software, and many penetrating comments.

Abbott (*Machine Tongues* II) proposes the axiom '. . . any programming effort is the result of posing a problem that someone wants to solve'. Before attempting to write a program it is important to be completely clear 1. exactly what you expect the computer to do, 2. whether the available hardware can do what you want (e.g. enough speed, memory, suitable **peripherals**), and 3. whether the language you intend to use is syntactically suitable for the problem you want to solve. If your problem involves intuitive and emotional components (and most music composition problems do), you may have to separate these essentially human decisions from the elements consisting of hard data that computers handle faster and better than we do. In music, synthesis and sound generating programs are often clear and unambiguous, but composition programs are another matter, see **computer music composition techniques**.

As time goes on, more and more people are computer users, but very few, in comparison, write programs. We buy (or, regrettably, steal) software to solve our problems, but particularly in very personal areas like the way we approach composing music, disappointment is frequent – not surprisingly, because someone else decided what problems to address. The first choice, therefore, is whether to hope that some available software will do the job, or learn enough programming to attempt it yourself. A new breed of computer-trained composers (and arts-educated programmers) is arising, and there have been many fruitful co-operations between composers and computer scientists.

High-level languages are inefficient because many of their features are designed for user-intelligibility rather than running the program. A given programming goal can be reached in several ways, just as different conversational ploys can arrive at the same end. For example my limited programming skills are likely to give the compiler more trouble (and hence lead to less efficient object code) than those of my expert friends. Some computer composers work with assembly code (in some cases even machine code), because they can achieve more streamlined, efficient results this way, but they have to spend a lot of potential composing time in dialogue with the machine. A few composers with outstanding programming skills have designed their own languages, and one of these is Bill Schottstaedt of Stanford. Here is part of his Introduction to *Pla: A Composer's Idea of a Language*:

> What we really want, so we are told, is a musical data-entry system where composers need know nothing of the machine. But composers are expected to learn the rudiments of other instruments; why should the computer be different? None of the composers I have discussed

this with has groused about the need for a little programming, and many have pointed out that most compositional devices are actually little programs that happen to be expressed in an obscure notation (common music notation). (Schottstaedt, 1983)

This ready acceptance may not apply to composers in general, but those who do wish to use computers are well advised to study the syntactical mechanisms likely to be used by programmers, and present their problems in 'computer-compatible' form.

As computers get more precise, fast and 'expert' (see **artificial intelligence**), increasingly high levels of language can be used. Sitting at a modern microcomputer and moving a mouse to point at an icon, the user need have no idea of the possible complexities released by that one gesture, but there are dangers in this widening gap between the upper interface and the machine itself, because there is less direct control, less possibility of making personal modifications to the software, and more dependence on the person who wrote it. It may be that at an even higher level this tendency will be self-correcting. If the resources of the machines are a few orders of magnitude greater still, we should be approaching the kind of flexibilities we expect from other human beings; machines that will really 'listen' to us, mould their behaviour to our ideas, and accept inputs in ordinary, familiarly imprecise languages. The much-heralded Japanese 'fifth generation' project is taking this approach, but practical results have yet to reach the ordinary user.

At a modest level, programming is not difficult, and every computer magazine contains programs which are easily analysable, can be changed and adapted, and typed in by anyone. Only a very elementary knowledge of maths is needed for most of the types of program that interest musicians. Even though the list of ready-to-run music software for the popular computers grows by the week, there is a satisfaction about achieving an aim with one's very own program that transcends the excitement derived from running someone else's. See **computer music composition techniques** and **digital synthesis techniques**.

Computer Music Association See **International Computer Music Association**

Computer music composition techniques This entry considers computers as structural organizers of music, rather than as generators or controllers of the sound itself (though as we shall see the two functions are often inseparable). The term 'composition' can mean inventing a few notes of melody, but this study assumes that we have enough material to warrant some kind of formal organization. The end result may be either electronic or instrumental music, and in the former case the same computer may be used for both composition and production. For using computers to originate and manipulate sound, see **digital synthesis techniques**. Compositional problems are not specific to the means used, and articles like **musique concrète, tape composition techniques** and parts of **analogue synthesis techniques** are also relevant, as well as the wider discussion in the Introduction.

1. Overview

A future computer may be able to create a work of art, but the ones we have now certainly cannot. A phrase like 'this music was composed by a computer' may not be entirely meaningless, though, and we shall look at ways in which it might be partly true. To quote chapter 19 of Hofstadter:

> Question: Will a computer ever write beautiful music?
> Speculation: Yes, but not soon. Music is a language of emotions, and until computers have emotions as complex as ours, there is no way a program will write anything beautiful. There can be 'forgeries' – shallow imitations of the syntax of earlier music – but despite what one might think at first, there is much more to musical expression than can be captured in syntactical rules . . . (Hofstadter, 1980)

There can be no 'right' way to compose, whether for instruments or machines. There are hundreds of books about composing music, offering everything from lists of strict rules to advocacy of the totally anarchic. Some methods are analysis-based ('Bach did this, so you do it too'), and many composition teachers rely mainly on passing on their own techniques ('Do as I do'), which can work well, but only if those methods are effective and the student temperamentally in tune with them.

The wide variety of approaches to composing, and therefore to using computers in composition, makes neat categorization difficult. Dodge and Jerse (see Dodge, 1985, chapter 8) divide the subject into compositions using aleatoric or random methods and those using deterministic ones, and this is certainly an important distinction, but not the only one. There are differences in strategy, for example, between using small, specialized systems and large, generalized ones. Score programming began some years before computers were powerful enough to be effectively used for synthesis, and the next section looks at some of the great variety of work going on in the 1950s and 1960s. Section 3 discusses changes in the computer music environment since *c.* 1970, and section 4 examines developments in composing software and the musical applications of it.

Apart from composing and sound analysis/synthesis, there are other uses for computers in music. Musicological applications are mentioned in the following section. Cataloguing is now computerized in most music libraries, and the publishing world is turning increasingly to music printing by computer.

2. Pioneer work up to *c.* 1970

The performance of music by machines (tune-playing clocks, musical boxes, etc.) has been commonplace for centuries, but automatic 'composing' needs much more processing power than a clockwork motor. The first reference to its possibility seems to have been made by Lady Ada Augusta Lovelace (1815–52). In her notes on Charles Babbage's Analytical Engine, she proposes the idea that the engine could operate on objects other than numbers '. . . were objects found whose . . . relations could be expressed by those of the abstract science of operations . . .'. She suggests that if 'relations of pitched sounds . . . and musical composition were susceptible of such expression and adaptations, the engine might compose elaborate and scientific pieces of music of any degree of complexity and extent' (Morrison, 1961). This remarkable achiever at a time when female enterprise was heavily discouraged is remembered in ADA, a computer language developed for the US Department of Defense.

Lady Lovelace was quite aware that the analytical engine was not capable of thought or emotion, but may have believed that music can indeed be reduced to a syntactical code, and composed by rule. This belief has resulted in a good deal of sterile work in computer music, the main problem being that, particularly in the early days, computing experts tended to be musically naive, and most of the composers who could have asked the right questions were not at all interested in computers.

A notable exception was the composer Lejaren Hiller, who has been very active in the field since the earliest days of computer music. With Leonard Isaacson, a mathematician, Hiller started a series of experiments in 1955, which resulted in a computer-produced string quartet called the *Illiac Suite* (Illiac was the name of the computer then installed at the University of Illinois). Their methods are fully described in *Experimental Music* (Hiller, 1959), and the book was of much wider influence than the suite itself, because it established certain methods as practicable, presented a balanced analysis of the aesthetics involved, and a forecast of what might follow. Most of the suite's music is founded (deliberately) on well-known traditional rules such as those of strict counterpoint, and the computer made successive selections by testing randomly generated notes against the rules and accepting only those which were 'legal'. The general form of this generate-and-test procedure is shown in fig. 34. The composer, by writing the rules, decides the general shape and character of the piece, but the details are variable, and the computer occasionally comes up with something really surprising and interesting.

Computer systems can have built-in **random number generators** (see also **pseudo-random**), and we should distinguish two different kinds of output: the continuous and the discrete. A continuous output is any number at all (within the possible **resolution**) between given limits, thus an unmeasured (arhythmic) or 'texture' piece might call for the durations of its components to be completely unrelated, and the rules might only specify a minimum and maximum length and perhaps something like 'no two successive durations to be the same'. If the music is conventionally notated, however, the composer might decide that the range of

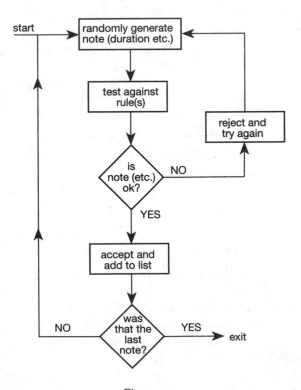

Fig. 34

durations is semibreves to semiquavers, in which case the choice will be made from a list of such discrete, prescribed note values.

Another way of generating notes (also used in the *Illiac Suite*) is not to have rigid, yes/no rules, but loaded chances of certain outcomes – light odds against events you wish to favour, heavy against those you wish to discourage, but not completely exclude, because the occasional surprising event is desirable. A well-known strategy is the Markoff Chain. Fig. 35 shows a 'transition table' for five notes assumed to be in ascending order, with the various probabilities controlling the next choice. Outcomes can also include certainties (o=never, 1=always). In fig. 35, repeated notes cannot occur at all, small intervals are favoured over large, and the note five will always be followed by three. Using the table, we can also calculate the probability of a given three-step sequence occurring, by multiplying the odds. Thus in fig. 35 the probability of 4–2–1 is .22 × .33 = .0726, or 7.26%. By suitable selection of the current, or first-order transition table, we can calculate the influence of previous transitions, and in this process their effect rapidly diminishes as the order number increases; thus the chance of 3–4–2–1 occurring is

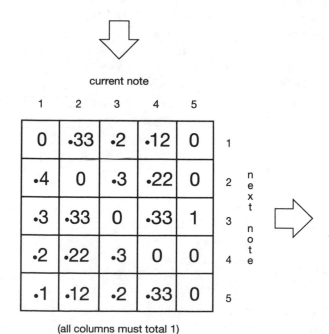

current note

1	2	3	4	5	
0	•33	•2	•12	0	1
•4	0	•3	•22	0	2
•3	•33	0	•33	1	3
•2	•22	•3	0	0	4
•1	•12	•2	•33	0	5

next note

(all columns must total 1)

Fig. 35

.2 × .22 × .33 = .01452 (*c.* 1½%).On the other hand, since 5–3 is a certainty the probability of 5–3–5–3 is high at 20%. Further, we have ruled out any such successions as 1–2–2–4 or 5–1–2–3, by making any repeated notes and 5–1, 5–2, 5–4 impossible. For a fuller discussion of Markoff Chain procedures, including a special case called the 'random walk', and analyses of other techniques, with compositional examples, see Dodge (1985) chapter 8.

Probabilities are loaded by applying suitable algorithms to randomly generated numbers to weight distributions in the desired way. There are a number of well-known curves of distribution such as uniform (no loading), exponential, Poisson, Gaussian. To take one example, a Gaussian distribution has a bell-shaped curve, favouring middle numbers over extremes. A practical non-computer implementation, used in my piece *Trios,** is to throw three dice together. The range is from 3 to 18. The middle range numbers (9–12) can result from any of six different face combinations, and are much more likely to occur than the highest or lowest numbers, which can only be thrown in one way.

So far we have discussed selection of 'notes', 'intervals' and other parameters of conventional instrumental music. About the same time as the experiments in Illinois, Iannis Xenakis was also working towards computer-aided composition in Paris, but his aims were different. Xenakis's training as an architect gave him an interest from the beginning in the mathematical basis of music, and he expounded his theories in *Musiques Formelles* (Xenakis, 1963), published in 1963 and later translated and enlarged as *Formalized Music* (Xenakis, 1971).

In the 1950s Xenakis developed a theory of 'free stochastic music'. *Stochos* (Greek) means 'goal' or 'target', the idea being that large numbers of random events tend towards a target of stability. In ordinary use, stochastic is another word for random, and Xenakis was interested in large clusters of similar events – 'clouds of sounds' – which he generated using random and probabilistic processes. The work *Achorripsis*, for twenty-one instruments, was composed in the mid-1950s using non-computer implementations of formulae such as Poisson's law, which predicts the probable densities of single, discrete events in a specified time/space, given a mean density of such events. Xenakis later programmed *Achorripsis* in Fortran for the IBM–7090, a state-of-the-art computer at the time. He also generated a number of other pieces, many designated as stochastic by the prefix ST, for example, ST–48–1,240,162 for forty-eight instruments. All these pieces are for instrumental rather

*Cary, Tristram *Trios for VCS3 synthesizer and turntables* (2 records & score), Electronic Music Studios, London, 1971.

than electronic realization, and the scores themselves are determined, i.e. there is no choice in performance.

Work at Illinois continued and grew through the 1960s. One piece of note is *HPSCHD* (1969), a collaboration between John Cage and Hiller, and written for up to seven harpsichords and up to fifty-one tapes. John Cage's *Silence* (Cage, 1961) had been published in 1961, and his use of dice, the Chinese I-Ching and other chance processes had stimulated many composers. By this time a composition language, Musicomp (1963), existed at Illinois, and Hiller wrote a new routine, Iching, to generate material for *HPSCHD*. The album issued later included another innovation, a unique (or at least, 1 of 10,000) print-out of a program called Knobs, by which the user is instructed to change the settings of the hi-fi as the piece plays.* At this time, also, the University of Illinois School of Music was publishing periodic technical reports, some of which are particularly relevant, such as the Musicomp manuals, and a historical overview (Hiller, 1963–8) of work in this field up to that date.

Meanwhile another significant research stream, initiated in the 1950s by Max V. Mathews, J. R. Pierce and others, was developing at Bell Labs in New Jersey. Of direct interest to a telephone company were experiments in speech processing (see **vocoders**), but musical material was also researched. Mathews is best known for a series of sound synthesis programs culminating late in the 1960s with Music v, a language still current twenty years later. His book *The Technology of Computer Music* (Mathews, 1969), a landmark in the subject's literature, includes a manual for Music v. The preceding version, Music iv, was a model for such languages in the mid-1960s. Production of computer-synthesized sound was then a lengthy process, requiring several 'passes' and tedious delays for the composer before anything was actually heard.

To begin with, the researchers at Bell Labs were concerned (as they were at Illinois) with manipulating conventional intervals, harmonies and so on, and as early as 1962 a record, *Music from Mathematics* (Mathews *et al.*, 1962), appeared. This contains a number of short pieces and arrangements, some of them amusing, by Mathews, Pierce and others. That these composers were quite aware of their relationship to the machine is indicated by the sleeve note, by Mathews and Ben Deutschman: 'The new techniques and tools of computer music are not meant to replace the more traditional means of composition and performance. Rather, they are designed to enhance and enlarge the range of possibilities available to the searching imagination of musicians . . .'

*Cage, John and Lejaren Hiller *HPSCHD for harpsichords and computer-generated sound tapes* Nonesuch Records, New York, H71224–A.

An important series of papers, given at a computer conference in 1966, were later published under the title *Music by Computers* (von Foerster, 1969), and one of them (by Mathews and L. Rosier) describes the use of graphic inputs and plots, which are, intuitively, a more natural way to work for most composers than lists of numbers. Using this technique, Mathews and Rosier devised a combining procedure by which two inputs could be averaged, gradually converted from one to the other, or algebraically manipulated in other ways. On the record supplied with the book, there is an example in which 'The British Grenadiers' (metre $\frac{2}{4}$, key F) changes to 'When Johnny Comes Marching Home' (metre $\frac{6}{8}$, key E minor) and back again. The transitions are of great interest because they do not consist of either tune but something new. Computer transformation techniques, as opposed to the random or loaded odds methods we discussed above, include not only those commonly used in serial composition – inversion, retrogression and transposition, but complex new ones as well which would be hard to implement without a computer.

In 1964 Gottfried Michael Koenig, who was a pioneer of tape music in the early Cologne days (see **electronic music**), was appointed artistic director of the Institute of Sonology at Utrecht State University in the Netherlands (now absorbed into the Royal Conservatory at The Hague*), which rapidly became (and still is) one of the major European teaching and composing studios, offering multi-lingual courses in a wide range of related topics. Koenig was an experienced composer of both instrumental and electronic music, and had studied computer programming. His first major program was Project 1 (1964–6). Like Musicomp (but unlike Music IV and V) it was essentially a composing rather than a synthesis program, designed to produce instrumental scores.

Towards the end of the decade Koenig completed Project 2, which greatly extended the general plan of Project 1. The idea was to allow composers maximum freedom to choose their own method of composition by providing a number of options at each stage, from the initial material to the final score. It was also meant to be a research base to probe the possibilities and limits of compositional procedures. Like Project 1, its main thrust was towards instrumental rather than electronic music. As Koenig said in an interview: 'Project 2 . . . is actually a questionnaire of more than 60 questions. According to [the answers to] these questions, the program would combine or compose a piece.' The overall flow is shown in fig. 36.

*Royal Conservatory, Juliana van Stolberglaan 1, 2595 CA The Hague, The Netherlands.

Project 2 was published as no. 3 of *Electronic Music Reports* (Koenig, 1970). Its features are too numerous to discuss in detail here, but an example is the selection programme, which allows the composer to decide how an ensemble is to be put together from tables of parameters, and how the score is made up from the ensemble data. In the first case

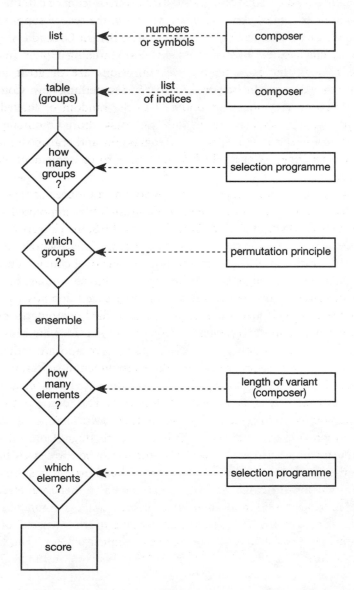

Fig. 36

the composer can choose three options, and in the second from six. These are: ALEA (chooses elements of a given supply at random, allowing repetition); SERIES (similar but does not allow repeats, so chooses elements till the supply is used up); RATIO (makes a loaded selection, allowing different numbers of repetitions to different items); GROUP (repetitions in groups); SEQUENCE (ordering of elements); TENDENCY (isolation of chosen areas, then selection within areas by ALEA).

Computer programs tend to be attached to the hardware they are designed to run with, and a lot of good software has died when a particular machine has become obsolete. But if a program shows signs of durability, it can be re-written for newer machines, and usually runs more efficiently as well. Project 2 has been updated, and Music IV and V have been translated many times, e.g. Barry Vercoe's Music 360 and Music 11.

The 1960s saw the arrival of the first mini-computers, including the PDP series by Digital Equipment Corporation (DEC), which made small, low budget computer studios a practical possibility. Electronic Music Studios (London) Ltd was started in 1968, the three founder directors being Peter Zinovieff, David Cockerell and myself. The computers we used were not powerful enough for sound synthesis, but hybrid systems were developed, in which the computers drove voltage controlled equipment (see **analogue synthesis techniques** 6). From the composing point of view Musys, the EMS language, did not offer the complex composing facilities of Project 2, but a good range of manipulations was possible. The portion of a file shown in fig. 37 refers to a set of computer-generated variations on a Haydn sonata, which Zinovieff named *A Lollipop for Papa*.

Hybrid systems offered another important innovation – real-time computer-controlled analogue synthesis. For the first time computer composing could be extended by improvisation, provided the computer was furnished with suitable quasi-analogue inputs such as knobs, joysticks, keyboards etc.

Another active hybrid system (from 1968) was Groove (Generated Real-time Output Operations on Voltage-controlled Equipment), developed at Bell Telephone by Max Mathews and F. R. Moore, who wrote: 'In the composing mode of the Groove system, a human being is in the feedback loop. Thus he is able to modify the functions instantaneously as a result of his observations of their effects' (Mathews, 1968). Groove, like Musys, allowed real-time control, and looked forward to the improved interactive possibilities which came later with high speed pure digital synthesis.

"AN EXAMPLE OF A MUSYS III PROGRAMME"

"HAYDN: SONATA XXXIV"

"THE FINAL VERSION IS ON 3 TRACKS EACH BEING VARIANTS
OF THE SAME PROGRAMME. THIS IS FOR TRACK 1."
"THIS PROGRAMME PLAYS THE FIRST PART OF THE FINALE TWISTING
AROUND VARIOUS PARAMATERS TO MAKE VARIATIONS ON THE EXACT DATA
PROVIDED BY PAPER TAPE. THE PROGRAMME MAKES SOME USE OF ALL THE
USUAL MUSYS III COMPILER FACILITIES. THIS EXAMPLE HAS
LAVISH COMMENTS."

"PATCH: O1-E1,O2-E2,O3-E3. E1+E2-A4,E3-A5.
A4-F2,A5-F3. F2-MA1, F3-MA2. A4-MA3,A5-MA4.   MA-OUT."

"INITIALISATION"
1! W1.0. T1.60. W1.1. U1.0. "MELODY VOICE ON BUS 3, REST ON BUS 1"
2! W2.0. T1.60. W2.1.
3! W3.0. #FLT2 1; #FLT3 1; T1.60. W3.1.

"MAIN PERFORMANCE PROGRAMME"

"#SM AND #SA (MELODY AND ACCOMPANIMENT) REQUIRE 6 PARAMETERS"
"NOTE VALUE, TIME VALUE, ATTACK, DECAY, LOUDNESS AND FILTERING LIST NUMBER"
"#SM ALSO SPECIFIES THE SEVENTH PARAMETER OF INTERRUPT RATE"
COMMENTS FOR EACH VARIATION DO NOT INDICATE EACH PARAMETER CHANGE."

"MAIN THEME PLAYS IT MACHANICALLY STRAIGHT"
 #SM -,-,5,3,15,1,8; #SA -,-,5,3,15,1;
"VARIATION 1: RANDOM NOTES IN ACCOMPANIMENT"
 #SM -12,-,6;3,15,2,6; #SA -*0 63;-,6,7,14,2;
"VARIATION 2: MOVES BASS UP TREBLE DOWN"
 #SM #ZE -24;,-,5,3,15,3,8; #SA #ZE 24;,-,5,3,14,3;
"VARIATION 3: POSITIONED RANDOM NOTES IN BOTH CLEFS"
 #SM #ZE -6↑+6;,-,6,2,14,4,7; #SA --14↑,-,6,2,14,4;
"VARIATION 4: STRAIGHT WITH WOODWIND FILTERING"
 #SM -,-,5,3,14,5,8; #SA -,-,5,3,14,5;
"VARIATION 5: A SORT OF INVERSION WITH ILLOGICALITIES"
 #SM 64--12,-,5,3,14,6,5; #SA #ZE 13;,-,6,5,15,6;
"VARIATION 6: SLOW AND TRANSPOSED"
 #SM #ZE -7+3↑;,-,4,2,15,7,12; #SA #ZE 5↑;,-,4,4,15,7;
"VARIATION 7: SWAP ALTERNATE HIGH AND LOW OCTAVES"
Y=0 #SM #INV ;,-,4↑+3,4↑+3,14,7,9;
 #SA #INV ;,-,4↑+3,4↑+3,13,9;
"VARIATION 8: MUDDLED TIMES"
 #SM --29,- #PROB 30;,5,3,15,8,8;
 #SA --12,- #PROB 8;,5,3,12,8; #ADJ ;
"VARIATION 9: RANDOM NOTES WITHIN THE CORRECT RANGE"
 #SM -*0+24↑+12,-,5,4,15,8,9;
 #SA -*0+13↑+22,-,5,3,15,10;
"VARIATION 10: SEPARATE PARTS WITH DIFFERENT RALLENTANDOS"
Y=0 #SM -,- #COND 55;,5,1,15,7,11;
Y=0 #SA -,- #COND 20;,5,3,13,11;

1! T1.63. T1.63.   "WAIT FOR A BIT AT THE END"

Fig. 37

At this stage very little computer music of more than trivial interest existed (with some notable exceptions, such as the work of Herbert Brün and James K. Randall), but the scene was set for developments in the 1970s. Some younger composers, whose work was to flourish later, had published research, again mainly in sound analysis and synthesis. Prominent among these was Jean-Claude Risset, whose analyses of sound (see **digital synthesis techniques** 3) were to form the basis of his later compositional methods. Risset was a member of the Bell team in the mid-1960s, before returning to pursue his own researches in France (see section 4 below).

Computers were also being increasingly used in musicology. A good cross-section of these applications, covering a range which includes cataloguing, special notations, melodic analysis, thematic indexing, and solutions to one of Bach's riddle canons, is the collection *Elektronische Datenverarbeitung in der Musikwissenschaft* (Electronic Data Processing in Musicology) published in 1967 (Heckman, 1967). Although the title is in German, more than half the articles are in English.

By 1970 a number of computer music studios were active, mostly but not all in the USA. Apart from Utrecht and London, interesting developments were afoot in Italy, Sweden and elsewhere. The primary research had been done, and the technology was preparing for rapid growth.

3. Since 1970 I: Environments and facilities

As we have seen, computer music research had been going on for fifteen years or more in selected places, but by this time established non-computer studios around the world also began to realize that computers were their future, even if their main output was still analogue tape music. Computer acoustic research was also seen to have industrial potential, and some of the bigger studios attracted serious funding. Among the most important was Stanford University's Center for Computer Research in Music and Acoustics (CCRMA). It acquired this title in 1975, when it was properly set up and funded, but the team had been doing important development work for some years before, for example, Leland Smith's original composing program Score dates from 1971 (there is now a new Score by Dr Smith, which is music printing rather than composing software), and John Chowning's definitive FM paper was published in 1973 (Chowning, 1973) (for FM synthesis see **digital synthesis techniques** 6).

About the same time as CCRMA was set up, L'Institut de Recherche et de Coordination Acoustique/Musique (IRCAM) was getting to work in Paris. An underground complex, physically connected to the Centre Pompidou, this is one of the best equipped studios anywhere. Pierre Boulez, director of IRCAM, made sure from the beginning that CCRMA and other leading US studios would be involved, and the group forms a co-operative consortium, aiming to make composer and synthesis software portable between these large facilities, and co-ordinating research in an effort to prevent unnecessary duplication. An outline of these intentions is given in an overview published by the Stanford studio in 1977 (Chowning *et al.*, 1977), and followed, with a few deviations, till now. Also about this time the continuing series of annual International Computer Music Conferences began, and a selection of ICMC papers, plus other articles, appeared in *Computer Music Journal* which was first published in 1977 (there are many references to *CMJ* in our reading list).

While the major research centres were getting into their stride, and providing massive programming and synthesis power for composers who had access to them, the technology was moving very fast (as it still is), and beginning to offer new options. Digital music hardware became cheaper and better, and at Dartmouth College, New Hampshire, also in the mid-1970s, the composer Jon Appleton and others pioneered a small machine, of deliberately limited capability and cost, but offering open-ended programming, FM and additive synthesis etc. – in fact a complete small-scale composing facility. A version of this machine was commercially developed and sold by New England Digital Corporation as the Synclavier I,* which allowed live performance from a keyboard as well as non-real-time composing using a terminal. At the same time, the prototype of what was to be the Fairlight Computer Music Instrument (CMI) was being developed in Australia.† Both these machines were capable of sampling real sounds as well as internally generated synthesis, but the CMI offered sampling as its primary technique. Both formed the basis of quite powerful and versatile studios that were within the budgets of most music departments and quite a few individuals.

By 1980, therefore, the choice for a composer was to apply for time in one of the big studios, or to work with a facility that was less comprehensive but more accessible and personal, and still a serious composing tool. Both have a valid place, of course – just as in instrumental

*New England Digital Corporation, Box 546, 49 N. Main St., White River Junction, Vermont 05001, USA. Manufacturers of the Synclavier II and other products.
†Fairlight ESP Pty Ltd, 30 Bay St., Broadway, Sydney, NSW 2007, Australia.

composition one line can sometimes say everything, but large pieces need large resources.

The early 1980s saw the digital **keyboard synthesizer** replacing the analogue types of the 1970s, and universally adopted by the rock music industry – indeed the large manufacturers (most but not all Japanese) did not enter the field until a mass market was assured. To start with, none of these machines offered composing facilities, but as performing instruments the best were immediately successful, being versatile, portable and very good value for money. Digital recording was also getting cheaper, the **compact disc** was on the way, and sound sampling (see **digital synthesis techniques** 1–3) of adequate quality was soon available at prices comparable to synthesizers (see **samplers**). From 1983 both performance and composition possibilities were enhanced by the introduction of the Musical Instrument Digital Interface (see **MIDI**).

By the late 1980s the growing ownership of popular microcomputers had caused the 'serious' end of the composing fraternity to enter the small system field as well, and today small studios exist within large ones. There is liaison between manufacturers like Yamaha and studios like Stanford, and a growing library of interesting compositional software (see below). A possibility for the 1990s is the decay of the big studios, which are already seriously embarrassed by costs, and their gradual replacement by 'network composing' – small studios, linked electronically, to create temporary facilities of any desired computing and synthesizing capability. To a degree these links, by telephone line, radio or satellite, already exist, but they should become cheaper and more efficient, offering international composite set-ups of almost unlimited scope and variety.

4. Since 1970 II: Software and music

The distinction between composing and synthesis programs became fuzzier when sound synthesis began to be efficient enough to give composers immediate feedback. In instrumental music we are used to keeping the piece and the instrument separate – when writing violin music we do not worry about the design of the violin itself. But two of the distinguishing features of electronic music from the beginning were 1. the composer did indeed 'design the violin' as well as write for it; 2. the compositional method allowed continuous feedback in audible sound, instead of the composer hearing nothing until the first rehearsal of the completed work. By the 1970s it was clear that computers could offer a powerful extension of the techniques already well proved in analogue studios.

The idea of the 'sound object' ('l'objet sonore') was formalized in the

1960s by Pierre Schaeffer (Schaeffer, 1966), but aspects of 'sound as structure' and 'form as sound' were explored much earlier by such techniques as running tape loops at a very wide range of speeds, producing timbres at the fast end, and series of discrete events at the slow (see **musique concrète**).

The smallest sound object in computer music is smaller than the 'note' – it is the intangible 'pre-note', the ingredients from which the chef will concoct the dish. Formally, some pieces work upwards and outwards by combining these minimal units, others are conceived as broad outlines and work down to the detail. Most of course, lie somewhere in between.

A good description of the sound object as it relates to computer music is given by William Buxton and others, who point out that any kind of piece can be thought of as made up of interdependent 'chunks', a 'chunk' being any separately identifiable object from the smallest to the largest (Buxton, 1978). Cycle, note, phrase, section, movement, symphony are all objects, arranged in a hierarchy with each layer referring only to its upper and lower neighbour. In a 'note-by-note' type of piece successive objects are relatively close together, but in an unstructured 'grain density' composition there may be no separable objects between the tiny individual units of sound and the millions of them that make up the whole piece (compare the description of granular synthesis in **digital synthesis techniques** 7).

Although the 'chunk' concept unifies a number of compositional positions, it is only one way to slice the cake. To give some idea of the complexity of the programming problem, let's list, A, some of the formal strategies available to composers, B, some types of piece in which computers can play a role, and C, types of sound source that may be used (bearing in mind that the sounds may also be part of the structure).

A   *Types of compositional approach*

1. Traditional tonal or modal methods (which may include unusual temperaments, microtones, etc.), with melodic and/or harmonic links and developments and 'classical' formal structures, such as binary, ternary, variations, rondo, canon, fugue.
2. Modifications of 1. by including non-traditional sections, for example, unstructured or random passages in otherwise traditional structures.
3. Computer versions of serial procedures on Schoenberg/Webern models, i.e. transformations of motivic material. The computer can apply such transformations precisely to non-pitch parameters such as durations, dynamics, spatial position (difficult

in a purely instrumental environment). Serial methods may also grow out of traditional structures like 1. and 2.

4. 'Process' methods in which a chosen algorithmic procedure is progressively applied to 'seed' material specified by the composer or generated by the computer under the composer's rules. Can include versions of 1., 2. and 3., but may be random – it depends on the algorithm.

5. Small-to-large hierarchies, where the music builds either from the sounds themselves or from some aspect of them (e.g. localization or reverberation), which becomes the structural motivation for the piece.

6. 'Montage' pieces in which several streams of music are combined, randomly or strictly, to produce rich textures. The mix might involve several piece-types simultaneously, for example, Bach-type counterpoint added to cloud-like masses, added to treated natural sounds.

B   *Types of piece*

1. Conventional instrumental/vocal pieces, with computer-aided score production. No performance variables involving computer.

2. Straight 'tape music' (or possibly live from a computer/synthesizer). The composition process may be a mixture of several techniques, but the result is a playback with no human performers and no performance variables.

3. As 2., but with performance variables, i.e. the composing process is in two parts, one of them consisting of real-time performance instructions.

4. Combinations of instrumental/vocal performance with a computer synthesized part, live from machine or on tape, with no specific performance cross-influences.

5. As 4., but with performance variables and interactions, for example instrumental dynamic patterns (input via ADC) might affect the tempo of synthesized music, or the computer part might operate through **transducers** to modify the sound of the instruments.

6. Music for use with other media, with resulting constraints (and possibly real-time interaction), including film, video, ballet, theatre, radio music, multi-media events.

C   Types of sound source

1. Instrumental/vocal, direct acoustic performance.
2. As 1., but with electronic modifications (not necessarily involving a computer).
3. Any real sound (including instrumental/vocal or a generated sound from another source such as an analogue synthesizer), input to a computer (sampled via ADC), and treated as part of a composition, i.e. not in real time. In effect computer **musique concrète**.
4. As 3., but with real-time components (different types and range of treatments).
5. Synthesized sound, by direct digital or hybrid methods.
6. Mixtures of any of the above, for example, the modulation of a natural sound by a synthesized one.

This by no means exhausts the possibilities, but assuming a given piece to be a choice of one item from each list (e.g. A2., B4., C6.), there is clearly a great variety of ways in which a computer composer can go to work, though in practice some of the combinations would be rare.

The largest category in numerical terms is A1. – conventionally composed and notated music, using a twelve-note equally tempered octave, normal key and time signatures, staff notation etc. Because this is the chosen syntax of nearly all the popular styles of music, it is well catered for in the commercial field, and **sequencers**, storing mainly pitch and duration data, existed well before the digital synthesizer era. One should distinguish composition packages based on sequencers from the kind of compositional manipulations discussed in section 2 above, which attempt to explore new ways of making musical statements. The basis of most composer modules is the song format, and the expected input and musical result is conventionally notated harmonized melody, created by the composer in the same way as instrumental music, but organized (and possibly played and printed as well) by the machine. In a typical case, a piece is entered by placing notes one by one on a displayed blank stave, or directly from a piano-type keyboard. The stored song data is built up layer by layer and output to a synthesizer. Tempo of replay can be adjusted, and the actual sounds that emerge depend on the timbres selected – a process independent of the sequenced data.

The earlier composer modules were attachments to particular systems by one maker, but **MIDI** opened up new possibilities by allowing a composer to link together all sorts of diverse equipment. The orientation was still towards keyboards, but MIDI greatly increased flexibility and individual choice.

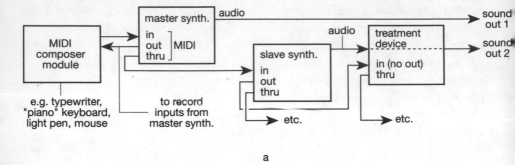

a

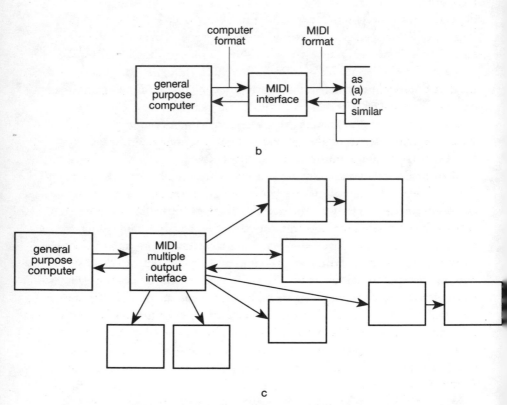

b

c

Fig. 38

Fig. 38 shows some composer set-ups using MIDI (see the **MIDI** entry for the functions of IN, OUT and THRU). As MIDI caught on, it was clear that dedicated composer packages were not necessary; any general purpose computer could be used provided suitable software was available and the machine was equipped with a hardware MIDI interface. Shown in fig. 38b and c, these are the most generally useful and flexible modes; 38b shows a simple interface initiating a chain of events as in a, and 38c shows a multi-output MIDI interface which allows devices to be operated in parallel (configured as a star rather than a chain). All the other peripherals and programs available on a general purpose computer can be called in as well, so composers can program in a wide range of languages, use graphics, print scores etc.

For many composers in the 'serious' field transferring instrumental syntax into computer music has no appeal, and for them most of the composer packages currently provided by synthesizer manufacturers have little to offer. The way these composers will choose to work depends on 1. the computer music options available (anything from a large, well-equipped studio, to a medium-grade university teaching studio, to a home computer with MIDI link to modest music hardware), and 2. the composer's skills as a programmer and grasp of the possibilities that do exist. Imaginatively used, a very limited studio can produce interesting work, as I attempted to show in *Quarts in Pint Pots* (Cary, 1985), given at the International Computer Music Conference, Paris, which describes some of the synthesis and programming work at the University of Adelaide in the early to mid-1980s.

Most of the best computer music is produced by composers who are not only sensitive musicians but thoroughly conversant with the programs and machines that produce it. There are really no effective shortcuts to this expertise, just as one cannot write properly for an orchestra without a thorough knowledge of the instruments that make it up. However, as soon as MIDI interfacing brought the resources of the popular computers within reach, programmers began to develop software offering much more than storing and sequencing a note input, and the list grows all the time. (For one popular machine (Apple Macintosh), the 1988 Australian Macworld Software Guide listed eighteen music programs. And this was only a small sample, available in a relatively small market, of the numerous packages now on offer in the main American, European and Oriental markets.)

Nearly all these programs lean towards conventionally notated music, some are designed more for score printing than performing or composing, and some have particular applications, for example, to commercial recording studios or drum machines (see **percussion generators**). But two programs in the list, Jam Factory and M (Intelligent Music),* are specially designed for a free, gestural approach to composing. Specific recommendations quickly get out of date, programs are updated

*Intelligent Music, 116 North Lake Avenue, Albany, NY 12206, USA.

NONET
SOURCE SCORE

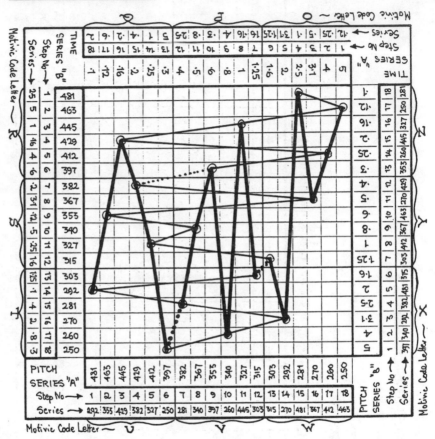

BASIC PITCH DIVISIONS

$\sqrt[18]{2}=1.0392592$ (⅔ eq. tempered semitone). 18 notes/octave. Middle octave 250-500 Hz, shifted in 17 steps by basic multipliers 1.346 and 1/1.346.

BASIC TIME DIVISIONS

Range 5" - 1" in exponential decrements (t/1.26, rounded to max. 3 figures). Shifted in 9 steps by basic multipliers 1.26, 1/1.26.

EVENT DISTRIBUTION

in Source Score is constant in all relevant directions

1	2	3
3	1	2
2	3	1

Fig. 39

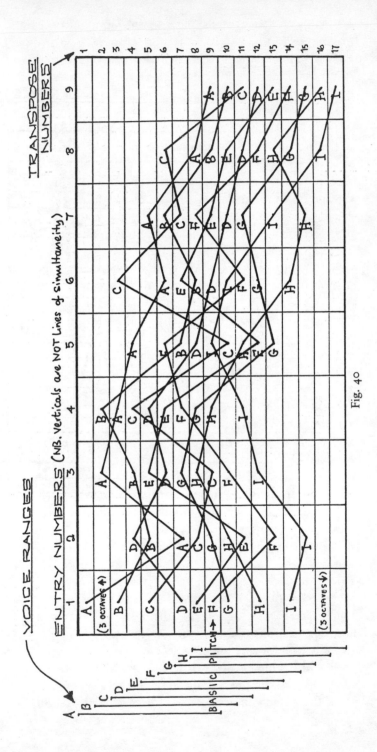

Fig. 40

frequently, and new ones appear, so one must consult current lists before making decisions. But M is a good example of a program by a well-known composer (Joel Chadabe) who has written his own software for many years, participating in the writing of a generalized user package that is intended to have wide appeal (an earlier program from the same source was Play).

To make composer software more saleable and appealing to users who want quick results without too much effort, the tendency (particularly since MIDI) has been to narrow rather than widen the options. M aims to go the other way, towards openness and flexibility, and to get the composer as much as possible out of boring note-by-note specification and into interesting and varied manipulations. There is a choice of precise control or extempore gesture. In such an open field as composing, however, it is impossible to make rules, and for some composers getting to grips with multi-option programs and choosing the correct path for the job in hand are difficult and inhibiting. It is a matter of working preferences, and in many cases there may be no alternative to designing a program specifically for one job. Composers know their own thought processes better than those of others, so I illustrate the kinds of decision to be made by two examples from my own work.

Nonet (compositional type A3., B2., C5.) (Cary, 1979) was composed at Stanford University (CCRMA) during a short stay of two months in 1979. I was keen to exploit the powerful resources of the then newly installed 256-voice synthesizer (Samson Box) by writing a multi-voice contrapuntal piece. My choices were: 1. Learn enough Sail (Stanford Artificial Intelligence Language) to write my piece program from scratch; or 2. Use existing, resident software, if necessary adapting my idea to suit it. After attending some Sail tutorials, it was clear that I would not acquire adequate skills to compose anything complex in the short time available. Turning to 2., I studied Leland Smith's Score (Smith, 1978, see section 3), and found that it had a motivic manipulation feature by which I could build the kind of structure I had in mind. So *Nonet* was written in Score, and completed in a few weeks. Fig. 39 shows the source score of the piece. The compressed notation shows two invertible eighteen-term series, applied both to an octave of eighteen equal steps and to an **exponential** time series ranging from 0.1 to 5 seconds. Time and pitch multipliers are used to create eighty-one unique entries (nine voices with nine entries each), and fig. 40 shows one of the graphic scores (pitch multiplier), indicating a generally downward pitch trend.

All the graphic material was gathered together, translated into Score code and typed in. The sample in fig. 41 includes a silent instrument

```
REVRB 0 0 1;    <Instr 1
P2 550;
P3 .04; P4 .056; P5 .047; P6 .058;
END;

DUMY;           <Instr 2
P2 NUM/O(.12/.25/.5/.1/3.1/1.25)/  P(1.6/.16/4/.3/.8/2.5)/
Q(5/1/.4/.2/.6/2)/  R(2.5/5/1/.16/4/.6)/  S(.2/3.1/.12/.5/
.25/1.6)/  T(1.25/.1/.4/2/.8/.3);
P3 NUM/U(291.6/353.5/428.6/381.9/327.3/250)/  V(280.6/340.2/
396.9/259.8/445.4/303)/  W(315/270/481/367.4/412.4/462.9)/
X(396.9/340.2/291.6/381.9/481/315)/  Y(303/412.4/367.4/
462.9/270/428.6)/  Z(353.5/259.8/445.4/327.3/250/280.6);
P5 F6; P6 1;
END;

TA 0,540;       <Instr 3  -  VOICE A-1
P2 NUM/eT .4/eQ .4/eO .4/eR .4/eP .4/eS .4/  eP .5/eQ .5/eR .5/
eS .5/eT .5/eO .5/  eR .63/eT .63/eP .63/eO .63/eQ .63/eS .63;
P3 NUM/eZ 10.8/eW 10.8/eU 10.8/eX 10.8/e-V 10.8/eY 10.8/
eU 1.81/eV 1.81/eW 1.81/eX 1.81/eY 1.81/eZ 1.81/  eV 8/eX 8/
eZ 8/eY 8/eU 8/eW 8;
P4 MOVX/19 1.3,1 1,.8/24 .7,.4 .8,.5/30 .7,.4 .3,.05;
P5 .6 "F29" .2 "F19" .2 "F6";
P10 .4 "45" .2 "135" .2 "225" .2 "315";
P11 1 3,6;
P12 .07;
P13 FUNC/31/33;
P14 DF 1.3;
END;
TA 73.1;
P2 NUM/-17/eT/eP/eO/eR/eQ/eS/  eP .794/eO .794/eR .794/
eT .794/eQ .794/eS .794/  eR 1.26/eO 1.26/eT 1.26/
eP 1.26/eQ 1.26/eS 1.26;
P3 NUM/0/eW 5.95/eY 5.95/eX 5.95/eU 5.95/eZ 5.95/eV 5.95
/eX 4.42/eW 4.42/eZ 4.42/eV 4.42/eY 4.42/eU 4.42/
eY 2.44/eV 2.44/eU 2.44/eW 2.44/eX 2.44/eZ 2.44;
P4 MOVX/65 .05,.2 .1,.4/38 .1,.2 .2,.1/59 .1,.05 .1,.1;
END;
TA 236;
P2 NUM/-12.28/e-T 1.59/e-R 1.59/eO 1.59/e-P 1.59/eQ 1.59/
eS 1.59/e-P 2/eO 2/e-R 2/e-T 2/eS 2/eQ 2/e-R 2.52/
eS 2.52/e-P 2.52/e-T 2.52/eQ 2.52/eO 2.52;
P3 NUM/0/eZ 3.28/eX 3.28/e-U 3.28/eV 3.28/e-W 3.28/e-Y 3.28/
eU 1.35/e-Z 1.35/eW 1.35/eY 1.35/e-X 1.35/e-Y 1.35/
eV/e-W/eZ/eX/e-U/e-Y;
P4 MOVX/88 .4,.1 .3,.1/95 .2,.3 .4,.1/120 .2,.5 .4,.8;
```

Fig. 41

('dumy') that contains all the motivic data. When the piece plays, this data is 'looked up' by the performing instruments (e.g. /@T .4/ in Instr. 3 means find motive T (in dumy) and multiply it by .4).

Finally, with sound to listen to, some editing decisions were made (such as relative voice levels, which are hard to judge before the actual counterpoint is heard), and the piece was ready. It would have been impossible to realize *Nonet* with keyboard/stave software, but an existing program with the necessary features was available.

The other example is *Trellises* (A4., B3., C5.), composed in 1984, and realized on a small system (Synclavier I, made by New England Digital),* using a general purpose language (Scientific XPL). Apart from calls to 'instruments' there is nothing specifically musical in the program, which creates textures rather than melodies or structured harmony. These textures are limited to the sixteen available voices, and absolute pitch values are subordinate to general pitch area and intervals between pitches (spacing), so pitch is specified by giving an upper and lower limit which defines a 'pitch-space' to be filled by a specified number of notes. These are selected either randomly or on an equal interval basis – go from here to there in *x* steps. Sometimes the upper and lower limits are very close, tending towards unisons or small undulations, sometimes wide apart, giving 'points in space' or arpeggio-like spread chords. Once established, a texture is changed progressively by replacing part of it, so there is always some of the old remaining with the new. Attacks vary in hardness but no note ends abruptly – there is an overlapping 'tail' of varying length, called the 'smudge factor' in my notes.

Formal aspects of the piece are self-regulating, i.e. my program decides the rules, but within these the piece re-writes its own score after so many events, plays a new variation, re-writes etc., and this process can continue indefinitely. The odds against exact repetition are millions to one, but the music is not formless because there is evolution in the successive variations (lasting about three minutes each). It is intended as a piece to visit from time to time rather than listen to continuously, and it also writes its current pitch data in real time to a visual display, painting a moving score which renews at each variation.

The programming strategy is to take a group of graphically input functions and read the curves progressively to provide data for all the variables (pitch area, event duration, sound duration within event, type of pitch selection, instrument (timbre), attack, voice density, smudge

*New England Digital Corporation, Box 546, 49 N. Main St., White River Junction, Vermont 05001, USA. Manufacturers of the Synclavier II and other products.

factor etc.). As the first version plays, the values selected for some parameters are fed back to the functions and added to them. These additions are non-linear in the sense that a large disturbance creates a disproportionately larger one. After a 'laundering' routine which smooths the now-roughened curves, the second version runs from the new functions, and so on. Because the new values are added to the old (+ and − from a mid-point) any undulations in the curves get larger in amplitude and more disturbed, which in the music means more sudden surprises and general activity. The self-correcting element in the program ensures that when any curve reaches certain set limits (beyond which the music may become unacceptably random and undisciplined) it is drastically corrected to a more central position, or 'calmed'. This calming operation takes place at different times for different functions, preventing the entire texture suddenly becoming too flat and boring. The general effect is that the music moves between calmness and excitement in slow waves. The 'launder' and non-linear adder/corrector sub-routines are shown in fig. 42. *Trellises* involved writing two programs because the graphic manipulation process is separate from the piece itself, and in the university studio where the piece was composed the graphics package was put into the system as generally available software – in this way a library of utilities is built up.

I have examined these two pieces in some detail because methods of work are best seen by citing real examples. To take some other categories, A2. and A6. are variants of schemes already discussed. In a typical A2. program, the piece is written in two stages, the first of which is to create blocks, each comprising a complete sub-program for part of the piece. The second, performing program calls the blocks in the desired sequence, arranges timing and any second stage manipulations etc. In any studio not able to mix digitally (which is still most studios) A6. may involve an analogue mix, the computer generated music being taped and mixed down. A good example, referred to in section 2, is *HPSCHD* (Cage/Hiller*) where a number of computer tracks are mixed and played back with live performers.

A5. (small-to-large) is well exemplified by the work of Jean-Claude Risset (see also section 2), who has made some of the most subtle and sensitive pieces in computer music literature. His sound sources include real sounds treated in the computer, live performance combined with such sounds or with synthesized sound, and pure synthesis.

---

*Cage, John and Lejaren Hiller *HPSCHD for harpsichords and computer-generated sound tapes* Nonesuch Records, New York, H71224–A.

```
1350
1360        /* Function smoothing routine. Effect depends on number of
1370        TIMES through the wash */
1380        LAUNDER:PROC(TIMES);
1390          DCL HOLD(63)FIXED;
1400          DCL(TIMES,W)FIXED;
1410          DCL INC FLOATING;
1420          DO I=1 TO TIMES;
1430            K=0;
1440            /* Take average of groups of 4 points and put in holding buffer */
1450            DO B=0 TO 63;
1460              W=0;
1470              DO A=0 TO 3;
1480                W=W+TEMP(K);K=K+1;
1490              END;
1500              HOLD(B)=INT(W/4);
1510            END;W=0;K=0;
1520            /* Draw straight lines between the average points and put in scratch pad buffer */
1530            DO A=0 TO 62;
1540              INC=(HOLD(A+1)-HOLD(A))/4;
1550              TEMP(K)=HOLD(A);W=HOLD(A);K=K+1;
1560              DO B=0 TO 2;
1570                W=W+INT(INC);TEMP(K)=W;K=K+1;
1580              END;
1590            END;
1600            K=251;DO A=252 TO 255;TEMP(A)=TEMP(K);K=K-1;END;
1610          END;
1620        END LAUNDER;
1630
```

```
1760
1770        /* Non-linear adder */
1780        DO A=0 TO 255;
1790          DCL(DIV,FAC)FIXED;
1800          IF (C+1) MOD 7=0 THEN FAC=512;
1810          ELSE FAC=1000-(((C13)+1)*80);
1820          /* The further out the old point was the more it is moved in the same direction */
1830          DIV=INT(FAC/(ABS(OL-512)+1));
1840          IF OL>=512 THEN DO;
1850            OL=OL+INT(NL/DIV);
1860            /* If it hits the top, bounce it down twice as far (more instability) */
1870            IF OL>1023 THEN OL=1023-((OL-1023)*2);
1880          END;
1890          ELSE DO;
1900            OL=OL-INT(NL/DIV);
1910            /* Ditto the bottom - bounce it up twice as far */
1920            IF OL<0 THEN OL=(-OL)*2;
1930          END;
1940        END;
1950
```

Fig. 42

His delicate micro-manipulations of timbre, beginning at Bell Labs in the 1960s, have produced a whole series of pieces in which the large structures in effect evolve from the detail of the sounds themselves. *Mutations* (1969) is entirely synthesized, *Inharmonique* (1977) is for tape and soprano, and *Songes* (1979) takes recorded instrumental fragments and treats and blends them with synthesized sounds. Needless to say, Risset develops his own software approach for each case. *Mutations*, *Inharmonique* and other pieces are available on disc,* and Risset is also represented on *IRCAM – Un Portrait*,† referred to below.

Real sound sources can of course be used in a much simpler way than Risset does. From one point of view sound sampling is simply another way to produce A1. or any other type of piece, and sampling synthesizers such as the Fairlight‡ have composing routines to organize sampled sounds into complete pieces. In recent years a wide range of sampling machines has appeared (see **samplers**), and they are all MIDI-equipped. Small systems cannot handle the massive sound files needed for large-scale pieces, however, and an even more complex situation arises when several types of sound source are used together. An excellent example of such a piece is Michael McNabb's *Dreamsong* (1978).

Dreamsong (A6., B2., C6.) comes to the hearer as a rich montage of diverse sounds, but it differs radically from a conventional tape montage, in that 1. most of the combined sounds result from merging or modulating in subtle ways, not simple mixing; 2. there is no post-computer montaging – the piece plays directly from the system with no further processing. To quote McNabb's analytical study *Dreamsong: The Composition*:

> The basic intent of the piece was to integrate a set of synthesized sounds with a set of digitally recorded natural sounds to such a degree that they would form a continuum of available sound material ... The essential sound elements in *Dreamsong* can be divided into five categories: simple frequency modulation (FM), complex FM, sung vocal processing and resynthesis, other additive synthesis, and processed crowd sounds and speech. (McNabb, 1981)

*Risset, Jean-Claude, *Mutations, Dialogues, Inharmonique, Moments Newtoniens* INA-GRM Records, Paris, AM564.09, 1978.
†Barrière, Jean-Baptiste (artistic director) *IRCAM: Un Portrait* (Record with booklet), IRCAM 0001, IRCAM, Centre Pompidou, Paris, 1983.
‡Fairlight ESP Pty Ltd, 30 Bay St., Broadway, Sydney, NSW 2007, Australia.

Short samples of soprano voice were processed to make long sounds and choral textures, and combined with a synthesized voice-like instrument. At the end, a digital recording of a crowd is processed to follow the nuances of the voice of Dylan Thomas (taken from a 1950s recording), and is eventually transformed into Thomas's voice. There are complex FM bell sounds, deep drones which merge into vocal sounds, and several significant thematic fragments that recur at various points in the piece.

The complex programming is detailed in *Dreamsong: The Composition* (McNabb, 1981), and reinforces the point made above, that most of the best computer music is through-programmed uniquely for the one work. *Dreamsong* is a good example of computer music that is convincing in its own right – it could only be computer music, but it succeeds as music without any explanation of its origin or mechanisms being necessary. A recording is available.*

5. Conclusion

Only a few names and pieces have been mentioned from what is now a very extensive literature – compared with the conventional field, in fact, computer composers are also prolific writers about the subject, and conference papers, articles and books abound, as well as a growing number of recordings. From the composer's point of view, the three main changes in the last fifteen years or so have been: 1. the removal of actual synthesis from software specification to digital hardware – a gain in convenience but a loss in flexibility; 2. the arrival of MIDI – also a gain in many ways but not without problems; 3. the increased accessibility of computer composing, albeit often at a restricted level, as prices of adequate computing and synthesis facilities drop.

Choosing recommendations for further study from the mass of material is difficult, but here are a few suggestions in addition to references given above. A useful general starter book is Adams's *Electronic Music Composition for Beginners* (Adams, 1986), and Manning's *Electronic and Computer Music* (Manning, 1987) contains a good technical and historical survey. Curtis Roads's collection of essays and interviews with a number of computer composers, *Composers & The Computer* (Roads, 1985), gives interesting insights into thought and method. There are many relevant articles in *Computer Music Journal*, and, in addition to those already cited, *Symposium on Computer Music Composition* (Roads, 1986) is of particular interest, and *Composing with Computers:*

*McNabb, Michael *Computer Music* 1750 Arch Records, S-1800, 1983.

A Progress Report (Hiller, 1981) is a very interesting survey by Lejaren Hiller of his own work over the years – a large span going right back to the *Illiac Suite*. In fact this whole issue of CMJ (vol. 5 no. 4, 1981), which also contains the McNabb article noted above, is devoted to aspects of composition. Bill Schottstaedt's article on his own composing language, 'Pla', is also relevant (Schottstaedt, 1983), and naturally the references I have given contain their own further references.

Finally, a number of studios run teaching programmes and will respond to enquiries. Many have house publication lists and/or issue records, some on direct sale (not available in record stores). To mention just one informative disc, *IRCAM – Un Portrait** gives many examples of different synthesis methods, and extracts from a number of works realized at this Paris centre. The copious sleeve notes and enclosed leaflet (in French) give the history of the studio and details of what the record contains.

Computer music studio design   See **studio design**

Condenser microphone   See **microphones**

Conduct/ance, -ive, -ivity   The reciprocal of **resistance**, i.e. 1/R. Former unit the mho (mild joke!), now replaced by the siemens (SI unit).

Conductor   A material which contains some electrical **charge** carrying particles (e.g. free electrons in metals) allowing electrical **current** to flow in it.

Cone   See **loudspeakers**

Console   The central control desk in a studio, often synonymous with **mixing desk**, but it may include more than this, for example **patches**, **remote controls** and assorted ancillary equipment grouped for easy access by studio operators. See also **control room**.

Consonance   See **dissonance**

Constant   1. (adjective) Not changing with time or varying when other parameters of a system change; e.g. a constant **current** is one designed

---

*Barrière, Jean-Baptiste (artistic director) *IRCAM: Un Portrait* (Record with booklet), IRCAM 0001, IRCAM, Centre Pompidou, Paris, 1983.

not to change even though its operating environment does (see e.g. **oscillators,** voltage controlled); 2. (noun) in mathematics, a fixed value. Algebraic expressions normally contain a mixture of constant and **variable** quantities.

Contact microphone   See **microphones**

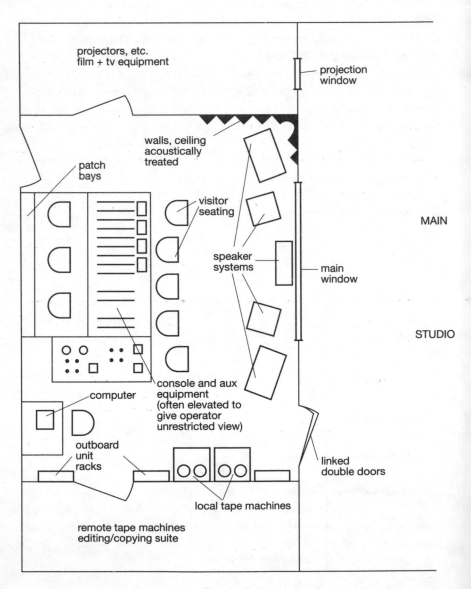

Fig. 43a

Control room   (control cubicle) The operational centre of a studio, preferably sound-proofed, acoustically treated and air-conditioned to constant temperature and humidity, which contains everything required to make a studio function (though not necessarily the recording machines). It need not be large, but must allow operators to be adequately distanced from monitor loudspeakers (even 'close field' speakers, which are designed for optimum sound balance at low output levels, should be some feet away from the listener).

The actual contents of the room depend on the function of the studio, for example, music recording only, music and dialogue/commentary recording, full drama studio, news broadcasting, disc jockey (DJ) broadcasting, TV sound, film sound, theatre stage playback etc. As many essential controls as possible are grouped in a central console so that they can be reached by one or two seated balance engineers. Traditionally, the cubicle is connected with one or more recording/broadcasting studios by heavy double doors and double-glazed windows, but today remote operation via closed-circuit TV is common.

Fig. 43a shows the layout of the cubicle for a typical music recording studio. Principal lines in and out are shown in 43b. Control rooms for the other functions mentioned above must contain appropriate

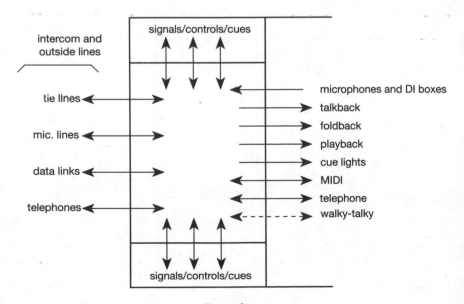

Fig. 43b

equipment – TV monitors, film projectors, transmitter lines etc. See **acoustic treatments, direct box, foldback, loudspeakers, MIDI, mixers and mixing desks, studio design** and **talkback**. A detailed study of the whole subject, with recommended building methods and many examples, can be found in chapters 5 and 6 of Ballou (1987), and more concise comments in Nisbett (1970), Runstein (1989) and Nisbett (1983).

Control voltage   See **analogue synthesis techniques** 4 and **oscillators**

Copy editing   Editing a programme without physically cutting tape. See **tape composition techniques.**

Core   A non-**volatile** magnetic fast **memory**, expensive to make and now obsolete (though the term still sometimes used). Replaced by **random access memory**, which is volatile but with power back-up can be made retentive.

Corner reflector   See **loudspeakers**

Cosine wave   Identical in shape to a **sine wave** but out of **phase**, described as leading it by 90° (or lagging by 270°). See fig. 44.

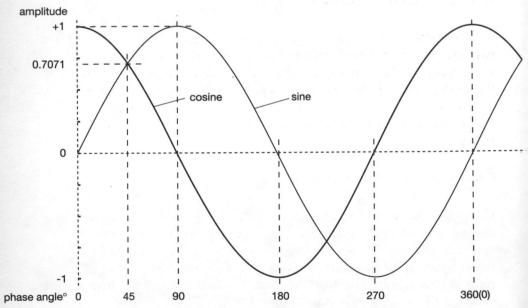

Fig. 44

Cottage loaf response See **microphones**

Coulomb An **SI unit** of charge, symbol C, defined as the quantity of charge which passes through a conductor in one second when a current of one **Ampère** flows in it.

CPU See **central processing unit**

Crab To move a camera or microphone, for example, along a linear sideways path. Compare **panning** (horizontal rotation about an axis).

Crash A computer system failure. A 'hard' crash is sudden and catastrophic. A typical 'soft' crash is preceded by warning symptoms, giving time for appropriate action (e.g. saving work in progress) to be taken. See **graceful degradation**.

CRO See **oscilloscope**

Crossfade The sound equivalent of a visual dissolve, i.e. the gradual replacement of one signal by another, the two signals combining in varying proportion during the change.

Cross-modulation A usually undesirable intermodulation between two signals, an unwanted strong signal influencing a wanted weaker one. Because modulation may cause new **inharmonic** frequency products, the result is often a bad type of **distortion**. It can also be used deliberately as a synthesis technique, and to test performance of **amplifiers**. For modulation principles, see **amplitude modulation** and **frequency modulation**.

Crossover network See **loudspeakers**

Crosstalk In multi-channel systems, an unwanted leakage from one channel to another. In most stereo applications a certain amount can be tolerated because the two signals are versions of the same material, but crosstalk must be minimal when multi-track recording (see **sound recording techniques** 2) completely different signals, e.g. controlling a montage. Crosstalk is expressed as decibels 'down' (− dB) at the adjacent track. For good equipment −70 dB, or better, would be expected. Low crosstalk is also referred to as good 'separation'.

CRT See **cathode ray tube**

Crystal movements See **microphones** and **pick-ups**

Crystal oscillator See **oscillators**

Cubicle See **control room**

Current A flow of electric **charge**. In a **circuit** this is caused by a potential difference or **voltage** in some part of the circuit and always has electrical energy associated with it. The size of a current in a circuit depends not only on the applied voltage but also, in a **DC** circuit, on the total **resistance**, and in the case of **AC** on the total **impedance** in the circuit. Algebraic symbol I, **SI** unit the **Ampère**. See also **Ohm's law**.

Cut editing Editing sound recordings by physically cutting and joining the tape. See **splice** and **tape composition techniques**.

Cut-off 1. In a transistor or valve (tube), condition where the restrictive effect of the control **electrode** stops the current flow altogether. Opposite condition to **saturation**; 2. **frequency** at which a **filter's** slope reaches maximum steepness. Also called 'break', or 'turnover'.

Cycle A regularly repeating set of changes, in which all values return at the end of a **period** to those obtaining at the beginning. See **frequency** and **hertz**.

D

DAC See **digital-to-analogue converter**

Damping The progressive draining of energy from a mechanical or electrical **oscillatory** system, because of an external force opposing its motion. Damping may be uncontrolled, e.g. a pendulum allowed to swing until it stops, or controlled, e.g. the dampers in a **piano** (*acoustic*) or a car's shock-absorbers. The 'damping factor' is the ratio of the amplitude of one oscillation to that of the following one. A potentially oscillatory circuit or mechanical system is 'critically damped' if it returns to its equilibrium state in the shortest possible time when disturbed, without actually oscillating, i.e. all the energy is absorbed in the first half-**cycle**. Correct damping is very important in electro-mechanical devices like **loudspeakers** and **microphones**. See also **hunting** and **resonance**.

Dash Digital Audio Stationary Head. See **sound recording techniques**.

DAT See **digital audio tape**

Data base A collection of information, preferably organized in an accessible and unambiguous way. In **computer music composition**, for example, the total data base required to realize a piece is a combination of that already resident in the computer and that supplied by the composer. For a successful outcome, everything must be logically ordered under the control of an **operating system**.

dB See **decibel**

dbx See **noise reduction**

DC See **direct current**

D.C. amplifier   See **amplifiers**

Dead room   A nearly **anechoic** room used in radio drama, for example, to simulate outdoor conditions. See **acoustic treatments**.

Dead side   See **microphones** (fig. 123b), and **stereo**

Debug/ging   The process of removing 'bugs' or errors which are almost certain to be initially present in any but the simplest new system or program. A bug is a problem in the programming of a system and is not the same as a fault, which is something that goes wrong with a debugged and proved system, and may be revealed by a **diagnostic routine**.

Decade   The relationship (up or down) between adjacent **powers** of 10, e.g. 55 to 550, 1234.56 to 123.456. See **logarithm, octave** and **order**.

Decay   1. The progressive dissipation of energy as a sound dies away. If decay is free and uncontrolled (e.g. in a percussive sound or in the air of a **reverberant** space), it follows an **exponential** law. 2. The name of segment(s) in an **envelope shaper**'s cycle where amplitude is usually falling (see **analogue synthesis techniques** 4).

Decibel   (symbol dB) One tenth of a Bel (named after Alexander Graham Bell), and being of a more convenient size in practical applications almost always used instead of it. A measure of relative electrical or acoustic energy levels, decibels usually refer to the relative size of two sound **intensities** or their equivalent in electrical power, both measured in **watts**. The unit can be adapted to compare voltages (or where appropriate, currents or sound pressures), but this entry is concerned with the decibel as a measure of relative power. By a lucky chance, one decibel represents about the smallest change in loudness we can perceive, so it is a convenient unit for sound engineers.

Our ears can handle an enormous range of levels (around $1-10^{12}$ from the barely audible to the noticeably painful), and **logarithmic** changes are perceived as roughly **linear**, i.e. doubling the power will result in a certain increase in perceived loudness, but doubling it again (four times the original) will only cause the same increase as before. Intensity relationships are expressed in decibels as $dB = 10 \ (\log_{10} I_2/I_1)$; for example, if intensity doubles, $I_2/I_1 = 2$, and the dB difference is thus $10 \times \log_{10} 2$. $\log_{10} 2$ is very nearly .3, so $+3$ dB represents a doubling of power (−3 dB a halving of it). 18 dB therefore means a power increase of ×64, and the vast range of a trillion to one mentioned above becomes reasonably manageable when expressed as 120 dB (see **phon**).

The dB in its basic form is a 'floating' unit, signal A being referred to as, for example, 7 dB up, or 20 dB down, on signal B. There are also various 'zero reference levels' for different purposes, o dB being given a specific value to which + or − departures are referred. In audio electronics a unit called the decibel milliwatt is used (dBm). o dBm is set at 1 milliwatt in 600 **ohms**, or .775 V (see **Ohm's law** and **watt**), and signals of around this value are said to be at 'line level', chosen as a comfortable working mean between small and large signals (see **lining up**). Professional equipment normally runs at +4 dBm (see **volume unit**), and domestic at −10 dBm.

Fig. 45 illustrates the typical range of dBm encountered in audio work.

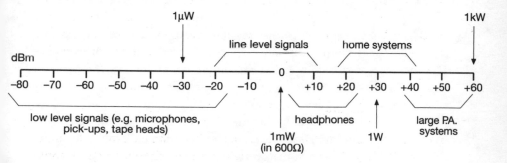

Fig. 45

Deck   The mechanical part of a tape or cassette recorder – i.e. motors, heads, braking systems etc., as distinct from the amplifiers or other electronics. Sometimes used, however, to denote a complete machine without cabinet (e.g. for rack mounting). Also used to refer to record players. See **tape recorder design**.

Decoding   The automatic re-conversion to normal of a signal previously encoded by a similar but opposite process. Analogue decoding is a stage in **noise reduction** systems. Digital decoding may involve several changes of format, see **compact disc, pulse code modulation, sound recording techniques** and **video cassette PCM**.

Default   (value) In a program, the value that will automatically be used if no other is specified. Chosen by the programmer as the 'most likely to be useful', but users have the option to change it.

Degaussing The process of demagnetizing, i.e. rendering a material magnetically neutral, named after J. K. F. Gauss. See **sound recording techniques** 2.

Demo tape A recording made for demonstration purposes. An important aid to public relations for performing groups, composers etc. Good demo tapes make the maximum impact in the shortest possible time. Sometimes the tape is excerpted from existing recordings, but often arrangements and songs are made specially for the demo, and large sums of money may be spent, particularly if video is included. Some studios make a speciality of demo recording, and master tapes are often of good enough quality for a commercial release if things go well.

Demodulat/e, -or To restore a wave to its original form after a previous modulation. This occurs in radio sets, for example, to recover the audio signal from the transmitted modulated **carrier**. Older usage (in AM radio) was detector. See **amplitude modulation** and **frequency modulation**.

Detent/ -ed A method of identifying a point (often the mid-point) in the travel of a continuous control, such as a spring locating in a notch. Typical uses are in tone and balance controls (for 'level' and 'central' positions).

Deviation See **frequency modulation**

Diagnostic routine In computers, an internal checking procedure, often automatically run when a system is activated, designed to reveal problems and advise the user. In an analogue context, **patching** not for musical results but to test some aspect of the system.

Diagonal cut See **tape composition techniques**

DI box See **direct box**

Dielectric The name for an insulating material (which may be solid, liquid or gaseous) placed between two conductors, for example, in a **capacitor**, where it reacts to the electric field. The Greeks noticed that when amber (*elektron*) was rubbed, it attracted small objects; electrical science thus takes its name from this ancient observation of a simple **electrostatic** phenomenon.

Difference frequency The **frequency** obtained by subtracting one frequency from another. This and the sum frequency occur in a pure form when the instantaneous amplitudes of two **sine waves** are multiplied, as in a suppressed **carrier**, or **ring modulator** (see also **analogue synthesis techniques** 5). Fig. 46 illustrates the result of multiplying two signals at 500 **hertz** and 600 Hz. Note that the output (100 and 1100 Hz) contains neither of the original frequencies.

A difference frequency in the sub-audio range is produced by the addition of two audio signals only a few Hz apart in frequency. In this case it is heard as 'beats', caused by the alternate cancellation and reinforcement of the two waves. If beats are slow (up to about 3 Hz) the effect is quite pleasant, but faster beats are a major cause of **dissonance**. See also **combination tones**.

Digital Literally 'of the fingers' (appropriately because fingers are the basic human counting device), this refers to systems which operate with discrete numbers rather than continuous functions (**analogue**). Digital methods are discussed in many entries, for example, **digital audio tape**, **digital synthesis techniques**, **sound recording techniques**, etc.

Digital audio tape (DAT) A high quality **pulse code modulation** digital recording system, using cassettes about three-quarters the size of standard compact cassettes, but the same width of tape (3.81 mm). **Sampling rate** is 48 kHz, **resolution** sixteen **bits**. Only high quality tape stock is suitable for this exacting application, and the cassettes have a locking shutter to protect the tape from dust and damage. For the general principles of digital sampling, see **digital synthesis techniques** 1.

DAT brings to domestic recording the same order of advance in high fidelity, low noise and user convenience over the analogue cassette that the **compact disc** showed over the vinyl LP as a play-only medium. In the professional field the appearance of portable, battery-driven DAT machines in 1988 signalled the probable replacement of analogue portables, in both open reel and cassette formats, for reportage and location recording of music, film dialogue, etc. It is too early to make firm predictions, though, because although DAT machines are now available in many countries, the industry itself is still indecisive about how best to develop and market the new medium.

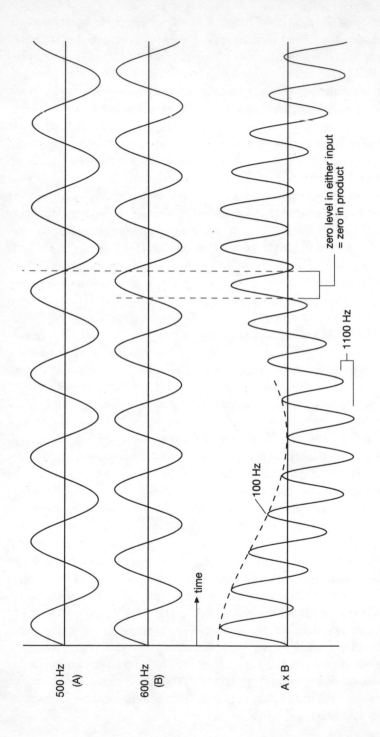

500 Hz
(A)

600 Hz
(B)

A x B

time

100 Hz

1100 Hz

zero level in either input
= zero in product

Fig. 46

As long ago as 1983 two formats were proposed for evaluation, S-DAT, or stationary head DAT, and R-DAT, in which the record/replay head rotates at an angle to the tape path (see **helical scan** and **video cassette PCM**). R-DAT has so far been the winner in this contest, because although mechanically a more complicated design, the industry has much experience in making reliable rotating head mechanisms for the huge video cassette market, and the method combines a tape-to-head speed adequate for high density recording with a very slow spool-to-spool speed (8.15 mm/sec, against 47.5 mm/sec for analogue cassettes), allowing extended play from relatively short tapes.

An unusually long time elapsed between their development and the first market appearances of DAT machines in 1986–7. Some of the delay was due to design problems, but much of it was caused by legal and commercial wrangles, principally over fears that DAT would produce a flood of contraband tapes copied from CD. Piracy was already a billion-dollar problem with analogue cassettes, even though most illegal copies are of very poor quality. Unless steps were taken, it was thought that DAT copies of impeccable sound would seriously threaten the enormous investment in CD plant and marketing.

Anti-copying strategies for CD, DAT and computer software are continually being reviewed. Some, for example, allow one digital copy but no more. In the case of DAT, the chosen copy protection measure was the adoption of the professional digital recording sampling rate of 48 kHz, deliberately incompatible with the 44.1 kHz of CDs. This does not prevent copying via an analogue link, however, and the quality of such copies is still very good. Playback at 44.1 kHz is allowed for and some machines also offer 32 kHz, a lower quality sampling rate used in the Video 8 format, and proposed for **PCM** radio, which also permits a long play mode, giving four hours of recording at reduced quality.

Digital copies of one's own digital recordings, at 48 kHz, are identical in quality to the original. Absence of signal deterioration or added noise on transfer are features of digital recordings because analogue noise is not recognized in the digital domain – it is only necessary for the code to be copied with sufficient accuracy to be recovered intact.

All magnetic media are subject to faults and drop-outs, however, and DAT uses a system of error detection/correction and interleaving codes similar to those used in the other digital media (see **compact disc**). Added to the signal are 'sub-codes' which include identification codes for locating items on the tape, and parts of the track are reserved for special pilot signals to ensure perfect tracking (area-divided track following or ATF).

DAT has so far been marketed as a domestic format, and rigorous tests have shown that when professional standards are expected there are problems, for example of compatibility – tapes recorded on one machine do not always play reliably on another. There is some doubt, too, about the long-term stability and accuracy of these tiny helical scan recordings, and S-DAT may still be the eventual winner. A new fixed-head system, Digital Compact Cassette (DCC), had not yet reached the market at the time of writing, but shows considerable promise.

It is likely that R-DAT will be the prevailing compact recording method for some time to come. In studio work the position is different, because the requirements are for multi-track recording, and in some cases for the possibility of **cut editing**, not feasible with helical scan tapes. See **sound recording techniques**, and for a complete technical analysis see chapter 8 in Watkinson (1988).

Digital multi-effect unit   A type of digital signal processor (DSP) which offers a wide range of effects instead of being dedicated to one only. The principle is to convert the incoming signal to the digital domain (by **analogue-to-digital converter**) manipulate it in this form and reconvert (by **digital-to-analogue converter**) at the output. At the heart of the device is a programmable delay line (see **reverberation**), which is controlled by a **central processing unit** and can be made to apply a variety of time-dependent treatments.

The advantage in studio use is that different effects can be called up without re-**patching**, and often remotely by **MIDI** for example. A problem is that one often needs to apply several effects together, such as reverberation, **filtering** and **compression**, and in these cases several units are needed (though some of the newer devices can run several programs together). A compromise is to have single-use modules for the most-used effects, and several multi-effect units as supplements.

Fig. 47 shows the block diagram of a well-designed multi-effect unit, the Yamaha SPX90II (for a general description of the conversion process, see **digital synthesis techniques** 1).

To give an idea of the versatility of this unit, thirty pre-set effects with re-writable default values reside in **ROM**, and the user can store re-written and re-named versions of any of these in sixty non-volatile (i.e. battery-backed) **RAM**s. The original (ROM) versions are always available as well. Memories can be MIDI-selected, so that, for example, a synthesizer player can automatically select a new effect by pressing a new SELECT INSTRUMENT button. In some cases parameters within the effect can be MIDI-controlled as well.

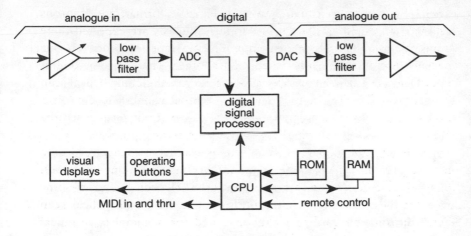

Fig. 47

The menu includes **echo** and reverberation of various kinds, **chorusing,** compression, **equalization, flanging,** freeze (record and loop blocks of samples), **gates, pan, pitch changing, vibrato** and other effects. See also **samplers.**

Digital recording See **compact disc, digital audio tape, digital synthesis techniques, pulse code modulation, sound recording techniques** and **video cassette PCM.**

Digital signal processor (DSP) A general term covering a wide range of hardware modules for high speed processing of audio and other types of digital data. DSPs may be fitted within computers as part of their standard complement, or be supplied as stand-alone units with or without input and output converters to receive/send analogue signals. **Digital multi-effect units** and digital **reverberators** are examples of DSPs.

Digital synthesis techniques Quite early in the history of the digital computer – around the mid-1950s – experiments were made in producing musical sound by operations on numbers. At the time analogue devices sounded better and were much cheaper and easier to use, and real time digital synthesis was far in the future, but it was realized even then that number machines could provide a level of precision, repeatability and multiple task handling very difficult to achieve by analogue methods.

A computer can be used both to generate sound and to organize and control complete pieces of music; the two functions are separable and require different types of programming. Set up as a performance instrument, a computer can produce sound much as an organ does, with the musical output entirely in the hands of a human performer. At the other end of the scale from live performance is a piece programme which produces an instrumental score. This entry deals with the microtemporal area of sound generation and manipulation. For macrotemporal or piece generating problems see **computer music composition techniques**. In fact the two temporal areas overlap. Phenomena between about 1 and 20 **hertz** can affect the quality of sounds (e.g. **vibrato**), or be discrete formal events (e.g. a rapid scale), and this ability to interchange sound with formal structure is one of the fascinations of electronic composition.

1. Input/output

Fundamental to digital synthesis is the principle of 'sampling'. A digital device can only work if the relevant data is represented as numbers, even if it is not 'naturally' numerical. Pressure waves in air are hard to visualize, so most people probably think of sound as something like the wavy groove on a record. Using that analogy, if we had a clock and a measuring device which took regular readings of the voltage in a pick-up, we would have a list of numbers telling us what the amplitude was at the time of each reading, and a plot of this list would show the general shape of the original wave. It is fairly obvious that the more points we have the better the representation, but how many is enough?

If you had never seen a film, but were told that flashing twenty-four still pictures in front of your eyes every second would give the illusion of continuous motion, you might not believe it, but, as we know, it works. In an article on the mathematics of digital sound processing, F. R. Moore uses as his main example a cinema illusion that doesn't quite work – wagon wheels that appear to stop and go backwards even though we know they are turning smoothly in one direction (Moore, 1978). In this case, the **sampling rate** (SR) of 24 frames per second is too low to follow the wheels' spokes accurately.

Fig. 48 shows an analogue waveform over a period of a hundredth of a second, starting at just under 200 Hz and swooping up to a much higher note. We sample it every millisecond (1 kHz), list the numbers we get on a scale of −5 to +5, and plot these out. Even if we assume that the output can be smoothed, it is clear that while the low **frequency** is quite well represented, the high frequency has disappeared altogether, and there is no way it can be retrieved. For a given sampling rate, then, the conversion will get worse as the frequency gets higher. What is the relationship between frequency and SR?

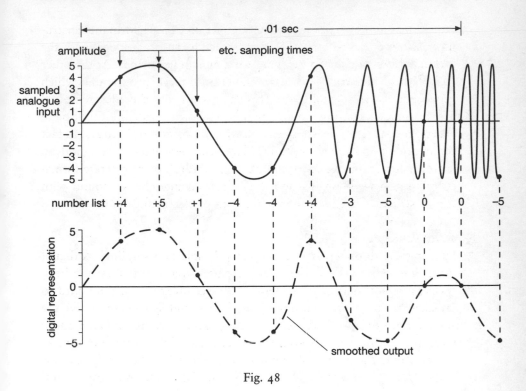

Fig. 48

It would be convenient to find that the minimum sampling rate for a given frequency is the same as that frequency (f), but the result (fig. 49a) is still uninformative – it could even be zero. **Cyclic** events can be seen as positive and negative departures from a mean position. Such a cycle may swing like a pendulum, bob up and down like a weight on a spring, go round like a wheel, etc. – a point on the rim of a wheel effectively goes forwards for half the time and backwards for the other half. The minimum number of samples to detect this alternation is 2, and fig. 49b shows that SR=2f does satisfy the basic condition (except in the special case of sampling exactly at the zero crossing). Let's test what happens when SR is somewhat above or below this value of 2f.

Fig. 50 shows an input f of 1000 Hz, so 2f is 2000 Hz. Sampling at 2500 Hz produces an improvement on 2f – if we continue in this direction the wave shape will get increasingly better. Sampling at 1250 Hz, on the other hand, produces a new and spurious frequency which is not present in the original and will certainly be heard if translated into sound. This is 'foldover' or **aliasing**, and results whenever the

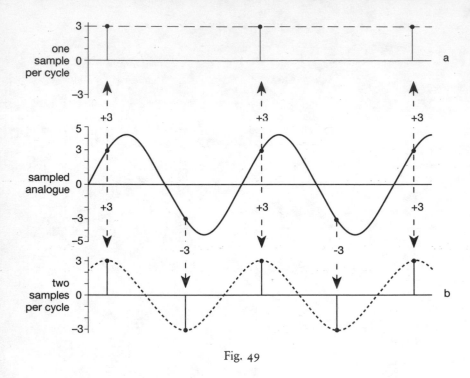

Fig. 49

highest frequency present exceeds half the SR. The foldover frequency is found by subtracting the input frequency from the sampling rate (in fig. 50: 1250–1000=250 Hz).

SR/2 is called the **Nyquist frequency**, the highest that can be converted without aliasing. In practical systems, SR is made somewhat higher than twice the top frequency desired, and frequencies above Nyquist are blocked by an anti-aliasing low-pass **filter** so that they never reach the sampling process. Fuller explanations can be found in numerous books and articles, including the Moore article referred to (Moore, 1978), Max Mathews's classic book *The Technology of Computer Music* (Mathews, 1969) and Appleton (1975), Dodge (1985) and Chamberlin (1985).

Also affecting the accuracy of conversion is the precision of the number. The value of the original analogue input varies continuously of course, but if our measuring device only has large divisions we have no way of representing small changes – you don't use a surveyor's tape to check a spark gap. In digital code the steps are of known and finite precision; a 'word' of eight binary digits (see **binary code**) can represent 256 different numbers (0–255), but no more, however you juggle it around (for example it could be scaled in tenths to 25.5, or in 10s to

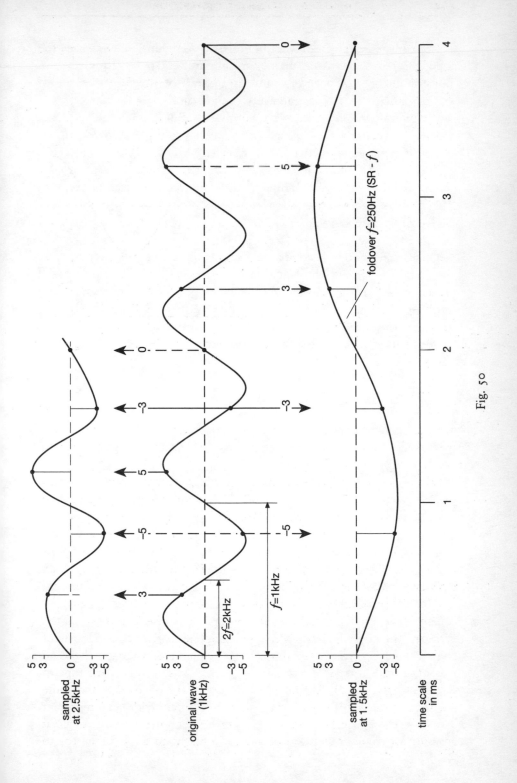

Fig. 50

2550, but there are still only 256 numbers). Assuming that we scale the analogue input so that at maximum amplitude it never converts to a higher number than 255, we would have a scale of integral values which corresponds to 256 steps, and every sample can only have one of those 256 values – nothing in between is possible. But it might still be vital to musical accuracy that a particular sample should be 163.134. In an eight **bit** representation this number, in fact everything between 162.5 and 163.5, would have to be 163. This kind of inaccuracy is called a 'quantizing error', and its audible result 'quantization noise'. For reasonable musical quality at least twelve bit precision (0–4095) is necessary, and high quality sampling is at fourteen (16,383) or sixteen (65,535) bits.

Quantization noise is comparable to analogue tape hiss, system **noise** etc., and an equivalent **signal-to-noise ratio** (and therefore useful **dynamic range**) can be estimated from the precision of the conversion processes, at roughly six **decibels** per bit. On this basis even twelve bits gives a theoretical 72 dB, better than most analogue recordings, and sixteen bits should yield a very satisfactory 96 dB. In practice other factors reduce these figures, but a genuine 90 dB is quite achievable. The

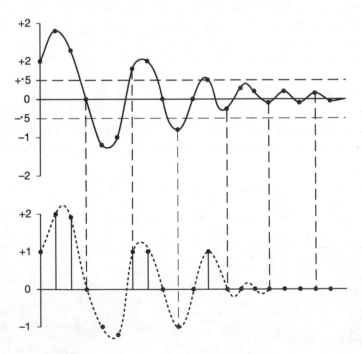

Fig. 51

worst problems when precision is low occur when the input amplitude is also low, because small signals will not be converted at all – they are simply not noticed. Fig. 51 shows a falling amplitude being sampled with a minimum incremental step of 0.5. Any input between +.5 and −.5 will be read as 0.

I have dealt at some length with the sampling process because the concept is fundamental to all types of digital music processing. For principles of sound-to-sample devices see **analogue-to-digital converter** (**ADC**). The complementary device, a **digital-to-analogue converter** (**DAC**), reads numerical samples and turns them into voltages. At the output stage low-pass filters are used again, not for anti-aliasing – it's too late for that – but to smooth the waveform and generally tidy up the analogue output signal.

To give an idea of the amount of data to be handled, let us take a high quality sixteen bit music system with an upper frequency limit of 20 kHz. If we sample at 50 kHz (comfortably above twice the maximum frequency to avoid aliasing problems) the data rate, which is the sample rate multiplied by the number of bits in each sample, will be 800k per second for each channel. Stereo would therefore involve a stream of 1.6 million bits per second, plus whatever the computer needs to process it, and in practical recording systems an 'overhead' of coding and error correction data. Fig. 52 is a diagrammatic summary of the input/output chain we have been discussing (see also fig. 162).

2. Real sound manipulation
Samples can either be generated internally (synthesis) or input via an ADC, stored and treated by digital versions of the kinds of manipulation described in **tape composition techniques**. Processing real sounds is one

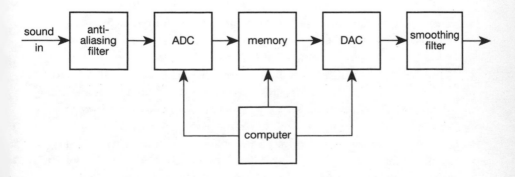

Fig. 52

of the earliest electronic composition techniques (see **musique concrète**), but in its newer digital form is also increasingly applied to performing instruments (see **percussion generators, pianos,** *electronic* and **samplers**).

We have just given the example of 800k bits (=100k **bytes**) per sec for high quality sound, so at around one megabyte for ten seconds of sound it is clear that ample storage is needed if the sound to be treated is longer than a fragment. Storage in the **giga**-byte range is certainly possible (see **tapeless studio**) and becoming cheaper, but in practice many useful manipulations only involve short passages of sound. The limitation for treatment is the fast memory (**random access memory (RAM)**) rather than the mass storage medium (**hard disk, floppy disk**) because only material actually in RAM can be addressed directly by the processor, and treatment of any complexity may involve many transfers to disk and back as work progresses (fig. 173 in **samplers** shows a typical arrangement).

Assuming we have captured and stored some sound, a few possible manipulations are: 1. Changing speed by making the output sampling rate different from the input. 2. Running the sample block backwards, retrograding the sound. 3. Arithmetic operations, creating **filters**, echo effects, various kinds of **modulation**, etc. 4. Chopping out parts of the block and reassembling them in different orders and directions, like editing tape but much more precise (for illustration see fig. 174). 5. Cross-cutting, mixing etc. between different blocks. 6. Changing the sound's character by rewriting groups of samples with selective omission or interpolative gap filling. 7. Looping to extend parts of sounds indefinitely. Compared with tape loops, these can be microscopically tiny. 8. Combining real sound with internally generated sounds and treatments. 9. Analysing the sound (see below).

There are further possibilities, but the above list already gives digital equivalents of all the main tape manipulation techniques. In some cases they are somewhat cumbersome to implement compared with the visual and tactile immediacy of tape editing, but set against this is the precision and absence of signal degradation that the computer offers.

The key feature of any usable manipulation program is an effective editor, and fortunately sound lends itself readily to visual representation. A block of samples can easily be displayed in a quasi-analogue, graphical form by plotting successive samples on a screen, and with a little practice one can extract a lot of information by merely looking at waveforms.

One problem when joining or looping sounds is the likelihood of clicks and thumps because of discontinuity in waveforms at joins. Fig. 53a shows a forward signal cut on to its retrograde. By taking out a

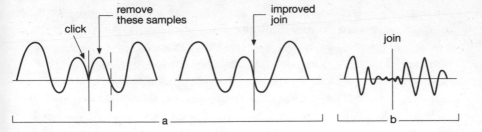

Fig. 53

few samples on one side of the join the waveform is cleaned up. Joins are in any case more likely to be click-free if made at a low amplitude part of the signal (fig. 53b). Some sound programs provide for generating special joining pieces which interpolate new samples smoothly over the join. This kind of micro-editing can be easily performed on digital signals, but is quite impossible with tape. By the same techniques it is possible to clean up signals, removing unwanted noises and leaving only the relevant material.

These relatively simple procedures are often used by composers in the same empirical ways as the earlier tape techniques: listen, trial edit, play again, second trial etc. Studio systems and all but the cheapest **samplers** have interactive facilities for working like this, but another important result of being able to represent sound as a list of numbers was a new approach to acoustic research. Because a block of samples is 'frozen' out of the time domain it can be examined repeatedly and in detail independently of the sound's real duration. These computerized analytical methods not only revealed more about natural and instrumental sound, but showed the way to improved synthesis techniques.

3. Analysis and re-synthesis

Animal ear/brain systems (including ours) routinely decode a mass of confused sound input, sort it out and make important judgements about actions to take etc. The **psychoacoustics** of this process are being intensely studied, and until recently it was thought that analysing musical tone must be a simple task in comparison. Earlier analyses of musical tone only attempted precision in the steady-state, or the least rapidly changing, part of a note, and **timbre** charts of instruments found in the older books on musical acoustics are of very limited value, because the steady state is usually the least informative part of the note. Try this: record the same middle range note on tape using as many different instruments as you can, then cut off the first half second (i.e. the **attack**) of each, leave a second or two of sound, cut the end off, and splice them all together with a second of spacing between each. Now play it to a musically knowledgeable friend and ask for the identities of the instruments. It's very unlikely that all the answers will be right.

In instrumental music there is no need to know about the constituents of a sound, because musicians use a traditional and familiar range of timbres, and can converse about them almost non-linguistically. But when composers began to move into electronics it became necessary to describe sounds like 'a heavy thumping noise', 'a sort of trumpet/horn timbre' or 'a giant harpsichord' to a machine instead of a person, and though simple, intuitive trial and error can produce brilliant results on occasion, it can be a time-consuming method, and much too imprecise to serve every kind of piece and composer. The first step in making a 'trombone-like' sound is therefore to find out what happens in a real trombone note.

The French mathematician Jean Baptiste Fourier (1768–1830) showed that any **waveform**, however complex, can be uniquely expressed as the sum of one or more **sine waves** (the waveform of simple harmonic, or single frequency motion). Music displayed on an **oscilloscope** as amplitude against time (a 'time domain' plot) shows an ever-changing, complex waveform, but unless it is very simple (e.g. only one or two notes

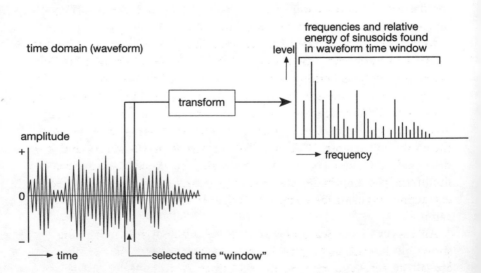

Fig. 54

together) even euphonious music looks 'noisy' and jumbled, showing no clear **periodicity**. Fourier devised a mathematical 'transform' by which a time domain plot could be converted into a **spectrum** or 'frequency domain' representation, showing all frequencies present at a given instant or during a selected span of time, and their relative energy content. Fig. 54 shows the relationship between the two types of plot (see also **analogue synthesis techniques** 5). The significance of 'window' is discussed below.

Fourier transformation was until recently an elaborate and slow process, but in a computer, operating on a list of time-related samples instead of a continuous function, it is called a discrete fourier transform (DFT), and in the 1960s an algorithm for efficient and rapid computer evaluation was devised, giving the fast fourier transform (FFT), which is now a standard facility in many synthesizers and computer music programs.

FFT is one way to extract the **harmonic** content of a sound (another method is by filtering, see **vocoder**). To illustrate how the spectral content correlates with the waveform, take an easily generated wave, the **ramp**, useful in many applications because it contains a complete **harmonic series**.

Fig. 55 shows an 'ideal' ramp form, and 55b how the ramp shape emerges as we sum successive harmonics. For this function, the amplitudes of the harmonics follow a simple progression: half the fundamental's amplitude for the second harmonic, a third for the third, a quarter for the fourth, and so on. The first eight harmonics are shown, with underneath, 55c, the corresponding spectrum.

Many books state that if we continue this progression to an infinite number of harmonics, the result will be the perfectly straight line and instantaneous discontinuity of fig. 55a. In fact this is not so, and I am grateful to Professor W. Moran (Professor of Pure Mathematics, University of Adelaide) for pointing it out. However many harmonics are used, applying the above amplitude rule, the 'humps' at each end of the ramp will remain. This is called the Gibbs phenomenon, and it is discussed in Kufner (1971). A better ramp shape can be achieved by modifying the amplitude rule, but in general we are more interested in extracting and using the components than in additively building a perfect ramp.

An aspect of the waveform not yet referred to is its **phase**. Fig. 55 shows all the partials 'in phase', i.e. at the start of each major cycle they are all at zero and moving in the same direction. Although relative phases between partials are sometimes of great importance, they make

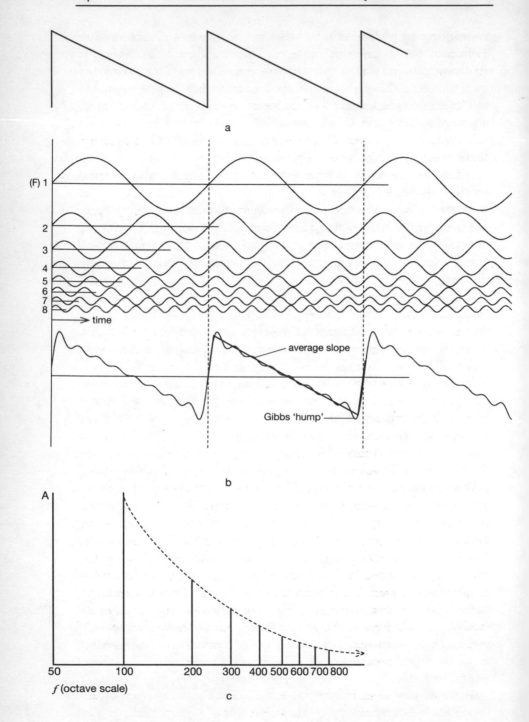

a

(F) 1
2
3
4
5
6
7
8
→ time

average slope

Gibbs 'hump'

b

A

50   100   200   300   400 500 600 700 800
f (octave scale)

c

Fig. 55

surprisingly little difference to what the ear hears – a fact noted by Helmholtz (1862) and since observed more accurately. (Try, however, re-drawing the waveform with different partial phases, and it will *look* quite different.) Where acoustic phase relationships really count is in low frequency phenomena such as 'beats' (see **dissonance**), and in our ability to localize sounds (see **stereo**). Various aspects of phase relationships, and further points about spectra, are discussed in **analogue synthesis techniques**. For more detailed comment on Fourier analysis of sound see Moore (1978), Dodge (1985), Taylor (1965), and many mathematical textbooks.

So far we have assumed that the waveform being analysed is neatly periodic, with characteristics that remain constant for long enough to provide an analysable sample. Unfortunately this is rarely true, because, as we have noticed, musical sound is vibrant with rapid change. The dilemma is that if we reduce the waveform sample to so short a time that all parametric changes are excluded, we finish up with nothing to transform. On the other hand, if we analyse, say, a complete note lasting several seconds, the spectrum will merely reveal what partials occurred during the note and their average energy, which is not very useful either.

A compromise has to be found, and the researcher tries to choose a block of samples which is long enough to provide adequate material, but short enough to reveal musical character. In the attack of a note every millisecond may show dramatic changes. Pioneer work on this was done by Jean-Claude Risset as long ago as 1966. He divided the sample block into 'windows' or 'frames' of 5–50 milliseconds (see again fig. 54), depending on the density of information required (Risset, 1966). A complete picture is built up by juxtaposing or overlapping windows and computing the composite data. Windowing improves our chances of examining the dynamic characteristics of a sound accurately, but introduces a new problem as well. Chopping out a block of samples causes the waves (especially those with longer time periods) to be truncated arbitrarily, giving a wrong impression of themselves to the analysis program, particularly in how much relative energy is contained in the partials. For analysing complex tones the best answer is to taper the window so that the amplitudes decrease towards the truncated ends, making these less important to the analysis procedure, and giving a better balance of average amplitudes. Various window shapes are offered in FFT programs.

The best way to judge the success of an analysis is to synthesize a sound based on its parameters and compare it with the original. A three-dimensional plot of time, amplitude and harmonic number can show the complete 'history' of a note at a glance, and the most informative flat paper (or screen) representation is often called a 'waterfall' display. Fig. 56 shows two such plots, of an oboe tone and a clarinet tone (taken from Moorer and Grey's *Lexicon of Analysed Tones*, Moorer, 1978). Even to the casual eye they are informative. The oboe's pungent tone is shown in a long, complete series of partials. Notice the fourth harmonic (double octave) developing at high speed to a peak, and the fundamental lagging behind the next four partials. The fifth harmonic (interval of a seventeenth, or compound major third above the fundamental) is actually more powerful than the fundamental except at the very end of the note, and its octave (tenth harmonic) is amazingly strong. Everything is on the move, with many short term variations in amplitude. The note is low for an oboe – E♭ above middle C (c. 311 Hz) – and to add to the already complex picture, the spectral content will change profoundly as we ascend the scale due to the **formants**, a fixed group of resonances depending on the physical construction of the instrument.

The clarinet note (at the same pitch) looks radically different (and of course our ears tell us this as well). It is not one of the lowest notes on the instrument, as was the case with the oboe, but well up towards the **break**. It is characteristic of a stopped cylindrical pipe to suppress even-numbered harmonics, and this is well shown here – vestigial second and fourth harmonics, a large third, and a fifth peaking nearly as high as the fundamental. The first even harmonic to make any reasonable showing is the eighth.

Re-synthesis of these sounds exactly as plotted would need 21 sine wave sources, each time/amplitude controlled to follow every blip and wiggle in the curves. The formidable amount of computing involved could be undertaken for a few experiments, perhaps, but hardly offers a practical and manageable composer's tool. It is quite likely, in any case, that many of the smaller events are random or spurious, so experiments were made in replacing the curves with a series of straight line segments, relatively trivial to compute. It was found that the ear accepted such 'piece-wise linear approximations' as surprisingly convincing re-creations of the original sounds (though with varying success for different instruments). Fig. 57 shows the principle applied to a single amplitude function.

Analysis-resynthesis of familiar instrumental sounds is not compositionally of interest to many composers, because in general they would rather use a real oboe than an imitation one, but it was important to demonstrate the validity of the approach. Using this (additive) method various studios have produced some very effective re-syntheses of fami-

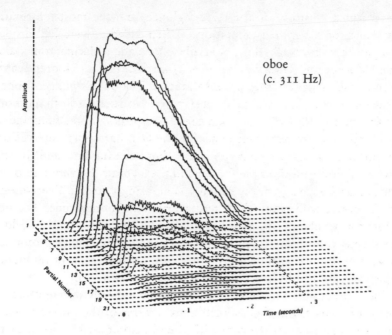

oboe
(c. 311 Hz)

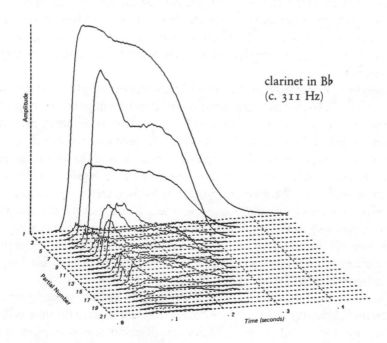

clarinet in B♭
(c. 311 Hz)

Fig. 56

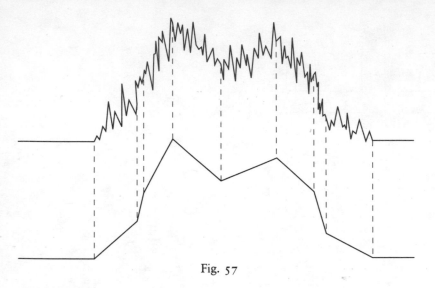

Fig. 57

liar timbres. Once set up, the technique can be extended to create completely new timbres by constructing arbitrary waveforms or by computing instruments that lie between different natural ones. Some of the synthesis methods discussed in the following sections can use analysis as the basis for new sounds, but others do not depend on analysis at all.

4. Additive synthesis

A general plan for additive synthesis is shown in Fig. 58a. In digital **oscillators** the amplitude control may be applied as an input to the oscillator (sine wave source), 58b, reversing the order of the stages, but the result is the same.

From the very beginning of electronic music there was strong appeal in the idea of building musical timbre from the simplest unit – the sine wave. With enough of them, any sound should be possible, but it was found to be difficult to apply this in an analogue environment, because: 1. Oscillator tuning tends to drift, distorting the ratios of the harmonics. 2. Oscillators must output very pure sines, or their own harmonics will pollute the synthesized spectrum. 3. For an effectively rich timbre (needing many oscillators) the number of controls is very large. Drift and sine impurities easily destroy the coherence of the sound, resulting in a chord rather than a timbre. These are not problems in the digital domain, but specifying parameters still can be (for a fuller discussion see **analogue synthesis techniques** 4).

An oscillator works by generating a function in time and repeating it

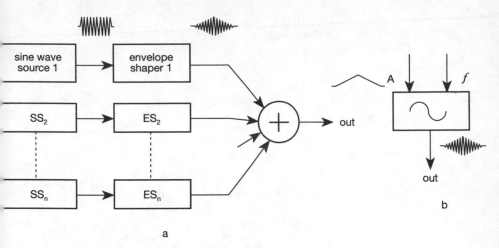

Fig. 58

indefinitely, and a computer can be made to do the same thing, generating not a function but a stream of samples, which are treated in exactly the same way as samples produced by digitizing an input, i.e. they are sent to a DAC to be converted into voltages and eventually sound. Straight-line waveforms such as the ramp can be generated by merely counting at a controlled rate. The computer is instructed to count to some number, say 100, go back to 0 and go on repeating the process. If we add an instruction to increment exactly every ten microseconds, the count will reach 100 in 1000 microseconds or one millisecond, and the frequency will therefore be 1 kHz. This is the way in which early computer sounds were generated, and the method is easily adapted to other linear shapes such as the **triangle** (count up then down), or **square** (switch between two numbers, repeating each the same number of times).

The timing can be changed to produce different frequencies, but this is a very limited design of oscillator. We need a general purpose algorithm that will generate any waveform, but particularly sine waves – the above method is cumbersome when a simple straight line becomes a curve that requires continuous non-trivial calculation. A solution is to do the calculation beforehand, and put the list of values for a complete **cycle** into a 'look-up table' or wavetable. Any point in a cycle can be identified by its 'phase angle' relative to 0° (see **phase** and **sine wave**). Listing the sines of selected angles between 0° and 360° gives a numerical representation of the waveform.

Take for example a wavetable of 256 (2^8) terms (**blocks** the size of powers of two give the most efficient storage for arrays, lists etc.). After dividing 360 into 256 parts, giving an angle of 1.40625° per step, the table consists of 256 addresses (like labels on boxes) and 256 values which are the contents of the boxes. We address a given box (e.g. 72 – standing for 101.25°) and extract the value, 0.9808 (i.e. sin 101.25°). The addresses are all integers, but the values are not. Supposing the sampling rate is 50 kHz and we read all the numbers, the frequency will be 50,000/256 = 195.3125 Hz.

Obviously a useful oscillator must generate not just one but any frequency, and this is where problems arise. To change 195.3125 to, say 200 Hz, we can either increase the sampling rate to 51.2 kHz, or scan the table in such a way that we read only 250 numbers. Variable SR is certainly possible, and is used in **samplers**, but in a sound generating system it tends to make more problems than it solves because the Nyquist frequency (SR/2) changes with it, and the design of other SR-dependent devices such as ADC and DAC filters becomes more complicated. So if we settle for a fixed SR we must read 250 numbers as evenly as possible from a table of 256, i.e. drop every 42nd or 43rd (256/6 = 42.66). This can be done by 'truncation': the 'correct' address increment is 256/250 = 1.024, so the address list should begin 0, 1.024, 2.048 etc., but these truncate back to the integers 0, 1, 2 (i.e. we disregard the decimal places in the numbers). Later on, however, 41 × 1.024 = 41.984, and 42 × 1.024 = 43.008, so after truncation the integer 42 disappears from the series and that address is omitted. The result will be the correct frequency but a slightly deformed waveform. Hardly more efficient than truncating is rounding to the nearest integer up or down – we still have 'rounding errors'. Much better is interpolation, by which the computer chooses an intermediate sample value by assessing the 'weight' of the fraction. This involves extra calculation, which may slow things down too much, so there is a trade-off between the advantages of better precision given by long wavetables, long words and high sampling rates, and the cost and complexity of providing these benefits.

As we increase the frequency the 'sampling increment' also increases, and there are places where the arithmetic is simple, such as when we scan exactly every other or every third angle. But inevitably there are fewer and fewer samples per cycle, and as we found in section 1 (fig. 49), the minimum number of samples is two. At first sight it might seem absurd that any system could recognize two values only as a sine wave, but non-sinusoidal waveforms must contain harmonics. Even the second harmonic should be filtered out on conversion as we approach the Nyquist frequency, and a wave without harmonics can only be sinusoidal. Nevertheless, as stated earlier, it is good practice to use sampling rates well above twice the required top frequency. Phase can be controlled by rotating the address list and starting somewhere in the middle, and amplitude is adjusted by scaling the wavetable appropriately. Many refinements are possible, for example one can use a half-wave or quarter-wave table and derive the rest by sign-changing or other manipulations. The general scheme of a basic wavetable oscillator is shown in fig. 59. For completely stable frequency, essential in music devices, the timing source is usually a rock-steady quartz oscillator, arranged to provide either a fixed or variable SR. We have described only two of many possible approaches to oscillator design – for more detailed reading see Dodge (1985), Chamberlin (1985), Snell (1977) and Moore (1977).

With adequately sinusoidal generators of very stable frequency, we have the main requirement for successful additive synthesis, but to construct musical sounds each oscillator's time/amplitude envelope must be

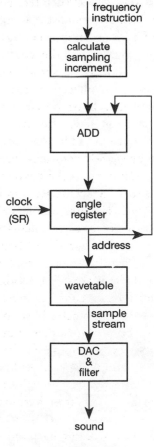

Fig. 59

shaped appropriately for its role in the timbre, and this is where parametric specification can get unwieldy. Even if we specify the envelope in straight segments (see fig. 57), we might need seven or eight segments to describe it fully enough. If each change of direction is given as a time and an amplitude, and assuming that the first and last amplitudes will be zero, a seven-segment envelope still needs thirteen numbers. We already have at least one instruction (probably more) for the oscillator, so we have a minimum of fourteen parameters. If we wish to have even a modest ten partials we must input 140 numbers to get one note! We may compromise (for example, by using the same envelope for several partials, or fewer segments), but getting interesting sounds can still be very time-consuming. One technique is to store a 'library' of envelopes that can be called up as complete modules.

There is another additive technique (fig. 60) which, although more of a compromise, is easier to use (the invariable trade-off in synthesis). Wavetables can be loaded with any function, not just sines, so a single oscillator can output a complex wave. Waveform is typically specified by percentage amplitude of harmonics, for example, fundamental – 80 per cent, second harmonic – 95 per cent, third harmonic – 43 per cent, etc. Percentages refer to a highest value of 100 per cent which may not actually occur, but the computer scales the correct proportions and loads the appropriate numbers into the wavetable. We may also be able to specify **inharmonic** partials (e.g. harmonic no. 3.06) and **noisy** sounds (for example by manipulating upper harmonics or randomizing the table). The next stage is to shape the envelope, and since the summing has already happened, we only need one shaper. This greatly reduces the amount of specification, but of course we have lost the internal articulation which can make the difference between a dull and an interesting sound. This cut-down additive method works quite well for some types of timbre, like percussive attacks and some woodwind sounds, but badly for brass and any sound that changes internal balance a lot during the course of a note.

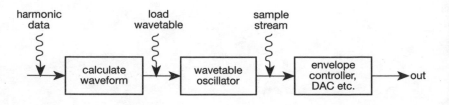

Fig. 60

In practical studios and synthesizers, both these methods, or a hybrid (a group of, say six oscillators with separate envelopes and different wavetable contents) may be used. So what we call an 'instrument', in working with a computer, is a temporary **patch** of more or less versatile units. The instrument may consist entirely of software talking to a general purpose processor, or computer control of hardware devices. High operating speeds allow a single device to offer the user what appears to be a bank of many separately controllable oscillators with simultaneous outputs.

5. Subtractive synthesis

This is the opposite process: instead of adding simple sources, a complex sound is treated by **filtering** to modify its structure. Included in the inputs shown in fig. 61 is the result of additive (or other, see following sections) synthesis, and although digital generators can often produce the required result without further processing, filtering is always an option. In fact anything except a sine wave (which has nothing to filter) may be suitable input material.

Even if it is voltage or computer controlled, an analogue filter has limited flexibility because its function is embodied in specific hardware, but digital filters consist of operations on numbers, capable of being re-specified as quickly and often as needed. This makes them far more powerful and adaptable tools than their analogue counterparts, particularly in rapidly changing situations like the internal structure of a note. In many cases, however, digital filters are required to behave in much

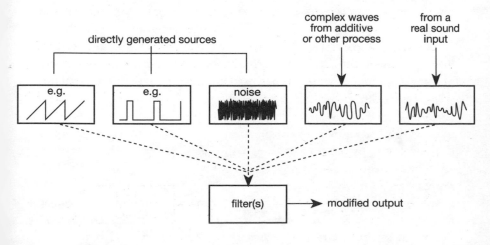

Fig. 61

the same way as their analogue equivalents (see **filters, equalizers**), and respond to the same type of parameter specification, such as centre frequency and bandwidth for a band pass filter.

Digital filters work by reading the sample stream and changing it in some way, thus if groups of samples were averaged this would reduce the effect of rapid fluctuations and cut high frequencies. Delaying samples by holding them in memory is an essential feature, because the operation depends on a combination of present and past samples. 'Non-recursive' filters work with inputs only and produce 'zeros' or reject mode responses, and 'recursive' types, computing from both inputs and past outputs, give 'poles' or peaks in the spectrum. Filter theory is complex and outside our scope here: a useful tutorial is Smith (1985), and detailed descriptions are given in Dodge (1985) chapter 5 and Chamberlin (1985) chapter 14. From the user's point of view the most important feature is usually the steady-state frequency response (spectrum), but the impulse response (see again **filters**) may predominate if the input is percussive or discontinuous. The 'order' of the filter is decided by the number of delay stages.

Spectrum manipulation is a very flexible synthesis mode because the generator (excitation) is separate from the spectral control and can be varied independently of it. Given a good variety of sources and filters, a wide range of sounds can be patched and heard relatively quickly, and empirical set-ups that are hard to repeat reliably in an analogue system can be securely stored and retrieved. The excitation + filter model is also much nearer to the way real instruments work than additive synthesis. The filter represents the physical properties of the instrument's resonating system, which causes **formants** (see fig. 92) or fixed peaks at certain frequencies.

The spectral envelope to be applied by the filter depends on the material being treated. The basic model for a pitched instrumental type of sound is shown in fig. 62a. The composer imagining the sound chooses a tone source in the right general area and adds a formant filter (or a patch of several filters) which may change little or not at all either during the course of a note or when the source frequency is changed. Noise-based sounds, 62b, on the other hand (such as cymbal-like crashes, wind-like swishing sounds) need a noise source such as a **random number generator,** and the filter becomes the frequency controller, in most cases changing its characteristics during the course of a sound in either centre frequency, bandwidth or both (this is called 'time-varying'). Just as important as the spectral envelope in all cases, of course, is the right amplitude envelope. The compound variants of these simple cases are

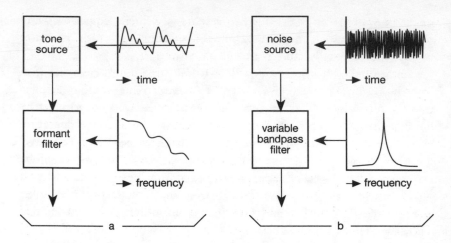

Fig. 62

virtually unlimited, for example a time-varying filter in addition to a formant filter on a pitched sound, several envelopes controlling different parameters, etc.

Analysis methods suitable for re-synthesis in this mode have been intensively studied for many years in the field of speech synthesis, a complete subject in itself which only partly overlaps with musical problems. We cannot go into this special area in detail (though aspects of it are discussed under **vocoder**), but the thrust of the research has been: 1. to find ways of reducing data transmission rates on telephone quality speech lines (speech is in any case quite acceptable at much lower bit-rates than music); and 2. to design low-cost, efficient artificial speech modules. Frequency domain analysis uses various methods to estimate the formants of a real sound, but the most successful (and musically useful) technique is linear predictive coding (LPC), which in a sense links the two domains because it operates in time but results in a filter specification.

A linear prediction estimates the value of the next sample from the present and a group of past samples, and computes the error when the next becomes the present sample. It can be shown that the error signal (time domain) provides the necessary spectral (frequency domain) data to model a filter more or less closely matching the formant structure of the sound being analysed. Prediction is done in frames, resulting in a series of filters which track the changing speech pattern. For detailed description of several forms of this technique see specialist speech synthesis books such as Witten (1982) and Linggard (1985). There are also good descriptions in Dodge (1985) chapter 6 (which discusses speech synthesis in general) and Chamberlin (1985) chapter 16.

The effectiveness of LPC varies with the material being analysed, but for musicians 'correct' analysis is usually less important than the exploitation of the technique as a fruitful source of interesting sounds, often by 'cross-synthesis', i.e. shaping one sound with the formants of another; one example is 'talking instruments' created by shaping an instrumental sound with formants derived from speech analysis. Pieces based on manipulated speech (such as those by Charles Dodge) often use LPC-modelled filters but change the excitation, sampling rate etc. to make new timbral effects. For other approaches to analysis/synthesis see granular synthesis, Vosim and FOF in section 7 below, and the speech synthesis references given above.

In analogue synthesis, because additive methods are difficult, filtering is often the main or only technique used, but in digital work, where the finished sound can often be generated directly, it is one option among many. We have seen that both summation additive and subtractive synthesis by filtering can be quite complicated to implement. Are there other, less cumbersome ways of generating complex sounds?

6. Synthesis by frequency modulation (FM)

See **amplitude modulation** (AM), **frequency modulation** and **ring modulation** for general descriptions of types of modulation. The main difference between any of these and summing (adding, mixing) is that they are multiplicative (non-linear) processes. Fig. 63 shows the basic patches for AM and FM. Fig. 63a shows that in AM the carrier's mean amplitude is varied at the frequency of the modulating oscillator at a 'depth' decided by the modulator's amplitude. In FM, 63b, the carrier's mean frequency is similarly varied, causing an excursion or 'deviation' above and below normal (f_c). A musical example where modulator frequency is far below that of the carrier is a string **vibrato**. The normal pitch of the note (say 500 Hz) is modulated at a low speed (say 5 Hz) by a deviation that can vary from none (senza vibrato) to a semitone or more (molto vibrato).

If both waves are in the audio range the arithmetic is the same but the effect on the ear is quite different, because there is an audible change in the carrier's shape on waveform. The definitive (and deservedly much cited) paper on FM is John Chowning's 'The synthesis of complex audio spectra by means of frequency modulation', which appeared in 1973. The phenomenon was known long before this (as a technique for broadcasting, for example), but Chowning grasped its far-reaching possibilities

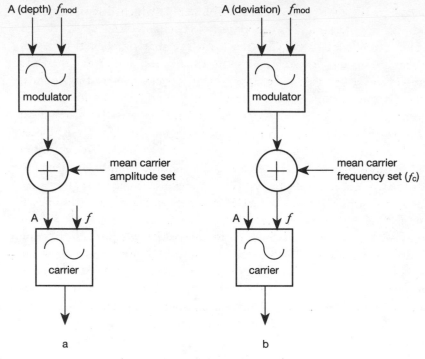

Fig. 63

for music synthesis (Chowning, 1973).

Assuming that both carrier and modulator are sine waves, suppose a carrier at 1 kHz and a modulator at 2 kHz. The carrier will go through its frequency deviation cycle twice for every one of its own periods, and this is hard to visualize as the usual wavy line. Instead, think of a light on the rim of a rotating wheel, observed from the side (fig. 64). The light will go up and down, appearing to be slower at the top and bottom than the middle, even though we know that the speed is constant – in fact this view converts the constant speed to an apparently sinusoidal oscillation. Frequency-modulating the wheel will change its speed from moment to moment above and below its normal or average speed, like a bad driver alternately braking and accelerating. If the deviation is symmetrical, the speeding up in one half of the cycle being matched by the slowing down in the other, the wheel will still take the same total time for each revolution.

What about the amplitude of the modulator? If it is zero there can clearly be no modulation, whatever its frequency; this does not mean no output – we simply have the carrier alone. But as we move the modulator level up from zero, the carrier frequency will swing symmetri-

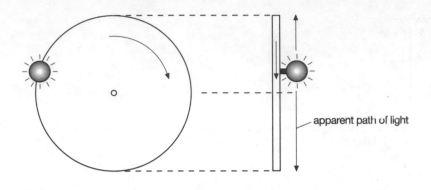

apparent path of light

Fig. 64

cally, above and below normal, by an amount proportional to the modulator's amplitude. The maximum departure from normal in either direction is called the 'peak deviation', thus a peak deviation of 100 Hz imposed on a carrier of 1 kHz will swing the frequency between 900 and 1100 Hz. So the modulator's frequency determines how often the deviations in frequency of the output occur, but its amplitude determines the actual range of variation.

By manipulating the modulator frequency and deviation a wide range of complex tones can be generated using only two sine waves, and without filter treatments. It only works reliably in a digital environment because high precision is essential – very tiny changes in frequency ratios, for example, can dramatically alter the sound.

The ratio of the peak deviation, d, to the modulating frequency, m, is called the modulation index, I (i.e. I = d/m), and the result of FM by two sinusoids can be completely predicted if we know this index and the frequency ratio, c/m, between the carrier, c, and the modulator, m. As a rule of thumb for the moment, the c/m ratio decides the degree of consonance of the output (simple ratios, i.e. of integers=harmonic spectra), and the modulation index decides the richness of the spectrum (higher I gives a denser spectrum). How do two sines produce all these extra frequencies?

The effect of FM on the carrier spectrum is to produce 'side frequencies' (often referred to in groups as **sidebands**), which occur above and below the carrier. These are always spaced at the distance of the modulating frequency and their density, i.e. the number of frequencies present, and relative energy depend on the index (fig. 65). It can be seen that as I increases the frequency spread, or bandwidth, also increases, and energy is progressively moved from the carrier and transferred into

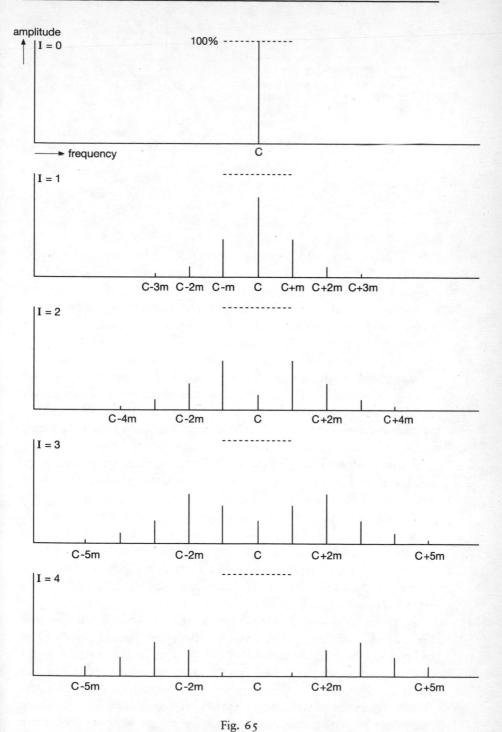

Fig. 65

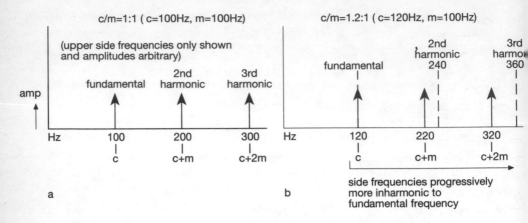

Fig. 66

the sidebands – the spectrum will get richer but at high indices the timbre will become harsh and gritty and the pitch less defined. Note that the new sound contains pitches lower as well as higher than the carrier.

Since the spacing of the side frequencies is at the modulating frequency, it follows that we will get a harmonic spectrum only if this spacing agrees fairly well with the natural harmonic series of the carrier. Fig. 66a shows the upper side frequencies (with arbitrary amplitudes) resulting from a c/m ratio of 1:1, which is commonly used when a complete harmonic spectrum is wanted. Changing the ratio to 1.2:1 results in an inharmonic spectrum, 66b, and such spectra are very useful too, for synthesizing inharmonic complex tones such as bell or chime sounds, or deliberately noisy effects. So varying I and the c/m ratio produces a wide range of richness and harmonicity – in fact even with simple FM it is all too easy for the spectrum to get out of hand and produce very unpleasant sounds.

What happens if deviation takes the carrier frequency below 0 Hz, for example, a carrier at 200 Hz deviating 250 Hz each way, giving −50 Hz at the low end? This is a normal occurrence, and the rule still holds. Our wheel doesn't merely stop (0 Hz), but goes backwards, and this is called 'negative' frequency – in effect the same as positive frequency but **phase** reversed (180° shift). In a wavetable oscillator this involves reading the table backwards, and one suitable for FM must have this capability.

There is another aspect of negativity. Spectral plots usually show 'magnitude' only on the vertical axis, i.e. amplitude independent of sign, because phase-inverted (negative) components sound no different from positive. But when (as quite often) the same frequencies occur both above and below o Hz (horizontal axis), the total effect is calculated by 'reflecting' those below o Hz to the right, with 180° phase change, and adding them to their counterparts at the same frequency. When this is done, some components increase (same signs) and some partly, even totally, cancel (different signs). This adds even more richness to the spectral envelope, but also makes exact prediction of the result more difficult. For complete evaluation, the relative amplitudes (+ and −) of the carrier and sidebands for any value of I can be found by plotting Bessel functions (see again Chowning, 1977, and also Moore, 1978, Moorer, 1977, Dodge, 1985, chapter 4, and Chamberlin, 1985, chapter 13). For comments on choosing c/m ratios, see Truax (1977).

A given index and c/m ratio produces a fixed (though possibly interesting) timbre; it can be amplitude enveloped, of course, but how do we alter its character within a note without using filters? Perhaps the most powerful feature brought out in Chowning's paper was that having reduced spectral control to one parameter (I), it would be an easy matter to change it during the course of a note. Enveloping I gives us dynamic control of timbre without the need for any filters. We could also change c/m, by applying a second frequency modulation to one or both inputs, but in simple, two-oscillator FM the easiest quantity to vary is deviation (by varying modulator amplitude). For a practical instrument, therefore, we need two separately controllable envelopes, one for each oscillator (fig. 67).

The exact behaviour of a time-varying spectrum is hard to predict − it is difficult enough to determine what all the components are doing when the index is steady. But so few parameters have to be changed that dozens of different envelopes and frequency ratios can be reviewed in a few minutes. FM does not lend itself to direct analysis/re-synthesis techniques (though one of its first applications was in producing very successful brass-like sounds), but it does offer easy access to a wide variety of timbres, even in the simple form so far discussed. The basic configuration can be extended in a large number of ways. Here are a few: 1. Multiple series modulation. Suppose two modulators, the second modulating the first, which modulates the carrier. If the first modulator and carrier are both, as normal, in the audio range, but the second modulator is sub-audio and of small amplitude, the effect will be a vibrato. Wide excursions will affect the index substantially, with more drastic effects on the output. 2. Parallel (additive) arrangements of various kinds, for example, a common modulator applying FM to several

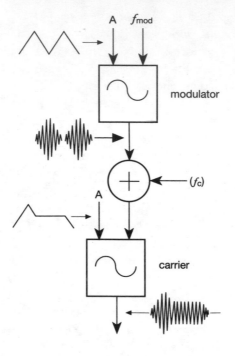

Fig. 67

summed carriers. 3. FM with complex waves. So far we have assumed sinusoidal inputs, but there is no reason why any waveform cannot be used, and the most favoured is probably a complex modulator with a sine carrier – the result of two complex waves tends to be over-rich and unmanageably noisy. 4. Big instruments with all the above features, plus refinements like noise inputs for percussive 'bow' or 'tongue' attacks, variable vibratos etc. The option of post-source filtering is always there as well.

In commercial **keyboard synthesizers** one of the most successful groups of instruments, the Yamaha DX series,* relies entirely on FM and additive synthesis, using no filters. The popular DX7, for example, reissued with improvements as DX7 II, uses six sine oscillators (called by Yamaha 'operators'), which can be patched in thirty-two different ways. Nine examples are shown in fig. 68 and though they look elaborate any operator can be disabled or set to zero if simpler set-ups are wanted. Only the bottom row in any patch actually outputs sound, and it can be seen that in general the higher patch numbers tend towards additive

*Yamaha, Nikkon Gakki Co. Ltd, Hamamatsu, Japan.

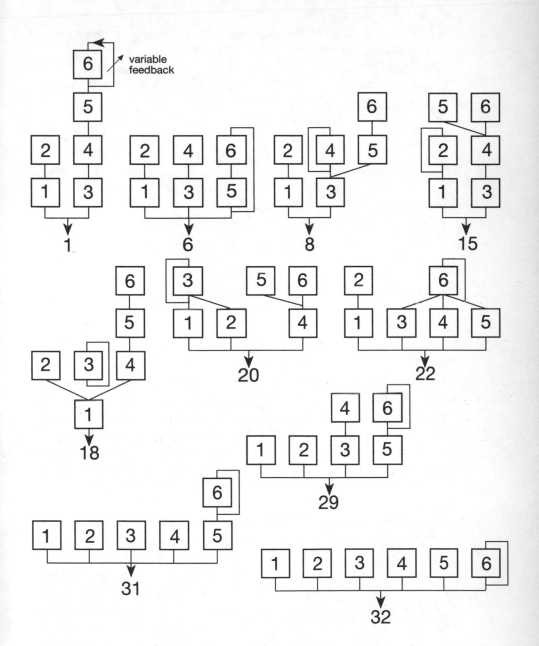

Fig. 68

only, with patch thirty-two being pure additive synthesis. There are many other features, but this illustrates a practical consumer approach to FM configuration. For studio use, the sound synthesis part of the DX7 can be supplied without keyboard and, in the form of a unit consisting of eight modules mounted together (TX802), provides powerful FM capabilities (in effect 8×DX7) in a very compact form. All these synthesizers have full MIDI facilities, and, via MIDI, can be computer controlled.

FM arrived when real-time digital synthesis was just becoming possible, and it was eagerly adopted as a very effective and economical technique. It is not the answer to everything, however, for example it is not a generalized method based on real acoustic models but an abstract mathematical process, a design approach that can be extended to other formulae than the Bessel function. In recent years there has been something of a swing to other methods after a decade of FM, but I have discussed it at some length because of its prominence and popularity. For compositional patches used in particular pieces, including some by John Chowning, see Dodge (1985) chapter 4.

7. Some other methods of synthesis
A large number of possible techniques have been tried over the years, and some oddities have become the favourites of particular composers or studios. Many are abortive for all sorts of reasons – maybe they just don't work well, are too expensive or slow, or work fine but turn out to produce the same result as some available, proven technique. Every issue of *Computer Music Journal*, every conference, adds new ideas or new views of old ones, and commercial synthesizers regularly claim technical breakthroughs with variable justification. The following comments cannot hope to be either complete or up to date, but briefly describe some alternative methods to those already discussed.

Waveshaping
Like FM, a non-linear technique, but it involves a quite different approach. When a signal is processed in some way (by an amplifier, for example), the relationship of output to input waveforms can be described by a 'transfer function'. Fig. 69a shows that a linear transfer function (which is what we usually hope for in amplifiers) does nothing to a wave except (possibly) alter its size. In 69b the function flattens at each end, and if the input amplitude is large enough to enter these regions the output will be 'clipped', adding an odd harmonic spectrum to the original sine. With a suitable function, the opposite (converting a non-sine waveform to a sine) can be done.

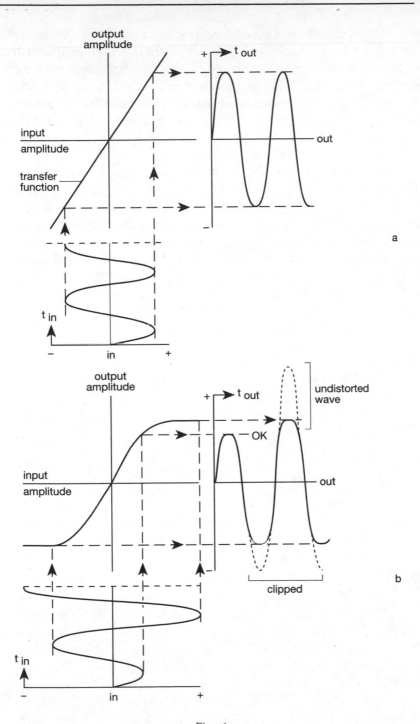

Fig. 69

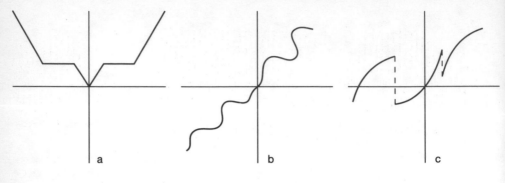

Fig. 70

Some functions can be specified algebraically, but an arbitrary, hand-drawn curve modified on a trial-and-error basis can also give interesting musical results. Certain general rules apply: assuming a sine input, functions symmetrical about the X-axis (like fig. 69b) give only odd harmonics, symmetry about the Y-axis (70a) produces an all-even series. Fig. 70b shows an arbitrary asymmetrical function which will result in some kind of complete series, and 70c a function with discontinuities, producing a theoretically infinite series (though in practice such waveforms must be band-limited to avoid aliasing). These are all series of harmonic partials, however. Waveshaping does not lend itself to inharmonic sound production (unlike FM), though this can be done with additional processing. Good introductions are Curtis Roads's *Tutorial* (1979), Dodge (1985) chapter 4 and Chamberlin (1985). A waveshaping technique using a high-pass filter is described by James Beauchamp (1979).

Granular synthesis

First outlined by Xenakis in 1971, this depends on viewing sound as a mass of separate quanta instead of a continuous phenomenon (Xenakis, 1971). Synthesis then becomes a matter of creating and organizing huge quantities of minute 'grains', of various waveforms, and with durations from very short up to about 50 ms (a length which seems to be the approximate **psychoacoustic** boundary beyond which discrete temporal events are perceived). To be effective as a tone source rather than a noisy click, each grain must be enveloped (see fig. 71).

Curtis Roads's short paper of 1978 proposed ways of generating grains and specifying control functions to create granular 'events' such as start time, duration of event, initial value and rate-of-change against time of waveform, centre frequency, bandwidth, grain density and amplitude (Roads, 1978). These can be graphically notated as slopes and

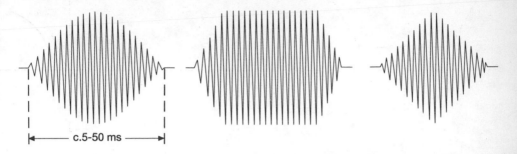

c.5-50 ms

Fig. 71

areas – grain structure can be thought of as frequency/time/amplitude activity planes of varying density, and like seeds in a field they can be drilled into neat rows or scattered broadcast.

The heavy computation required at first prevented much practical development of these techniques, and very few composers had a chance to work with granular synthesis. Recently, however, there has been a strong revival of interest, including real-time implementations and pieces of music. A new addition is the 'granulation' of sound sample inputs. For details of new work, an update and introduction by Roads, and two descriptive articles, by Truax and by Jones and Parks, see *Computer Music Journal*, vol. XII no. 2 (1988). A granular approach to analysis has also been developed by Richard Kronland-Martinet in France (Kronland-Martinet, 1988). For comments on graphic notations, see **computer music composition techniques**.

Vosim
(VOice SIMulation) As the name implies, this was developed for voice synthesis, and designed as a flexible but economical speech generator. It was conceived by Werner Kaegi (1973) and developed as hardware by Kaegi and Stan Tempelaars (1978) at the Institute of Sonology, University of Utrecht. Although speech synthesis as such is not a topic in this book, Vosim is an ingenious technique with useful musical applications. Instead of generating a continuous waveform, the oscillator produces controlled bursts of sinusoids each of which has the form of a falling train of pulses, displaced vertically so that the most negative point remains clamped to 0, as shown in fig. 72. This simulates the human voice box, and can be manipulated to produce a wide range of vowel formants. Each burst can be regarded as a complete event and controlled separately by changing very few parameters. Frequency is

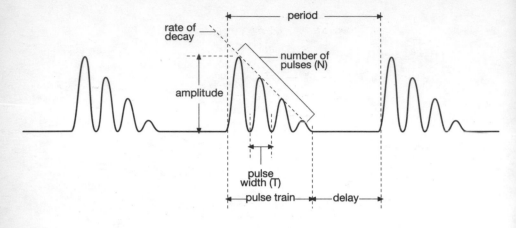

Fig. 72

altered simply by increasing or reducing the delay time between pulse trains, and it can be shown (and heard) that changing this delay has very little effect on spectrum, which is mainly controlled by N, T and the decay between successive peaks. A Vosim generator can be quite cheaply made, and though not suitable for every type of sound, the method can produce rich, time-varying timbres. For more detail see Chamberlin (1985) chapter 13, Dodge (1985) chapter 6, de Poli (1983) and Manning (1987).

FOF
(Fonctions d'Onde Formantique, i.e. formant wave functions) Another voice-simulating system with wide musical applications, developed by Xavier Rodet at IRCAM, Paris, and embodied in a general synthesis system called Chant.

Fig. 73 looks at first sight like the subtractive synthesis model discussed in section 5 above, or the filter bank illustrated in **vocoder**. In those systems the pulse wave source is separate from the filter. But in FOF each generating element is an oscillator which generates the waveform appropriate to one formant of the speech, singing voice or other timbre. The method simplifies parameter specification, and has been used for a wide range of vocal and instrumental sounds. For details see Rodet's exposition of the FOF module (Rodet, 1984), and the article on Chant (Rodet *et al.*, 1984), both in *Computer Music Journal*, vol. VIII, no. 3 (1984). See also Dodge (1985) chapter 6.

Reverberation
Time-delay devices, normally associated with the addition of **reverber-**

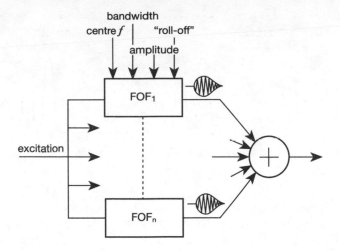

Fig. 73

ation effects to sounds, can be used as part of the sound synthesis process. They can be seen as filters with an 'all-pass' response, i.e. they do not affect spectra, only phase. Reverberation in the normal sense is an essential ingredient in music where movement and localization are involved (see **quadraphony**, and Dodge, 1985, chapter 7). But when used in the middle of a synthesis chain (i.e. when its 'tail' is likely to be cut off by later processes), the deliberate blurring of spectral boundaries by selective phase changing and recycling by time delays is a powerful timbre transformer in itself, capable of merging elements that would otherwise be perceived as separate. Delay arrangements, either electronic or electro-acoustic, are essential facilities in any composing studio (see **reverberation**).

Hybrid synthesis
This usually refers to digital control of analogue devices (see **analogue synthesis techniques** 6 and **computer music composition techniques**) but it may mean the opposite, for example, real sound used to control computers. With interfaces like MIDI all sorts of ad hoc composing arrangements can be set up, and though most **keyboard synthesizers** are now all-digital, hybrid designs still have their advocates. Hybrid synthesis was a popular technique when computers were less powerful, but on the whole has been overtaken by fully digital systems.

8. Conclusion

As I've said, some techniques are developed for a particular piece and may have little general application, for example a composer may be prepared to devote months of experiment to get one sound right, using labour intensive methods that have little attraction for others who want quick results and versatility without worrying very much about where the sound comes from. Interesting variants and developments frequently appear, see for example Dashow (1986) and Cavaliere (1988). Composers often write in detail about the methods used for their pieces (e.g. McNabb, 1981). See also **vocoder**.

In the past few years digital analysis, re-synthesis and synthesis of entirely new sounds have developed enormously in scope, efficiency and cost-effectiveness. At the time of writing, however, the fastest growing area, at least in commercial synthesizers, is that of real sound manipulation by **samplers**, which in a way bypasses most of the problems we have been discussing and suggests that in the end you can't do better than use real acoustic sources. The speed of development in digital technology shows no signs of slowing down, and we can expect rapid change to continue for some time to come. Many psychoacoustic aspects of synthesis – just why some artificial sounds are more convincing, 'musical' or just 'pleasant' than others – remain unsolved mysteries, and some very old analogue techniques still rival the latest digital methods when such qualities are compared.

Many references throughout this article have been to *Computer Music Journal*, which is strongly recommended for back-up reading. Good overviews are Moorer (1977), de Poli (1983) and the two books most cited, Dodge (1985) and Chamberlin (1985), are both readable and detailed.

Digital-to-analogue converter   (DAC) A device which accepts information encoded as **binary** numbers and outputs a voltage (or current) appropriately scaled to the size of those numbers. In the case of audio signals, many thousands of numbers are converted each second, but a DAC may also output slow changes or steady voltages, for control and other purposes etc. A DAC is the complementary device to an **analogue-to-digital converter** (ADC).

DACs work by generating a reference voltage or current, and tapping off that proportion of it which has the same relationship to its maximum as the number being converted has to *its* maximum. Music conversion would be at fourteen or sixteen bits, but let us take as an example a 6 bit word: 110101. Its decimal equivalent is 53 (see **binary code**), out of

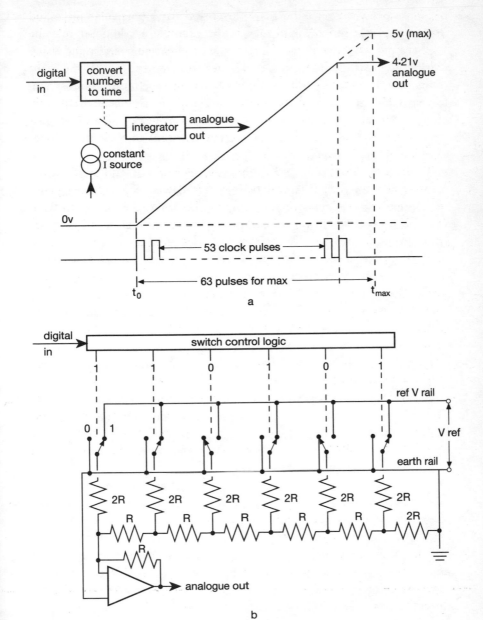

Fig. 74

a possible maximum for 6 bits of 63 (111111). So if the maximum output is five volts, 110101 should convert to $^{53}\!/_{63} \times 5 = 4.21$V. One method (fig. 74a) uses an **integrator** to generate a linearly rising voltage which is precisely timed, for example by counting the same number of clock pulses as the input number. The voltage reached at this instant is output and held. Other methods use a bank of switches in parallel, one for each bit, arranged so that when on (binary digit 1) each switch activates a current proportional to the significance of that bit. The total current will then be proportional to the number being converted. In 'weighted resistor' converters this is done by using **resistors** whose value doubles at each step down the number, but it is expensive and difficult to produce numerous values of R with the high accuracy needed. The 'R–2R Ladder' avoids this problem, and is shown in fig. 74b. The weighting is automatically achieved by the position of a switch in the ladder, and only two values of R are needed (only one if 2R is made up of R+R in series). Naturally the 'switches' are microscopic and non-mechanical, and the whole operation repeats at very high speeds, producing an output voltage which changes rapidly in steps.

During the actual conversion the output voltage may fluctuate widely, and the new voltage is only steady after a 'settling time' which varies with signal conditions. If these extra discontinuities ('glitches') on top of an already stepped **waveform** reach the final output they can cause very audible **distortion**, so the DAC is followed by a **sample-and-hold** (S/H) circuit which should pass on only the steady value of each step. The final component is a low-pass **filter** which smooths the waveform before sending it to audio equipment. In today's high speed, high **resolution** DACs most of the problems have been solved, and prices have fallen dramatically in the last few years.

For the principles of sampling, see **digital synthesis techniques** 1. For further reading see Pohlmann (1989), Barbeau and Corinthios (1984), Chamberlin (1985) and Watkinson (1988).

DIN (Deutsche Industrie Normen) A set of German standards and units, used widely, and particularly in the EEC. Probably best known for a range of plugs and sockets (including the universal plugging system for MIDI), and for a scale of photographic film speeds. See **cannon** and **jack**.

Diode A two-**electrode** device which allows **current** to flow in one direction only – the electrical equivalent of a valve in a pumping system. Diodes have many uses, including **demodulation** of an **amplitude**

modulated radio signal and **rectifying AC** mains to provide a **DC** power supply. The **resistance** of a perfect diode would be zero in the 'forward' direction and infinity in the 'reverse', but in practical devices neither of these ideals is met. A rising reverse voltage meets an almost constant high resistance, however, until at a critical point the diode goes into 'avalanche breakdown' and conducts heavily in the wrong direction. See also **amplifiers** and **semiconductors**.

Direct box   (direct injection or DI box) A unit **patched** into the line between an instrument (e.g. **electric guitar**) and its own **amplifier,** with an output which is a copy of the signal suitable for direct injection into a **mixing** system as an alternative to input via a **microphone**. Typically a DI box has a hi-Z (**impedance**) input and a lo-Z **balanced** output.

Direct current (DC)   An electrical **current** which always flows in the same direction, but not necessarily constantly or continuously, thus placing a **diode** in an **alternating current** will remove alternate half-cycles, leaving the other halves as discontinuous pulses of DC. Electronic devices require a steady DC power supply, i.e. one maintaining a constant voltage at its terminals.

Direct sound   See reverberation

Direct-to-disk   See tapeless studio

Disc manipulation techniques   These were used by early **musique concrète** composers to modify sounds in pre-tape days, and sometimes even after tape recorders became available. Examples from my first studio: 1. Looping by closed groove. 2. Turntables with large speed range. 3 Anti-clockwise turntables for retrograde playing, with appropriately modified pick-ups. 4. Echo effects by using a train of pick-ups in the same turn of the groove. Fig. 75 shows the modifications made to normal disc equipment for these manipulations. A simple type of disc 'lathe' was used for this work (for disc recording principles see **sound recording techniques**). Certain skills were needed to obtain reasonable results – cutting a loop in an **acetate** without cutting through to the aluminium base called for a very well judged lift of the cutter as the loop completed itself. Different improvisations were employed in different studios, and some remarkable effects were achieved.

A popular disc technique developed in the mid-1980s is 'scratching' or 'scratch-mixing', using normal disco turntables without special

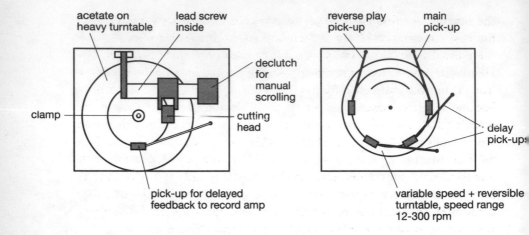

modified 78rpm cutting lathe   modified playback turntable

Fig. 75

modifications, but often swung forwards or backwards by hand rather than driven. By repeating, reversing, mixing etc. fragments of music from standard LP discs the disc jockey in effect improvises a new piece, and some scratch artists do this with considerable skill.

Disc recording   See **sound recording techniques**

Disk   The 'k' spelling is generally used for data storage media (e.g. floppy disk, diskette), the 'c' version for audio applications (e.g. vinyl disc, compact disc). In the USA the 'k' spelling is used for both types.

Dissonance   A perceived sense of roughness or jarring in the sound heard when two or more notes are sounded together. The term does not apply to **noise** phenomena, whose harshness, if any, is of a different character. As with all subjective qualities, opinions vary and no absolute values can be assigned, only comparative scales by which a particular listener judges chord A to be more or less dissonant than chord B.

   Most acoustic theorists from Helmholtz (1862) onwards agree that the main cause of the harsh effect is 'beats' (see **difference frequency**). Between two **sine waves** there can only be beats near the unison, but in real musical tones they will occur between any **partials** which are close in frequency, producing strong effects whenever two **harmonic series** nearly coincide. Since perfect coincidence occurs only at the unison and the octaves, we find the harshest dissonances immediately adjacent to the best consonances. Even if there are some **inharmonic** partials, and there usually are, the octaves will still be the most consonant intervals. Helmholtz concluded experimentally that beats became increasingly 'rough' up to a difference frequency of about 33 Hz, after which they became in effect tones and ceased to be irritating. On this basis he calculated a curve of dissonance based on violin timbre, in which one violin holds middle C (C_3), while the other glides slowly upwards. Fig. 76 is an adapted version of this plot (see Helmholtz, 1954, p. 193), with a musical stave for comparison. Modern theorists such as Taylor (1965) have made subjective tests with groups of students which generally confirm Helmholtz's curve, though wider variations occurred if subjects were asked to gauge 'unpleasantness' rather than 'roughness'.

Note that the positions of consonances also coincide with simple frequency ratios. This might lead one to conclude that complex, non-integral ratios always sound dissonant, but it is not so clear-cut as that. In equal **temperament**, for example, which we all hear every day, and in general enjoy, the frequency ratios used are extremely ungainly, and the actual pitches are offset from the 'best' consonances shown in fig. 76. Although the mistuning is quite noticeable, even Bach found it tolerable, and it is certainly not harsh enough to merit the description 'dissonant'. The explanation seems to be that if a mistuning causes beats low enough in the 'roughness' scale, the interval is musically usable – indeed very slow beats are quite pleasant, and are sometimes used deliberately, for example when a piano tuner offsets the three strings of

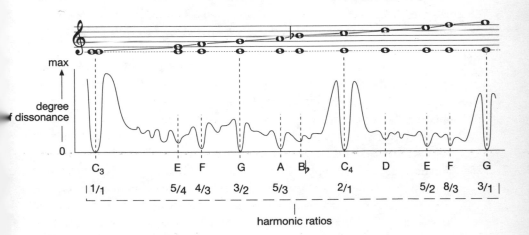

Fig. 76

a note slightly, to give more liveliness to the sound. In recent years computer acoustic research has contributed much new knowledge about the physical behaviour of sound, but there are still many unanswered questions in the **psychoacoustic** area. See also Wood (1962), Olson (1967), Roederer (1979) and Deutsch (1982).

Distortion   A change in the waveform of a **signal** (apart from **amplitude**). This can occur as a signal passes through any system and is usually unwanted, but may be deliberately introduced, as in waveshaping synthesis (see **digital synthesis techniques** 7).

Distortion is an ever-present problem wherever **amplifiers** are involved, because transistors and valves (tubes) only behave linearly within strict limits of signal amplitude. When driven outside these limits, **harmonic distortion** results.

Other types of distortion include crossover distortion (lack of symmetry in an amplifier's complementary circuit), delay distortion (frequency dependent delays), intermodulation distortion (see **cross-modulation**), and **phase** distortion. Encoding and decoding circuits can also introduce distortion (see **noise reduction**), as can conversions to and from the digital domain (see **analogue-to-digital** and **digital-to-analogue converter** and **glitch**). Some of the worst distortions in an average system occur not in the electronics but in the associated **transducers**.

Dolby   See **noise reduction**

Doppler effect   Named after the Austrian scientist Christian Johann Doppler (1803–53), this is the apparent change in frequency of a wave due to relative motion between its source and its receiver. In the common experience of a police car wailing past you, the perceived drop in pitch is greatest if you are standing very close to the path of the car – i.e. when the rate of change of angle between you and the moving source is rapid. You have no criterion by which to judge that the pitch is unnaturally high as the car approaches, but it may fall by as much as a minor third or so during the pass if the car is travelling fast. Only at the instant when the car is exactly opposite you is the true pitch heard. To sum up, typical Doppler is an almost steady pitch which drops very quickly to a lower steady pitch. If you are some distance away the change of angle is small and the rate of change fairly constant, so little or no effect is observed (none at all if the source is circling you). The simple formula, for a stationary listener and a directly approaching source, is $f_p = f(c/(c-v))$, where f_p is the perceived frequency, f is the true frequency of the source, c the speed of sound in air and v the speed of the source towards the observer, expressed in the same units ($-v$ becomes $+v$ when the source is receding).

Doppler is one of the many cues we use to locate ourselves and judge the behaviour of our surroundings, and its absence where expected immediately takes away 'naturalness', even if we don't quite know why. In electronic music the use of apparently moving sounds began quite early, but many of these artificial movements, using two or four tracks and carefully planned by their composers, lacked conviction because Doppler was technically too difficult to apply. To simulate sounds passing rapidly overhead or in changing curves a simulation of the Doppler effect is essential for realism, and must also be combined with changes in **reverberation** as the sound moves.

The only effective way to generate and control the necessary data is with a computer, and the problem was tackled by John Chowning in the early 1970s. His paper 'The simulation of moving sound sources' describes a method of calculating both Doppler effect and reverberation changes in a field of four speakers (Chowning, 1977). See also **quadraphony**, fig. 164, and Dodge (1985) chapter 7.

Double head A mute film and its associated sound track set up to run separately but synchronized in lock (see **selsyn**). A film in production is projected thus until the final 'married print'.

Drift Usually occurring in **oscillators**, drift is the tendency to wander off the desired frequency setting, due to thermal or other causes. A common problem in analogue music equipment.

Drop-out A gap in a recording, usually due to poorly manufactured, worn, dirty or damaged magnetic medium. In digital recordings, such faults can also result in drop-in, or spurious additional data.

Drum machine See **percussion generators**

Dubbing The process of combining several pre-recorded (or recorded plus live) sources into a new composite recording, often in synchronism with a film or video. Also described as 're-recording'. See **mixdown, mixers and mixing desks** and **rock and roll**.

Duplicate (dupe) A copy of a recording as nearly as possible identical with the original, or **master tape**, but, in analogue tape recording, inevitably noisier. Two 'dupes' made on the same machine from the same master are very nearly identical, however, apart from variations in tape stock. Important masters are carefully archived and only played to make dupes or sub-masters from which further copies are derived. In **cut editing** operations it is always wise to cut a dupe first, then match cut the master. See **noise reduction** on duping coded tapes.

Dynamic/s   1. Loudness instructions in a musical score, and the result of these, i.e. the actual loudness contour of a performance. 2. The adjective 'dynamic' is used to describe the characteristics of a device in action, responding to changing **parameters** (not necessarily concerning loudness), which may be quite different from its static or inactive behaviour. 3. 'Dynamic' also means 'self-powered', as, for example, in **loudspeakers** and **microphones** which use permanent magnets as sources of energy.

Dynamic range   The difference, usually expressed in **decibels**, between the lowest and highest intensity levels present in a musical performance, a natural or man-made environment, or a recording. In equipment speci-fications it represents the range of levels between the system's **noise** floor (the quietest **signals** must be significantly above this to be clearly aud-ible), and the onset of noticeable or unacceptable **distortion**. Depending on the context, various degrees of distortion may be tolerable – very little for high quality music recording, a great deal, in comparison, for an amplified speech in a public square.

   Musical instruments vary greatly in their dynamic range, from very limited (e.g. clavichord) to very large (e.g. trombone, particularly if muted sounds are included). Composite instruments (e.g. organ, orches-tra) have wider ranges still. No recording system can handle as wide a range as human ears, and various compromises are adopted to improve the naturalness of recording and broadcasting. See also **compressor, noise reduction, signal-to-noise ratio** and **sound recording techniques**.

E

Earphones See **headphones**

Earth (US ground) 1. (noun) The surface of the earth, being a good conductor of electricity, is effectively at the same electrical potential everywhere. It is therefore used as a reference level for potential in circuit electricity and defined as zero potential. The earth acts as a virtually infinite 'sink' which will absorb any charge connected to it. If the earth itself cannot be used (as in the case of an aircraft) the largest available mass of conducting material (the aircraft itself) is used as the 'earth' for electrical systems. 2. (verb) To connect something to earth or to a virtual earth point. See **hum**.

EBU European Broadcasting Union. The European standard-setting body for broadcasting, video etc. See **NTSC** and **time codes**.

Echo 1. A reflected sound, distinguished from **reverberation** by having only one or a very small number of reflecting paths, so that the returning sound is clearly heard as a delayed version of the original. The nature of an echo depends on many factors, but mainly a) the hardness and flatness of the reflecting surface, b) the size of the reflecting surface in relation to the **wavelength** of the source sound, c) the distance of the reflector from the source, and d) the presence or absence of other reflecting surfaces which may distort the main echo.

Fig. 77 shows a typical echo-producing situation. Added to the real source A, the reflecting surfaces give rise to apparent sources B, C and D. Electronically, single or multiple echoes can be produced by tape-head delays or digital delay lines (see **reverberation**). See also **acoustic treatments**. 2. In computers and communications systems, 'echo' is an accuracy check in which transmitted data is returned to its source for comparison with the original.

Editing 1. Re-arranging recorded material, by selective copying or

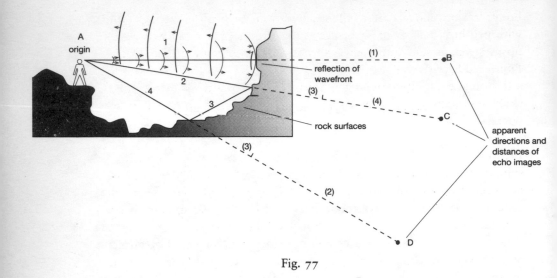

Fig. 77

physical cutting (see **tape composition techniques**). 2. Changing the form of computer software, usually to improve its performance. A new program of any complexity will almost certainly need **debugging**, after which it will be refined by successive edits.

Effects unit   See **digital multi-effect unit**

Efficiency   Of a single device or a whole system, the ratio of desired output energy to total input energy (signal + power supply). In general, the higher the efficiency the better (because inefficiency usually takes the form of unwanted heat), but high efficiency is not always a design aim. For example many good **loudspeakers** are very inefficient in terms of the electrical energy supplied compared with the acoustic energy delivered, because they are heavily **damped** to improve their response.

Eight-track   See **tape track configurations**

Electret   Any material capable of holding a permanent **electrostatic charge**, the electrical equivalent of a permanent **magnet**. Some natural waxes have this property, but synthetic materials (e.g. Teflon) are used in devices like electret **microphones**.

Electr/ic, -onic bass   Not the same as bass guitar (see next entry), but a version of the conventional orchestral double bass with a much reduced body. Various models are available, with four or five steel strings, and with peg box, finger board, bridge etc. as normal but fitted with pick-ups. As well as standard repertoire, it is capable of many special effects. Pioneered by virtuoso bassists such as Bertram Turetsky, whose book is a thorough exploration of contemporary double bass techniques (Turetsky, 1989), the electric bass is also used in jazz and rock, where its portability is an added advantage.

Electric guitar In its simplest form, a normal guitar fitted with a suitable air or contact **microphone** and amplified. The true electric guitar, however, does not use a microphone but **electromagnetic** pick-ups which generate a current in response to the vibrations of the guitar's steel strings. This type of instrument was developed in the 1950s by Leo Fender and Les Paul. Groups of pick-ups corresponding to the number of strings are made up in blocks and mounted under the strings near the **bridge**. In most cases two or three such blocks are fitted, an arrangement which gives a choice of tone qualities since the nearer to the bridge a pick-up is sited, the greater the upper **partial** content in the ouput. Selector switches, volume and tone controls are fitted near the bridge, and there may be foot operated treatments in the amplifier chain as well. Amplifier and speaker requirements are different from normal hi-fidelity applications, and equipment is specially designed for guitars (see guitar amplifiers in **amplifiers** and guitar speakers in **loudspeakers**).

No acoustic chamber or sound board is needed, so the body is a solid block of wood or other material which is hollowed out to receive the electrical components, and because the acoustic performance is unimportant electric guitars are made in a wide variety of shapes to suit a particular maker's style or the inclinations of the owner.

'Lead' guitars are tuned to the same six notes as the standard Spanish guitar (i.e. perfect fourths except the major third between strings four and five). The bass guitar (sometimes called the Fender Bass after its originator) has only four heavy strings and is an electric equivalent of the pizzicato string or double bass standard in popular instrumentation. In fact, with its shorter, stiffer strings and lack of bowing capability, the bass guitar is a completely different instrument from the string bass, and has found uses in serious orchestral music when rapid, firm articulation is wanted in the deep bass. As well as instruments with the normal fretted guitar fingerboard, fretless versions are made and often favoured for jazz. Tuning is the same as for the double bass i.e. an octave below the first four strings of the standard guitar. See also **electric bass** (previous entry).

The electromagnetic type of pick-up is suitable for any instrument with steel strings (e.g. mandolin, and see **pianos** *electric and electronic*). Because the guitar has enjoyed enormous popularity in recent years, a large number of designs have been tried, and various forms of the modified acoustic instrument remain popular as well as the Fender/Paul type described above. There are many specialist books and magazines on guitar design and performance, such as Kamimoto (1975), which contains constructional drawings of many different types of instrument.

Electric piano   See **pianos** *electric and electronic*

Electro-acoustic   One of the terms denoting the whole field of **electronic music** and electrical techniques in music, including composition, but sometimes distinguished from 'electronic' to refer specifically to amplified devices with acoustic generators. Not an elegant word, but widely current (see e.g. **EMAS**), and in French as *électro-acoustique*.

Electro-chemical   Describes a phenomenon in which either a chemical process has electrical consequences (e.g. a battery) or an electric current results in a chemical reaction (e.g. electro-plating).

Electrode   A general term for an interface between current in a wire and current (or charge) in a vacuum, gas, liquid, **dielectric** or **semiconductor**. If an electrode's **polarity** is known or relevant, it may be described as a cathode (negative (−) or **electron** source), or anode (positive (+) or electron sink). Normally a wire, plate or coil of metal, sited so as to make optimum contact with the other medium.

Electromagnet   A **magnet** which is only energized when current flows in a coiled wire adjacent to, around or through it. At **audio frequencies** the magnet is normally a core of ferro-magnetic material inside a current carrying coil. The principle can be applied in both directions, so that either 1. an applied current results in a magnetic and mechanical output (e.g. a **relay**), or 2. a continuously varying magnetic field produces an analogous output current, as in a tape replay head (see **sound recording techniques**). The changing magnetic field on the tape is transferred to the magnetic core and thence to the windings around it. Devices using **moving coils** normally contain permanent rather than electromagnets. See also **electric guitar** and **transformers**.

Electromagnetic radiation   Wave propagation of energy through free space at the velocity of light, electric and magnetic fields being mutually at right angles. The phenomenon can occur over an enormous range of **frequencies** from very long wave radio at *c.* 10^4 Hz (overlapping the audible band), through all the radio bands to microwaves (*c.* 10^{11} Hz), followed by infra-red, visible (*c.* 10^{15} Hz) and ultra-violet light, X- and finally gamma rays (*c.* 10^{20} Hz).

Electron A negatively charged elementary particle of constant and stable characteristics (e.g. weight, charge). It is found within all atoms, but also as an independent 'free' charge, in which form it is the basic energy carrier of all electric and **electronic** operations. It was first identified by J. J. Thomson in 1897.

Electronic music This expression was coined in the early 1950s to denote a method of composing which derived its sounds entirely from electronic origins such as **oscillators**, excluding all acoustic sources, even sounds recorded through microphones. It also excluded keyboard instruments like the electronic **organ**, which had appeared many years before, referring specifically to studio-realized music, and in the beginning to the products of one studio only.

A few years after Pierre Schaeffer produced his first experimental **musique concrète** in Paris (1948), a new studio was founded in Cologne by Herbert Eimert, and like Schaeffer's it was based on a radio station (Nordwestdeutscher Rundfunk). It sprang from earlier research by Werner Meyer-Eppler and Robert Beyer, and began producing in 1952. Its principal composers were Eimert himself and the young Stockhausen, who had worked in Paris but had different ideas from Schaeffer. The expression 'Elektronische Musik' was used to distinguish Cologne's product from that of the French studio.

The proponents of electronic music argued that by using only 'pure' sources, i.e. **sine wave** oscillators, it should be possible to build any complex sound in a completely predictable way. Compositionally, the aim was to extend the **serial** techniques already well established by composers like Schoenberg, Berg, Krenek and Webern, but with a degree of control and accuracy unattainable by human performers on acoustic instruments. To all appearances this was radically opposed to the way Schaeffer was working, and in those early days a heated battle of words ensued, polarizing opinion between Paris and Cologne (though the public thought little of either). The history is well described in books like Ernst (1977), Russcol (1972), Manning (1987) Griffiths (1979). Some interesting essays by Meyer-Eppler, Eimert, Stockhausen and others who had joined the movement were published in 1955 as *Die Reihe*, No. 1 (see Stockhausen, 1958), and by this time several other European countries and America were also active in the field.

Before long it was obvious that the argument about method was somewhat artificial. The new studios and composers made use of any source they felt like, and electronic music, in its English form, became (like electro-acoustic music) a generic term covering a wide range of genres, but still excluding otherwise conventional music that happens to be played on an electronic instrument.

The first electronic works were clearly different from instrumental ones because they used no performers and were always played from tape, but by the 1960s it became important to distinguish taped electronic music (see **tape music composition techniques**, **sound recording techniques**) from **live performance electronic music**, though recorded and performed elements often figure in the same piece. Sub-dividing in another way, **analogue synthesis techniques** were later joined by **digital synthesis techniques**, and computers also opened up new approaches to composition not possible in the 1950s (see **computer music composition techniques**). Many articles throughout this book are relevant to some aspect of electronic music, and for comments on studio environments see **studio design**.

Electronic music studio design   See **studio design**

Electronics   The area of physics concerned with the behaviour of free **electrons** in a vacuum, a gas or a **semiconductor**. The basic devices upon which the science rests are the **diode**, which conducts in one direction only, and the triode **amplifier** (in either semiconductor or **thermionic** form). In triodes a stream of electrons is caused to pass through one of the above media by an applied **voltage**, and controlled during its passage.

Electronic switch   A switch without moving parts, usually a **semiconductor** device arranged to cut off current completely when the OFF state is required. Widely used in computers and music devices. See **flip-flop** and **patch**.

Electrostatic charge   As the name implies, this is a charge arising between unmoving rather than moving objects. Typically the energy held in a charged **capacitor**, and comparable to a spring compressed but not released. **Electrets** are materials able to hold a permanent static charge.

Electrostatic speaker See **loudspeakers**

EMAS Electro-acoustic Music Association of Great Britain, 174 Mill Lane, London NW6 1TB. Tel: (071) 794 5638. In May 1990 EMAS amalgamated with the National Studio Project and the combined group became the Sonic Arts Network, but EMAS is retained as the name of the equipment hire company operated by the organization.

Emphasis The process of strengthening a chosen part of the audio **spectrum** by suitable **filtering**. See **pre-emphasis** and **presence**.

Enclosure An acoustic environment with known and usually controllable boundaries, typically for a **loudspeaker**. Another example is a closed, **damped** and non-**resonant** box into which very quiet sound sources (e.g. small insects) can be placed with a microphone to record them.

Encoding See **decoding**

Enharmonic 1. In ancient Greek music, describing a scale containing some intervals smaller than a semitone. 2. In modern notation, the same note written in different ways (e.g. $G\times=A=B\flat\flat$, $B\sharp=C$, $D\sharp=E\flat$). The identity is only strictly true in equal **temperament**, but in tonal music the grammatically correct version should be used. In twelve-note serial music, unless the notation refers to a fingering, as it may in string music for example, 'sharp' or 'flat' notation is used at convenience, but it still helps to be consistent – a perfect fifth, for example, looks wrong if notated as if it were a doubly augmented fourth (e.g. $D\flat–G\sharp$) or a diminished sixth ($C\sharp–A\flat$). Easily confused with, but quite different from **inharmonic**.

Envelope 1. In **amplitude modulation**, the shape imposed on a **carrier** by a modulating wave, symmetrical on each side of a centre zero (see e.g. figs. 3, 13, 16b). 2. In a musical context, the intensity of a sound plotted against time, and one of the three most important determinants of its character – the other two being **pitch** and **spectrum**. See **envelope shaper** and **analogue synthesis techniques** 4. The term is also used of an amplitude/**frequency** plot ('spectral envelope'), see **formant** and fig. 92.

Envelope follower A device which detects the **envelope** of an incoming signal (e.g. from an amplified instrument), and outputs an

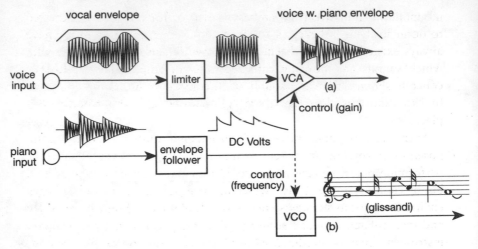

Fig. 78

analogous voltage/time curve which may be used to modulate another device. A typical application is to introduce electronic cross-influences in live performance.

Fig. 78 shows a piano envelope converted by an envelope follower and applied (78a) to a voice input, using a voltage controlled **amplifier** to impose the piano envelope on the voice signal. In 78b the same envelope modulates a voltage controlled **oscillator**, resulting in a series of glissandi synchronized exactly with the pianist's performance, of a range depending on the piano's dynamics.

For a discussion of voltage control, see **analogue synthesis techniques 4–6**. For the operating principles of limiters, see **compressor**. See also **live performance electronic music** and **pitch follower**.

Envelope shaper   An **amplitude modulating** device or computer procedure which applies an **envelope** to a continuous signal from, say, an **oscillator**. The simplest shaper for a single event (silence-to-silence) has three main segments – Attack, Steady State and Decay, but the commonest 'instrumental' type, has four – Attack, Decay, Sustain, Release, and is thus called an ADSR shaper. Shapers normally operate from a **trigger**, and behave as **one-shot oscillators**. See **analogue synthesis techniques 4**, **digital synthesis techniques 3**, Dodge (1985) chapter 3 and Wells (1981) chapter 5.

Environmental music   Outdoor performances in places chosen either for their acoustic/visual/historical/political or other character (a lake, a mountain, a slum street, an embassy lawn) or for the sounds expected to occur in them (a beach, a forest, a zoo). Street and field music have always existed, but have been given a new dimension by the ease with which sounds can now be captured, altered, amplified etc. **Musique concrète** showed that any sound at all could be musical material, and by extension it is clear that there are no strict rules about performing places.

There are three main kinds of environmental music: 1. Sounds composed for normal or unconventional instruments which are taken to the performing place, i.e. the music could also be set up in a concert hall, but by choice is not. 2. Music which in some way depends on the chosen environment for its very existence – sounds of the place may be recorded and manipulated to make some or all of the performance, or ordinary instruments may be modified by aspects of the environment. 3. Sounds from specially built artifacts which are usually designed to be visually interesting as well, and may be either part of a larger structure or self-contained, moveable sound sources. These are discussed under **sound sculpture**.

In the first category there are many examples of music scored suitably for open air conditions, from Handel's 'Water Music' and 'Royal Fireworks', through the **son et lumière** performances popular in the 1950s, to contemporary spectaculars put on for special occasions, and encompassing anything from a park to a whole town.

Music which actually grows from the environment can also take a variety of forms, but does not necessarily involve large, or even outdoor spaces. One example of a deceptively simple but musically original idea is *I Am Sitting In A Room* by Alvin Lucier (b. 1931).* A short passage beginning as the title is spoken in an ordinary, fairly bare room containing a microphone and a loudspeaker, connected to a tape recorder in the next room. The recording is then played back into the same room, re-recorded and played back again, etc. With each recording generation the natural acoustics of the room become increasingly influential because they are added to themselves, and the original line of speech is gradually replaced by long humming and singing sounds – the acoustics of a huge, imaginary room which is the original space blown up to enormous dimensions. There are often visual accompaniments to environmental pieces, and *I Am Sitting In A Room* may be heard while slides are shown, but they are not really necessary to enjoy the piece.

*Lucier, Alvin *I Am Sitting In A Room* (record) Lovely Music VR 1013, New York; 1981.

A composer who uses large scale environments is David Dunn who prefers the term environmental 'language' to 'music' and aims at interaction between people and not only environments, but the creatures that inhabit them. An example of Dunn's work is *Entrainments 2*, described in Dunn (1986), which began with pre-recorded descriptions and observations of the surroundings of three mountain peaks around the chosen performance site in Cuyamaca State Park, California, mixed with drones derived from astrological chartings of the location. These tapes were played at specific positions near the centre (everything is clearly mapped on a diagram), and at the centre a digital **sampler** recorded and immediately played back blocks of 3 seconds' duration of the signal from a microphone carried by a performer along an orbital track. Three other performers carried **oscillators**, adjusting tuning to what they judged the appropriate frequency for the overall sound environment. The performance went on for 45 minutes, and apart from the participants about fifty people walked about in the site while it was going on. Other pieces are also described in *Music, Language and Environment*, and Dunn gives his theories on music and animal communication in Dunn (1983–4).

A notable series of performances was put on for several years (late 1970s–early 1980s) by Martin Wesley-Smith (and many others) at Wattamolla Beach near Sydney, Australia. Spectacular water effects, floating ballets, light projections onto airborne objects etc. were combined with electronic music in several highly successful shows. The whole community was involved: 'Blokes from the Bundeena Bush Fire Brigade coordinated performances with their walky-talkies . . . they used their fire truck to create a huge water-sculpture that suddenly erupted from the lagoon to provide yet another projection screen. This was true community art, where participation was its own reward.'*

In *The Tuning of the World*, R. Murray Schafer looks at the whole 'soundscape' of the world, and the book, which came into being as part of a large World Soundscape Project in the mid-1970s, provides a good starting point for the musical aspects of a study that can easily extend to cover noise pollution and other topics outside the scope of this book (Schafer, 1977). It became clear in the 1950s that in the loudspeaker age serious musical performance could take place in many places apart from conventional concert halls, and we have even now only scratched the surface of the environmental presentation, not only of music, but visual, dramatic, operatic and balletic arts.

*Wesley-Smith, Martin *Wattamolla* Descriptive document available on request from Dr Wesley-Smith, NSW State Conservatorium of Music, Macquarie St., Sydney, NSW 2060, Australia.

The coming of **MIDI** and compact micro-computers has made possible a wide range of real-time interactions, and mixed media environmental performance is found at all levels from spectacular and very expensive productions to simple but imaginative schemes using pipes, bottles, pieces of wood etc., and designed to be accessible to anyone. The pioneer of this 'natural' approach was Harry Partch, who constructed a large number of instruments, and whose ideas are embodied in his book *Genesis of a Music* (Partch, 1974). A good example of an imaginative contemporary artist in this field is the Australian composer Ros Bandt (b. 1951), whose booklet *Sounds in Space* contains numerous good ideas (illustrated with photographs) and suggestions for further reading (Bandt, 1985). See also **bio-music, live performance electronic music, sound sculpture.**

Environmental recording   Some remarkable early open air recordings were made under great difficulties, when bulky equipment had to be transported to each location, for example the bird recordings made by Ludwig Koch in the 1920s and 1930s. Nowadays, with the improvement of miniature battery driven tape machines, first analogue and more recently digital, the recording itself is easy.

The main problem remains the actual collection of the sounds, particularly separating wanted signals from unwanted interference by wind, traffic and other obtrusive noises (unless of course the deliberate aim is a total sound picture). In recording shy creatures like wild birds and animals this is made even harder by the difficulty of getting close to the target sound source. For successful results in this very rewarding field, careful choice and protection of equipment is essential, a gift for improvisation is useful, but the main ingredient is and always has been endless patience.

For methods of achieving high sensitivity and directivity of sound collection, and minimizing wind noise, see **microphones** 4.

EPROM   Erasable Programmable **Read-Only Memory**. A type of computer memory erased by removing it from the circuit and treating it with ultraviolet light. Electrically EPROM (EEPROM) can be re-programmed in situ.

Equaliz/ation, -er   Colloquially 'EQ'. A type of **filter**, the word having two applications: 1. Fixed or switchable equalization built into the input circuit of a playback amplifier for discs or tape to compensate for the deliberately non-linear characteristic applied during recording (see **sound**

recording techniques). This type of EQ is only user-variable by switch selection, in, for example, a pre-amplifier with positions for different types of pick-up, or cassette recorders with selectors for different tape types. In professional open reel tape machines at least two input/output EQ curves are needed – CCIR (Europe) and NAB (USA). 2. Variable equalizers, which can be set to do the same job as 1. but are usually supplementary to fixed compensation circuits. Though they are intended to allow corrections to be applied as necessary, for example reducing the bass on a boomy recording, the term 'equalizer' is often a misnomer because they are frequently used to apply deliberate non-linearity, i.e. as 'colour controllers'. The bass and treble lift/cut controls on any hi-fi are a simple equalizer, but more comprehensive control of **response** is needed in a music studio.

A graphic equalizer (now also common in home and car equipment) is so called because the setting of the controls gives a visual indication of the filter's current response curve. Fig. 79a is a sketch of the front panel of a typical eight-octave graphic equalizer, which consists of eight parallel band pass/reject filters tuned to fixed frequencies an octave apart,

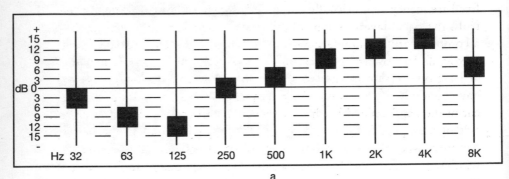

a

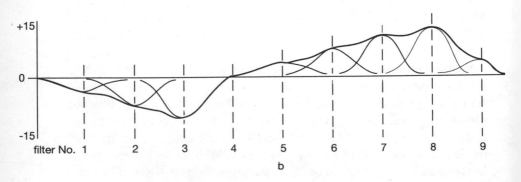

b

Fig. 79

and with **linear pots** controlling the amount of boost or attenuation for each filter. Fig. 79b shows the response of the filter bank at the setting shown, which is similar to the pattern made by the slider knobs.

As well as the frequencies being fixed, the sharpness of tuning (Q, see **filters**) of each filter is also pre-set so that the total summed response will be reasonably smooth. If tuning is too flat (low Q, wide **bandwidth**) there will be excessive overlap between filters; if too sharp, the overall response will be a 'comb' with local ripples and resonances. The cheaper three- or four-band graphic equalizers are intended for quick by-ear adjustment of a signal. At the top end of the range, accurately calibrated ⅓ octave equalizers for studio use can be very expensive, and are often combined with spectrum analysers. Apart from their general utility as signal improvers, these devices are useful for composers as fine-tuners of synthesized timbres. Some instruments also offer a separate output from each filter channel as well as the summed output, enabling a musical texture to be **spectrally** split into pitch regions.

Another type of equalizer in common use is the parametric equalizer, so called because there are more user-controlled variables than in the fixed frequency type. Usually fitted with rotary rather than linear controls, the panel layout is typically a row of up to ten calibrated knobs, a compact format suitable for installing as part of a 'channel strip' in a **mixing desk**. Detailed specifications vary widely, but to justify the name at least one section of the spectrum (if only one, the mid-range) must have continuously variable centre frequency as well as variable boost/cut of the band defined by that frequency, i.e. response falls off on each side of the centre frequency at a slope determined by the Q. The better parametric equalizers also have control of Q (usually labelled 'bandwidth'), to adjust the sharpness of the peak (or trough) at the chosen frequency. An application for high Q is when a signal is corrupted by a hum, whine or whistle at one frequency; it may be possible to substantially reduce or even remove it without seriously affecting the wanted signal.

Fig. 80 shows the response of a possible four-filter equalizer, which, for illustration, uses three different types of filter. The extreme bass and subsonic **high pass** filter (labelled LO) has a fixed slope and a switched roll-off frequency. The two middle filters have three controls each (centre frequency (CF), bandwidth (B/W) and boost/cut (B/C)), and the high treble (HI) is controlled by a fixed frequency, variable slope filter, which is also band pass/reject – but with the upper end of the band in the supersonic region. Because of the overlapping of the filters' ranges and the comprehensive controls provided, very complex curves can be

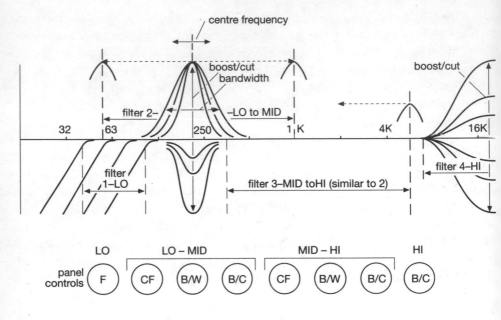

Fig. 80

created, but, by the same token, precise settings are difficult to repeat. Equalizers are usually provided with by-pass switches so that a whole pre-set curve can be switched in and out. In computerized studios a complete equalizer 'map' can be stored and retrieved at will. Parametric equalization is also offered in some **digital multi-effect units**, enabling particular equalizer settings and complete pre-sets to be similarly stored.

Most studios have several sets of differently specified equalizers. All input channels of the main **mixing desk**, and usually output groups as well, are likely to have parametric equalization available as an inbuilt facility. As well as this, additional units of various types (see again **filters**) can be **patched** in as required.

Equal temperament See **temperament**

Erasing The process of removing a recorded signal from magnetic tape, usually with a supersonic **AC** signal, which leaves the tape magnetically neutral. See **sound recording techniques**.

Error correction and detection In digital systems transmitted data can include codes which enable the receiver to check and/or correct the accuracy of the data. The commonest error detection method is a continuous 'parity check' in which an extra bit is added to a word on transmission to make the total number of '1' bits odd or even ('odd' or 'even' parity). Parity is checked at the receiving end, and any 'parity error' signalled. In digital recording various strategies are used to ensure a continuous performance even if the code is corrupted. See **compact disc, sound recording techniques**, Pohlmann (1989), Runstein (1989) and Watkinson (1988).

Even harmonic   See **harmonic series**

Expert system   A type of **data base** management used in **artificial intelligence** programming – a computer might, for example, be 'expert' in the rules of classical harmony. By suitable programming not only can information be intelligently deployed, but the computer can 'learn' for itself by noting the results of certain courses of action.

Exponent/ial   The number denoting the **power** to which another number is raised, i.e. n in X^n. In an exponential **function** one quantity varies as the power of another $(y=a^x)$ – see fig. 81. The energy in

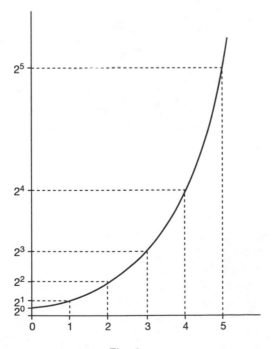

Fig. 81

percussive sounds **decays** exponentially when the energy source is removed.

Exponential horn   A tube shaped so that the area of its cross-section expands **exponentially** with unit length. This is an efficient shape for sound radiation, and a near approximation of it is used for the bells of many **brass instruments** and for some **loudspeakers**.

F

Fade/r   A fader reduces the level of a signal, ultimately to zero (fade out). Faders are the main controls on **mixing desks,** and are usually sliders, i.e. **potentiometers** with linear movement rather than rotary knobs (for two different meanings of 'linear' in this connection, see **linear pot**). Rotary faders are still found, however, and a third design is based on a pivoted quadrant. The **resistive** track of a fader is designed to follow a **logarithmic** law, so that equal decrements of perceived loudness more or less correspond with equal distances along the track. See also **analogue synthesis techniques** 5.

Farad   See **capacitance**

Fast fourier transform (FFT)   A method of converting the description of wave characteristics from the format showing the variation of amplitude with time (time domain) to the format showing the variation of amplitude with frequency (frequency domain) and vice versa. See **digital synthesis techniques** 3.

Feedback   1. The condition when the output of a process affects its input thus creating a looped system which partly controls itself. Most human activity except the simplest decisions involves some degree of looping, giving rise to expressions like 'turning over in the mind', see **analogue synthesis techniques** 2. 2. In an **active** electrical or electro-acoustic system, feedback is a connection from output to input, forming a loop which may either increase or reduce the system's total **gain**. Fig. 82a shows that positive (in-**phase**) feedback adds to the original signal, negative feedback in 82b opposes it.

Positive feedback tends towards instability, and is used purposely when this condition is sought, in, for example, 'regenerative' feedback in some **oscillator** circuits. Uncontrolled positive feedback causes a rapid build-up of power to the limits of a system. It is the cause, for instance, of the electro-acoustic **howl round** when a **microphone** is brought too

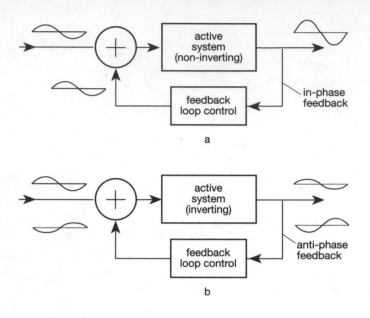

Fig. 82

near the **loudspeaker** it is feeding. Negative feedback, correctly applied, has the good effect of reducing **harmonic** and **phase distortion**, thus improving **linearity** (though at the expense of **gain**). Used widely in power, operational and other **amplifiers**, and **frequency** dependent feedback loops can form the basis of **filters**.

Ferrites   A group of man-made ceramic **magnetic** materials, used both in permanent and electromagnet applications. More efficient than iron or steel, they also have the advantage of being non-conductors. Used for example in tape heads, **loudspeakers**, **microphones** and **transformers**.

FET   See **field effect transistor**

FFT   See **fast fourier transform**

Fibonacci sequence   The series of numbers, first explored by Leonardo Fibonacci (*c.* 1170–1230), in which each successive number is the sum of the two previous numbers: 1, 1, 2, 3, 5, 8, 13, 21, 34 etc. As Hofstadter (1980), p. 173, points out, the sequence cannot be inferred from the first two numbers alone. Its interesting mathematical properties have been exploited by some composers.

Fibre optics Rapidly developing method of signal transmission based on light being transmitted down a very thin, pure glass filament. The nearly total internal reflection keeps the light within the filament, provided it is not bent beyond a certain angle. Increasingly used instead of electrical currents in wires for mass, high-speed data transmission, optic fibre systems have a huge **bandwidth** and, being insulators, do not transmit or receive electrical **interference** and cannot form **earth** loops (see **hum**).

Field effect transistor (FET) A type of **semiconductor amplifier** with different operating principles from the junction transistor, a commoner device which is always referred to when the word 'transistor' is used alone. An FET's three electrodes (though some have more) are called Source, Gate and Drain, and compared with junction transistors they have a very high input **impedance**. A common use in audio is for high-**gain** pre-amplifier stages, such as **microphone** head amplifiers. See also **MOS**.

Figure-of-eight See **microphones**

Filters These are signal modifying devices whose input/output relationships are a function of **frequency**. Filtering is essentially a subtractive process, but the description can be misleading because **active** filters (i.e. containing **amplifiers**) may actually boost signal power, and some filters are generators as well as treatments. In general, though, comparison with a water or oil filter is valid – an electrical filter is placed in a signal path and removes something from that signal. The numerous uses of filters in audio and electronic music include **compensation**, **equalization**, **loudspeaker** crossover networks, **AC** mains smoothing and **subtractive synthesis**. Delay lines, used in **reverberators** etc., are also classed as filters, called 'all-pass' because they do not affect frequency **response**, only **phase**.

Analogue filters work by passing signals through frequency-dependent networks, usually based on **capacitors** (f-dependent) and **resistors** (not f-dependent) in various configurations. **Inductors** (f-dependent conversely to capacitors) can also be used, but are usually avoided because they are relatively inefficient, space-consuming and subject to **interference**. Digital filters operate on numbers rather than audio signals, and digital equivalents of all the main analogue types exist, plus features not available in analogue technology. Filter design is an enormous and complex subject. This entry discusses their use rather than their

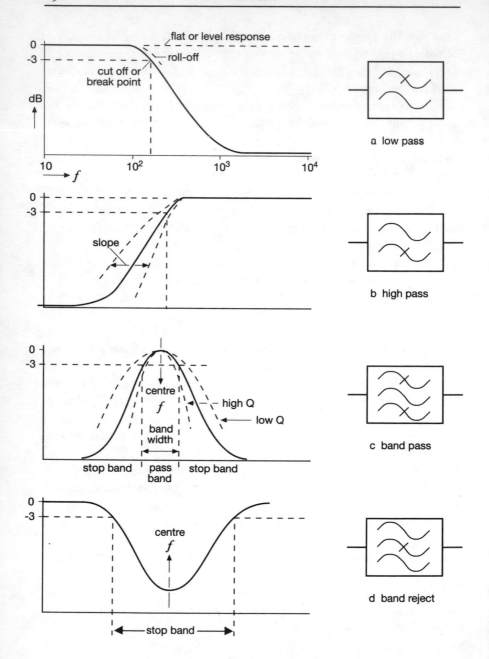

Fig. 83

construction. For more detail see, for analogue: Wells (1981) chapter 6, Strange (1983) chapter 9 and **analogue synthesis techniques** 4; for digital: Dodge (1985) chapter 5, Chamberlin (1985) chapter 14 and **digital synthesis techniques** 5.

Filters come in a large variety of specifications, but all (except all-pass) employ variants of four basic shapes of response curve: low pass, high pass, band pass and band reject. Typical curves for each are shown in fig. 83, together with a generally accepted symbolic notation. A filter does not suddenly begin to act fully at a certain frequency. Attenuation gradually increases until a more or less straight-line 'slope' is reached. By convention the 'roll-off' portion ends when signal power is reduced by half (the −3 **decibels** level), and this 'break', 'cut-off' or 'turnover' frequency is also regarded as that at which filtering begins. The slope of the straight-line portion is expressed in dB/octave or decade. Using only one simple filter network (a 'first-order' filter) the maximum attenuation obtainable is 6 dB/octave, but steeper slopes (12, 18 dB/octave etc.) can be achieved by cascading several filters (second-, third-order etc.). For some applications (e.g. timbre control) a gentle slope is generally desirable, but for others the slope should be as steep as possible − such designs are sometimes called 'brick wall' filters.

All the responses in fig. 83 depend on attenuating part of the **spectrum**. A 'boost' response can be achieved by adding an amplifier to a filter, as in fig. 84.

A familiar example of high and low pass first-order filters is the tone control circuitry of a domestic hi-fi amplifier, typically designed to roll off from a central position in the spectrum (c. 1 kHz), and provide both boost and cut for each end (treble and bass), with a 'level' position halfway through the travel of each knob.

Band pass and band reject filters operate somewhere in the middle of the audio range − if set close to either end they may become in effect high or low pass because the 'return' part of the response will be

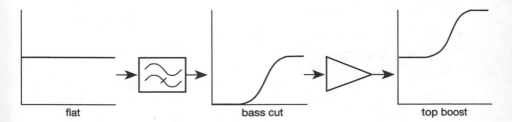

flat   bass cut   top boost

Fig. 84

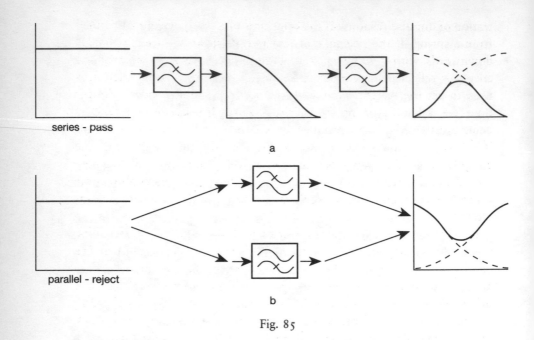

series - pass

a

parallel - reject

b

Fig. 85

sub- or supersonic. Fig. 85a shows that a band pass filter can be made by connecting low and high pass filters in series, and the same pair in parallel (85b) form a band reject combination.

Centre frequency of the resultant filter is adjusted by shifting the break points of the constituent filters up or down in frequency by the same amount, and bandwidth by moving them closer or further apart symmetrically around the centre f. By suitable design the pass mode can be made to change smoothly to the reject mode, providing a continuous boost/cut with one control. This versatile type of filter is the basis of the parametric **equalizer**. For a **voltage controlled** version see below and fig. 88.

So far we have looked at filters in terms of steady-state frequency response only, but the process involves many time sensitive operations, capacitors charging and discharging, frequency-dependent phase shifts, etc. For continuous signals like most music these time characteristics are not important because the filter can be assumed to reach a steady state rapidly, but the position is different if the filter is strongly attacked from rest (such as music starting with a very loud drum beat) or a signal is changing rapidly, in which case the impulse and transient responses of the filter become relevant. These are similar, but 'impulse' assumes that the filter is without stored energy before the attack, 'transient' that we wish to change the energy contents very quickly. A mechanical illustration of impulse response is the behaviour of a heavy weight suspended from a spring. If the system is at rest and we strike the weight sharply downwards with a hammer, very little happens because most of the energy is reflected back into the hammer, and only a small fraction is used to get the weight moving. A smaller force applied over a longer time (e.g. a hand pushing the weight down) will result in more energy being transferred to the system, which will then **oscillate** when the weight is released. In an electrical system the mass of the weight and the compliance of the spring become respectively inductance and capacitance, and a circuit consisting of both of these (plus inevitably some resistance) is called a **tuned circuit,** whose action is the basis of resonant filters.

Fig. 83c showed two response curves with the notation Q. In filters, the Q ('magnification', UK, 'quality', US) factor is a measure of the bandwidth in relation to the sharpness of the peak, and for band pass filters is defined as the ratio of the centre frequency (o dB) to the difference between the frequencies on each side at -3 dB – see fig. 86.

The higher the Q, the sharper the peak and the more frequency selective the filter. Apart from being one way to achieve high Q, a **resonant** circuit behaves as the name suggests – like a bell, with a **ringing**

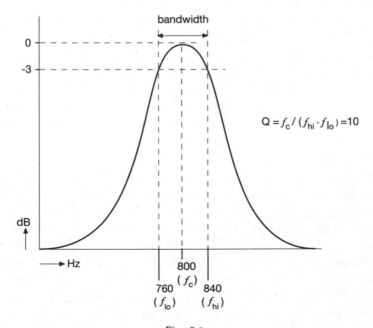

Fig. 86

impulse response. A single pulse of energy will cause the filter to ring at the frequency it is tuned to, the length of decay depending on the amount of **damping** (resistance) in the system.

One example of the use of resonant filters is in **percussion generators,** where a suitably tuned filter is 'struck' with a sharp pulse to simulate the **envelopes** of bongos, marimbas, etc., typically a very large first half-cycle and very rapid decay thereafter (see fig. 87a). If the oscillatory output of a tuned circuit is amplified and applied in-phase to its input (positive **feedback** or regeneration) it has the effect of sharpening the Q further and increasing the length of the ring (b). Eventually, when enough energy is fed back to overcome all the resistance in the tuned circuit, the whole system **oscillates** continuously (c).

The filter oscillator combines both effects. Its response can be varied from low Q through increasingly sharp tuning to the oscillatory state. Inputs can still be applied when the device is oscillating, but it has now become a type of **modulator.** If **noise,** for example, is applied to an oscillating filter, various kinds of whistle and siren ('windy tone') sounds can be produced.

There are many further types of filter. Although inductors are conven-

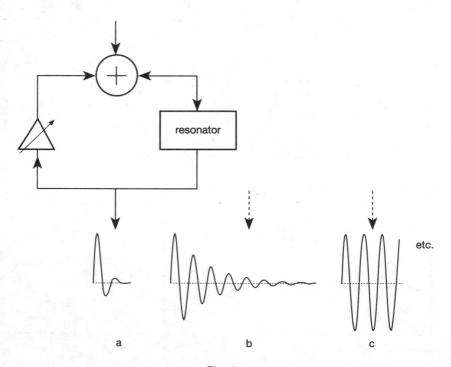

Fig. 87

tionally used in tuned circuits, we have noted that they can cause problems, and high Q circuits can be designed without them. One method
uses an **operational amplifier** in a + and − feedback configuration called
a 'gyrator'. High Q reject filters are sometimes called notch or slot filters.
In fixed frequency form such filters are little use as timbre controllers
because they are too limited and drastic, but they have many special
uses as, for example, 'traps' to block off an unwanted signal which is
principally at one frequency only. A good example is the **bias** trap
fitted in tape recorders to prevent high frequencies from the bias/erase
oscillator entering the audio circuits (see **sound recording techniques**).
Fixed resonant peaks at low Q are characteristic of instrumental **formants,** and the most flexible filters for responses of this type are voltage
controlled band pass filters (based on **VC amplifiers**) in which both
bandwidth and centre frequency are voltage controllable (see fig. 88a).

If a VC filter is of the two-filter type shown in fig. 85 the slope of
each is fixed while the bandwidth is controllable by adjusting cut off
points as described above and shown in fig. 88b, and a series/parallel
switch may be fitted to select pass or reject. If the filter is the resonant
type, the bandwidth is varied by changing Q (88c). Using a band pass

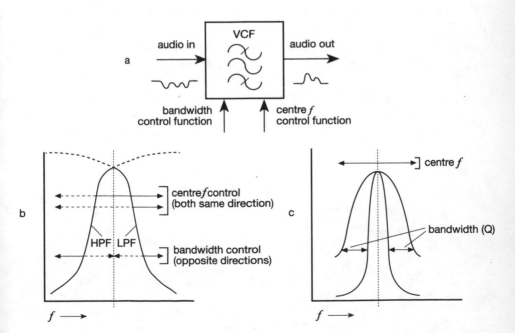

Fig. 88

VCF, subtle real-time timbre control is possible, only rivalled by the greater precision and repeatability of digital equivalents (see above).

A group of fixed notch filters can be arranged as a parallel 'bank' (in the same way as a graphic **equalizer**, but with higher Q than that device). This is called a 'comb' filter, whose characteristic is to divide the spectrum into alternating pass and stop bands. A special type of comb filtering is 'phasing', where a signal is split between a direct feed and a series of networks which produce a **phase shift** whose angle can be varied by, for example, a low frequency oscillator. The result is a set of varying nulls and peaks, not necessarily in any harmonic relationship with the signal. Light phasing adds a mobile sheen to a sound, and heavy applications (less direct sound, more phased) produce a 'rotating' effect as different parts of the spectrum are selectively distorted.

Another way to generate a comb is by using delay lines. If a complete spectrum is delayed, and the delayed signal mixed with the original, frequencies which exactly complete whole cycles (or integral multiples of whole cycles) in the delay period will be doubled in amplitude, those that complete (odd multiples of) half-cycles in the given period will be in anti-phase and cancel to zero, and for intermediate values varying proportions will pass. The resultant signal contains a series of harmonically related nulls and peaks, and their positions can be adjusted by changing the delay time and/or inverting one of the signals before mixing. Fig. 89 shows the method, and a typical output comb response. In use, the effect is called **flanging**, and produces anything from a slight 'churning' of the sound to swishing and 'aeroplane' effects.

Delay lines in various configurations are now commonly employed for many types of treatment, some of which are not normally regarded as filtering (e.g. **echo, frequency shifting**). Delays are difficult to implement by purely analogue means, but the arrival of reasonably

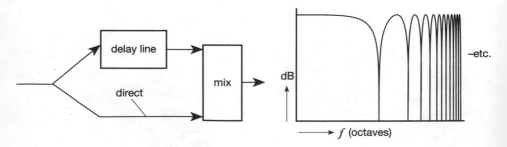

Fig. 89

priced high quality ADCs and DACs has made it easy to do this kind of processing digitally. Many **digital multi-effect units** offer several kinds of filter as part of their menu.

The list of different filters is endless, ranging from simple **networks** of two or three cheap components to elaborate modules with multiple variables. Many filters are fixed, but when adjustable they can be controlled manually by voltage control, by direct computer instruction or via a **MIDI** link. From the main types outlined, a suitable compound device can be put together for almost any purpose. Fig. 90 shows typical uses within a patch of some of the filters described or referenced above, and two that have not been specifically mentioned. Rumble and scratch filters are high and low pass respectively, designed to improve results from poor turntables, pick-ups and discs.

Firmware   Software (program instructions) in permanent or semi-permanent electronic storage (e.g. integrated circuits) rather than on paper or disk. Storage is usually **ROM (PROM, EPROM)**. See also **hardware.**

Flanging   An effect caused by small and varying time delays between two otherwise identical signals. The term is derived from a tape engineer's trick of running two copies of the same material simultaneously and braking one machine with a hand on the spool's flange. Flanging is

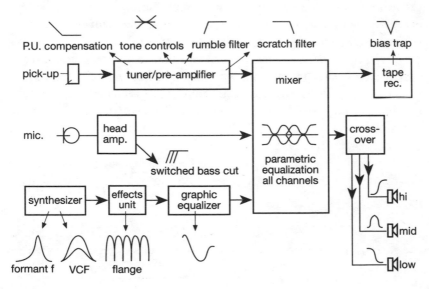

Fig. 90

now produced in a controlled way by digital delay lines. See **filters**, **phasing** and **reverberation**.

Flip-flop A two-state electronic switching device widely used in computers for storage, arithmetic and logic operations. The commonest type is **bistable** – effectively two linked switches, one on and one off. When 'flipped' by a **trigger** it switches to the opposite stable condition until 'flopped' back again. A **monostable** flip-flop has only one stable state. An astable (neither state stable) form of the device is an **oscillator** (multivibrator) with a **square wave** output. See also **Schmitt trigger**.

Floppy disk Thin plastic disc coated with a magnetic material and permanently encased in a paper or plastic envelope, suitably lubricated for smooth rotation when placed in a disk drive. Cheaper than **hard disk** (though not necessarily cheaper per **bit** stored), and the preferred mass storage medium for most micro-computers. Commonly referred to by size as 8in floppy (203 mm), minifloppy (5¼in/133 mm), microfloppy (3½in/89 mm). Also rated by density of data storage capacity (single, e.g. 48 tracks per inch, or double, e.g. 96 tracks per inch) and usage of sides (single, double).

Flowchart Software equivalent of a hardware **block diagram**, showing procedural steps in a system or program in a logical sequence, but not executive methods. Can be drawn at nested levels from broad outline to fine detail, and different conventions may be used to distinguish, for example, questions needing answers, actions to be taken, people, processes, objects. In planning, say, a **computer music composition**, flowcharts are valuable in revealing mental jumps which are quite natural in human thought but incomprehensible to a computer. Fig. 91 shows an example from *Introduction to Computer Science* by Levison and Sentance, which breaks down an everyday sequence of events into logical steps (Levison, 1969). It would be easy to extend such a sequence by adding a power cut, a faulty frying pan and so on. For a simple musical flowchart see fig. 34.

Flutter Relatively rapid fluctuations in signals from tape recorders, due to vibration of tape itself or mechanical faults in tape transport. See **wow** and **tape recorder design**.

Flutter echo 1. A type of **reverberation** decay with regularly spaced repeats, characteristic of small, bright rooms with parallel walls.

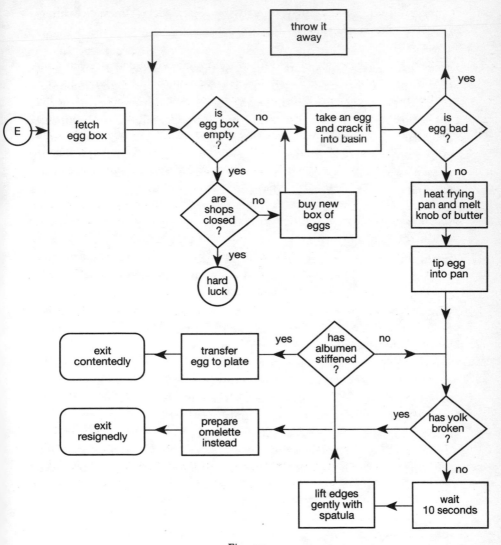

Fig. 91

2. Artificial creation of 1. by rapidly switching between **stereo** or **quad** channels and simultaneously applying time delays.

Flyback   See **oscilloscope**

FM   See **frequency modulation**

Foldback   The provision for playing sound back to musicians during performance. Used in rock and jazz concerts, backward-facing foldback speakers being placed on stage so that performers can hear either themselves (such as vocalists otherwise drowned by loud instruments behind them) or quieter instruments sited at a distant part of the stage. In a recording studio there are two main applications: 1. In **overdubbing**, foldback of previously recorded tracks is fed to headphones for synchronization of new tracks (see **sound recording techniques**). 2. Foldback of **equalized, reverberated** etc. sound is fed to loudspeakers or headphones so that artists can hear the control room mix, and also in order to take away the deadness of the studio. See **acoustic treatments, control room** and **mixers and mixing desks**. Compare **talkback**.

Foldover See **alias**

Formant Peak in a **spectrum** at a particular **frequency**, caused by the physical characteristics of an instrumental or vocal sound source. All instruments, because of their shape, dimensions and the materials from which they are made, are more efficient at certain frequencies than others. More than this, each individual example of a given instrument has unique formants whose exact placing is an important factor in the quality of that one instrument. The human voice is different because we can change the shape of certain **resonant** cavities in our heads, and thus to some extent control formants. This ability allows us, among other things, to form different vowel sounds. The pattern of formant peaks can be plotted as a spectral **envelope** (fig. 92).

As discussed in **bowed string, brass** and **woodwind instruments**, each sounded note begins life at the generator – string, lip and mouthpiece

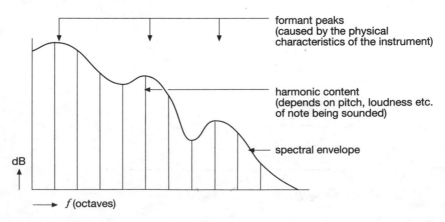

Fig. 92

or reed. At this stage it has the spectral content or **timbre** appropriate
to that generator and pitch, which varies in different parts of the compass
and with the way it is produced, thus the same note on different strings
of a violin will be different timbrally. The sound then passes to the
resonator or acoustic amplifier – the body of violin, tube of clarinet or
trumpet – and is modified in turn by the formants imposed by that
structure in a way that depends on the relationship of the note's pitch
to the formant envelope. Fig. 93 illustrates this in a highly simplified
way. The two notes shown (low and high) are assumed to have a
complete **harmonic series** with regularly diminishing amplitude (only the
first four harmonics are shown). Fig. 93a shows the spectra if we assume
a level **response**. In 93b a simple formant envelope with only one peak
is imposed, and it can be seen that the relative level of harmonics within
a note as well as the relative amplitude of the two **fundamentals** is
altered.

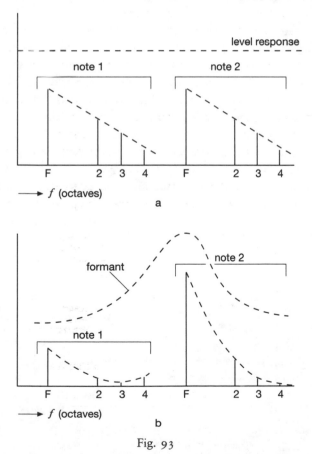

Fig. 93

The formant pattern is one of the strongest 'thumb-prints' of an instrument, not only accounting for much of the perceived quality of an instrumental type but helping to identify a particular instrument (e.g. a 'wolf' note on a bad violin is caused, at least partly, by an unmanageable formant peak).

In synthesis of instrumental sounds a formant **filter** is designed to imitate the spectral envelope of the instrument being synthesized. For designers of electronic **organs,** the existence of fixed formants makes it possible to use filters which do not have to be retuned for different parts of the compass, though tunable filters may be used as well. In computer music, formants are simulated in various ways, and formant 'tracking' is an important technique in speech synthesis. See **digital synthesis techniques 5, vocoder** and Dodge (1985) chapter 6.

Forth   See **computer languages**

Fortran   See **computer languages**

Fourier analysis/synthesis/transform   See **digital synthesis techniques 3**

Four-track   See **tape track configurations**

Frame   1. One complete scan of a TV screen (25 frames per second, UK, 30 frames per second, US). 2. One picture of a movie film (24 frames per second). 3. A reading across a multi-track data tape, at one **bit** position. 4. A **gated** group of pulses. 5. A block of samples selected for analysis (also 'window'), see **digital synthesis techniques 3**. 6. A defined block of code in a digital recording system, see **compact disc.**

Frequency   The number of occurrences of a repetitive phenomenon per unit of time. Mathematically it is the reciprocal of **period** – SI unit the **hertz** (Hz), replacing the older expression 'cycles per second' (cps). Oscillations at frequencies below 1 Hz are often more conveniently described by their period, for example 0.02 Hz has a period of 50 seconds (1/.02). If a wave contains one frequency only it must be a **sine wave.** In a complex wave two or more frequencies are present together, and if they are members of the same **harmonic series** the frequency of the longest wave (lowest frequency) present (**fundamental**) is also the same as the frequency interval between each wave in the series, as well as being the repetition frequency of the complex as a whole.

Frequency divider/multiplier A divider derives lower **frequency** electrical oscillations from signals containing higher ones (commonly a 'divide by two' giving the **octave** below). It is used in electronic **organs** for example, to derive a whole keyboard range from only twelve **oscillators** covering the top octave. Some organs have only one oscillator and use a $^{12}\sqrt{2}$ (see **temperament**) divider to produce the top octave. Also used in digital timing devices to divide down a high frequency quartz oscillator output to produce a required period (one second, for example). A frequency multiplier is the converse device.

Frequency meters Instruments which measure frequency. They come in several forms: 1. A calibrated **Helmholtz resonator** or **vibrating reed** is set into vibration by the sound to be tested. If **resonance** occurs the calibration frequency must be present in the sound. They are accurate, but limited because each calibrated device can be used for only one frequency. 2. Digital counter/timers, in which a quartz **oscillator** provides the timing standard, and the number of **cycles** in a precisely **gated** interval (typically one second) is counted. These timers are read directly in **hertz** (or kHz) from a display, with a possible error of one cycle because the gate may open/close just before or after a cycle begins. They can sometimes be confused by rich **waveforms** and read a **partial** rather than the **fundamental**. These useful tools also read **period** (reciprocal Hz), and often have other timing modes as well. 3. Some analogue tuning aids, as well as giving standard frequencies to tune to, receive input from instruments and indicate 'flat' or 'sharp' in **cents**.

Frequency modulation (FM) The process by which the frequency of one wave (the carrier) is changed at the frequency of another wave (the modulator) by an amount, called the deviation, above and below its unmodulated frequency.

Fig. 94 shows an analogue **patch** for FM using two voltage controlled **oscillators** and a VC **amplifier**. The result of FM with two **sine waves** can be predicted if the modulating frequency, m, carrier frequency, c, and amplitude of deviation, d, are known. See **digital synthesis techniques** 6.

The term is generally familiar as FM radio, in which the audio signal modulates the transmitter (carrier) frequency instead of its amplitude (see **amplitude modulation**, AM). Because most interference and other unwanted signals are AM phenomena they have little effect on FM transmissions. On the other hand the **bandwidth** required is much wider than in AM, so FM is broadcast at frequencies in the order of 100 MHz (100 times higher than medium wave at *c.* 1 MHz). This higher frequency

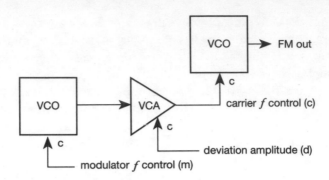

Fig. 94

gives greater bandwidth but a more limited transmitter range.

In instrumental music, **vibrato** is an FM where the modulator is at a much lower frequency than the carrier, but when the carrier and modulator frequencies are both in the audio band, FM changes the **waveform** (hence **timbre**) of the carrier. In digital synthesis, FM is a powerful and cost-effective tone-generating technique, and in some synthesizers is the only method employed. Developed in the early 1970s by the Stanford University team **CCRMA**, particularly John Chowning, it makes possible the synthesis of complex tones (containing both **harmonic** and **inharmonic partials**) with only two sine oscillators (though more can be used) (Chowning, 1973). For uses of FM in analogue work see **analogue synthesis techniques** 4ff.

Frequency response   See **response**

Frequency shifter   A device for shifting a complete **spectrum** linearly – i.e. in which every component wave within the spectrum is increased or decreased in **frequency** by the same amount. The device is, in effect, a suppressed carrier or **ring modulator** with only one **sideband** (hence sometimes SSSCM – Single Sideband Suppressed Carrier Modulator). A natural **harmonic series** is a set of simple frequency ratios, and the linear shift, by changing these ratios, creates **inharmonic partials** which have a strong effect on **timbre** and harmonic balance.

Fig. 95a shows the first four harmonics of a tone whose **fundamental** is the A at 110 Hz. If we use the shifter to lower the A by 12 Hz to G (98 Hz), the partials will also move down by 12 Hz. But fig. 95b shows that the partials (solid lines) have now become inharmonic in relation to the new fundamental. They are in fact much sharper than the frequencies of the natural harmonics (dashed lines). For discussion of

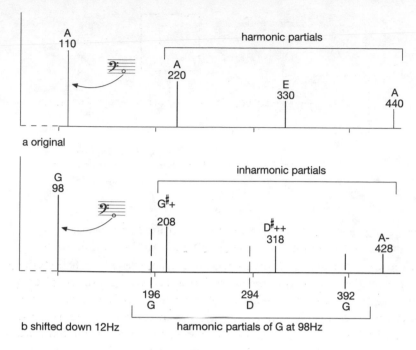

a original

b shifted down 12Hz   harmonic partials of G at 98Hz

Fig. 95

suppressed carrier modulators (SCM) see **analogue synthesis techniques**
5. In a shifter one sideband of a normal SCM is removed.

For proportional shifting, i.e. preserving the correct internal ratios of
the spectrum, see **pitch changer**.

Frequency shift keying (FSK)   See **time codes**

Function   The relationship between two **variables** such that for every
possible value of one, the independent variable, a unique value exists
for the other, or dependent variable. This may be expressed as a verbal
statement (for example that a variation of amplitude with time is an
exponential function), as an algebraic expression (e.g. $y = x^2$) or as a
graphical plot. See also **quantization, resolution**.

Fundamental   The word is used alone, but the complete expression is
fundamental **frequency** or **tone**. In a **complex wave**, it is the frequency
corresponding to the **period** of the complete repetition of the **waveform**,
i.e. the lowest **sine wave** present (fig. 96).

The word fundamental implies that the wave is not a single sinusoid
but accompanied by **partials** or **harmonics** above it, and in a practical

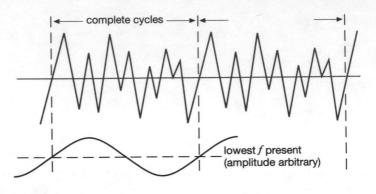

Fig. 96

vibratory system most of these are integral multiples of the fundamental, or nearly so (see **harmonic series**). Because the first harmonic's frequency is twice that of the fundamental (and successive further ones are ×3, ×4 etc.) it is convenient to give it the number of its multiplier and call it number 2. The fundamental, though not really a harmonic at all, is therefore by convention called harmonic number 1.

In some musical notes, and in many small **loudspeakers**, fundamentals of low notes may be missing or very weak, but if enough of the harmonics of these notes are there, the ear/brain system will supply the missing fundamental. This **psychoacoustic** phenomenon is called fundamental tracking, and was discovered and used many centuries ago by organ builders to give the illusion of low notes by supplying part of the appropriate series. Many explanations have been suggested, and a good survey is given by Juan G. Roederer in *Introduction to the Physics and Psychophysics of Music* (Roederer, 1979).

Fuzz box   See **clipping**

G

Gain The amount by which a signal is magnified by an **amplifier**. Opposite of **loss**, and usually measured in **decibels**. Depending on the type of amplifier, it may be expressed as **voltage, current** or **power** gain. When it affects loudness, a gain control is usually called a volume control.

Gang/ed, -ing A linkage, usually mechanical, of two or more variable components so that they move together, for example, **panpots** or tuning **capacitors** in radios.

Gap width The distance between pole pieces in certain magnetic devices, of critical importance in tape heads and moving coil **transducers**. See **loudspeakers** and fig. 113, **microphones** and fig. 124, and **sound recording techniques** and figs. 183 and 184.

Gat/e, -ing 1. Switching device that allows a signal to pass only under certain conditions of, say, time or level. See **noise gate**. 2. A digital logic circuit such as an *and* gate or an *or* gate. See **Boolean algebra**. 3. The control **electrode** of a **field effect transistor**. 4. An alternative name for one type of **trigger**.

Giga A standard prefix for one thousand million (10^9). Symbol G. It is a useful shorthand for frequencies in the microwave region (for example 4.1 GHz = 4,100,000,000 Hz), or massive data storage (G-bytes).

Gliding tone A **sine wave** of continuously changing **frequency** covering the whole audio **spectrum**. It may be taken directly from an **oscillator** or recorded on disc or tape. It is used to test the overall **response** of a system, thus if recorded on disc and played it will reveal **resonant** peaks in **pick-up** and **loudspeaker**. With suitable measuring instruments it can provide the input for a response plot.

Glitch A discontinuity in what should be a smooth waveform, especially when caused by errors in converting discrete number steps to voltages. The term is also used of the audible **distortion** arising from such errors. See **digital-to-analogue converter**.

Golden section Division of a line so that the proportion of the smaller part to the greater is the same as that of the greater part to the whole.

There is no exact expression for this in decimal arithmetic, but .618:1 is near enough for practical purposes, in fact the even less accurate 8:13 is often used. Endowed with almost magical properties by renaissance architects, etc., it has been incorporated into numerous artifacts, including the dimensions of the violin family (see **bowed strings**). Fig. 97 shows how the basic proportion can be extended into a number series, which has been used by composers as a basis for pitch and time divisions, formal structures, etc.

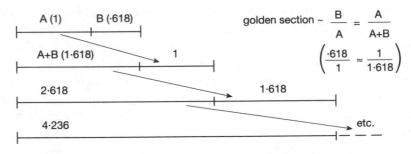

Fig. 97

Graceful degradation Computer-talk for a gentle and progressive collapse with predictable levels of inefficiency, as opposed to a **crash**. Systems that must not fail (e.g. vital radio links) can be designed with enough redundancy (duplicated or alternative circuitry or modes of operation) so that they continue running even when partly faulty.

Graphic equalizer See **equalizers**

Graphic scores Notations for music fall into three main groups, descriptive, tablature and graphic. Descriptive scores may be verbal, numeric or a mixture of the two, but in general they are texts giving instructions for making or playing the music.

Tablatures (for example seventeenth-century lute scores, modern guitar chord charts) contain no absolute pitch information and often no time information, but are a type of map, usually of fingering. For example a guitar tablature indicates the frets behind which the fingers should be placed, but the actual notes can only be deduced if the tuning of the open strings is known. In practice tuning is either standard or given at the head of the score, but the chord is read as a fingering rather than as pitches.

Graphical notations, if properly calibrated, do give absolute information, and conventional music notation is a graph of sorts, with pitch on the Y axis and time on the X. But both are dimensionally non-standard. Pitch increments are not uniform; even within one stave the next note up or down often means the next but one, and in a full score the pitch representation is a wild zig-zag. Time notation is also non-linear – relative duration depends on the way the note is drawn, not the horizontal space it occupies.

True graphs, in which time is shown on a prescribed scale (such as 2 cm/sec) result in overcrowded fast passages and wastefully empty paper in slow ones. Nevertheless proportional (sometimes called 'proportionate') notation has the advantage of allowing time relationships to be seen at a glance, and will automatically result if sounds are recorded by a constant speed device such as a motor-driven plotter.

Non-conventional graphical scores are particularly attractive when gestural rather than precise indications are wanted, because a general tendency can be shown by a freely drawn line instead of a mathematical expression (meaningless to most musicians) or a verbal description (often long and even then inefficient).

Such non-conventional notations have been used in many contemporary instrumental scores, and from the earliest days for electronic music. 'Workshop' scores for studio use include computer input instructions (see **computer music composition techniques**), and an interesting earlier example of an automated graphic input method was Oramics, a system developed by Daphne Oram in the 1960s which read shapes drawn by hand on clear 35 mm film. It is fully described in Oram's *An Individual Note* (Oram, 1972). Performing scores have to be simple and clear enough to execute in real time, and in a typical 'tape plus' piece (see **live performance electronic music**) a graphic 'technical' score might be combined with a conventional instrumental one.

See Hugo Cole's *Sounds and Signs* (Cole, 1974), which itself contains a list of further references.

GRM   See **Groupe de Recherches Musicales**

Groove   1. The spiral track of a gramophone record. 2. An interactive program developed at Bell Laboratories. See **computer music composition techniques** 2.

Ground   See **earth**

Group   In a mixing system, an output channel to which any input may be sent. Thus a 16–4 mixer has sixteen input channels any or all of which may be routed to any of four output groups, controlled by group **faders**. Usually two or more groups may be selected for each input channel, with the facility of **panning** between them. See also **analogue synthesis techniques** 5.

Groupe de Recherches Musicales (GRM)   Now part of the Institut National de l'Audiovisuel, 5 Avenue du Recteur-Poincaré, Paris 75016. Formerly part of the Service de la Recherche of ORTF. For historical comment see **musique concrète**.

Guide track   A recording, usually one track of a multi-track tape (see **tape recorder design**) carrying synchronization information rather than programme material. It can take various forms, such as clicks or pips for human interpretation, or tones, pulses or digital codes for automatic timing control. See **time codes**.

Gun microphone   See **microphones**

H

Half-track See **tape track configurations**

Half-tube A term applied to **brass instruments** whose lowest usable note is not the **fundamental** but the second **harmonic**, i.e. in effect half the length of the tube is not exploited. Most narrow-bore instruments are half-tube (e.g. trumpet). Trombones and horns have limited access to the fundamental. True whole-tube instruments are the wide-bored tuba and euphonium, which sound consistently and securely down to the fundamental.

Hammond organ The most ingenious and long-lived of the pre-1939 electric organs. Until the late 1960s, instead of **oscillators**, it used shaped wheels which rotated in front of **electromagnetic** heads. See **analogue synthesis techniques 4**.

Hand-held See **microphone placement**

Hard disk As opposed to **floppy disk**, a rigid platter for magnetic storage, single or layered in 'disk packs', and removable or fixed. Hard disks are often used in conjunction with floppies. They are more efficient than floppies because their closer tolerances, greater writing area and faster rotation speeds allow higher density storage and much faster access times. Reductions in price and physical size plus improved reliability have brought them within reach of the modest user, and capacities are increasing all the time. Useful for space-hungry sound storage, but not suitable for rough handling in performance conditions. When hard disk **crashes** do occur they are abrupt and destructive, and back-up floppy storage of important material is always advisable.

Hardware The physical components in a system, such as circuit boards, integrated circuits, wires, plugs, disk drives etc. Paper documentation and its electrical/magnetic equivalent are classed as software.

Firmware, being software stored in hardware, lies somewhere between the other two. The electric currents that make the computer hardware perform are difficult to classify. Indispensable 'services' like power supplies would normally be considered part of the hardware, but data and signal currents are functions of the program, i.e. software.

Harmonic 1. (adjective) Relating to harmony, that aspect of music concerned with the effects of two or more simultaneous sounds, as opposed to the melodic or rhythmic (i.e. time-related) analyses of musical material. 2. Member of a given **harmonic series**. 3. Note produced on string or wind instrument by dividing the whole of the string (or air column) into an integral number of segments, producing higher notes without shortening its effective length. See also **bowed string, brass, harmonic series, woodwind instruments** and **partial**.

Harmonic analysis The process of breaking down a complex wave into its component **sine waves**, which can then be plotted as a **spectrum**. For digital analysis methods, see **digital synthesis techniques** 3. Analogue techniques include: 1. Using fixed **filters** (e.g. a ⅓-octave filter bank, see **equalizers**) to separate the components of the wave (see also **vocoder**). 2. Sweeping the relevant **band** with a variable tuned **filter** and plotting its output **amplitude** against **frequency**.

Harmonic distortion The corruption of a signal by adding harmonics not present in the original, one of many types of **distortion**. Take, for example, a pure **sine wave** (no harmonics): if an **amplifier** or **transducer**, in transmitting the signal, favours one half of the **cycle** over the other, the result will be an asymmetrical wave, indicating the presence of the second and other even-numbered harmonics (see **harmonic series**). Fig. 98a shows the lop-sided result of adding 15% (relative amplitude) of the second harmonic to a pure sine. Alternatively an amplifier overdriven into the non-linear regions near **saturation** and **cut-off** may distort symmetrically, and this is characteristic of the addition of the third or higher odd harmonics (98b). The level of second harmonic distortion tolerable in a 'high fidelity' system (expressed as a percentage), is higher than that of third and other odd harmonics.

In **timbre** synthesis, processes such as waveshaping involve deliberate non-linear transmission of a **waveform** (see **digital synthesis techniques** 7), and in rock music, overdriving amplifiers is one of a range of intentional distortion effects (see **clipping**), but in general the aim is to make amplifiers that do not distort. One way of rating the performance of

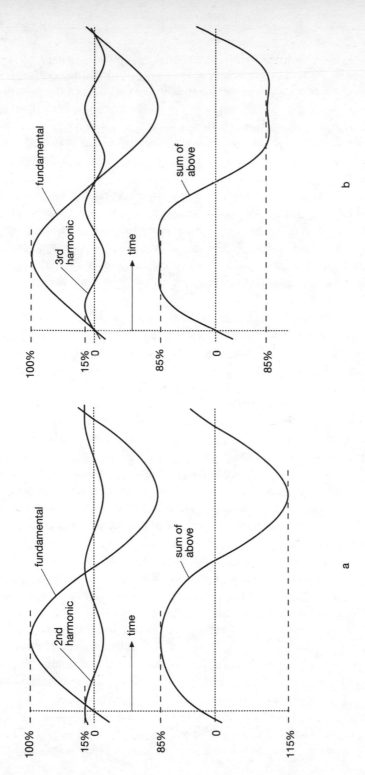

Fig. 98

sound systems is to combine the various harmonic distortions as Total Harmonic Distortion (THD). A pure sine is injected at the input, then removed from the output by a notch **filter**, leaving the distortion as a residue which is analysed, and individual harmonic content measured and squared. The squares are summed, and THD is the square root of this figure, usually converted to a percentage of the amplitude of the original sine input, for example, THD (20 Hz–20 kHz)=0.05%.

Harmonic series   A phenomenon of vibrating systems which in certain physical forms is the basis of all acoustically produced music, and when it occurs in electrical circuits is an important component in electronic music. The series consists of integral multiples of the system's own fundamental (lowest possible) frequency. (Strictly a mathematical harmonic series is based on inverse integral relationships, for example, 1, ½, ⅓, ¼ etc.)

Certain objects (such as taut strings, air in pipes, metal bars) vibrate easily and periodically because they possess a combination of mass and **compliance** that allows them to **resonate**, and the very elasticity that permits this also encourages them to flex internally and vibrate in a complex manner.

In some cases (e.g. a bell) this complexity almost defies analysis, but in the relatively simple case of a string it was noticed very early that if it was lightly checked at exactly the halfway point, both halves continued to vibrate and the sound was one octave higher than that of the 'open' string. Continuing the process, preventing movement one-third of the way along automatically produced another **node** at the two-thirds position, and the pitch went up again, but only a perfect fifth this time. The effect continues to work (within practical limits depending on the length, tension etc. of the string) provided that the nodal points are at precise integral divisions of the string, but not otherwise.

In this example the series (1/2, 1/3, 1/4 etc.) in pitch terms applies to the **period** (time) of a **cycle** of vibration. We usually talk about the reciprocal of period, however, or **frequency**, and since the series reciprocal is a simple arithmetic series, the calculation of a given position in frequency terms is also very simple. If we call the **fundamental** mode, or whole-string vibration, number 1, half the string, or number 2 (second harmonic) is twice the frequency, and so on – the eighteenth harmonic will be eighteen times the fundamental frequency.

Fig. 99 shows the first ten harmonics on a fundamental of 55 Hz (standard pitch A), and the frequencies given are those of a natural series, not the standard equal temperament pitches, which are all

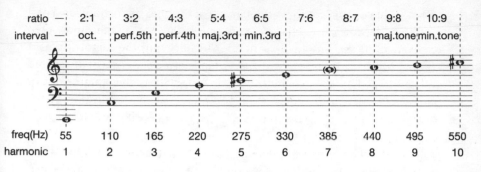

ratio —	2:1	3:2	4:3	5:4	6:5	7:6	8:7	9:8	10:9
interval —	oct.	perf.5th	perf.4th	maj.3rd	min.3rd			maj.tone	min.tone

freq(Hz)	55	110	165	220	275	330	385	440	495	550
harmonic	1	2	3	4	5	6	7	8	9	10

Fig. 99

different except the As (for reasons see **temperament**). Several points arise from the illustration: 1. The harmonics on powers of 2 (2, 4, 8 etc.) are the octaves of the fundamental. Octaves correspond to a frequency ratio (2:1) rather than a constant frequency difference – our perception of pitch is **logarithmic** rather than **linear**. 2. The difference in frequency between successive harmonics is equal to the frequency of the fundamental. 3. All the common intervals except the tritone (which is an intervallic odd man out) and the semitone (which occurs higher up, between 15 and 16) are represented in diminishing order in the series (sixths are inversions of thirds). Number 7 is bracketed because it does not 'fit' with the tonal/modal system used in the West – the interval 6–7 is a 'thin' minor third, and 7–8 is a 'fat' major second.

It is worth noting that the degree of consonance of intervals in the series corresponds to the simplicity of ratio of its frequencies – 2:1 is the perfectly consonant octave, 5:4 is the less perfect but still consonant major third, and so on. A scale made by combining these simple ratios is said to be in just intonation (again see **temperament**). The harmonics number 8, 9 and 10 are the first three notes of the major scale (in just intonation), and from this point upwards conjunct scales are possible using only notes from the series (see **brass instruments**).

Because this series (of which at least the first twenty terms are musically important) has been recognized as the cornerstone of music for so long, several names for it are in use concurrently. The word 'harmonic' should refer only to a member of the natural series. 'Overtone' is another word for harmonic except that the second harmonic is the first overtone, etc. **Partials**, on the other hand, can be **inharmonic** as well as harmonic, and in practical instruments many of the partials are slightly inharmonic, and some completely spurious tones may be present – indeed they are often a necessary and welcome part of the instrument's **timbre**.

It is important to distinguish two quite independent manifestations of the harmonic series: 1. Every instrument, all the time, is sounding many harmonics at once, some strong, some weak. Possibly little or no fundamental is present, and some sound generators cannot produce even-numbered harmonics at all, making an odd series instead (3, 5, 7 etc.). **Noise** and inharmonic partials are also present. This ever-changing mass is the timbre of the instrument, and is perceived as a single complex sound, not as a chord of separate pitches. 2. Particularly in wind instruments, the series natural to a particular length and bore of pipe is utilized to change pitch, i.e. to form a new quasi-fundamental (with the series above it creating the timbre). In **woodwind** this is called overblowing, the upper octaves being played in the pipe's second, third or fourth harmonic mode. In the **brass**, the natural series is used up to harmonics 8 or 16, and may or may not be supplemented by valves or slides. For example, most bugle calls are played on harmonics 3, 4, 5 and 6; running passages in eighteenth-century natural horn parts lie between harmonics 8 and 16.

We have been referring to the series as an acoustic/musical phenomenon, but it occurs in electrical resonant circuits and throughout nature in all media and at all frequencies, wherever something is vibrating. See also **sub-harmonic**.

The literature on the harmonic series, tuning and temperament is enormous and growing, particularly as new technologies are leading to new discoveries. For the first time in history, computer instruments allow us to tune with assured precision and change the entire tuning system instantly. New studies are showing that the behaviour of the series is not the matter of simple arithmetic that our predecessors believed, but part of a complex and interlocking physical/aural/neural system that we are only just beginning to understand. See also **analogue synthesis techniques 4**, **bowed string instruments**, **digital synthesis techniques 3**, **dissonance**, **formant** and Taylor (1965), Wood (1962), Olson (1967), Hutchins (1978), Roederer (1979), Carlos (1987) and Lloyd (1978).

Head   1. A **transducer** to convert electrical energy to its magnetic or mechanical equivalent and vice versa. Different applications are identified by prefixes, thus: erase head, playback head, R/P (record/play) head, cutting head (disc recorder) etc. The 'head block' is a machine's complement of two, three or more heads mounted as a unit. A 'head stack' is a vertical assembly of four, eight, sixteen etc. active elements for multi-track tape machines. See **sound recording techniques** and **tape recorder design**. 2. The beginning of a recorded tape or film, as opposed to **tail**.

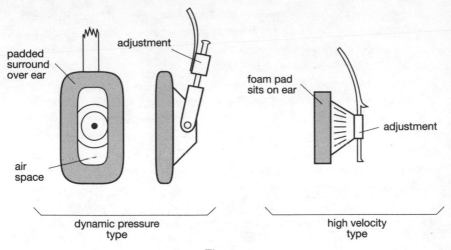

Fig. 100

Headphones   A personal listening device, pre-dating **loudspeakers**, and colloquially called 'cans'. They were originally of poor quality but have greatly improved in recent years. Their driving systems are miniature versions of those used in speakers, including some with separate bass and treble units. Because of the small enclosed body of air, even deep bass can be accurately reproduced, though it lacks the direct sensory reception of 'real' bass, which is felt through the body as well as heard. There is great variety in detailed design, including **electrostatic** as well as magnetic drivers, and **quadraphonic** models with two units per ear-piece. The two main types most commonly found are illustrated in fig. 100.

The more traditional type fits completely over the ear, largely excluding external sounds and creating a private world, but needing a fairly large and heavy headset. The newer design, which many prefer, is the lightweight, high-velocity type, which 'projects' the sound across a foam pad resting on rather than around the ear. This type is 'transparent' and allows much of the external sound to mingle with the headphone signal. In many professional situations, e.g. conducting a radio discussion while wearing cans so that the producer can communicate, transparency is essential.

Ultra-lightweight headphones, using tiny but extremely powerful magnets of special alloys, were developed for personal hi-fis like the Walkman, and perform remarkably well considering their small size. The smallest type of all is the single earphone, fitted directly into the external canal of the ear, and even these are now made to deliver surprisingly good quality. See Borwick (1988).

Headroom The difference (in **decibels**) between a system's normal operating level (usually set to o **volume units** (VU)) and the level above which **distortion** becomes unacceptable. In modern systems this is set at around 20 dB. Most signal level meters in tape recorders are **VU meters**, which read the average programme level. **Transient** peaks may be much higher than this, and a well-designed system must have enough head-room to accommodate them. See **peak programme meter** and **sound recording techniques**.

Helical pot A **potentiometer** with a screw-shaped track giving much longer travel than the normal flat, circular or linear track. Because full travel requires many rotations it is often called a 'multi-turn pot'.

Helical scan A method of achieving high head-to-tape speeds with relatively slow reel-to-reel speeds, used in all video cassette recorders. The tape is led round a rotating drum with active head gaps on its surface. The tape path is tilted with respect to the drum's axis, resulting in a long diagonal track. The tape moves forward relatively slowly so that tracks are recorded side by side as in fig. 101.

  In digital audio, helical scan is used for **video cassette PCM**, the form in which master tapes for **compact discs** are supplied. The principle is also used in **digital audio tape** recording. The main disadvantage in

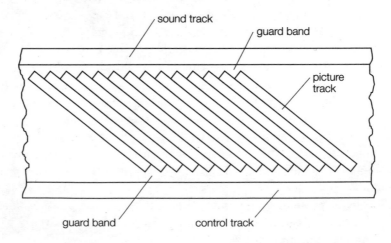

Fig. 101

professional use is the impossibility of **cut editing**. See **sound recording techniques**.

Helmholtz resonator   An acoustic device, shaped rather like a bottle, designed so that sound waves entering it at one particular frequency build up to large amplitudes, other frequencies being absorbed. It is traditionally spherical in shape. The air in it oscillates – the air in the neck corresponding to the mass in a mechanical oscillating system, and the air in the body being the **compliance**. They were used in numerous sizes to pinpoint particular **frequencies** in a **spectrum,** but have now been replaced by electronic methods (see **frequency meter**). In studio or concert hall design, sound absorbing panels with carefully measured slots or holes are like batteries of Helmholtz resonators, which can be tuned to absorb selected frequencies. See Helmholtz (1862), Taylor (1965), Wood (1962), Olson (1967) and Ballou (1987).

Hertz   Named after Heinrich R. Hertz (1857–94), whose work was the foundation of radio. It is the SI unit of **frequency**. 1 Hz=1 **cycle** per second (cps), which it replaced. Higher audio frequencies are usually expressed in kiloHertz (kHz), and radio frequencies in MegaHertz (MHz). See **SI units.**

Heterodyn/e, -ing   The addition of two signals at different **frequencies,** resulting in a signal at a new, **difference frequency** which is usually lower than either original. This is the principle on which the beat frequency **oscillator** operates, and also (in radio reception) the supersonic heterodyne, or superhet, in which a local oscillator tracks and beats with the incoming signal to produce a constant 'intermediate' frequency.

Heuristic   From the Greek for 'find', a trial and error approach to programming as opposed to an **algorithmic** one. It can involve random and probabilistic methods. Computer programs for composing can be of both kinds, but are often heuristic. See **artificial intelligence** and **computer music composition techniques**.

Hexachord   Any six adjacent notes, but specifically in music a group having as successive intervals **tone,** tone, semitone, tone, tone as in the white keyboard notes from C to A. The basis of diatonic scale construction in tonal and modal music. See **mnemonics.**

Hexadecimal (Hex)   The number system based on 16 (2^4) different symbols: 0–9, plus the letters A–F representing 10–15. Long strings of **binary** digits are difficult for human beings to remember and deal with, whereas Hex and **octal** are compact and convenient shorthand notations. A binary number is broken up into groups of four digits for conversion to Hex, thus 0101|1100|1111|0111 becomes 5CF7. All that needs to be remembered is binary numbers up to 15.

High fidelity (hi-fi)   A popular term with no absolute meaning. It replaced the 'perfect tone' of the 1920s and 1930s about the time that undoubtedly better equipment appeared around 1950, and was mainly set up by the industry as a goal for buyers of equipment, particularly in the upper domestic market. It could perhaps be defined as 'record/ reproduce chain in which the output is as nearly as possible identical to the input', but the real question is 'fidelity to what?'. You can't have a symphony orchestra in your living room, so the aim must be something like 'the most acceptable artificial version of the real original'. The term 'hi-fi' has become almost totally debased by the very poor equipment often dignified by the label.

High level language   See **computer languages**

High order (bit)   Leftmost 1 in a **binary** number or **word**, also called the Most Significant **Bit** (MSB). Contrast **low order**.

High pass filter   One that attenuates low but passes higher **frequencies**. See **filters**.

Hill and dale recording   In cutting discs, a vertical rather than lateral groove modulation, used by Edison in the first phonograph recordings, and tried again, combined with lateral, as a technique for stereo in the 1950s. Abandoned for the current 45°/45° groove (see **pick-ups**).

Hole   The place in the molecular structure of a solid where a (negatively charged) **electron** would normally be found but is not. The absence of the electron leaves the location in effect positively charged. In **semiconductors,** a movement of holes through the medium is called a hole current.

Horn speaker   See **loudspeakers**

Howl round   Uncontrolled positive **feedback** caused by an input **transducer** (usually a **microphone** but sometimes a **pick-up** on a resonant surface) picking up its own amplified signal from a nearby **loudspeaker** thus increasing the input signal and causing a progressive increase in levels. This rapidly builds up to **saturation**, the whole electro-acoustic circuit becoming a crude **oscillator**, giving a piercing output tone (the 'howl') whose power can easily damage equipment and ears. If close proximity of microphone and speaker is unavoidable, feedback can sometimes be reduced by including a **frequency shifter** – a shift of only a few Hz between input and output will ensure that most output signal components are out of **phase** with their input equivalents.

Hub See **spool**

Hum The audible effect of interference from a mains supply. The mains is **alternating current** at 50 **hertz** (US 60 Hz) and rich in second **harmonic**, giving a hum frequency of 100 (120) Hz, well into the musical band and a serious nuisance if present. The interference may occur internally due to poor power smoothing for example, or be induced into lines by stray fields, perhaps from **transformers** or fluorescent lighting. Once the bane of the audio engineer's life, it is now a comparatively rare problem. The commonest cause is 'earth loops' made by earthing (grounding) equipment at several points. These are prevented by using only one common earth point for a given complex of equipment, especially avoiding earthing at several power points, whose 'third pin' potentials may in practice differ.

Hunting Behaviour of a controlled device (such as a motor) whose controller continually overshoots the desired value in both directions. Type of instability usually symptomatic of insufficient **damping** in the system.

Hybrid synthesis See **analogue synthesis techniques 6, digital synthesis techniques 7.**

Hydrophone See **microphones**

Hygroscopic Of materials that readily absorb moisture, particularly some insulators that absorb atmospheric humidity, becoming less effective insulators. The usual remedy is to pack hygroscopic components with 'teabags' of silica gel, which soak up moisture avidly and can be easily replaced or removed for drying out.

Hypercardioid See **microphones**

Hysteresis From the Greek for 'be late', the delay between the production of an effect and its cause. **Magnetic** hysteresis is an important factor in devices where magnetic flux inside a magnetic material is being continuously changed in amount and direction by an applied magnetic field (which is in turn usually created by current flowing in a coil, see **electromagnet**). The way in which the magnetism of a particular material lags behind the changes in its magnetizing field is illustrated by a graph called a hysteresis curve. See fig. 102.

The curve shows the effect of taking an applied field through a cycle of values starting at zero, going on to maximum positive, back through zero to maximum negative, then back through zero to maximum positive again. The magnetic material's magnetization rises as the applied field strength rises but, as the arrows show, the magnetization of the material

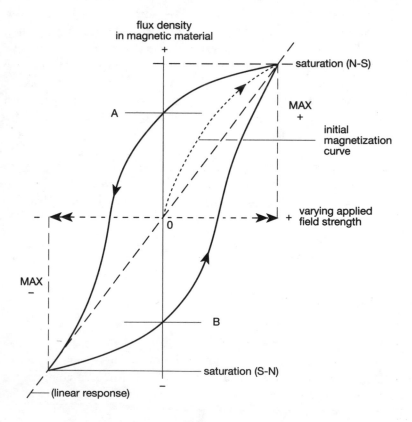

Fig. 102

does not change proportionally with the applied field (this would follow the linear response line) but lags behind, and continues (at A and B) even when the applied field falls to zero.

In tape recording (see **sound recording techniques**) 'hysteresis loss' (i.e. energy lost as materials are continuously magnetized and demagnetized) can seriously affect performance. Magnetic materials for tape heads should have the opposite characteristics from those for permanent magnets – low retentivity (i.e. poor ability to retain applied flux), and high permeability (i.e. accepting and losing a magnetic charge easily thus wasting less energy). Special materials such as **ferrites** fulfil these requirements, having very 'slim' hysteresis loops.

I

IC See **integrated circuit**

ICEM International Confederation for Electroacoustic Music/Confédération Internationale de Musique Electroacoustique (CIME), Place André Malraux, F-18000 Bourges, France.

ICMA See **International Computer Music Association**

Idiophone A self-sounding instrument, i.e. one in which generator and resonator are not separate. See **musical instruments, types of.**

Impedance The measure of the total effective opposition to the flow of current in **AC** circuits, symbol Z. Defined as $Z=\frac{V}{I}$, i.e. applied voltage/current in a circuit or group of components. Its **SI unit** is **ohms** and its value relates sizes of applied voltages and currents together in AC circuits in the way that **resistance** does in DC. Its value actually depends on several factors, resistance, **inductance, capacitance, frequency** of current and **phase** differences between currents and voltages in components. Theoretical calculations of Z are thus complex. See Ballou (1987), Young (1983), Capel (1988) and Grob (1987).

Impedance matching Arranging the **impedances** (Z) of two connected devices to produce optimal operating conditions. True 'matching' (such that the output Z of the first device is exactly equal to the input Z of the second) is only used when energy transfer is to be maximized (e.g. in **transformer** coupling and transmission lines) and not always then – a source driving **loudspeakers**, for example, should have a lower Z than the speakers. In most audio applications, particularly **amplifier** chains, the aim is to maximize **voltage** only, with minimum loss of energy. True 'matching' would have the bad result of halving the voltage at each connection since source and load are effectively in **series**. The rule of thumb for voltage transfer is that an input Z 'seen' by the previous output should be at least ten times that output's Z value (e.g. 500 ohms to 5 K-ohms), and this order of ratio is provided for in connecting most store-bought equipment. There are many complexities, however, particularly in connecting **frequency**-dependent components. Apart from transformers, a typical Z-changing device is a **direct box**.

Induct/ance, -ive, -or The property of current in a wire (usually a coil of wire), and the magnetic field associated with the current, which causes an induced voltage in the wire when the current changes. This induced voltage opposes the change in current, and inductance is thus an inertial property, behaving similarly to mass, which resists sudden changes of speed in mechanical systems. Most practical inductors are coils of wire with many turns and, in audio frequency applications, ferrous cores are normally used to increase the inductive effect.

Inductance (symbol L) is measured in Henrys (H), the **SI unit** named after Joseph Henry (1799–1878). The opposition effect described is to the change of current, not the current itself, and it is therefore a property of **AC** circuits, in which the current is continually changing and reversing. The effect is called inductive **reactance** (X_L) and measured in **ohms**. X_L increases with increasing frequency, the complementary opposite of capacitive reactance (X_C), which decreases as frequency rises.

Inductors always contain some (often considerable) **resistance** because of the long coils of wire involved, and **capacitance** also exists between the turns of the coil, so they are not usually very **efficient** or **linear** devices. They are, however, the operating components in tape **heads**, most **loudspeakers**, many **microphones**, and **relays**, etc.

Inductance can also occur between neighbouring coils which share the same magnetic field, see **transformers**.

Information theory The mathematical analysis of the process of transmitting messages, also called communication theory. First seriously studied in the context of telegraphy/telephony, it distinguishes acoustic/electrical from semantic/linguistic content, and calculates the probability of adequate transmission under differing conditions. The primary source text is *The Mathematical Theory of Communication*, by C. E. Shannon and W. Weaver (Shannon, 1949). A study of its application in music composition can be found in Hiller (1959) chapter 2.

Infra-red The part of the **electromagnetic spectrum** between the shortest radio waves and the longest visible light waves. Used in **remote controls**, night vision devices, etc.

Infra-sonic   Of sound waves at **frequencies** below about 20 Hz, see **sub/-, super/sonic**.

Inharmonic   Usually as a qualification for a **partial** which does not belong to the natural **harmonic series**, i.e. does not have a simple integer relationship with the **fundamental**. Partials created when a real string or pipe vibrates may depart from the theoretical harmonic series, particularly if irregularities in materials or construction are present. Additional foreign inharmonic components may occur for various reasons. See also **analogue synthesis techniques 5, enharmonic** and **frequency shifter**.

Input/output (I/O)   Anything concerned with access to and/or retrieval from a device, but I/O is used particularly in computer terminology when a single unit (e.g. a terminal) handles both input and output.

Insertion loss   Loss of power (which may or may not be **frequency-**dependent) caused by placing a **network** between the source and a **load**. In audio, the loss caused by simply connecting a device into a circuit, apart from any intended action it may have.

Instruction   Minimum syntactically complete unit in a chain of commands, either one of a built-in instruction set that the computer 'knows', or a specifically 'taught' command.

Insulat/or, -e, -ion   A material, such as rubber, ceramics, most plastics, dry air, and glass, that is for practical purposes a non-**conductor** of electricity, i.e. it does not contain any charged particles which are free to move through it. It is used to isolate conductors, protect people and equipment, and as **dielectrics** in **capacitors**.

Integrat/e, -or   To make a whole from discrete parts. A practical integrator – the simplest circuit is **resistor** and **capacitor** connected as in fig. 103a – converts discontinuities into smooth transitions by applying a fixed or variable **slew rate**. Fig. 103b shows the principle applied as a pitch slide (portamento) for a keyboard, and c to smooth a stepped waveform.

Integrated circuit (IC)   Many components packaged as one device, either hybrid (several sub-assemblies joined in manufacture) or monolithic (complete circuit on one **chip**). ICs vary in complexity from fairly simple circuits to Very Large Scale Integration (VLSI) and E(Extra)LSI,

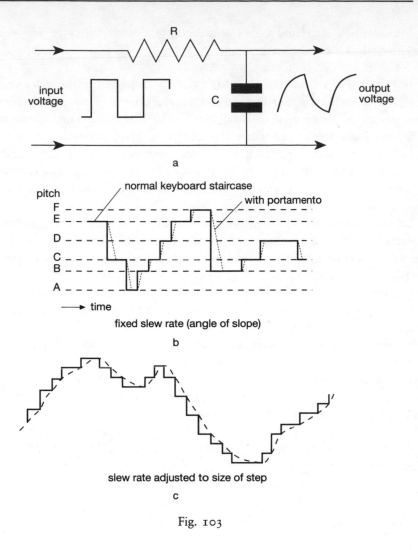

Fig. 103

comprising circuits with many thousands of individual components.

Intelligent Also 'smart'. Used to describe **interface** devices such as terminals which contain their own computers, and can therefore make decisions and perform certain functions independently of the main computer.

Intensity A measure of the energy content of a sound wave. It is defined as the rate of energy transfer per unit area and measured absolutely in **watts** per square metre (W/m^2). Relative intensities are expressed in **decibels**. It is related to the **amplitude** of a wave (intensity is proportional to the square of the amplitude) and to the perceived **loudness** of a sound which is measured in **phons**.

Interactive systems   Those that operate in a real-time, 'conversational' mode, giving immediate feedback to users. Computer systems have become increasingly interactive over the years, because faster operation and increased memory allow greater amounts of data to be on immediate call, and give more space for 'extras' like friendly messages, while improved input/output devices allow instant display and modification of material.

Computer composition was a tedious process before it became interactive (see **computer music composition techniques** 2). Some music systems are real-time but not interactive – a computer controlling a synthesizer simply instructs, there is no conversational feedback. Non-interactive processing is still widely used, particularly for large, repetitive jobs such as working out pay sheets.

Interface   The point where different modes of behaviour must communicate. For example, a **microphone** converts air pressure to an electric current and so is the acoustic/electric interface. In computers a terminal, for example, or a **mouse,** is the human/machine interface. Various kinds of **distortion** can occur because interfacing is inefficient or inaccurate – a message may become garbled at any change point: voice to ear/brain, hand to paper, paper to eye/brain, hand to telex machine, machine to transmission system, and so on.

Interference   1. Unwanted pollution or disturbance of a signal, either man-made (such as **hum** interfering with music, a car's ignition affecting TV reception) or natural (lightning, wind sounds), and generally more intrusive and intermittent than **background noise**. 2. Interaction of wave motions, particularly light waves, giving new products which can be utilized – in holography, for example, where interference patterns form the image.

Interlace   A TV scanning system in which, to reduce flicker, the field is scanned twice on alternate lines, two scans completing the **frame**.

Intermodulation   The effect of mutual interference of two or more sounds or audio signals (see **cross-modulation**).

International Computer Music Association   Suite 330, 2040 Polk
St., San Francisco, CA 94109, USA. Journal: *Array*. ICMA organizes
the annual International Computer Music Conference, and publishes its
proceedings and other material. The ICMA Source Book lists individuals,
studios, activities etc. (Harris, 1987).

Interrupt   A signal (from a key on a terminal, for example) which
stops current program execution and causes the computer either to wait
for the next instruction or go into a prepared sub-routine, after which
it returns to the point of interruption in the main program. In **computer
music composition** interrupt processing allows pieces to be changed
while running – for example a piece might be arranged to run through
to the end if no interrupt is received, but switch to a selection of prepared
events at any time during the run. Compare **poll**.

I/O   See **input/output**

IRCAM   Institut de Recherche et de Coordination Acoustique/
Musique, 31 rue St Merri, Paris 75004, France. See **computer music
composition techniques** and **studio design**.

J

Jack (plug and socket) A two- (or more) way connection system, originally designed for telephony. The **poles** are arranged concentrically (rod within tube) and therefore compactly, the central rod (live) terminating in a rounded tip and separated from the sleeve (earth) by an insulating washer (in three-way jacks – 'tip, ring and sleeve' – a further conducting section is placed between tip and sleeve). See **patch** for illustration and **analogue synthesis techniques** 3. Plugs may be used to make internal connections within a device or to link two devices via a 'patch cord'. Depending on the complexity of the socket design, a number of other circuits may be controlled by inserting a plug. Jack strip: a single unit consisting of twenty or more jack sockets. Jack field: a group of jack strips mounted together to make a 'patch bay' of any desired size. See also **cannon, DIN** and **normalling**.

Jitter Instability of **synchronization** due to short-term changes in **phase** or **frequency** of a signal or timebase (see **oscilloscope**), small fluctuations in tape speed etc. In visual media like TV, jitter makes the picture jump or vibrate. In digital recording jitter is always present and must be allowed for in decoding routines, see Watkinson (1988) chapter 6.

Joule An **SI unit** of energy and work, symbol J. Defined in relation to the energy converted when a force does work moving an object. See **volt** and **watt**.

Joystick A device capable of controlling two **parameters** simultaneously, usually via **potentiometers** (pots).

Fig. 104a shows the commonest design. A more elaborate form allows a third control by rotating the stick, and provision for certain stick positions to operate switches may also be included.

Joysticks are useful for various kinds of gestural control, and also as **quad panners**. One problem if accurate positioning is wanted is the difficulty of arranging calibrated scales that are easily read in

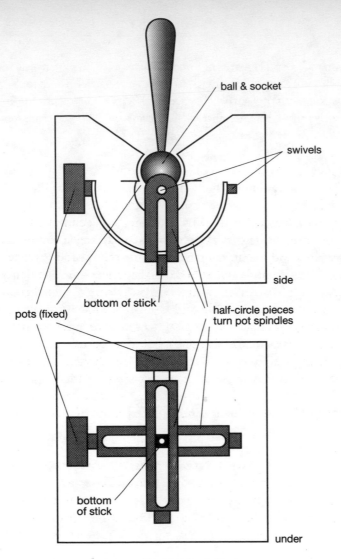

ball & socket

swivels

side

pots (fixed)

bottom of stick

half-circle pieces
turn pot spindles

bottom
of stick

under

n.b. mounting details omitted

a

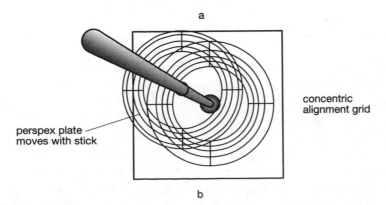

concentric
alignment grid

perspex plate
moves with stick

b

Fig. 104

performance conditions. One method uses two sets of rings, the move-able ones on a transparent plate, fig. 104b. With practice the stick can be located with surprising accuracy. Another technique is to have secondary measuring circuits which read out the co-ordinates for the stick position and show them on an **LED** display.

Jump cut   In sound and visual media, the removal of a portion of a **take** resulting in a jump in time in the remaining track. Often a desperate measure used when part of a recording is destroyed or unusable, it is rarely a complete success. In film or video, a 'cut away', however short, will often save the situation. In **musique concrète**, a similar technique, of inserting a short contrasting sound into a broken long one can create the illusion that the long sound continues uninterrupted behind the insert.

Jumper   1. Wire bridging several tracks of a **printed circuit**, either soldered in for permanent connection or moveable to select different configurations. 2. Wire with 'crocodile' clips at each end, for making temporary, test or emergency connections. Also called a jump lead.

Just interval   See **temperament**

Just noticeable difference (jnd)   See **psychoacoustics**

K

Keyboard design   The first **organ** keyboards, replacing wooden sliders to open the pipes' airways, appeared in the thirteenth century. The idea of a 'normal' scale with occasional 'foreign' notes soon evolved to become the familiar pattern of seven wide and long keys and five narrow and short ones in use now for more than five centuries. We still call the wide notes 'naturals' and describe the others with reference to them as 'sharps', 'flats' or 'accidentals'.

Numerous alternative layouts have been tried, but none so far has been more successful than the traditional 7/5 pattern. It works well because 1. the asymmetrical layout of the two shapes of key helps in locating any note; 2. asymmetry also suits music itself, which is full of non-linearities of pitch, harmony, time etc.; 3. the front/back arrangement suits the short/long design of human thumbs and fingers; 4. the wide lower keys allow fingers to drop between them when depressed, while the narrow short keys fall only to a position flush with the wide keys, giving security and control; 5. it offers a compass of at least an octave (with all intermediate notes available) from one hand position for all but the smallest hands; 6. centuries of keyboard literature have been composed to suit the present layout, so any new design would have to co-exist with the old.

A symmetrical layout (6/6) was proposed as early as 1708, and is tidy but musically unnatural, giving the two possible whole tone scales on each colour, fig. 105. It was never adopted generally.

Special keyboards are used, however, for any application in which the

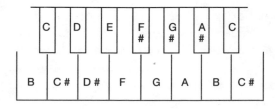

Fig. 105

octave is divided into more than twelve parts. These include variable **temperament** keyboards, in which alternative tunings are provided, and microtonal keyboards, which may have twice as many notes as normal. Many experiments have been made, some of them with four or more rows of keys or buttons, but in general such keyboards are complicated to learn and hard to play fluently, and none have been adopted on a large scale. Harry Partch, himself a tireless experimenter, illustrates and comments on several (Partch, 1974). See also Helmholtz (1954), p. 423.

Although the layout of the keyboard itself is standard, there is great variety in the mechanisms that lie behind the key. The simplest is the clavichord action, merely a lever pushing a metal 'tangent' against a pair of strings, making a temporary bridge. Harpsichords are more complex, with a loose 'jack' thrown against and past a string to give a plucking action. For comments on piano actions, see **pianos** *acoustic*. There is a clear distinction between instruments like the harpsichord and organ, in which loudness does not depend on the velocity of the key, and those in which it does, such as the piano and clavichord. Another factor important to the 'feel' of the key is whether it is gravity or spring returned.

The same distinction applies to keyboards for controlling electronics. For some types of instrument a simple keyboard is adequate, but if the intention is to synthesize a piano-type instrument, velocity sensing must be provided, see **pianos** *electric and electronic*.

Computer control of sound production allows a completely different approach to temperament adjustment, microtonal intervals etc., because the function of any key can be instantly changed. Provided that twelve choices per octave are sufficient at any one time, the keys themselves can be assigned in any way – allowing several notes or **noise** mixtures to be sounded with one key. In addition to the velocity sensing mechanism, a facility to detect sideways or up and down shaking to produce **tremolo** or **vibrato** may be part of a key's action. Extra pressure on the key when it is depressed ('after-touch') can provide yet another form of output. See **keyboard synthesizers.**

Keyboard synthesizers Self-contained portable **synthesizers** (colloquially 'synths') intended primarily for real-time performance rather than studio work, containing a keyboard controller as well as the sound synthesis electronics. Some are almost interchangeable with organs, but the development history and intended markets are different (see **organs** *electronic*). Synthesizers, even if many pre-set voices are provided, must always have the possibility of constructing a sound from basics.

Keyboards were features of packaged synthesizers from the start, but the early voltage controlling keyboards were restricted in live performance by lack of polyphony, the difficulty of combining a good variety of sounds with ease of programming, and oscillator 'drift' (see **analogue synthesis techniques** 4 and **oscillators**). During the 1970s integrated circuit technology made the essentials of voltage controlled **subtractive synthesis** – VC oscillators, **amplifiers** and **filters** – increasingly smaller and cheaper, so polyphony became easier to implement. At the same time digital techniques were racing ahead, and the scene was set for the development of a wide range of accessibly priced live performance synthesizers. The main selling point of all these instruments is 'plug in and play' – at a basic level you need know nothing of the technical side. At another level, the better machines have many features that can only be exploited with time and patience – in the composing studio rather than on stage. In this highly competitive market the rate at which instruments appear, flourish briefly and become obsolete is very rapid, and any survey quickly outdated. The following paragraphs cover the main operating principles.

Pure analogue   Now obsolete as commercial live performance instruments, though a number survive from earlier days (and are essential, of course, to perform pieces written specifically for them). This is also a simple and inexpensive means of synthesizing sound for the home constructor – popular electronics magazines still publish design details, and a number of kits are available.

Digital/analogue hybrid   Analogue synthesis has great appeal not only because it can make sounds that people like, but because voltage control circuitry is straightforward and reliable. For live performance, however, foolproof switching and **patching**, memory facilities for storing prepared voices, and possibly **sequencing**, are all desirable features and much easier to provide with microprocessor controlled logic than by analogue methods. A number of successful machines use hybrid technology, and repeatability and drift problems (again see **oscillators** and **analogue synthesis techniques** 6–7) are overcome by automatic frequency checking/correction, for example.

Pure digital   This is steadily replacing all other types. Its design strategy can be completely open and any (or several) of a number of synthesis methods used (see **digital synthesis techniques** 4–7), because unlike analogue synthesis, which depends on dedicated hardware, a digital machine can be configured in any way desired. Most live performance instruments, however, are restricted to one or two synthesis methods. If all the operations of the synthesizer are in the digital domain, precision and repeatability are not problems, exact parameters are displayed, and a variety of number-based manipulations can be used.

Sample-based digital   See **samplers** for the general principles of these machines and their operation. They are not strictly synthesizers because the basic source of the sound is real rather than constructed, but samplers may include synthesizer modes as well. The same sample replay principle is also used in some electronic **organs** (sampled pipe organs) and **pianos** (which are, in effect, dedicated synthesizers).

Storage for instrumental sounds, sequences etc. has improved greatly in all types of synthesizer, and built-in disk drives are becoming the norm as a supplement to **ROM** and **RAM**, with full computer **interfacing** a further option.

The live performance picture was profoundly changed in 1983 by the introduction of **MIDI**, which has tended to dominate design philosophy ever since, because it allows one player to control a whole 'orchestra' of different types of synthesizer, as well as organs, pianos, drum machines etc., simultaneously. Although a great deal of pre-patching may be needed, the problem of changing configurations rapidly during a performance is largely solved – you simply switch to another pre-set on a different instrument. MIDI has also extended the range of devices used as performance controllers – e.g. wind-, brass-, guitar-type controllers as well as keyboards are used. Because one keyboard can perform many functions the set-up is often changed so that sound generators and processors are mounted separately in racks instead of with the keyboard. MIDI-equipped computers are also increasingly used, with sequencing software controlling a whole spread of equipment.

A careful review of what is available is necessary for an intending buyer, and in this field the potential of the machine itself is sometimes far ahead of the often inadequate and obscure software that comes with it. Even price is not a good criterion – some of the cheaper machines offer both good sound and surprising versatility. Books such as Horn (1988) are updated fairly regularly, and publications like *Keyboard* magazine* contain regular surveys of equipment and useful practical guidance for the performer. See also **computer music composition techniques** and **live performance electronic music**.

Keyboard Magazine, GPI Corporation, 20085 Stevens Creek, Cupertino, CA 95014, USA.

L

Ladder A circuit containing a series of **attenuating** components, usually **resistors**, dividing a total **voltage** into discrete steps. Used for example in keyboards (fig. 106) to send appropriate voltages to a voltage controlled **oscillator**. See also **digital-to-analogue converter**.

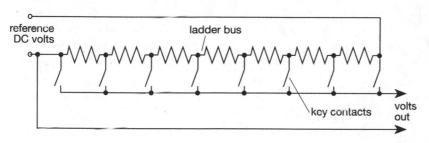

Fig. 106

Lag See **phase** and fig. 154. The amount by which one wave is delayed in relation to another, usually expressed as a phase angle. Opposite of **lead**.

Language See **computer languages**

Large scale integration (LSI) See **integrated circuit**

Laser A light source using the principle of Light Amplification by Stimulated Emission of Radiation. Compared to more conventional filament or gas discharge (fluorescent) lamps, the laser produces light of one wavelength only as a continuous, monochromatic, coherent (in-**phase**) wave. The two main types are the gas laser and the **semiconductor** laser (see **compact disc**).

Laser discs Digital optical recording and retrieval systems based on **laser** technology. They have audio, video and data applications of which the **compact disc** is the most familiar in a musical context. See also **CD-ROM, WORM**.

Laser printers   Paper printers using **lasers**. These produce very high quality print, ideal for music printing and **graphic scores**.

Lattice   1. The regular arrangement of atoms or molecules forming the stable structure of a crystal. This involves shared outer electrons (co-valency bonds) (fig. 107a). See **semiconductors**. 2. Cross-linked circuit configuration, also known as a ring or bridge circuit (fig. 107b), used in **ring modulators** for example. See also **network**.

Lavalier microphone   See **microphones**

LCD   See **liquid crystal display**

Lead   1. A connecting wire, terminated with a connector or with bare ends. It is usually external to a device and often described by its function (e.g. mains lead, speaker leads). See **jumper**. 2. In relating two waves together, lead is the opposite of **lag**. In fig. 44 the cosine leads the sine by a **phase** angle of 90° (or lags by 270°). See also fig. 154.

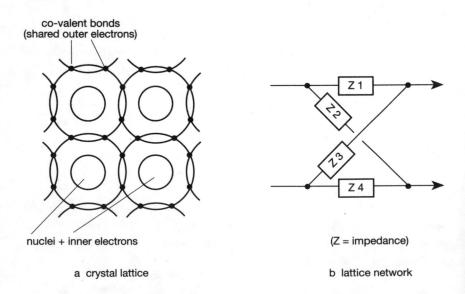

co-valent bonds
(shared outer electrons)

nuclei + inner electrons

(Z = impedance)

a crystal lattice

b lattice network

Fig. 107

Leader   1. In UK orchestras, the principal first violin. In the USA the term is often applied to the conductor, and 'concertmaster' (from the German 'Konzertmeister') describes the first violin. 2. Plain plastic or paper tape with no magnetic **oxide**, spliced to beginning of active tape and often coloured and/or lettered to indicate, for example, **tape track configuration**, speed and contents. See **spacer** and **trailer**.

Lead-in   1. The outer spiral of a record groove. 2. The wire joining an external aerial (antenna) to a receiver.

Leading edge   The first **modulations** of a tape recording. This is identified by moving the tape backwards and forwards across the tape **head** listening for the change from silence to sound. It is often a cut point in **editing**. See **trailing edge**.

LED   See **light emitting diode**

Level   1. Of signals, the relative magnitude of sound **intensity**, or electrical power, see **decibel**. 2. (adjective) Of **response**, unvarying over a given **frequency** range.

Light emitting diode (LED)   A **diode** which emits light when passing current in the 'forward' direction. Universally used device for low-level, low-voltage, compact illumination, much more efficient and reliable than the small incandescent or neon lamps they replaced. Stacks of LEDs can be arranged as 'thermometer'-type level indicators, see **peak programme meter** and **volume unit meter**. Compare **liquid crystal display**.

Light pen   A manual, pen-like device with a lead attached to it, which when touched to the glass screen of a **cathode ray tube** interacts with the electron beam inside. It is used as an input (by touching displayed messages), also for direct graphical interaction with computer by 'drawing'. A main control tool in series I and II of the Fairlight Computer Music Instrument.*

Limiter   See **compressor**

*Fairlight ESP Pty Ltd, 30 Bay St., Broadway, Sydney, NSW 2007, Australia.

Line   In full 'transmission line'. A cable for carrying **signals**. Transmitting signals along lines requires careful co-ordination of the lines with the rest of the system. See **decibel** (for line level), **impedance matching** and **unbalanced line**.

Line amplifier   An intermediate **amplifier** to optimize **signal** for insertion into a **line,** by e.g. adding **gain,** changing **impedance**.

Linear   1. Arranged in a straight line. 2. The relationship between two varying quantities such that their corresponding values plotted on a graph produce a straight line, for example the input/output plot of a perfect **amplifier**.

Linear pot   1. A **potentiometer** with a uniform **resistive** track, i.e. a given change in wiper position alters the output R by the same amount at all points. 2. A potentiometer (not necessarily linear in sense 1.) with straight-line rather than circular track. See fig. 108, also **logarithmic pot**.

Lining up   A drill for optimizing performance, particularly of analogue tape machines, which in any case need frequent cleaning, head-demagnetization and checking. The procedure involves adjusting the tape recorder so that a line level (see **decibel**) input signal, recorded on tape, produces the same level output when played back. This should be done each time a new tape is loaded because tapes can vary considerably, even of the same make and batch.

A short-form line up uses a **sine wave oscillator** with output approximately at line level tuned to a suitable middle range **frequency** or 'tone' (typically 400, 700 or 1000 Hz), and fed into the system as shown in fig. 109 (only record and play heads shown connected). Many **mixing desks** include built-in oscillators for this purpose.

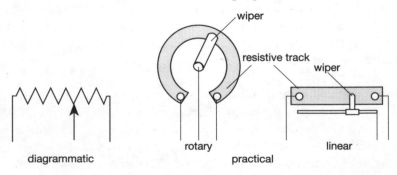

Fig. 108

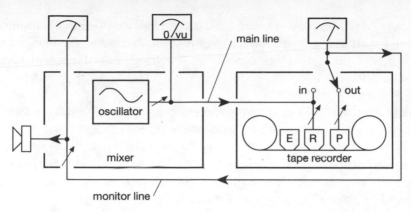

Fig. 109

The tone's level is adjusted to read zero **volume units** (VU) at all relevant points (desk meters, tape recorder inputs etc.), and a length of it recorded while the machine is set to playback and its output level adjusted until it is the same as the input. Placing a line up tone at the head of any recording is important for two reasons: 1. It allows another user or studio to be aware of the 0 VU level used in the recording (which may not be standard if the calibration is incorrect but can still be satisfactory); 2. For future copying of the tape, in which case the recorded tone, not the oscillator, is used to line up the second machine. This drill also ensures that the signal to tape and the signal off tape are at exactly the same listening level. For procedures in digital recording see **sound recording techniques**.

Even for domestic equipment, lining up is worthwhile to ensure the best **signal-to-noise ratio**, though it cannot be properly done with machines using a single (R/P) head for record and playback (which includes most **cassette** machines).

A full line-up uses a number of frequencies to check performance throughout the music band. A typical series is 40 Hz, 400 Hz, 1 kHz, 10 kHz, 15 kHz. The higher frequencies are useful for checking head **azimuth**. See **tape recorder design**.

Liquid crystal display (LCD) A visual display system which uses a grid of separate cells containing liquid crystals (organic compounds which display both solid and liquid characteristics). Each cell is normally transparent but turns 'dark' when a voltage is applied to it. By activating groups of individual cells within the grid different letters, numbers etc. are formed. LCDs use tiny amounts of power but unlike **light emitting**

diodes are not self illuminating. A reflective backing allows them to be seen in ambient lighting or a separate back light may be provided.

Lisp   See **computer languages**

Lissajous figure   The pattern obtained when two oscillations at right angles to each other are added together, for example by connecting **AC** signals to the X and Y inputs of an **oscilloscope** (with the normal X timebase switched off). If two **sine waves** are in an integral **frequency** relationship, the shape of the figure is characteristic of the ratio, as shown in fig. 110, and any **distortion** appears as irregularities in the pattern. In the top row of 110 the same wave has been sent to both inputs and the shape indicates the **phase**, a line indicating in-phase (0°) or **antiphase** (180°) and a circle 90° or 270°. If the frequency ratio is non-integral the figure is not steady, but rotates either vertically or horizontally.

  A Lissajous display can also be used as a **stereo** signal **monitor**, with left and right channels on the two co-ordinates. When there are no signals the picture reduces to a central spot, and signals on only one channel result in a vertical or horizontal line of varying length. The

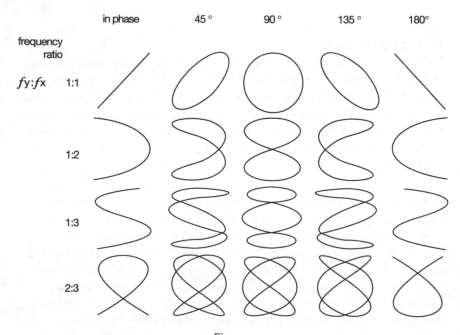

Fig. 110

picture indicates the left/right phase relationship, perfectly in-phase signals producing a diagonal line. A more elegant display is obtained by rotating the tube 45° (left and right are diagonals and in-phase line vertical).

Live performance electronic music This entry deals with music whose studio-realized component, if any, is only contributory to its performance, and does not constitute the piece itself. Performing instruments may be acoustic and/or electronic, but conventional instrumental music that happens to be realized electronically is not included. For other types of compositional approach, see **computer music composition techniques, musique concrète** and **tape composition techniques.**

Live electronic music preceded any other kind. In the 1920s, before efficient magnetic recording, specialist electronic instruments like the **Ondes Martenot** and the **Theremin,** though often used for conventional musical statements, were also capable of exploring new compositional ideas. Some composers, such as Edgard Varèse, imagined music for which the technology was not yet ready. Although few adventurous experiments were made until after 1945 an exception was John Cage's *Imaginary Landscapes* of 1939 and 1942, which made musical use of test and laboratory equipment such as **gliding tone** recordings made for calibration.

1. 'Tape plus' music

From the very beginning of electronic music it was seen that combining live and pre-recorded sounds could be musically interesting, and the pioneer work was Varèse's *Deserts* (1949–54). Early electronic music tended, mainly through technical crudity, to be unsubtle, and live voices or instruments added a human element as well as providing a stage presence. The scheme of a typical 'tape plus' piece is shown in fig. 111a.

Musically, the main problem in pieces of this type is to allow performer(s) interpretative freedom – trying to synchronize a performance with a running tape can be very inhibiting. In practice a tape part is easier to perform with if it is not continuous, and clear cues (and in the case of vocal music pitch cues) should precede live entries, in the same way as a conductor's upbeat. Noise caused by starting and stopping tape can also be a problem. Cueing is sometimes done by special tracks fed to headphones worn by the performer. Another technique is to use two play-in tapes with flexible overlaps. In some scores, of course, these problems do not occur because instruments and tape are not meant to synchronize in any case.

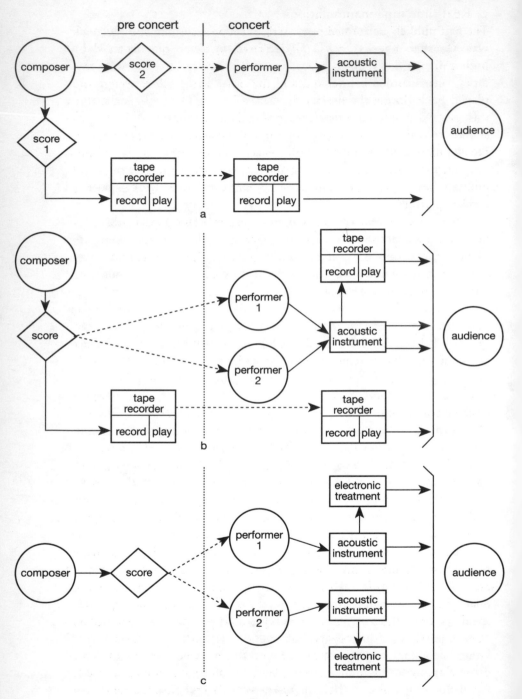

Fig. 111

2. Real-time tape manipulations

The first publicly performed piece with live tape recording and playback was Mauricio Kagel's *Transición II* (1958–9), for a piano played by both a pianist (keys) and a percussionist (hitting strings), and with two tapes, one recorded beforehand and the other recorded, rewound and played back during the performance (see fig. 111b). Compositionally, this piece depends on altered repetition, later in the performance, of sounds recorded earlier, exploiting the uniqueness of each playing and the cumulative effect of delayed playbacks. Manipulations already familiar in the studio, like tape looping and delays, variable speed drives and multiple heads (see **tape composition techniques**), were brought to the concert platform.

Such pieces often involve constructing or improvising mechanical set-ups which are notoriously accident-prone in performance. Delays and loops are now much easier to do with digital delay lines (see **digital multi-effect unit, reverberation**), but mechanical processes have considerable audience appeal, and remain popular.

3. Analogue live performance without tape

In tapeless live electronics the first really successful piece was Karlheinz Stockhausen's *Mikrophonie I* (1964), which explores very small sounds (as well as normal and loud ones) by amplifying and **filtering** them, using hand-held microphones on each side of a large tam-tam (non-pitched gong), and striking or stroking it with a number of different objects. It was followed by *Mixtur*, using four **ring modulators** to modify instrumental sounds, and *Mikrophonie II* which included a tape and exploited modulated voices. By that time purpose-built, reasonably compact treatment devices were available and, as with tape manipulation, some techniques migrated on occasions from the studio to the concert hall. Works with several performers on one instrument are in fact quite rare; a more general form of this type of piece is shown in fig. 111c.

Some composers made ingenious use of simple electro-acoustic phenomena to make music without performers in the ordinary sense. Steve Reich's *Pendulum Music* (1968), for example, uses three or more microphones swinging from their cables over upward-facing loudspeakers, amplifier **gain** being adjusted so that positive **feedback** occurs as each passes over its speaker. The sounds are short when the swing is large, becoming longer as it diminishes, and different lengths of cable cause a changing rhythmic pattern. Another effective automatic piece is Alvin Lucier's *Music On A Long Thin Wire* (1979), using a tensioned wire carrying a high audio **AC** current and passing between the jaws of a large magnet. The wire 'sings' continuously and with varying pitch and intensity (see also **environmental music**, for Lucier's *I Am Sitting In A Room*).

The post-war years saw a wave of small ensemble instrumental pieces, and a number of virtuoso composer/performer groups formed, many of them inventing their own electronic techniques, ranging from simple amplification of small, unusual sounds to elaborate audio-visual performances with lighting, TV screens, choreography, etc.

From 1966 or so, voltage-controlled **synthesizers** made live electronic performance comparatively easy, but the early ones were cumbersome to **patch** and possessed only monophonic keyboards or touch-pad controls. For the first few years they were mainly used in studios, but they brought more musicians into electronic music by making it possible for anyone to participate at some level without special knowledge or training in electronic engineering. Automatic **sequencers** were also a feature of some of the new machines, a halfway stage between the early mechanical ones and digital storage. There were also some non-commercial machines, built in very small quantities, the most notable of which was the Synket, designed by Paul Ketoff in Rome, and intended specifically for live performance. The American composer John Eaton was the main user of this small but comprehensive synthesizer, writing a number of pieces using one or several Synkets, or combining them with voices, instruments and/or tape. By about 1970 there were portable commercial machines with more compact patching (see **analogue synthesis techniques** 6), and very soon a number of new pieces using them. Electronic music concerts were now likely to include works of all types already mentioned, as well as tape-only music.

4. Hybrid and digital live performance

The first public musical performance by a computer was in January 1968 at the Queen Elizabeth Hall, London, when Peter Zinovieff played his *Partita for Unattended Computer* from a hybrid system consisting of a PDP–8/S mini-computer linked to a voltage controlled **oscillator** and a **percussion generator**. The hybrid systems of the day (see again **analogue synthesis techniques** 6), even though they usually provided for real-time control, were more suited to studio than live realizations, though devices like **sequencers** and **reverberators** were increasingly using digital circuitry. What follows should be read in conjunction with **computer music composition techniques** 3 and 4, which gives background on, for example, **Groove**. See also **keyboard synthesizers** for types of commercially made instrument, and **MIDI**.

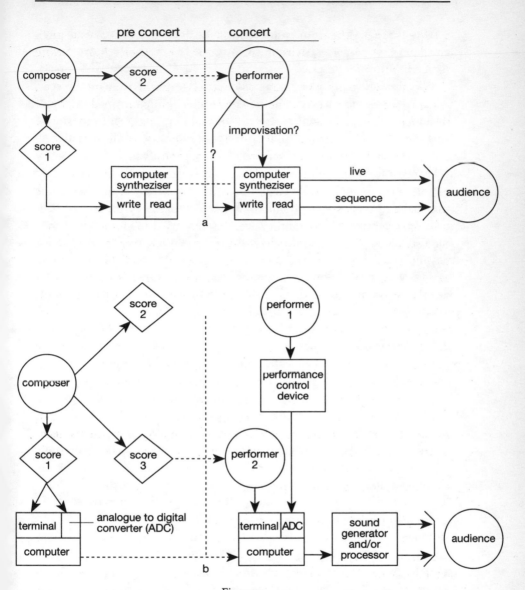

Fig. 112

The four main modes of real-time computer performance are neatly summarized by Dodge and Jerse, as 'electronic organ', 'music minus one', 'player piano' and 'conductor' (Dodge, 1985). 'Organ' performance, i.e. conventional instrumental performance, is what most commercial synthesizers are intended for, and their effectiveness depends largely on keyboard expertise and the range and interest of the sounds in the machine's memory.

'Music minus one' is an enhancement of 'organ', still requiring key-board or other performance skills to complete the piece, but having most of the composition pre-sequenced and stored. The larger synthesizers such as the Fairlight* and the Synclavier II† are well suited to 'M−1' mode; alternatively, linked combinations of MIDI-equipped machines, including real-sound **samplers**, can be used. As fig. 112a shows, there is a parallel with 'tape plus', but the 'tape' part is re-programmable in real time, and other live cross-influences (e.g. using **envelope** and **pitch followers**) can be included.

In 'player piano' and 'conductor' traditional performance skills are not needed, because the music itself is played by the computer. 'Player piano' performances may be fixed in the same way as tape-only pieces, but can have program features that ensure a different piece at each playing.

Max Mathews's 'Conductor' program (controlling a **groove** system) was the forerunner of a number of experiments and on-going projects in live performance control of machine-generated music, or 'conductor' mode. Fig. 112b shows one of many possible arrangements. Since 1983 such patches nearly always include MIDI control, which now offers alternatives to keyboard inputs. One of these, percussion interfacing, was pioneered in pre-MIDI days by Mathews and Curtis Abbott, as the 'sequential drum' (Mathews, 1980). A rectangular drum-like pad is struck, producing four outputs: 1. Trigger (each time hit), 2. Amplitude (how hard hit), 3. and 4. Co-ordinates of point on surface hit. These outputs could be harnessed in numerous ways, and since then a number of MIDI drum kits have appeared (see Vilardi, 1985). A good contem-porary example of a MIDI percussion piece is Greg Schiemer's *Mono-phonic Variations*.‡ Using a Roland‡‡ 'Octapad' MIDI drum set control-ling an Akai§ **sampler** and a special computer sequencer, the drummer has considerable influence over the development of the music. There are now MIDI interfaces for guitar, saxophone, trumpet and other instru-mental players as well as keyboard performers and drummers. Another composer who uses analogue devices to control computers is Joel

---

*Fairlight ESP Pty Ltd, 30 Bay St., Broadway, Sydney, NSW 2007, Australia.
†New England Digital Corporation, Box 546, 49 N. Main St., White River Junction, Vermont 05001, USA. Manufacturers of the Synclavier II and other products.
‡Schiemer, Greg *Monophonic Variations* NMA 6, pp. 31–7. NMA Publications, PO Box 185, Brunswick, VIC 3056, Australia.
‡‡Roland Corporation, 3–7–13, Shinkitajima Suminoe-ku, Osaka, Japan.
§Akai Electrical Co. Ltd, 12–14, 2–chome, Higashi-kojiya, Ohta-ku, Tokyo, Japan.

Chadabe; *Solo*, which passes hand movements to the computer via antennae, is an example.

An elaborate 'conductor' project was the Structural Sound Synthesis Project (SSSP) developed by William Buxton at Toronto University, which was both a live performance and a generalized composing tool. With computers now universally affordable, new performance projects, cheap and expensive, good and bad, appear every few weeks. The staged audio-visual performance with special instruments and visual/dramatic/choreographic components is also alive and well (see **bio-music, environmental music, sound sculpture** and **ultrasonics**), but now almost invariably controlled at least partly by computers.

5. Conclusion and references

All the techniques described above are still in use, and there will always be a place for the simplest as well as for complex and expensively mounted performances. Most people can buy or borrow an array of reasonably priced MIDI equipment, but the commercial market is rock orientated, and for some kinds of composer and performances many of the commercially available machines are unsuitable. For the ingenious musical and mechanical improviser there is a large range of technology to choose from, and almost all composers who use electronics at all have been involved in live performance projects. They include Appleton, Ashley, Cardew, Davies, Gehlhaar, Ichiyanagi, Mumma, Neuhaus, Smalley, Souster, Subotnick, to give only a few, and the list grows continually. An important organization devoted to developing live performance interfaces and performing electronic music is STEIM, in Amsterdam. In popular styles (apart from the electronics normal to the genre), one could note Laurie Anderson, Brian Eno, Pink Floyd, Tangerine Dream, and Tomita as particularly imaginative, but in this field too there are new arrivals all the time.

For further study, David Ernst's *The Evolution of Electronic Music* (Ernst, 1977), Gordon Mumma's chapter 6 in Appleton (1975), and Paul Griffiths's *A Guide to Electronic Music* (Griffiths, 1979) all contain detail about pieces and groups up to the middle 1970s. For more recent developments both Dodge (1985) and Peter Manning's *Electronic and Computer Music* (Manning, 1987) are recommended – this last covering the earlier part as well. See also Introduction and **tape recorder design**.

Load 1. A power drain (see **watt**) from a source. 2. A device absorbing (see **watt**) power (e.g. a **loudspeaker**), or its **impedance** (Z). 3. To transfer data from a disk store, for example, into a computer's **memory**.

Log/arithm The **power** to which a 'base' must be raised to represent a given number, e.g. $10^{.30103} = 2$, or $\log_{10} 2$ (log to the base 10 of 2) = .30103. Adding logs is equivalent to multiplying ordinary numbers, and on a graphical 'log scale' equal distances represent, for example, **decades** or **octaves**. Such scales are commonly used for plotting audio **frequency** because although the **hertz** is a **linear** unit, human perception of **pitch** is naturally logarithmic. Loudness (see **phon**) and audio power, to which our response is similarly non-linear, are conveniently expressed in **decibels**, a logarithmic unit.

Log(arithmic) pot A **potentiometer** whose **resistive** track follows a **logarithmic** rather than **linear** law. Used, for example, in volume controls so that equal movements of the knob cause roughly equal changes in perceived loudness at all points. See **linear pot**.

Logic See **Boolean algebra**

Longitudinal wave A back-and-forth wave motion, such as that of air pressure waves in a pipe, as opposed to the lateral motion of a **transverse wave**. See also **travelling wave**.

Long play(ing) record (LP) A term redundant since 78 rpm records were discontinued in the 1950s, but still surviving as LP. It was introduced in the USA in 1948 (UK 1950) and brought three innovations – slower speeds, microgrooves and low noise vinyl pressings which revolutionized disc quality. LPs were **stereo** from 1957 (see **pick-ups**). **Quadraphonic** discs were developed but abandoned soon after their unsuccessful launch in the 1970s. LPs are now rapidly giving way to the **compact disc**.

Look-up table A stored list of numbers, either permanent (e.g. in **ROM**) or calculated as required. Because many **functions** call for complex (therefore slow) calculation, it is more efficient to prepare such lists in advance than at **run time**. For digital **oscillator** look-up, see **digital synthesis techniques 4**.

Loop 1. A portion of sound, a sampled signal or a sequence which repeats indefinitely. This can be arranged by using tape loops or closed grooves in analogue recordings, or by using digital delay lines in digital systems. See **cartridge player, digital synthesis techniques 2, disc manipulation techniques, Möbius loop, samplers** and **tape composition tech-**

niques. 2. In programming, self-contained series of **instructions** in a computer program that repeats until some condition is satisfied, for example: 'Play phrase 2 four times then go to phrase 3', 'Do while x is greater than y'. Many loops of different length and type can be 'nested' within each other, and find frequent uses in music programming.

Loss(y)   The dissipation of energy from a signal due to the **resistance** and/or **reactance** present in any circuit through which it passes. A **passive device** is always lossy, because there is no power supply to replace losses. See also **active device**.

Loudness   See **phon**

Loudspeakers   **Transducers** which convert electrical oscillations in **alternating currents** into sound waves in air. In the electro-acoustic chain, loudspeakers are the hardest to design, the most **distortion**-prone and the most subjectively assessed of any component.

The sound output of a reproducing system is arguably the most important part of all, and although there have been many improvements in loudspeakers, the basic principles have not changed much in fifty years or so, and speaker design has still to catch up with the striking advances in other areas. Market forces encourage a degree of advertising hyperbole that further clouds the issue. The enormous literature can be compared to that for motor cars, with books, journals, popular magazines and manufacturers' pamphlets all contributing their advice. This brief survey can only serve as a guide to the nature of the problems, and some of the strategies for solving them.

Loudspeakers are never easy to choose because so many factors affect judgement. Good speakers cannot be very cheap, but price alone is no guide because one can pay a lot of money for non-acoustic cosmetics. The internationally renowned makers of drivers and housings are widely imitated, and some of these clones are very good – for example a plainly finished low-cost kit for home assembly can give excellent results if the drivers are of good quality and the enclosure well designed. At the end of this entry there is a list of at least some of the manufacturers whose products are generally respected in the industry. Of course no one system can be called the 'best' because of the great variety of jobs that speakers are required to do.

The wide scope of applications demands a flexible approach to design, and the different methods are found in an almost endless variety of mixes and matches. Objective assessment is very difficult – even in similar high quality applications there are differences in coloration and 'feel' not accounted for by paper analysis. As an indication of the fallibility of tests, Clifford A. Henriksen in his seventy-page assessment of the whole subject in Ballou (1987) chapter 14, states at the outset that he will not be using response curves as a criterion, and illustrates why by printing four different curves, all from the same speaker, all justifiable as 'honest', but tailored by changing measurement methods and graph scaling to obtain a 'good' response – described by Henriksen as a 'marketing curve'.

The word loudspeaker can refer to the complete instrument or to the transducer part only, but 'driver' clearly distinguishes the latter from its associated transmission system, and this active element of the two essential parts is discussed first.

1. Types of driver

A number of ways of converting electrical waves into analogous air waves have been tried, but by far the most successful to date has been the moving coil.

The voice (or speech) coil is wound on a light, accurately made cylindrical 'former' and suspended in a strong magnetic field so that it can move in both directions from its rest position (see fig. 113). The former is firmly glued to a stiff conical radiator so that the whole assembly moves together. The throat suspension is often called the 'spider' because of its shape in some speaker designs. The second suspension is a flexible 'surround' between the rim of the cone and the rigid frame. The coil's two ends are led up the lower part of the cone and joined by flexible leads to a connection block on the frame. To protect the fragile coil from dust and damage a cap is fixed across the throat of the cone, and the interior space is vented either by making the cap porous or providing vents somewhere in the magnet assembly.

When an audio signal is applied, the current flowing in the coil interacts with the strong magnetic field produced by the permanent magnet, creating a force which moves the entire coil/cone assembly back and forth in a mechanical copy of the electrical input.

This mechanism has remained essentially the same since the early 1930s, but there have been numerous improvements, due to new materials and manufacturing techniques, and to design criteria being better understood. Early moving coil speakers, for example, used **electromagnets,** requiring an energizing **DC** power supply, but new magnetic alloys have made this unnecessary.

For ordinary applications moving coil speakers can be made cheaply

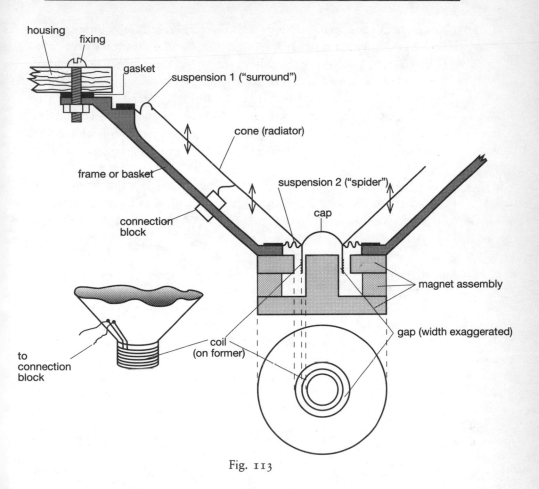

housing

fixing

gasket

suspension 1 ("surround")

cone (radiator)

frame or basket

suspension 2 ("spider")

cap

connection block

magnet assembly

gap (width exaggerated)

to connection block

coil (on former)

Fig. 113

and are reliable and robust, but for the designer of high quality systems there are inherent factors that tend to compromise performance. Some of the most important are:

Resonance The mass of the coil/cone assembly with its **compliance** (suspension) form a **resonator,** peaking in the lower part of the speaker's range. If not too prominent and below the main musical bass, this can actually be used to advantage when controlled by a suitable housing (see section 2).

Physical dimensions For good bass reproduction one needs a large air-moving surface, flexible suspension and a fairly long cone excursion, and for treble a light, small amplitude movement with a stiff suspension. The usual way to satisfy both requirements is to divide the spectrum between two or more differently specified speakers, and supply them

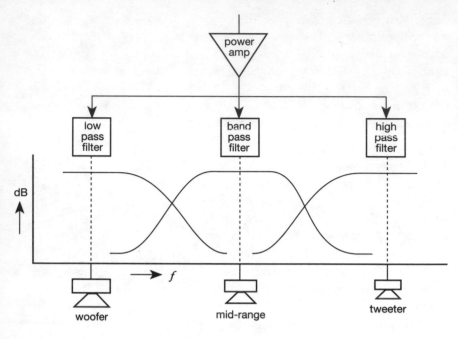

Fig. 114

through a 'crossover network' or special **filter** which splits the signal into frequency bands, providing suitable overlaps to ensure smooth transitions from one speaker to another. The two ends of the spectrum are covered by a bass 'woofer' and a treble 'tweeter', and if there is a third it is the 'mid-range' speaker. Woofers are nearly always moving coil, but some alternative tweeter systems are mentioned below. Most crossovers are **passive**, using the signal energy as it comes from the amplifier (see fig. 114).

Another approach is to use columns or batteries of identical all-range speakers (which means that both ends would be fairly deficient) working together in **phase** (the Bose 802, with eight speakers, is an example).* They are driven through a compensating network, however, to create an even frequency **response** by tailoring the signal rather than the mechanical/acoustic system. A crossover network is not involved, because all speakers handle all frequencies.

Cone 'break-up'   To reproduce faithfully, the coil/cone assembly should move as a true piston – in one rigid piece. In practice this only happens

*Bose Corporation, The Mountain, Framingham, MA 01701, USA.

in the bass because any cone light enough to be useful 'breaks up' in a very complicated way as the frequency increases, generating spurious **harmonics** and cancelling or stressing legitimate ones. The traditional cone is of high grade paper stiffened with concentric ribs, but numerous cone materials and different shapes of radiator, including flat, have been tried, some of them giving marked improvements in cone performance. Nisbett (1970) chapter 13 shows some curves obtained with different cone materials.

Coil impedance (Z) and heating problems   To make the coil light, the amount of wire is kept to a minimum, and power is delivered as a high **current** at a relatively low **voltage**. Speakers are rated at a 'nominal' impedance (a sort of effective average), typically 4 or 8 **ohms**, and if leads are long it is advisable to use thick, low **resistance** cable to avoid power loss. The actual Z, however, varies all over the frequency range, and in most moving coil speakers is at a maximum at or near bass resonance. Z variation not only causes non-linear response, but if the minimum Z is over-estimated, excessive current may heat up, even burn out the coil. It is not easy to provide adequate cooling in the very confined gap, and some tweeters use 'ferro-fluids' – magnetic liquids, conducting heat much better than air, and retained in the gap by their magnetic properties. Many systems also have overload protection to prevent accidental burn-out.

Transient response   Sounds like loud drum beats or pistol shots test the ability of the coil/cone assembly to move a lot of air quickly. The compromise here is between flexibility and lightness for rapid response but enough damping to prevent 'hangover' – unwanted movement after a transient (or a continuous signal) had ceased. Delays at either end can spoil the clarity of the sound, and in practice are more likely to be caused by the housing (see next section) than the driver.

Distribution   As frequency increases the angle of effective radiation reduces, very high frequencies being concentrated along the axis of the speaker. In single whole-range speakers various types of diffuser may be fitted to help widen the high frequency angle, while moving coil tweeters typically use a dome radiator with a single suspension and no cone. A common arrangement is to mount several tweeters at different angles, and horns are also widely used for treble distribution (see section 2).

Although the moving coil dominates the field, other methods have their advocates, and one of the most successful rivals is the **electrostatic** speaker. This is in effect a **capacitor** of which one **electrode** is a thin, flexible foil. A **polarizing** voltage is applied, charging the capacitor and creating an electrostatic field in the air space between electrodes. The signal is applied on top of the polarizing voltage, causing the charge to fluctuate above and below its steady value, and the foil electrode responds by vibrating. Practical designs are quite complex, but the idea is that a thin, nearly flat radiator held at the sides moves to produce a spherical wavefront of much larger area than is possible with a cone driver, and system resonance is at a minimum. Several manufacturers offer all-range electrostatic speakers, but the most consistently successful has been the QUAD electrostatic.* Their original model (mid-1960s) was outstanding for its time, and updated versions have recently appeared. All-range electrostatics remain fairly rare, however, one of the problems being the high (therefore potentially dangerous) polarizing voltages needed for electrostatic woofers – typically 5000 volts. The principle is much more commonly used in tweeters, and also found in some **headphones** (for comments on moving coil flat radiators see section 3).

Another alternative to moving coils for tweeters is the 'ribbon' movement, in which a thin aluminium foil is mounted between magnet poles – in effect a single-wire coil is both conductor and radiator (compare ribbon **microphones**). A further type uses the **piezo-electric** effect, which depends on the ability of some materials to bend when a voltage is applied. Rochelle salt is a naturally piezo-electric material, but much more efficient piezo-ceramics have been developed. The principle is also used in ultrasonic transducers (see **sub/-**, **super/sonic**), and for underwater loudspeakers, using a vibrating diaphragm in direct contact with the water. For fuller details of these and other principles, a good source is Ballou (1987) chapter 14.

2. Housings and horns

The majority of speakers are direct radiators, i.e. the surface of the cone directly excites the free air in contact with it. Both the front and the back of the cone radiate, but in opposing phases. If the speaker is unmounted, high end radiation is little affected, but at lower frequencies (longer **wavelengths**), waves from behind leak round to the front, selective **cancellation** occurs, and the sound is thin and 'tinny'. The primary object of any housing is to separate the bodies of air on each side of the cone, and the simplest form of separation is a flat 'baffle', which is effective, but only if large enough. A diameter of at least a metre is

*QUAD Electroacoustics Ltd, 30 St Peter's Road, Huntingdon, Cambridgeshire PE18 7DB.

needed, twice that for really deep bass. A virtually 'infinite' baffle can
be achieved by mounting the speaker in a solid wall. A baffle should be
as heavy and 'dead' as possible – its purpose is to separate, not to
vibrate, and a thin board with its own resonances only adds to the
problems. Baffles of adequate size are not convenient, however, and
most people prefer the alternative of some kind of box.

The obvious way to reduce the overall size of a baffle is to fold it,
and in ordinary radios and TVs the speaker is mounted in an open- or
perforated-backed box containing other components as well, resulting
in an unstable, hit-or-miss bass response, though if properly designed
and solidly made the open-backed box can be quite successful. Most
speaker housings, however, fall somewhere between an open back and
a totally sealed box, the choice depending on factors such as the performance of the drivers, the allowable size of the box, the power handling
requirements of the system, etc. The one firm rule is that (as with all
baffles) the box should not itself vibrate. Much design effort goes into
making boxes that are completely inert without being too heavy. At one
time there was a vogue for brick or concrete sand-loaded enclosures,
but today dense particle board, braced inside and heavily lagged with
rock-wool, for example, is the material most often used.

In a completely closed box, movement of the woofer cone compresses
trapped air creating a sort of 'air spring', and if the box is large and the
air spring weak enough to approach the free air condition, the box acts
as an infinite baffle (see fig. 115a). Small closed boxes can work well

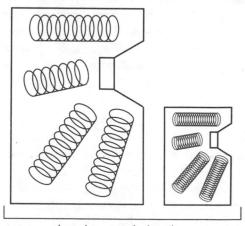

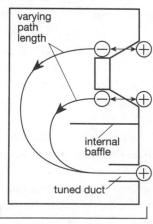

large box – weak air spring   bass reflex effect
small box – stiff air spring

a   b

Fig. 115

but only if the driver (which is necessarily small as well) has the flexible suspension and long cone travel necessary to move enough air for adequate bass response, and the amplifier has the power to drive the cone against the stiff air spring. All closed boxes are inherently inefficient, however, in that half the speaker's output is deliberately lost. The alternative is the vented or ported box, also known as a bass reflex enclosure.

By strategically placing a hole (port) in the box, a **Helmholtz resonator** is formed, assisting bass response and improving efficiency. The path length from behind the speaker to the port varies according to the point on the cone (and the position at the port, which can be quite large) from which it is measured. The idea is to construct a 'flatly' tuned (low Q, see **filters**) resonator that will approximately reverse the phase of sounds from the back of the speaker for a band of low to middle frequencies, so that they emerge from the port in phase with the direct radiation (see fig. 115b).

The resonator is tuned by taking all the known parameters into consideration, and calculating an optimum size for the box. Path lengths can be increased by internal baffles, and a tuned duct behind the port is a further adjustable option, as well as various resistive materials, lagging etc. to adjust the Q of the box. Designing housings is a mixture of careful calculation (nowadays with sophisticated computer techniques) and individual flair. Subjective listening tests are always the final arbiter of any speaker system.

Horn loading, or indirect radiation, was one of the earliest methods developed, being used in the 1920s with moving iron diaphragms. The restricted air in the throat of the horn is compressed by the driver, and as the horn flares out it gradually approaches the free air state. Just as a tuba is larger than a trumpet, a long horn with a wide opening is needed for good bass reproduction. An **exponential** horn gives the best results, but practical constraints often dictate a less than ideal shape.

A horn couples the driver to the air much more efficiently than a direct radiator, i.e. a louder sound can be produced for the amplifier power supplied. For this reason and the fact that they are robust and easily weatherproofed horns are used for rugged, speech-quality applications like public announcements, megaphones etc. Fig. 116a shows the 're-entrant' method of folding such horns for both compactness and weather protection.

With some differences in detail, the same types of driver are used for horns as for direct radiators, for example moving coils with cones for bass and domes for treble. A popular combination, producing a good

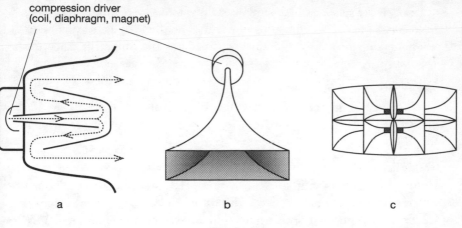

compression driver
(coil, diaphragm, magnet)

a   b   c

Fig. 116

full-range loudspeaker, is a horn tweeter with a direct radiator woofer.
It is not particularly important to distribute the sound vertically (as all
listeners are usually at approximately the same height), so a horn tweeter
is usually flared to a rectangular mouth (fig. 116b). Another favoured
design is the 'cellular' horn, in which one driver is loaded by a cluster
of square-section horns, flaring out to give very efficient transmission
over a wide angle (fig. 116c).

Bass horns are very bulky if a straight horn is used, so they are
often folded labyrinths of wooden construction. Some designs employ a
mixture of horns and vented boxes, and may use several drivers. Typical
locations for these systems are large cinemas and concert halls, and they
may work with several cellular horn treble units.

3. Some practical implementations

We have seen that loudspeaker design is a matter of steering the best
course through a number of intractable problems. Building speakers
comes nearer to being an art form than any other branch of audio
engineering, and some of the most successful designs have been inspired
hunches. Good speaker manufacturers always keep firmly in touch with
the actual user – 'never mind the figures, what does it sound like?' The
variations are endless, but here are just a few, noting that whatever
selection is made a great many are necessarily omitted.

Active crossovers and speakers   Crossover circuits designed as part of
the **active** electronics rather than as passive devices in the speaker housing, though more complex and expensive, have great potential advantages because they can be adjusted in several ways to fine tune the

system. Active speakers contain their own amplifiers and therefore accept **line** level inputs. These are convenient in domestic use to convert headphone equipment (e.g. Walkman) into general entertainment, and professionally as quickly connected, one-piece reproducers.

Bookshelf speakers   One of the most striking recent advances is the production of quite acceptable low bass from small enclosures. Closed or vented housings are fitted with long excursion drivers, giving a somewhat 'tight' but very clean response at moderate listening levels. Small speakers are also used as 'close field' monitors in studios.

Co-axial speakers   Split speaker systems also mean spread out sound sources, which may among other things lead to a poor **stereo** image. A clever idea combines horn tweeter and cone woofer on the same axis, and this co-axial or dual concentric construction has been implemented by Altec Lansing in the USA and Tannoy* in the UK. Fig. 117 shows the Tannoy principle – the bass cone is also the flare of the treble horn, whose throat is formed by drilling out the centre pole piece of the woofer's magnetic assembly.

   Certain problems of time and phase alignment occur with this arrangement, but in a well-designed housing the Tannoy gives a very clean sound; although it came out many years ago it is still the preferred monitor speaker in many control rooms, and is also a good concert speaker.

Corner reflector speakers   A number of enclosures are designed to use indirect sound reflected from the corners and walls of rooms (after all most of the sound you hear in a concert hall is indirect). Many shapes and placings of boxes encourage this method, with rear or side ports, multiple tweeters, rear-facing direct radiators, etc., though some people dispute the validity of this approach.

Flat radiators   The panel radiator pioneered by QUAD in their 1960s electrostatic speaker has long been recognized as an acoustically efficient design, and various makers (e.g. KEF) have used flat radiators with versions of the moving coil for some time. However, it has been difficult to find materials that are both very light and very rigid – most solutions are sandwiches of cellular panels between thin plates. Ultra-thin panel woofers developed by Sony and Technics have large surfaces driven by multiple coils, and are claimed to give smooth, full-range bass while taking up very little floor space. This seems a promising line of research,

*Tannoy Products Ltd, High Fidelity Division, Canterbury Grove, London SE27 0PW.

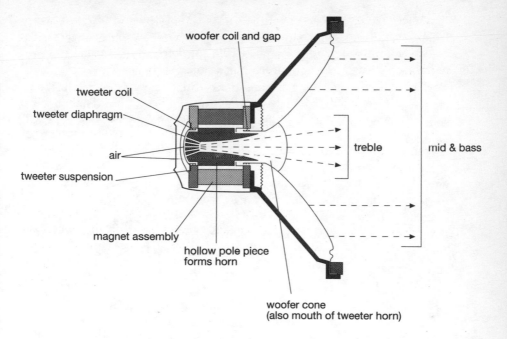

woofer coil and gap

tweeter coil

tweeter diaphragm

air

tweeter suspension

treble

mid & bass

magnet assembly

hollow pole piece
forms horn

woofer cone
(also mouth of tweeter horn)

Fig. 117

and Sony have been successfully marketing flat radiator speakers with four voice coils in more conventional housings for some years.

Guitar speakers   In **electric guitars** the speaker must be considered part of the instrument, and is chosen for the sound the player wants, in combination with an amplifier that is also tailored to specific requirements (see *guitar amplifiers* in **amplifiers**). Speaker(s) are either mounted in the same portable box as the amplifier, or in 'stacks' of boxes containing several speakers each. Two well-known makes are Fender and Marshall. Bass guitar systems may use very large (e.g. 18 inch) drivers.

Rotating speakers   These are a speciality of the Leslie company and can be purchased as an optional system with **Hammond** and other organs. In them, the drivers themselves are fixed, but rotating components distribute and modify the sound in several ways, including **amplitude modulation** and **Doppler effect**.

Satellite and wall speakers   The demand for the best possible sound in today's small living rooms produced bookshelf speakers, and the thin panels discussed above are another approach. A third is to take advantage of the fact that deep bass is virtually non-directional, and separate it completely from the mid and treble end. The bulky woofer box, fed by a summed left and right signal, can be placed out of sight almost anywhere in a room, and only the treble speakers, in very small boxes, need be on view in the normal front position. Several makers offer such satellite systems, including a very successful one by Bose. A further method which combines high quality listening with low demand on room space is the flat, wall-hung speaker – a leader in this field is Duntech.

Judging speakers is not unlike judging wine – in fact much the same descriptive imagery is used for both. The way to study loudspeakers is to start by listening to the very best you can find – probably in a recording studio or a broadcasting **control room,** and judge others by these. For some years the speaker industry has been ringing fairly small changes on firmly established techniques, and though this has undoubtedly brought many improvements, one feels that before long a major breakthrough on quite new principles may bring the same kind of advance at the reproducing end as has already occurred with recording techniques – maybe some kind of direct digital-to-air converter.

As mentioned at the beginning of this article, the literature on loudspeakers is extensive and continually expanding, just as new products (with fresh claims to excellence) regularly appear. I have referred several times to Ballou (1987) chapter 14 as a useful general resource. Another, more recent book is Borwick (1988), with contributions by fourteen authors on a wide range of speaker and headphone topics. A complete list of makes would run to hundreds, but the following includes some widely respected names in speaker research and manufacture: Acoustic Research, Altec Lansing, B and W, Bose, Celestion, Dali, Duntech, Dynaudio, Electro-Voice, Fender, Goodman, JBL, KEF, Klipsch, Leslie, Magnavox, Marshall, Mitsubishi, Motorola, Pioneer, QUAD, Sony, Tannoy, Technics, Wharfedale, Yamaha.

Low level language See **computer languages**

Low order (bit) The digit on the right-hand end of a number or **word,** also known as the Least Significant Bit (LSB). Contrast **high order.**

Low pass filter See **filters**

M

Machine code   See **computer languages**

Macro   As a prefix, macro means 'large-scale', the opposite of micro, but it is also used alone as short for 'macro-instruction', a single command initiating a prepared series of actions on a computer.

Magnet/-ic, -ism   A piece of a material in which enough of the miniscule current loops formed by spinning **electrons** can be aligned to combine and produce an appreciable external energy field (see **inductance** for the magnetic effect of current). Such materials are called ferromagnetic because iron was observed to be easily magnetized, or permeable. An **electromagnet** uses, for example, 'soft' iron which is easily magnetized but has poor retentivity or remanence, i.e. the field collapses as soon as the energizing current is removed. Permanent magnets, made of steel or other more efficient special alloys, demand more energy to magnetize them, but are highly retentive. Both types are widely used in music electronics. See also **hysteresis**.

Magnetic cartridge   See **pick-ups**

Magnetic field   The region around a **magnet** or a current-carrying wire or coil in which another magnet, etc., will experience a force. Magnetic fields are conventionally described by patterns of field lines (also called lines of magnetic flux) whose concentration represents the shape of the field. Fig. 118 shows that the concentration is greatest near the magnet's **poles**. In practical magnetic devices the magnet is shaped to concentrate the maximum field where it is needed. In tape heads, for example, the magnet is horseshoe-shaped, bringing the poles very close together. In moving coil devices like **loudspeakers** and dynamic **microphones** the poles are arranged concentrically (see fig. 113).

Magnetic recording   See **sound recording techniques**

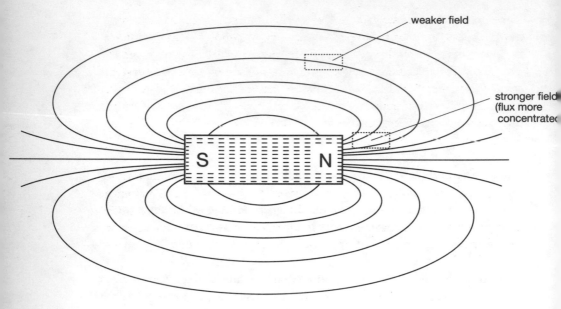

weaker field

stronger field
(flux more
concentrated

Fig. 118

Magnetostriction The change in shape that occurs when some materials are placed in a **magnetic field**, typically lengthening or shortening of a rod. The principle can be applied in loudspeakers and microphones, but the **piezo-electric** effect is more popular.

Mainframe A survival from the days of physically very large computers, this referred to the housing for the **central processing unit** and main **memory**. Today the word refers to any large, fixed computer system as opposed to desktop, home, lap, micro, mini, personal, pocket etc. computers.

Main gain Master **fader**, the final level control of a complete mixed signal before it goes to a radio transmitter, a tape recorder, etc.

Mains supplies Where a public supply exists at all, **AC** is now more or less universal, which obviates the earlier necessity for compromise AC/DC equipment power units. Mains **voltages** are generally speaking in two ranges, the American of $c.110$V and the European of $c.220$V (in Britain 240V). Both have their advantages – the lower voltage is safer but requires heavier cable because twice the **current** is needed for the same **power**. Mains supplies, however, do fluctuate and designers must always allow for the behaviour of circuitry if supply voltage is higher or lower than normal or polluted with spikes, surges, poor waveform etc., by such means as fitting regulators and suppressors. Equipment with clocks, memories etc. can be battery backed to avoid tedious resetting and reloading, and vital installations can be arranged to switch automatically to emergency supplies when public services fail. See also **earth, hum** and **root-mean-square**.

Make-before-break A type of switch in which the new contact is made before the old is broken, used when it is important to maintain circuit continuity, or simply to avoid clicks and pops. It cannot be used, however, when momentary paralleling of two paths would cause problems such as a **current** surge.

Marking-up Any kind of preparatory/rehearsal work on scripts, scores etc., but particularly reading and marking a magnetic track (with a wax pencil on the inactive side) to identify starts, ends, cuts etc. Contrast 'marking' – see **slate**.

Markoff chain See **computer music composition techniques 2**

Mark/space ratio Derived from the trace left by the vertical pen recorders used for telegraphy, this term is one way of describing the time relationship of the 'high' to the 'low' parts of a **pulse wave**. In the case of a **square wave** the ratio is 1:1. An alternative description is 'duty cycle', which gives the percentage of the 'up' portion to the whole cycle (e.g. 70% duty cycle = 7:3 mark/space).

Mask/ing 1. The obscuring of a quiet sound by a loud one, particularly when both are at similar **frequencies**. Our ears automatically desensitize as loudness increases, so quiet sounds, easily audible alone, recede in the presence of louder ones, thus footsteps heard across an empty street seem loud, but cannot be distinguished if the street is busy. 2. A procedure used to select part of a number and ignore the rest. For example, any **binary** number '*anded*' (see **Boolean algebra**) with 7 (binary 111 at the least significant end, the rest 0s) will result in zero for all but the three lowest **bits** because *and* 0 always gives 0. The three low bits will remain unaffected, because *and* 1 passes a value unchanged.

Master tape The original, 'top copy' analogue or digital recording in a given tape format, i.e. in a music recording the first master may be on 24-track two-inch tape (see **tape track configurations**), but there will also be a ¼-in stereo master after **mixdown** to two tracks. Master tapes are normally run only for copying purposes, never edited, and wound and stored carefully (see **print-through**). When an occasion is important and re-takes not possible (such as single live performances at public events) duplicate masters (two machines in parallel) are usually made, one being retained after checking.

The masters of tape music pieces may well have many joins, because the composer minimizes noise by eliminating unnecessary copying, and works in sections between cut-editing points. Performance copies made from the joined master are, of course, join-free.

Mastering tape   The best quality magnetic tape, the most rigorously tested for **drop-out** and other faults, therefore the most expensive, and guaranteed for quality by reputable makers. Not all tape so labelled merits the description, however.

Match   See **impedance matching**

Mellotron   A keyboard instrument (from 1977 officially renamed the Novatron) in which each key initiates the playing of a piece of prepared tape (maximum time ten seconds). On key release a spring quickly resets the tape. Any material (e.g. recordings of instruments) can be loaded. It dates from the mid-1960s, and was widely used for music and effects for some years, but digital techniques (see **samplers**) have overtaken the technology.

Memory   This usually denotes 'main memory', the high-speed, quick-access internal store that every computer needs in order to function. It is also loosely used for other types of storage. **Core** memory was magnetic and non-volatile (contents preserved when power off) but expensive and slow compared with today's **semiconductor** memories, which are volatile but quickly loaded from a mass storage device (e.g. tape or disk). Part of the memory is occupied with running the **operating system**, and part is user-programmable. Some computers have expansion slots for add-on memory. Today's equivalent of core is bubble memory, in which tiny magnetic 'bubbles' are created by conductors. Hailed as a great advance, it has so far not proved as cheap or successful as was hoped. See **random access memory** and **read-only memory**.

Metronomes Tempo indicators, devices which mark musical beats visibly and/or audibly. A pendulum with sliding weight was proposed and drawn by Galileo in the sixteenth century, and although that model was not made, many simple metronomes have been built on these lines when visual indication is enough. Johann Maelzel (1772–1838), who made many musical automata, designed the upside-down, clockwork-driven pendulum with moveable weight and loud click familiar to this day. His friend Beethoven (for whom he also made an ear trumpet) was the first prominent composer to use metronome marks as a matter of routine. Today various types of electronic metronome are available, but clockwork models, both standard and in pocket watch form, are still made and preferred by many.

Microfarad See **capacitance** and **SI units**

Microfloppy or microdisk. General name for the smallest sizes of **floppy disk**. Sizes can vary from 2.8 in (71 mm) to 4 in (102 mm), but the 3.5 in (89 mm) size has become the effective standard.

Micron A thousandth of a millimetre (10^{-6}m or .00003937 in or .03937 **thou** (in US mil)).

Microphone placement (If necessary see **microphones** before reading this entry, for types of microphone, technical terms, etc.) Other relevant articles are **acoustic treatments**, **control room**, **filters**, **quadraphony**, **reverberation**, **sound recording techniques** and **stereo**. 'Microphone' is usually abbreviated as 'mic', but the 'k' spelling is used for the verb – 'to mike', 'miking'.

There can be no firm rules about microphone placement, only suggestions. Recording/broadcasting balance is a mixture of firm data – what the mics and other equipment can do, the known behaviour of the acoustic environment etc., and empirical decisions based on experience of what is likely to work and (sometimes) on inspired hunches. The best sound engineers are valued as much for their creative flair as for their technical skills.

Preliminaries
First of all it is necessary to learn your equipment thoroughly, including your own ears – many people have a slight imbalance in their hearing. Try all the mics you have in every position, even obviously bad ones, with every source, and listen with great care to the result. Test your

speaker/headphone system with all types of material. If you know where your monitor speakers are deficient you can train yourself to compensate for this in recording balance. Before placing any mics, decide exactly what sound you want, for example, warm and expansive, detailed and delicate, punchy and aggressive. Obviously this depends a lot on the music you are recording, but there are many ways to record any material, from pointing a mic vaguely in the direction of the source to elaborate set-ups needing hours to deploy and rehearse. Set out your mics with a sound in mind, and in all but the simplest cases keep a sketch of what you did so that successes can be repeated, failures avoided.

Some references cited in **microphones** are useful here, particularly Clifford (1986), Nisbett (1970) chapter 7, Nisbett (1983), Ballou (1987) chapter 13, but there is no shortage of articles in journals etc. with recommendations for microphone placement based on personal experience. Apart from the full **tonmeister** course available at some universities, there are studio technique courses in most cities, of varying quality and cost. The many problems of speech recording (e.g. radio and TV drama, talks, conferences, film dialogue) are not discussed here, and the following can only be brief guidelines. In this area, as with learning an instrument, there is no substitute for plenty of practical experience.

Overall approach

First think through the whole process to the final sound. Two opposite extremes of recording style are: 1. To use only one mic (two for stereo) in the optimum audience listening position, and record direct to master, with no intermediate processing. The aim in this case is to produce a sound like a real concert in a real acoustic – the total ensemble that an audience hears. 2. To use many mics and record onto multi-track tape, with processing (**compression, equalization, reverberation** etc.) being applied during **mixdown**. In this case the final sound, including stereo image, is a completely artificial construction. The first is a good way of recording, say, a string quartet if the natural acoustics are friendly. Balance must be achieved by first placing the mic(s) in the best position for all players (probably above and in front of the group), then rehearsing for correct internal balance among the musicians. The second procedure would be normal for a jazz or rock group where each voice needs separate emphasis, and where even in live performance the sound is amplified, i.e. artificiality is 'natural' to the medium. On the other hand recording a jazz concert by method 1 can be very effective, and string quartets are frequently recorded with four close mics and balanced on mixdown.

There are many compromises in between, such as close miking some players (e.g. soloists only), using section mics for, say, woodwinds, upper strings, and placing distant omnidirectional mics to fill in the natural ambience of the hall. The aim (as with composing) is first to hear the sound in your head and then try to capture it in reality. If possible, even in a home studio, this is best achieved by isolating playing from recording rooms, and listening only on speakers/headphones, rather than 'live', which is less confusing than continually switching between the real and the reproduced.

Miking: single instruments

Decide how much reflected sound from the 'room' you want mixed in with the instrument. An omni mic will pick up all the reflected as well as the direct sound, and for adequate direct/indirect balance must be placed closer to the source than a cardioid, whose directional pattern gives longer 'reach' but less general atmosphere. Try bi-directional and hypercardioid mics as well. With small area sound radiators (e.g. flute, violin, trumpet) try placing the mic in the path of the instrument's most efficient output (usually obvious) and if this sounds wrong try different positions (off the direct line, nearer or further back, placed to catch indirect sound bouncing off a wall etc.). Listen for the room's acoustics (**flutter echoes, resonances** etc.), and possibly move the instrument to another place. If you are using a properly equipped studio make use of reflecting or absorbing screens to tailor the sound. Large, multi-source instruments are more difficult – for example there are dozens of ways of miking pianos, and fig. 119 shows some recommended by Alec Nisbett in Nisbett (1983). Although bi-directional mics are shown in the sketches, cardioids would also be satisfactory – it depends how much indirect sound you want to use. Adapting Nisbett's caption: 1 and 2 are on the same arc, any part of which may be good, though 1 is a favoured position; 2 discriminates against the heavy bass of some pianos; 3 favours the bass, and a mix of 2 and 3 is often effective; 4 is a close balance for multi-tracked ensembles with other instruments separately miked; 5 and 6 are for a self-accompanied singer; both discriminate against the piano, and 6 has the mic tilted down towards the singer/pianist; 7 and 8 are other possible positions, 8 looking diagonally down on the strings; 9 uses reflection from under the lid; 10 picks up reflections from the floor.

The pressure zone microphone (PZM, see **microphones** 3) is another good mic for pianos, placed on the floor underneath the instrument or taped under the lid. Again, it is a matter of deciding what kind of piano

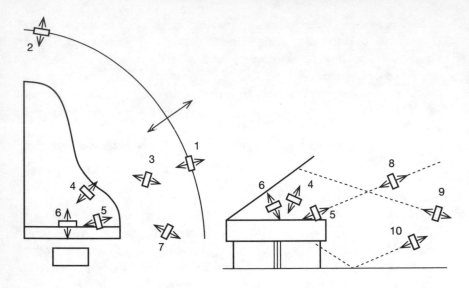

Fig. 119

sound you want, trying a set-up that looks promising, and modifying it until you are satisfied. Apart from the musical effect desired, other factors such as the hardness of the piano's felts, the style of playing etc. will all contribute to the final decision.

Miking: small groups

This covers a wide variety of musical styles and types of sound, for example jazz groups, brass quintets, instruments plus voices, electronic sources plus live performance, a cappella (unaccompanied) vocal groups etc. Having decided on the overall approach, the next thing is to place the group for the best acoustic effect in the recording space. If instruments are to be individually miked, test each separately for the best mic type, angle and distance, and minimize 'spill' to neighbouring mics by placing adjacent mics for the least mutual pick-up. If necessary screens can be put up to separate individuals or sections.

In fig. 120a the drums (the loudest and most likely to spill into the string and woodwind mics) and the harp (the most likely to be swamped by the others and hence to need extra mic boost) are screened off in such a way that everyone can see the conductor. Small vocal groups can be arranged in a line with a mic for each, or in various curved or circular patterns, allowing them to cue each other, as in fig. 120b, using two coincident (see **microphones**) bi-directional mics but not at right angles.

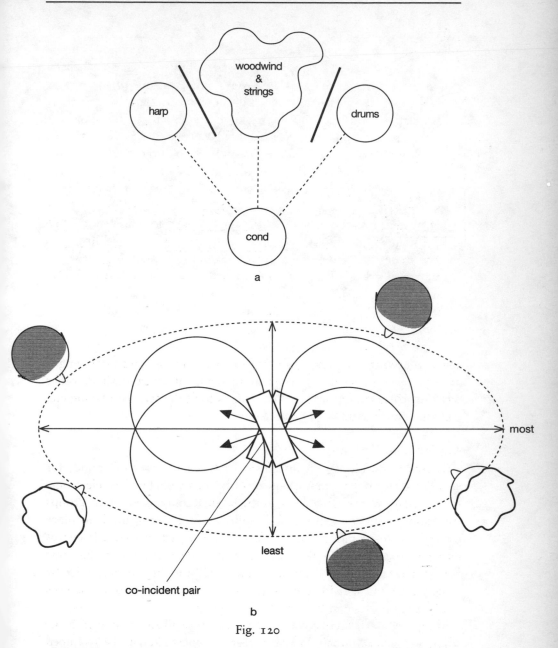

Fig. 120

This gives a slight variation of sensitivity around the mics, allowing weak and strong voices to be balanced by small sideways adjustments, though there may be problems with phase **cancellations**. In miking a drum kit or percussion section, up to eight mics may be used for one player, depending on the variety of instruments.

Miking: large groups

With luck, recording an orchestra can be simple – in the right hall one or a pair of mics carefully positioned by trial and error during rehearsal can give excellent results providing the internal balance of the players is itself good. However, if this method doesn't work, no post-recording rebalancing is possible. Fig. 121a shows two such simple set-ups – spaced omnis (1) and coincident cardioids (2), known as X–Y miking because the axes are at or near a right angle. Both of these arrangements can be extended for **quadraphonic** recording (see fig. 163). See **stereo** for further discussion and a third technique (M–S), using two dissimilar mics.

Fig. 121b shows the opposite approach, with section mics (not necessarily as shown), a soloist mic, an overall stereo pair, plus PZMs and distant omni to add some extra hall ambience if wanted. Such a set-up may be mixed live to air or tape, but if multi-tracked it can be rebalanced during mixdown. Miking an orchestra with a chorus and solo singers is a challenge to any recordist, in fig. 121c the orchestra mics are omitted. Gun mics have been successful for a rear-seated chorus, and another favoured arrangement is a group of high, suspended bi-directionals tilted down towards the chorus for minimum orchestra pick-up. The rear faces of the mics will add reflected sound and give acoustic spaciousness, but in a very live hall or church the time delays can lead to mushiness and it may be better to use cardioids instead.

Conclusion

There is no 'right' way to broadcast or record music, because we are dealing with an artificial and subjectively viewed technique (even if 'naturalness' is the declared aim). At every stage – placing musicians and microphones, recording, mixdown, if any, and listening to the finished product – individual views differ widely. The art of a good balance engineer, like that of a first-class chef, lies in its subtle details. Small touches like moving one mic 3 cm can make all the difference to the final result.

Microphones **Transducers** which convert sound waves in air into their electrical analogue. They perform the converse operation to **loudspeakers,** and in some cases (e.g. intercom systems) the same device does both jobs.

There are hundreds of designs for microphones with thousands of applications, but this entry is mainly about those suitable for music recording/broadcasting work. Good overviews of the whole subject are

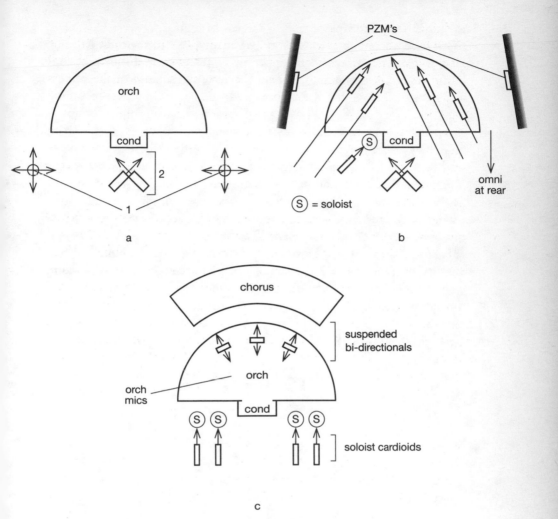

Fig. 121

Clifford (1986) and Ballou (1987) chapter 13. Small books with useful information are Pawera (1981) and Nisbett (1983). Nisbett's larger book (1970) also has sections on microphones and studio technique, as do Olson (1967) and Runstein and Huber (1989). Many books on mics (and loudspeakers) are written by people with particular trade interests (an example is Pawera, 1981, which relates to the excellent products of AKG),* but that doesn't make the information less useful, it is just that the field of choice may be wider than indicated. Good microphones are

*AKG Acoustics, Akustische u. Kino-Geräte GmbH, Brunhildengasse 1, A-1150 Wien, Austria.

reviewed more in the professional than the hi-fi press, because few home users are equipped for high quality live recording. A list of some of the leading names in microphones is given at the end of this article. For music balancing techniques, see **microphone placement**, **quadraphony** and **stereo**.

1. Sound waves in air and microphone response

Sound waves are **longitudinal** waves which involve air particles vibrating backwards and forwards in such a way that regions of compression and rarefaction (increased and decreased air pressure) are created in the air as the wave travels outwards from its source. At a given point in the wave's path, therefore, air particles are moving to and fro locally, but their mean positions do not change.

Fig. 122 shows that the pressure of the air at such a point, and the velocity of its movement, are 90° out of **phase**, i.e. when at maximum compression or rarefaction the air is momentarily stationary, and its maximum velocity occurs half-way between the two states (when it is momentarily at normal, undisturbed pressure).

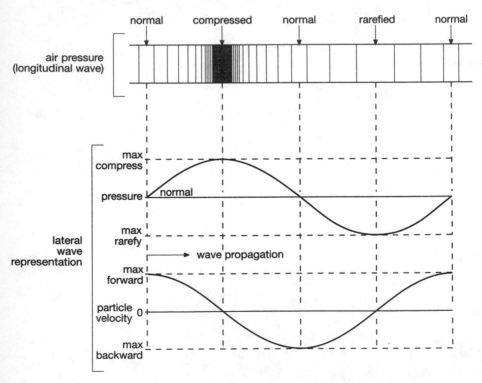

Fig. 122

All microphones have some sort of diaphragm arranged so that sound waves can move it in both directions from a rest position – either a thin membrane that itself bends, or a rigid plate flexibly suspended. A microphone whose diaphragm is open to the air on one side only responds mainly to pressure, which is a non-directional effect – a submarine is equally squeezed at all orientations in the water. This is illustrated in fig. 123a by a circular 'polar pattern', indicating an omnidirectional response. On the other hand, if a diaphragm is mounted with access to free air on both sides it responds mainly to the velocity of the wave, which does have a direction (from source to microphone).

The basic 'velocity' mic (sometimes called 'pressure gradient' because it detects the pressure difference at the two sides) responds equally (though oppositely) to sound arriving at either face, but hardly at all to

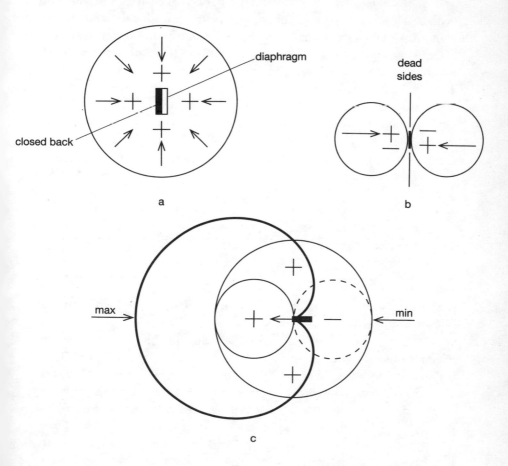

Fig. 123

input from the sides because the wavefront reaches both faces simultaneously, causing a net cancellation. The result is a figure-of-eight or bi-directional response (fig. 123b). The polar patterns shown are idealized and two-dimensional – real ones are not only more irregular, but three-dimensional and dependent on the **frequencies** in the wave.

The human ear is basically a pressure device. It has some directional properties of course, given by the shape of the ear's outer part (pinna) and the position of the head in relation to the sound source etc., but in general we hear a complete picture of all the sounds around us – direct, reflected, refracted, diffracted, diffused. The most 'natural' sound will be picked up by a pressure (omni) mic, therefore. A mic with a figure of eight response not only suppresses important side reflections, but the diaphragm's equal and opposite behaviour can lead to total **cancellation** at certain **wavelengths**. In studio recording, however, naturalness is not necessarily the aim (see **microphone placement**), and for music the most used mic of all has an even less realistic uni-directional response.

One way to achieve a response from one direction only is to combine pressure and velocity movements in one housing, and add the outputs. The 'back' face of the velocity mic is effectively subtracted from the omni output, and fig. 123c shows the heart-shaped ('cardioid') polar pattern that results if we assume that the maximum sensitivity of the two mics is the same. By changing the relative sensitivities different patterns are obtained. The distance between the mic and the curve represents the mic's response to incoming waves from different directions.

2. Magnetic transducers

Two types of magnetic transducer have been found suitable for high quality microphones, the ribbon and the moving coil.

Ribbon microphones

A thin strip (ribbon) of aluminium, corrugated to give lateral stiffness but longitudinal flexibility, and supported at both ends, is placed in a magnetic field. The ribbon is both diaphragm and conductor, and when it vibrates a very small current (see **electromagnet**) is induced in it by the magnet (fig. 124a). A simple, open ribbon with no acoustic treatment is a pure velocity mic with a figure-of-eight response. For many years these were the best studio mics available, and most of the old recordings now being re-issued on digital media owe their quality to them. Their frequency **response** is not particularly flat, and by today's standards both bass and high treble are deficient, but for earlier recordings and **AM**

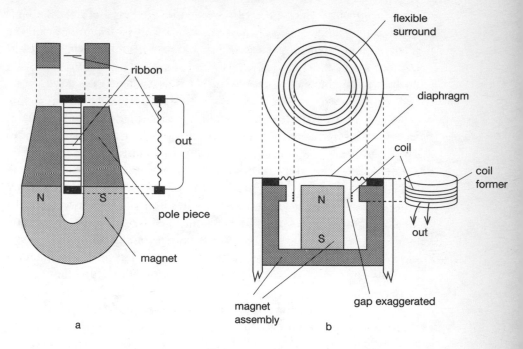

Fig. 124

broadcasting this was actually an advantage, and their performance in the main speech and music band is incisive and clear. There are various other types of ribbon movement, such as double ribbons, variable polar pattern ribbons (with an adjustable baffle blocking off all or part of the ribbon on one side), and miniature ribbons built into stick-type housings with acoustic treatments (see below) to give them a cardioid or omni response.

The traditional ribbon velocity mic is still a favourite with some engineers, but ribbons are fragile, output is low (therefore needing a high ratio step-up **transformer** to lift the signal to usable levels), and there is a pronounced bass emphasis when working close. As a general studio mic the ribbon has tended to fall out of favour as other designs have improved.

Moving coil (dynamic) microphones
As with the ribbon mic, the output of a moving coil mic is a current induced when a conductor moves in a magnetic field, but the diaphragm is separated from the conductor, which is a coil wound on a cylindrical former suspended in a magnetic gap (fig. 124b). Because the gap is

narrow compared with the necessarily wide one of the ribbon, the magnet can be much smaller, and although a transformer may still be used the whole assembly fits easily into a barrel of convenient size for hand-held work.

Early dynamic mics were chosen more for robustness than good performance, but nowadays the best ones, with diaphragms made of tough, bounce-back plastics instead of metal, better suspension and internal **damping** and **resonators** to smooth out response, are excellent music microphones, as well as retaining their rugged qualities. A stage mic, for example, is expected to handle huge sound levels at close range and survive repeated shocks and falls – dynamic mics designed for these conditions can still have more than adequate frequency response.

The basic moving coil is a pressure mic, just as the basic ribbon is velocity sensitive, and we saw (fig. 123c) how a combination of the two could produce the useful cardioid polar pattern. A single moving coil movement can be given a cardioid response, however, by suitable acoustic treatment.

Fig. 125a is a sketch of a diaphragm and body only of a mic with ports in its casing (shown towards the lower end of the barrel for clarity, but often part of the head assembly). These ports allow sound to enter behind the diaphragm. The + signs indicate compression maxima and the − signs rarefaction. The ports are so placed that sound arriving from the front has a longer path to travel to reach the rear of the diaphragm, and is further delayed by an acoustic resistance packed into a hole in the magnet. If this process can completely reverse the phase of the rear input, it will assist diaphragm motion (arrows) and improve response from the front. Sound arriving from behind has much the same distance to travel to the two sides, and is intended to be *in* phase at the diaphragm. The resulting self-cancelling effect will reduce response from behind.

Fig. 125b shows the idea in more practical form, but this is the 'phase shift' method of response control at its simplest. Ports at one position in the barrel only can work efficiently at certain frequencies only, and properly designed cardioid mics typically have multiple ports, complex acoustic labyrinths, resonant chambers etc. to extend the effect over a wide band of frequencies. Response can also be controlled electrically, for example, two back-to-back moving coil movements may be interconnected so that their mutual phases can be adjusted to give a variety of response patterns.

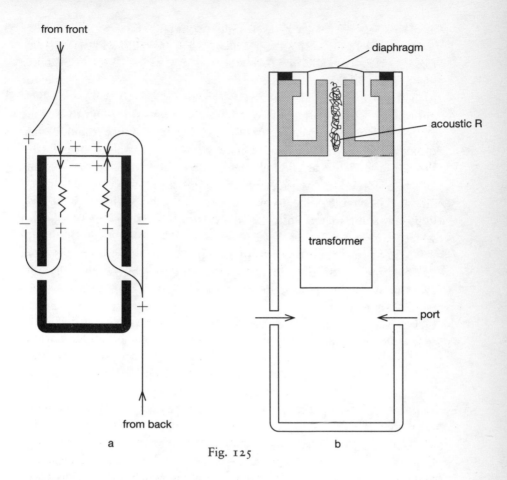

from front

diaphragm

acoustic R

+

+ +
− +

+   +

−   −

+

transformer

from back

port

a   b

Fig. 125

3. Non-magnetic transducers

The two main types are **piezo-electric** and **capacitor**. Crystal or ceramic piezo-electric elements, whose output is the current generated when a wafer of Rochelle salt or special ceramic is bent or twisted, are used for contact microphones (see section 4) and for some high frequency air mic applications, but are in general not high quality devices. Capacitors, on the other hand, are the basis of the very best music microphones. There are two main categories of capacitor-based mic, the 'condenser mic' which uses an external power source to charge its capacitor, and the **'electret'** mic which has a permanently charged capacitor.

Externally powered condenser mics

'Condenser' for capacitor is now an obsolete usage, but still current for mics using the principle (condenser microphones). A thin flexible diaphragm of metal or metallized plastic is fixed very close to but insulated from a much thicker rigid backplate, forming a capacitor whose value varies as the distance between diaphragm and plate fluctuates (see fig. 126a). Compared with the moving coil, which is fairly massive and whose **inductance** tends to oppose movement, the capacitor is light, responsive and sensitive. Because of the capacitor's very high **impedance (Z)** the output is derived in a different way from those of the magnetic types. One method uses the varying capacitance to **modulate** a radio frequency wave, but the commonest way is to charge (or **polarize**) the capacitor from an external **DC** source, and amplify the currents which result when the changing capacitance admits or expels small amounts of charge – like an open plastic bottle full of water: squeezing it pushes some out, releasing it makes room for the same amount of water to go in.

To the extent that it needs a power supply, the condenser mic is more troublesome to use than the self-powered types, but it has very low inherent **noise** (total noise depends on the quality of the mic's electronics), is magnet-free, and its thin diaphragm gives smooth response, high sensitivity and good **transient** performance. For digital recording, where **signal-to-noise ratios** of 90 dB or better are expected, the best

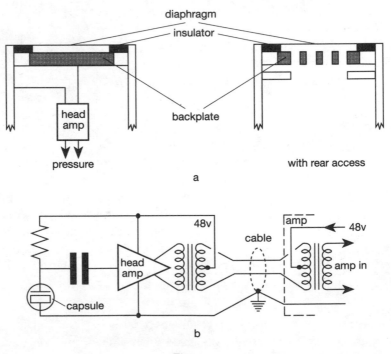

Fig. 126

condenser mics are almost always chosen for studio work. In multi-mic recordings a mix of dynamics and condensers will probably be used, and on stage a predominance of dynamic mics.

The high Z capacitive capsule output is first fed to a suitable amplifier (see **field effect transistor**) called the head amp in the body of the mic, creating a second need for a power supply. For some condenser mics special power units are necessary, but most use 'phantom' powering, an ingenious method of carrying power 'invisibly' on the same wires as the signal. Fig. 126b shows a popular phantom circuit. DC is supplied to centre taps on transformer windings at each end of the cable, so the power voltage appears equally on both sides of the balanced signal circuit and does not affect it. The DC is isolated from the signal path in the microphone, and power is supplied both to the amplifier and through a high value resistor (typically 20 million **ohms**) to the capsule. Most **mixers** include a switchable phantom power facility to simplify matters even further.

Another advantage of capacitive transducers is that they can be made very small and still produce a healthy output. Too large a diaphragm allows high frequency sounds (short wavelengths) to cancel themselves out because both peak and trough of the wave can be present at the same time. The ideal size is around that of the human ear drum (a little over 1 cm). The acoustic network required for a cardioid or other response can be similarly scaled down, and many condenser mics have removable capsules so that response can be altered merely by changing the capsule.

Similar acoustic treatments to those for moving coils can give the basic pressure capacitor other polar patterns, but response can also be controlled electrically by using two diaphragms, one on each side of the backplate, and varying the size and polarity of the charge. One assembly of this type can produce several patterns at the turn of a switch. A favourite studio microphone, the Neumann U87, has three patterns selected in this way.* Fig. 127 shows that the three responses are selected by cancelling or changing the polarity of one diaphragm, and some models have intermediate positions as well – an offset omni pattern and a 'cottage loaf' (an unbalanced figure-of-eight with one side more sensitive than the other).

Note the following points about polar patterns generally: 1. They are very frequency-dependent – at high frequencies the shapes should be

*Audio Export Georg Neumann GmbH, Badstrasse 14, Postfach 1180, D-7100 Heilbronn, Germany.

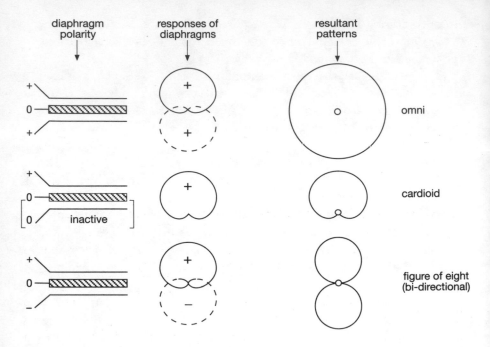

Fig. 127

imagined as more directional than shown; at low frequencies all microphones are virtually omni. 2. The two dimensional drawings in general relate to the behaviour of a mic mounted horizontally (i.e. with the diaphragm in a vertical plane) and show the response for the horizontal plane around it. True omnis should have a spherical response, but obstructions invariably change it to something else. Mics tilted on boom stands, for example, or pointed at the floor may have odd, asymmetrical characteristics. A full discussion is outside our scope here, but when choosing a mic always look at the manufacturer's claimed polar patterns and frequency responses.

Electret condenser mics

A phenomenon studied many years ago was reapplied with the advent of new synthetic materials, to produce capacitor mics that need no external power supply. Electrets are substances able to retain a permanent electrostatic charge in a similar way to permanent magnets. Used in mics, the electret is incorporated into the backplate, and the capacitor is self-polarized. Early electret mics were disappointing compared with the externally powered types, tending to lose their charge and become very noisy, particularly if dropped or roughly handled, but nowadays

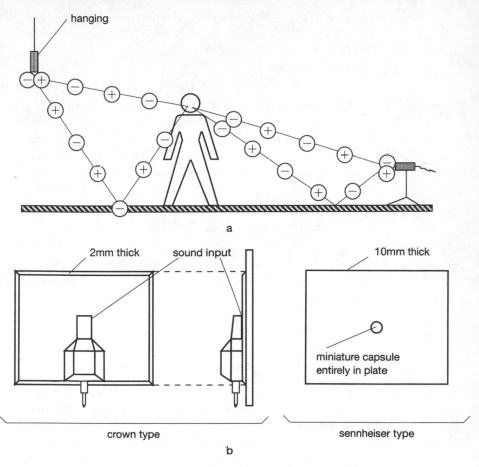

Fig. 128

many very good microphones are electrets. A head amplifier is still involved because the basic characteristics are the same as for standard condenser mics, but the low voltage power needed for this can be supplied by a small battery in the mic body as an alternative to phantom powering.

An important new approach in mics (from 1978) which uses an electret movement is the pressure zone microphone (PZM), commercially developed by Crown International.* PZMs operate on the principle that sounds at a point on an environmental boundary such as a floor or wall cannot be out of phase. Fig. 128a shows that with a normally positioned mic direct and reflected waves may cancel each other out at the micro-

---

*Crown International, 1718 W. Mishawaka Rd, Elkhart, Indiana 46517, USA.

phone. Whether this happens depends on the dimensions of the direct/ reflected paths and the **wavelength** of the sound; over the audio band the effect is a 'comb' response (see **filters**). This cannot happen at a point on the boundary itself, however, where all waves must be in phase and response can only be pressure, not velocity. The PZM (fig. 128b) is a small downward-facing electret mounted very close to a flat metal plate placed on a floor, wall or any plane surface. If the plane is large (such as an unbroken room wall) the mic has a smooth, wide frequency response and a hemispherical polar pattern. If the boundary size is reduced (say, by placing the mic on a table), the bass response falls off, but in applications like speech recording this may be desirable. Directivity can be given by placing the mic at corners where two or three boundaries meet, or blocking certain directions with absorbers. The PZM's enthusiasts claim advantages in almost any situation, but I think we shall need the complete range of existing kinds of mic for some time to come, as well as new varieties not yet invented.

4. Other types of mic, accessories etc.

The main mic types we have discussed appear in a variety of sizes and modified forms, and other transducer principles can also be used. The following is a selection of mics and accessories of interest in music and speech recording/broadcasting, taken alphabetically.

Carbon mics   depend on variations of current through loosely packed carbon granules. They are useful only for low quality speech, for example in telephones. Carbon throat mics (a type of contact mic, see below) worn on a neckband outside the larynx, can be used in very noisy conditions (e.g. aircraft), but are now rare.

Contact mics   should really be described as **pick-ups** rather than mics, since they are sensitive not to airborne sounds but the vibrations of solid bodies. Piezo-electric types, which vary greatly in quality and price, are useful for instrumental pick-up (they can be taped or Blu-tacked to soundboards, etc.), but are fragile, easily overloaded and sensitive to mechanical shock. A high quality device using a capacitor made as a flexible tape is the versatile 'C-ducer', available in various lengths and types, including one for single reed instruments (saxophone, clarinet). (The magnetic pick-ups used in **electric guitars** respond only to vibrating ferromagnetic objects (e.g. a steel string), not to mechanical movement within the pick-up itself.)

Dummy heads   are models of the human head, including a simulation

of the ear as far as the drum, in which omni mics are placed, approximat-
ing human aural conditions. With each 'ear's output fed separately to
headphones on the ears of a real human listener, the resemblance to a
natural **binaural** effect can be startling.

Gun mics are highly directional mics with many uses, such as picking
out single voices from an audience, recording dialogue from a distance
and 'spotting' particular effects on stages, sports grounds etc. They are
designed to cause deliberate phase cancelling, and consist of a long tube
with slots cut in it fixed to a cardioid (so already directional) mic. Sound
on the mic's axis passes directly up the tube, but even a few degrees off
axis the slots cause multiple delays, which increase to a maximum at
and beyond the right-angle position, so that most waves cancel out at
the plane of the diaphragm (see fig. 129). Gun mics have a very unnatural
response and are not always successful. To be effectively directional at
low frequencies a gun would have to be impracticably long (several feet).
This is not attempted in practice, so as frequency reduces the polar
pattern gradually approaches that of the mic without gun. Guns work
best in the open air, because the numerous reflected sounds in a room
are multi-directional and tend to negate the cancellation effect.

Hydrophones are waterproof mics (usually piezo-electric) that have

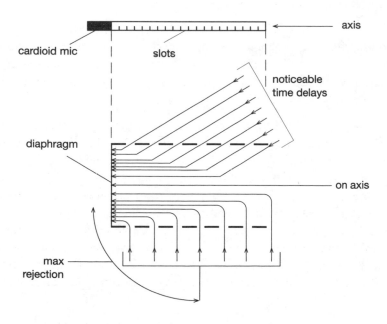

Fig. 129

diaphragms in direct contact with the water. Passable results, but not as good as from purpose-built hydrophones, can be got by wrapping an ordinary air mic in a very thin waterpoof bag (such as a condom), stretching the rubber tightly over the diaphragm end.

Lapel and lavalier mics   are small units on clips or neckbands designed to be unobtrusive and typically used by commentators, newsreaders etc. ('Lavalier' is from (Mme de) la Vallière, who wore pendant jewellery at the court of Louis XIV.) They are usually omni pattern because the source/mic orientation varies, and a bass cut filter is used to minimize clothing noise and the boomy effect of the chest cavity. Conversely, they have treble lift in the main speech high band to give good definition from the voice given the mic's bad pick-up position (almost at right angles to the ideal, and with the direct path obstructed by the speaker's chin). Mics clipped on to instruments can also be used effectively for music recording.

Noise cancelling mics   are designed for very close work, hand-held with the speaker's upper lip against a guard which holds the lips about a quarter of an inch from the mic's diaphragm. They have a phase-cancelling network to reduce noise from the rear, while the speaker's head almost covers the front. They are used for commentating in noisy conditions etc.

Parabolic reflectors   A technique for achieving highly directional recording using a mic mounted facing back into a parabolic bowl (see fig. 130). With the mic at the focus of the parabola, there is strong rejection of off-axis sound.

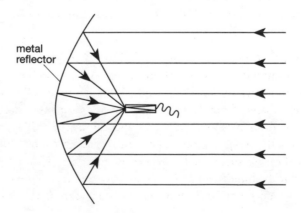

metal
reflector

Fig. 130

Reflectors must be large for directional bass response, but a 1 m diameter bowl gives good results from middle frequencies upwards. They are excellent for some **environmental recording**, especially for high sounds such as birdsong.

Radio mics (also called wireless mics)   These combine microphone and radio transmitter in one unit. The radio signal is picked up by a receiver at some distance, and communication is thus achieved without connecting cable. These are one-way, short range systems as opposed to two-way intercom, telephone and walky-talky applications, which require only speech intelligibility, but often have long ranges. This is a busy research area and the quality of radio mics has improved greatly in recent years. It is now standard for entertainers to have radio mics as an option and a typical fixed stage system has transmitters, mic amps and batteries all built into the mics themselves, and use a high radio frequency allowing hidden or short stub antennae, with careful suppression of local interference from stage lighting equipment etc. Some use several receivers with automatic selection of the best signal as performers move about. There are also 'no hands' radio mics for actors/commentators (i.e. miniature clip or lavalier mics with belt-pack transmitters) which can have longer wavelengths because antennae can be concealed in clothing. All radio mics have automatic **compression** to keep the system within acceptable distortion limits, because in stage conditions it is impossible to anticipate unexpected peak levels. A detailed study of this specialist area is outside our scope, but Ballou (1987) chapter 13 has a good survey, and it is not difficult to obtain manufacturer's data. Good radio mics are expensive, and local conditions are so variable that disappointment is frequent. Always demand a full demonstration in situ (with deliberate worst-case conditions) before buying.

Shock absorbers, stands, suspensions   The need for a mic to be protected from mechanical shocks, vibration etc. varies with its function and location, and mics intended for rugged use are internally cushioned to isolate the capsule from shock. External shock protection mounts include resilient links between the stand and the mic, flexible couplings in the stand itself, or space-consuming but efficient rubber band type mounts with the mic suspended within a circular or cylindrical frame. Mics designed to be hand-held need the minimum external shock mounting, and stands can be fitted with a quick-release clip to facilitate stand or hand use.

There are many designs and sizes of stand, from small table types through straight or cranked floor stands to the very large booms used in film and TV studios, mounted on moveable dollies with a platform for the operator, who can control boom angle and extension, as well as microphone tilt and orientation, from that position. The most adaptable stand for general studio use is the small boom, with vertical extension to about head height and maximum boom extension of about 1 m. A boom can be set up as a vertical stand when required, or just as readily hold mics over tables or inside instrumental groups. For orchestral/choral work, ceiling suspension isolates mics completely from floor vibration, and though two or three guy lines may be needed to position a cardioid correctly, most omni mics can hang by their own cables. There are also medium-sized booms with counterweighted or back-stayed arms and a reach of 2–3 m, which can be positioned around the periphery of an orchestra and reach in to cover particular sections.

Sound powered mics   A dynamic mic can be made to generate enough current to operate headphones without an amplifier, at some sacrifice to quality. Such mics are used in situations where communication must be maintained when power fails.

Stereo mics   **Stereo** recordings require a minimum of two mics, and the commonest arrangement is 'X–Y' miking (see **microphone placement**). To avoid cancellation effects the two diaphragms should be as close together ('coincident') as possible. There are various designs offering two mics in the same housing for convenient stereo recording, but the most satisfactory is a coincident pair mounted on the same vertical axis with provision for mutual angle adjustment. The best of these have selectable polar patterns (as described in section 3, fig. 127). Apart from reducing cancellation effects, another advantage of sound arriving at both mics in-phase is that the combined signal is mono-compatible (see **pick-ups** and again **stereo**).

Windshields and pop filters   Wind pushing against a diaphragm, apart from the obtrusive noise it makes, can seriously affect performance, and the internal screen built into most mics is often not enough. Windshields aim to break up and slow down moving air with minimum loss of sensitivity. The simplest and cheapest is a 'sock' of polyurethane foam pushed on to the head of the mic, which is reasonably effective in moderate conditions.

More elaborate windshields are made of fine weave mesh covering a wire or plastic frame, large enough to leave a space of quiet air all round the diaphragm. Such windshields for gun mics (often used by TV crews) are large 'sausages' around the mic, which is held in a pistol grip. Another hazard for microphones is close vocal work, when plosive consonants (especially 'p') cause powerful wavefronts that 'pop' the diaphragm and cause bad distortion. A flat, circular disc of two nylon membranes with light foam filling placed between voice and mic helps considerably. Special close-working mics like noise-cancelling types have built-in pop filters.

Microphone manufacturers are being remarkably successful in coping with the challenges of digital recording, and the demands of the rock music industry etc., but new types of transducer are continuously being researched and new models announced. Digital microphones are now appearing in which the analogue transducer output is converted to digital code in the microphone itself. A complete list of reliable makers would be impossible, but some names regarded as industry standards include: AKG, Beyer, Bruel & Kjaer, Calrec, Crown, Electro-Voice, Milab, Neumann, RCA, Schoeps, Sennheiser, Shure, Sony. Good mics will always be expensive, but the standard of the cheaper dynamics and electrets has improved greatly, and surprisingly good results can be obtained with units in the low price bracket provided their limitations are understood.

MIDI (Musical Instrument Digital Interface)   A microprocessor-based system of communication between music devices which enables hardware of different manufacture and design concept to exchange operational messages, not to be confused with the quite unrelated trade description of medium-sized hi-fi systems as 'midi'. MIDI carries control, not musical data, and its codes may be adapted to other purposes than music (e.g. lighting). All MIDI-equipped machines respond in the same way to MIDI data, though some can only recognize a small part of it. MIDI is not a two-way **bus** – a device cannot 'talk back' to the origin of the message on the same line.

The MIDI 1.0 specification of 1983 was orientated towards live performance instruments (particularly keyboards) using conventional musical formats, but its applications have since been greatly widened to include, for example, non-keyboard controls such as guitars and wind instruments, and non-real-time composition. Development is very active, and the following can only outline the salient features of a system whose details are under constant review. Complete specifications and current updates may be obtained from the International MIDI Association.*

*International MIDI Association, 5316 West 57th St., Los Angeles, California 90056, USA.

Hardware

A five-pin **DIN** plug and socket is standard for MIDI (only three pins
are actually used), and only one type of **lead** pluggable either way, of
which the length is not critical up to about 20 m. There are three types
of MIDI port: IN, OUT and THRU, with only two valid connections: OUT-
to-IN and THRU-to-IN. IN ports are not **earthed** but the signal is passed
through an **opto-isolator** to provide electrical isolation of each device.
This removes the possibility of earth-loop **hum** or other unwanted interaction with audio lines.

Fig. 131 shows the main connections of a typical MIDI-equipped
instrument. THRU passes on incoming MIDI data unchanged except for
the necessary **buffering**. OUT carries data from the local processor, and

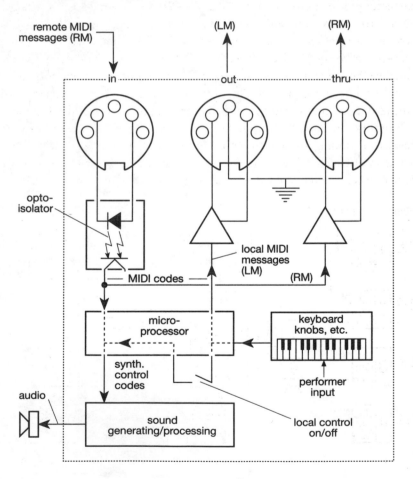

Fig. 131

the sound generator/processor may be influenced by local and MIDI input simultaneously. If local control is switched off (itself a MIDI command), the sound generator responds only to MIDI messages and the local manual input generates only OUT messages to remote devices.

Fig. 132a shows the 'daisy chain' method of connecting several music machines by one OUT (master or controlling synthesizer) and several THRUS. Machines 2, 3 and 4 may or may not have performers as well. Daisy-chains tend to become inefficient if more than three or four 'slaves' are attached because of data corruption in successive IN-to-THRU processes, but MIDI lines cannot be directly paralleled because data becomes unreadably confused. Switching boxes can select alternatives, or if two OUTS are required to feed one IN simultaneously, a 'MIDI merger' will correctly police and pass on the data. One OUT to several INS is managed by a 'THRU box', and the 'star' connection of fig. 132b, using such a box, is more efficient than the daisy-chain. Fig. 132c is a 'ring' using OUT–IN: each synthesizer receives MIDI messages from the previous machine and transmits its own to the next. Some machines provide a switched internal connection to allow input data to be merged with output data so that the output port is carrying both OUT and THRU data.

Building on such basic patches, elaborate 'tree' structures can be devised. If timing is involved, MIDI provides for this as well, clock data being interleaved with event data (see sequencers and fig. 176). Each device accepts what data it can respond to and ignores the rest, thus

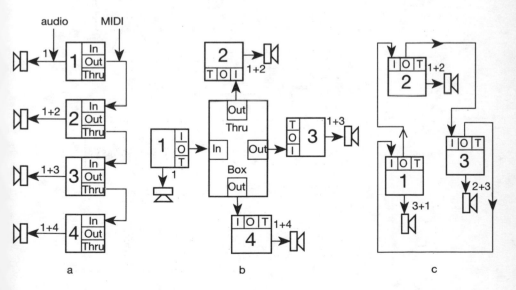

Fig. 132

clock data would be irrelevant to a receiver with no temporal function. The MIDI networks needed for a live performance, in a recording studio and by a composer will all be different, and many MIDI control and **patch** devices are now available. In selecting any MIDI device, study the MIDI implementation chart (which tells you which specific MIDI functions the device deals with) in the handbook. If none is given, beware. Fig. 133a shows a typical set-up for laying down tracks, each being played separately from the master synth into the sequencer, and all tracks played back together through an array of MIDI-linked instruments. For MIDI as a composing and performing tool, see **computer music composition techniques 4, live performance electronic music.**

Software
All MIDI messages are carried in one serial **bit** stream. Parallel processing (one or two **bytes** at a time) would be more efficient, but much more expensive and fault-prone, and the MIDI specification is deliberately aimed at ease of implementation at modest cost plus reliability in rugged

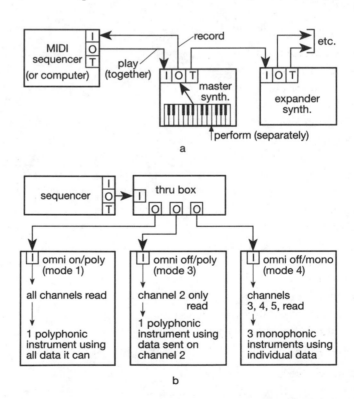

Fig. 133

performance conditions. The stream consists of eight bit bytes (plus start and stop bits), at a speed of 31,250 bits/second – an average three byte message takes about 1 millisecond to transfer. A leftmost (**high order**) bit of 1 indicates a status byte, which identifies what type of message will follow it. The message itself consists of data bytes (leftmost bit 0). Messages fall into the following categories:

Channel (voice and mode) messages
In the status byte the remaining seven bits are split into a word of three bits (0–7) indicating the action expected (e.g. note ON or OFF, control change, pitch wheel change) and a word of four bits (0–15) identifying one of the sixteen channels. In the case of a note ON, the following two data bytes give the note's pitch (0–127) and velocity (1–127). Note ON, velocity = 0 has the force of note OFF, and can be used instead of it. This makes possible a 'running status', which is very useful to save data when (as often happens) a long string of notes occurs with no variables except pitch and velocity (loudness). If note OFF can be given as a note ON command, no status byte is needed after the first, and the series is sent a third more efficiently as pairs of data bytes only. As soon as a new status byte arrives normal coding is resumed.

A synthesizer is set to a 'channel mode' which dictates how it will respond to these channel messages. The mode names often cause confusion. The default mode to which the device is in most cases automatically set when switched on is OMNI ON/POLY (mode 1) – the instrument responds on all sixteen channels **polyphonically**, using the same sound(s) for all voices. Mode 2 (OMNI ON/MONO) receives on all channels but assigns all data to one voice only. This mode is not much used, but causes a polyphonic instrument to behave like a **monophonic** one. Mode 3 (OMNI OFF/POLY) assigns data to selected channels only, but plays instruments polyphonically. This is a powerful mode, allowing different machines to select individual data by channel number – the instant orchestra. Mode 4 (OMNI OFF/MONO) is interpreted in different ways according to the capabilities of the instrument. Fig. 133b, which illustrates modes 1, 3 and 4, shows mode 4 as three mono instruments on different channels, but on many multi-timbral instruments it is given polyphonic possibilities along the lines of mode 3. (This is one area where the MIDI specification falls short of what the actual instruments can do.) For more details see books such as Casabona (1987).

System messages
These are for data without channel significance. The high end of the status byte is always 1111, and the lower four bits indicate the type of

command. 'System common', with features like song position pointer, is used with sequencers and controllers, to select pieces (or parts of them) for performance. 'System real time' is concerned with clocks (start, stop, continue) and with relative timing, which can be internally or externally controlled (see **sequencers**). For MIDI Time Code (MTC), which is an absolute timing system, see **time codes**.

So far all the commands we have looked at apply equally to any MIDI device, but there is also a 'private line' mode – 'system exclusive' – called by Gareth Loy (1985) the 'great escape hatch' of MIDI. This allows MIDI messages to be sent to machines of one make only. The status byte (11110000) is always followed by a manufacturer's ID code which tells each device whether or not to respond to what follows. Anything which doesn't fit conveniently elsewhere, such as patch commands unique to one instrument, can be put here. Unlike the other message types, system exclusive ends with a special 'off' status byte telling other equipment to stop ignoring the data. In each area of data assignation, undefined groups of numbers allow for future expansion.

MIDI's architects, a consortium of five manufacturers, were well aware of the limits of the specification, but may not have envisaged how soon those limits would be tested by MIDI's success and rapid expansion. The most criticized aspects of MIDI are: 1. Serial streaming prevents any group of musical events being truly simultaneous, and 'traffic jams' can happen if too much data is sent. 2. There is no two-way communication. This becomes serious with large set-ups like MIDI recording studios, because there is no way of checking centrally that all remote devices have successfully accepted commands until the musical result occurs, by which time it is too late. 3. It is not fully automatic. Although, once set up, a MIDI performance should run without problems, there is still a great deal of manual preparation needed at each station. Beyond the simplest levels, MIDI is demanding to use, and making mistakes is easy. In recent updates a number of informal procedures have been cleaned up and more consistency brought to different manufacturers' MIDI implementations. With an increasing number of sound **samplers** on the market, a MIDI sample dump protocol has been added to the range of options. A full discussion of the speed question is impossible here, but one important point is that MIDI's delay is often not as great as other delays in the system, for example it takes 5–7 ms for most synthesizers to process a keystroke into audible sound. The performance effect of MIDI itself depends on many factors, including the type of musical material.

There are many books and articles on MIDI. Apart from the International MIDI Association and Loy's excellent analysis quoted above, helpful guides are De Furia (1986), Baird (1986), Casabona (1987) and Boom (1987). Adams (1986) has a section on MIDI for beginning composers, and F. Richard Moore (1988) takes a critical look at timing and other problems.

Mid-lift   The boosting of levels in the central part of the **spectrum**, a facility offered by most parametric **equalizers**. See also **presence**.

Minifloppy   The middle size of **floppy disk** (5¼ in/133 mm), used in many micro-computers.

Mixdown   The process of reducing many tracks to two (for **stereo**) or one (for **mono**), by re-recording. May be done in more than one stage, by intermediate pre-mixing. See next entry.

Mixers and mixing desks   Signal summing devices for combining and controlling a number of audio inputs. In practical form a mixer may be anything from a simple **passive** network of **resistors** to very large panels with hundreds of controls and many features, including computer control. 'Mixer' implies a transportable, self-contained unit with a limited range of features. A 'mixing desk' or console, on the other hand, is the operations centre of a studio, containing additional facilities not directly connected with mixing. Reducing a few tracks to one, adding amplifiers where necessary and controlling input and output levels is not in itself a difficult operation, but if there are sixty tracks and sixteen outputs, and many ancillary functions as well, **noise, distortion, crosstalk, interference** etc. can become serious problems. It is the solving of these which partly accounts for the high cost of good mixers. Variations of design are too numerous to catalogue here, and the following is a selection of features and recent developments relevant to composing and recording work. For general background see **analogue synthesis techniques** 5. Other entries of relevance are **control room, decibel, lining up, MIDI, panpot, patch, peak programme meter, stereo,** and **volume unit.**

Ancillary equipment in mixing desks
Fig. 17 (in **analogue synthesis techniques**) shows the main functional routing of a typical small to medium mixing desk, described in the associated text. Among other features that can be expected, depending on price and intended use, are:

Compression, limiting Automatic **level** control of various kinds (see **compressor**) may be part of the internal facilities or accessed by insert points or auxiliary sends (intermediate outputs to route signals).

Foldback This is similar to auxiliary sends but has no corresponding return (see **foldback**).

Line-up tone Generated by an internal **oscillator** (with an ON/OFF switch and possibly a frequency selector) sending **sine** tone to all output **buses** for **lining up** purposes.

Phantom power A switchable **DC** supply to microphone input sockets (see **microphones**).

Pre-fade listen (PFL) The facility for sending any input direct to monitor speakers/headphones even with the **fader** closed, and bypassing all other desk functions. Important in broadcasting, for example, to check material on a channel before it is cued to air.

Quad controlling See **quad panners**.

Solo A similar facility to PFL, but one that does not bypass main functions, i.e. a soloed signal retains its current level and position in the stereo image. It is useful to isolate and fine tune **equalization** etc. on one input during a session. (Other channels are muted when one is soloed.)

Splits The capacity to divide desk functions in order to allow more than one simultaneous process.

Sub-groups Fig. 17 shows limited switching to master or 'group' faders, but on larger desks any input can be routed to any or all output groups. Sub-groups are an additional, intermediate stage, a group of inputs being first assembled to a sub-group fader, and sub-groups further routed to output channels.

Talkback and cue A local microphone activated by a button on the mixing desk, used to communicate with the performers in the studio and other locations (such as the studio manager or tape recorder room). 'Slates' (i.e. music number, take number) can be announced on studio mics via talkback. To avoid **howl round**, the button also operates a muting **relay** to disable monitor speakers in the control room while the talkback is active.

Mixer control
Most mixers are built in modular units so that extra channels etc. can

be added, and internal architecture optimized for the intended tasks. With the increasing use of sixteen and twenty-four track tape machines, consoles have expanded to meet the need for more inputs, outputs and modes, and some time ago exceeded the modest limits of one human being with two hands, a narrow field of good vision and a fairly slow reaction time. The traditional answers to this are either to use more operators (problem: who is in control?), or to mix by stages, pre-mixing a group of signals then mixing the pre-mixes (problem: once a pre-mix is made, its internal levels are fixed in a way that might not suit the next mixing stage; also, every recording generation means an increase in tape noise). The way to keep the flexibility of many separate channels as far along the process as possible, and allow an operator to keep track of the mass of data involved, is partly or fully to automate the mixing operation.

Automated mixer control

There are two main types of function to consider: switched and continu- ously variable. The hundreds of two- and multi-way switches in a large mixer must be set correctly, but most are pre-set for a given take or session, and the complexity and expense of operating them automatically is not usually attempted (but see **patch**). Instead, a computer takes a 'snapshot' of the current state of everything, and this set-up is memorized until needed again. On recall, indications on the desk itself or on a computer screen show which switches need resetting, and when they have been correctly readjusted. This method can be used for variable controls also, by showing the position to which a knob or slider must be moved (for example, a **LED** which glows to show when the correct position is reached).

The most important continuous controls are channel and group faders, and the essence of good automation is to allow the operator to retain full manual control but supply any level of automatic back-up on demand. In a recording session the mixer's actions are time-linked with those of the tape recorder(s), and the whole operation is subject to a master timing source, originating from the mixer's computer or received from, for example, a videotape. This **time code** is laid down on the tape as a primary operation, and all future changes are related to it. In a typical session the first pass is manually controlled but all fader changes noted and stored. On replay the previously manual actions are repeated auto- matically but can be overridden and modified, and the new version written to a new file (the old settings are always retained until deliber- ately erased).

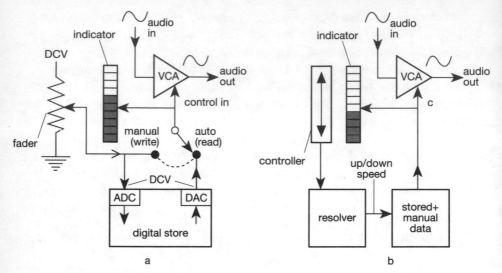

Fig. 134

Practical design approaches are numerous, and to give an idea of the choice of consoles, the May 1988 issue of *Studio Sound*,* in a survey, listed ninety-two professional consoles from thirty-eight manufacturers, most of which have partial or complete automation facilities. Many desks are built to special order, and with today's computer resources almost any combination of features can be provided.

For any of these systems to work, faders must be responsive to either manual or automatic control. Two control methods for faders are dominant, the most popular being to make signal control indirect by using the faders to control voltage controlled **amplifiers** (VCA) or digitally controlled **attenuators** (a form of **digital-to-analogue converter**) instead of the signal itself. Fig. 134a shows a semi-automatic arrangement in which a manual input is stored, but no manual interference is possible on playback – the slider is disabled. Current level status is indicated by meters or **LED** bar graphs reading the VCA's **DC** supply.

In fig. 134b the manual control is 'endless', i.e. with no position-defining knob. Alternatives include a belt on rollers, a touch-strip or a rotating ball (as in the computer **mouse**). In such cases the manual input is permanently in the read/write loop and the VCA is controlled by a combination of stored and manual data.

*Studio Sound (and Broadcast Engineering), Link House, Dingwall Avenue, Croydon CR9 2TA, UK.

The other popular control method is the motor-driven fader, introduced in the late 1970s by Neve* as part of a pioneering automated
system. By physically moving the knobs, these faders give a direct (and
decorative) indication of channel status. Neve's 'Necam' system has been
refined over the years, and is the basis of their present Necam 96 (up
to ninety-six channels). Motorized faders are also used by some other
makers, and work on the principle that they read data and operate
automatically unless manually moved, in which case the new data is
received and stored. Computerized mixing systems with very comprehensive facilities, and using VCA fader control, are made by Solid State
Logic.†

Digital mixing
Handling multiple signals in the digital domain presents complex problems, among them the need for ultra-fast computing, but even by the
early 1980s it was shown to be feasible by such ambitious projects as
that developed for Lucasfilm in California (Moorer, 1982, and Snell,
1982). Some aspects of mixers (e.g. microphone pre-amplifiers) are likely
to be analogue for a long time, but in today's digital recording environment there is strong pressure to produce cost-effective digital mixing
systems, and all-digital processors are now available which offer conversion from one digital format to another, as well as mixing, etc. Because
digital manipulation involves storage in any case, full automation is
much easier than with analogue mixers, and recent tendencies are
towards 'software' mixers, which in theory have unlimited capacity
because they are not bounded by physical construction to certain techniques and features. A 'soft' fader is typically a picture on a screen
whose 'knob' is moved by a mouse or **light pen**.

Though many amplifiers now accept direct digital inputs (from **compact disc** or **digital audio tape** players for example), most signal handling
and mixing will continue to be analogue for some time to come, and a
compromise is the digital mixer with analogue inputs and outputs, such
as the Yamaha DMP7.‡ This unit accepts analogue inputs, but immediately converts them and carries out all processing digitally. As well as
normal mixing (eight into two) and equalizing, there are built in **digital
multi-effect units**, full **MIDI** control, motorized manual/automatic
faders, and the ability to cascade (digitally) several units for up to thirty-

*Neve Electronics International Ltd, Cambridge House, Melbourn, Royston, Herts SG8
6AU, UK.
†Solid State Logic, Begbroke, Oxford OX5 1RU, UK. Manufacturers of mixing consoles.
‡Yamaha, Nippon Gakki Co. Ltd, Hamamatsu, Japan.

two channels. Conversion is linear 16 bit at 44.1 kHz (standard for CD), and the desk will run automatically from a MIDI **sequencer**. Its main problem is rather high **noise** levels, but this is being improved, and the makers also offer an all-digital model for use with digital recording systems.

The era of enormous consoles with large **jack** fields and tangled **patch-cords** is rapidly passing. Using small computers, time codes and/or MIDI sequencers, the tendency is to automate patching completely, remove most hardware from the console to racks, and present the operator with a small, human-sized **work station** containing perhaps six or eight sliders, twenty or so knobs and some buttons and switches, plus a typewriter keyboard, mouse and display. The status of the whole system or any part of it can be displayed on demand, and the local controls assigned only to those parameters that call for immediate real-time control. The most stable of the older designs are likely to be the smaller types, which are already convenient to use, and because they are usually employed for one purpose only (such as microphone mixing, disco playback, public address) do not benefit much from automatic control. For a fuller study of the technical aspects of mixers, see Dove (Ballou, 1987, chapter 22), Runstein and Huber (1989, chapter 9), which has illustrations of the Neve system mentioned, and Watkinson (1988), who analyses the arithmetical problems of digital mixing.

Mnemonics   (memory aids). These have been used in music from at least the time of Guido d'Arezzo (b. 990?), who adapted the first syllables of an eighth-century hymn by Diaconus: UT (queant laxis) RE-(sonare fibris) MI-(ra gestorum), FA- (etc.), SOL-, LA-. Sung to a certain tune (possibly written by Guido) these syllables fall on a rising **hexachord**, and have become a way of representing the tone/semitone pattern of the Western major scale that is still used today. Guido also used the finger joints ('Guidonian hand') to teach the correct use of hexachords in practical music. Mnemonics are widely used in music software to clarify computer procedures, choosing terms familiar to musicians and therefore easy to remember.

Möbius loop (strip)   A flat strip twisted once (180°) and joined. (fig. 135). It has the strange property of being an object having only one surface and one edge. The implications of this were first investigated by A. F. Möbius (1790–1868). A Möbius tape loop rolls over completely in two passes, playing both sides and swapping tracks each time the join crosses the head (see **tape composition techniques**). See also the dis-

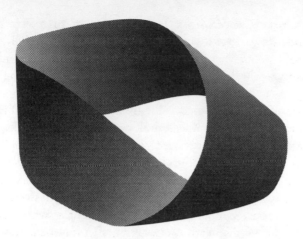

Fig. 135

cussion of strange loops in Hofstadter (1980), and the ingenious Möbius strip drawings by M. C. Escher reproduced in the book.

Mode 1. A type of scale formation. A modal system uses the same note series (e.g. the white keyboard notes) but starts on different degrees for different modes (e.g. Dorian starts from D, Aeolian from A). 2. The configuration of a device for a certain task, e.g. record mode (tape recorder), **mixdown** mode (**mixing desk**). 3. Patterns of vibration exhibited by a string, a pipe or a flat radiator like a drumhead. Thus the third **harmonic** is a higher mode than the **fundamental**.

Modulat/e, -ion(s) 1. In tonal music, a process of changing key by intermediate steps, rather than simply 'going there'. 2. In audio, 'mods' is used loosely and unqualified as synonymous with 'recorded signal', particularly when this is visible (on disc or film). For meanings when qualified, see **amplitude modulation, cross-modulation, frequency modulation, phase modulation, ring modulation, spatial modulation**.

Module A separable unit of hardware or software, possibly viable alone but designed to fit with others to make a system. Modular construction is common where one type of unit is used repeatedly, for example in the electronics of multi-channel **mixers** and **tape recorders**. Modular software is separable in terms of clearly defined tasks such as instrument definitions, formal time structure etc.

Monaural   Hearing with one ear only. The term refers to a human characteristic and is not to be confused with **monophonic**.

Monitor/ing   Checking a signal for optimum quality, and the equipment for doing this. **Volume unit meters** etc. are types of monitoring device, but in audio the sound is the most important factor. **Amplifiers, loudspeakers** and/or **headphones** should if possible be the best available without compromise, though 'best', of course, depends greatly on individual preference. Room acoustics, listening levels etc. are also important and, ideally, the person monitoring should be aware of, and make allowances for, any personal deficiencies in hearing. On occasions very high sound quality is not the aim, for example, when dubbing a TV programme the sound being monitored will eventually be heard on a small speaker, and this condition can be mimicked in the studio. Monitoring is independent of the main signal path, and switchable to any part of it. Fig. 136 shows a typical recording chain and the points where monitoring might take place. During the **take** itself listening should always be 'off-tape' to pick up **drop-outs** and system faults at the end of the process. Visual monitoring of sound (by means of **Lissajous figures** on an **oscilloscope** for example) can also be useful. See also **loudspeakers, mixers and mixing desks.**

Mono/-, phon/y, -ic (mono)   1. An audio signal with all the information on one channel, which remains mono even if sent to many speakers and/or **panned** from one to another. Compare **binaural, monaural** and **stereo**. 2. Of instruments, capable of playing only one note at a time.

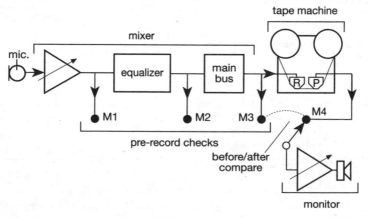

Fig. 136

Monostable Of a switching circuit having two states only one of which is stable, i.e. when 'flipped' into state 2 it automatically returns to state 1, typically after a programmed time delay. See **flip-flop**.

Montag/e, -ing A term borrowed from multi-image, slow dissolve techniques used in film (the audio equivalent of a dissolve is a crossfade). It usually refers to mixtures of disparate sounds rather than the normal layering of musical textures (in a sense any music not a solo is a montage). Effects mixing began with radio drama and talking pictures, but it was not until **musique concrète**, when composers explored other types of sound manipulation, that montages began to have some creative direction and coherence. Sound mixtures have a lower level of 'confusion tolerance' than visual ones, and apart from having a creative reason for making a montage, simple guidelines are: 1. Keep each individual track fairly spare, avoiding thick, smudgy sounds. 2. Choose tracks in different spectral bands to ensure clarity when mixed. 3. Make one track the rhythmic 'master' and either avoid strong rhythms on the others or ensure that their interaction is meaningful. Fig. 137 shows a typical cue sheet for a short four-track montage. See also **tape composition techniques**.

MOS (Metal-Oxide Semiconductor) The operating principle of many **capacitors, integrated circuits** etc. MOSFETs (MOS **Field-Effect Transistors**) are widely used as power **amplifiers** and switching devices. See **patch**.

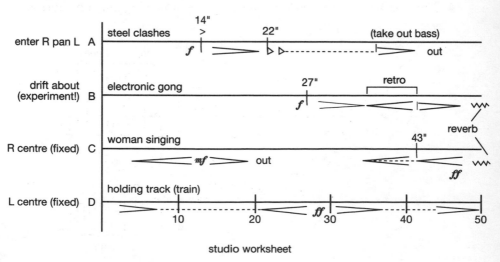

studio worksheet

Fig. 137

Mother   One of the steps in the production process in vinyl disc manufacture. See **sound recording techniques.**

Mouse   A computer input device with freely rolling ball and one or more buttons, usually linked to a visual cursor (arrow, blinking character etc.) on the computer monitor's screen. Alternatives are track balls, paddles, joysticks, arrow keys.

Moving coil   The operating principle of most **loudspeakers** (see figs. 113 and 117) and meters, many **microphones** (fig. 124) and some **pick-ups.**

Multimeter   A testing/measuring device with internal switching arrangements enabling several different electrical properties to be measured. Typically **ohms, DC volts,** DC **amps, AC** volts and **decibels** are catered for, with several ranges for each. Ohms (**resistance**) ranges are powered by an internal battery. An ideal voltmeter has infinite resistance (R), while an ideal ammeter has zero R, but neither of these criteria is met in practice, though modern digital types (with **LCD** or **LED** numeric displays) come much nearer than the traditional moving coil meter. Some types select range automatically, and most have fuses or cut-outs for overload protection. As with any equipment, you get what you pay for, but some sort of multimeter is essential equipment in even the smallest studio.

Multiplexing   A way of carrying many signals on a single transmission channel (e.g. wire, radio, optical fibre) so that they retain their identity. Coding may be by frequency or time division. Long distance telephone services (see **vocoder**), stereo radio, **video cassette PCM** are examples of multiplexed systems.

Multi-track tape recorders   See **sound recording techniques** and **tape recorder design**

Multi-turn pot   See **helical pot**

Multivibrator   See **oscillators**

Music   In Greek 'the muse's art', because the purest and most abstract. Music communicates directly – it doesn't have to tell stories about anything or look like anything. Definitions in the standard dictionaries do not seem adequate, and it is noteworthy that Grove and other standard musical lexicons do not have an entry for music at all – presumably because they assume that anyone using such books already knows what it is.

Most primary definitions in the standard dictionaries say something like: 'the art of combining sounds (tones) in (coherent) melody, harmony, rhythm and colour (timbre), so as to produce compositions (structures) which elicit an emotional response in the listener; the study of the laws and principles involved in this art'. The Oxford English Dictionary adds 'with a view to beauty of form', which has all sorts of difficult implications, since even if we can agree on what beauty is, it is clear that any art form makes use of deliberate harshness as well as beauty, for example, the oxymoron effect of certain cadential devices. And if there are 'laws and principles' involved, are they at all related to the 'rules' of Western harmony?

When electronic music was a new experience to most people, a frequent comment was: 'You've got some interesting sounds there, but of course it's not music.' If music can only be an arrangement of pitches in melodies, harmonies and rhythms, they were right, but plenty of undoubted music has no tune (e.g. drums), and much has no clear beat or harmonic structure (e.g. plainsong). It seems that a wider definition is needed.

To be 'music' rather than chance sounds, a sonic event must be the result of a conscious human decision, but the sound itself and the composing process can take a wide variety of forms. We should certainly not judge the composition process by the skills or effort involved. Someone vocally moulding a tune to the acoustics of a bathroom (mainly by choosing a pitch and tempo) is, in a proper sense, creating music. And while improvisation is certainly not the same process as the control of the complex set of variables involved in a fully-worked score, a good improvisation may be much better music than a dull 'composed' piece. Birdsong may be beautiful, but is not music unless a deliberate decision is made about it – even the simple act of choosing a passage. People will listen to long tracks of recorded steam trains with as much attention as to a symphony, and they are without doubt enjoying a musical experience. If the train is not recorded, and the hearer is lying in a field listening to a real train go by, the listener is the composer – choosing which train, where to lie, how long to listen, and thus creating a personal emotional experience.

In *The Tuning of the World*, R. Murray Schafer quotes John Cage as saying 'Music is sounds, sounds around us whether we're in or out of concert halls' (Schafer, 1977). In the same paragraph Schafer says, '. . . I am going to treat the world as a macrocosmic musical composition.'

In any definition we have to notice one class of organized sounds as special, and that is speech. An actor speaking Shakespeare affects our emotions in two quite different ways – through Shakespeare's words and his interpretation of them, and also through the beauty (or strength, harshness, etc.) of the sound of his voice. The possible value of this sound as music is assessable quite separately from the verbal message. In **musique concrète**, for example, it is often wise to remove the semantic content (by garbling it or by using an outlandish language which nobody can understand) if you want your audience to pay attention to the sound for its own sake. Otherwise they'll be worrying about what it means.

Taking the foregoing points into consideration, this writer offers a definition of music as 'the art of ordering sounds so as to convey an emotional experience by non-verbal means'. This does not exclude a verbal meaning as well, but indicates that the musical symbolism is separate from the verbal. 'Convey' implies a listener, and no description of artistic activity can be complete without a suggestion of communication.

Musical instruments, types of In 1914 Erich M. von Hornbostel and Curt Sachs published a classification of world musical instruments (von Hornbostel, 1914), and although others have been proposed (see under 'classification' in Sadie, 1984), the Hornbostel and Sachs listing by generator type has remained the most effective. Their approach was ethno-musicological, and included a large variety of local and primitive instruments which are outside the scope of this book – for example they distinguished four main kinds each of idiophone and membranophone, whereas I give only two.

The following is not meant to be a rigorous classification, but the listing shows the great variety of sound producing methods used in the various families of Western instruments, and includes a group of electric and electronic ones. The class of idiophones ('self-sounding', in which generator and resonator are not separate) includes instruments (e.g. vibraphone) whose principle is idiophonic but which may have added resonators, etc. Only one or two examples of each sub-class are given, and an overall view such as this cannot include every possible variety of mechanism and power source.

A Idiophones

1. Pitched
a   metal
    single pitch (crotale, gong)
    multi-pitch (glockenspiel, musical box)
b   wood/plastics
    single pitch (temple block, log drum)
    multi-pitch (xylophone)

2. Unpitched
a   metal (cymbal, wind chimes)
b   wood/plastics (castanets, woodblock)
c   miscellaneous (maracas, rattle)

B Membranophones

1. Pitched (timpani)

2. Unpitched (snare drum)

C Chordophones

1. Bowed (violin)

2. Plucked
a   non-keyboard (guitar, harp)
b   keyboard (harpsichord)

3. Hammered
a   non-keyboard (dulcimer, cimbalom)
b   keyboard (piano, clavichord)

D Aerophones

1. Mouth-blown
a   open hole (flute, panpipe)
b   whistle or fipple (recorder, swannee whistle)
c   single reed
    cylindrical bore (clarinet)
    conical bore (saxophone)
d   double reed (oboe, bassoon)
e   lip 'reed' (cup or cone mouthpieces) – metal tube
    cylindrical bore (trombone)
    conical bore (tuba)

f   lip reed – wooden tube (cornetto, serpent)
g   metal reed (harmonica)
h   perforated disc (siren)

2. *Reservoir-blown*
a   non-keyboard (bagpipe)
b   keyboard
    pipe (organ)
    metal reed (accordion, harmonium)

E Electric/electronic

1. *Amplified acoustic*
a   non-keyboard (electric guitar)
b   keyboard (electric piano)

2. *Electronic*
a   non- (or optional) keyboard (Ondes Martenot, Theremin)
b   keyboard (electronic organ, synthesizer)

3. *Not directly sound-producing*
a   non-keyboard (computer music software)
b   keyboard (MIDI controller)

See also **bowed strings, brass instruments, organs, pianos, woodwind instruments**, and the numerous entries referring to electronic instruments. An excellent book on percussion is James Blades's *Percussion Instruments and Their History* (Blades, 1984).

Musique concrète   As opposed to ordinary or 'abstract' music, this term, coined by Pierre Schaeffer in 1948, describes music made '. . . not on the basis of preconceived sound abstractions, but from concretely existing sonic fragments, . . . considered as defined and complete sound objects, even, indeed above all, when they don't conform to basic definitions of musical grammar' (from *A La Recherche d'une Musique Concrète*, a book in diary form in which Schaeffer describes his pioneering work) (Schaeffer, 1952).

Experiments in modifying recordings of ordinary sounds to make meaningful compositions were going on in a number of places in the late 1940s (including by this writer in London, see Introduction and **disc manipulation techniques**), but Schaeffer was the first to develop his thoughts into a coherent theory and persuade an organization (French National Radio – then RTF) to provide a rudimentary research facility.

At first called the Studio d'Essai, it became the Club d'Essai ('experimental club'), and later the **Groupe de Recherches Musicales** (GRM). It remains one of the most influential studios in Europe, and, with **IRCAM**, one of two Paris studios of world significance.

This book is concerned with technologies rather than personal histories, and good accounts of the early concrete concerts, broadcasts etc. can be found in Russcol (1972), Ernst (1977), Manning (1987) and elsewhere including the studio's own records, but Schaeffer is important, apart from his own writings, for inspiring a number of other composers to experiment in the new medium. His passionate belief in the 'objet sonore' as compositional material extended to fierce rejection of the electronic instruments then available and being advocated in some quarters – for example the **Ondes Martenot**. 'I am suspicious of the new instruments ... what the Germans pompously call "Elektronische Musik" ... I seek direct contact with the sonic material, without electrons in between.'

The German reference is to experimental work which soon afterwards resulted in the foundation by Herbert Eimert of a new studio in Cologne (see **electronic music**). Later in the 1950s, Eimert attacked Schaeffer's position when the first recordings of Cologne's electronic music productions were issued: 'These creations have nothing to do with experiments, neither are they produced by cutting or montage procedures, or similar tricks' (Eimert, 1957).

The concrete approach was to take intrinsically interesting real sounds and present them in a new sonic context, just as pop visual artists of the time surprised by changing the scale or colour of something familiar. Musique concrète selected, altered and re-arranged already complex sounds, and some primitive but effective manipulation techniques were developed by the Club d'Essai, see **phonogène**. Electronic music took the simplest sounds (**sine waves**) and built them up stage by stage, arguing that unlike empirical concrete techniques, the method gave the complete control necessary for the total **serialism** then sought by many composers. Within a few years the distinction between microphone- and electronically-sourced sounds was acknowledged but no longer regarded as something to quarrel about, and composers often used both freely in the same piece.

Although electronically generated sound has come far, concrete sources have never lost their popularity, and are flourishing now in the new digital **sampling** environment. A paper on a recent computer-realized piece (*Leviathan*) by its composer, Bill Schottstaedt, reads almost like Schaeffer forty years on: '... synthesized sounds are ugly, they lack life; they cause fatigue, they suggest nothing. What is it about a real sound that gives it its richness? . . . even after years of experimentation, most real sounds remain a mystery' (Schottstaedt, 1988). It is the mystery that attracts – in this case Schottstaedt's main source sound was the 'groaning and creaking of a mast on a sailing ship', which on being dissected with the minuteness nowadays possible, yielded a whole world of detailed complexity.

Concrete composition easily becomes an undisciplined affair because there is often too much material to choose from. The first necessity is to be aware of the character of sounds and look for ones that are compositionally helpful. I have found it useful to divide sounds into **envelope** types and **spectrum** types as follows:

Envelope types

A Constant continuous e.g. mains **hum**
B **Periodically** changing continuous e.g. helicopter
C **Aperiodically** changing continuous e.g. traffic
D Regular discontinuous (repeated identical or nearly identical events) e.g. footsteps
E Irregular discontinuous (repeated non-identical or single unique events) e.g. door slam

Spectrum types

1 Mainly on a single **harmonic series**
2 Mainly multiple-series but tone-based
3 Mainly **noise**-based
4 Complex (1 + 3 or 2 + 3).

Some examples:

A1 whistle; A2 electric motor, A3 slipstream of travelling car (from inside); A4 jet plane in flight (from inside)

B1 police car; B2 air raid siren; B3 pebbles in revolving drum; B4 car engine idling

C1 child crying; C2 cloud of insects; C3 surf on beach; C4 cocktail party

D1 squeaky wheel; D2 bell tolling; D3 clock tick; D4 compressed air hammer

E1 scream; E2 breaking glass; E3 thunder; E4 gunshots with ricochets.

The planning of a piece entails considering not only what type of sound to look for, but the degree of control open to the composer in collecting it. Voices and instruments may also be part of the plan. Consider these levels of composer direction:

Random found sounds

No composer influence is possible with these sounds except a sensible choice of venue – you might go to a shop, a park, a railway station because you expect certain sounds there. I have collected interesting night sounds by simply leaving a sound-actuated machine switched on in a garden.

Selected found sounds

Derived either by editing random found sounds or by encouraging sounds to happen in the right environment, for example, in busy traffic, making sure that a car door is slammed, or that the tape includes a close-up of a bus drawing away.

Unscored prepared sounds

In this case the recording is specially set up, but the actual performance is ad lib. For example, you might want metallic percussive sounds in a reverberant room, so you arrange the room and an assortment of objects, but leave open details of what to use and how to play.

Scored prepared sounds

The most controlled type of recording, this includes sounds like an object being struck using a written rhythm part, vocal fragments rehearsed beforehand but sung in a special way and a special place, or fully scored instrumental segments, which might be used unchanged or treated.

The finished product may, of course, consist only partly of concrete material. Voices were used very early because they helped to bridge the gap between the known and the strange, and added emotional warmth to what many people found a rather mechanical and dehumanized form of expression. Vocal or instrumental parts may be ingredients in a tape-only piece, or live parts to be sung/played with the tape. Today, using stored samples, real-sound performances need not involve tape at all (see **live performance electronic music** and **samplers**).

Fig. 138 shows an imaginary working plan using the four recording categories above plus the further type, treated sound. Sometimes a sound exists in many different stages of transformation all of which must be retained for later inclusion. In the original concrete realizations few treatments were available, and most of them were mechanical

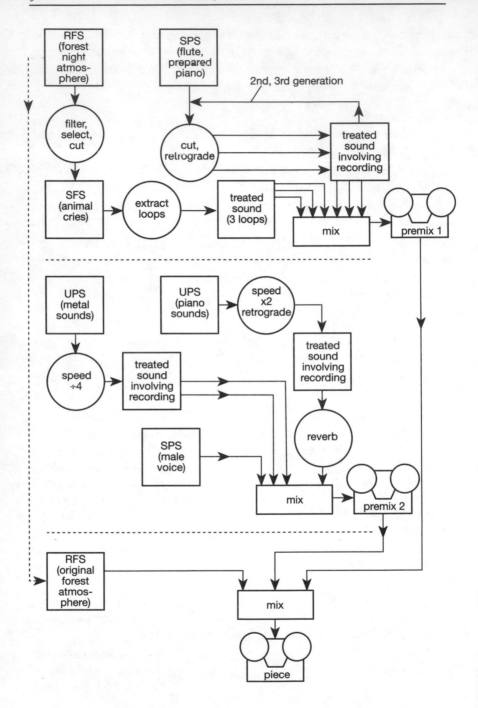

Fig. 138

(deliberately so in Paris). Today, of course, numerous electronic treatments can be applied – a microphone-recorded signal has exactly the same possibilities as an electronic one.

Tape treatments such as retrograding, cutting and looping are discussed in **tape composition techniques,** and electronic treatments in **analogue synthesis techniques, digital synthesis techniques, compressors, equalizers, filters** and **reverberation.**

One historical aspect of looping should be mentioned here. The first loops were made on disc, by disabling the tracking mechanism and cutting a complete circle (not easy to do without clicks). Schaeffer examined the philosophy of the 'closed groove' ('sillon fermé') carefully, with its implications (like a short film loop) of 'freezing time'. Tape loops are much more flexible as to length and speed than closed grooves, and the technique has been much over-used, but some striking loop-based pieces have appeared, among them Steve Reich's *Come Out* (1966). Tape loops are an example (but not the only one) of electronics influencing instrumental practices. The hypnotic effect of an exactly repeated sound (or one subjected to a slow change by running several loops of slightly different lengths) has been applied instrumentally by Reich himself and others such as Terry Riley and Philip Glass. A notable loop artist in a more popular genre is Robert Fripp.

Speed-changing, another basic technique of early concrete music, also opened a door to the 'timbral continuum', first seriously explored by Stockhausen. In conventional music we are used to thinking of 'events' which last for seconds or minutes as different in character from 'notes', whose internal timing is measured in milliseconds. But by progressively changing speed this gap can be bridged – one gradually becomes the other. A 4 sec loop containing a group of different sounds can be thought of either as an event lasting 4 secs or a complex sound with a (sub-audio) **fundamental** frequency of .25 Hz. If we speed up the loop 256 times (the method of the 1950s was to double speed and re-record eight times) its frequency becomes 64 Hz (well into the audible range) and the original constituents have (at eight octaves higher) changed character profoundly – indeed some of the higher sounds in the original will have disappeared out of the audible range. Later on this kind of transformation was more easily done with **sequencers,** and more recently with computers. This is an example of how musique concrète experiments led to interesting developments not directly connected with concrete composition. In this case the transformation of the original sound removes all 'reality' from it. In true (Schaefferian) concrete music the character of the original sounds is always recognizable.

Choosing anything from the extensive repertoire is bound to be unfair, but a classic merger was the co-coperation of Schaeffer and Pierre Henry to produce *Symphonie pour un Homme Seul*, premiered in 1950. Some of the most outstanding pieces in the genre were not produced in Paris, for example Edgard Varèse's *Poème Électronique* (Eindhoven, Holland, 1958). Luciano Berio's vocal piece *Thema – Omaggio a Joyce* (Milan, 1958) is still fresh and original thirty years on. It is entirely composed of transformations of Cathy Berberian's speaking voice. Another noteworthy concrete composition was Hugh LeCaine's *Dripsody* (Ottawa, Canada, 1955) which was made exclusively of water drip sounds. To supplement this inadequate list, reference to the *International Electronic Music Catalog*, compiled in 1967 by Hugh Davies (another important real-sound composer) will show the remarkable volume of studio activity and composition going on by that time (Davies, 1967).

Today many composers use real sounds, either in their original form or transformed in some way, because they can have a subtlety and complexity which, as Schottstaedt observed, is absent from most synthesized sounds – indeed in many cases has so far eluded analysis (see **computer music composition techniques** 4). For readers wishing to research the original musique concrète movement, Schaeffer's large *Traité des Objets Musicaux* is a detailed exposition of his theories (Schaeffer, 1966), and three very interesting discs were published (1967) to supplement this study.*

As microphones and recording techniques improve, and **samplers** get cheaper and more powerful, the future use of real sound as composing raw material is likely to increase rather than diminish.

---

*Schaeffer, Pierre *Trois Microsillons d'exemples sonores (Guy Reibeil/Beatriz Ferreyra) illustrant le Traité des Objets Musicaux* Groupe de Recherches Musicales de l'ORTF, Editions du Seuil, Paris, 1967.

N

NAB (NARTB) The National Association of (Radio and Television) Broadcasters. The short version is more common. It is a standardization body, and NAB **equalization** curves for recording/playback, for example, are used in the USA and Japan. See **CCIR** and **sound recording techniques**.

Nano- A billionth of (10^{-9}). Most commonly as 'nanosecond' – a useful unit for very rapid operations, e.g. in computers, radars. See **SI units**.

Negative feedback See **feedback**

Neon An inert gas which glows red when ionized, i.e. when electric current flows in it. Apart from its ubiquitous appearance in illuminated signs etc., miniature neon lights are useful indicators in equipment, though they are now largely replaced by **LEDs**. See also **oscillators**.

Nesting In a computer program, the use of one complete routine (often a recursive **loop**) within another. Frequently used in music programming, nests can be set up like sets of Russian dolls, one inside the other many times over.

Network/ing 1. An arrangement of components linked together in some way. Fig. 139 shows a group of different networks. See also **lattice**, and fig. 107. 2. A complex of radio/TV/computer stations with unified operational control.

Nibble Half a **byte**, i.e. four **bits**. See **time codes** (MIDI time code).

Node (Latin 'nodus' = knot) In a **standing wave** system, a point of minimum or zero activity. A point of maximum amplitude is an **anti-node**. See also **bowed strings**, **brass instruments** (fig. 26) and **woodwind instruments**.

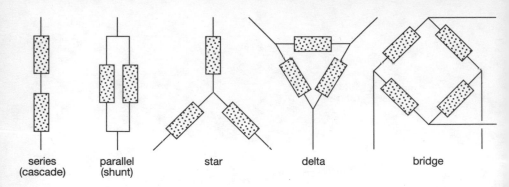

series   parallel   star   delta   bridge
(cascade)   (shunt)

Fig. 139

Noise 1. Any unwanted interference with a desired programme. In this sense even a pitched tone may be noise, see **background noise**. 2. A sound which contains so many unrelated components that the ear fails to recognize any **periodicity**. Many percussion instruments, the consonants in speech, and the majority of natural sounds are noise rather than tone sources, and **noise generators** are essential equipment for electronic music.

Noise has a 'distributed' **spectrum**, i.e. there is some energy in all (or a very wide spread of) frequencies in the audible range, as opposed to a 'discrete' spectrum, with energy at specific frequencies only, which is exhibited by a pitched tone. 'White' noise is defined as having equal energy content per unit band of frequencies on a **linear** scale (see **analogue synthesis techniques** 4). In the continuum between a simple **sine** tone and the complex white noise, the point where noise begins is impossible to place accurately, because it varies with both person and source. If we take white noise and gradually narrow the **bandwidth** by **filtering**, it at first becomes 'coloured' and then goes through a series of 'noisy tone' states before reaching (if a sharp enough filter is available) a clear tone. Whistling wind is a good example of noisy tone.

For a more detailed discussion, and a definition of 'pink' noise, see **analogue synthesis techniques** 4. See also **random number generators**.

Noise-cancelling microphone   See **microphones**

Noise gate   A circuit which cuts off or substantially reduces signals which fall below a pre-determined level. This effectively suppresses quieter (but obtrusive) sounds and leaves the higher-level wanted components in a signal.

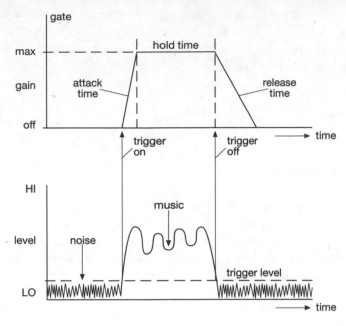

Fig. 140

Fig. 140 shows the principle. A typical noise gate has, as well as an adjustable **trigger** level, provision for varying attack, hold and release times. Hold time may be signal-controlled, release beginning as soon as the signal falls below trigger level, or time-controlled, i.e. on for a preset time even if the signal is not continuous. Triggering may also be independent of the signal, for example it could be **MIDI**-transmitted from one instrument to another whose output is wanted for a certain part of a piece. Noise gates are sometimes included as a feature of **compressor**/limiters, but work the opposite way – i.e. they are expanders (see **noise reduction**).

Gating speech produces unnatural silences between words, but in noisy conditions it may improve intelligibility. In music, gates work most reliably with instruments having clear, percussive attacks such as guitars or drums. If the noise itself is varying in amplitude and the musical attack slow and gentle, triggering is likely to be haphazard and the result unpredictable. Gates can be used effectively to reduce system noise and the possibility of **howl round** when many microphones are in use for, say, conferences, by closing channels completely and automatically when a given microphone is not being used. See also **schmitt trigger**.

Noise generators The converse of tone generators (see **oscillators**), noise generators are designed to produce a distributed **spectrum** containing all frequencies. Generating literally all frequencies (zero to infinity) would require infinite power, so a practical noise source is 'band limited' to the range of musical interest (slightly greater than the audible band itself).

Random thermal activity is inherent in every electronic device, and usually this is a nuisance that designers try very hard to minimize. A typical noise generator is based on a transistor circuit configured for maximum noisiness, and its output amplified to a suitable level. See **analogue synthesis techniques** 4 and **noise**.

In digital **synthesizers** noise generators as such are not usually provided, but 'coloured' noise outputs can be obtained by combining together a group of **inharmonically** related low tones with rich spectra. Such additively produced noise is shaped to the desired colour by adjusting the frequencies of the oscillators and the relative amplitudes of their **harmonics**, a different process from the subtractive one of filtering white noise. In computer music the basis of a noise source is a **random number generator**.

Noise reduction Designing audio equipment is a constant battle against unwanted noise. In electronic circuitry most of the problems have now been reduced to insignificance, but a continuing bugbear in analogue recording remains the noise introduced by the medium itself. Noise reduction (NR) is also used in disc and optical recording, but this entry is concerned with tape. Studio machines with relatively high speeds and wide tape tracks do not generate as much noise as low speed, narrow track formats like cassette, but much higher quality is demanded in professional than domestic formats, and the problem is exacerbated by the several generations of tape involved in the production process, each adding another layer of noise. Tape noise does not arise in digital media (though they have noise problems of other kinds) because the signal and the noise are expressed in different terms (see **sound recording techniques** 3), but once an analogue signal is mixed with noise the playback circuitry has no way of distinguishing the desired from the unwanted. The best design approach, therefore, is to process the signal before the stage at which noise is added to it.

Tape noise is not a problem when the music is loud, because it is effectively **masked** by the programme signal. Fig. 141a shows the dynamic contour of some recorded music, with louder parts well clear of the tape 'noise floor', but with quiet passages severely contaminated.

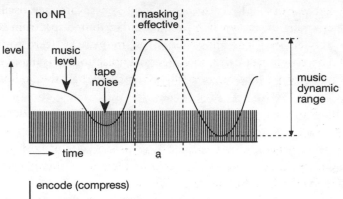

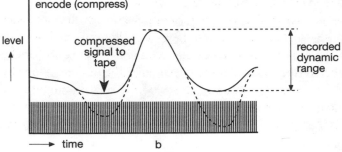

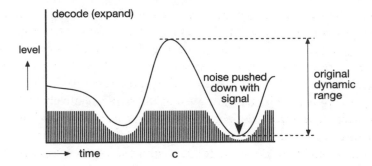

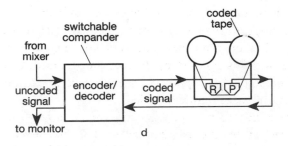

Fig. 141

The principle of NR is to lift low level signals before recording (fig. 141b), so that the tape carries music with compressed dynamics. On playback (fig. 141c), an opposite and complementary process restores the original dynamics and, in reducing the gain on quiet passages to do this, reduces tape noise with it. Fig. 141d shows how the **compressor/ expander** ('compander') is connected. Because a single compander can only be in one mode at a time, two are needed (four for stereo) if continuous **monitoring** is required, and companding has the further advantage of increasing the musical **dynamic range** that can be recorded.

There are a number of systems, but the first and still biggest name in NR is R. M. Dolby,* whose 'Double-D' trademark appears on millions of domestic and professional recording machines throughout the world. Noise disturbance is a function of **frequency** (noise in the same **band** as the music is less obtrusive than that outside, while high pitched noise is generally worse than low), and programme material varies in sensitivity to noise. So in his 'A' system, brought out in the late 1960s, Dolby divided the **spectrum** into four regions, each with its own encoder/ decoder. High level programme signals (which do not need processing) are left untouched. Dolby A quickly became the industry standard, but it was unsuitable for home use because, apart from being expensive, it needed regular **lining up** to work properly. It was soon joined by the simpler Dolby B, which operates only on higher frequencies (where noise is most troublesome) and was designed for the mass-duplication market. Dolby B became standard equipment in all but the cheapest cassette machines.

The recently introduced Dolby Spectral Recording (SR) system has taken professional noise reduction further still. In brief, the system constantly examines the spectrum of the incoming signal and dynamically adjusts 'sliding band' circuits to optimize noise reduction at each instant. Dolby SR is claimed to give noise figures for analogue recordings comparable to sixteen bit digital recording (see again **sound recording techniques**). Just as Dolby B offered some of the features of A, a new nofrills system, Dolby C, now widely used commercially, shows a marked improvement on B, varying the gain of a sliding upper frequency band – i.e. with some of SR's features.

Another popular system is dbx, which is an all-frequency compander giving 2:1 compression on to tape and 1:2 complementary expansion

*Dolby Signal Processing and Noise Reduction Systems, 346 Clapham Rd, London SW9 9AP, UK.

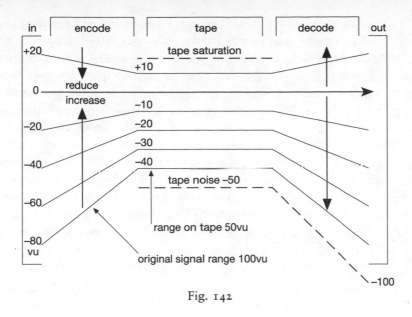

Fig. 142

on playback. Fig. 142 shows the dbx operational sequence. Lining up is minimal, because provided that the o VU (see **volume unit**) level is correctly transmitted without change, the other levels are automatically correct.

Without NR the performance of the smaller multi-track machines – e.g. eight tracks on ¼ in tape – would be unacceptably noisy, so Dolby C or dbx is a built-in feature (see **tape track configurations**). Many cassette decks have a choice of two or three types of NR.

All NR systems are likely to colour the signal to some extent, if only because complementary companding circuits are never perfect, however carefully set up, and splitting and reassembling a complex spectrum is a surgical operation that can leave scars. Some problems are similar to those mentioned in **compressors** – the 'pumping' of dynamics and 'breathing' as noise levels rise and fall. Sub-audio inputs such as air-conditioning can upset some NR systems, and if coded tapes are played back in different studios, bad lining up at either end can result in faulty decoding. Coded tape can be directly copied (**duped**) without any processing, but for **monitoring, mixing** or any signal treatment decoding is essential. In normal recording operations this is not a problem, but in traditional **tape composition**, with many re-recordings, cuts, loops etc., using NR throughout can make working very cumbersome, and it may be practicable only at certain stages, such as recording the original material and the final master.

Compander NR deals specifically with tape noise. Any other noises, acoustic or electric in origin, which find their way on to the tape with the programme signal, remain there on decoding. Another approach is single-ended NR, which operates only on the signal coming off the tape to remove as much as possible of any noise it finds, of whatever origin. With the improved tape and recording machines now available, some studios record without compander NR, often at the high speed of 76 cm/s (30 inches per second), which itself improves noise performance. This school of thought argues that the remaining noise content is a small price to pay for the naturalness of a clean, unprocessed signal. Single-ended NR – in effect the expander half only – is an option in these cases as a general signal improver. The principle is similar to that of **noise gates**, reducing the signal (and the noise) when it falls below a set threshold, and suppressing noise in spectral areas where no signal is present.

Detailed literature is published by manufacturers such as Dolby, and descriptions of different systems can be found in Wells (1981) chapter 8, Runstein (1989) chapter 10 and Ballou (1987) chapter 23. See also **cassette recorders** and **decibel**.

Normalling   Of a **jack** field or patchbay, the process of permanently wiring some sockets to make a pre-set 'normal' **patch** when no plugs are inserted (see fig. 152). Plugging in to a normalled socket breaks the normal and allows whatever is plugged to enter the circuit. See **analogue synthesis techniques** 3.

Notch filter   See **filters**

NTSC   The National Television Standards Committee, responsible for setting US TV and video standards. The NTSC colour TV system was developed in the 1950s and is still current, though now an ageing standard. See **EBU**, **PAL**, **SECAM** and **video cassette PCM**.

Nyquist frequency   The highest **frequency** that can be digitally enco-ded without ambiguity at a given **sampling rate** (SR). It is, in theory, equal to half that rate (SR/2), or conversely the SR must be at least twice the Nyquist frequency. In practice, because of **filtering** and other problems, an SR well above the theoretical minimum for the intended frequency limit is desirable. See **alias** and **digital synthesis techniques** 1.

O

Octal   The number system based on 8, and using only the figures 0–7. A shorthand method of notating **binary code** which is easy to memorize because only numbers up to 7 (binary 111) need be learned. To convert it a binary number is divided into groups of 3 digits from the **low order** end, for example, 11│100│010│111│101 becomes 34275 in octal. See also **hexadecimal.**

Octave   1. The interval between two notes in the **frequency** ratio 2:1. Called 'octave' because diatonic and modal scales divide the distance between any two such notes into eight (inclusive) steps of five **tones** and two semitones. 2. Two notes an octave apart sounded together. 3. By extension, any measuring scale arranged in increments of 2:1 (e.g. 3 **decibels** = 1 octave of level). See also **decade** and **logarithm.**

Odd harmonic   See **harmonic series** and **partial**

Ohm   An SI unit of **resistance, reactance** and **impedance.** Symbol Ω. See also **conductance, Ohm's law** and **SI units.**

Ohmmeter   See **multimeter**

Ohm's law   Georg Simon Ohm (1787–1854) showed that the **resistance** (R) of a metallic conductor is effectively constant whatever the current flowing through it, provided that its temperature stays constant. Electrical **current** (I) flows in conductors because of a **voltage** (V) applied to them, and for a given V the flow of I is inversely proportional to the value of R. Thus $I = V/R$ (Ohm's law).

Fig. 143 illustrates the above three quantities in a **DC** circuit (current flow in one direction only). Note that the circuit must be completed by a path through the source of the voltage (or **potential** difference). The formula given above expresses I in terms of R and V, but can be rewritten as $R = V/I$ or $V = IR$. Ohm's law underlies all electrical theory

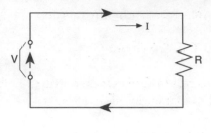

Fig. 143

and is its most important single rule. In practice R (SI unit the **ohm**) is almost always not one but a number of elements in **series, parallel** or complex **networks**, but the total can be regarded as a single lumped R.

The **SI units** for voltage and current, the **volt** and the **ampère**, together with the ohm, permit calculation without the use of constants, i.e. one volt will send one amp through a load of one ohm. In **AC** circuits Ohm's law cannot be applied simply because frequency-dependent **reactances**, together with resistance, must all be evaluated to arrive at a total circuit **impedance** (Z) which varies with the frequency of the AC. See also **capacitance, inductance, root-mean-square, power** and **watt**.

Omnidirectional   See **microphones**

Ondes Martenot   A **monophonic** electronic instrument with a tone generator similar to that of the **Theremin** but played from a keyboard and/or a continuous controller for producing glissando and **vibrato** effects. Brought out by Maurice Martenot in 1928, and at first called 'ondes musicales', it was one of the most successful and long lasting of the early electronic instruments. It is still in regular use today, particularly for performing certain works by Olivier Messiaen. See **analogue synthesis techniques** 1, **oscillators** and **Trautonium**.

One-shot oscillators   1. Devices like **envelope shapers** and **monostable** flip-flops, which execute one cycle only in response to a **trigger** (though in many cases they are designed to be capable of 'free-running' as well). 2. Also used of **resonating** circuits designed to be 'rung' by a short burst of energy, the oscillations being left to **decay** naturally after that. The length of the 'ring' depends on the amount of **damping**, but basically this is a single cycle effect. A circuit used in this way is not strictly an oscillator because no continuing energy is supplied to maintain the output. See also **oscillators** 2 and **percussion generators**.

Open air acoustic   See **acoustic treatments**

Open circuit (O/C)   See **circuit**

Open reel   Also 'reel-to-reel'. Of tape that is handled directly by the user, as opposed to that enclosed in a cassette.

Operating systems   Software to control the internal operations of a computer, the essential link between the user's instructions and their efficient execution by the machine. Operating systems include programs for handling input and output, data management, multitask scheduling, organizing jobs, translating etc., and generally supervising the smooth running of the machine. Normally hidden from the user, operating systems occupy large amounts of reserved space in the internal memory. A system popular with computer musicians is UNIX, written in the programming language 'C' (see **computer languages**), and developed by Bell Laboratories, who have been active in music research and composition for many years. See **computer music composition techniques.**

Operational amplifier   See **amplifiers**

Optical fibre   See **fibre optics**

Optical discs   Record/play systems using **laser** technology. See **compact disc, CD–ROM** and **WORM.**

Opto-isolator   A device which transfers an electrical signal without a direct electrical connection. In the usual type a **light emitting diode** illuminates a photo-conductive transistor, which passes a current proportional to the light falling on it. An important musical application is in **MIDI** systems, where its use at each IN port ensures that each device is electrically isolated from the others.

Order   1. In filters, for example, the number of times the operation is performed (thus in a 'second-order' filter the signal is passing through two separate filtering circuits). 2. In numbers, the 'weight' or significance (**high order, low order**) indicated by their position. 3. 'Order of magnitude' implies difference by a factor of ten. See **decade.**

Organs   *electronic* The history of electronic organs goes back to the turn of the century and Cahill's 'telharmonium' (see **analogue synthesis**

techniques 1), but this entry is restricted to a brief description of recent developments in the field. A good general and historical survey is Hugh Davies's article on electronic instruments in Sadie (1984). For technical descriptions of analogue circuitry used until fairly recently, see Douglas (1976). For some electronic instruments not classed as organs, see **Ondes Martenot, oscillators, Solovox, Theremin** and **Trautonium**.

Many of the features of today's electronic organs are shared with **keyboard synthesizers**, but there are important differences because they are aimed at different markets. 'Synth' users expect to be able to construct any type of sound from first principles, and although 'factory' voices are always supplied, it must be possible to rewrite them. Organs have a large number of 'stops' – different tone colours or 'voices' that can be mixed into a variety of ensembles, but offer limited or no facilities for changing voice parameters. Synthesizers are typically 'restricted **polyphonic**' – up to a limit of, say, eight or sixteen simultaneous voices. Organs are 'all notes together' polyphonic, so a separate tone must be generated or derived by division from a master oscillator, for each note. A synthesizer is normally a unit in a **patch** – outboard amplifiers and speakers are necessary to produce sounds. Most electronic organs, on the other hand, contain everything necessary for performance, though outboard equipment can also be attached.

Electronic organ users divide roughly into those looking for an adequate alternative on which to play the concert and church organ repertoire, and those who want a versatile entertainment machine. Church and other skilled organists seek an instrument with the same general 'feel' and console layout as a pipe organ – stops, full pedal board, combinations, several manuals, swell and tremulant etc., but do not expect either the tactile or the acoustic quality of the pneumatic instrument (see **organs** *pipe*). The electronic organ is an independent, different instrument with valid arguments for its existence, including convenience of installation and relatively low cost. A number of hybrids and compromises also exist, such as electronic sections added to pipe organs to provide, for example, very low notes (where large pipes would be too expensive or space-consuming), or an extra range of solo voices not available on pipes at all.

Electronic organs intended for light entertainment may not offer everything the skilled player wants – for example pedal boards are typically monophonic and have a range of one octave only. However, all but the simplest have automatic features that make it easy to play in a variety of popular styles and produce a full, 'orchestrated' sound without too much training and keyboard dexterity. Accordion-like push-button chord basses appeared many years ago, and automatic 'walking' basses and rhythm sections were added in the 1960s (at the same time as the first synthesizer 'explosion'). By the late 1970s digital generators had been established, and with microprocessor control memory facilities were added as well.

Today's electronic organs are digital, and either use waveform synthesis (see **digital synthesis techniques**) to model organ sounds, or stored, digitally recorded **samples** of real pipe sounds, sometimes recorded at different pitches and levels, and selected for replay according to the dynamic being used. The general console layout is still recognizably traditional, however, and some digital organs retain features that go back many years, such as drawbars for selecting harmonic mixtures, familiar from the early days of the **Hammond** organ, and Leslie (rotating) **loudspeakers**.

The question of whether an electronic instrument produces a good imitation of its acoustic counterpart does not always arise with organs, because some stops are meant to resemble their pipe equivalents – a pipe organ 'flute' or 'trumpet' stop does not sound like those instruments in any case. There is already a long tradition of organs for different purposes – church, theatre, jazz organ etc. – each having different types of stop. The modern instrument aims to supply groups of appropriate sounds with pre-programmed ease, plus newer 'synthesizer' voices that are intended to sound like the acoustic instrument named (such as harpsichord, guitar, string bass pizz, accordion). Many electronic organs now have **MIDI** facilities, allowing external sound sources (such as an electric piano) to be played from the organ as well (see **pianos** *electric*).

Complete specifications of the large range available cannot be listed here, but the following are some of the features one might expect to find on a modern electronic organ:

Keyboards   At least two polyphonic manuals and possibly a monophonic 'solo' manual as well, plus a pedal board of one or two octaves, also probably monophonic. There may also be velocity and 'after-touch' sensing, i.e. a response to the speed of depression (usually converted to loudness) and to the pressure used to hold the key down.

Instruments   As mentioned, traditional organ stops (including variable mixtures) plus synthesizer-type 'real' sounds and a selection of specials – 'space' noises, effects etc. These can be poly- or monophonic as appropriate – **chorused** sounds such as strings or brass choir, and keyboards (e.g. celesta) are obviously polyphonic, while solo voices needing note-by-note articulation (such as a solo trombone) are monophonic. 'Detuning' (i.e. slight pitch deviations) for increased chorus effect, controllable **vibrato** and **reverberation** etc. may also be options.

Rhythm **Percussion generators** are standard, and vary from simple 'play along' drum rhythms to highly complex, programmable units comparable to stand-alone drum machines.

Memory Internal memories and/or **RAM** cartridges for storing registrations (i.e. selections of organ stops in pre-set patterns) and often the possibility of recording complete multi-layered sequences. An example might be: pass 1 – record 'orchestral' backing, percussion and all support material, pass 2 – (live or also recorded) melodic solo parts needing more 'expression' input. **Floppy disk** drives may also be built in or available as extras. For serious recitalists, portable memories allow complete programme registrations to be instantly set on any organ of the same type, a great asset when touring.

MIDI Ports (IN, OUT and THRU) for MIDI interfacing are now virtually standard, and larger machines have full interfacing with any other MIDI equipment including computers, so any appropriate music software, composer and performer programs etc. can be used with the organ.

User aids Comprehensive visual displays like **LED**s on buttons, LED volume setting indicators and LCD multi-message panels are now expected features. There may also be pre-set combinations allowing one-touch re-patching of the whole instrument, automatic chording and orchestration, arpeggiation, bass rhythms etc.

Speakers and microphones Electronic organs are designed to be complete, and include wide-range speaker systems, but they can also be line-connected to further speakers, **mixers** etc. Outputs are at least stereo, sometimes multi-channel. An output for headphones may be provided for private practice, while microphone inputs allow live voice to be added to the general mix.

Electronic organs are in the main designed for a traditional, mature-age market with a fairly conventional musical outlook. Younger customers, and those exploring rock, jazz and contemporary concert music are more likely to look for synthesizers, which are unashamedly high-tech. The preference in organs is for layouts, names of instruments, controls and procedures etc. to be chosen for immediate recognition by the traditional organist, who will then be tempted to try some of the newer features. As a salesman in a large music store said to me: 'Mention the word computer and some of our best prospects fly out of the door.'

Organs *pipe* The organ fraternity worldwide is perhaps the largest club in music, and forms a special enclave with its own body of musical literature, books and periodicals. The history of pipe organs goes back to at least the third century BC (Csetibius of Alexandria), and the gradual development of the instrument is well documented in many books. (See Rowntree, 1975, Barnes, 1959, and Sumner, 1973 for a small sample.)

The approach to pipe organ design is quite different from that of the electronic instrument, not only in the principles of their operation but because a full-scale pipe organ is a major investment which both buyer and maker expect to last a long time. Most builders, when designing and constructing pipes, airways, moving parts etc., think in terms of 100 years of reliable service. Consequently a very wide spread of technologies

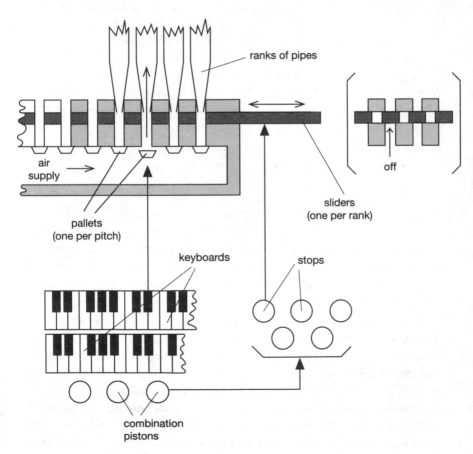

Fig. 144

needs to be in working order and daily use at any given moment. This entry aims only to single out a few recent developments in a field that has always been notable for complex and ingenious engineering.

Fig. 144 shows three essential control paths in an organ. There are others not shown, such as the swell pedal, which operates shutters or doors enclosing the swell organ, and couplers, by which keyboards can be linked together.

The word 'stop' is applied both to a given rank (or 'register') of pipes and to its console controller (usually a cylindrical plunger). The control path from stop to slider activates a rank of pipes when the organist draws (pulls) the stop associated with it. The mechanism shown is a long strip with as many holes as pipes in the rank, which lines up with two identically drilled stationary boards to open the airways to the whole rank. A given pipe will not 'speak', however, till a second control path joins a key to a pallet which lifts off its seating to admit air to the path opened by the slider. One pallet may operate the same note in several ranks, but naturally only those with sliders set to the open position will respond.

There are sliderless systems in which each pipe is treated individually, but the principle of selecting the stop and the key separately still applies. Originally both control paths were fully mechanical, but for many years now alternatives for both have included mechanical/pneumatic, electric/pneumatic and fully electric. A common arrangement is a fully electric performing console combined with electro-pneumatic slider and pallet mechanisms, using **solenoids**, switches etc. working with small bellows (motors) powered by the organ's wind supply. A fully electric console gives a great advantage in flexibility because, being joined only by wires to the organ, it can be sited anywhere, moved about and/or duplicated, but there is also a strong lobby for traditional 'tracker' or all-mechanical key mechanisms.

Almost as important as these is the third path shown – combination pistons to stops. This allows the organist to pre-set stop combinations before playing and change registration (i.e. whole groups of stops) by means of a single hand or foot switch. In all but the shortest pieces several changes of registration are likely, and even with the facility of combinations an assistant is sometimes needed. Without it the extra person is indispensable.

For multiple stop control to be possible, the rows of stops on the console had to be automated, and this was first done electrically many years ago by adding two solenoids (one for each direction). In older instruments with mechanical linkage between stops and sliders the stops had to move as much as 10 cm, and bulky, long-travel solenoids of considerable power were required. Pushing a combination piston causes groups of stops to change position and operate all the linkages exactly as if it were being done manually. In modern organs the stops are simply switches, but are still usually implemented as moving plungers giving the same visual indication (though travelling a much shorter distance). If the break from tradition is tolerable, the same job can be done more simply with rocker or tab switches, possibly backed up by indicator lights.

The main recent change in the stop and combination department is the elimination of mechanical solenoids, switches etc. at the console end, and their replacement by microprocessor controlled electronic switching. Once this is done, provision of a memory is a relatively easy step, allowing settings for complete programmes to be stored and retrieved as required. Registration memory is invaluable for multi-user organs because each player can have favourite combinations up and running without delay. A typical organ specification today lists memory levels or channels as part of the built-in features, for example, a recent organ built by Walker for the Royal Scottish Academy of Music and Drama, Glasgow,* lists the following accessories: 6 pistons to great, 6 pistons to swell, 6 pistons to pedal, 6 general pistons, 3 coupler pistons, 8 levels of memory.

Performance memory (i.e. complete playback facilities) can also be provided, using **sequencer** technology similar to that used in **MIDI** instruments, but naturally it involves automating not just the stops but the entire keyboard system, and providing output arrangements so that keystrokes can be recorded in a time frame. One way of doing this is to fit magnetic send/receive drives to the keys themselves (so that in playback mode they actually move), but a much simpler approach is to automate the pallet system. Performance memory is a great asset to organists when preparing work, because one of the long-standing difficulties of organ playing is not being able to hear one's own performance properly – consoles are rarely sited in good listening positions, and playback from the organ's memory allows unhurried appraisal of both the performance and the balance of the organ from an audience position.

With the advances in control flexibility outlined, organ designers now have a large choice of strategies. The baroque revival in organs began in the 1920s as a movement in favour of the low pressure, mechanically operated organs that Bach knew, and many modern organists still prefer

*J. W. Walker and Sons, Brandon, Suffolk IP27 ONF, UK. Advertisement in *Organists' Review* for July 1988.

the direct 'feel' of a tracker action. Nowadays this can easily be combined with automation at various levels – the Walker organ mentioned above, for example, has mechanical action.

Another aspect of organs which has been changing during the last few decades is the layout and appearance of the instrument. Eighteenth-century organs were often cased in highly decorated woodwork, and intended to be beautiful objects in themselves. As organs grew in power and size during the nineteenth century, they were increasingly hidden away behind screens or in lofts and galleries, and many of them were (are) extremely difficult to reach for servicing, whole sections having to be dismantled to cure small faults. The tendency today is to return to the architectural approach, with visually appealing casework and pipe layout. Modern woodworking tools can cut intricate curves and patterns that are now too expensive to carry out by hand, and metal, even plastic decorations are also popular. The electronic technology is concealed behind a traditional facade, and since it also takes up little room compared with the cumbersome electro-mechanical systems it replaces, there is more space in a given site for the acoustic aspects of the instrument.

This entry has not attempted to cover the manufacture and theory of the different types of pipe, of which the main categories are 'flues' (basically large whistles) and 'reeds' (which work on the same principle as the clarinet's single beating reed – see **woodwind instruments**). In this area, too, technology is providing help in design, tuning, voicing and analysis of the results. Many mechanisms are now made of carefully chosen plastics instead of wood, either because of their better temperature and humidity performance or better self-lubricating or wear properties. One reason for continually investigating new materials is the steady disappearance from world markets of good timber at affordable prices. Pipes (apart from wooden flues) are still made of the traditional metals – tin, lead, brass etc. – and although they are becoming expensive, there is currently no supply problem. It might have been predicted thirty years ago that the increasingly efficient electronic organ would eventually make the pneumatic instrument obsolete, but in spite of the high (and exponentially rising) price of even a modest pipe organ, the industry is booming, order books are full, and there is also a very large business in the restoration of antique organs previously written off as beyond repair.

For comparisons between the development of the organ and that of electronic music studios, see the Introduction. I am grateful to several people listed in the acknowledgements for help in preparing this entry.

Oscillators   Electronic devices for generating **alternating current** from a **direct current** supply, as compared with alternators which do the same thing electro-mechanically. Audio frequency (AF) oscillators (range *c.* 20 **hertz**–20 kHz) are the source of tone for nearly all pitched electronic musical instruments, but oscillators working outside this band are also relevant in musical applications. Control oscillators, for example, may operate at very low frequencies, having **periods** up to the order of 1 min/**cycle** (.017 Hz). Clocking devices in computers, **sequencers** etc. use oscillators running in the megahertz (MHz) range. This entry is concerned with analogue devices. The principles of digital oscillators are described in **digital synthesis techniques** 4.

1. Basic oscillator principles

There are two main types of oscillator design – harmonic and relaxation.

Harmonic oscillators

These work by maintaining the vibrations in a naturally **resonant** device or circuit, in which the oscillations would normally die down because of **damping** if energy were not put back into the system. The **frequency** maintained by the oscillator is still that of the natural system. A tuning fork, for example, will ring for a time after being struck, but frictional forces soon weaken and stop the sound. In fig. 145a a fork is rigidly clamped at the foot and a small **electromagnet** placed near each of the tines. If the fork is vibrating, current at the same frequency will be

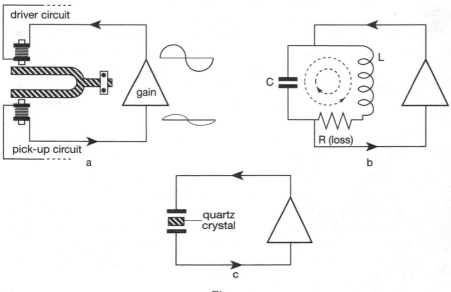

Fig. 145

generated in the coils, and if current from one of them is **amplified** and returned to the other in the correct **phase** (180° or antiphase in this case because the tines vibrate equally and oppositely), the loss can be replaced and oscillation maintained. Although we described the fork as already vibrating, there is always enough random disturbance for the system to start itself as soon as power is applied. I chose this as a good demonstration of the principle of regenerative **feedback**, but in fact electromechanical oscillators are rarely used today.

The electrical equivalent of the tuning fork is the **tuned circuit**. In fig. 145b the circuit on the left, consisting of **inductance** (L), **capacitance** (C) and **resistance** (R), behaves like the fork without the maintaining energy. Ignoring R for the moment, let's suppose that C is fully charged (if necessary see **inductance** and **capacitance** to help clarify the following). With C charged the circuit has an energy imbalance, and C must discharge through it. If there were no L or R present, discharge would be instantaneous, but here the discharge current causes an opposing induced voltage in L, which slows down the process. As C continues to discharge through L, the energy changes from being an electrostatic charge in the capacitor, to an electromagnetic one round the coil. When C is discharged current stops and at that instant all the energy is magnetic. L then discharges in the opposite direction, reversing the next charge on C, until the current again momentarily stops. After another C-to-L and L-to-C transfer, the position is as at the start, and one cycle is complete, the next one begins, and so on.

Resistance, of which there must certainly be some and may be a lot, enters the picture because at each interchange of energy R dissipates some of it – each successive cycle is weaker and the process eventually stop. In oscillators energy is supplied (righthand side of fig. 145b) to keep the system going.

Fig. 145c shows the LCR circuit replaced by a quartz crystal. In effect the crystal is between the plates of a capacitor and, when driven, its **piezo-electric** properties allow it to deform and bounce back at an extremely stable frequency – the accuracy of quartz clocks is exploited in thousands of devices, including computers. Crystals may also be used to regulate the frequency of a conventional tuned circuit. Their limitation is that a given crystal runs at only one frequency or **harmonics** of that frequency, but since this is high (typically many mega**hertz**), **frequency dividers** can derive any lower frequency required (such as fractional seconds, seconds, minutes, hours, days, months for a watch).

LC circuits are less efficient at audio frequencies than the higher radio frequencies because **inductors** for low frequencies need ferrous cores and many turns of unavoidably resistive wire. A laboratory **sine wave** source is the beat frequency oscillator (BFO), which derives an audio output by **heterodyning** the outputs of two radio frequency oscillators, one fixed and the other variable. The audio output is the **difference frequency** resulting from this combination; a crude form of the effect happens when a faulty radio goes into oscillation and produces whistles by beating with an incoming signal.

Sinusoidal audio oscillators can avoid inductors altogether, however, by using a **phase shift** method. Regenerative feedback only works if the renewed signal is exactly in phase (0° or 360°) with the old. Fig. 146 shows one of many circuits exploiting the fact that a CR network causes a phase **lag**, the voltage waveform across the resistors (R_1, R_2 and R_3) being delayed at each stage. The angle of lag depends on C, R and the frequency, so only one frequency gives a total circuit phase change of 360° and oscillations build up at that frequency only. If oscillations are at a single frequency the output must be sinusoidal.

Any electronic music composing studio must have sine wave sources, for example to implement **additive synthesis,** and harmonic oscillators are one way of providing them. The regenerative principle can also be used to give extra sharpness to a resonant circuit without causing it to oscillate (see **filters** and fig. 87). In most musical applications, however, we don't want sine tone but a richer waveform. Sine outputs can be

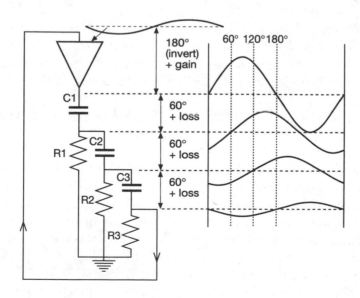

Fig. 146

shaped (**square waves** can be produced by **clipping** the sine, etc.), but some oscillators are naturally non-sinusoidal.

Relaxation oscillators

These work by exploiting CR circuits in a different way from the phase shift circuit above. The regular repetition of a cycle essential to all oscillators is achieved in this case by controlling the rate of charge or discharge of a capacitor through a resistor. CR circuits behave very predictably, and the product CR is known as the **time constant,** i.e. it is a measure of the time C will take to charge or discharge through R in given conditions.

The most musically useful basic waveform for subtractive treatment is the ramp or sawtooth, which contains all harmonics in a predictable progression. A basic sawtooth relaxation circuit is shown in fig. 147a. If a rising voltage is applied to inert gases like neon, no current flows until a critical 'striking' voltage, when the gas suddenly ionizes and passes a large current, short circuiting and instantly discharging C (this is the 'relaxation' part of the cycle). The oscillator exploits the fact that the short circuit condition still obtains even if the voltage drops considerably below the striking point (in fluorescent lighting a special starting circuit 'hits' the tube with a high voltage on switching on). Fig. 147b shows how after the initial charge the neon discharges C only to the point of gas extinction, when C charges again, and so on. This simple neon circuit does not produce the desired **linear** sawtooth because C's charging current drops as the charge increases. A more efficient design replaces R with a 'constant current' device which forces C to charge linearly, and replaces the neon with a 'unijunction' transistor, having similar switching properties but much more controllability. Fig. 148 shows the improved circuit and the output waveform.

There are many other relaxation circuits, and at one time an oscillator called the multivibrator was popular. This is a symmetrical arrangement

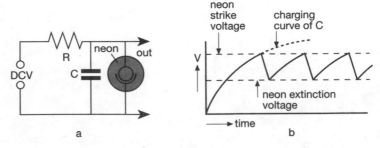

Fig. 147

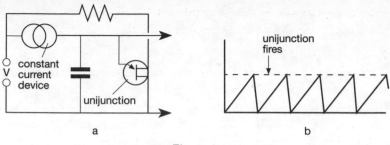

Fig. 148

with two CR circuits discharging alternately through transistors, giving a roughly **square wave** output, but its waveform is poor and is in any case less useful than a ramp. It is rarely found as an audio generator today, but the same type of circuit is the basis of bistable and monostable **flip-flop** switching devices.

2. Oscillators for music

Although most new equipment now uses digital tone generators, analogue techniques are by no means obsolete, and will be useful and common for many years to come. This section should be read in conjunction with **analogue synthesis techniques**, already referred to, where the musical applications of oscillators are discussed.

Electronic **organs** pre-dated electronic music composing by many years, and dozens of oscillator circuits have been used besides the few described above, including LCR designs using efficient **ferrite** inductors. By the time electronic music began seriously in the 1950s, therefore, a good deal of experience in designing stable, reliable music oscillators had been gained (frequency stability being of paramount importance because, however aptly the timbre is tailored, a note is musically useless unless it stays in tune). But composers wanted a different kind of control from organists – mainly the ability to choose any frequency instead of a fixed range of pre-tuned ones, and to shape and build waveforms minutely at every stage instead of selecting from pre-set 'voices'.

Shaping methods
Non-sine waveforms cannot be derived from sine wave oscillators by filtering alone because there are no harmonics to filter, so the basic sine must be **harmonically distorted** first (fig. 149a shows the general plan). One system produces square waves by clipping, as mentioned above, and these can then be **integrated** to produce **ramp** and **triangle** waves. **Diodes** in various configurations can introduce other distortions. Fig. 149b shows the same waveforms derived from a basic ramp.

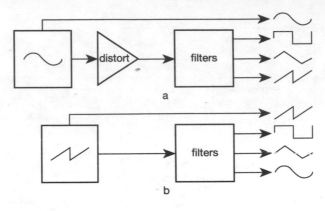

Fig. 149

A true sine can be produced by feeding a suitable non-sinusoidal input (e.g. a triangle) to a resonator tuned to the same frequency, but musically adequate quasi-sines can be made without using resonance. A useful oscillator is one with continuously variable waveforms, as shown in fig. 10, and an advantage of single-source multi-waveform devices is that phase relationships derived from one source are stable with respect to each other. The result is that waveforms can be reliably added in any proportion to produce a large variety of stable complex shapes. This is apart from any subtractive treatment that may follow, such as **equalization, formant** filtering, **reverberation** etc.

Tuning methods
We have seen that most music oscillators are based on RC circuits, and that changing R and/or C will alter the frequency. The usual method in a wide range oscillator is to combine a continuously variable resistor with range switching by selecting different fixed capacitors. Calibrated dials are not accurate enough for setting precise frequencies, and a **frequency meter** is a useful accessory, as is a cathode ray **oscilloscope** (CRO) for checking waveforms. Even with such aids, however, manual oscillator tuning is cumbersome, and a new dimension in versatility was added when voltage control was introduced in the 1960s, notably by Robert Moog (1965).

Voltage controlled oscillators (VCO)
The classic Moog VCO (fig. 150a) is a development of the circuit of fig. 148. Frequency depends on the firing point of the unijunction and the value and charging rate of C. The charging source is a constant current generator whose output is **exponentially** dependent on its input voltage,

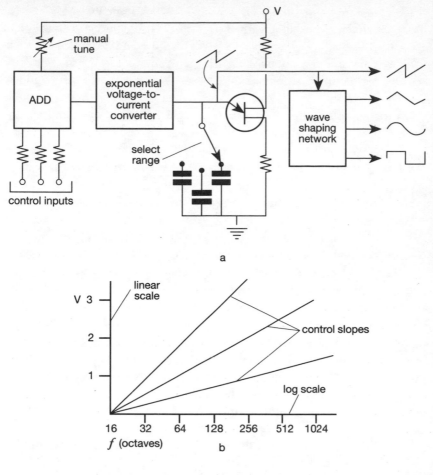

Fig. 150

and the value of that voltage determines the frequency. Exponentially because in musical terms equal increments of frequency are ratios (e.g. **octaves**), and it makes musical sense if **linear** volts become **logarithmic** frequency (VCOs are therefore rated in **volts** per **octave**, see fig. 150b).

Some advantages of the VCO are: 1. Frequency control is entirely in the electrical domain, and the control and oscillator functions are separate. No manual control is necessary, but if one is provided it affects control voltage, not the oscillator itself. 2. Oscillators can control each other, so that **frequency modulation** (FM), which with conventional oscillators can be difficult or impossible, becomes a simple and reliable operation. 3. System noises like crackles and clicks do not affect the signal directly – they will be heard as random FM, not as crackles. In fact deliberate filtered **noise** modulation is a common VC technique. 4. VCOs can be 'tracked' together if the control slopes are linear and properly aligned, thus complete chords can be bodily moved in pitch and remain internally correct. 5. In general, once the principle was established, and VC amplifiers (VCA) and VC filters (VCF) were added to the VCO (all these devices appeared at the same time), a whole vista of complex musical interactions opened out, far exceeding the possibilities of manual control.

A problem with VCOs is frequency 'drift'. For musical purposes the best arrangement is a wide frequency range with a small control voltage range, but this results in even the tiniest voltage changes, such as those caused by small temperature or supply variations, being audible as a change in frequency. For example, in an oscillator with a control slope of .5 volt/octave a change of .005V (5mV) will move the frequency by a very noticeable 12 **cents** (more than $\frac{1}{10}$ of a semitone). In synthesis work a good example of a drift problem is the difficulty of holding unisons (or octaves, fifths) between several oscillators without small drifts causing beats. This can be solved by **synchronizing** – one oscillator is chosen as the master control, and the others are locked to it in unison or a low number **harmonic** relationship. If drift occurs they will all move together and at least the internal ratios will be maintained. VCOs (unless, for example, they are digitally monitored) are not suitable for applications needing long term pitch stability, such as electronic organs, but for analogue composition work the advantages easily outweigh the drawbacks, and good regulation ensures reasonable stability for an average working session. Even today, when digital equipment offers similar facilities (and more) with quartz accuracy, VC is very appealing for some modes of composing.

Super- and sub-audio oscillators

Frequencies in the two or three octaves above the limit of hearing (say up to 100 kHz) would not seem to be useful for music, and on the whole are not, but I (and possibly others) have found that **ring modulating** supersonic outputs to produce audible difference tones gives sounds of unusually intense structure when suitably treated (e.g. in my piece *345*, Cary, 1970), in which only the frequencies 3, 4, and 5 Hz and their multiples by 10, 10^2, 10^3, 10^4 – fifteen in all – are used, the last three being supersonic). See also *tape erase* below.

Sub-audio oscillators at about 1–10 Hz have long had a function as vibrato and tremolo generators in electronic organs, but with the arrival of VC a need arose for very slow voltage changes to be applied to audio

VC oscillators, amplifiers and filters. A 30 second ramp control input to a VC filter, for example, might transform a timbre gradually as a sound proceeds. Fig. 11 shows two low frequency and one audio oscillator being used together to produce note patterns, and fig. 21 shows a large VC **patch** for a piece. VC opened up new explorations of the continuum between sub-audio and audio regions (discussed in **musique concrète**).

Requirements for sub-audio oscillators are different from audio, because they are often needed only intermittently, and possibly for one cycle only, but the timing of their application is vital. For this reason slow generators may have two modes – free-running and **one-shot**, with the one-shot mode requiring a timed **trigger** to execute a single cycle. An **envelope shaper** is an example of a special purpose one-shot oscillator with internal timing control as well as triggered onset, and normally applied to a VCA. Sub-audio oscillators can be synchronized in the same way as audio, and waveforms added to produce complex control functions.

3. Other applications

To conclude, here are a few further types of oscillator relevant in music and associated equipment:

Atomic oscillators   Using the natural resonances occurring in rubidium, caesium or hydrogen atoms, these are competition for quartz in the timing and high precision areas.

Line-up tone   These are sine wave oscillators for **lining up**. They often have only one frequency (e.g. 400 Hz or 1 kHz) and one level (e.g. 0 VU), but may offer a choice of both. They need to have reasonable frequency stability but excellent amplitude stability.

Quadrature oscillators   A sine oscillator with four outputs arranged to differ in phase successively by 90°. These are applied to control four VCAs which in turn feed four loudspeakers spread around the listener. The result is that the sound appears to rotate round the space at the oscillator's frequency. Automatic **quad panners** can be complicated if they involve slowing down to stationary sound (0 Hz), and reversing (changing direction of phase angles).

Speed control   Tape recorders with continuously variable speed are essential in **tape composition**. Most modern machines use **servo** controlled motors (see **tape recorder design**) and speed variation is by a form of voltage control; older machines usually have semi-synchronous capstan motors speed-controlled by the mains frequency of 50 Hz (UK) or 60 Hz (US). A way of controlling such motors is to replace the mains with an oscillator and power amplifier suitably terminated to drive a motor instead of a loudspeaker. A reasonably pure sine wave is needed to give smooth results from the motor, and a typical frequency range is 25–100 Hz (UK), 30–120 Hz (US), giving a two octave speed range. Usage should be regarded as intermittent, because motors are designed (iron content, windings) to run optimally at one frequency only, and may overheat or otherwise object if run continuously at another.

Tape erase and bias Supersonic oscillators (typically 100 kHz or higher) switched on in RECORD mode supply a high level signal to the ERASE head, plus a lower level 'bias' which is added to the audio input and sent to the RECORD head (see **sound recording techniques** and figs. 185 and 186).

Timebases A sawtooth oscillator of wide frequency range and good linearity 'paints' the horizontal X-axis line in an **oscilloscope** making the spot move steadily across the screen and fly back again (once each cycle). A synchronizing input allows it to be locked to any reasonably steady 'Y' signal to give a jitter-free picture. A TV has two timebases, line (fast) and frame (slow).

See Wells (1981) for fuller descriptions of oscillator circuits, shapers etc. Moog's original VC paper (1965) was presented in 1964, but he later (1967) published an explanatory article for the more general reader. Numerous alternative VC designs have appeared since, and today complete VC synthesizers are available on **chips**.

Oscilloscope, cathode ray (CRO) A visual display instrument, whose main component is a **cathode ray tube**. A versatile item, useful for measurement and analysis as well as display. In 'drawing' a **waveform**, the spot on the screen is moved from left to right across the horizontal (X) axis at a constant speed by an internal 'timebase' generator, the signal being applied on the Y axis. If there is also a facility for brightness modulation, this is known as the Z input.

The ideal timebase is a perfect **ramp wave**, the vertical part becoming the almost instantaneous 'flyback' of the spot. Because flyback can never be completely instantaneous, the spot is suppressed during this time to prevent it spoiling the picture (as in TV). Timebase frequency is adjusted to an integral relationship with the input waveform's frequency (e.g. to display four **cycles** of a 1 kHz wave, the timebase must run at 250 Hz).

The timebase is controllable and calibrated over a wide frequency range, and switched off completely if signals are to be applied to both X and Y inputs (see **Lissajous figure**). For displaying very slow phenomena, long persistence screen phosphors can be obtained. Input amplifier **gain** is also accurately calibrated, and synchronization can be applied to hold the picture steady under changing input frequency conditions. Spot deflection is measured in volts per centimetre, and read on a graticule (grid of lines etched on a glass or plastic plate mounted in front of the tube).

Modern CROs have digital storage arrangements and many other refinements, but a comparatively simple, low cost instrument is still very useful in a composing or recording studio. It is certainly worth paying for a double beam CRO, allowing two different waveforms to be compared, but unless it is to be used for digital diagnostics there is no need to spend money on extended high frequency response. An adapted TV set does not make a good CRO, but a video camera can be used to pick up the small CRO picture and display it on a large TV screen, a technique that can also be used with computer screens, and is useful in lectures and in performances of computer pieces that contain visual elements.

Output impedance   Impedance (Z) of a device as 'seen' by the input of another device to which its output is connected. See **impedance matching**.

Overblow   To raise the effective **fundamental** of a wind instrument by 1. increasing lip and air pressure and/or 2. opening an **octave** or 'speaker' key which creates an **antinode** at the main **node** point of the original fundamental, preventing its generation. The first overblown series of notes is commonly at the octave (second **harmonic**) but sometimes (e.g. clarinet, see **break**) at the twelfth (third harmonic). See **brass instruments** and **woodwind instruments**.

Overdubbing   Assembling a complete recording by adding new tracks to previously recorded ones on the same multi-track tape. **Foldback** of the previous tracks to musicians recording new ones is done from the RECORD head used as a 'sync' playback head, rather than from the normal PLAYBACK head, so that precise timing is maintained. Otherwise each overdub would lag by a time dependent on tape speed and the distance between R and P heads. See **dubbing** and **sound recording techniques** 2.

Overflow   A problem in, for example, a computer's **memory** which

happens when a number is too large to fit the storage space provided
for it, with the result that the most significant end disappears. In digital
music processing this a potential source of serious distortion (see **sound
recording techniques**).

Overlap   Of recording or playback, the procedure of starting a new
one on a second machine before the old is finished, usually as a safety
precaution. Overlapped recordings can be cut together, or played by
synchronizing the overlap and changing over at a suitable point. In
digital playback the process can be automated, the computer searching
for a match between the two sample files.

Overload   1. (Analogue) Too large a **signal** for a given device, causing
distortion at least and, if gross, **paralysis** or damage. 2. (Digital) Too
much data for a system to handle in the allotted time, causing errors,
slowdowns and possibly **crashes**, for example a **MIDI** 'traffic jam'. See
also **overflow** and **sound recording techniques**.

Overmodulation   1. In radio, **modulating** the **carrier** with a larger
signal amplitude than the transmit/receive system can process without
unacceptable **distortion**. See **amplitude modulation**. 2. In tape recording,
too high a signal, which will **saturate** the **oxide**. In disc recording, gross
overmodulation can cause grooves to join or cross, making the disc
unplayable. See **compressor, sound recording techniques**.

Oversampling   A technique for improving the **resolution** of **digital-to-
analogue conversion** in devices such as **compact disc** players, by converting each sample many times (for example, oversampling a signal four
times at the standard CD **sampling rate** of 44.1 kHz gives an effective
rate of 176.4 kHz). More data is provided for processing refinements,
and output **filtering** is simplified. For the theory of this see Watkinson
(1988) chapter 2.

Overshoot   See **hunting** and **ringing**

Overtone   See **harmonic series**

Overwrite   To replace previously recorded digital data with new data,
destroying the old, as against **erasing**, which leaves the storage medium
'clean'.

Oxide A general term for a material (e.g. ferric oxide, chromium dioxide) used as the active magnetic medium in recording tape, floppy disks etc., even if (as in metal tape) it is not chemically an oxide. Rated according to particle size, magnetic properties, resistance to wear etc., oxide is fixed to the 'base film', usually polyester, with an adhesive 'binder'. A good illustrated survey of modern tape manufacture and characteristics is Barry Fox's article in the *New Scientist* (Fox, 1986). See also **cassette recorders** and **sound recording techniques**.

P

PA   See public address

Pad   A signal **attenuator** with fixed **loss** which may also act as an **impedance** changer. Normally small resistive **networks**, they can be wired into **patch** cords, fitted to **jack** strips, **mixing desks** etc. as necessary.

PAL   (Phase Alternate Line). A colour TV system used in the UK and many other countries. The **phase** of the colour signals is reversed on alternate lines and the pair averaged, resulting in stable colour compared to, say, **NTSC**. See also **video cassette PCM**.

Pan/ning   From 'panorama', and a camera term adopted for audio use. The apparent horizontal movement of a sound source with respect to a stationary listener. The illusion cannot be maintained beyond about 90° with only two speakers, but complete 360° rotation is possible with three or more. Compare **crab**, and see next entry.

Panpot   A **PAN**oramic **POT**entiometer, usually two **ganged** pots with complementary (e.g. **log**, antilog) tracks. Fig. 151 shows a common arrangement, but there are several methods, including some using a single pot. Panpots, also called panners or pan controls, are used to create the illusion of horizontal sound source movement in **stereo** systems by means of adjustments to the relative levels of the signal in the two channels. The effect is subjective and depends on local conditions, speaker spacing etc., but in general continuous adjustment of both pots as in fig. 151b results in a drop of apparent level towards the centre. The arrangement of 151c, where the 'down' side is brought up to a standing level on the 'up' side, is more successful. Panning is a technique for placing **mono** sounds in a 'field', as opposed to stereo proper, which requires an initial recording using at least two microphones. See also **quad panner** and **quadraphony**.

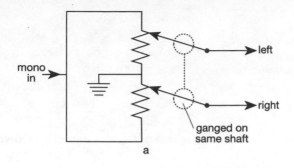

a

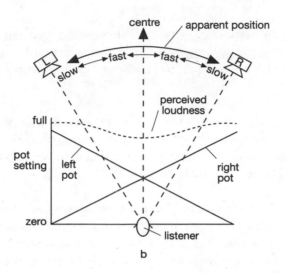

b

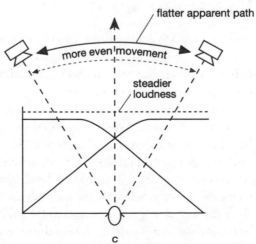

c

Fig. 151

Parabolic reflector See **microphones**

Parallel 1. Used to describe a **circuit** (or part of one) which is divided into two or more paths, such that the main **current** splits to pass through them in inverse proportion to the ratio of the **impedances** in each path. Also known as a 'shunt' connection. See also **Ohm's law**, **series** and **tuned circuit**. 2. In digital systems, the processing or transmitting of two or more **bits** of data simultaneously (commonly eight or sixteen). See **serial**.

Paralysis A 'latch-up' of, for example, an **amplifier** caused when a gross **overload** or accidental **DC** input fully charges and disables the coupling **capacitors** as signal carriers. It is usually self-clearing without damage.

Parameter Originally an exclusively mathematical term, but now often a vague buzzword, imprecisely used in almost any context. Any object can in theory be described in terms of separate properties, but in practice even simple objects (physical or abstract) defy complete and exact description, either because they are more complex than appears, or because our understanding is too limited to be able to describe them anyway. The parameters of an object or system can be listed in two ways: 1. by separating **constants** from **variables**, or 2. by arranging them in a hierarchy of importance. These two lists themselves alter in different contexts. If an owner describes his car, for example, the constants will include body, engine etc., while the contents of the sump, fuel tank, passenger seats etc. will be variables. The designer of the car, on the other hand, would list body and engine as variables. Body colour would be at the bottom of the variables list for an engineer, but possibly at the top for a person buying the car. When complex phenomena are studied, the parameters tend to get more numerous and change in order of importance. In the case of musical sounds, parameters once unknown, ignored or immeasurable have turned out to be materially important.

Parametric equalizer See **equalizers**

Parasitic oscillation An additional signal, usually of much higher **frequency**, 'riding on the back' of the wanted signal. A supersonic (and therefore in itself inaudible) parasite can seriously contribute to **distortion**. If it cannot be cured at source, a 'stopper' (usually a rejector **tuned circuit**) helps to prevent contamination of the audio signal.

Partial   A constituent of a **complex wave** which is at a higher **frequency** than the wave's **fundamental**. Helmholtz (1862) used the word to describe the fundamental as well ('prime partial tone'), because it is indeed a part rather than the whole of a total complex vibration, but in ordinary use 'partial' always means 'upper partial', and does not include the fundamental.

When the term refers to upper tones which are integral multiples of the fundamental it is synonymous with 'harmonic' or 'overtone' (see **harmonic series** and fig. 55 in **digital synthesis techniques**), and in this case may be called a 'harmonic partial', but there are also **inharmonic partials** in complex waves whose ratios with the fundamental are not integral.

From the musical point of view inharmonic partials fall into two kinds: 1. those that are near enough to integral harmonics to be regarded as mistunings of them, for example, a ratio like 3.05:1; and 2. frequencies that appear to have no rational connection with any other in the complex.

It was once assumed that 'good' musical tone resulted from a perfectly tuned harmonic series, but it is now known that much of the timbral character of instrumental sound is due to 'mistuning' of some or all harmonics. In a typical string or pipe playing a steady tone, the lower harmonics will be nearly perfect, but the higher numbers are often out of tune by easily measurable amounts, and this causes beats which add to the internal mobility of the sound. The inharmonicity derives from many small factors in design and construction – the bridge and body of a violin are slightly flexible, the diameter of the string is not perfectly constant, etc. In a wind instrument, the theoretically ideal position of **nodes** is modified by, for example, the shape of the bell, irregularities of bore caused by finger holes, acute bends in valve mechanisms, the presence of obstructions such as mutes, etc.

One reason for the dullness of much early synthesized tone was that perfect harmonicity was aimed at. (One of many ways of introducing inharmonic partials is illustrated under **frequency shifter**.) In practical music, of course, several tones are usually heard together, and this adds another dimension to the inharmonicity of the total – a mistuned unison or octave, for instance, will produce beating of partials right through the **spectrum**. Inharmonicity is deliberately introduced in piano tuning to add liveliness to the sound, apart from the fact that instruments or ensembles tuned in equal or any compromise **temperament** must contain inharmonic components. A bell is an example of a single sound source with several fundamental tones, and its characteristic **timbre** is the result of the multiple beating of a large number of upper partials, as well as a 'hum' tone which is typically about an octave below the main fundamental.

Noise producing instruments (e.g. most percussion) have dense clusters of partials with no obvious relationship, but some noise phenomena can be analysed as the upper harmonics of an absent and very much lower fundamental.

For further comment on the acoustics of partials, see Taylor (1965), Wood (1962) and Olson (1967). For synthesis and control of inharmonic partials, see Wells (1981) for analogue techniques, and Dodge (1985) for computer methods.

Pascal   See **computer languages**

Pass   1. Used, in contrast to 'reject', to describe devices that selectively transmit certain part(s) of the frequency **spectrum** (see next entry). 2. An identifiable sequence of events forming part or the whole of a process, typically the completion of one aspect of a total process. Realization of a piece of music typically needs at least four passes: mental processes, sketch, score, and performance, whereas a keyboard improvisation is complete in one. Computer music usually calls for several passes, each addressing different aspects of the piece.

Pass band   The **band** defined by giving its lowest and highest **frequencies**, passed by, for example, a band pass **filter**.

Passive device   One that uses only the energy contained in the **signal** (i.e. it has no power supply), and must therefore cause an overall **loss**. Compare **active device**.

Patch/ing   1. A configuration of a number of devices to perform some function as a group, often represented as a **block diagram**. 2. The adjustable hardware arrangements by which 1. is effected are also called patches, and they must combine facilities for easy disconnection and re-routing of signals with electrical and mechanical reliability. Patching does not imply an emergency repair, and many patches are permanently in place. 3. In software, a program sub-routine inserted to replace part of an existing program (not covered in this entry).

Certain connections in any system are invariable and can be 'hard-wired' (such as that from a monitor power amplifier to its speaker), but most links must be optionally variable, for example a treatment unit such as a **filter** may be needed anywhere in the chain, and it must be easy to 'patch it in'. Patching may be internal, such as that within a synthesizer, where configurations are usually changed by buttons, switches, sliders, knobs, plug-in memories etc. In the case of external patches each device, however complex internally, is regarded as a **black box** with so many outputs and/or inputs, all of which are brought for interconnection to a conveniently placed panel, often called a 'patchbay'. See **analogue synthesis techniques** 3 for a discussion of block diagrams and an introduction to two common types of manual patching, the **jack** plug and socket, using 'patch cords' to bridge between sockets, and the pin matrix, in which two adjacent planes of contact strips at right angles, one carrying inputs and the other outputs, can be joined at any intersection (fig. 8).

Of the two approaches described, the matrix is the more logical and elegant, but the time-tested jack field has shown remarkable persistence in the face of increasing automation in other areas of audio electronics, in spite of its bulk and proneness to faults caused by accumulated dirt, broken patch cords etc. Matrices can be made very compact, but if too small can have **crosstalk** problems caused by inter-channel **capacitance**. They also contain a varying amount of redundancy because many intersections are meaningless in practice. On the whole, therefore, the rugged adaptability of a jack field is preferred for main patchbays, even in studios being equipped today.

Jack plugs and sockets may be two-way for **unbalanced** working (fig. 152a), or three-way (152b) for balanced signals, and sockets may have a number of extra contacts which make or break when a jack plug is inserted. Fig. 152c shows a single break contact used to make a **normalled** patching, i.e. the most used connection is made with the socket empty, and broken by the insertion of a jack plug carrying a new input. In a fully normalled patch a complete default configuration is automatically set up by removing all patch cords.

In recent years the tendency has been to shift much of the routine patch changing from the patchbay to the **mixing desk**. Large consoles are fitted with local patches (often using compact, miniature jack fields) so that most running operations can be done without changes in the main patch, which may only be adjusted at the beginning of a session when decisions about the number, type and input assignment of microphones, and the output routing to chosen recording machines etc., are made.

The simplicity and easy servicing qualities of the traditional patch will probably ensure its survival for many years, at least for configuring the

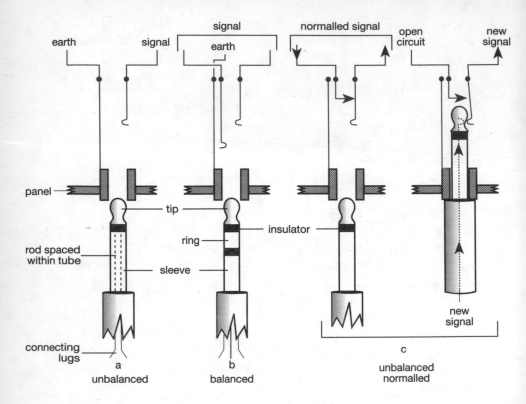

Fig. 152

larger aspects of studios and for inter-studio ('tie line') links, but for applications such as electronic music composition new technology is offering great improvements in speed and convenience. Over the last twenty years the number of signal types which need some form of flexible routing has been increasing. Apart from normal audio signals, there was (from the 1960s) a need to patch low frequency and **DC** control signals, and recent developments have added **MIDI** and other digital data streams, as well as digital audio. In the 1990s, more and more wire links will be replaced by optical fibres. All these factors, as well as the development of many new music devices, have increased the need for efficient automated patches, eliminating cords or pins, and containing patch memories from which a complex configuration can be instantly recalled and implemented.

The logical patch format for automation is a matrix, because each possible connection possesses a unique map reference – once channels are assigned and connected, there can be no confusion. For a time the

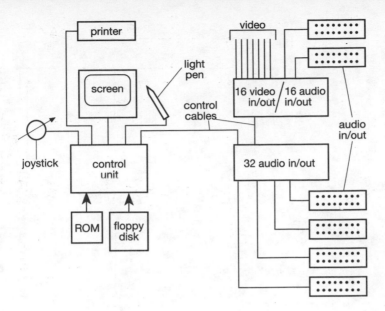

Fig. 153

problem was to design an electronic switch for high-grade audio signals as efficient as a simple cord or pin – ideally a device offering zero resistance in both directions when triggered ON, infinite resistance when OFF. The current solution is to use complementary pairs of **MOSFETs** (Metal Oxide Semiconductor Field Effect Transistors). The performance of such switches (complementary MOS or CMOS) meets professional standards of quality, and they form the basis of computer controlled matrices.

Fig. 153 shows a simplified block diagram of an automated audio-video patching system by Akai.* The control module, with visual display and printer, can support additional interface units to give up to 112 inputs and outputs, plus the sixteen audio circuits normally associated with video. A version of this system adapted for use in a MIDI environment is installed at the BBC's Radiophonic Workshop in London, where a large group of music devices, mixed and routed by several Yamaha DMP7 units (see **mixers**), is controlled from a computer screen without a patch bay in sight. The Macintosh II software for this system was designed by Mark Wilson.

For further comments on CMOS applications in mixers and patches,

*Akai Electric Co. Ltd, 12–14, 2–chome, Higashi-Kojiya, Ohta-ku, Tokyo, Japan.

see Ballou (1987) chapter 22. For patchbays in conjunction with mixing consoles, see Runstein (1989) chapter 9.

Patchbay See **patch**

PCM See **pulse code modulation**

Peak See **root-mean-square**

Peak programme meter (PPM) One type of audio signal level indicator. Originally a BBC broadcast standard specification, the needle of a PPM is designed to rise very rapidly so as to capture the **transient** peaks, and fall back slowly to allow time for the peak to be read. Not as useful as the **volume unit meter** for general programme level, but more accurate in following fine detail. In recent years the 'thermometer' type **LED** indicator has tended to replace the traditional mechanical meter, and can be arranged so that it works as either PPM or VUM. Engineers are divided as to the type of indication they prefer, but in critical applications such as **mixing desks** it is useful and perfectly feasible to have both.

Percussion generators Electronic sources specially designed or adapted to simulate drums, cymbals and other percussion instruments. When combined with **sequencers** percussion generators are usually called drum machines, and today are made in a large variety of designs. Electronic drum simulators were pioneered in the 1930s, but the first commercially successful artificial drum kits appeared in the early 1960s, notably the Wurlitzer 'Side Man', which was available either as part of an organ or as a stand-alone 'rhythm box'. A coded wheel with spring contacts was driven by a variable speed motor to produce popular dance patterns in any tempo. With its heavy power amplifier, speaker and motor, it was barely portable, but equipped with such a rhythm box, plus a small monophonic add-on keyboard (such as a **Solovox**), a single pianist could produce a reasonably full and band-like sound. Each effect could also be produced manually by pressing a button, with or without the rhythm sequence running, and the sounds themselves varied from very poor (snare drum) to strong and effective (bongos).

Unpitched percussion sounds can be synthesized using a **noise generator** with its output **filtered** to stress the spectral **band** of interest, and **modulated** by a percussive **envelope** (except in cases where the appropriate attack is gentler, such as wire-brushed cymbal, maracas). Narrow band noise can produce quasi-pitched click (such as claves) and thump (such as tom-tom) sounds, but for pitched drums like timpani a **one-shot oscillator** is more appropriate, designed to produce one large half-cycle followed by a rapidly damped train of oscillations, which is in essence the behaviour of a real drum.

By the late 1960s the **sequencer** had become electronic and the sound generators transistorized, greatly reducing the size of the unit. However, the facilities offered were much the same or even less versatile than those of the earlier machines, and there remained the severe musical limitation of a rigidly metronomic beat with no 'give' or human flexibility, though as before the sounds could be manually played, either with or instead of the automatic sequence. But serious musicians and particularly percussionists showed little interest in what they regarded as a poor substitute for good drumming, and this situation obtained till the late 1970s, when the demands of heavily amplified rock music began to exceed the output of unamplified or conventionally amplified live percussion, and a firm, unyielding beat had become fashionable in any case.

In the past decade artificial percussion has developed dramatically, and today's drum machines often have resources that greatly exceed what is normally regarded as percussion. Complete compositions have been realized using a suitably programmed drum machine as the sole electronic resource. The most important recent changes are:

Multi-tracking   With digital sequencing and logic control, many simultaneous tracks can be run together, each with its own rhythmic features and instruments, separately adjustable for level, accent etc. A block building facility allows small units – 'patterns' – to be built into 'songs', with full editing capability at all stages.

Sampling   This has made possible the replacement of generated sounds by real percussion digitally recorded and stored, either supplied by the manufacturer or input by the user. Not only does this give more variety and flexibility to the sounds available – several versions of similar types of stroke on the same drum, for example, all subtly different – but once the principle is established, it also allows other sampled sounds, not just standard percussion, to be included in the menu.

MIDI   (For general information see the entry on **MIDI**.) A drum machine, like any other music device, can be designed to receive and send MIDI data. It can then output data (including timing), be driven by a MIDI sequencer, controlled using a **time code**, or played live from a performance input device. Provision can be made, either in the drum machine itself or the computer/sequencer driving it, for small tempo irregularities, adding 'naturalness', and for any kind of sudden or gradual speed change.

Increased choice of input types   Most drum machines are intended for automatic operation, live performance being possible only via the instrument buttons or from a MIDI keyboard. But there are also input devices purpose-built for percussionists. These are played by striking pads which are position- and velocity-sensitive, as well as sending a trigger each time they are struck. Drummers can thus combine acoustic percussion with a drum machine or any other MIDI-accessible sounds and perform using techniques they are familiar with. The pioneering drum interface was Max Mathews's 'sequential drum' of the late 1970s, see Mathews (1980) and **live performance electronic music 4**. There are also computer programs specially designed for drum machines, for example UpBeat (Intelligent Music).* One of UpBeat's features is a variable 'fill' instruction that can select computer-generated fills (sub-beats between main beats) on a percentage basis.

Drum machines range from simple rhythm boxes to expensive units with many features. There are specialist books (e.g. Vilardi, 1985) but they tend to date quickly in this fast-moving field. Most MIDI books (e.g. Casabona, 1987) have sections on drum machine interfacing.

Perfect pitch   See **absolute pitch**

Period/ic   A periodic variation is one which shows a regular repetition of a **cycle** of values. The time taken for one whole cycle is called the period (short for 'time period') of the variation. It is related to the **frequency**, f, of the variation by the expression period (in seconds) = $1/f$ (in **hertz**). See also **aperiodic** and **fundamental**.

Permanent magnet   See **magnet**

Permeability   See **hysteresis** and **magnet**

PFL   (Pre-Fade Listen) See **mixers and mixing desks**

Phantom power   See **microphones 3**

Phase   A term used to identify positions within the **cycle** of a **periodic**

*Intelligent Music, 116 North Lake Avenue, Albany, 12206, USA.

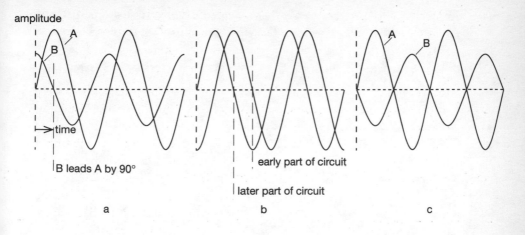

amplitude

B leads A by 90°

→time

early part of circuit

later part of circuit

a

b

c

Fig. 154

variation. Position is usually expressed as an angle, the entire cycle being represented as 360° (see **sine wave** and fig. 178b).

In the case of two waves out of step with each other as in fig. 154a, one is said to lead or lag the other by a certain angle. In the figure A leads B by 90°. The phase of a single wave may shift as a result of processing (see, for example, fig. 146) and this shift is also expressed in degrees of lead (fig. 154b). If two waves are 180° out of phase with each other, i.e. one is the inversion of the other (fig. 154c), they are said to be in antiphase. See **digital synthesis techniques** 3 and **cosine wave**.

Phase inverter   A device (for example, most single stage **amplifiers**) which causes a 180° (half-cycle) **phase** shift, i.e. its output is in **antiphase** to its input. See **oscillators** 1 and fig. 146 for a practical application (phase shift oscillator).

Phase modulation   The process of varying the **phase** of a **carrier** at the **frequency** of a modulating input. Frequency can be expressed as a rate of change of phase angle, and in practice the results are similar to **frequency modulation**.

Phasing   A **spectrum**-distorting effect, not unlike **flanging** (and the words are sometimes used interchangeably), but the operating principle is **phase** shifting rather than the time delay techniques used in flanging. See **filters**.

Phon   A unit of perceived loudness, related to the physical quantity of intensity, which is measured in **decibels**. One phon is made equal to one decibel at the arbitrarily chosen **frequency** of 1 kHz, but modified at other frequencies to allow for the sensitivity characteristic of the human ear.

Any unit arrived at by taking the average perception of a number of individuals must be imprecise, and the relationship of absolute sound levels to perceived loudness is confused by the difficulty of measuring anything accurately. Because of the **logarithmic** nature of loudness perception, it is convenient to convert absolute intensity (in **watts** per metre^2) to decibels, 0 dB being taken as 10^{-12}W/m^2. This is the 'threshold of audibility' at 1 kHz (for an 'average' person). On this scale, the 'threshold of pain' is at *c*. 120 dB (also at 1 kHz). Fig. 155 shows the curves published by Fletcher and Munson in 1933, and still regarded as a standard (Fletcher, 1933). The dip (indicating peak response) at around 3.5 kHz is thought to be due to **resonance** in the ear's external canal.

The family of curves are lines of equal phons, arrived at by asking a number of subjects to compare the loudness of a tone with that of a reference tone at 1 kHz – not necessarily a good test, as noted by many

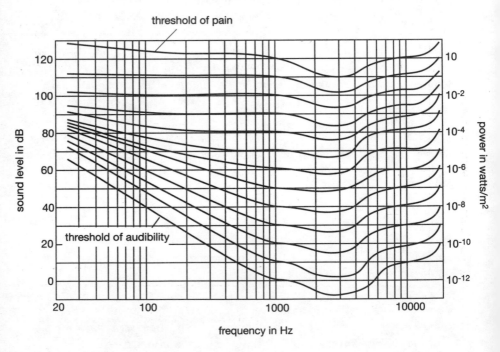

Fig. 155

observers. However, in the 'musically most active' area bounded by
c. 400 Hz–4 kHz and 40–90 dB, the curves are reasonably flat and
phons not very different from dB. Neither the dB nor the phon scales
match subjective loudness response well, however; for example an
increase of about 10 phons is required to obtain a sound heard as only
twice as loud. A further unit, the sone, was devised by S. S. Stevens in
an attempt to provide a more accurate human perception scale (Stevens,
1955). Making 1 sone equal to 40 phons (reasonably quiet), a sound at
a level of 5 sones should seem about five times as loud. Fig. 156 shows
sones compared to phons. Note the logarithmic scale for sones.

For further reading in this important but subjective area, see Roederer
(1979) chapter 3, Wells (1981) chapter 2, Olson (1967) chapter 7 and
several articles in Deutsch (1982). See also **psychoacoustics, sub/-, super/
sonic.**

Phonogène A special tape machine with variable speed tape transport
developed by the Club d'Essai (Paris), in the early days of **musique
concrète.** Two models were made, one continuously variable and the
other changing speed in semitone steps. Another pioneering tape machine

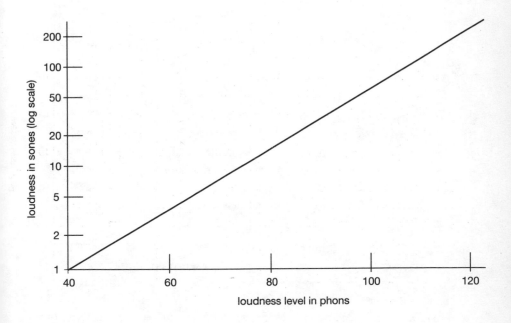

Fig. 156

was the morphophone, which had multiple heads for delays and echo effects. See also **tape composition techniques**, Schaeffer (1952) and Manning (1987).

Photo-electric cell (photocell)   A **transducer** which converts light to electric current, the term being loosely applied to both self-generating types and photo-conductive cells which require an external power source. Their main musical application is as detectors of modulated light in film sound projectors.

Photo-transistor   A transistor whose base current (see **amplifiers**) is light-dependent. They are used, for example, in **opto-isolators**. See **MIDI**.

Pianos   *acoustic*   The piano's great period of development was the nineteenth century, culminating perhaps in the years just before 1914. Since then there has been little change of significance in piano design, and much has been made of small improvements. The only major innovation (apart from electric pianos – see next entry) has been the appearance, from the 1930s, of the miniature upright, and even the best of these exist more for convenience than quality.

It took nearly a hundred years, from the mid-seventeenth to the mid-eighteenth century, to produce velocity-sensitive hammer actions that gave the player any real control of dynamics, and even then the pioneer instruments (Cristofori, Silbermann) hardly rivalled the well-tried, powerful harpsichords of the time. But within half a century Beethoven was writing music unthinkable on the harpsichord, and Chopin and Liszt flourished only a few years later. The piano improved with amazing speed during that period.

There are many specialist books on piano construction, and excellent illustrated studies in musical encyclopaedias such as Sadie (1984). This entry seeks only to highlight a few important points in the technology of what must be, by a large margin, the most successful and widely used **polyphonic** musical instrument ever devised.

Strings and frames
The musical use of both iron (or steel) and brass (or bronze) strings goes back to medieval times, and early pianos used a combination of both. But as more and more power was required from the instrument higher string tensions had to be used, and special new steel wire alloys were introduced and became standard. Frames were originally wooden, but as both the tension and the number of strings per note increased (to three except in the bass), frames began to be strengthened with iron

braces. A complete one-piece iron-cast frame had been suggested quite early, but it was opposed by many who thought it would spoil the tone of the instrument. It proved to be the only satisfactory answer, however, and was combined with 'overstringing': pianos up to the mid-nineteenth century had all strings parallel, like a harpsichord; crossing the bass strings over the treble not only allowed an increase in the length of the bass strings, but distributed string tension in two directions, the cross-bracing effect adding to the stability of the whole system and the load-bearing capacity of the frame. The total string tension in a modern piano is many tons.

Actions

The first percussive keyboard instrument was the clavichord, in which the finger connects with the string(s) directly via a metal 'tangent'. This gives great delicacy of touch and some dynamic control, but very limited power because the tangent is in effect a bridge – the tone results wholly from displacement of the string at its extreme end. The essential break-through of the piano was to let a hinged hammer 'escape' from the finger key mechanism and fly free at the string – it is literally thrown. The greater the acceleration applied to the key the greater the velocity of the hammer on striking the string and hence the louder the sound. Neither the plucking action of a harpsichord's jack or the opening of an air valve (pallet) in an **organ** is sensitive to finger velocity. The flying hammer principle brought with it the problem of how to control the hammer after it has struck and strongly bounced off a taut string, so that it can be re-engaged quickly with the finger key (early pianos had severe problems with rapid repeated notes). This was solved by providing a 'check' or brake that instantly took the energy out of the returning hammer. The numerous ingenious mechanisms made between *c.* 1700 and 1900 gradually reached designs of such reliability that modern actions, though made only of wood, small springs and pins, fragments of leather and felt and (in upright pianos) a piece of tape, work faultlessly for millions of operations.

Dampers and pedals

In grand pianos the damper simply rests on the strings, is lifted by the rear end of the seesaw finger key, and returned by gravity when the note is released. In upright pianos the dampers (and hammers) are not only vertically mounted so that gravity is ineffective, but dampers and hammers are on the same side of the strings, so a more complex, spring-assisted damper mechanism must be used.

The two pedals have traditionally been called 'piano' and 'forte', but 'loud' is a misnomer apart from the slight extra volume given by sympathetic vibrations. From 1770 or so a pedal to lift all dampers simultaneously began to be fitted, adding sustaining power (rather than loudness) to held chords etc. The 'soft' pedal, as with dampers, demands a different approach in grands and uprights. In a grand piano the pedal pushes the whole action (on a board beneath the strings) sideways so that the hammers strike two instead of three strings, leaving the dampers above in their original positions, but still responding to the appropriate keys. Uprights cannot use this method because the dampers and hammers are inseparably part of the same mechanism. The most successful of various techniques is for the pedal to bring all the hammers nearer to the strings, limiting the velocity they will reach at a given performance dynamic. A third or 'sostenuto' pedal was invented in the 1860s, by which a player can sustain the notes currently depressed while allowing full damping on subsequent ones. Some piano music cannot be properly played without this pedal, and from being a comparatively rare fitting it is now standard on nearly all concert grand pianos.

Keyboards

The familiar repeating pattern of seven white keys and five black was in place long before pianos appeared (see **keyboard design**). Special piano keyboards have been built from time to time, but in general the key size and spacing have become standardized. Lightness of touch is a matter of individual preference, and makers vary in the amount of lead weighting added to keys and in the overall stiffness of actions. Experiments with microtones, alternative **temperaments** etc. are more easily carried out with organ-type instruments than strings, but a number of microtonal pianos have been made, either with two or three normal keyboards or a single specially designed one (again see Sadie, 1984).

Experimental pianos

Historical mention should be made of 'sostenente' pianos – a generic term applied to a number of experimental instruments. In any percussion instrument control of the note is lost as soon as it is sounded. This can be regarded as a disability or not. Piano music, which contains some of the greatest works ever composed, allows for it by including trills, arpeggios, repeated notes and patterns etc., and such note-extending devices are part of the character of the music. But over the years dozens of attempts to produce sustained tone from pianos have been made. Some directed streams of air at the strings, others used mechanisms to produce rapid repetition of a held note, and others again invented ways of bowing the strings. Some of these ingenuities worked quite well, but attracted little interest from composers of note. The coming of electronics has finally solved the problem for anyone who wants a solution. Electronic pianos can easily be arranged to prolong the original percussive sound indefinitely, and acoustic pianos can be fitted with electric sustaining mechanisms (see next entry).

The future of pianos may well be electronic, simply because it may eventually be impossible to produce the traditional instrument. Already the increasing shortage and ever higher cost of first grade seasoned timbers is forcing piano makers to use lower quality woods or synthetic substitutes, and even with automated factory methods a good piano needs a great deal of skilled human input. In spite of the already high cost of good instruments, however, there is no lack of demand, order books are full, and the many thousands of children who begin learning the piano each year can still expect to spend at least part of their time playing an instrument with hammers and strings.

Pianos *electric and electronic* The term 'electric' should properly be reserved for electro-acoustic instruments in which the output of a string, bar or other mechanical generator is amplified to produce the finished sound. 'Electronic' pianos have electronic sound generators and no mechanical parts except the keyboard mechanism, switches etc. In practical usage, however, 'electric piano' is often used to denote both kinds.

Electric pianos

Numerous electrified versions of pianos were made from the late 1920s onwards, many of them described in Sadie (1984). The most famous of these was the Neo-Bechstein Flügel (1932). Resembling an ordinary grand piano, but like other electric pianos needing no soundboard because there was no acoustic amplification, the Neo-Bechstein used **electromagnetic pick-ups**, one for every five strings. At the time such instruments were regarded as novelties rather than serious contributions to musical art, and few of them were made in more than experimental numbers.

The best known of the post-war electric pianos is the Rhodes (or Fender–Rhodes), which was developed in the 1950s and is still popular today, improved but still essentially the same. Pop and jazz groups were the ideal media for a piano that sounded unashamedly different from a conventional instrument, because such groups are interested in 'different' sounds, and need varying amounts of loudness according to the venue. Harold Rhodes designed a machine based on amplified steel bars, which stayed in tune, responded dynamically like a piano, and was tough and transportable. Its distinctive sound has earned the Rhodes piano a well-loved place in small group jazz. Later models use an ingenious quasi-tuning fork, one tine of which is a thin wire that is actually struck by the hammers, and the other a flat resonating bar whose vibrations are amplified.

Some electric pianos use strings with **piezo-electric** pick-ups; another type employs steel reeds as generators, either struck or plucked. The Hohner Duo combines both bars and plucked reeds in one instrument. Alternative **timbres** can be obtained by **filtering** the output in different ways, and some string-based pianos have several pick-ups along the string to favour different groups of **harmonics**.

A different kind of piano electrification is to automate the action rather than (or as well as) amplifying the sound. The modern equivalent of the pneumatically operated player piano or pianola (with paper roll recording) is a normal keyboard fitted with **solenoids** for automatic playback – one example is the Marantz Pianocorder. The keystrokes of a performance can be recorded on a storage medium, and played back by the instrument (or via **MIDI** by another one). An expansion of the Pianocorder system, using three pianos with computer manipulations, MIDI interfacing and other features has been built by Richard Teitelbaum (1985). Another type is the Yahama Disklavier,* which uses optical velocity sensing at both key and hammer positions, and also features MIDI.

Several new approaches to computer-controlled pianos have been developed in Melbourne by Alistair Riddell (Riddell, 1988). One of these pianos has its action replaced by solenoid-actuated hammers which strike the strings directly. They can either rest on the strings as dampers, or strike once, bouncing off and staying clear of the string like a normal piano hammer stroke, or deliver repeated strikes at various speeds, the highest of which produces a virtually continuous though slightly buzzy note, an effect aimed at by some of the much earlier 'sostenente' pianos (see **pianos** *acoustic*).

Automated pianos, including the earlier ones, offer some interesting possibilities to composers, since the number of simultaneous notes, the complexity of rhythms, the speed of execution etc. are not limited by manual skills. The most celebrated 'piano roll' composer is the Mexican Conlon Nancarrow.

---

*Yamaha Nippon Gakki Co. Ltd, Hamamatsu, Japan.

Electronic pianos

Until recently electronic pianos were in effect adapted analogue organ or synthesizer designs with timbres and percussive envelopes approximately modelled on piano sound, and some kind of velocity sensing to give a dynamically sensitive touch. Without this no instrument can claim to be a piano, and ways of providing this include optical sensing (mentioned above) and fitting two switches which close in succession as the key is depressed, the time interval between closures being a measure of velocity. But even with velocity sensing an organ-type keyboard feels nothing like a piano to play. One instrument that was sometimes also used as a piano was the **Mellotron**. This was fitted with tapes carrying recordings of real piano sounds, and the idea has been revived in a much improved, digital form (see below). The early electronic pianos were much inferior to the electro-acoustic pianos in power, crisp sound and piano-like performance characteristics, but neither group sounded much like real pianos.

However, today's electronic pianos (now often called 'digital pianos') are quite another matter. This is partly because the problems were at last properly investigated. A team set up in 1983 to develop the Kurzweil 250 synthesizer,* decided to concentrate on the piano because its sound is not only extremely complex but well known to millions of people. They argued that 'if you can do a convincing piano, you should be able to do almost anything' (introduction to Byrd (1986)). Apart from noting that the timbre alters many times as one ascends the keyboard and changes string type and number etc., the team observed that strongly played notes are not just louder than gently struck ones, but substantially different in harmonic content. In brief, the stored piano sounds in the Kurzweil far outnumber the eighty-eight notes of the keyboard, and velocity sensing includes provision for changing the basic sound as well as the loudness in response to different key strikes. Combined with a wooden-keyed weighted action designed to give a natural piano 'feel', both performers and audiences agreed that a new level of realism had been achieved.

By the late 1980s a number of more modestly priced electronic pianos were offering comparable facilities, some using synthesis and others stored **samples** of real piano sounds (compare **percussion generators**). A typical choice of sounds on one instrument's menu might include two or three 'acoustic' pianos, electric pianos, harpsichords and sometimes mallet instruments (such as vibraphone). Some require external **ampli-**

*Kurzweil Music Systems Inc., 411 Waverley Oaks Rd, Waltham, Massachusetts 02154, USA. Manufacturers of the Kurzweil 250 Digital Synthesizer and other products.

fiers and **loudspeakers** and others are self-contained. Nearly all have piano-like key actions, and extras may include **MIDI** interfacing, built-in effects like **reverberation**, and recording/playback facilities from an on-board **sequencer**. At the same time a range of electro-acoustic instruments still continues to be available, also in updated form with **MIDI** and other facilities.

Apart from offering relative cheapness, portability and maintenance-free reliability, it is likely that future digital pianos will equal all but the very best conventional instruments in tonal quality as well. Tuning is permanently correct, but pitch adjustments may also be offered, including fine-tuning for working with ensembles or non-standard instruments, shifting the whole keyboard to a different pitch standard (see **A**), automatic transposition, microtonal tuning and a choice of alternatives to equal **temperament**.

Piano *prepared* This refers particularly to the type of preparation made famous by John Cage, in which bolts, screws, wedges, rubber erasers etc. are placed at carefully specified positions between certain strings, radically modifying the sound of the notes affected. Some of these techniques (particularly loose bolts) only work with grand pianos, and there is also the problem that as the internal dimensions of pianos vary considerably, an absolute measurement may not accurately define the point aimed at, for example a particular **antinode** might have to be found by measuring off seven-tenths of whatever happens to be the string's length. A number of composers besides Cage have used these methods; the San Diego composer David Ward-Steinman, for example, writes music for 'fortified piano', which refers not to amplification but to the use of several techniques in one piece – keyboard, inside plucking, preparation and percussion effects on the case. An excellent handbook, giving full practical details and a list of prepared piano works, is Richard Bunger's *The Well-Prepared Piano* (1981).

Pick-ups **Transducers** that respond to mechanical or magnetic changes, rather than sound waves. Contact pick-ups are dealt with under **microphones 5** because that description is usually (but incorrectly) applied to them. Magnetic pick-ups that respond to string vibration are described under **electric guitar**. This entry deals specifically with pick-ups for playing records. For disc recording and manufacture see **sound recording techniques**.

For a century the analogue disc recording dominated music reproduction (Emil Berliner demonstrated a flat disc system in 1887), but the digital **compact disc**, while still in a state of development, has rapidly won over both professional and home users. Although advocates of the **LP** are fighting a strong rearguard action, the familiar vinyl is certain before long to join the 78 rpm disc in the archives and museums. This article is therefore confined to a broad outline of the problems encountered in pick-up design, but there is no shortage of accessible and detailed material for interested readers, see the comprehensive survey in Ballou (1987) chapter 23 and useful comments in Nisbett (1970) and Runstein (1989).

A pick-up consists of the transducer (cartridge) into which a needle or stylus is inserted, and the 'tone arm' (a quaint term surviving from the days when it was a hollow tube carrying the sound itself). Since the late 1950s most discs have been **stereo**, using a symmetrical system (45°/ 45°), so pick-ups must be able to detect two distinct sound streams while still being 'compatible' (i.e. able to reproduce the older – and some new – mono recordings). Fig. 157 shows the difference between mono and stereo groove modulation. Arrows show the direction of stylus movement and the dotted lines approximate limits of travel. In the stereo example modulation is assumed to be on the righthand channel only. Groove walls are at 90° and in stereo each channel is modulated perpendicularly to its respective wall. Recording is arranged so that the in-**phase** components of the stereo signal sum to produce a lateral stylus movement, which is how the groove is made compatible (see **stereo**).

Pick-up cartridges
Stereo pick-ups use two transducers whose axes of maximum sensitivity are set at right angles to each other. The main types are **piezo-electric**,

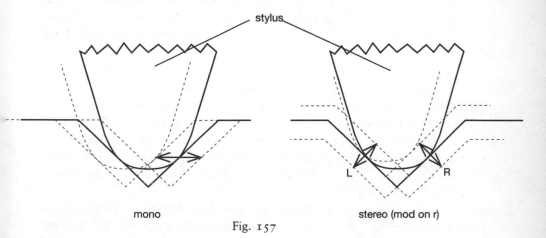

mono   stereo (mod on r)

Fig. 157

with crystal or ceramic elements, and **magnetic**, which can consist of moving iron, moving coil or moving magnet. **Capacitor** and **semiconductor** pick-ups are also made. In general the crystal types are cheaper, and produce high outputs which are easy to handle and amplify, and the magnetics are more accurate, less noisy and cause less wear because low tracking weights can be used. The best magnetics are expensive, not only to make but because their low outputs demand a well-designed 'front end' **amplifier** to give of their best.

A mono groove (lateral) should be detected equally by both transducers, but there can be problems with unequal response, phase cancellation and unwanted vertical information. Stereo channel separation is not good compared with tape, but because in music recording the two channels are normally carrying versions of the same material, poor separation may well be tolerated in favour of other, desirable features of a given design. Because of the vertical component, mono pick-ups playing stereo discs must have some vertical **compliance** or they will damage records.

Considering the numerous pitfalls in disc reproduction, the real surprise is that it works so well. Take, for example, just two of the problems that beset pick-ups: tracing distortion and pinch effect. Tracing problems arise because the polished, rounded diamond that plays the record is a different shape from the sharp V-pointed tool (see fig. 179) that cut it. Fig. 158a shows that the cutter can incise **wavelengths** too short for the playing stylus to follow. The problem gets worse towards the centre of the record because all wavelengths on the disc become shorter as the groove-to-stylus velocity decreases. The distortion shown in 158b occurs because the undulating groove's shape is incorrectly transferred to the motion of a round stylus tip constrained to move only laterally, and the error increases with amplitude.

Pinch effect is shown (greatly exaggerated) in 158c. Cutting lateral modulations as the disc rotates results in the groove width being narrower in the central portion of a **cycle** than at the peak. This imparts a vertical movement to the stylus at twice the frequency being traced (second **harmonic** distortion). The problem in 158b can be electronically compensated to some extent by applying an opposite pre-distortion in recording, and both tracing and pinch errors are helped by using an elliptical rather than a round stylus (shown in 158c).

Tone arms
For correct tracking a pick-up should follow the same radial path as the cutter did before it (see again fig. 179), and a normal pivoted arm cannot

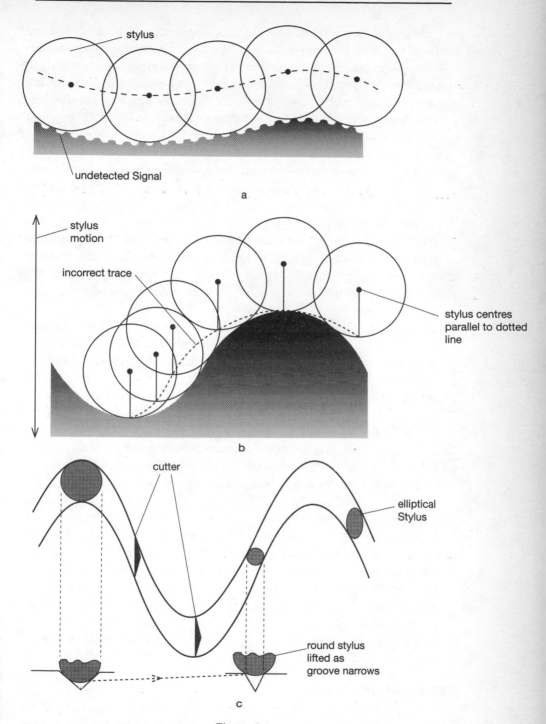

stylus

undetected Signal

a

stylus motion

incorrect trace

stylus centres parallel to dotted line

b

cutter

elliptical Stylus

round stylus lifted as groove narrows

c

Fig. 158

do this. It is, however, achieved by the 'tangential' type of tone arm, in which the head assembly rolls sideways along a track. With 78s the large groove and heavy tracking weights made such a pick-up feasible with no energy source except the turntable, but with microgroove discs radial tracking must be power assisted. Position sensors and a **servo** mechanism move the pick-up so that it precisely follows the groove. This expensive method is used in a few high quality record players, but it is difficult to make reliable under all conditions (for example with warped discs and 'swingers' – off-centre discs), and changing and cueing records is often a slower process than with conventional pick-ups. In spite of the compromises involved, the pivoted arm remains by far the most popular type.

However well an arm performs in having low pivot friction, adjustable height and tracking weight, an absence of mechanical **resonance**, and correct inertial damping etc., there must always be some 'tracking error'. Fig. 159a shows that a straight arm mounted reasonably close to the turntable can only track accurately at one point in its travel, and is badly out at the extremes (very long arms are ruled out for practical reasons). By offsetting the head, 159b, a longer arm can be sited at the same point, and track very much better by gradually changing the radius followed as the record is played.

Unfortunately the offset itself introduces a new problem, a 'skating' force (fig. 159c) which at best pushes the stylus against the inner groove wall, and at worst sends the pick-up flying across the record. In low cost equipment this is usually overcome by increasing the tracking weight and/or tilting the turntable slightly. High quality tone arms have anti-skating devices using magnets, springs, or strings with pulleys and weights.

There are numerous approaches to pick-up design, each with its advocates, but most assume level and stable conditions, and use the weight of the pick-up as the tracking force, counterbalanced by weights or springs. There are also dynamically balanced systems, originally developed for ships, in which all forces are first balanced out and the tracking force applied with a spring. Used in many juke boxes, this method allows a record to be tracked in the vertical position, and, with suitably designed components, to be played on both sides without turning.

Picofarad   See **capacitance**

Piezo-electric   (from the Greek *piezein* 'to press') A property of some

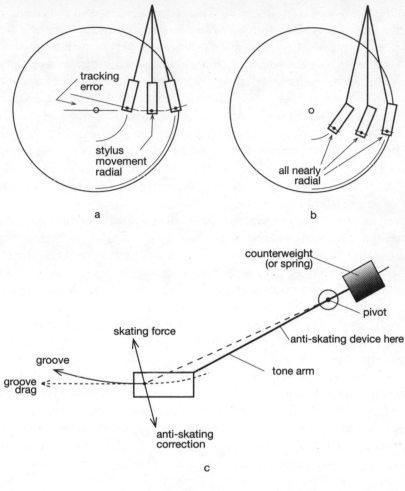

tracking
error

stylus
movement
radial

a

all nearly
radial

b

counterweight
(or spring)

pivot

anti-skating device here

skating force

groove

groove
drag

tone arm

anti-skating
correction

c

Fig. 159

crystalline and ceramic substances that become electrically polarized when deformed by compressing, bending or twisting. Such materials include quartz (natural crystalline silicon dioxide), Rochelle salt (artificially grown from sodium potassium tartrate tetrahydrate), barium titanate (ceramic), various lead compounds etc. The material is cut on critical axes and often assembled as a 'bimorph' sandwich with metal foil between, and on each side of, two crystal wafers. Deforming the crystals produces a **voltage** between the metal foil **electrodes**. This principle is used in **microphones, pick-ups**, and also in reverse (applied voltage deforming the crystal) in **loudspeakers**. It is the electrostatic equivalent of **magnetostriction**. See also **oscillators**.

Pilot tone   A synchronizing or **phase**-controlling signal, separate from the audio signal. One type is used in filming to lock camera and tape recorder together (also called 'pulse'). In stereo **frequency modulation** broadcasting, a pilot tone (usually 19 kHz) is used to separate LEFT and RIGHT information, and can generate spurious products when combined with the **bias/erase** frequency of a tape recorder. A reject **filter** can be used to remove it before recording.

Pinch roller   See **tape recorder design**

Ping-pong (stereo)   A pseudo-**stereo** effect in which sound is continually flipped from channel to channel. It has been used effectively by composers as a deliberate technique, but is usually a crude way of producing 'stereo' from mono sources.

Pink noise   Noise with energy distributed as the inverse of **frequency** ($1/f$). See **analogue synthesis techniques** 4.

Pitch   1. The human perception of the 'highness' or 'lowness' of a sound. In ordinary use it is synonymous with **frequency**, but it is modified by pitch standards (see **A**), i.e. C$\sharp$ as a pitch can mean different things as a frequency. As with perceived loudness, however (see **phon**), there are variations in sensitivity in different parts of our hearing range. For example, an **octave** interval is easily perceived in the middle ranges, but most untrained people would find great difficulty in tuning the lowest A octave of the piano (27.5 Hz–55 Hz) accurately from a randomly tuned condition given only middle A (440 Hz) as a guide.

A similar uncertainty occurs if an oscillator is tuned to 5 kHz and a person is asked to tune another to exactly 10 kHz, because although we can clearly hear 10 kHz it is hard to relate it to a particular 'note' – it just sounds 'very high'. Another common phenomenon is that complex **harmonic** structures can lead us to perceive the wrong **fundamental** or supply a non-existent one.

Many ingenious tests have been devised to challenge our sense of pitch, and although attempts have been made to find a parallel unit to the phon, tailored to human aural characteristics, the **hertz** continues to be the accepted unit for both pitch and frequency. The study of pitch perception is a branch of **psychoacoustics**. See also **absolute pitch** and Dodge (1985), Risset (1966), Olson (1967), Roederer (1979) and Deutsch (1982). 2. The distance between successive turns of a screw thread or spiral track. For example, a record's 'pitch' is measured in lines per unit of radial length.

Pitch changer   A **digital** device using delay line techniques (see **reverberators**) to change the frequency of all constituents of a signal while preserving their internal ratios. These devices allow the **pitch** of a musical line to be changed without changing the speed, and vice versa, by changing the speed and then correcting the pitch back to the original (an earlier related analogue device was the tempophon, see **tape composition techniques**). A pitch changer is often one feature of a **digital multi-effect unit** or of a 'harmonizer', which offers a choice of pre-set interval changes and other facilities. Compare **frequency shifter**, which applies a linear rather than proportional shift.

Pitch follower   A device which detects and tracks the changing **frequency** of an instrumental or vocal performance, and outputs a voltage or equivalent **MIDI** data dependent on it. Its effectiveness varies with the nature of the sound input: detached, firmly attacked steady pitches are read much better than, for example, continuous glissandi with heavy **vibrato**. It is used in **live performance electronic music** to provide cross-influences, for example making the pitch contour of a sung melody affect the **timbre** of an electronic instrument. It is often combined in one unit with an **envelope follower**.

Pixel   (Short for 'picture element'.) The minimum 'dot' size in a given visual display, represented by one **bit** in the computer. Pixels/cm² (the more the sharper) are a measure of picture **resolution**.

Point source   (effect) In single loudspeaker listening, the reduction of the natural sound stage to a single direction and source location (the higher the **frequency** the more pronounced the effect). It is particularly noticeable in, for example, opera on mono radio, but is to some extent relieved by secondary room reflections. Correct **stereo** imaging does not merely add a second point source, but fills the space in between and around.

Polar pattern   See **microphones**

Pol/e, -arity, -arization   The terminal (negative or positive) of an electrical source such as a battery, or an area of maximum flux (North

or South) in a magnet. Something is 'polarized' if it is **charged** in one
direction, or if it must be connected in a stated direction to function,
for example some devices require + power rails, some −, and some both
(relative to a reference **potential,** usually **earth (ground)**). Polarization is
the process of aligning an unorientated system in one direction or the
other.

Poll/ing   A procedure in which a number of 'stations' are scanned
repeatedly and rapidly in an infinite loop, so that any new data from
any of them can be implemented. In a digital **keyboard synthesizer,** for
example, all control points are polled continuously and the appropriate
actions initiated whenever any new instruction (e.g. keys pressed, sliders
moved) is found.

Polyphon/y, -ic   From the Greek meaning 'many voices', as opposed
to monophony (one voice), and used, with different connotations, of
both music, 1, and musical instruments, 2. 1. The term can be applied
to any music in two or more parts, but particularly when voices are
rhythmically independent, i.e. polyphony is a horizontal, multi-melodic
view of composition, and in historical studies refers especially to the
period from roughly the eleventh to the sixteenth century in Europe. The
polyphonic music of the baroque period is usually termed counterpoint
(contrapuntal), and the **serial** polyphony of the twentieth century is
'linear counterpoint'. Music in several parts which all sound together in
a progression of chords (e.g. many hymns) is called homophonic and
analysed harmonically (vertically) rather than contrapuntally. 2. Polyphonic musical instruments can sound several notes simultaneously,
either up to all possible notes together (e.g. **piano**), or 'restricted polyphonic', such as many **keyboard synthesizers,** which allow up to a
certain number of voices (typically eight or sixteen) but no more, and
instruments like the pedal harp which can only sound one pitch for each
note name, i.e. if G♯ is set, all Gs are sharp and G♮ and G♭ cannot be
played.

Positive feedback   See **feedback**

Post-sync   A process of recording and synchronizing film dialogue (and
occasionally also music) that is recorded after a scene has been shot.
Actors speak short sections of dialogue to match picture loops of themselves run with matching loops of magnetic film. This is necessary where
original 'sync dialogue' is unusable, for example when microphones

cannot be properly sited, or when conditions are noisy or windy.

Potential   As an absolute electrical quantity, the energy possessed by an object compared with that possessed by the same object if removed an infinite distance from the field. More commonly used in the relative term 'potential difference' (PD). The PD between two points, such as between the terminals of a battery or a charged object and **earth**, is expressed in **volts**. PD and voltage are often treated as synonymous.

Potentiometer (pot)   As its name implies, a device for measuring potential difference (in **volts**). A calibrated **resistive** track can be tapped at any point by a moveable slider or 'wiper', giving accurate voltage division of the source to be measured. In practice the word 'pot' is loosely used of any three-terminal variable resistor, and rarely refers to a measuring device. Pots are used for the majority of variable controls such as **faders**. They come in numerous shapes and sizes, with many different electrical characteristics. See also **linear pot, logarithmic pot** and **helical pot**.

Power   1. The rate at which energy is converted from one form to another, SI unit the **watt**. 2. The number of times the value of a number is raised by multiplication with itself, for example 1000 is the third power of 10 (10^3). See **exponential**. 3. 'Power' is used colloquially to refer to mains or battery electrical supply to equipment. See **mains supplies**.

Power amplifier   See **amplifiers**

PPM   See **peak programme meter**

Pre-amplifier   See **amplifiers**

Pre-emphasis   The treble boost applied in recording media and **FM** radio before the material is recorded/broadcast. It is **compensated** (or corrected) on playback/reception by a complementary treble cut to restore a level **response**. Because the most irritating noise and interference are at the high **frequency** end of the **spectrum**, pre-emphasis improves the **signal-to-noise ratio**. See also **equalizer** and **sound recording techniques**.

Pre-fade   1. To run a previously timed recording of, for example, a signature tune behind the last few minutes of a programme, with the

fader closed until the programme is over. This means that whenever it is faded up, the pre-faded material will finish at exactly the right time. 2. As in 'Pre-Fade Listen' (PFL). See **mixers and mixing desks**.

Pre-mix   A mix made before the main **mixdown**, often when there are too many separate tracks for the operator to handle. Thus in film **dubbing** it is common to make a dialogue pre-mix or an effects pre-mix. Although this is a convenient procedure it prevents any further adjustment of internal levels. Automated **mixing desks** and **patches** now allow many tracks to be mixed down without pre-mixing.

Pre-recording   A recording made in advance of a main session, where it will be played in with live performances and/or other pre-recordings, and re-recorded (**dubbed**) in the final **mixdown**, possibly preceded by **pre-mixes**.

Presence   The degree of apparent 'nearness' of a sound source. In a poorly balanced **pre-mix** of singer and orchestra for example, the vocal presence can often be increased by emphasizing an area of strong voice **partials**, found by trial and error, but usually in the 3–6 kHz region. Boosting the extreme highs will merely add shrillness and edge. Normally controlled by a built-in **equalizer** in the **mixing desk**.

Pressing   The final form of a mass-produced vinyl disc, made by squeezing soft plastic at high pressure between two 'stampers'. See **sound recording techniques**.

Pressure gradient microphone   See **microphones**

Pressure microphone   See **microphones**

Pressure pad   See **tape recorder design**

Pressure zone microphone (PZM)   See **microphones**

Printed circuit   A universally used circuit and component carrying medium, PC boards are prepared by printing, painting or dry-transferring the circuit in a corrosion-resistant material on to a thin copper layer bonded to a rigid non-conducting board. The uncoated copper parts are etched away, leaving only the circuit. Printed circuit boards (PCBs) can be double-sided or multi-layered. One of the many conveniences of PCBs (also known as 'cards') is the ease with which they can be made detachable by a multi-way edge connector and socket, not only simplifying replacement and servicing, but allowing alternative circuit elements to be inserted for different purposes, such as plug-in **RAMs** and **ROMs** for **synthesizers**.

Print-through   The transfer of magnetic flux between adjacent layers of wound tape, particularly likely when high levels are recorded on thin-based tape, and made worse by storage at high temperatures. For mastering, standard tape (1.5 **thou**) should always be used. Print-through occurs in both directions (as 'pre-echo' and 'post-echo'), but the effect is worse towards the next outer layer than towards the inner. Since pre-echo is usually more destructive than post-echo (which is often lost in the next signal or the decay of the echoed signal), storing tape 'tail out' ensures that the worse effect will be the post-echo. Finally, fast winding tape before use helps to disperse and reduce the stray fields, and tail-out storage compels a beneficial rewind before the tape can be played, also ensuring that the tape is neatly spooled afterwards instead of fast wound immediately before storage. Regular winding of all master and archive tapes helps to keep the plastic supple and reduce print-through.

Probability   See **random and chance procedures**

PROM   Programmable **Read-Only Memory**. A storage device with user-selectable contents but not erasable once programmed. See **EPROM**.

Pseudo-random   Of a series of numbers designed to exhibit adequate randomness for the purpose in hand, but arithmetically generated. A pseudo-random procedure takes any 'seed' (except o), and calculates a new, seemingly unrelated number from it, and another from that etc. At a time dependent on the speed of generation and the **word** length, the seed and hence the whole sequence is bound to repeat, but this may actually be an advantage. For example if random numbers are being used to generate versions of a musical texture, and a desirable event occurs once by chance, that event can be exactly repeated by seeding it with the number that began it. Pseudo-random generators are available as hardware modules or can be implemented by suitable **algorithms**, some of which are given in Chamberlin (1985) chapter 15 and Dodge (1985) chapter 3. See also **random number and voltage generators**.

Psychoacoustics A subdivision of psychophysics, which examines the way human beings perceive and respond to the phenomena objectively studied in physics. The aspect of psychoacoustics concerned with music also overlaps with another more general area, the psychology of music, which itself extends into non-acoustic issues such as how we measure musical time and the nature of the mental process of listening to a performance.

Psychoacoustic studies examine, for example, our **pitch** and **loudness** perceptions, our sense of direction and distance in hearing, how we analyse **timbre**, how we sort out detail from a mass of inputs (**cocktail party effect**), and the explanation of aural illusions, which are often just as puzzling as optical ones. Helmholtz made the first serious investigations of musical perception in the 1850s (Helmholtz, 1862) but most of the researchers in the half century or so following him showed surprisingly little sensitivity to musical problems (and many of Helmholtz's own conclusions have since been overturned, partly because adequate experimental methods were not available to him).

A problem with any subjective study is that the researcher cannot make precise objective measurements. Experiments have to be based on asking a group of people: 'Was that sound louder (or longer, higher, richer, more to the left) than the one before?', and statistically assessing the results. Criteria such as **just noticeable difference** (jnd) vary widely between individuals, and establishing norms for an 'average listener' or 'typical concert room' is almost impossible. As well as this, early investigators often used inappropriate tests, drawing conclusions on the basis of steady **sine** tones, for example, although no real music is ever in a steady state, and musical tones are never sinusoidal but usually very complex, even in seemingly simple music. Nevertheless some of the work done many years ago (e.g. the famous Fletcher–Munson curves of 1933, see **phon** and fig. 155) have stood the test of time well.

The picture has changed completely in recent years, however, because computers have brought new levels of precision to the physical investigation of sound, to the measurement of human response and to the mathematics of analysis. Contemporary researchers are moving further down the neural road into the brain itself, attempting to find the deeper secrets of musical interpretation, the workings of the mind's ear etc. Much is still mysterious, but a beginning has been made.

Practical impetus to the new psychoacoustics was given by early research into computer synthesis, notably by Jean-Claude Risset, whose paper on trumpet tones was published in 1966. Risset found that the 'classical' method of **synthesizing** tones by reconstructing a steady-state

spectrum (as shown in many acoustics textbooks) simply does not work. He showed that by studying sounds dynamically (how they develop in the first few milliseconds and how their **partials** change throughout) and using this new data as a model, much more convincing synthetic sounds could be made. This work began a continuing series of interactions between analysis and synthesis, and studies of how people reacted both to imitations of familiar instruments, and the new sounds that could now be made with computers. Composers using these new sounds and new compositional methods were thus, for the first time, offered criteria by which to judge their effect on listeners.

In *The Psychology of Music*, edited and partly written by Diana Deutsch (Deutsch, 1982), chapter 2 by Risset and David Wessel summarizes the work Risset began in the 1960s and is still engaged on (see also **digital synthesis techniques** 3 and **computer music composition techniques** 2 and 4). Another recommended book is Juan G. Roederer's *Introduction to the Physics and Psychophysics of Music*, in which objective and subjective aspects are developed side by side (Roederer, 1979).

The ear does not seem at first sight a promising piece of engineering – a collection of small bones knocking against each other and eventually disturbing a liquid reservoir containing hair-like sensors. Nevertheless, as more is discovered about the way we hear, interpret and create sounds and music, what emerges is that we possess an aural system of amazing complexity and accuracy. If we take only the basic act of hearing, our ears can handle an intensity range of a trillion to one (see **decibel**) but still detect small changes in level. In localizing sounds, consider the following: you enter an unfamiliar, dark hall, groping for light switches; your friend has gone in first but is invisible. You call 'Where are you?', he says 'Over here'. After this one exchange you each know within a few degrees in which direction the other is, can make a sensible guess at how far away and have a good idea about the size of the hall and whether it contains largely reflective or largely absorbent surfaces. The cues that give us all this information are extremely complex, and even if the mass of data could be quantified accurately it would take long and elaborate analysis to evaluate, instead of the fraction of a second it takes our brains (for further comment see **stereo**). Blind people continuously process a huge input of aural data as a matter of course to cope with everyday living.

Enlarging the scope of enquiry to include the whole range of musical activities, the ear/brain neural chain can be thought of as part of a looped **feedback** system.

Fig. 160 shows, in simplistic form, the process of a person composing

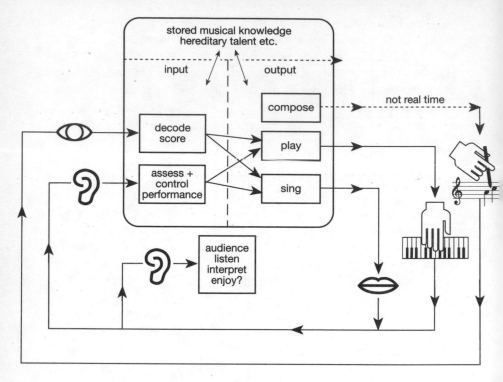

Fig. 160

a song with piano, and later performing it (for a slightly different perspective see **analogue synthesis techniques** 2). To write the song, the composer draws on a number of resources, some learned, some hereditary, some 'inspirational'. If the piano is used as a compositional aid, there will be preliminary loops not shown in the diagram. The 'composer' block is therefore very complex, and to date little understood – a dozen composers will give a dozen opinions about how it is done. Once the **real-time** loops are entered an elaborate series of mental decisions and physical acts must take place without hesitation: firstly eyes to hands and voice box, and then self-assessing/correcting feedback (is this the right tempo, is voice balance OK?). Meanwhile the audience, to whom the piece is a new experience, are applying a different set of criteria to interpret and understand the music. Studies have been done to test audience reactions to unfamiliar music – both in the formal and the sonic sense.

The above examples should illustrate the difficulty of researching psychoacoustic areas with objectivity. Overlaps with other fields occur,

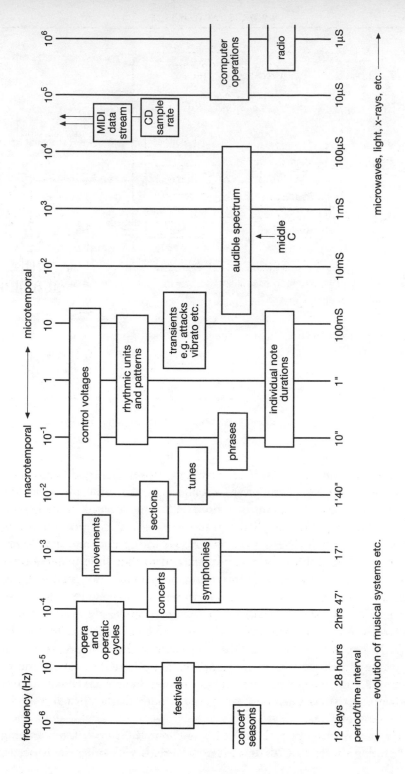

Fig. 161

of course, so that new knowledge about, say, visual processing may well open doors to aural equivalents.

An attribute generally useful in our lives, but vital in music, is an ability to distinguish a wide range of temporal events. Fig. 161 summarizes the range of time scales (often **cyclic** so given in **frequency** as well as time interval) relevant in musical contexts. Even in ordinary musical listening and appreciation our ear/brain system has to cope with a large part of the spectrum shown, from around 10^4 Hz for the highest sounds we can hear, to periods of an hour or more in assessing the shape and sense of a large work. Roederer summarizes what is believed to be the subjective process involved (Roederer, 1979, chapter 1). The microtemporal part (vibrations of sounds) appears to be processed in the inner ear, the middle range (attacks, vibrati, internal timbre changes) in the neural pathway between the ear and the brain, and the macrotemporal (anything from individual notes, through groups of notes in rhythms and tunes, to whole works) by the cerebral cortex. At the present time, the further along that chain we proceed the less is properly understood (see also Deutsch, 1982, chapters 6 and 7).

The psychology (rather than the neural process) of composition spills over into the philosophy of creativity, which is discussed in many of the recommended books, see for example, Roads (1985). A useful summary of typical psychoacoustic topics is appendix A in *The Technology of Computer Music*, by Max Mathews and J. R. Pierce (Mathews, 1969). Though it represents the state of exploration in 1969, it shows that the main areas of experiment were already very active. They include: loudness (**phon**), **masking, pitch, timbre, transients,** consonance (**dissonance**), **combination tones, reverberation, chorus effect,** direction and distance.

Public address (PA)   Originally applied to equipment specifically for open air speech amplification, 'public address' (always contracted as PA) now describes any array of **amplifiers** and **loudspeakers** designed for the information or entertainment of large audiences rather than for studio or domestic purposes. In speech-only applications fairly high levels of distortion can be tolerated without serious loss of intelligibility, and relatively small amplifiers coupled with high efficiency speakers can deliver high loudness outputs, provided that problems like **howl round** are solved. Ruggedness and weather-resistance are also primary considerations. For music or high quality speech (such as drama) high power must be combined with high quality, which involves large amplifiers and many speakers carefully placed to distribute output as evenly as possible in the environment (see **loudspeakers** for the directional properties of sound radiators). Live rock music, for which the PA is a fundamental requisite, is elaborately balanced for every venue used.

A special application of PA is in sound reinforcement, where time delays may be interposed between the source and the reproducing system. In a concert hall with unsatisfactory, woolly acoustics, for example, microphones suspended above the platform can pick up and re-distribute the programme with simulated **reverberation** (at one time done by using tape head delays, but now by digital methods) to provide the 'liveness' missing from the space. The fidelity must be good (the audience should not suspect anything 'artificial'), so the speakers are usually hidden and played at low level. A different example of a building needing help from reinforcement would be a cathedral with over-lively acoustics and such a long reverberation time that people distant from the pulpit hear an unintelligible jumble of mixed reflections. In this case speakers are mounted relatively close to the listeners, and the time delay adjusted so that the output from speakers arrives at the same time as the direct sound. Levels are set so that the speaker outputs are substantially louder than the confused indirect reflections. If the outputs from a line of speakers (perhaps mounted on pillars) are correctly delayed according to the distance of each from the pulpit, a clear sound should be heard from any position.

For fuller discussions of sound reinforcement and PA generally, see Capel (1981), Ballou (1987) chapter 26 and **microphones**.

Pulse code modulation (PCM)   A digital encoding system adopted for almost all digital music recording. Timed samples of the instantaneous amplitudes of the input analogue signal are converted to numbers, which are then encoded as pulses and recorded (see **digital synthesis techniques** 1 for a description of the sampling process).

Fig. 162 illustrates the principle using (for clarity) a very coarse scale in both timing and resolution (three bits – see **binary code**). In practical recording systems of fourteen or sixteen bits at **sampling rates** of 44.1 or 48 kHz, the basic PCM is converted into a more efficient 'channel code' for recording. See **analogue-to-digital** and **digital-to-analogue converter, compact disc, digital audio tape, sound recording techniques, video cassette PCM,** and Pohlmann (1989), Runstein (1989) and Watkinson (1988).

Pulse wave   A rectangular wave with one half short compared with the other. A **complex wave** containing the complete **harmonic series**, the energy content of each **partial** varying with the degree of asymmetry in

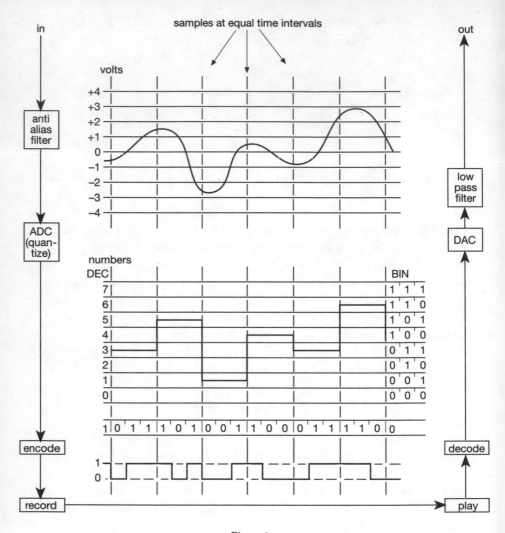

Fig. 162

the two parts of the wave's cycle. See **analogue synthesis techniques** 4.
Compare **square wave** (symmetrical rectangular) and **ramp** and **triangle**
waves.

Pure tone   See sine wave

PZM   Pressure Zone Microphone. See **microphones**

Q

Q   The magnification or 'quality' factor of a **resonant** system. See **filters** and fig. 86.

Quad panner   A manual control, commonly a **joystick** controlling a pair of **panpots**, which allows a mono signal to be 'placed' in a field bounded by four speakers roughly equidistant from and around the listener, by assigning different proportions of the output to each speaker. Controlling levels alone is effective with static locations or slow movement, but to simulate 'flying objects' **reverberation** changes and **Doppler effect** must also be considered (see next entry). Panners using four voltage controlled **amplifiers** (see also **oscillators** 3) can move a sound automatically, for example a slow **sine wave** control oscillator with outputs successively **lagging** by 90°, and applied to the four signals, will rotate the sound around the space (see the **phase** shift principle illustrated in fig. 146).

Quadraphony   Four-channel **stereo** listening which is, in theory, more realistic than two-channel, particularly for simulating movement, because direct sound can come from any angle instead of only from somewhere on a line between two speakers. Quad tape recording is a simple matter using multi-track machines, which have been available since the 1950s. No satisfactory way has been found of cutting four discrete signals into a single record groove, but coding methods can be used to combine and later separate the information. Quad discs were launched in the 1970s but were never a success. Many of them had poor sound quality and people resisted buying extra equipment for what seemed a small gain over normal stereo. Today's **surround sound** four-speaker systems are an artificial enhancement of stereo, not true quad.

There are two distinct approaches to quad: 1. 'natural' quad recording, made by placing four **microphones** in a space and recreating the image with four speakers; and 2. 'Creative' quad, which ranges from simply presenting four different signals (as if one were sitting inside a group of performers), through various kinds of **panning**, to a full simulation of 'natural' quad, which is complex and can only be done adequately with computers.

Quad recording and playback
One method of quad recording uses uni-directional (cardioid) microphones in a coincident cluster near the centre of the performing space, i.e. where the listener will sit in playback mode. The other uses spaced omnidirectional mics, which although theoretically a less valid approach (see **stereo**) can work well in practice (for different mic types, coincidence etc. see **microphones**). These methods are extensions of the two-channel set-ups shown in **microphone placement** (fig. 121a).

Fig. 163 shows that the pattern of direct and indirect paths (only a few shown of many, see **reverberation**) is different for each microphone. The playback environment should be as free of local coloration as possible, because its own acoustics, added to those of the recording, tend to confuse the listener's position cues. Recording a normally arranged group of musicians should result in a natural front/back orientation, but the directional effect given by the listener's head and the shape of the ears can be enhanced by slightly increasing reverberation and reducing level to the rear pair of speakers, and assigning the listener a definite direction to face.

'Creative' quad
Four- (or more) track working was used by electronic music composers very early, as a means of adding interest, spaciousness and mobility to sounds. The naturalistic creation of an image is not an issue because the whole acoustic basis of such music is artificial. Some multi-track pieces sound dense and dull when heard in stereo or mono versions on disc, but spring to life when properly presented.

With the general advance of computer music studies in the 1960s, more was discovered about the **psychoacoustic** cues that allow us to localize and track sounds. John Chowning, in *The Simulation of Moving Sound Sources*, proposed that it should be possible to give synthetic sounds the same position and motion characteristics as live quad recordings (Chowning, 1977). He analysed and simulated: 1. velocity cues – a combination of (a) angular (circumferential) velocity and (b) radial velocity (giving rise to the **Doppler effect**). He computed the changes of level required in each speaker, and the correct Doppler pitch shifts above and below the static pitch of the sound to be applied; and 2. reverberation cues – a combination of (a) 'global' reverberation (i.e. the acoustics of the imagined environment, therefore from all speakers and fairly

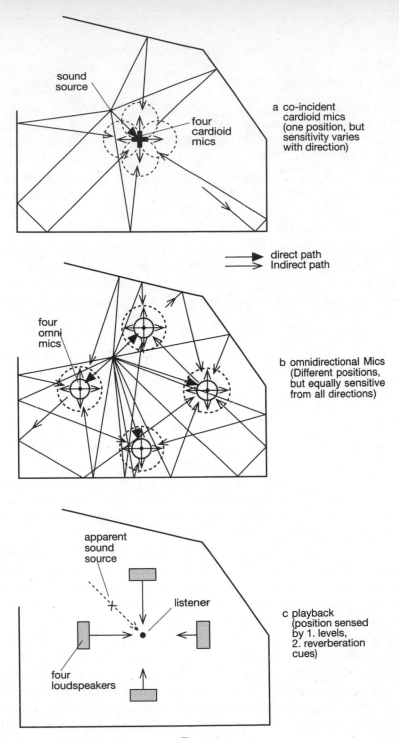

sound
source

four
cardioid
mics

a co-incident
cardioid mics
(one position, but
sensitivity varies
with direction)

→ direct path
⇒ Indirect path

four
omni
mics

b omnidirectional Mics
(Different positions,
but equally sensitive
from all directions)

apparent
sound
source

listener

c playback
(position sensed
by 1. levels,
2. reverberation
cues)

four
loudspeakers

Fig. 163

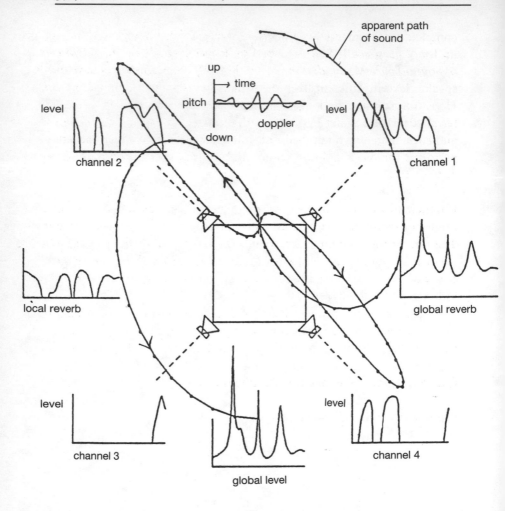

Fig. 164

constant) and (b) 'local' reverberation, which moves with the source and is distributed mainly between the pair of speakers currently radiating the sound. A striking example of the success of this exercise is Chowning's own piece *Turenas*, in which he makes use of the fact that we can detect motion more easily with trains of short sounds than with continuous ones.

Fig. 164 is the plot of a rapidly travelling string of percussive sounds from the opening section of the piece, with the functions of the various parameter changes involved. All the plots cover the same time interval, corresponding to the total length of the sound path if it were 'straightened out'. Even without the powerful resources Chowning used, less complex arrangements have also been successful, for example the set-up for *Voicespace I: Still* described by Roger Reynolds in *Explorations of Sound/Space Manipulation* (1977). Finally, some composers have used speaker layouts different from the usual square shape. In my piece *I Am Here*, for soprano and tape, the speakers are arranged in a regular tetrahedron (triangular pyramid) with one speaker flown high above the audience, matching a tetrahedral frame on stage within which the singer performs the piece. Sounds 'climb' and 'spiral', or a sound may rotate at floor level while a different sound is poised above.*

Quantization The process of dividing a continuous quantity into ranges or quantums, each represented throughout by the same number. The size of the quantums determines the **resolution** of the process (the smaller, the more precise). For example, in fig. 162 any voltage between 0 V and +1 V is represented by the number 4, and there is no way to indicate a voltage of, say, 0.3.

A 'quantization error' is caused by insufficient precision in, for example, an **analogue-to-digital conversion** process, and the error may give rise to 'quantization noise' (see also **digital synthesis techniques** 1).

Quarter track See **tape track configurations**

Quartz crystal See **oscillators** and **piezo-electric**

---

*Cary, Tristram *I Am Here for soprano and 4-track tape*, text by Peter Zinovieff, first performance by Jane Manning, St John's, Smith Square, London, 1981.

R

Radio control   See remote controls

Radio microphone   See microphones

RAM   See random access memory

Ramp wave   (Also known as a 'sawtooth' wave.) Ideally this waveform would show a **linear** change of **amplitude** over time followed by an instantaneous return to its starting point. Practical ramps, however, do not meet these requirements (the 'flyback' can never be instantaneous), but even imperfect ramps have wide uses in **synthesis**. The ramp is an asymmetric **complex waveform** containing a complete **harmonic series** with relative intensities diminishing such that the second harmonic has half the **fundamental**'s energy, the third has a third etc. (but see **digital synthesis techniques** 3 for further comment). See also **analogue synthesis techniques** 4 and relaxation **oscillators**. Compare **pulse**, **square** and **triangle waves**.

Random access memory (RAM)   A type of **semiconductor** fast memory universally used in computers, in which any location can be accessed directly and in the same amount of time, unlike types of storage that must be searched serially. RAM is volatile (it loses its contents when the power is switched off) but it can be made retentive by power backing. Battery-backed RAM is used in many music devices, sometimes in plug-in form. In this case the contents are virtually permanent, since batteries last several years, but also rewritable.

Random and chance procedures   A degree of indeterminacy is inevitable in any musical performance. One may like to think that a fully notated piece is determined, but even the most meticulously written score only provides guidelines. The input contributed by the player includes interpretative skills, knowledge of performing precedent, understanding of what the composer has left unstated etc., and each performer sees these things differently. In instrumental sound there are numerous random influences which ensure that even the 'same' note is different every time, and this is an important factor in making music interesting to listen to. The most completely determined music is pre-recorded **tape music**, which apart from variables like loudness level, listening conditions, tape wear etc. is exactly the same each time it is played.

Indeterminacy of varying degrees has always been a part of music, but in the past half-century many composers have introduced deliberate indeterminacy into scores, ranging from modest degrees of randomness, such as saying that a group of movements can be played in any order, to completely unnotated scores which contain only emotional cues, like: 'Sing "Oo", sadly and sweetly, choosing a note different from the one your neighbour chose.' A good survey of indeterminate methods is chapter 11 of David Cope's *New Music Composition* (1977), and some of the lectures and writings of that master of chance procedures, John Cage, can be found in his entertaining (but serious) books *Silence* (1961), and *A Year from Monday* (1968).

There is a great deal of imprecise usage in descriptions of randomness, for example 'aleatoric' (Latin *aleatorius* 'depending on a dice throw') properly refers to a strictly limited range of chances, not the complete randomness which it is often used to describe. The probability of a given outcome can be expressed as the ratio of that outcome to the total possibilities – with one die $1/6$ (or $5:1$ against). With two dice the possible throws rise to 36, and for extreme numbers (2 and 12) that figure represents the odds $(1/36)$. Middle numbers, however, can result from several different combinations, for example, 7 can be thrown in 6 ways, so the probability, at $6/36$ $(1/6)$ is much higher. This is called a Gaussian distribution, and is one of several ways of loading odds. Expressed in this way, probability ranges from 0 (never) to 1 (always). The single die gives a 'uniform distribution' (all chances equal), and in a **random generator** a selection is made from a uniformly distributed **spectrum**, or 'white' **noise** (see also **analogue synthesis techniques** 4). Very nearly white noise can also be numerically generated (see **pseudo-random**), and statistical loadings can be applied if a non-uniform output is wanted. In electronic music, random procedures are used in both synthesis and composition. For example, a **vibrato** (slow **FM**) that is slightly randomized will come much nearer to a natural vibrato than a boringly constant one. In composition, random numbers may be used to derive frequencies, rhythms, structures etc. Similar processes can also generate instrumental scores.

See **computer music composition techniques** 2 for a discussion of various probabilistic techniques in composition, including the pioneer work by Iannis Xenakis in random (he uses the word 'stochastic') processes, applied in the first instance to generate instrumental scores. That entry also gives references for further reading. A clear exposition of the whole probability field is given by Horace C. Levinson in *Chance, Luck and Statistics* (1963).

Random number and voltage generators   Random numbers have many uses in computer music (see previous entry, and **computer music composition techniques** 2). A truly random selection requires a random source such as 'white' **noise**, whose instantaneous amplitude is **sampled** to generate each random number and the value retained until the next sample is taken (see **sample-and-hold**). Converted to a number, the output is suitably scaled (to cover a user-specified range), and can be 'continuous' (limited only by the **resolution** of the system), or 'discrete', i.e. any number from a specified list. Time can be randomized by applying random numbers to a 'wait' routine. Easier to implement since it needs no hardware noise generator is a **pseudo-random** series.

In analogue random voltage (or **staircase**) generators the range is truly continuous because it is not converted to a number scale, but it can be made discrete by **quantizing** gates. Timing is randomized by applying a variable amount of a sampled voltage to the control input of a voltage controlled clock **oscillator**. Uniform distribution of numbers is the norm, but both computer and analogue random generator outputs can be loaded statistically (by **algorithmic** methods or by **filtering** the noise).

RCA synthesizer   See **analogue synthesis techniques** 6

Reactance   The property of **inductors** and **capacitors** to limit the size of **alternating currents**, defined similarly to **resistance** and hence measured in **ohms**. Reactance depends on the **frequency** of the AC as well as the inductance or capacitance of the reactive components. The combination of all the reactances and resistances in a circuit gives the **impedance** of that circuit.

Read/write   Terms used instead of PLAY/RECORD when referring to digital rather than analogue storage media.

Read-only memory (ROM)   A permanently programmed data storage device, non-volatile (i.e. the contents are not lost when the power is off) and not user-programmable. Usually a **semiconductor** device, but it may be optical (see **CD–ROM**). It is widely used in all computer-like devices, typically in **synthesizers** for storing 'factory'-programmed instruments etc. Compare **EPROM** and **PROM**, which are also non-volatile but user-programmable.

Real time The time taken to reach a point in or to complete some event, measured in actual time units but not necessarily related to clock (time-of-day) time. For example, a real-time tape counter (see **tape recorder design**) reading 2 mins 40 secs indicates that the tape would take that time to run to this point if rewound to zero. If a computer generating music samples can do all the necessary calculations by the actual time the next sample is needed, at the tempo set, it can play music in real time. If not, its output must be stored and later re-output in the intended time frame, just as writing out a score cannot be done in real time, but its symbols and tempo markings relate to real time.

Recording   See **sound recording techniques**

Rectifier   A device based on **diodes** for converting **AC** to **DC**. Used, for example, in conjunction with **transformers** to provide a DC power supply for electronics equipment from the AC mains supply.

Reed relay   See **relay**

Reel-to-reel   See **open reel**

Regenerative feedback   See **feedback** and **oscillators**

Register   1. The set of pipes associated with an **organ** 'stop' – hence 'registration', an organist's choice of stops. 2. A defined section of an instrument's range, such as 'low', 'upper' or 'top' register (see **woodwind instruments**). 3. In a computer, small (one **byte** or one **word**) high speed memory units with specialized jobs such as counting or temporary storage.

Reinforcement   See **public address**

Rejector   See **tuned circuit**

Relaxation oscillator   See **oscillators**

Relay A device which allows one circuit to influence (usually switch) another without direct connection to it, thus keeping control separate from the main 'executive' circuit. There are numerous types. 'Armature' relays (fig. 165a) use **electromagnets** to close/open contacts in secondary circuit(s) when the coil is energized. An alternative design giving fast, spark-free operation is the 'reed' relay (fig. 165b), in which the secondary contacts are enclosed in an evacuated glass tube. Most signal switching is now done by **semiconductor** relays with no moving parts (see **patch**). Fig. 165c shows the action of a **solenoid**, which may also be employed as a relay.

Remote controls Some remote control options are essential in a studio. Remoteness does not necessarily mean great distance, and some types of remote control actually require visual contact to work. The expression is also used colloquially as a verb – to 'remote' something.

The equipment to be remoted must be designed to make this possible. Earlier models of tape recorders, for example, where manual transport controls operate mechanical linkages directly, are not suitable. The next generation have switches with ON/OFF positions but **solenoid** operated linkages, and today's machines use momentarily-on feather-touch buttons which activate logic circuits. Both these types are easily remote controlled.

Tape recorders are a good example of remoting being almost an

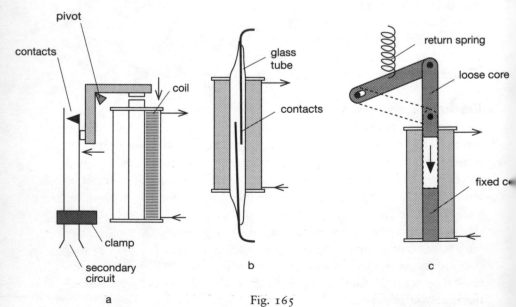

Fig. 165

ergonomic necessity, because a great deal of time is wasted if the **mixing desk** operator has to go to each machine for all functions. Modern multi-track machines have comprehensive remote control boxes which take care of **time codes**, track switching etc. as well as the main mechanical modes. One need only visit the machine itself to load and unload tape. There must be two-way communication so that the machine can tell the control station (for example by indicator lights) that it is acting on a command. Remotes can also be linked to allow for the simultaneous start of several machines.

Wired remote controls use either multi-core cable, with a separate circuit for each function, or a single circuit with appropriate encode/decode and logic arrangements. **MIDI** is a good example of the latter, and MIDI protocols now include transport control and time codes for audio and video machines. From this position it is a short step to the completely computer-controlled studio, with the current state of everything displayed on one screen.

Wireless remotes can be either radio controlled, with command codes similar to those used for model boats and planes, or the infra-red type now common for domestic TV and hi-fi, which sends codes of long and short pulses. Radio is interference-prone and not favoured for studio remotes, but has useful applications in live performance (for example the use of wireless **microphones** and radio-controlled 'magic' computers). Infra-red remotes now come with so many devices that a professional studio may well have some units sited so that the necessary line of sight contact can be made. When there are several infra-red controlled units, one can obtain a 'universal' controller, with many buttons and a **write** facility, which can be programmed with the codes of a number of separate transmitters.

Resist/ance, -ive, -ivity, -or   (symbol R) The property of an electrical conductor to oppose the free flow of **current** through it. Defined as the ratio of **DC voltage** to current through a conductor (see **Ohm's law**), it is measured in **ohms**. The resistance in any circuit converts some electrical energy into heat and is the electrical equivalent of friction. R is always present, but minimized when not wanted by making connecting wires of 'good' conductors such as copper and silver. R is deliberately introduced in known amounts, when needed, by manufacturing resistors with stated ohmic values. R is not frequency-dependent in an **AC** circuit (see **capacitance** and **inductance**). The resistivity of a material is its resistance per unit length and cross-section. See also **impedance, potentiometer** and **reactance**.

Resolution   1. In tonal music, the completion of a cadential process such as a change from the 'dominant' to the 'tonic' chord, or the resolving of 'suspended' chords from a discordant to a concordant state. 2. In calculations, the limit of possible subdivision in a given numerical operation, hence the precision with which continuous **functions** can be **quantized**. In general the more significant digits (in **binary code** the longer the **word**), the better the resolution. 3. Similar to 2. but referring loosely to particle size or 'grain'. Thus an important determinant of the noisiness and high frequency response of a tape stock is the size of its individual magnetic particles (the smaller the better). See also **pixel**.

Resonance   A phenomenon which occurs when a system which is able to **oscillate** naturally at a particular **frequency** is 'driven' (made to vibrate) by another oscillating system (the 'driver') oscillating at the same frequency. The result is a build up of **amplitude** in the driven system to abnormally large values at this one frequency (the driven system's natural frequency) and also sometimes at **harmonics** of it.

Resonance occurs in both mechanical (acoustic) and electrical systems. A tuning fork (driver) and milk bottle (driven system) can be used to demonstrate mechanical resonance. Blowing across the top of the bottle produces a note at the natural frequency of vibration for the air in the bottle. If a tuning fork is sounded over the top of the bottle there will generally be no sound except for the fork itself, but if water is poured into the bottle and its depth is adjusted, a loud sound will be heard as the natural frequency of vibrations in the bottle reaches the fork's frequency.

Electrical resonance is used in a radio receiver. Many **carriers** at different frequencies arrive at the radio's aerial (driver) where they cause oscillatory currents. A **tuned circuit** (driven system) is adjusted by the tuning knob until its natural frequency is the same as that of the particular carrier (station) we wish to tune to. A large amplitude current builds up at this frequency only, and all other carriers are rejected.

Resonance may be undesirable, for example in loudspeaker cabinets vibrating at certain frequencies, but in electrical form it is the design principle of many oscillators, **filters** etc., and acoustic resonators are essential features of nearly all musical instruments. See also **bowed strings**, **brass** and **woodwind instruments**, **formant** and **Helmholtz resonator**.

Response   The performance of some aspect of the whole or part of a system, measured by comparing the output with the input. Thus if the

frequency response of an **amplifier** is **linear** (also described as 'even', 'flat' or 'level') it means that all frequencies in the relevant **band** are being transmitted so that their relative **amplitudes** at the input are exactly reproduced at the output. Response curves are plotted for **transducers** such as **loudspeakers** and **microphones** by inputting a **sine wave** 'frequency run' (i.e. tuning its frequency continuously through the whole audio band – also known as 'squeaking') and plotting the output. Such curves are useful, but other types of response must also be assessed to get a complete picture, for example 'impulse' and 'transient' response, and **distortion** characteristics. See also **filters, reverberation** and polar patterns in **microphones**.

Retentivity   See **hysteresis** and **magnet**

Reverberat/ion, -ors   An effect closely related to **echo**, but used particularly when echoes are so numerous and along so many different paths that they cannot be individually distinguished. The 'early reflections', or initial echoes, of a sound made in an enclosed space (illustrated in fig. 163) are different in quality from the confused mass that follows. Consider two contrasting cases. Fig. 166a shows the behaviour of a space in which a continuous tone is played. The reflected sounds add to the direct sound and to each other, building up loudness until a steady state is reached when the energy absorbed by the surrounding surfaces balances the total energy of all the direct and indirect sources. When the note stops, the energy decays **exponentially** until it is quiet enough to be **masked** by the ambient noise present in any environment. The pioneer work in this field was done in the early 1920s by W. C. Sabine of Harvard, who based his research on a particular lecture hall at that university which was renowned for its ability to confuse lecturers' voices into unintelligibility. After many experiments with an organ pipe and dozens of cushions placed in different parts of the room, he concluded that the most important criterion in assessing the acoustic behaviour of a space was 'reverberation time', which depends on: 1. the volume of the enclosed space (the bigger the space, the longer the time), and 2. the sound-absorbing qualities of the wall surfaces (the more absorbent the surfaces, the shorter the time). His 'open window unit' (later called the 'sabin') is the amount of total absorption represented by a square foot of open window. Wall coverings can be rated by 'coefficient of absorption', small for hard surfaces like marble or concrete, and large for special acoustic felts, tiles and drapes.

Subjective judgements of reverberation time vary widely since they

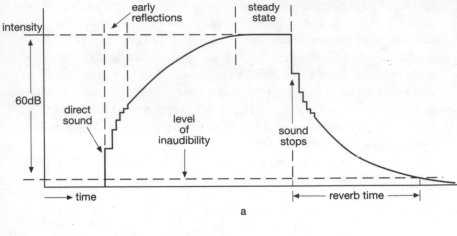

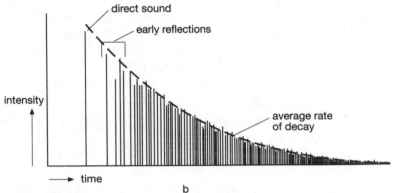

Fig. 166

depend on factors like the acuteness of your hearing and your position in the space. To overcome this uncertainty, reverberation time is defined as the time taken for the steady state (maximum) loudness to decay to a millionth (10^{-6} or -60 **decibels**) of its maximum intensity. Architectural acoustics is outside the scope of this book, but Wood (1962) has a good chapter on the acoustics of halls, and Nisbett (1970) those of studios. See also **acoustic treatments**, **control room** and **studio design**. For the general theory of reverberation see also Taylor (1965), Olson (1967) and Dodge (1985) chapter 7.

The second case is illustrated in fig. 166b. Here, a space is excited by a short, loud sound (such as a pistol shot or electric spark). This is its 'impulse response'. The important features in this case are the delay before the first reflection (often called 'pre-delay'), which indicates the length of the shortest indirect path, the following train of separable echoes, and the main mass of reverberation, which is heard as continuous and described in terms of 'density' (echoes/sec). The 'lumpiness' of the decay indicates the 'badness' of the acoustic, and varies with the **frequency** of the sound. Other phenomena may depend more on room shape than volume, for example **flutter echo** (caused by parallel walls), focusing by concave walls, and 'lopsided' effects due to unevenly distributed absorption. In cases like that of the dark hall described in **psychoacoustics**, our ear/brain systems decode all this data to tell us about the kind of environment we are in.

Different kinds of music require different reverb times, and spoken dialogue in radio drama, for example, demands the right 'feel' for various indoor ('live' acoustic) and outdoor ('dead') conditions. The effect of reverberation can also be a creative tool, see **additive synthesis** and **digital synthesis techniques** 7. Reverb content is a cue to distance – close sounds seem 'dry' because the direct sound is much louder than the reflections. We can thus simulate distance by adding reverb to a synthetic sound, for example, a **pan** during which reverb is added progressively will seem to take a sound further away as well as moving it sideways.

A means of adding reverb at will was seen as a necessity many years ago, and the oldest and simplest method is to use a real space, either an empty hall or a specially made 'echo room'.

A real room, with fixed dimensions, can only be effective within limits. The amount of reverb is controllable by varying the ratio of direct to indirect sound (see fig. 167a), but the only ways of adjusting the room itself are 1. trying different positions for the speaker and mic(s), and/or 2. modifying the acoustics by introducing absorbent objects or coverings. The final problem is that the room must be completely free of accidental noise input, which in today's crowded and heavily equipped urban buildings is virtually impossible to guarantee. Many methods of providing variable acoustics artificially in less inconvenient ways than using a real room have been tried, some of them exotic and elaborate, but only a few proved viable.

Electro-mechanical reverberators
Fig. 167b shows a simple tape echo set-up, with **feedback** of some of the playback head signal to the record head. The resulting 'echo delay' is a function of tape speed and the distance between heads. It is easily achieved on any machine with separate record and play heads, but it is not true reverb, merely a single train of echoes. Specially made echo machines with several playback heads (fig. 167c), were on the market in the 1950s and 1960s, but though a great advance on single head

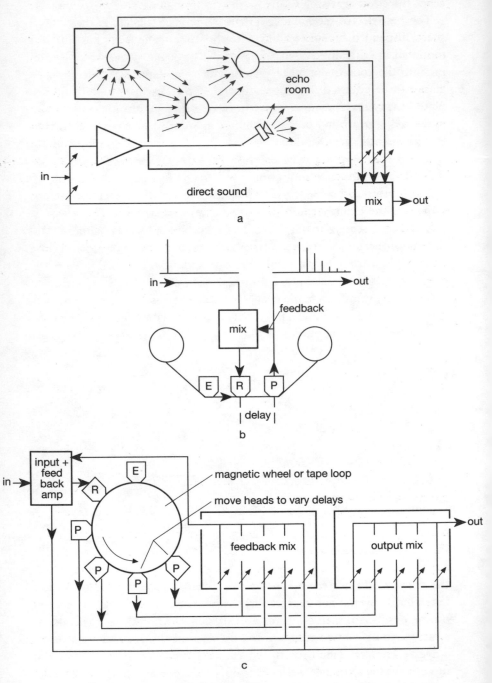

Fig. 167

echo, the effect was still a long way from natural reverb.

The best electro-mechanical system is the reverb 'plate', a large steel sheet suspended by springs like a trampoline on its side. **Transducers** mounted in critically chosen positions excite the plate in one place and pick up the consequent vibrations in others. A damping sheet of fibreglass can be adjusted (usually remotely) to different distances from the plate to vary reverberation time from as much as five seconds (an enormous hall) to around half a second. Good plate reverb is very clean though slightly metallic, and echo density is less than that of an equivalent real room (which may generate up to 1000 echoes/sec). A quiet, shock-free site must be found for this bulky item.

Much more compact, and cheaper, is 'spring' reverb, first used in the 1930s for the **Hammond organ** as a long, loosely hanging coil driven at one end and sensed at the other. Later types use two or more slightly different springs, sometimes tapered to reduce **resonant** peaks, and held under light tension. Even the best springs lack the 'ripples on a pool' effect of a plate, the linear mode of vibration giving a distinct coloration. Overdriven springs distort badly, producing unpleasant jangles and twangs. In recent years all the methods described have been steadily supplanted by digital ones.

Digital reverberators

For the general principles of sampling and conversion, see **digital synthesis techniques** 1. The necessary delay circuitry is very difficult to provide by analogue techniques, which is why compromise hybrid methods were devised, but digital delays are relatively easy to design, allowing more elegant, all-electronic solutions. Reverberation **algorithms** for implementation in large computer systems have existed since the 1960s, and take various forms (see Dodge, 1985, chapter 7, **quadraphony** and Chowning, 1977).

Fig. 168 shows two ways of organizing a 'queue' of memory units to make a delay 'line'. In 168a the numbers representing the samples are shifted one place along the queue as each new sample arrives, until they emerge at the other end. Fig. 168b shows a 'circular' queue in which the contents do not move, but at each sample time the oldest data is taken off as output and replaced by the new arrival. Delay time depends on the number of memory units and the sampling rate, for example, at a rate of 50 kHz a two-second delay would need 100,000 memory units.

Delay lines are employed in digital versions of the set-ups shown in fig. 167. Using feedback (fig. 168c), delay lines need only be long enough to bridge the longest reflection time (say 50 milliseconds), not the total

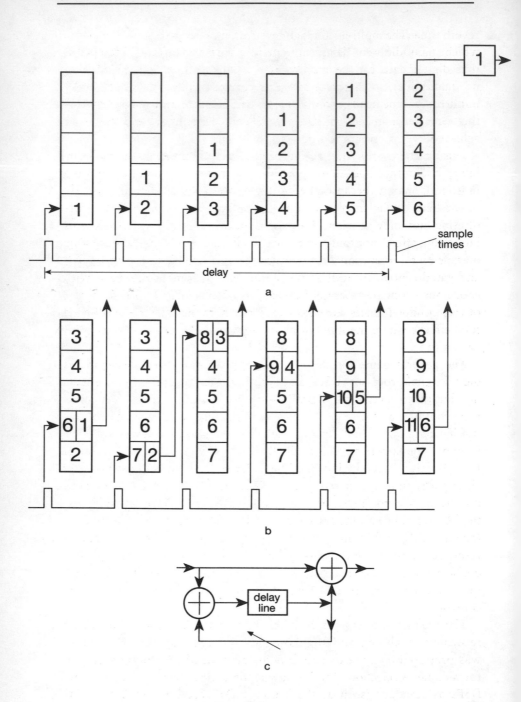

Fig. 168

reverb time. The multi-head machine becomes a 'tapped' delay line, from which many different delays are extracted. The important difference is that digital data can be manipulated as many times as needed with no quality loss, so that very complex configurations, the equivalent of hundreds of tape heads and dozens of machines, can be used to generate the very dense reflection patterns essential if 'naturalness' is to be achieved.

During the 1970s stand-alone digital reverb units, with analogue inputs and outputs, began to appear, at first expensive and disappointing in sound, mainly because the problem itself had not been properly researched. Today there is a range of reasonably priced reverberators offering not only a wide choice of 'typical' acoustics but numerous interesting effects not found in nature at all, such as reverse echoes (done on tape by reverberating a retrograde tape and then playing it normally), and **gated** echoes. As well as the sounds of vast, impossible halls with enormously long reverberation times, provision is made for the acoustics of very confined spaces like boxes, and special sounds like the 'cardboard tube effect', where the input is modulated at the resonant frequency of such a tube.

The general name for the type of unit we have been discussing is digital signal processor (DSP), and a given device may offer many effects in addition to reverb (see **digital multi-effect unit**). A typical user interface contains a choice of 'factory' treatments, with facilities for re-writing parameters and storing one's own versions for future use. For example, the factory settings in the Roland* SRV–2000 consist of: vocal I and II, large, medium and small halls, large, medium and small rooms, clear plate, tunnel, concrete pipe, large chapel, basin, outdoor theatre, non-linear and non-linear inverse (the last two are deliberately unrealis-tic). All relevant parameters are adjustable, for example, pre-delay time (giving early reflections), reverb time, equalizer (affecting general **response** contours), HF damp (giving shorter reverb time for high fre-quencies), density, attack gain and time (determining density build-up), ratio direct to reverb, and several others. **MIDI** ports allow remote control.

The idea of recreating a real hall known for its good acoustics by recording, analysing and simulating its impulse response (fig. 166b), was proposed many years ago, but the amount of computing was then formidable. A selection of well-known halls is now being offered in some DSPs as standard (such as the Yamaha DSP-100). See Dodge (1985)

*Roland Corporation, 3–7–13, Shinkitajima, Suminoe-ku, Osaka, Japan.

chapter 7, Chamberlin (1985), Runstein (1989) chapter 8, **surround sound** and **studio design**.

RIAA   Record Industry Association of America. The body responsible for defining recording curves and playback **equalization** for **LP** discs (see **sound recording techniques**).

Ribbon controller   See **analogue synthesis techniques** 6

Ribbon microphone   See **microphones**

Ringing   The **oscillatory** behaviour in switching waveforms such as **pulse** and **square waves**, caused by a circuit not settling instantaneously to the sudden change in condition, see fig. 169. See also **filters** and **resonance**.

Ring modulat/ion, -or   Also known as 'suppressed carrier modulation' (SCM), this is described with applications in **analogue synthesis techniques** 5. If input with two **sine waves** (the **carrier** and the modulator) the output is their sum and difference **frequencies** (**sidebands** above and below the carrier). Neither input appears at the output. The modulator produces this effect by multiplying the instantaneous **amplitudes** of both inputs (see fig. 46).

The traditional device for implementing this musically useful process is based on a **transformer**-coupled four-**diode** lattice or ring network (fig. 170a). In the absence of a modulator input (signal B) the carrier

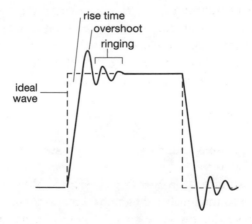

Fig. 169

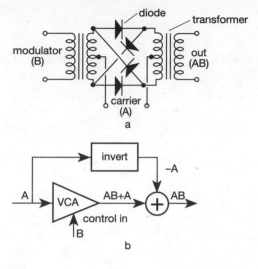

Fig. 170

input (signal A) is balanced out and does not appear at the output. The presence of a modulator unbalances the circuit and the output is the product of the two amplitudes AB, see **difference frequency**. SCM is more efficiently achieved using a voltage controlled **amplifier** (VCA), illustrated schematically in fig. 170b. Compare **amplitude modulation**. If one sideband is removed, the device becomes a **frequency shifter**.

RMS (rms)   See **root-mean-square**

Rock and roll dubbing   In film re-recording, the mechanism for rolling the picture and all sound tracks backwards as well as forwards, keeping in perfect lock (see **selsyn**) at all times and permitting retakes of small portions. At one time a mistake near the end of a reel entailed re-dubbing the entire reel from the head.

Roll-off   See **filters**

ROM   See **read-only memory**

Root-mean-square   (rms) A way of expressing the size of an alternating (therefore continuously changing) **current** or **voltage** which gives the numerical rms value the same effect in power terms (see **watt**) as a **DC** current or voltage of the same numerical value. Thus a domestic **AC**

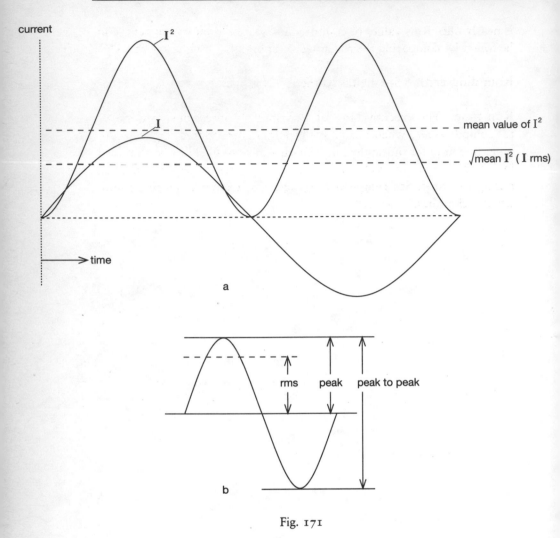

Fig. 171

supply at 240 **volts** (rms) will produce the same effect in lamps and heaters etc. as a 240 V DC supply (quoted values for AC quantities will be rms unless otherwise specified). Root-mean-square refers to the process of squaring individual values, taking the mean (average) of those squares and then the square root of the average. For an alternating current (I) this is illustrated graphically in fig. 171a (both half-cycles of I square to a positive value). Fig. 171b illustrates the three amplitude values commonly used to describe a **sine wave**. Rms = peak × .707. Peak = rms × 1.414. Peak-to-peak = peak × 2. In the above example 240 V (rms) represents a peak voltage of over 339, while peak-to-peak is nearly 680. Rms values of complex and aperiodic (noisy) currents can be found by comparing their heating effect on a load with that of a DC.

Rounding error   See **digital synthesis techniques** 4

Run time   The executive part of a computer's operations, as opposed to 'compile time', when the source program is translated for later running. In computer music the main instructions are likely to be compiled in advance, but any **real-time** performance instructions must happen during run time. See **computer languages** and **computer music composition techniques**.

S

Sample-and-hold (S/H) Circuits that sample the instantaneous amplitude of a wave and hold the sampled value until the next sample arrives. For the principles of sampling see **digital synthesis techniques** 1. For the correct operation of both **analogue-to-digital** and **digital-to-analogue converters** (ADC and DAC) it is essential to hold a sample value steady while conversion takes place.

Fig. 172 shows the action of a simplified S/H circuit. The **capacitor** is instantaneously charged to the sampled voltage and then isolated in a very high **impedance** (Z) circuit so that it does not appreciably discharge

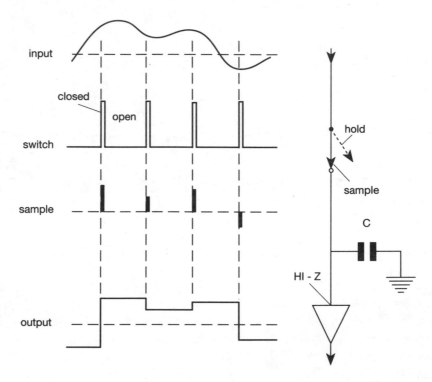

Fig. 172

('droop') before the next sample time. Practical circuits use two **semiconductor** switches, the second to discharge the capacitor before each sample. See also **random number generators** and **staircase**.

Samplers A general description of a range of units which digitally record sounds and offer various manipulations of them, usually including keyboard playback with appropriate pitch changes. They are sold under various names (such as digital wave-sampling synthesizer, digital sampling keyboard etc.).

Sound manipulation in computers has been possible for many years, but the dramatic fall in the cost of **random access memory** (RAM) and high quality converters (**analogue-to-digital**, ADC, and **digital-to-analogue**, DAC) has brought sound processing techniques out of the large studios and into the mass market. Samplers are the fastest growing area in digital sound, and though not strictly 'synthesizers', because they manipulate rather than generate, they can be used in many of the same ways, for example as 'switch on and play' keyboard instruments, supplanting the earlier **Mellotron**, which played pre-recorded tapes from a keyboard. In price and specification they range from cheap, almost toy units with very modest sound quality to large, high-priced studio machines that combine sampling with waveform synthesis facilities.

The following assumes an understanding of the principles of sampling, manipulation and analysis of sound given in **digital synthesis techniques** 1–3. In effect many of the processes described there are now available 'off the shelf', although samplers offer the features expected to be popular in the music market rather than precise research tools. Various design approaches are used, some having built-in keyboards while others interface with any **MIDI** keyboard. All have diskette storage, and visual aids vary from none, through small windows with cryptic messages, to detailed graphic displays of **waveforms** and **envelopes** etc. on full size monitor screens. MIDI ports enable any of these machines to be combined not only with other music devices but with external computers. This greatly expands the possibilities because sound files can be examined in detail, analysed by Fourier transforms etc., and modified in more subtle ways than is possible with the normal on-board features. A good example of sampler-extending software is Alchemy, an Apple Macintosh program by Blank Software.*

At one level, samplers are easy to use, and many companies are now selling diskettes of ready-prepared instrumental sounds that one can

*Blank Software, PO Box 6561, San Francisco, CA 94101–6561, USA.

simply load and play. Some instruments which use sampled sounds are not user-programmable except in a limited way (see **percussion generators** and **pianos** *electronic*). But for composers and performers who want to process their own sounds in detail samplers have the reputation of being hard to use compared with most synthesizers, and this is in general true because however carefully the manufacturer thinks out the user interface (and some of them do not do this well) there really cannot be a simple approach to an inherently complex procedure. Even with analogue tape fine editing calls for patience and skill. Digital sound files can be cut with a precision equivalent to shaving off microns of tape, but the same human qualities are still needed. Another problem is slowness. Compared with, say, **FM** synthesis, a massive amount of data has to be loaded, edited and moved around, and when this is done by a relatively slow means such as a diskette or a **serial MIDI** port, frustrating delays can occur.

Fig. 173 shows some typical features, not all of which may be offered in a given machine. Two routes for linking an external computer are shown, and systems with high-speed serial ports, by-passing MIDI for transferring sound data, can avoid the delays mentioned above. The diagram shows only one ADC and one DAC, but a number of samplers offer stereo sampling (two ADCs), and many have multiple outputs (several DACs).

To use a sampler to play music, the simplest procedure is to input a sound to RAM and immediately 'play' it from the keyboard, by-passing all the editing and treatment facilities. The essential principle is to vary the output pitch to produce a scale from the single pitch of the original, and two ways of doing this are by varying the playback **sampling rate**, or by using the same rate as the input but removing or interpolating samples – much the same technique as in digital oscillators (see **digital synthesis techniques** 4).

Interesting final sounds will not be achieved unless the original input is itself interesting and recorded at good quality and adequate **signal-to-noise ratio**. To this end the input sampling rate should be as high as possible, but there is a trade-off between the amount of RAM available and the rate, i.e. higher rates mean shorter maximum lengths. Most machines offer a choice of input rates, giving durations at different qualities from a few seconds upwards, the upper limit depending on the amount of RAM available (for example 16 bit sampling at 50 kHz (excellent quality) fills 100 K-bytes of RAM in one second; 12 bit sampling at 15 kHz (adequate for many purposes) fits over 4 seconds into the same space). Although word length is obviously an important

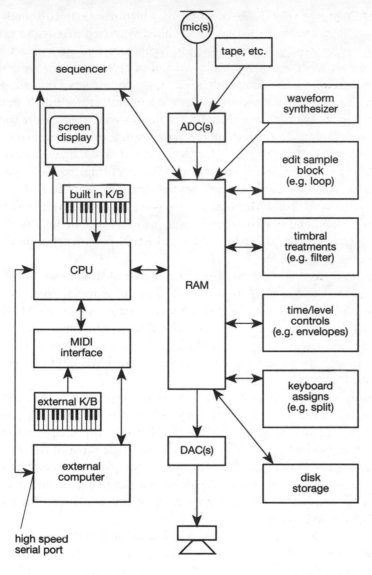

Fig. 173

factor in determining sound quality, it is not always a reliable guide because various compression techniques may reduce the effective precision internally. Some 12 bit machines sound better than others claiming a full 16 bits, and have the advantage of ⅓ greater storage capacity for a given memory size. Memory expansion is an optional extra on many samplers.

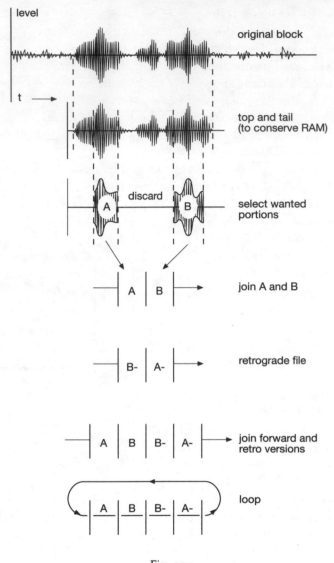

level

t →

original block

top and tail
(to conserve RAM)

discard

select wanted
portions

A   B

join A and B

B-   A-

retrograde file

A   B   B-   A-

join forward and
retro versions

A   B   B-   A-

loop

Fig. 174

Whatever other manipulations they offer, all serious samplers must have some means of editing the 'raw' sound file, and fig. 174 shows a typical sequence of operations, which are much easier to carry out if the whole file can be displayed on a computer screen, with zooming facilities to examine its contents right down to sample level. 'De-clicking' joins, for example, can be visually done by experimentally chopping out a few samples to give a smooth curve, or drawing in a portion of the wave (see **digital synthesis techniques** 2 and fig. 53). Some samplers have automatic de-clickers that look for matching zero crossings on each side of the join. **Crossfading** is another method – it does not remove discontinuities but obscures their effect; long crossfades also alter the character of the sound. Sometimes the original file may even be reduced to a single looped cycle, which leaves no trace of its initial character.

The treatment menu offered by a sampler depends not only on its price but the intended market, and new models appear frequently. A survey in the March 1989 issue of *Keyboard* magazine* lists thirty machines, varying from eight to sixteen bits (though the majority are twelve), and in price from US $795 (Akai† S612) to $250,000 (Synclavier II from New England Digital‡ with all possible options). There are also sample players which do not accept inputs but offer modest processing of pre-recorded sound files. In choosing one for personal use it is particularly necessary to test it for sound quality with the kind of material that interests you, and to check that it can manipulate sound in ways that suit your purpose. For full scale computerized **musique concrète** (see **computer music composition techniques** 4), the power, massive storage and comprehensive software of a large studio are still desirable, though a collection of several samplers, linked via MIDI to a computer with a hard disk and good sampler software, can be a serious rival.

Sampling rate   The **frequency** at which instantaneous readings of some continuous function are taken (in an **analogue-to-digital converter**), or the rate at which individual samples are read (in a **digital-to-analogue converter**), expressed in samples/sec or **hertz**. See also **digital synthesis techniques** 1 and **Nyquist frequency**.

Saturation   1. Condition of maximum output **current** or **voltage** from a given device (e.g. a transistor), such that it remains constant if the applied input voltage is further increased. It is usually avoided because **harmonic distortion** results, but it can be useful when this is sought (e.g. in a **clipping** circuit). 2. Condition of a magnetic material that is fully magnetized in one of two directions. This kind of saturation is also undesirable in, for example, analogue tape recording, again because of distortion, but it is common in digital recording where a maximum

Keyboard Magazine, GPI Corporation, 20085 Stevens Creek, Cupertino, CA 95014, USA.
†Akai Electric Co. Ltd., 12–14, 2–chome, Higashi-Kojiya, Ohta-Ku, Tokyo, Japan.
‡New England Digital Corporation, Box 546, 49 N. Main St., White River Junction, Vermont 05001, USA.

difference between only two states is the aim, and waveform distortion is not an issue (see **sound recording techniques**).

Sawtooth wave   See **ramp wave**

Scales   See **temperament**

Schmitt trigger   A type of **bistable** circuit, which is switched by signal level. It has many applications, for example, **noise gates** and timing pulses for **sample-and-hold** circuits.

Scratch pad   A computer memory set aside for the temporary storage of intermediate data.

SEAMUS   Society for Electro-Acoustic Music in the United States, 2550 Beverly Boulevard, Los Angeles, Calif. 90057, USA.

SECAM   SEquential Couleur A Memoire. A colour TV system used by a few countries, including France and Russia. It is not easily compatible with the much more widely used **PAL**, so material is usually originated in PAL and coded into SECAM for transmission. See also **NTSC**.

Selsyn   A **three-phase** master/slave **servo** system which accurately transmits angular position. It is used in film **dubbing**, for example, where a number of motors must run in precise lock. Not to be confused with selective synchronization (sel-sync) in multi-track tape recorders (see **sound recording techniques** 2).

Semiconductors   Crystalline forms of certain elements (e.g. germanium, silicon) which are 'doped' with impurity atoms of other materials to give them a small electrical **conductivity**. N-type crystals (with 'donor' impurities) have a surplus of 'free' electrons, P-type (with 'acceptor' impurities) a shortage of electrons called 'holes', which behave as if positively charged. See **amplifiers** and **lattice**. Fig. 107 shows how electrons are 'bonded' in a crystal. N-type material has additional 'free' electrons, and P-type has 'holes' in the bond pattern. Devices like **diodes** and transistors use conjunctions of N- and P-type crystals.

Sensitivity   The ratio of output to input of, for example, an **amplifier**, usually given as the **voltage** input required to give a stated output **power**, for example, 5 mV for 50 **watts** into an 8 **ohm** load.

Separation   See **crosstalk**

Sequencers   Devices that deliver a timed series of cues (such as the mechanism of a musical box or a 'moving' neon sign). Motor- or clock-actuated sets of contacts were used in early electronic music to automate short, repetitive pitch sequences, delayed tape recorder starts, etc. The most refined example from the pioneer era was used in the RCA synthesizer (in the late 1950s), which had a punched paper roll to sequence the machine (see **analogue synthesis techniques** 6), but most sequencers of that period were cumbersome to program, inaccurate and very limited.

The voltage controlled sequencers of the 1960s were more flexible because the output was not definitely assigned, but a series of control voltage steps that could be **patched** to perform a variety of tasks. Sequence length was hardware-limited, however, to a very small number of steps (rarely more than thirty, often as little as eight), and numbers of knobs had to be patiently adjusted. One interesting use for this type of sequencer was for **waveform** generation. A series of **voltage** steps, if looped and repeated at an audio frequency, produced a timbre which could be 'tuned' by adjusting step voltages. This was an improvement on earlier tape loop methods of achieving this slightly eccentric type of synthesis (see **musique concrète**).

Percussion generators involved rhythm sequencing from the beginning (in the early 1960s), but design requirements were confined to a small choice of sounds and steady, repetitive time patterns. At the same time computers (which are also sequencers) were developing fast, and software sequencing was an integral part of music-related programs (even if they did not then run in real time). By 1970 relatively powerful digital/analogue sequencers with front panel controls rather than typed-in programs were being made by, among others, EMS (London) Ltd. (see again **analogue synthesis techniques** 6).

In the 1970s time control in computer systems was further refined, and the first serious digital synthesizers on the market (Fairlight* and Synclavier I†) included editable sequencing. But the arrival of MIDI in 1983 changed the scene completely. Here was a ready-made protocol of digital commands including time controls, 'understood' by a wide spread of music machines, and with the ability to send as well as receive – a music device could cue the sequencer as well as accept cues from it (see

*Fairlight ESP Pty Ltd, 30 Bay St., Broadway, Sydney, NSW 2007, Australia.
†New England Digital Corporation, Box 546, 49 N. Main St., White River Junction, Vermont 05001, USA. Manufacturers of the Synclavier II and other products.

MIDI to clarify references to its features in the following). The important thing to remember is that sequencers deliver event timing and data, not the events themselves, so that major sound editing processes can take place after a sequence is recorded.

Hardware MIDI sequencers
A built-in facility in some synthesizers, or available as stand-alone units, these are available in a great variety of power and price. A selection of typical features is shown in fig. 175. Taking the 'boxes' shown in the sketch: INPUT TYPE SELECT allows data to be recorded as a performance, or in 'step time' i.e. event by event in time units and notes. The perform-ance can be slower than full tempo and speeded up later. TIMING SOURCE SELECT allows a choice of timing 'master' – sequencers may originate timing data, or be 'slaved' to an external clock source such as a recorded **time code**. TRACK/RECORD/PLAY SELECT decides the operating mode of each track. Sequencers are configured like multi-track tape machines, with a number of tracks some of which may be playing while others are recording. CLOCK RESOLUTION. Digital machines regard time as a series of discrete packages. Standard unit for sequencers is pulses per quarter-note (crotchet) or ppq. High ppq detects shorter events but uses memory more quickly. In fast music notes may be missed if ppq is too slow. A machine will 'correct' mis-timed performance notes to the nearest pulse

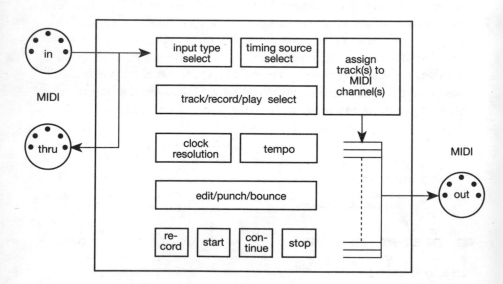

Fig. 175

(unless the performance is so bad that it corrects to the wrong beat!). There is a trade-off between low ppq giving good sync but a wooden, metronomic result and high ppq retaining human performance nuance but rhythmic inaccuracies as well. MIDI (system real time) standard rate is 24 ppq, which was considered adequate in 1983 but now well below the **resolution** offered by the machines themselves. Fig. 176 shows how timing and channel data are interleaved in the data stream.

Continuing the boxes in fig. 175, the next is TEMPO which gives control of the overall clock speed (musical tempo in beats per minute) adjustable either at the sequencer or the master timer. EDIT, PUNCH and BOUNCE are all editing modes. Editing may be done in real time by 'punching in' new passages, replacing part of the original track, or in step time by rolling down the sequence and editing individual events. Complete tracks may be 'bounced' to other tracks, or two may be 'merged' to a third (all these processes are similar to tape recorder operations). RECORD/ START/CONTINUE/STOP are all buttons which activate the unit (also MIDI-controllable). START means 'go from the beginning', CONTINUE means 'resume from where STOP was pressed'. ASSIGN TRACK(S) TO MIDI CHANNEL(S) allows any track to be sent on any or all sixteen MIDI channels.

Of course the size of the sequencer's memory limits the length and density of sequences it can deliver, but this limit cannot be assessed in terms of the number of events because it depends on how much data is contained in each. For example, MIDI messages for continuous controls like pitch-bend are very data-hungry. In general, most sequencers can hold at least 5000 average notes, and many a lot more than this. A useful MIDI feature in long sequences, when one device is clocking another, is the song position pointer (SPP). If the master is started from somewhere in mid-sequence, it can transmit an SSP which locates the slave (e.g. a drum machine) at the same place in the sequence.

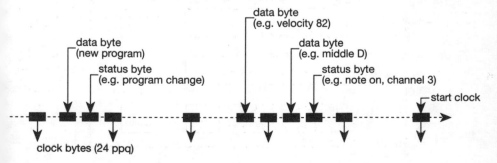

Fig. 176

Software MIDI sequencers

The units outlined above are easily set up and very useful for applications like live concerts. There are also dedicated 'music computers', and some sequencers have computer add-on features, but for studio use the most favoured course is to interface a general purpose computer with MIDI devices, and use the very powerful sequencer software now available.

Any interactive music program must have sequencing capabilities, and some composing programs are discussed in **computer music composition techniques** 4. In generalized sequencing programs, everything described above can be 'on screen', giving many extra bonuses such as 'bird's eye views' of whole event series and instant editing by moving icons, etc. For example, one Macintosh program popular with many professionals, Master Tracks Pro by Passport Designs,* includes the following features: 1. 64 tracks. 2. On-screen 'tape transport buttons' (PLAY, RECORD, PAUSE, STOP, REWIND, FAST-FORWARD). 3. Resolution can be adjusted at any time to optimize storage and accommodate varying note densities. 4. Elapsed time checks can be made on any or all sections. 5. There is timing correction as described above, but also a 'humanize' feature which adds small, random irregularities. 6. Continuously changing tempos are accurately fitted to a total available time. 7. There is provision for quick visual editing by mouse. 8. Graphical plots of relevant parameters can be displayed. 9. It is possible to make instant jumps to preset markers as well as fast-forward/rewind. 10. **Time codes** and SPP are available (see previous section). 11. There is storage not just for sequence data but for all MIDI data in a set-up.

Given adequate computer power and memory, there are really no limits to the possibilities except the ability of a person to handle all the decisions – one recent program offers 256 tracks. In a MIDI system the main limits are those of MIDI itself, but that is another problem. Sequencers have changed the whole process of producing songs, commercials, etc. The multi-track tape machine is still needed, but many of its traditional roles have been replaced by the modern sequencer's ability to store whole **polyphonic** complexes in digital form, allowing complete freedom of manipulation until a much later stage in production than before. Sequencers are on the whole designed to aid this kind of music and process, and their assumptions do not necessarily suit experimental composers. Also, they are only useful if the music is electronic or at least MIDI-translatable in some way. Sequencers can to some extent relate with live performers on non-MIDI instruments, however, by their

*Passport Designs Inc., 625 Miramontes St., Half Moon Bay, CA 94019, USA.

ability to output **metronomes**, click tracks, visual light cues and other timing aids useful to human musicians.

Serial   1. Of music composed using **series**. 2. Of the computer processing or transmission of data one **bit** at a time. Compare **parallel**.

Series   1. A list of pitches, note durations, dynamics or any other musical quality, in which the terms are given equal weight by being used serially and repetitively in a predetermined order, which may however be permutated in various ways. This is in contrast with tonal music, where a note's importance depends on its position in the tonal hierarchy – tonic, leading note etc. 2. Of circuit elements joined so that the same current flows through each in succession (also 'cascade'), the **voltage** across a group of such elements being split in direct proportion to the ratio of their **impedances**. See also **Ohm's law, parallel** and **tuned circuit**. 3. A numerical sequence yielded by the repetition of a particular mathematical procedure, for example **Fibonacci sequence** and **harmonic series**.

Servo   (motors) From the Latin for 'slave', servos are control systems by which a force, an angular position, a speed etc. is accurately transmitted to the slave(s) from a master control, often amplifying the effort if force is involved. Servo motors are used in film dubbing, for example (see **selsyn**), tracking pick-ups (see **compact disc** and **pick-ups**) and synchronizing and speed-controlling tape recorders (see **tape recorder design** and **time codes**).

Shifter   See **frequency shifter**

Short circuit   The by-passing of part or the whole of a **circuit** by connecting its ends together directly. 'Shorting' the terminals of a power source activates a current limited only by the internal **resistance** of the source.

Shunt   See **parallel**

SI units   Système International d'Unités. The set of internationally recommended scientific units, consisting of a short list of 'base' units on which a longer list of 'derived' units is built. The base units are:

QUANTITY	UNIT	
	name	symbol
mass	kilogram	kg
length	metre	m
time	second	s
current	ampère	A

Units for other quantities are derived from these and the derived unit is expressed as a combination of base units, thus the SI unit for speed is metres per second (m/s). Some derived units have special names, and the following are of relevance in music and audio:

force	newton	N
pressure	pascal	Pa
energy	joule	J
power	watt	W
frequency	hertz	Hz
charge	coulomb	C
potential	volt	V
resistance	ohm	Ω
conductance	siemens	S
inductance	henry	H
capacitance	farad	F
magnetic flux density	tesla	T

All SI units can be modified by the use of the standard metric prefixes, giving sub-multiples or multiples of the base or derived units:

sub-multiple	prefix	symbol	multiple	prefix	symbol
10^{-1} ($1/10$)	deci	d	10^3	kilo	k
10^{-2} ($1/100$)	centi	c	10^6	mega	M
10^{-3} ($1/1000$)	milli	m	10^9	giga	G
10^{-6}	micro	μ	10^{12}	tera	T
10^{-9}	nano	n			
10^{-12}	pico	p			

The above prefixes allow small or large values of SI units to be expressed without the need for long strings of zeros, thus: 3 kHz = 3000 Hz; $8\mu A = 8 \times 10^{-6}$ A; 0.6 MΩ = 600,000Ω.

Sidebands   In a wave **modulation** process, groups (**bands**) of modulation products (i.e. waves at other **frequencies** than the original) that appear above (upper sideband) and below (lower) the **carrier** wave. See also **amplitude modulation, digital synthesis techniques** 6, **frequency shifter** and **ring modulation**.

Signal An electric **current** or **electromagnetic** wave which conveys information (such as an audio, control, digital or radio signal) as opposed to a utility, such as a power supply.

Signal-to-noise ratio (S/N) At any point in a **signal**-carrying system, the ratio of the levels of wanted signal to unwanted **noise** in the same circuit, usually expressed as the **root-mean-square** level of noise (in −**decibels**) compared with a stated level (typically the maximum 'undistorted' level) of the signal. Because S/N gets worse as the signal level reduces against a constant noise level, it is also a measure of usable **dynamic range,** and the **lining up** of tape recorders, for example, is done to make the S/N as high as possible. See **digital synthesis techniques** 1 for quantization noise. See also **noise reduction.**

Simple harmonic motion See **sine wave**

Sine From Latin 'sinus', a bend. The sine of an angle can be illustrated by considering an imaginary wheel spoke moving away from a horizontal reference line. The sine of the angle at any point is the shortest distance from the end of the spoke to the base line, divided by the spoke's length (radius). The sine varies between +1 (90°) and −1 (270°) with 0 at 0°

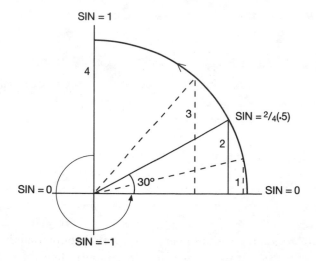

Fig. 177

(360°) and 180°, but not **linearly**. For example, .5 is SIN 30° not 45°. See **cosine wave**.

Sine wave   The waveshape resulting from a graphical representation of 'simple harmonic motion', as exhibited, for example, by a freely swinging pendulum. Fig. 178a illustrates the **cycle** of acceleration, deceleration, reversal etc. that a pendulum performs, and if the weight at the pendulum's end could be made to mark a strip of paper pulled underneath and at right angles to its swing at a constant speed (ignoring the friction of the pen and the curvature of the weight's path), it would draw a sine wave. Referred to many times in this book, the familiar shape represents **oscillation** at one **frequency** only, and occurs in both mechanical and electrical systems, though rarely in a pure form. Two or more sine waves constitute a complex wave.

Positions within a wave's cycle are called **phase** angles, and expressed in degrees or radians. Fig. 178b connects the angular (circular) concept with the sine waveshape by plotting the sine of the angle as it changes. A turn of the 'wheel' represents a cycle of the wave, and its speed (turns per second) represents the wave's frequency. See also **analogue synthesis techniques**, **bowed strings**, **digital synthesis techniques**, **harmonic series** and **woodwind instruments**.

Sink   1. Positive (+) destination of **electrons** originating from a source (negative). 2. Short for 'heat sink'. See power amplifiers in **amplifiers**.

Sinusoid/al   A description of anything in the shape of a **sine wave**, including **cosine waves**.

Slate   From chalked slates or 'clapper boards' used to mark the beginning of a film take, logging the number for a section of music to be recorded, which is not necessarily a complete piece. Recording the slate and **take** numbers is called 'marking'.

Slave   A device being controlled by a 'master', in, for example, a **MIDI** or **servo** system.

Slew rate   The maximum rate (usually in units per second) at which the output of a device can be forced from one limit (e.g. of voltage) to the other, taking all internal **time constants** into consideration. For example, the rise time shown in fig. 169 indicates the slew rate of a

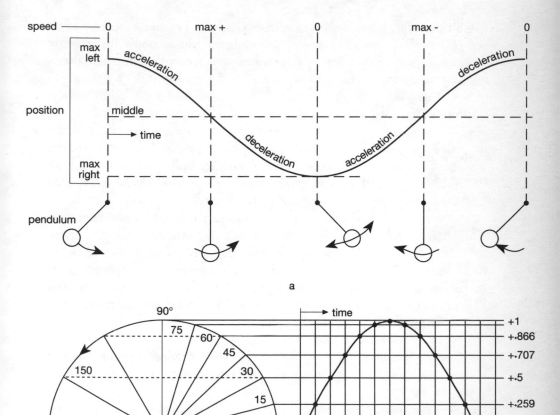

Fig. 178

device transmitting a **square wave**. Variable slew rates are used to produce effects like glissando in synthesizers.

Slope The angle with the horizontal (X-axis) of any plot. The angle of slope has varying significance, for example it can show the **response** of a **filter**, or, tangential to the curve of a wave showing amplitude, slope can indicate the wave's velocity at that point.

Slot filter See **filters**

Smart See **intelligent**

SMPTE Society of Motion Picture and Television Engineers. See **time codes.**

Software See **hardware**

Solenoid Literally 'tube-shaped'. A device based on the **electromagnet,** designed to do mechanical work when energized. In the commonest type a loose ferrous core is drawn into a hollow centre (see fig. 165c). Used in tape transports (see **tape recorder design**). Solenoids may also combine functions with those of a **relay**; in starting a car, for example, the low current ignition key circuit energizes a solenoid which engages the high current starter motor circuit. The term is also used as an alternative name for **inductor.**

Solovox One of a number of 'add-on' **monophonic** keyboards (another was the Clavioline) designed for attachment below the upper end of a piano keyboard, and to provide 'instrumental' solos accompanied by the pianist's left hand. The Solovox had a 3-octave keyboard but covered a pitch range of 5 octaves, and offered a range of **timbre** controls, **reverberation** etc.

Son et lumière Entertainments in impressive surroundings with programmed floodlighting accompanied by multi-track music and usually a spoken narrative. As a night-time open air spectacular it became popular in the 1950s, and still flourishes at many historic sites around the world. Computer-controlled indoor versions are now a feature of permanent 'realistic' exhibition displays, with full **montages** of music, sound effects and commentary. See also **environmental music.**

Sone See **phon**

Sonic Arts Network 174 Mill Lane, London NW6 1TB. Tel: (071) 794 5638. Formed in May 1990 by the amalgamation of the National Studio Project and the Electro-acoustic Music Association of Great Britain (**EMAS**).

Sonic (sound) sculpture The term is sometimes applied to natural objects which make interesting sounds because of their position and/or shape (such as a hollow rock that moans and whistles as the waves advance), but usually refers to human artifacts designed for both visual and aural appeal. In a sense any beautiful looking musical instrument is a sound sculpture, but in general the expression is reserved for objects (often of very complex construction) that are arresting visually and also have some deliberate noise-producing features. These can be operated by natural influences (such as wind, rain, tides), mechanically (by motors, levers, thermal distortions etc.) or electronically (for example by **oscillators** controlled by touch, invisible beams or proximity devices). Most works in this genre do not play music in the normal melodic sense, but output sound either randomly or when some kind of trigger is activated. Some sculptures use conventional sound generating principles but made on a huge scale, such as long wires whose **fundamental** tone is **subsonic** but which produce a changing complex of **harmonics**. Another example is tube sculpture, a set of enormous pan pipes made in London by Simon Desorgher and Lawrence Casserley.

A pioneer of elaborate mechanical sculpture in the late 1930s was the Swiss artist Jean Tinguely, but the explosion of kinetic art in the 1960s brought many sculptors and musicians together in joint exploration of the possibilities. A leading British sound sculptor is the composer Hugh Davies, and among the large number of sonic objects he has produced are a group of 'feelie boxes', in which Davies co-operated with John Furnival. These sensitive, tactile sound producers happen to be small, but many sound sculptures are enormous and publicly sited, often including an element of surprise in their action. A comprehensive survey of the field is Davies's article in Sadie (1984). See also **environmental music**.

Sound recording techniques This entry is mainly about magnetic tape recording, because with very few exceptions other media are secondary processes whose success depends on the quality of the tape master. For the mechanical (transport) aspects of tape recorders see **tape recorder design**. For comments on optical **laser** discs and pre-recorded cassettes, see **compact disc, cassette recorders** and **cassette duplication**. The first section is a brief description of disc cutting and manufacturing techniques, which after nearly a century of commercial dominance must now be regarded as obsolescent technology (see also **pick-ups**). Section 2 is concerned with analogue tape recording, and the final part with digital techniques.

1. Disc recording and manufacture

The essentials of a recording 'lathe' are shown in fig. 179a. A heavy turntable is used because its flywheel effect helps to keep the speed constant under varying loads. The recording blank of lacquered aluminium (see **acetate**) is seated firmly to the flat platter (turntable) by suction, and a rigid 'sled' (carriage) is driven along a track radial to the disc by a lead screw as cutting proceeds. The thread of 'swarf' or 'chip' thrown out by the stylus is removed by a further suction device. Fig. 179b shows the main parts of a magnetic cutting head – in effect a pick-up in reverse, but much more massive. The left and right signals drive the stylus at a mutual angle of 90° to cut a 45°/45° **stereo** groove (again see **pick-ups**). Precise control of the cutting depth ensures that the groove is correct under all signal conditions. **Feedback** coils generate a current which is used to **damp** the movement, and the use of a hot stylus smooths the cut and improves frequency **response**, particularly towards the disc's centre where the stylus-to-groove speed is slower and high frequency information more densely packed. The stylus, 179c, is usually of sapphire. Diamond would be harder-wearing, but sapphire can be shaped and polished more easily and is less fragile.

The disc is normally cut from a tape master, though direct-to-disc mastering (DDM) enjoyed a vogue recently. DDM eliminates tape **noise** and offers a theoretically greater dynamic range, but only suits artists who prefer a 'real' performance to one that can be edited, retaken etc. – any wrong notes or stray noises at the session are there to stay. But the rapid growth of noise-free digital recording (see below) has effectively made DDM obsolete (if artists prefer not to edit performances this option is still available, of course).

Assuming the use of a tape master, therefore, there are some features of the copying process that we should note. Magnetic cutting heads (and pick-ups) have a 'constant velocity' characteristic. This is illustrated in fig. 180a, which shows that different frequencies with the same maximum velocity (angle at zero crossing) show increasing amplitude with decreasing frequency, i.e. at the bass end the cutting stylus ampli-

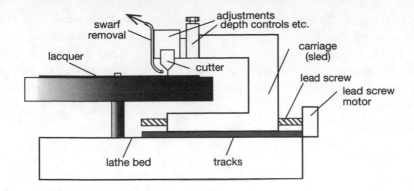

a

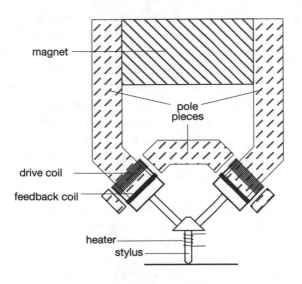

b

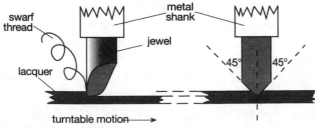

c

Fig. 179

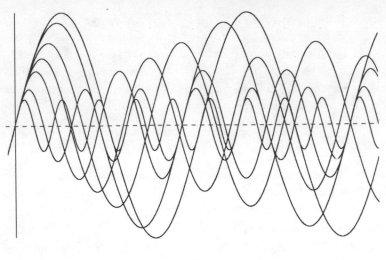

a

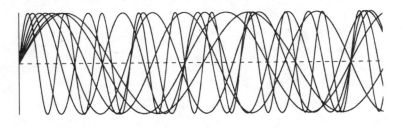

b

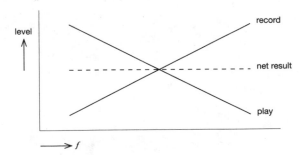

c

Fig. 180

tude will be much greater than in the treble. A recording curve which progressively reduces low frequency amplitude results in something nearer to 'constant amplitude' (180b) at this end of the spectrum. In practical curves (e.g. **DIN, RIAA**) the top is boosted as well (pre-emphasis), producing the general form shown in 180c. On playback a complementary **equalization** curve restores the original bass response and also reduces high frequency noise such as needle crackle. This process evens out frequency-dependent amplitude changes, but there is still a wide range of amplitudes between silence and the loudest passages. If the pitch of the groove's spiral is set so that the loudest sounds do not cross-cut to adjacent turns, the spacing will be wastefully wide on quiet passages, reducing possible total duration. The answer is variable pitch cutting, which is achieved by varying the speed of the lead screw motor (fig. 179a) to match the strength of the signal.

Fig. 181 shows a tape deck with a 'preview' head followed by a long tape path to give a substantial delay between heads. Lefthand signals, which are cut into the inside groove wall, do not affect the turn outside the current one, so can be read from the programme head, but righthand signals must be detected in advance by sampling the preview head. Samples are taken several times a turn, and a computer judges from a group of three (the current and two before) which way and how much each signal is moving, and what action to take to optimize the groove pitch for the coming signals. A digital delay line (see **digital multi-effect unit** and **reverberation**) with output providing the programme signal can also be used to allow 'previewing' for this purpose.

Having cut a lacquer (or metal, see below) master, a series of plating and pressing stages transforms it into the record you buy in the store.

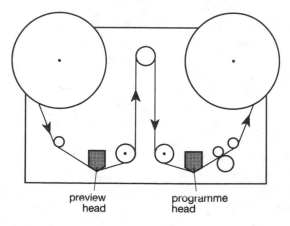

preview   programme
 head   head

Fig. 181

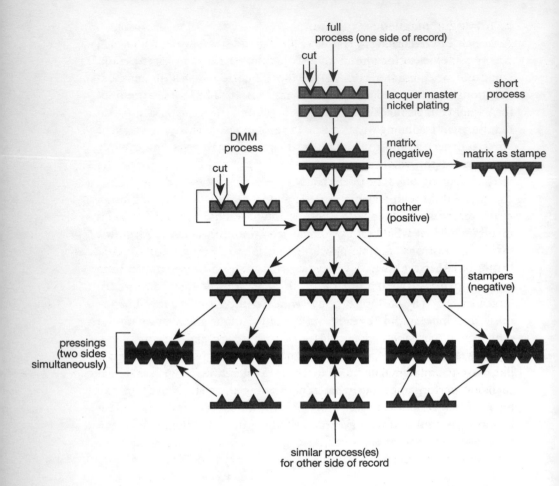

full
process (one side of record)

cut

lacquer master
nickel plating

short
process

DMM
process

cut

matrix
(negative)

matrix as stampe

mother
(positive)

stampers
(negative)

pressings
(two sides
simultaneously)

similar process(es)
for other side of record

Fig. 182

Fig. 182 shows the various steps involved (see **compact disc** for the similar series in that medium). Of the two shortened processes, the one using the matrix as the stamper is only suitable for runs of up to 200 copies or so, after which it is too worn. The lacquer was destroyed in the plating process, so further copies can only be made by cutting a new lacquer. Direct metal mastering (DMM), featured by a few companies, is a high quality process in which a cold, supersonically vibrated stylus cuts a copper blank and directly produces a mother, eliminating two stages with a consequent gain in quality and low noise. For fuller details and more illustrations of the foregoing, see Runstein (1989) chapter 14 and Ballou (1987) chapter 23.

2. Analogue magnetic recording

Although disc recording was an excellent mass production medium, it was very inefficient for routine studio operations. The expensive acetates could not be re-used or even played more than a few times, unbroken durations were limited, and no editing was possible. The arrival of high quality tape machines in the late 1940s (after half a century of development beginning with Valdemar Poulsen's 1899 patent for a piano wire recorder) removed all these restrictions at a stroke, and quickly transformed the whole technology of broadcasting and recording, as well as opening the door to electronic music.

The breakthrough was the replacement of solid steel wire or ribbon as the recording medium with a suspension of minute magnetic particles in a 'binder' that would set like paint, and bond this mechanically weak 'oxide' to a strong, flexible plastic 'base'. From the coarse oxides and brittle bases of the early days (again see **acetate**), many improvements have been made over the years. New magnetic materials can contain larger signals. They can be divided into ever smaller particles for lower noise and more rapid response, and bonded more efficiently to bases with better mechanical properties. The best tapes are very costly and difficult to manufacture, and are used mainly in small, low-speed formats like **cassette** and **digital audio tape,** where excellent **resolution** is essential for good performance, but the actual quantity of tape is small. 'Metal' tape contains microscopically fine particles of deposited pure metal and is not to be confused with earlier solid media. For further comment on tape stock see **cassette recorders**, and for a recent assessment of current materials and manufacturing techniques see Fox (1986).

Record and play

The magnetic particles or 'domains' in the oxide are lined up during manufacture along the path of the tape, and in unrecorded stock their fields are random and self-neutralizing. Fig. 183 shows the process of recording and playing back a **triangle wave**. As the polarity changes the domains are lined up first one way and then the other, leaving a magnetic pattern corresponding to the input, though some **noise** is also added to the signal. In practice not all the domains would be lined up as shown, or the tape would be **saturated** (see fig. 185). The heads are designed so that the maximum flux (see **magnetic field**) is concentrated in the gap (not of air but a magnetically inert filler), and the tape responds to changes and reversals in the flux as it crosses the gap. At a point near the 'trailing edge', however, a 'trapping plane' is reached, where the flux already in the tape is stronger than the magnetizing flux in the head gap and the recording is fixed.

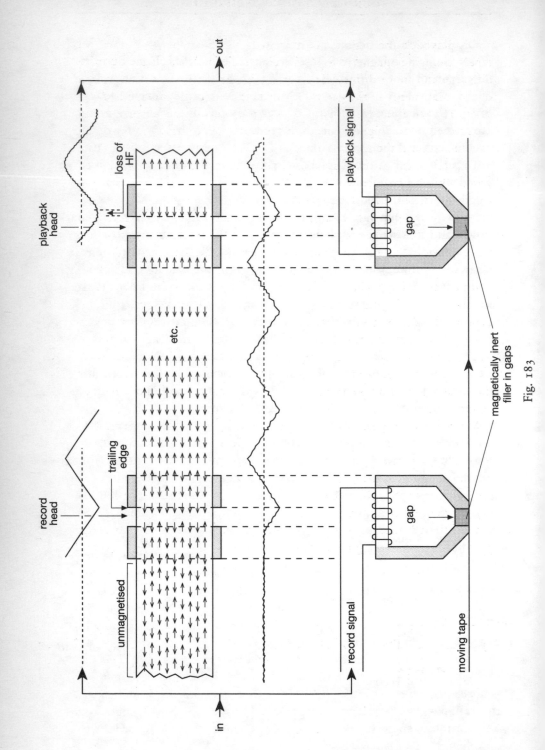

Fig. 183

On playback the action, apart from being the opposite one of the tape's changing magnetic field inducing current in the head's coil, is different and more diffuse. The current in the coil is now the average of the total energy in the gap at any instant, and in the exaggerated gap of fig. 183 the effect is to 'blunt' the sharp corners of the triangle, which are created by the higher **partials** in the wave – in other words the wide gap has reduced the top response.

To analyse this more closely, imagine a simple tone (**sine wave**) recorded while its frequency is gradually increased, and therefore its **wavelength** shortened. At low frequencies, when the wavelength is long compared with the gap (fig. 184a), the average gap flux changes relatively slowly and follows the waveshape well. As the wavelength approaches the gap width (184b) increasing amounts of cancellation occur until, when wavelength = gap (184c) there is no output at all. This 'extinction' point can be made higher by increasing tape speed (and hence all wavelengths), which is one reason why high speed machines have a greater **bandwidth**. If speeds must be slow (as in cassette decks) the narrowest possible gaps are combined with very fine grain tapes. When the wavelength is even shorter (past the first extinction point) output recommences and as frequency rises there is a series of peaks and nulls, but the design aim is to keep the audio high frequencies below the first extinction point.

Many more properties of the system can be varied to optimize performance, although the effects of design changes are often in conflict; for example, narrow gaps and high speeds are good for treble response but may be bad for the bass end. For a detailed study of the complexities see Runstein (1989) chapter 6 or Ballou (1987) chapter 24. In a practical design, the best compromise is worked out for a particular application. One of the advantages of tape recorders is the similarity of record and play heads (unlike the great differences between, say, a cutting head and

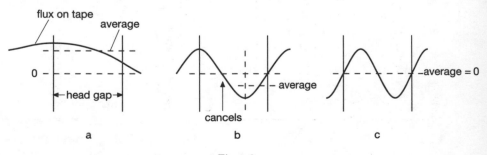

Fig. 184

a pick-up). On cheaper open reel machines, and on most cassette recorders, a single record/play (R/P) head is used for both, and the gap is chosen to be wide enough to inject a strong signal when recording, but narrow enough to give adequate treble response on playback. In professional tape decks and three-head cassettes, with separate R and P heads, less compromise is necessary and the record head gap is substantially larger than that of the play head. A studio machine normally running at 15 in (38 cm) per second might have a record head gap of 20 **microns** and a play head gap of 2 microns (.000079 in or about twenty times thinner than the average human hair). In high quality cassette machines (1⅞ ips) the play head gap may be as little as .8 microns (.0000315 in). For head alignment parameters see **tape recorder design**.

Erase and bias
Some early recorders used permanent magnets to erase tape, but this left it saturated in one direction, a bad condition from which to begin a new recording. To ensure a magnetically neutral tape, the most effective way is to apply a strong alternating current and gradually weaken the field so that domains retain a fixed polarity at randomly different times. A bulk eraser, which wipes an entire tape on the spool, uses a powerful mains **inductor**, the spool being slowly removed either manually or automatically, or the tape left in position and the field slowly reduced to zero. The erase head of a tape recorder, placed before the R or R/P head in the tape path, is fed by a supersonic **oscillator** at a frequency of 100 kHz or more. In the same way as in a bulk eraser, the field weakens as the tape leaves the influence of the head, and a wide gap (often two gaps in succession) is used to ensure a good 'soaking'.

Tape does not have a **linear** magnetization curve (see **hysteresis**). As well as flattening out at each end due to saturation, it has a kink in the middle where the collective magnet switches direction (each small portion of tape, even though made up of many particles, is behaving like a magnet overall). Even if the tape is magnetically neutral before recording, an input will be distorted as shown in fig. 185a. Bias consists of a supersonic signal added to the audio one to offset it into the two linear regions. Fig. 185b is an approximation of the result, assuming that the tape is fully demagnetized at each reversal, which in practice it would not be (see again **hysteresis**). The action is therefore quite complex, but it certainly works. The sinusoidal bias signal is distorted in the process, but this has no effect on the audio.

Apart from being inaudibly high, very little bias finds its way to the

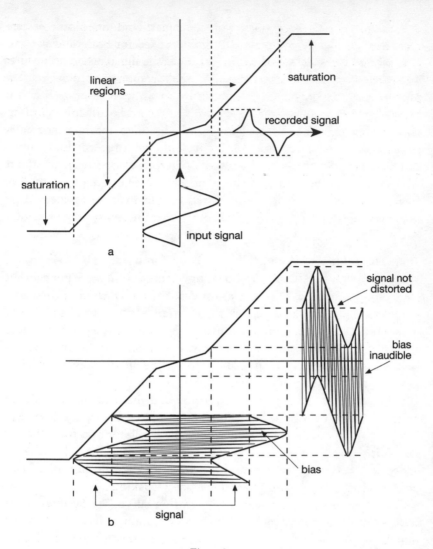

Fig. 185

output, because head geometry and circuitry are not designed for efficient operation at these high frequencies (a problem in **tape composition** can arise, however, that when tape is greatly slowed down bias may become audible). Bias setting is critical because the signal must be placed correctly in the linear regions, which vary with different tapes and speeds. In professional studios bias checks are part of the regular service routine, and are made at least for every new batch of tape (even of the same make and type, which is no guarantee of uniformity). In cassette

machines, which use several types of tape with different magnetic properties ('normal', 'chrome', 'metal' etc.), bias and equalization (see below)
are selected by switches, or automatically if the machine is equipped to
read the coded tape shells now used. A few tape decks even have a self-
setting bias feature, which automatically runs the beginning of a new
tape, injects a test signal, optimizes bias and rewinds ready for recording.

Conveniently, the same oscillator can be used for both bias and erase
(with bias at a much lower level). To prevent high frequency interference
with the audio amplifiers, 'bias trap' rejectors (see **tuned circuit**) are
always fitted in the record circuit, and sometimes in the play circuit as
well (see fig. 186, which also shows the other main components of a
tape recorder).

Equalization (EQ)
Both heads (inductors) and tape are highly non-linear in behaviour, and
correction circuits are used in both input and output, as shown in fig.
186. In practice the EQ curves are not dissimilar to those for disc
recording (fig. 180c), and the main world standards are **NAB** (USA) and
CCIR (Europe). Like bias, EQ must be properly set up for tape speed
and type of tape. Some machines have switched provision for both CCIR
and NAB, useful when exchanging tapes with studios calibrated to the

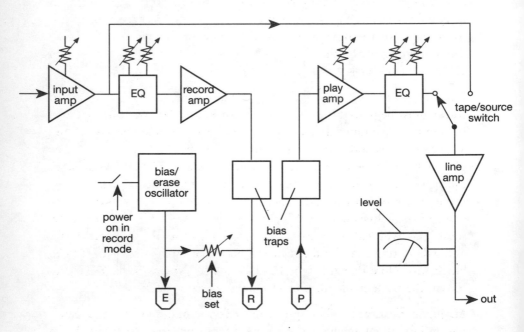

Fig. 186

other standard. Tape, like any granular medium, is inherently noisy, though modern fine-grained, polished tapes are remarkably quiet, and the top boost added on RECORD followed by cut on REPLAY also helps to reduce noise. The effective **signal-to-noise ratio**, hence the **dynamic range** of tape depends on the stock itself and also on proper **lining up**, and can be improved by using a **noise reduction** system.

A few further points about analogue magnetic recording require brief comment:

Cross-field bias Some designers prefer to feed bias separately to the tape (instead of mixing it electrically with the audio signal) by using a separate bias head on the base side of the tape. This is claimed to improve flux concentration in the tape. (Another technique for doing this is the 'focused gap', where a silver 'flux blocker' is placed in the gap to force more flux out into the tape.)

Degaussing Heavy **overloading** may effectively apply **DC** to the record head, permanently magnetizing it. Apart from adding noise, 'magged-up' heads can ruin recordings. Regular degaussing with a small mains **electromagnet** cures this problem, and the same device will demagnetize cutting blades, tools etc.

Punch-in/punch-out Entering and leaving record mode 'on the fly' is essential for electronic editing (cut editing is hardly ever used for multi-track tape, for the obvious reason that it cuts through all the tracks). The erase/bias oscillator must be activated rapidly but without causing clicks, so its onset is a controlled but fast build-up on punch-in.

Selective synchronization When **overdubbing**, previously recorded tracks must be played back from the record head (fig. 187), or they will be late by an amount determined by the head spacing/tape speed, and as each track is added the music will get progressively out of sync. The playback quality will be poorer than off the playback head (because of the wider gap of the record head), but this playback is for cueing only – the final **mixdown** is done from the playback head. In sel-sync mode (sometimes 'self-sync' or just 'sync' – it depends on the manufacturer) some bias will leak over from the active segment of the record head, and a bias trap may be fitted in the playback circuit (see fig. 186) to block this. Note that this tape head switching process is not related to **selsyn**, the trade name for a master/slave motor system.

Magnetic film stock Film optical recording is outside our scope, but a few points about magnetic 35 or 16 mm sprocketed stock should be

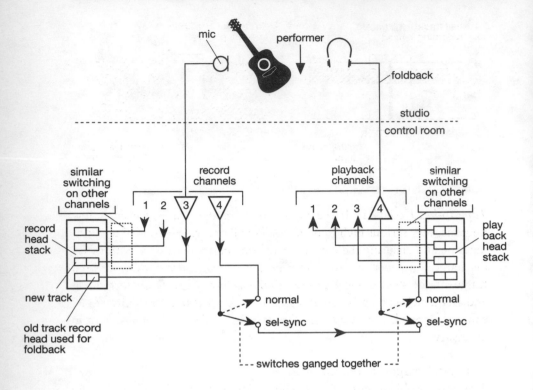

Fig. 187

noted. Sprocketing enables a magnetic sound track to be precisely synchronized with the picture, and the oxide may be applied all over ('fully coated') or as a 'stripe', i.e. with a recording track down one side and a narrow balancing track on the other to ensure even spooling. Film stock is much thicker than the base used for normal audio tape, and the high tension necessary to keep good head contact makes for rapid head wear. Increasingly, film sound is prepared and dubbed using normal tape and electronic synchronization with the picture, see **time codes**.

Stereo and multi-track heads   For common formats see **tape track configurations**. The different sections of multi-track heads are magnetically shielded from each other, and the tracks on the tape are separated by unrecorded 'guard bands'. Playing back tape on a head with a different track width from that used for recording is often done, but may produce unsatisfactory results. Fig. 188a shows that a half-track recording played on a full-track head will be unduly noisy, and 188b that half-track playback of full-track material produces 'fringing' or leakage into the head of flux from outside the gap plane.

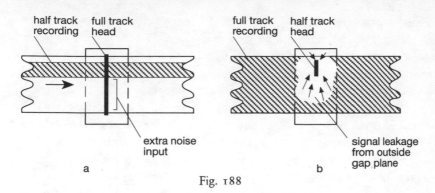

Fig. 188

Tape-to-head contact If the tape lifts from the head by even a few microns, very serious high frequency loss will occur. Methods of tensioning tape and ensuring the correct head contact are discussed, with other mechanical aspects of tape machines, in **tape recorder design**. Dirt, fragments of shed oxide etc. can similarly ruin a head's performance, and frequent cleaning is essential. Head faces that are worn into 'flats' can be relapped, but eventually the gap will widen and replacement is necessary.

3. Digital magnetic recording

A serious problem with all analogue media is that **noise** enters by the same door as the signal, and the two can never be completely separated. Everything in the chain from microphone onwards is to some extent noisy, including of course the recording medium itself, and this noise can only be reduced, not eliminated. Every generation of copying adds still more noise, and in most media the problem also increases with use and age. A digital recording chain still has some analogue stages, such as a microphone amplifier and a final amplifier, but the recording itself is noise-free because the process simply does not recognize analogue phenomena – it can only respond to code. Noisy tape, **drop-outs** etc. may corrupt the code and cause errors, but that is a different problem. Copying cannot add noise either: provided the code is readable the thousandth copy will be identical with the first.

This tremendous advantage is offset by some problems of course, one of them being **quantization** noise, not in the recording but the conversion process. This and the basics of sampling, resolution etc. are discussed in **digital synthesis techniques** 1–3. We are concerned here with digital tape recording (i.e. the moving linear medium), but of course digital sound is also stored in magnetic **hard** and **floppy disks** and **semiconductor** memory like **random access memory** (see **samplers**), as well as optical media like **compact disc** or **WORM**. The **tapeless studio** is already a reality, and the next major step will be to eliminate tape transports altogether and store either in solid state (at the moment limited by the cost of the huge capacities needed for long pieces of music) or by a simpler mechanical method, such as optical storage on a stationary 'card' scanned by a moving **laser** beam. No one can be certain what the position will be in a few years, and the notes below are confined to the two main current digital tape recording methods: rotating head and fixed or stationary head. See **pulse code modulation** (PCM) and fig. 162 for a description of the primary encoding system used for both.

As fig. 162 shows, the PCM signal is a series of pulses of varying length, and although it is further modulated before recording (see below) its general form remains. The recording ('writing') process aims to near-**saturate** the tape in both directions, giving maximum discrimination between the two states of the pulses. The impressed pattern is therefore much simpler than the continuous variations of an analogue waveform, but the required **bandwidth** is very much greater – where 20 kHz is a satisfactory upper audio limit, a high quality digital signal may contain a million or more transitions per second for every track recorded.

The electronics for digital recording are much more complex than for analogue: 1. There are two conversions – in (**ADC**) and out (**DAC**) of the digital domain, with associated **filtering**. 2. Error detection/correction codes and interleaving must be added (the general principles are discussed in **compact disc**). 3. The 'raw' PCM is optimized for recording by conversion to a 'channel code' which minimizes transitions and hence bandwidth. The one used for compact disc (EFM) is mentioned in that entry, and several types are in use. 4. Depending on the medium, **multiplexing** of channels and/or provision for many channels, buffer memory to allow for discontinuous recording, conversion to video format etc. may be needed. 5. The timing of processing must be serviced by suitable clock **oscillators**. A generalized scheme of a digital record/playback system is shown in fig. 189.

Rotating head machines

By the time that consumer digital audio became a serious possibility, the bandwidth problem had already been solved for video recording (which needs an even greater bandwidth – c. 5 MHz). The first reliable digital audio systems to appear simply adapted the well-proven **helical scan** technology by replacing the video recording with a digital audio one. Considerable encoding complexity is involved, because as well as the normal 'overhead', the stereo signal must be multiplexed on to one

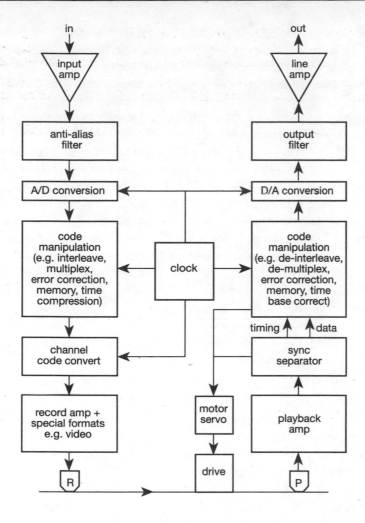

Fig. 189

track (see **video cassette PCM**). Moreover the music code is not continuous so memory buffering is needed, and the signal must be made video-compatible. When all this has been done, however, any type of video cassette machine can be used, and it is a very convenient format. The **sampling rate** is the same (44.1 kHz) as compact disc, and the **resolution** is 14 or 16 bits, which makes it a suitable CD mastering medium. Helical scan is also used in the **digital audio tape** (DAT) format currently available.

Because the scan is diagonal and the tape is held in a cassette, cut editing is impossible and all editing must be done on the code itself. The track format of standard video machines also restricts the number of tracks to two. It is therefore an excellent medium for storing finished stereo material, but unsuitable for studio work involving **overdubbing**, **editing** and **mixdowns**. This is why fixed head systems were evolved, but these are both bulky and costly, and before leaving helical systems we should note an ingenious format developed by Akai,* which offers no less than twelve tracks using the miniature Sony Video 8 cassette, and gives professional multi-track recording at very reasonable cost.

A-DAM (Akai Digital Audio Multi-track format) uses a special rotating drum fitted with three record and three playback heads, each carrying the data for four channels instead of the two possible with normal video machines. The separate playback heads allow off-tape monitoring, and resolution is sixteen bits at sampling rates of either 48 or 44.1 kHz. Two analogue (non-helical) tracks are also provided, one of which can be recorded with SMPTE timing data (see **time codes**). This allows two or more A-DAM units to be locked in sync, thus extending the track capacity to 24 or any further multiple of 12. Cut editing is still not possible, of course, and mixdown involves conversion to analogue unless the studio is equipped for digital mixing, but the quality of the reconverted signal is still very high.

Fixed head machines

Studios have large investments in equipment and the design philosophy behind fixed head digital recorders was to produce studio machines that could replace their analogue equivalents with the minimum of expensive installation costs. With fixed heads, of course, the large bandwidths offered by the helical scan process are not available. Other methods of expanding bandwidth are: 1. Increasing the density of signals by improving tapes and heads. 2. Paralleling data by using more than one digital track per audio channel. 3. Using wider tape and/or reducing track widths on the tape. At the time of writing there are two widely used systems: Digital Audio Stationary Head (DASH) and Pro-Digi.

DASH is a format agreed by a consortium but mainly implemented by Sony, using the same speeds – 76, 38, and 19 cm/sec (30, 15, 7½ ips) as in standard analogue practice, and two standard tape widths, 6.35 mm (¼ in) and 12.7 mm (½ in). Sampling rate at these speeds is 48 kHz, but a slightly slower version of each gives 44.1 kHz, the SR for compact disc. The channel code devised for DASH, HDM–1, gives a 50 per cent longer minimum wavelength than basic PCM. At all but

*Akai Electric Co. Ltd., 12–14, 2–chome, Higashi-kojiya, Ohta-ku, Tokyo, Japan.

the fastest speed parallel digital tracking is used, and the number of audio channels with normal heads ranges from 24 (½ in, 76 cm) to 2 (¼ in, 19 cm). Analogue tracks are also provided, and they are useful for editing, recording **time codes** etc. Sony's very successful twenty-four-track machine (PCM-3324) has recently been joined by the PCM-3348, which uses 'thin film' heads to double the density and offer an astonishing forty-eight tracks on ½ in tape. Mitsubishi's Pro-Digi system has user features not unlike DASH. Quarter-inch Pro-Digi is a stereo format with speeds of 15 and 7½ ips, and there is a thirty-two-track version using 1 in tape, both having a number of ancillary tracks as well. The coding of DASH and Pro-Digi is significantly different, however.

Fixed head machines provide everything that analogue multi-track offers, including the possibility of cut editing and punch-in/punch-out. Both inevitably cause discontinuities in the codes, but ingenious techniques such as those used in **samplers** optimize joins by **crossfading** or interpolation.

An important difference between analogue and digital technique is the effect of too large an input signal. Running 'into the red' is quite normal in analogue recording – distortion worsens gently as the level increases, and the occasional over-high peak will not necessarily ruin the recording. Digital systems, on the other hand, have a strict limit set by the word length, for example in a 14 bit 'frame' the maximum number (14 1s) is 16,383. The 'next' number is not 16,384 but 0, so at worst a large signal would be inverted to the other end of the frame, at best 'hard **clipping**' would cause immediate and drastic distortion. In practical systems such 'overflows' are optimized in various ways, but the best course is to make sure they never happen. Fortunately the absence of tape noise permits clean recording down to levels that would be below the noise floor in an analogue system, and **lining up** is typically to around −15 dB (average maximum signal), not the 0 of analogue recording. This gives greatly increased **headroom** to accommodate heavy transients.

There are many aspects of digital technique which we cannot discuss here, such as details of coding, thin film heads, vertical and other special magnetic formats, but excellent illustrated descriptions are given in Pohlmann's *Principles of Digital Audio* (Pohlmann, 1989) and Watkinson's *The Art of Digital Audio* (Watkinson, 1988). *Newnes Audio and Hi-Fi Engineer's Pocket Book* (Capel, 1988) contains a useful guide to all aspects of tape recording. See also **mixers and mixing desks, patch** and **print-through**.

Sound reinforcement   See **public address**

Spac/er, -ing   Non-active tape **spliced** into magnetic recording tape to separate two items, as opposed to **leader** and **trailer** at each end. All three types use the same sort of tape, generally known as 'leader tape', which is sometimes colour-coded to indicate the type of material on the adjacent tape, and/or printed with time markers to simplify the timing of silent inserts.

Spatial modulation   A general term covering any manipulation of the apparent motion or position of a sound source in a space, either manually by, for example, a **panpot** or **joystick**, or automatically, and particularly when it has some compositional function. See also **quadraphony** and **stereo**.

Speaker key   A key fitted to clarinets (and oboes, when it is called an octave key) to force an **antinode** and facilitate playing in the upper register. See **woodwind instruments** and Baines (1962).

Spectr/um, -a, -al   A plot showing energy in relation to **frequency**. The word can be used loosely to indicate a broad general **band** (for example, fig. 161, a small part of which is labelled 'audible spectrum'). Musical notes have energy at specific frequencies (**partials**) and, in more precise usage, a spectrum details the instantaneous energy in each partial of a **complex wave** (or the one frequency of a **sine wave**). Plotting a 'distributed' spectrum such as that of **noise** shows energy per unit **bandwidth**. This 'frequency domain' plot is one way to describe a sound. Another is a **waveform** or 'time domain' plot (energy/time). See **analogue synthesis techniques** 4 for some waveforms and their spectra, and **digital synthesis techniques** 3 for analytical methods and the Fourier transform, which converts one domain to the other. See also **formant** for the idea of spectral **envelopes**.

Speech coil   See **loudspeakers**

Speech synthesis   There is no specific discussion of this complex subject in this book, but see **digital synthesis techniques** 5 (subtractive synthesis) and 7 (Vosim, FOF) and **vocoder**.

Spider   See **loudspeakers**

Spill Unwanted input to a microphone. See **microphone placement**.

Splice In **cut editing**, to join tape. The tape is usually cut at an angle to minimize clicks on replay, and joined with special 'non-bleeding' adhesive tape on the non-active side. Occasionally an overlapped and glued join is used. See also **tape composition techniques**.

Spool (Reel) A container for tape, made of plastic or non-ferrous metal. Small sizes (17.8 cm (7 in) and smaller) are often called 'ciné' spools because their centre is similar to the 8 mm film type. Some professional spools (26.7 cm, 10½ in) are made with ciné centres, but most are made on the **NAB** (USA) pattern with 7.6 cm (3 in) holes. They usually consist of three parts, a 'hub' and two detachable 'cheeks'. The cheapest way to buy tape is as 'pancakes' – bare tape on hubs to which cheeks are fixed when the tape is used. There is also an extra large (35.6 cm, 14 in) size which some machines can accommodate. The **CCIR** (Europe) system uses no spool cheeks but a single platter above which the bare tape, on a hub, is clamped to the centre spindle.

Spurious signals The unwanted results of signals interacting with themselves or an external source. They may be audible (as an **alias**, for example) or outside the audio band, like most **parasitic oscillations**. See also **cross-modulation**.

Square wave A symmetrical rectangular wave containing only odd **harmonics**, which diminish at a rate of a third of the **fundamental**'s energy in the third harmonic, a fifth in the fifth, and so on. See **analogue synthesis techniques** 4 and **ringing**. Compare **pulse**, **ramp** and **triangle waves**.

Squawk box A small amplifier and speaker used in cutting rooms for editing and laying sound tracks.

SR See **sampling rate**

Staircase A stepped **waveform**, not only in the regular form of fig. 190a; that shown in 190b is also a staircase, i.e. a series of steady amplitudes with instant transitions from one to another. A staircase is distinguished from a **square** or **pulse wave** by having multiple levels of steady state. At audio frequencies, this pattern is typical of the output of a **sample-and-hold** circuit (see fig. 172). At lower frequencies, the

a   b

Fig. 190

output of, for example, a voltage controlling keyboard is also a staircase (see **analogue synthesis techniques** 6). A random staircase generator derives a staircase by sampling **noise**, and provides variable probability in both amplitude and time domains (see **random number and voltage generators**).

Stamper   See **sound recording techniques**

Standing wave   (or stationary wave) A **travelling wave** confined within a closed system (such as a pipe, bottle, string, or room) or in a two-dimensional medium such as a drum or gong. Such a wave reflects back onto itself from the boundaries of the system, and the two oppositely moving waves set up a positionally stationary (though continuously vibrating) wave pattern, as shown in fig. 191.

The **nodes** and **antinodes** thus formed are characteristic of **resonance**. Standing waves do not occur much in free air because, although there are plenty of reflections, conditions are too random for the necessary cancellations and reinforcements to take place, though special environments such as parallel surfaces (see **flutter echo**) may cause them. The formation of standing waves is the fundamental operating principle of all pitched musical instruments (see **bowed strings, brass instruments** and **woodwind instruments**).

Static charge   See **electrostatic charge**

Steady state   1. A state of equilibrium in some aspect of a system (such as **level** or **frequency**) which is maintained for some time. The condition reached after disturbance by some unsettling effect, thus, for example, the 'flat' part of the waveshape in fig. 169, after the **ringing** has stopped. 2. A less precise usage refers to the middle portion of a musical note, after the attack and before **decay** begins. This 'steady state' is largely

positions where travelling waves always cancel ⟶ are the node points of the standing wave

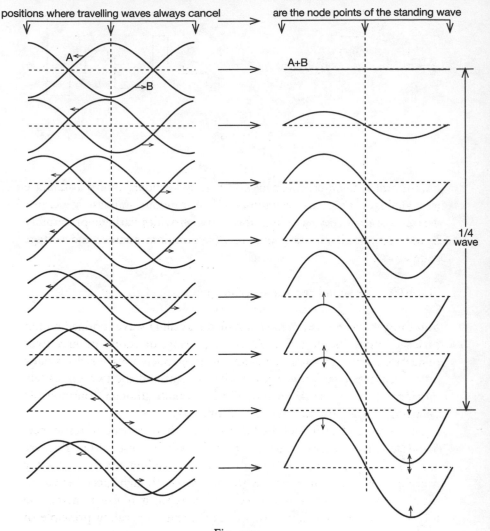

Fig. 191

illusory because, though it is sometimes difficult to detect, continuous dynamic activity is occurring.

Step/-down, -up See **transformers**

Stereo/phony From Greek *stereos* meaning 'solid'. The artificial construction of a sound field having aural cues similar to those in a real environment, and thus appearing 'solid' to the listener. The word used alone implies the use of a minimum of two channels, which is the subject of this entry, but **quadraphony** is also stereo, and some of the points made in that entry apply here as well.

Human beings can localize sounds surprisingly well. Some of this ability is undoubtedly learned – although an important cue to distance is loudness, we know whether someone is speaking quietly nearby or loudly from afar by our experience of the way people project their voices. To judge direction, we decode the different inputs to our two ears, which although separated by only the width of the head, are also shielded by it so that 'far side' sounds must go round it. In the case of low **frequencies**, whose **wavelength** is long compared with the distance between ears, the head is hardly a barrier at all. The sound flows round it, and we detect time – in effect **phase** – differences between the two signals to decide the sound's direction. At high frequencies (short wavelengths), the head materially obstructs the sound, and loudness difference appears to be the main criterion.

The design of the external ear (pinna) is also directional (though only slightly compared with the huge focused collectors of some nocturnal animals), which helps us to distinguish front from rear (sounds from both are in phase and of equal intensity). But the decoding of sounds involves much more than this. Most of the sound reaching us (except in a completely open space) is reflected in any case, and therefore coming from the 'wrong' direction, so there is a mass of additional input to decode, and the mechanisms are still not fully understood. A stereo sound system aims to provide these depth and position cues, and recreate either the 'natural' effect of a real space, or to construct similar effects artificially in the recording/mixing process.

Stereo listening
For serious assessment and monitoring the listener should form a roughly equilateral triangle with the **loudspeakers**. But in ordinary use good results should be possible from anywhere more or less equidistant from them and giving two distinct paths to the ears. There are various ways, advocated by different speaker designers, of using wall reflections etc. to widen the image, and a number of different approaches are discussed in the entry on **loudspeakers**. Whatever system is used, the speakers should be matched, and must be connected in **phase** (fed with the same signal, the cones must move simultaneously and in the same direction).

Local acoustics should be fairly dead to avoid extra reflections and colorations being imposed on those arriving with the signal. Headphone listening, advocated by some, removes the local environment entirely, but apart from its inconvenience and social isolation it adds new kinds of artificiality. In listening to speakers, for example, deep bass is felt with the whole body as well as heard, an effect not possible with headphones. In both recording and listening there are so many variables in stereo that words like 'accuracy' and 'naturalness' have little meaning – subjective impression prevails over precise theory, even where one can be propounded. The whole notion of recreating an orchestra (let alone an opera house) in one's living room demands a certain suspension (willingly given) of reality.

Stereo recording

(See **microphones** for explanations of 'omni', 'cardioid' etc.) In **microphone placement** two methods of collecting a general stereo image are shown (fig. 121a). The 'spaced omni' technique follows the theory of early experiments using many channels.

The row of speakers in fig. 192 corresponds to an input array of microphones, and the matching delay and level patterns allow the listener to place the origin of the sound. Unfortunately (as Nisbett, 1970, chapter 1 points out) this technique does not hold up well when reduced to two channels. If omni mics are placed close the result will hardly differ from mono, and if widely spaced their inputs have little coherent relationship with each other or to the ears of the listener. In addition, sources near the middle tend to fall back compared with those near either of the mics. If this is compensated by adding a centre mic feeding both channels (the usual remedy), the image is even further from 'real'. All the same, as said above, good results do not necessarily conform to theory, some undoubtedly excellent recordings have been based on spaced mics, and the method can work well when there are more channels, as in quad (see fig. 163).

The other arrangement shown in fig. 121a is the coincident X–Y pair of cardioids, which is reliable, theoretically sound, and the most widely used. Whether two separate mics are used, or a pair mounted one above the other on a common rotatable axis (see stereo mics in **microphones**), the idea is to place the diaphragms as close together as possible, so that inputs at both are in phase. Pick-up is directional because of the offset polar patterns, arranged so that equal response occurs only from the front (fig. 193a). One great advantage over the spaced omni arrangement (whose signals bear no consistent phase relationship) is that the signals can be added to make a coherent mono signal, essential in applications such as radio and commercial recording where many users do not have stereo equipment. In fact both the sum $(A+B)$ and difference $(A-B)$ signals are used when stereo is coded for radio transmission, and in

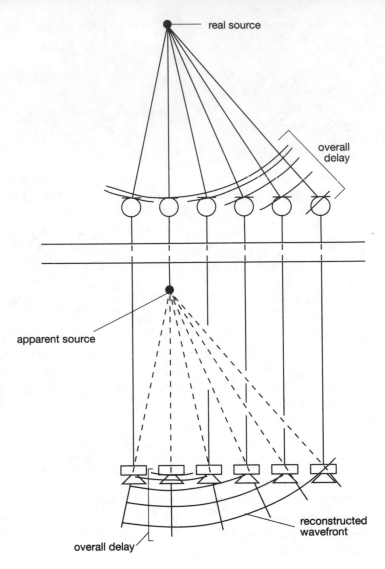

real source

overall
delay

apparent source

reconstructed
wavefront

overall delay

Fig. 192

mono-compatible stereo discs the lateral component is A+B, the vertical
A−B (see **pick-ups**).

A further mic arrangement is the 'M–S' technique, standing for Main
(or Mid) and Side. Fig. 193b shows a main cardioid (though other
patterns are sometimes used) which is in effect a front facing mono mic,
and a side mic which is bi-directional with a 'dead side' on the axis of
the main, so that it collects mostly indirect sound and room ambience.

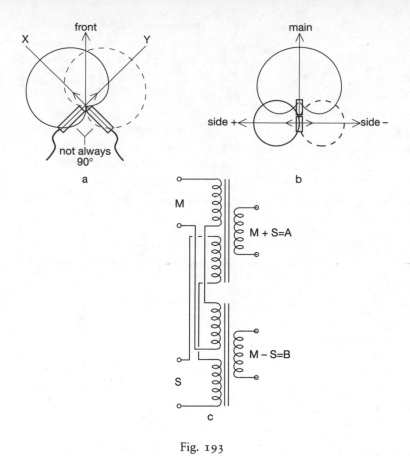

Fig. 193

A bi-directional (velocity) mic responds in antiphase on the two sides, so reversing the phase of the output from S simulates an input from the reverse side (these antiphase outputs are called +S and −S signals). Combining the output from M with +S gives a signal for one stereo channel, M and −S the other. Fig. 193c shows how mixing is done with a **transformer** matrix (the direction of connections deciding the polarity of output). If a mic pair with variable polar pattern is used (see fig. 127 and condenser mics in **microphones**), the same mic can be configured as X–Y or M–S, and by manipulating mutual levels and polar patterns the apparent width of the image can be electrically controlled.

Mixdown, panning etc.
(See **mixers and mixing desks** for general information.) In practice a simple two mic stereo balance is rare. In most cases the sound you hear is a highly artificial product, and may have no true stereo imaging at

all. A mono source (from a solo instrument's mic, for example) can be moved in the stereo field by adjusting A and B levels with a **panpot** and **equalization, reverberation** and other treatments added to give it depth and **presence**. Sometimes delays are used on single mics to take a sound further back. Fig 194 shows some steps in a typical recording production. The multi-track tape stage may be omitted and all balancing done at the first pass – as it must be in live broadcasting.

Many solo and small ensemble recordings need little or no processing, but for most recording the constructional approach to stereo is a necessary and efficient part of audio production. The art of the balance engineer, whether dealing with a symphony orchestra, an opera, or the

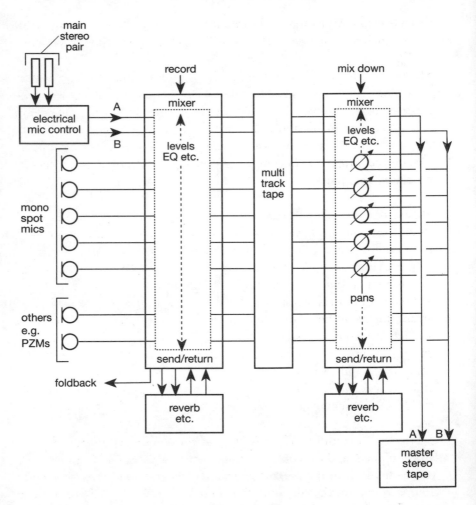

Fig. 194

electronic instruments of a rock group, is to deliver a final recording in which all relevant strands and textures are clearly heard, in a stereo image that is convincing and effective for the intended listening environment, which is likely to be very different from the original one. If after all this the result seems 'lifelike', the job has been well done.

Stochastic   See **computer music composition techniques** 2

Stop band   The **band,** defined by stating the lowest and highest **frequencies,** excluded by, for example, a reject **filter.** The opposite of a **pass band.**

Storyboard   A pictorial substitute for a script, often the raw material from which a composer works in media such as animation, or ballet.

String   1. The sound generator in a large group of musical instruments ('chordophones' – see **musical instruments, types of**). Strings may be made of brass, bronze, iron, steel and other metals, or silk, gut, nylon and other man-made fibres. To increase their weight per unit length, they may also be spirally covered with, for example, silver or copper. (See **bowed strings.**) 2. In computers, a group of **bits, bytes** or **characters** processed as a unit.

Studio design   This entry is concerned particularly with the design of studios for composing electronic and computer music, but in most cases such studios can also be used for normal recording purposes.

In providing a work environment for electronic composing, the only rule is that it should be efficient and comfortable for those who use it. Some composers work best when organization is not too tidy and arrangements ad hoc. For others, a neatly labelled **patching** system and a planned layout are essential for clear thinking. A studio for multiple use (for example in a university) should accommodate as many different approaches and techniques as possible, as well as providing teaching and research facilities. It is most important in planning a new studio to decide in advance exactly what it is intended to do, and many fail because designers and users have different expectations.

Provided a studio works efficiently at the level to which it is funded and equipped, and the composer fully understands its limits, good music can be made with the humblest resources. There are also magnificently equipped studios that do almost no effective work at all. To take some examples, fig. 195 shows one of many possible ways of configuring a

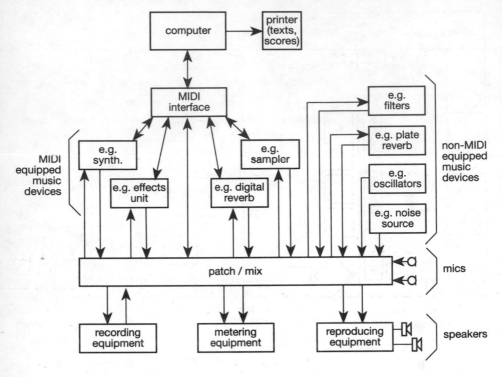

Fig. 195

low-budget personal composing studio. In this case it is envisaged that the composer wants to work mainly with the computer and associated **MIDI** equipment, but if traditional tape techniques are to be included also, the tape recorder section must contain equipment suitable for this type of work (see **tape composition techniques**). The physical layout can be arranged in many ways, from a temporary, easily dismantled hook-up to a permanently wired studio allowing for future expansion. If any of the equipment is needed for performance also, it must obviously be portable enough to take to a concert room.

Fig. 196 shows a typical medium-sized educational studio, designed for several types of use including professional and student composition, teaching, general music recording and musicology studies. This is a flexible combination of fixed and moveable items, with some permanent patching, but with selected suites of equipment which can be moved to a work station when needed, and a lecture room doubling as a recording studio. The emphasis is on careful allocation of space so that functions can be changed in the minimum time. It is very important that compos-ers, who need to work undisturbed, should be separated from the lecture

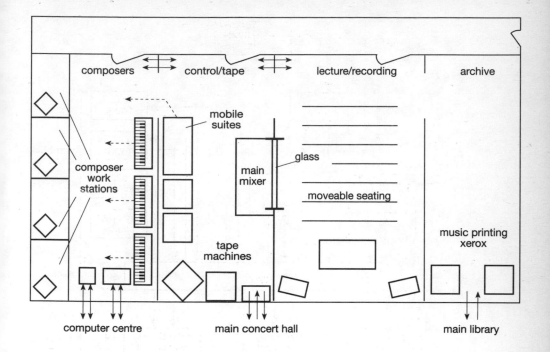

Fig. 196

area, but how this is done depends on local conditions.

Large, well-funded and well-equipped studios can take many forms, and often reflect the way they were started and grew. Some result from an individual's research leading to the formation of a team which attracts funding. Some spring up within an existing industrial or cultural organization (e.g. a radio station or a university), and some are created whole by single large funding grants.

To take an example of what amounts to a national studio, the Institut de Recherche et de Coordination Acoustique/Musique (**IRCAM**) in Paris was constructed as part of the Centre Pompidou, and is directed by Pierre Boulez, heading an international committee of respected composers and researchers. The organization aims to cover every aspect of musical and acoustic research, composition, instruction and concert-giving. Its details are continually under review as technology changes, but the original establishment of facilities gives an idea of the scope intended:

7   studios
1   **anechoic** chamber
1   computer room

    6 laboratories
    1 conference room
    1 library
   32 offices
    1 mechanical workshop
    1 experimental concert hall with service areas.

This last, L'Espace de Projection, is an elaborate essay in variable acoustics. To quote from an IRCAM brochure: 'This experimental hall is the only one of its kind in the world. It measures 375 m² and is unique in that its acoustical properties can be altered; **reverberation** time can be changed from 0.5 to 4.5 seconds, depending on the configuration of the ceiling, divided into three mobile panels, and the acoustic prisms installed in the walls and the ceiling. Each prism has three sides: reflective, absorbent and diffusing.' (IRCAM, c. 1981)

There are 171 of these prisms, arranged in groups of three and electrically controlled. The three heavy (24 ton) ceiling panels can be adjusted to give a height variation from 1.5 to 11.5 metres, and all these numerous variables can be reset quickly by computer control.

As discussed in **computer music composition techniques** the decreasing cost of both computing power and sophisticated music equipment, and the flexibility offered by MIDI, have today brought serious, professional composing into the home studio, in contrast to the earlier position when composers had to find a place in large, institutional studios to produce finished work of any scope and quality, or face a huge financial outlay. The big studios are still very necessary, of course – they and the large manufacturers conduct the research and marketing from which the small studios benefit, and there is much high level, expensive work that the small studio cannot attempt, needing powerful computers and specialist staff. A trend already started is to combine home work stations with electronic access to large facilities, backed up by personal visits when necessary.

A good plan for beginners in this field is to attend one or two of the courses offered by the larger institutions, and learn a range of composing techniques before deciding which direction of development suits them best, and making a choice of personal equipment. It is worth remembering, too, that alongside the relatively expensive high-tech composing and performing machines and software that are now becoming the norm, there is still a place for good musical ideas which can be realized very cheaply and with simple equipment (see **tape composition techniques**). See also **analogue synthesis techniques, control room** and **digital synthesis techniques**.

Stylus   See **pick-ups** and **sound recording techniques**

Sub-harmonic   The integral sub-multiple of a given **frequency** (½, ⅓, ¼ etc.), the converse of a normal **harmonic**. Sub-harmonics can occur naturally, for example a strong, low note may cause a piece of furniture to vibrate at half its frequency, but extended sub-harmonic series must be generated artificially. They have the 'unnatural' but interesting characteristic that the **partials** become more crowded as the pitch descends (see fig. 197). Compare fig. 99, illustrating the **harmonic series**, and note that the converse of the seventh harmonic (bracketed) is also 'out of tune', but sharp rather than flat. Sub-harmonic tones, particularly the octaves at the half and the quarter of a **fundamental** frequency, can add attractive richness to a sound.

Sub/-, super/sonic   These terms can refer to the velocity of objects (e.g. 'supersonic' flight), but in the context of this book they indicate **frequencies** below (and above) the range of human hearing. There is not a clean boundary at either end, because low sounds (below *c*. 20 **hertz**) do not disappear at once but become variously described throbbing sensations, 'felt' with the body rather than heard. At the upper end authorities differ in what they consider 'normal' for young, healthy ears – 10–20 kHz (Taylor, 1965), 25 kHz (Wood, 1962), 15 kHz (Olson, 1967). An earlier book, Percy C. Buck's *Acoustics for Musicians* of 1918, claims 38 kHz (Buck, 1918)! Whichever limit is chosen (and it is quite easy to perform personal tests with an oscillator and headphones) all are well above the high end of musical **fundamentals** (*c*. 4 kHz), though not of **partials**, and all of us must expect a considerable high frequency loss with age. More important than actual limits is our sensitivity to small changes of pitch and loudness, which is greatest in the middle, musically most relevant zone. Plots like the Fletcher–Munson

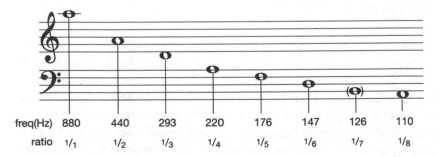

freq(Hz)	880	440	293	220	176	147	126	110
ratio	1/1	1/2	1/3	1/4	1/5	1/6	1/7	1/8

Fig. 197

curves (fig. 155) are sometimes adapted to form a loop indicating upper and lower frequency limits as well as intensity boundaries but, for the reasons mentioned above, the accuracy of such diagrams is suspect. Sub-sonic sounds are also described as 'sub-audio' or 'infra-sonic'. See **ultrasonics**.

Subtractive synthesis   A group of synthesis techniques based on refining a rich source such as a **complex wave** or **noise** by removing unwanted components until the desired sound is reached. Compare its opposite, **additive synthesis**, and see **analogue synthesis techniques** 4, **digital synthesis techniques** 5 and **filters**. In practice the process often involves several methods of refining the source, used concurrently or in succession.

Sum frequency   See **difference frequency**

Superhet/erodyne   See **heterodyne**

Supply spool   The **spool** from which tape is fed to the record/playback **heads** – normally a tape machine's lefthand spool. See **tape recorder design**.

Surround sound   The local (listening room or auditorium) processing of a mono or **stereo** signal to produce pseudo-**quad**. Simpler systems apply small **phase** changes to generate new signals, but the best are based on digital **reverberators**, programmed to give a choice of pre-set and user-adjustable hall acoustics. The process requires extra amplifiers and speakers which are fed with the processed output.

Sustain   1. Of sounds used in **keyboard synthesizers**, electronic **organs** etc. The part of the **envelope** of long sounds (in wind, string-type instruments etc.) nearest to **steady state**, maintained as long as a key is held down. The term does not apply to staccato and percussive envelopes, which die away even if the key remains down. See also **analogue synthesis techniques** 4. 2. The effect of the 'sustaining' pedal of a piano, which lifts all the dampers together (see **pianos** *acoustic*).

Swarf   (chip) The thread of plastic (or metal) cut from the groove during disc recording (see **sound recording techniques**).

Symmetrical waveform   One whose positive and negative half-cycles are symmetrical, for example **square** and **triangle waves**, which contain only odd harmonics, or **sine waves**, a special case with no harmonics. Asymmetrical waves such as **ramp** and **pulse** waves have complete **harmonic series**. See also **analogue synthesis techniques** 4.

Synchronization (sync, synch) Human life and the natural world in general depend a great deal on recurrent time patterns that are free-running and not precisely synchronized at all. Pulse rates, sleep cycles, menstrual cycles, lifetimes etc. are not measured or correlated exactly but thought of as being 'within a normal range', or not. Fig. 161 in **psychoacoustics** shows part of a wide periodic range to which we are sensitive, and the life blood of musical performance is the elastic approach to precision which gives rhythmic 'spring' and drive. An interesting analysis of this aspect of music is chapter 7 ('Timing by skilled musicians', by Sternberg *et al.*) in Deutsch (1982).

In order to preserve these very nuances, and for other reasons too, techniques for ensuring temporal precision are essential. In recording, good **distortion** figures, low **noise** etc. are a waste of time if events that should start simultaneously do not. Synchronizing tasks may be continuous (time-locking two running tapes) or discrete (sending a **trigger** at a precise time). Some applications are purely electrical: see **MIDI** (system messages), **oscillators** (voltage controlled), **percussion generators**, **sequencers** and **time codes**; others electro-mechanical: see **selsyn**, **servo**, **sound recording techniques** (selective synchronization), **tape recorder design** and **time codes**.

Once precision has been established, freedoms within it can be implemented, such as the 'humanize' feature mentioned under **sequencers**. The dangers of the boringly metronomic are discussed in **computer music composition techniques**. Computers must be very precisely controlled at the microsecond level, but the operator need not be aware of this. Musical 'precision' is of much lower resolution than electronic, so in many cases the pseudo-synchronism offered by a serial data stream such as **MIDI** is perfectly adequate and, in computer music, complex calculations may happen between the onsets of two 'simultaneous' events.

Synthesiz/ers From the Greek for 'putting together', the act or the result of combining separate ingredients into a whole. The word 'synthesizer', though sometimes used for specific single-purpose devices (such as a stereo synthesizer, which generates pseudo-stereo from a mono source), usually means a self-contained package of generator and treatment modules **patchable** in various ways to produce musically useful sounds, and has been used in this sense since the mid-1960s when such packages first appeared (see Introduction, **analogue synthesis techniques** 6 and **computer music composition techniques**). By far the largest group today, and the subject of a separate entry, is **keyboard synthesizers**. For the internal requirements of synthesizers, see also **digital synthesis techniques**.

Apart from live performance (the main use for the keyboard group), synthesizers are used in composition, teaching and research, and people have widely diverse ideas about what they need for each purpose. In this situation, there is a choice between trying to design one do-everything device, or a number of smaller, more specialized machines. Attempts were made in the 1950s to build 'total' music machines, notably the Siemens Synthesizer (Munich) and the RCA Synthesizer (New York, see **analogue synthesis techniques** 6). But apart from being overtaken by voltage control and digital technology a few years later, the 'universal' concept never quite works – however many possibilities have been thought of, there are always some that have not. The voltage controlled synthesizers that followed offered compact and adaptable set-ups that could be configured for different jobs as needed, and as computers became smaller and cheaper, hybrid synthesizers with computer control of analogue devices were another alternative (and still are, see **keyboard synthesizers**). From the beginning, though, it had been seen that the most elegant synthesis would be purely digital.

Synthesis that exists only as software is in theory unlimited – any sound should be possible if the right program is input. For the first few years of computer synthesis (see **computer music composition techniques**) this was the only method available, i.e. synthesis software was directly implemented in a general purpose computer, the only specialized hardware being a **digital-to-analogue converter** to output sound (fig. 198a). The problem was that people didn't know how to instruct the computer beyond a certain point, music of any subtlety needed large, cumbersome programs, and the whole process was very slow. By the mid-1970s digital music hardware and faster processing made **real-time** interactive synthesis possible, and most studios from then on have used a mixture of hardware and software techniques (fig. 198b). As portable, performing digital machines became available, the field tended to divide between large studios which aimed at the 'total' approach for composers and researchers, and small synthesizers offering a limited range of options designed to fill the needs of particular markets.

The position has changed, however, because the small studio is

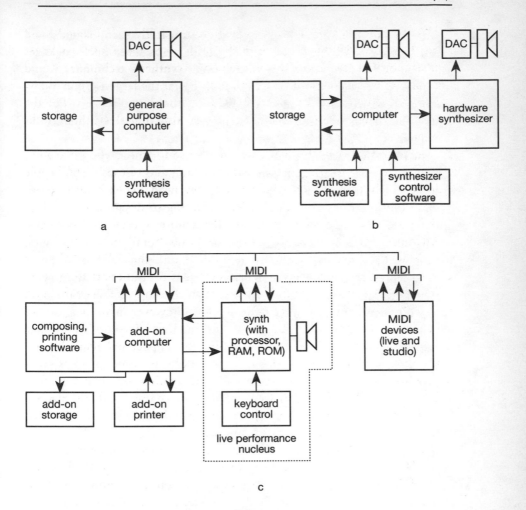

Fig. 198

increasingly adaptable and open-ended. Keyboard synthesizers can be used on their own for live performance, but have a number of 'add-ons' for studio composition work (fig. 198c). Also the range of music software is growing all the time (see again **computer music composition techniques**). Several **MIDI**-linked devices with computer interfacing can make the home studio a very powerful tool, and many computers today have built-in synthesizers as well. More powerful, and found typically in university studios, are dedicated, very high speed signal processing computers such as the DMX 1000 by Digital Music Systems.* This

*Digital Music Systems Inc., P.O. Box 1632, Boston, Mass. 02105, USA.

comes close to the 'universal' concept because the hardware is as generalized as possible, and (working with another, controlling computer) it can be configured in almost any way desired.

There are excellent studio synthesizers which can be ordered as manufactured products, but some of the best studios have developed their own unique systems and devices, such as the Samson Box at Stanford University's CCRMA, the 4X synthesizer at IRCAM in Paris – the list is growing. Alongside all these developments work on direct software synthesis, with no specifically musical devices except output DACs, has continued because it is still acknowledged as the purest approach, and with faster machines and better software its techniques continually improve.

There are still many analogue machines in use, and some composers continue to prefer them, but today the word synthesizer almost always means 'digital synthesizer'. Descriptions of both processes and machines can be found throughout *Computer Music Journal* (see note at the start of the Bibliography), and in specialist magazines such as *Keyboard*.* An excellent survey of design strategies is chapter 19 of Chamberlin (1985). Descriptions of the large systems can be obtained from the studios themselves, some of which, such as IRCAM, offer courses and issue recordings.†

Keyboard Magazine, GPI Corporation, 20085 Stevens Creek, Cupertino, CA 95014, USA.
†Barrière, Jean-Baptiste (artistic director) *IRCAM: Un Portrait* (Record with booklet), IRCAM 0001, IRCAM, Centre Pompidou, Paris, 1983.

T

Tachometer   (tacho, tach) From the Greek *tachos* meaning 'speed'. A device to measure the speed (usually angular or rotational) of, for example, a motor. See **tape recorder design**.

Tail   The end of a recorded tape, as opposed to the 'head'. Tape stored 'tails out' must be rewound before playing. See **print-through**.

Take   One of (possibly) several versions of a given **slate** or music number (e.g. music 6, take 4). To make editing possible, the piece of music being recorded, whether or not it has an 'official' title, should always be clearly distinguished, in announcements, from the take number, for example 'horn ad libs 2, take 3'.

Take-up spool   (reel) The **spool** onto which tape winds after record/ playback. It is normally a tape machine's righthand spool, see **tape recorder design**.

Talkback   An inter-studio link for communication rather than signal feed (which is **foldback**). See talkback and cue in **mixers and mixing desks**.

Tap   In electrical circuits, an intermediate entry and/or exit point in, for example, a **transformer** winding or a digital delay line (see **reverberation**).

Tape composition techniques   In tape music the initial material may be natural or performed sound, or generated by **analogue** or **digital synthesis**. Subsequent treatment may be by electronic processes such as **filtering**, **reverberation** etc., and/or physical and manual processes. It is these mechanical rather than electronic manipulations of sound which are the subject of this entry.

When synthesis techniques were primitive, modifying the recording and/or the machine was the principal or only electronic composition method, and it might be thought that with today's advanced equipment manual tape treatments were now obsolete or irrelevant. This is far from the case. Even in studios using the latest technology, tape procedures still have a place. There are also thousands of creative musicians who, for economic reasons, must use simple techniques, and many more whose needs are not met by the design approach of most manufactured composing devices and for whom direct tape techniques are a practical – sometimes the only – way to realize their thoughts. Analogue tape recording does have quality and noise problems, but even with the equipment of the 1950s these were not serious enough to prevent many fine tape pieces from appearing, and both tape and machines have improved greatly since then. The studio of those days (separate analogue modules plus tape machines, and no automation) has come to be called the 'classical' studio.

Examples of a simple assembly of tape music material is shown in fig. 137 in **montage**, while fig. 138 in **musique concrète** sketches the processes that might go to make up a finished tape. Books giving historical background on tape composing include Appleton and Perera (1975), Ernst (1977), Russcol (1972), Manning (1987) and Griffiths (1979). For studio electronics and tape techniques, Wells (1981) and Strange (1983) are recommended, and a good basic guide to studio practice, organizing a piece etc. is David Keane's *Tape Music Composition* (1980). In this book, knowledge of the information in **sound recording techniques, tape recorder design** and **tape track configurations** is assumed. See also **studio design, electronic music** and **live performance electronic music**. Of the selection of manipulations given below, many can be done more efficiently by electronic means (such as retrograding and looping blocks of digital samples), but the essence of tape work is the direct interaction between composer and material.

Basic tape manipulations

The usual medium for this work is quarter-inch tape, with a single analogue recording, preferably across the full width of the tape. Half-track mono, with either an empty side or two programmes in opposite directions, is not suitable. Multi-track is obviously very limited from the cutting point of view (all tracks are cut) and when retrograded the tracks change position. Cassette formats are inaccessible for manipulation (though it has been done) and normally offer no choice of speeds. Digital fixed head recordings can be cut, but for several reasons this is an unsuitable medium for this type of work.

The best recording format, therefore, is full-track **mono** (**stereo** imaging is a later process), but if recording on a twin-track machine both tracks should be identical from a mono feed. The master tape should never be handled repeatedly or cut etc. Indeed all important source material, vital intermediate mixes etc., should be kept separately on a master spool from which duplicates are made as necessary. See **noise reduction** for comments on using it in tape manipulation work.

Retrograding

This is a simple process, provided the tape is recorded as above. The method of leading the tape the wrong way through the capstan assembly to reverse tape travel is not recommended. Both spool torques are incorrect for reverse running, and the capstan is at the wrong end of the head block. At best head contact and speed regulation are poor, and at worst the tape may be stretched or damaged. Turning the tape over is the only reliable way, and to simplify this obstructions like head covers are best removed from the tape path. A passage to be retrograded in an otherwise forward recording can be cut out, reversed and spliced in again. The perceived effect of retrograding musical notes depends on the **envelope** type. Gentle attacks (such as a flute playing legato) change very little in reverse, but percussive attacks (such as piano or drum) change radically. The reversed **exponential decay** (which does not occur in natural sounds) can produce a powerful accelerating crescendo (a good example is a slowed down, retrograded cymbal crash).

Speed changing

This is also very simple in essence, but limited to shifts of one octave up or down on typical two-speed machines. Any studio should have one or more three-speed machines so that two-octave shifts are possible without re-copying (the only way of extending range with two speeds only). There should also be at least one machine with a fully variable capstan (see **tape recorder design**), so that any intermediate speed can be obtained (the importance of this was noticed in the pioneer days when the **phonogène** was developed for the Paris **musique concrète** studio). A problem with speeded-up tapes is that if the original recording has any low frequency fault like hum it will sound worse when transposed upwards. Also, as noted in **sound recording techniques**, **bias** tone may become audible when tape is slowed down several octaves, but this can usually be filtered without trouble because it is so much higher than the (now slowed down) wanted signal. As with retrograding, the effect of speed changing varies with the material, for example white **noise** (if truly 'white') does not change at all. Apart from the obvious effects on pitch and speed, internal modulations like vocal vibrato change character completely. With simple speed changing of this kind pitch and speed must necessarily increase/decrease together, and making them independent calls for more complex arrangements using either electronic means (see **pitch changer**) or a rotating head machine (see extended techniques below).

Cut editing

This is the primary skill in tape work, and expertise can only be acquired with practice, first in normal speech and music editing, and then in constructing inventive sequences of sounds. Cut editing remains the simplest way to bring sounds from any source at all into juxtaposition. **Sequencing**, however advanced the method, is **patch**-orientated, i.e. it is easy to implement a sequence of similar sounds with changes to pitch, **envelope** etc., but to produce a succession of completely different colours – say one note each of flute, drum, cello, vibraphone, piano, trumpet – calls for lengthy preparation, a separate sequencer track for each sound, track switching to change them, etc. With a recording of each and simple tape editing gear such a sequence can be cut together in two minutes.

Step-by-step editing instructions would occupy undue space here. Nisbett (1970) has some good advice on normal cut editing, but there is no substitute for hands-on experience and adventurous experiment.

The basic tools are: 1. A machine with playback head active in all modes, and visibly sited (not hiding in a slot or well). 2. A jointing block with at least two cutting slots, 90° and either 60°, 45° or both. 3. A razor blade or trimming knife, which should be demagnetized if it has been near a strong field (see degaussing in **sound recording techniques**). Bronze knives or scissors were once specified, but are unnecessary in practice. 4. Splicing or joining tape, normally slightly narrower than the magnetic tape, and with a special 'non-bleeding', medium strength adhesive, allowing a join to be peeled off easily. 5. Wax pencils or spirit-based fibre pens for marking and labelling. 6. **Leader** tape, preferably in several colours. 7. A calibrated ruler, such as a table or bench edge marked off in 'tape seconds', i.e. with main marks 15 in apart, and subdivisions at 7½, 3¾ in etc., is useful.

Obviously a stationary tape produces no output, so in 'reading' the tape in order to find the spot at which to edit it, the trick is to manipulate the two spools so as to jerk the tape sharply back and forth over the playback head, travelling very short distances each time, without stretching it or losing head contact. One learns to identify internal fragments of a sound in either direction and at very slow speeds. The difficulty of doing this varies – the leading edge of a spoken 't' or 's' is easy to find, but the junction between 'n' and 'm' in 'elfin music', or the very end of a long string diminuendo, may not be. The slower the recording speed and hence the more densely packed the modulations, the harder it is to make accurate cuts, but it may be easier to identify low speed material because the 'hand shuttling' can more readily be brought to more or less the original speed.

Marking a cut point is often done at the head itself, but unless a separate editing machine is used, whose performance is not important, care must be taken not to scratch the head or deposit pencil wax or finger grease on it. A safer way is to mark at a tape guide, measure the offset and mark the cutting block accordingly (fig. 199). The sketch also shows that for very exacting cuts it may be necessary to move the point slightly to include a whole leading edge attack or exclude a following sound (when cutting a trailing edge). Joining tape must be placed centrally and exactly parallel – joins with sides protruding will leave adhesive deposits on heads, guides etc. and may even jam in the transport.

Fig. 200 shows one step in a possible musique concrète piece, where two 40 second passages, exclusively of metallic sounds, are cut together, then played from two machines for montaging. Note: 1. All sounds are 'dry', which is necessary for this kind of close cutting – reverberation (if wanted) and other electronic treatments are added at the montage stage or possibly later. 2. The starred sounds have been prepared for this sequence by previous treatments. 3. All material must have been

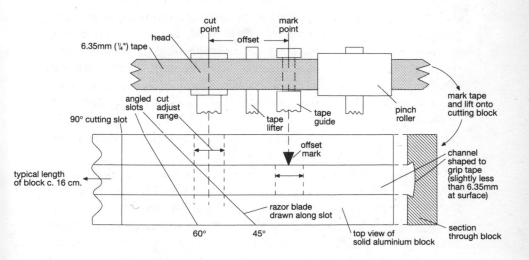

Fig. 199

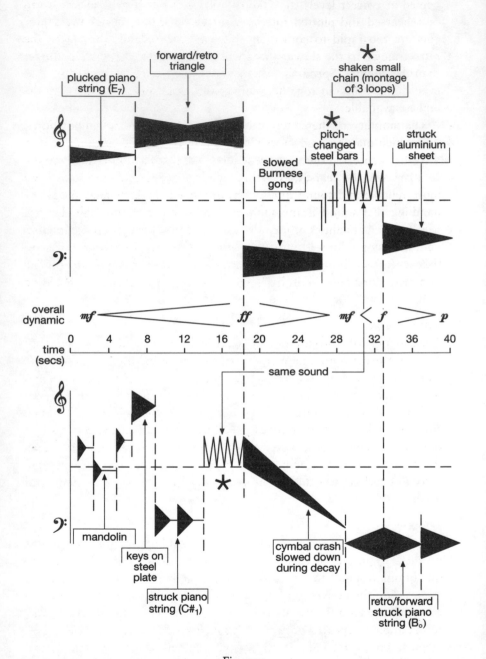

Fig. 200

copied at correct levels to make the cuts effective – general levels can be rehearsed and plotted for the montage recording, but changes over cuts are too rapid to control in this way, for example the cut of the retro triangle to the slowed gong will not work if the triangle is louder than the gong. 4. Speed-changed sounds must have been copied so that everything to be cut together runs at the same speed – preferably the highest available.

The montage of these two tracks then becomes a new compositional unit which may be used in its present form or become a component in a further process. Low cost procedures like this have not substantially changed over the years, except that tapes are quieter, capstan speeds are more reliable and sound quality has improved. Today's technology for handling real sound is the **sampler,** but no store-bought sampler has nearly enough facilities or memory to handle the above example. It could be done using a large computer studio and the quality would be better than with tape but the cost would be enormous by comparison. The humble razor blade, skilfully handled, is still an important composing tool.

Copy editing

The assembly of a programme by selecting the items and recopying them in correct order onto a new tape. Used widely in broadcasting, it avoids cutting tapes and although it can be accurate to a fraction of a second if done well, it does not offer the precision of cut editing and is not widely used in tape composition except for assembling material. Crossing from one take to another (both being run simultaneously) can also be done in the course of a piece, and without physically cutting the tape, by 'punching-in/out' a new section on a running tape (see again **sound recording techniques**), and a **time code** may be used to ensure **synchronization.**

Looping

This was one of the earliest methods of extending material (first done on discs by means of closed grooves, see **musique concrète**). The way our brains respond to repeated groups of sounds depends not only on the sounds themselves but the rate of repetition. Short loops (up to about three seconds) are roughly equivalent to beats or bars in music, for example a repeated group of four or five notes on a piano. Medium lengths, up to around twenty seconds, are like complete small-scale musical statements. Long loops could be defined as those which contain too much material to memorize as a whole until repeated several times, and very long loops (a minute or more) may not be heard as loops at

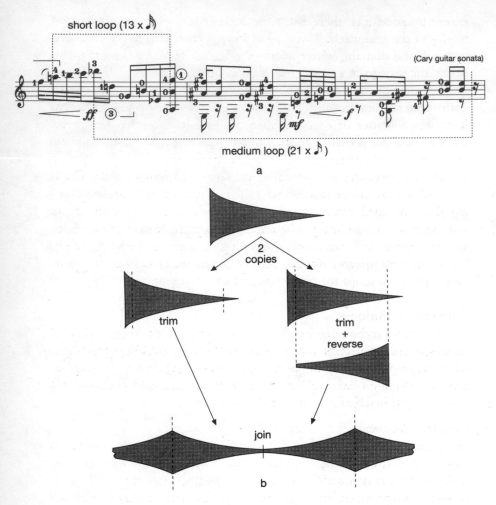

Fig. 201

all, particularly if mixed with other, changing sounds.

Random cutting of any disparate group of sounds into short or medium loops cannot fail to produce a rhythmic sequence, sometimes metrically complex. Fig. 201a shows a line of guitar music with a short loop of thirteen demisemiquavers and a medium one of twenty-one semiquavers selected from many possible alternatives. The opposite of the 'busy' loop is shown in fig. 201b, where two copies of a single piano chord are cut and reversed on to themselves, resulting in a gently undulating continuous sound. Looping single sounds, even if apparently unvarying, almost always produces a click or thump at the join, because except by good luck there will be a discontinuity – at the millisecond level – of the tone itself. This type of loop is more effectively produced in the digital domain, where micro-editing (not feasible with tape) can match the waveform exactly (see again **samplers**).

To run loops, any auto-stop mechanism must be disconnected, and both spool motors disabled, either electrically or by taping them down. It is then a matter of ensuring adequate back tension for good head contact (now not provided by the supply spool motor), and small spools taped to the deck, arrangements of jars weighted with sand, microphone stands as loop guides etc. are called into play depending on the length involved. Loops can be labelled with their contents and an arrow showing their intended direction, and sometimes also a start mark if the starting place is significant. The photograph in the Introduction of my studio in the early 1970s shows loops filed on hooks in the background. See again **musique concrète** for further comment, including the use of very high speed loops for tone generation.

Extended techniques

All the above techniques can be used in combination of course, and supplemented by electronic treatments, sequencers, **remote controls** etc. where appropriate. They can be further extended in various ways, sometimes involving special machines. Some of these extended techniques and non-standard machines are discussed below.

Compound loops

Sometimes the endless repetitiveness of a loop is what the composer seeks, but in any case there are few ways of varying this condition with a single loop. It is possible to change its speed gradually or to alter its contents progressively by injecting 'spots' of new material (entering record mode for very short periods). But with two or more loops, or loops combined with continuous material, the possibilities are much greater.

Fig. 202a shows a 'nearly the same' set-up, with three loops cut to slightly different lengths so that their mutual positions shift with each pass, generating a changing metrical pattern. The sketch shows the same material on all three, but it could well be different. Fig. 202b shows a continuous track montaged with four loops of different lengths, faded in and out during the course of the recording, and a **ring modulator** connected to produce an output only when loops one and three are active together (to illustrate combining electronic with manual treatments).

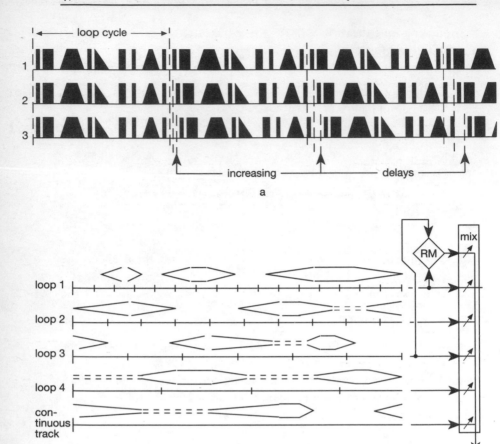

Fig. 202

Möbius loops

(See **Möbius loop** and fig. 135.) With a half-twist, one cannot avoid placing joining tape on the oxide surface. If the tape contains two signals recorded twin-track, the tracks will be flipped at every pass, and the oxide and base sides will play alternately. Thin tape should be used so that the inevitable high frequency and amplitude losses when the base side is being played are minimized, and the heads etc. should be cleaned afterwards. This is an example of numerous special techniques which are only used occasionally, but are exactly right on those occasions.

Shared capstans

Provided a row of decks has been lined up to the same height, a given capstan can be made to draw tape over the heads of any machine to its left, producing long delays (canons, for example). For maximum versatility, the rightmost machine should have fully variable speed.

Modified decks

There can hardly be too many tape machines in a tape studio, and one at least should be a battery powered portable for location and environmental recording (today this could be a **digital audio tape** machine, from which chosen sounds can be transferred to quarter-inch analogue tape for studio treatment). Only a few studio machines need to record, however, and play-only decks can be modified freely since erase and record heads can be removed. A useful deck for shorter delays than are possible with the shared capstan method is one with three or four closely spaced playback heads, with separate switching so that any track(s) on any head(s) can be selected. For increased flexibility heads can be fitted in slots to allow their positions to be changed, and for longer delays the scheme shown in fig. 181 can be extended, with several adjustable tape guides. For **feedback** effects, of course, a record head is necessary (see **reverberation**).

Special decks

Of the many decks constructed over the years, one noteworthy device was the German-designed Zeitdehner (time-stretcher), known also as the Tempophon or Springer machine. In pre-digital days this was the only method of changing pitch without changing speed and vice versa, and it was not a complete unit but an add-on to a main tape transport. The

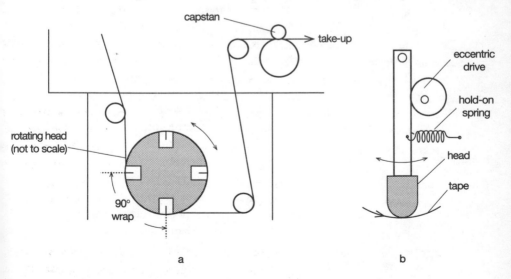

Fig. 203

tape is led off the main deck and guided to give a precise 90° wrap round a rotating head with four gaps (in effect four heads treated electrically as one), as shown in fig. 203a. A constant tape speed is maintained by the capstan, but the rotating head turns in either direction to vary the tape-to-head speed. Thus if the tape speed is 15 in/sec (ips) and the head is rotated so that its surface moves at 5 ips against the flow of the tape, the effective tape-to-head speed is 20 ips and the signal frequency goes up by ⅓. This can only be done by 'cheating', of course – as one gap leaves the tape the next one enters at a different place, so slowing down is done by playing material twice and speeding up by omitting some. The effect is very poor on some signals, and always somewhat 'bumpy', but the device was widely used in the 1960s and 1970s, both for music and for speech compression/extension, though it has now been made obsolete by digital **pitch changers**. A simpler idea using the same principle is the oscillating head (fig. 203b), which I (and possibly others) used to **frequency modulate** a signal. It is interesting to note that both these techniques can produce reverse playback from a forward moving tape.

There are no firm rules for tape (or any other) composition, and the techniques discussed are merely a sample of many processes that can be used between the initial ideas and the finished music. Some tape pieces are simply recorded directly from a synthesizer, with no intermediate processing at all. Others go through elaborate studio treatments, and others again, with live performance components, are partly processed in **real time**. Even if the advance of digital techniques eventually ousts tape manipulation as a composing process (which has not happened yet), the means of performing such pieces should still be available. Skills like tape editing have produced their own virtuosi, and have much in common with performance. As noted in other entries, musical history is full of instruments (such as harpsichords and tracker **organs**) that are rejected as obsolete, only to stage a comeback later when their special qualities are missed and needed.

Tape counter   See **tape recorder design**

Tape echo   See **echo** and **reverberation**

Tape guide   See **tape recorder design**

Tapeless studio   The trade name of a New England Digital Corporation* 'direct-to-disk' recording system using massive disk storage combined with optical (**WORM**) disks. Up to eight **giga**-bytes can be stored. There are now a number of such direct-to-disk facilities in main centres around the world, and more are certain to appear as mass storage becomes cheaper and optical recording methods are refined. The logical next step will be to eliminate mechanically driven disks and carry out all processing in solid state or optical memory without any moving parts at all.

Tape music   See **tape composition techniques**

Tape recorder design   A tape machine has two main parts, the 'deck' or mechanical transport, which is the subject of this entry, and the electronic/magnetic systems, for which see **sound recording techniques**. Video recording is not covered in this book (but see **helical scan** and **video cassette PCM**). For audio cassette formats see **cassette recorders** and **digital audio tape**.

Most professional recording is still done on analogue open reel machines, which vary greatly in size and price. They may have one to twenty-four tracks, and may use tape widths varying from ¼ in (6.35 mm) to 2 in (50.8 mm). However, the basic tape handling problems are common to all, and many are shared by stationary head digital, a format which deliberately borrows some features from analogue practice (see **sound recording techniques**).

A tape transport must be able to perform two very different functions. In play mode the thin, sprocketless and fairly slippery ribbon of tape must be held at a constant speed and tension, behaving as nearly as possible like a solid bar as it crosses the heads. In fast wind mode the same fragile medium must be shifted as quickly as possible and without danger of being damaged.

In cheaper decks various compromises are used to reduce the problems, including the obvious one of using slow winding speeds. But open reel tape has almost disappeared as a domestic medium, and the following mainly concerns studio machines, where price is less a consideration than performance and reliability.

Open-loop transports
Fig. 204 shows the main parts of an 'open-loop' tape transport, which

*New England Digital Corporation, Box 546, 49 N. Main St., White River Junction, Vermont 05001, USA. Manufacturers of the Synclavier II and other products.

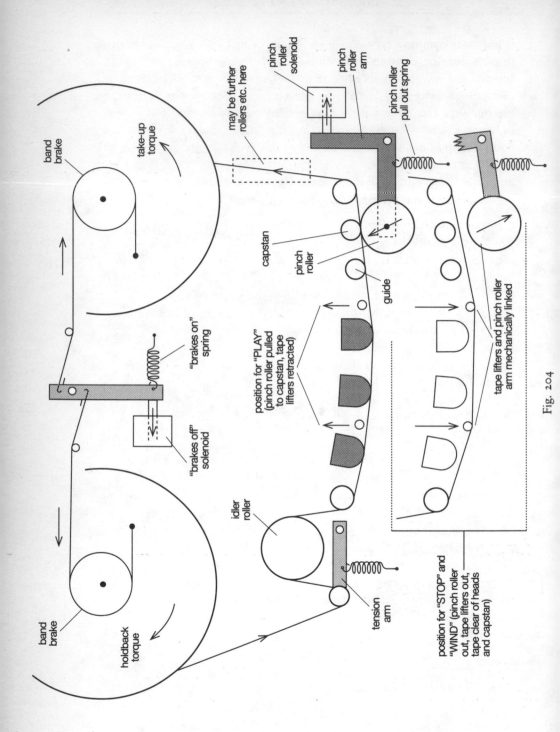

band
brake

take-up
torque

may be further
rollers etc. here

pinch
roller
solenoid

pinch
roller
arm

pinch roller
pull out spring

capstan

pinch
roller

guide

"brakes on"
spring

"brakes off"
solenoid

position for "PLAY"
(pinch roller pulled
to capstan, tape
lifters retracted)

tape lifters and pinch roller
arm mechanically linked

band
brake

holdback
torque

idler
roller

tension
arm

position for "STOP" and
"WIND" (pinch roller
out, tape lifters out,
tape clear of heads
and capstan)

Fig. 204

is the most common type. Some earlier decks had only one motor, used directly for the capstan and through slipping clutches to control the spools, but except in cassette machines three motors (one for each reel plus the capstan) is the norm. Details of tape guides, tensioning mechanisms etc. vary with different designs, and the diagram shows only the essential components for running and winding the tape. For additional features see below. Note that the deck is designed so that the 'power off' state is safe, i.e. with the brakes on, and the pinch roller and tape lifters out. It is fundamental to good design that the tape is not damaged if the power fails.

Capstan and pinch roller

The tape is gripped very firmly between these two components, and the capstan with its motor, being the transport's prime mover, is the most important item in the deck. Not only must the tape not slip, but its linear motion must conform precisely to one of the standard speeds (see **tape track configurations**) or tape recorded on one machine could not be played on another. Earlier and domestic grade recorders mostly use(d) mains frequency-dependent synchronous motors driving a heavy flywheel through an idler or belt (fig. 205a). Given a clean, well-regulated mains supply this works well, especially if the capstan is allowed to reach thermal stability by running continuously and not just when playing tape. But the long term accuracy of mains synchronous capstans is only moderate, and most machines now use one of a variety of self-monitoring **servo** systems, with asynchronous motors whose speed can be controlled by voltage changes.

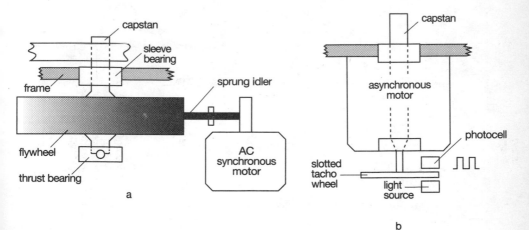

Fig. 205

Fig. 205b shows a **DC** motor whose shaft is extended to become the capstan. If speed control is accurate, and the motor powerful enough, a flywheel is not necessary. Mounted on the same shaft, a slotted **tachometer** wheel generates an AC whose frequency is directly dependent on motor speed (the system shown is optical but they are often electromagnetic). A nominal drive voltage is applied at a value which, under ideal conditions, would give correct speed. In a 'phase-locked loop' the tacho output is compared with a quartz-generated (see **oscillators**) reference frequency (usually 9.6 kHz) by a phase **comparator**, and any **lead** or **lag** converted into a + or − correction to the drive voltage, thus locking the capstan speed to the crystal reference. If a variable oscillator is substituted for the crystal, the capstan speed can be made fully adjustable. This is essential in **tape composition** work (for varying the speed of synchronous capstan drives, see speed control in **oscillators**). The capstan itself must be finished with the greatest possible precision, and its surface may be roughened (e.g. by sandblasting) to grip the tape better. Another advantage of DC capstan (and reel) motors is that they do not induce **hum** into the tape heads, a common problem with AC mains motors.

The pinch roller is held off the capstan by a spring when not in use, and linked with the tape lifter, so that in STOP or FAST WIND the tape is clear of heads, capstan and roller. This also ensures that the roller is never pressed against a stationary capstan, which can form 'flats' on its compliant (rubber or synthetic) surface and seriously affect performance (see flutter and wow below). Opinions vary about the best design for rollers – narrow or wide, ribbed or plain – but most are somewhat wider than the tape, allowing the tape's thickness to squash in the central part of the roller for maximum grip. When the play mode is entered, the powerful pinch roller **solenoid** locks the roller and tape onto the capstan with considerable force (typically one to two kilograms for quarter-inch tape, more for wider gauges). At the same time the tape lifter is withdrawn and the reel brakes released. Because of the high roller pressure the bearings of both capstan and pinch roller mountings must be designed to withstand heavy side thrust. In applications involving spot cueing (such as tape inserts in broadcasting) a quick start is essential, and a good machine should reach speed and tape stability in less than half a second (the slower the tape speed, the faster everything settles). In poor tape transports the capstan feeds out tape before the take-up spool has begun to roll properly, causing a loop which is then snatched up, and speed may be unstable for several seconds. A way to overcome this is to apply a burst of extra power to the take-up spool on starting.

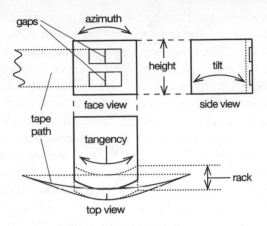

Fig. 206

Head block geometry, tape tension etc.

The three heads must be mutually angled so that under light tension the tape makes ideal contact with each active face. This can only work efficiently if the tape guides, heads and capstan are all perfectly aligned, and tension maintained within certain tolerances.

Five head adjustments are shown in fig. 206, and though all are critical most only need occasional checking: the *height* of all heads and associated guides must be set so that tracks line up perfectly with head gaps; if the *tilt* is incorrect the tape will tend to ride up or down; *tangency* is set so that the tape enters and leaves the back-to-front plane of the gap at precisely the same angle, and with the *rack* determines the wrap or 'insertion', i.e. the displacement tape-to-head pressure that ensures good head contact. In ordinary use, the *azimuth* is the most critical – if either the record or play gap is not precisely at right angles to the tape path there will be loss of treble on playback. Play head azimuth error affects only one machine, but record head misalignment makes any tape recorded on that machine useless for playback on any other. To reduce the necessity for so many precise adjustments, cheaper machines (and nearly all cassette decks) use sprung 'pressure pads' to push the tape against the heads (in fact a pressure pad is built into every cassette shell), but in high quality machines good head contact is maintained entirely by careful design of the tape path, and the tension supplied by the spool motors.

The path of the tape from one spool to the other is designed to stabilize the tape mechanically. Frequent changes of direction at guides and rollers are deliberate, though too many can cause drag and 'scrape flutter'. (This can be compared to the action of a violin bow, and occurs to some extent at the heads in any case.) The job of the spool motors is to keep just enough tension on the tape to control it firmly, particularly over the heads, but not so much that the constant speed traction of the capstan assembly is disturbed. Holdback tension (from the supply reel) was applied in some earlier machines by a slipping clutch or light braking, but using reverse torque is much more reliable. In this method the supply reel is arranged so that it is trying, but fairly weakly, to rotate in the opposite direction to the flow of the tape. It thus applies controlled back tension, and a spring-loaded tension arm mounted in the supply path helps to absorb irregularities due to poorly wound tape, reel eccentricity etc. Similar but opposite take-up torque (with the motor moving in the same direction but slower than it wants to) is used to gather up the tape delivered by the capstan.

Until recently the choice of torque values was a compromise, because the actual tensile forces on the tape change with the changing diameter of the tape packs on each spool. Capstan assemblies had to be designed to cope with at least a doubling of back tension during the run of a tape, and with take-up tensions unduly high at the beginning and weak at the end of a reel. The level of compromise is reduced by fitting a 'reel switch' to adjust tension for 'ciné' and **NAB** (see **spool**) sizes, but this is a fairly blunt instrument. The arrival of logic circuitry has changed all this, and modern machines use tension sensors (which can be incorporated into tension arms) combined with motion sensors (tachometers on the reel motors) to get a complete picture of the tape's behaviour, process it continuously and apply running torque corrections. This in turn allows more moderate pinch roller pressure because high back tensions need not be catered for, resulting in gentler tape handling and less wear. An idler roller between the supply tension arm and the head block is not always fitted (or may be in a different place), but as well as smoothing tape motion as it enters the active area, it is driven by the tape and is therefore an accurate motion and position sensor, capable of providing a tachometer output or driving a real-time tape counter (see below).

Fast wind modes

In professional studios high speed winding is essential, but the safety of valuable recordings is equally so. If tape is being wound off the spool completely, the basic method of releasing brakes and applying full power to the appropriate motor is satisfactory – the inertia of the system prevents over-rapid acceleration, and controlled deceleration is not necessary. Stopping a tape in the middle, however, does need a controlled slowdown, and with a simple system the result of pressing STOP (or a power failure) at full speed depends on how well the brakes are adjusted. It can be disastrous. Careful operators go into the opposite wind mode to slow the tape electrically before braking, and with experience it is possible to cue tape exactly by manipulating the two wind buttons.

As with control of the play mode, however, motion sensing and logic have taken over this role also, controlling acceleration, applying electrical braking to slow the tape smoothly and under correct tension, and putting on mechanical brakes only when the reels have actually stopped (like a parking brake). This type of control is almost essential when winding wide format, multi-track tapes – a spinning fourteen-inch metal spool loaded with two-inch tape is a formidable weapon. With logic control PLAY can be pressed during a wind mode; the machine reads the command, stops the tape smoothly and goes immediately into the play mode. If the deck has tape position sensing, auto-locate can be an added feature, for example, 'Go back to 2 min 43 sec and replay from there' might be executed by pressing two buttons together: MEMORY 1 and PLAY (see also **time codes** and **remote controls**).

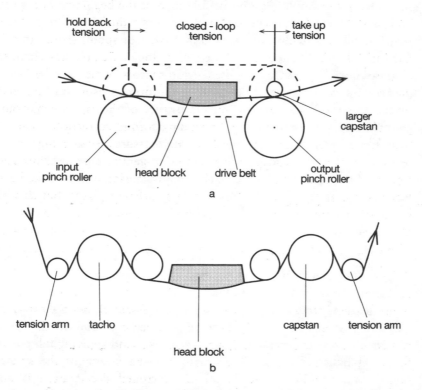

Fig. 207

Closed-loop transports

Before logic circuitry arrived, various ways of controlling tension in the active part of the tape path were tried. One method is the closed loop, which controls tape tension in the head block region by isolating this part from the less critical supply and take-up portions.

Fig. 207a shows two capstans linked by a belt and driven at the same speed by one motor. The diameter of the output capstan is made slightly larger than that of the input one, and the effect of this is to tension the tape precisely and constantly over the head block, utilizing the tape's natural elasticity by stretching it slightly. The ingenious 'Isoloop' transport made by 3M for many years used two pinch rollers on a single grooved capstan, arranged so that the tape made two passes, one at the lower (smaller diameter) groove level (input) and one at the upper groove level (output), with the same effect on tension as two separate capstans. The closed loop is still featured on some decks, and in a few of the best quality **cassette recorders**, but the trend today is towards eliminating pinch rollers rather than doubling their number.

Zero-loop transports

It was realized some years ago that if the capstan were made with a large diameter and the tensioned tape well wrapped round it, enough grip might be obtained to dispense with the pinch roller altogether. Unfortunately the earlier designs had problems with different reel sizes and other tension-affecting variables, and under adverse conditions even higher tensions than those used in open-loop transports were needed to ensure adequate traction. With logic control, however, the whole tape path can be held at the same ideal tension under all conditions, and the method becomes practical and elegant. Fig. 207b is a sketch of the deck layout of the pinch-rollerless Otari MTR-90 series, which also has auto-sensing of reel size.*

Other features

Editing facilities   For cut editing procedures see **tape composition techniques**. Only machines with visibly sited heads are convenient for reading and marking tape, and some otherwise excellent decks are poor in this respect. Some decks have cutting blocks with built-in guillotines or scissors, and most have an 'edit mode' in which the tape lifters (but not the pinch roller) are set into the play position, allowing tape to be manually pulled across the heads. Another useful facility is 'tape dump',

*Otari Electric Co. Ltd, 4–29–18 Minami-Ogikubo, Suginami-ku, Tokyo 167, Japan.

which runs tape normally but disables the take-up motor, enabling tape to be run on to the floor or into a bin. This is also useful for discarding unwanted parts of a tape on which material is otherwise in the correct order.

Flutter and wow These are the commonest transport problems. 'Flutter' covers a range of fairly rapid vibratory effects which blur and roughen recordings. 'Scrape flutter' was mentioned above, and there are other types, caused by instability and resonance in unsupported lengths of tape, dirty or worn guides, rattling roller or capstan bearings, etc. 'Wow' is lower frequency modulation caused typically by an unevenly worn or faulty pinch roller or large diameter capstan. Test kits for recorders include wow and flutter meters, which measure the frequencies of these effects and their percentage deviations from true speed.

Head shielding Play (and to a lesser extent record) heads are very sensitive to stray fields from **transformers,** motors, fluorescent lights etc. The whole head block can be shielded, but usually each head is fitted into a can of 'mu-metal', a highly permeable (see **magnet**) alloy of nickel, iron and copper, and in some cases chromium and molybdenum as well. The front edges of the shield overhang the head face so that the tape runs in a deep channel, and there may be an additional hinged or sliding front cover activated manually or by the play button. Erase heads do not need shielding.

Non-standard decks Many experimental transports have come and gone over the years, and some special modifications are noted in **tape composition techniques.** By the late 1960s, before new electronic developments started to overshadow tape manipulation as a composition method, several ingenious but short-lived tape transports appeared. For historically interested readers, a whole issue of *Electronic Music Review* (for April 1968) was devoted to a symposium on tape recording. Among other innovations, there is a description of the 'MRS' transport (by Magnetic Recording Systems) which had a voltage controlled capstan motor giving a speed range of 32:1 (from 60 to 1⅞ ips). Another was the Newell Tape Transport (by C. W. Newell), in which unsupported tape is eliminated: tape is led round a large drum to each side of which the supply and take-up tape packs are pressed (Weidenaar, 1968).

Portable machines Miniature battery-operated recorders must necessarily lack some of the space and power consuming features of studio decks, but this need not compromise recording quality. The Nagra is the industry standard in this area, producing tapes of the highest quality in exacting applications like location film work.* The all-important capstan is tacho-servo controlled along the lines already described, and the user is warned of imminent battery failure in good time. To enable the transport to be used in any position, the clamped spools are limited to small sizes, and the tape path highly controlled by very precise components. To conserve the battery, fast wind in the studio sense is not attempted – in fact the usual procedure in the field is to run tapes off forwards and rewind them later in the studio.

Pause   This is an intermediate mode, not always fitted, which has different interpretations. In one type the first press of the button removes the pinch roller a very short distance from the capstan, halting the tape but otherwise leaving the transport in play mode, which is fully restored on the second press. Another type requires the button to be held down as long as the mode is engaged.

Tape counters   The simplest way of logging tape movement is to drive a zero-resettable decade counter from a spooling motor. The reading from such a counter is arbitrary because being tied to the varying motor speed it cannot be related to time or absolute tape footage, but it is useful for noting cues within a spool. A refinement is a 'memory' mode that triggers STOP when o is reached. **Real-time** counters need a free idler driven by the tape, a count of whose revolutions is directly proportional to the length of tape passing. Real time is computed from this count and the tape speed, and the clock reading is automatically adjusted when the speed is changed. Auto-locate (mentioned in Fast wind modes above), memory and other features may be included as well.

Tape run-out switches   These are devices to stop the transport at the end of a tape or in the event of a break (such as a faulty join parting). The two main types are mechanical, such as a micro-switch in a tension arm (which also ensures that incorrectly laced tape will not run), or **photo-electric** – a lamp or infra-red source and a photocell separated by the tape. Both work well, and the optical type is also useful in, for example, **live performance electronic music** or stage work, because inserts of transparent leader can be made to stop tape at the end of cues. When running loops (see **tape composition techniques**) auto-stop devices must be defeated.

Tape stocks   New types of tape are in development all the time, and

*Kudelski S.A., 1033 Cheseaux, Switzerland. Manufacturers of Nagra tape recorder and other products.

the need to set bias and equalization for each type is discussed in **sound recording techniques**. It is the physical rather than magnetic properties of tape that affect transport mechanisms, and tension settings may need changing for different types (it is not enough to consider only currently available tapes, a machine must be able to play old tapes). Apart from being made in three thicknesses (standard, long and double play – 1.5, 1 and .5 **thou**) which may behave differently at the capstan, some are smooth on the base side with a relatively rough oxide surface, others (most professional mastering tapes) have a roughened base side (for good traction) and a polished live surface (for smooth performance on the heads). There are also specialized tape stocks, for example lubricated tape for loop cassette use.

Though digital tape recording is now well established and advancing fast, and other magnetic and optical media are on the increase as well, the analogue tape machine will probably remain the studio workhorse for a long time. Apart from being a proven and reliable tool, there is a vast world investment in analogue equipment and in tape already recorded. Moreover most of the refinements added over the years to analogue tape transports are also applicable to fixed head digital machines.

Runstein and Huber (1989) has a good section on tape transports. See also Ballou (1987) chapter 24, Nisbett (1970) and Wells (1981). Some very good machines are made in small quantities by local engineering workshops, and a complete list would be impossible, but some industry leaders in professional recording are: 1. (top end): Ampex, MCI (Sony), Nagra, Otari (top models), Scully, Studer and Telefunken. 2. (less expensive, excellent value): Fostex, Otari (budget range), Revox (made by Studer), Tascam and Technics.

Tape speed   See **tape track configurations**

Tape track configurations   In spite of numerous developments over the years, some aspects of tape recording have not changed. Tape widths have been standardized in inches and sub-multiples of inches since the beginning of recording on coated plastic tape, and there has been no good reason to change this system. Apart from the large investment in producing the current sizes, there is the great advantage of being able to play tapes of any date on modern equipment. However, cassette tape does not conform to the division rule since it is 3.81 mm wide (⅛th inch would be 3.175 mm).

Tape speeds have tended to get slower as tape and electronics improved, but they have continued to be based on submultiples of sixty inches per second (ips), a standard set when early recorders achieved reasonable quality by using high speeds. It was probably not envisaged then that speeds such as 1⅞ths ips (i.e. 60/32) would be usable, or a base of sixty-four might have been chosen for its tidier arithmetic!

Because the standards for both width and speed are expressed in inches the metric conversions are somewhat unwieldy, and to save giving equivalents repeatedly, here is a conversion table for the main widths and speeds now current:

Tape widths		Tape speeds	
in	mm	ips	cm/s
2	50.8	60	152.4 (now rare)
1	25.4	30	76.2
½	12.7	15	38.1
¼	6.35	7½	19.05
(¹⁵/₁₀₀)	3.81 (cassette)	3¾	9.525
		1⅞	4.7625
		¹⁵/₁₆	2.38125

The lowest speed of ¹⁵/₁₆ ips is mainly used for logging transmissions at radio stations (a legal requirement). A large reel of tape gives many hours of recording at adequate quality for this purpose. Domestic equipment typically runs at 3¾ ips, but may offer a choice. Professional music recording is done at a speed of 15 ips, but 7½ ips is often used, and is standard for speech. On many quarter-inch and most large format machines 30 ips is also provided, giving a significantly quieter performance at the expense of rapid tape usage (see **noise reduction**).

This degree of uniformity does not apply to the division of the tape's width into tracks, however, and machines using all sorts of formats have been made. This is satisfactory if one is always recording and playing back on the same machine, but for general use a set of agreed configurations is obviously desirable. The following is a summary of common analogue track formats (for digital tapes see **digital audio tape, sound recording techniques** and **video cassette PCM**).

Cassette tape
Fig. 208a and b show the normal cassette track layouts. For **mono/stereo** compatibility, the placing of the left and right tracks next to each other on one side ensures that mono heads play the sum of both tracks, and that a mono tape will play from both speakers in a stereo system. Speed 1⅞ ips only.

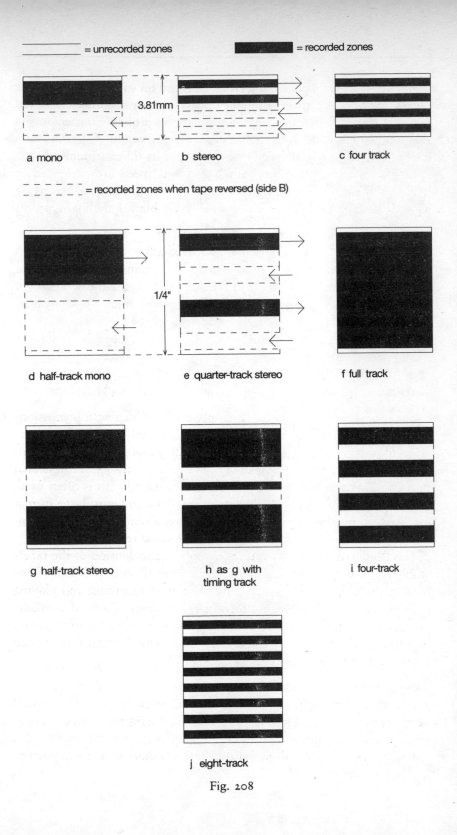

= unrecorded zones   = recorded zones

a mono   b stereo   c four track

3.81mm

= recorded zones when tape reversed (side B)

d half-track mono   e quarter-track stereo   f full track

1/4"

g half-track stereo   h as g with timing track   i four-track

j eight-track

Fig. 208

Fig. 208c shows a non-standard format found in four-track 'mini-studios' (see **cassette recorders**). Six- and eight-track cassette recorders are now available and many of these multi-track machines run at 3¾ ips.

Quarter-inch tape

This is by far the most widely used tape on open reel machines. The 1950s and 1960s were the heyday of the home quarter-inch tape recorder – there were about 120 low cost models on the British market in 1959 (Briggs (1960)). But with the rise of cassettes, open reel recording is now largely confined to professional use. Machines using the two-way mono and stereo formats shown in figs. 208d and e are still made, however, and some studio recorders are also fitted with an extra head for playing quarter-track tapes. Full-track, fig. 208f, is used in mono media (most films, TV and AM radio), and half-track stereo (or twin-track), fig. 208g, is the expected format for professional machines. These usually have a similar twin-track erase head but may (if both tracks are always recorded together) have full-track erase ensuring complete erasure of all previous material (erase heads in any case cover a wider track than record and play heads). For comments on fig. 208h see **time codes**.

Tracks are separated by unrecorded 'guard bands', and the narrower these are the more **crosstalk** will occur. Multi-tracking involves a trade-off between adequate guard bands and **signal-to-noise ratio** (the narrower the tracks the worse the noise problem). Early four-track recording was done on one-inch tape, and half-inch is still a favoured gauge, but with modern tapes and heads quarter-inch four-track, fig. 208i, is now a fully professional format. The sketches are only approximately to scale, but note that four-track (fig. 208i) tapes will not play successfully (as 2+2) on stereo heads (fig. 208g) because there is almost no pick-up from the two centre tracks.

Eight-track quarter-inch tape, fig. 208j, involves very narrow tracks, but it has been successfully implemented by Fostex* and Tascam.† Using built-in **noise reduction**, these compact machines are serious rivals to the more expensive large gauges.

Because all quarter-inch tape looks the same, it is very important to label it with the speed and configuration used. At one time there was an attempt to establish a **leader** colour code for this, but general agreement was never reached.

*Fostex Corporation, 3–2–35 Musashino, Akishima, Tokyo 196, Japan.
†TEAC Corporation, Musashino Center Bldg, 1–19–18 Nakacho, Musashino-shi, Tokyo 180, Japan.

Wider tapes

With wider tracks and more comfortable guard bands the large tapes still offer better quality for a given number of tracks, but costs rise sharply, not only of the tape itself but of the transports. Half-inch transports are only a little heavier than quarter-inch (in fact some machines have dual-gauge decks), but for the one-inch and two-inch sizes every component of the deck is much more massively built, and the large multi-tracks are major investments in precision engineering. Half-inch tape is sometimes used for stereo, but more commonly for four or eight tracks, and by Fostex and Tascam for sixteen tracks (a larger version of the eight-track quarter-inch machine). One-inch tape for four tracks may still be found on surviving older machines, but is standard for eight and increasingly used for sixteen and even twenty-four tracks. Other sixteen-track and most twenty-four-track machines at present use two-inch tape.

Tape width   See **tape track configurations**

Temperament   The compromise tuning of instruments, particularly of fixed-pitch, pre-tuned ones like the organ and piano, to produce the maximum concordance from the available intervals. It is noted in **harmonic series** that the most concordant intervals result from **frequency ratios** of small integers – see fig. 99, a natural series in which consonance, for most ears, reduces as numbers get higher. These intervals are called 'just', and over the years many attempts have been made to construct musically useful scales which employ only the just intervals. Nearly all share certain features: 1. They repeat at the octave. 2. They contain intervals of at least two sizes. 3. They have enough notes for melodic variety, but not so many that intervals are hard to pitch. 4. They are arranged so that combinations of intervals yield as many concords as possible. Some cultures have favoured the pentatonic ('black note') scale with no semitones, but from ancient times Western music has used variants of the tone/semitone pattern familiar as the keyboard 'white notes'. The 'mode' can be changed by starting on different notes, but the pattern of adjacent intervals remains. The 'Pythagorean scale' is formed by successively folding back 'just' fifths and fourths into one octave and the 'Just scale' uses more of the just intervals, including both the whole tones shown in fig. 99 and the just semitone (16:15), which occurs at the fourth octave in the natural series. Details of the arithmetic can be found in the larger studies mentioned below, but the important point is that however the intervals are deployed there are always some 'unjust' ratios. Temperament is the modification of some pitches to give an acceptable result, and arguments about it have raged for centuries and still continue. The literature is voluminous, and we can only note a few main points here. Mark Lindley's excellent survey in Sadie (1984) includes a large bibliography, and Lloyd and Boyle (1978), Taylor (1965), Wood (1962), Olson (1967), Roederer (1979) and Ellis (Appendix xx to Helmholtz, 1954), all contain analyses of different temperaments.

Serious tuning problems only occur in some kinds of music. Voices and many instruments can make running adjustments to intonation. **Timbres rich in inharmonic partials** are less sensitive to pitch errors than simple ones, and short, rapid notes pass so quickly that small mistunings are hardly noticed. Worst are **polyphonic** instruments whose tuning the player cannot control in performance, like harps, pianos and organs. Much early work in temperament was directed to making organs sound 'purer'.

Fig. 209a shows a succession of twelve perfect fifths including every semitone. Taking the lowest note shown (27.5 Hz, bottom A on a piano) and multiplying it by 1.5 (3:2) twelve times, we reach another A (or G$\times$) at 3568.024295 Hz. But seven octaves from 27.5 (by repeated doubling) gives 3520, so the fifths come out sharper than the octaves by a ratio of 1.013643266:1. This 'Pythagorean comma' may seem small but it is 23.5 **cents** or nearly an eighth of a tone – far from trivial. Fig. 209b shows the comma of Didymus (or 'syntonic' comma) which is the amount by which a succession of four fifths exceed two octaves plus a major third (5:4), and is a somewhat smaller difference at 1.0125:1 or 21.506 cents.

Difficulties arose when music became more harmonically adventurous, and when modes were transposed to different pitches. The Pythagorean scale, for example, begins with two major tones (9:8), which add up to a very sharp major third, not serious in a melody but far too large in a harmonic context. In the just scale both sizes of tone (9:8 and 10:9) are used (the difference is a syntonic comma), so the third is just (5:4). But if we transpose the scale one tone up the new first degree will be too small. 'Mean-tone' temperaments, once widely used, keep the major third just by compromising the more dissonant (and therefore less critical) tones, making them both the average (or 'mean') of 9:8 and 10:9. This tuning gives very acceptable concords but in a few keys only, suiting music that is modal or does not move far from 'home' – in fact most early music. The penalty for good chords in some keys was unusable 'wolf' tones in others, and instruments were tuned to suit the music in hand.

When composers began to **modulate** freely to all keys, the only logical course was to divide the octave into twelve identical intervals, and this 'equal temperament' gradually replaced the others. Equal temperament

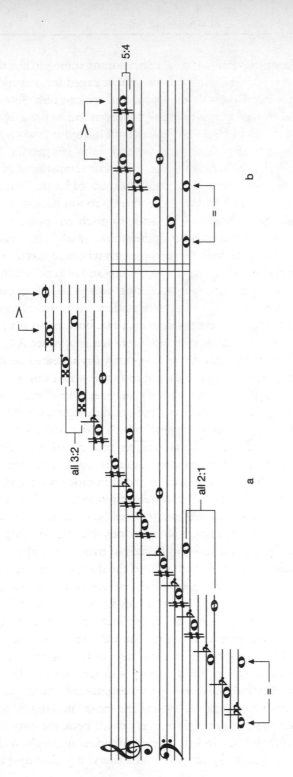

Fig. 209

involves eliminating the Pythagorean comma by flattening all the fifths by a twelfth of a comma (thus enlarging the fourths to match). The semitone is $^{12}\sqrt{2}$ (a ratio of 1.059463094) which is ungainly enough, but to most ears the worst feature of the system is the bad thirds (major too large, minor too small). Convenience outweighed shortcomings, however; this became the standard tuning for Western music, and the cent was designed for it (100 cents per tempered semitone). Tempered frequencies are currently based on middle A = 440 Hz, giving a middle C of 261.6 Hz (see A).

In practice temperament is only roughly equal, and some distortion is deliberate, for example pianos are usually tuned with 'stretched' octaves to heighten brilliance. Special keyboards with extra keys to reduce the errors have been tried from early times (see **keyboard design**), but departures from the familiar pattern are strongly resisted by performers. The way our harmonic systems have developed demands total mobility of key, and twelve-note **serial** music further entrenched equal temperament. In general we make the best of the compromise, especially with keyboards, and break into just intonation whenever we see a chance, for example in a cappella choral music, string quartets, etc.

Today, for the first time in music's long history, computers allow us to set up any tuning system instantly, and get an immediate aural comparison between different temperaments. This ability has also sparked a new interest in microtonal composition, which has always been inhibited by the difficulty (often impossibility) of sounding small intervals precisely on existing instruments, and the delay and expense of making microtonal keyboards. There have been some notable enthusiasts such as Harry Partch who made many special microtonal instruments (Partch, 1974), but nowadays (at least in synthesized music) any system, traditional or not, is readily accessible. (For example in my piece *Strands* for two pianos and four synthesized tracks, the octave is divided into seventy-eight parts.) In temperament, equal divisions can in fact provide what is needed if there are enough of them. The minimum effective extension of twelve is nineteen, thirty-one is better still and fifty-three allows all the just intervals to be used. Nobody can make a fifty-three notes per octave keyboard that is easy to play, but a computer can be programmed to select the optimum tuning for each note of the normal twelve in context. Several ingenious approaches have been made, see for example Wendy Carlos's 'Tuning: at the crossroads' in *Computer Music Journal* (Carlos, 1987), a whole issue devoted to microtonality and new attitudes to tuning problems. See also **hexachord** and **mnemonics**.

Tempophon See **tape composition techniques** and fig. 203

Test recordings Recordings (on discs, vinyl and compact, or tapes) which are specially made to test equipment. They have carefully calibrated levels of **tone, pink noise** etc. and to preserve their accuracy must be used with great care, for example test tapes should never be fast wound or run over magnetized heads (see **sound recording techniques**).

THD Total Harmonic Distortion. See **harmonic distortion**

Theremin An early non-keyboard monophonic electronic instrument (first model 1920) made by the Russian inventor Lev Termen (whose name was gallicized to Leon Thérémin). See **analogue synthesis techniques** 1. The term is now often applied to unusual input **transducers** rather than complete instruments. See also **Ondes Martenot, Trautonium**, Appleton (1975), Russcol (1972) and Manning (1987).

Thermal noise Noise that originates from the random vibrations of molecules and electrons in electrical conductors. It is one of the main noise sources in any circuit and increases with temperature. When it occurs in, for example, the windings of a tape replay head, the noise is inseparable from the signal and is amplified with it.

Thermionic See **amplifiers**

Thou (also 'mil') One thousandth of an inch or 25.4 **microns**.

Three-phase An **AC** supply system which uses three supply lines such that the currents in each are exactly 120° out of **phase**. This produces an efficient four-wire (three live and a common return or neutral) power distribution system which is used, for example, in **selsyn** motors.

Threshold The level at which a given effect begins to operate; see, for example, **compressor**.

Timbre A French word whose commonest meaning in that language is 'stamp'. Its musical connotation is near to 'stamp' in the sense of 'individual imprint', but its usage is imprecise, conveying a personal impression of a sound's character. It is often translated as 'tone colour' or 'quality', but these terms are also vague and imprecise. Helmholtz (1862) regarded **spectrum** and amplitude **envelope** as the factors which chiefly determined a sound's character. The narrowest definitions refer to spectrum only, and acoustics textbooks commonly give spectral plots of the relative energy in the various **partials** for different instruments. But it is easy to show that more is needed: 1. The timbre of a given instrument changes with **pitch**, but even if we change pitch artificially (say, by slowing down a tape) thereby retaining the internal proportions, the timbre is altered. 2. Not only the ratios of partials but their absolute loudness is relevant – the same sound has different timbres at different distances. 3. In the rare case of a virtually steady tone, static spectra can be meaningful, but the vast majority of musical sounds change continuously, so the temporal component must be included, not just as a global envelope but in order to describe the amplitude/time behaviour of every component present. Comprehensive descriptions must also include other aspects of the sound such as the **reverberation** conditions, its spectral envelope (see **formant**), and **intermodulation** with other sounds in the environment.

Timbre is not a physicist's but a musician's concept. The same sound might be 'bright' in one piece and 'aggressive' in another, but with experience musicians can learn to translate timbral descriptions into an expected **harmonic** content and envelope type (and hence into a strategy for synthesis). Thus 'bright' tones are likely to contain high level upper partials, 'bell-like' sounds to be rich in **inharmonic** partials, percussive timbres to have short, spiky envelopes and a high **noise** content, etc.

See **analogue synthesis techniques** 4 and **digital synthesis techniques** 3ff, for aspects of timbre, methods of analysing etc. In the Bibliography Helmholtz (1954), Taylor (1965), Wood (1962) and Roederer (1979) have slightly different approaches, and some avoid the equivocal 'timbre' altogether. A good survey of historical views and present computer-aided research is in Dodge (1985) chapter 2.

Time codes   In audio production of any complexity and for all film and video work a reliable means of **synchronizing** different machines is essential. Methods have evolved from direct mechanical linkage, through **selsyn** electrically locked motors used with sprocketed film and magnetic sound stock, to today's digital control of sprocketless audio and video tape, and the time-locking of sound tape to sprocketed picture film. To be effective, any timing system must have an adequate **resolution** for the intended purpose – a one-second clock tick cannot time events in the millisecond range. The resolution of 35 mm sprocketed film sound stock, for example, is $\frac{1}{96}$ sec (four holes per frame, twenty-four frames per second).

Simple clocks

A metronomic 'click track' has long been used to help conductors record
film music to accurate lengths, and the idea was adopted for multi-track
recording, a clock reference being laid down on one track and used for
subsequent timing. The limitation of simple pulse trains is that there is
no information about elapsed time – the first and the millionth pulse
are exactly the same. However, given a device that can count, and by
selecting a particular pulse as zero, both cueing and timing can be
arranged. Suppose, for example, that we use the 50 Hz mains as the
time source, a **sequencer** started at 0 could be told to stop at clock pulse
7050 or 2 min 21 sec. If the same clock controls a number of machines
they should stay in sync, but with a simple pulse any error, however
late in the take, involves returning to 0, as the only usable start reference.
Some devices may also have different 'timebases' which respond differently to the same sync input (see **sequencers** for comment on ppq, pulses-
per-quarter-note, clocks).

Frequency shift keying (FSK)

Square wave clock pulses do not record reliably on analogue audio
machines. The system tends to **integrate** the waveshape (see fig. 103) so
that it loses definition, leading to errors, **drop-outs** etc., which are fatal
in clock tracks because the count is lost. FSK is a simple form of
frequency modulation (see fig. 210a) in which the two states (no-pulse,
pulse) are converted to high and low tones in the middle of the audio
band, giving a much more stable recording.

MIDI (system real time)

(See the **MIDI** entry and **sequencers** for fuller details of this system.)
MIDI is designed for interfacing music devices, and its **baud rate** of *c.*
31 kHz is too high for recording on analogue audio machines (which
have a top limit of around 20 kHz). The MIDI clock supplies relative,
not absolute timing – its rate depends on the tempo set. The standard
MIDI system real time code (as opposed to the MIDI time code, see
below) only provides for a clock at 24 ppq, three commands (START,
STOP, CONTINUE) and a song position pointer (not always implemented)
which refers to the current sequence zero. MIDI time-related devices
often accept FSK or other inputs and convert them to MIDI, however.

SMPTE/EBU time code

The Society of Motion Picture and Television Engineers/European
Broadcasting Union time code (colloquially 'simty code') was originally
developed for video production, but has proved so useful that it is

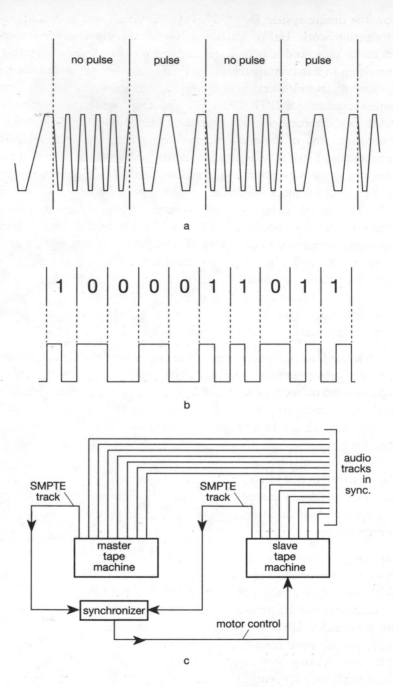

Fig. 210

now the timing system for all audio-visual media and most audio-only production work. Unlike MIDI, it is specifically designed for recording on audio tape, and it is an absolute time format – every fraction of a second up to a maximum of twenty-four hours carries a unique address. Because of its video origins it counts in 'frames' and comes in several timing standards: SMPTE (US video), 30 frames per second; 'drop frame' (US), 29.97 frames/sec; EBU video, 25 frames/sec; and film speed, 24 frames/sec. Any of these can be used for audio-only work. SMPTE is generated and stored as eighty bit words, containing not only the time data but space for optional user code. The time readout is very clear: 02:14:35:11 means 2 hours, 14 minutes, 35 seconds, 11 frames. The SMPTE rate of 2400 (30×80) bits/sec records reliably on audio machines, and the encoding system marks each 'bit cell' boundary with a polarity transition, 1s being distinguished from 0s by having a central transition as well (fig. 210b). Once 'striped' on to a tape, the code provides an absolute location reference independent of speed changes, bad tape etc., which can also be read in either direction.

A code reader/synchronizer has two main jobs: controlling tape transports, and initiating various actions at pre-selected times:

Controlling tape transports   Fig. 210c shows two multi-track machines synced together, effectively doubling the number of available tracks (for capstan control, see **tape recorder design**). The synchronizer (which may be the same unit that previously generated the code for both tapes) reads the two SMPTE tracks and adjusts the capstan of the slave machine so that time readings are always identical. Alternatively it can hold an 'offset' – you might want to mix a signal starting at 10 min 20 sec on the master with one located at 25 min 06 sec on the slave. Stereo quarter-inch tape machines cannot spare a track for a time code, but some are equipped with an additional centre track for the purpose (see **tape track configurations**).

Initiating actions   As an example of event cueing, suppose the offset described above allowed two takes of the same music to run together. With the output of the master pre-**patched** to the input of the slave, the synchronizer can be programmed to switch from one to the other at a given moment. At the chosen time the synchronizer 'punches-in' record mode on the slave machine, and the changeover is made. (However, a safer way, leaving both originals unerased, would be to copy both to a third machine.) Depending on how much of a studio's equipment is capable of automation, complete **mixdowns** can be carried out entirely under SMPTE control. Many synchronizers can output MIDI code as well, so a SMPTE cue can start a MIDI sequencer running an independently timed series of MIDI-linked events, and so on. Another important feature of SMPTE is its portability. A composer working in a home studio with only a few tracks can build up work on a number of tapes, stripe them with SMPTE, and be sure that they can all be run in sync on a larger system. See also **mixers and mixing desks**.

MIDI time code (MTC)
The success of SMPTE prompted an extension to the original MIDI 1.0 specification of 1983 (see **MIDI**), so that SMPTE-encoded data could be sent down MIDI lines, enabling both musicians and engineers to work in their preferred format. For a full description see Meyer and Brooks. MTC's main 'running' code is sent in eight quarter-frame 4 bit **nibbles**, i.e. a complete time code every two SMPTE frames. The nibbles are assembled into **bytes** to give the frames, seconds, minutes and hours count, plus the frame standard in use (24, 25, 30, 29.97 frames per second). There are also set-up messages corresponding to SMPTE's event cues, enabling a large variety of different devices to be controlled by a single event list.

The precise control systems now available actually allow more freedom rather than locking the musician into a rigid time frame, because the elements in music production that must synchronize can easily and repeatably be made to do so, leaving performers free to concentrate on interpretation and ad hoc timing decisions.

Time constant   Circuits containing **capacitance** and **inductance** cannot change instantly from one state (of current flow, charge etc.) to another. The time constant for such circuits is a measure of the speed with which they can change and is defined as the time taken for the circuit to make 63% of the total change (in current, charge etc.). For **capacitor/resistor** networks (used in **filters** and **oscillators**) the time constant (in seconds) = capacitance (in farads) × resistance (in ohms). See also **slew rate**.

Timers   See **frequency meters**, which usually include a **period** timing mode. There are many types of clock in music devices, see, for example, **percussion generators**, **sequencers** and **time codes**.

Time sharing   In larger computer systems, including multi-**work station** music studios, each user seems to have exclusive use of the computer, but in fact each job is being allocated a series of 'time slices', with other jobs interleaved.

Tolerance The maximum allowable error in a mechanical part or electrical property, given either as an absolute quantity, for example a capstan (see **tape recorder design**) of diameter 8 mm +/− .001 mm, or a percentage, for example a **resistor** of 27 kil**ohms** +/− 10%.

Tone 1. Sound of sufficient **periodicity** to exhibit **pitch**, as opposed to **noise**. 2. A musical interval, also called a 'whole tone', comprising two semitones. In equal **temperament** a whole tone is 200 **cents** or one sixth of an **octave**, but its size varies according to the tuning system. 3. Short for a **lining up** or reference **sine** test tone. 4. Imprecise description roughly equivalent to **timbre** – e.g. 'flutey' tone. 5. An imprecise description of frequency **response**, as in 'tone control' (see **filters**).

Tone burst A **sine wave** modulated with a **square wave envelope**, which is useful for testing the **transient** behaviour of, for example, **amplifiers**, and the **reverberation** of spaces.

Tonmeister A balance engineer/operator in music recording and broadcasting. German studios have always insisted that engineers controlling music recordings should be properly educated in music, and the word is used in other countries, as well as Germany, to describe music degree courses with a strong technical component.

Toroid/, -al See **transformers**

Torque The turning force of, for example, a motor shaft. See **tape recorder design**.

Total harmonic distortion (THD) See **harmonic distortion**

Tracing distortion See **pick-ups**

Tracker See **organs** *pipe*

Tracking error See **pick-ups**

Trailer Apart from its meaning as an advance sample advertising, for example, a film, a 'trailer' is a length of non-active tape joined to the tail of a tape, or in the middle of a composite tape to show where a programme ends. Sometimes coloured red. See **leader** and **spacer**.

Trailing edge   In **editing**, the final **modulations** of a given sound, often harder to 'read' than the **leading edge** because effects like **reverberation** may die slowly into the **noise** floor.

Transducer   A device which converts one form of energy to another. In audio applications they are used to change air pressure waves, mechanical movement or magnetic energy into electrical energy, and vice versa. Transducers like **headphones, microphones, loudspeakers, pick-ups,** tape heads etc. are the most difficult links in the electro-acoustic chain to design satisfactorily. See also **sound recording techniques** and **tape recorder design.**

Transformation   In composition, a word rather loosely used for various manipulations of musical material. In computer music it can be applied to **algorithms** for performing such manipulations. In general one would not use the word for small departures from an original (such as simple variations, inversions, new harmonies), but for changes that can be structurally attributed to the original but sound very different.

Transformers   These are **passive** devices working on the principle that if two **inductors** are arranged so that an **alternating current** flowing in one of them (the primary) produces a magnetic field which passes through both, then a **voltage** at the same **frequency** will be **induced** in the other (the secondary), without any electrical connection between them. Transformers for the audio **band** use coils wound on ferro-magnetic cores, and fig. 211a shows the most usual symbolic representation (though in some diagrams the coil shapes are replaced by solid bars). Figs. 211b and c show two of many types of core.

The rule for voltage transformation is simple – the voltage ratio between coils (inductors) equals the ratio of the number of turns in each. In fig. 211a 2:1 is given as an example of such a 'turns ratio'. If we input 100 V at the primary coil the secondary will output 50 V (or would in an ideal transformer). The action works both ways. If we reverse the roles of primary and secondary coils 100 V will be 'stepped up' to 200 V. In a passive device there can be no energy gain, so if the voltage, V, increases then the current, I, decreases while maintaining the same power (V × I remains constant in an ideal system, see **watt**).

In the power grids of national supply systems, long distances are covered efficiently by using very high voltages at comparatively low currents (hence low energy loss, see **resistors**) and transforming them down in steps to the final domestic voltage. Transformers are a ready

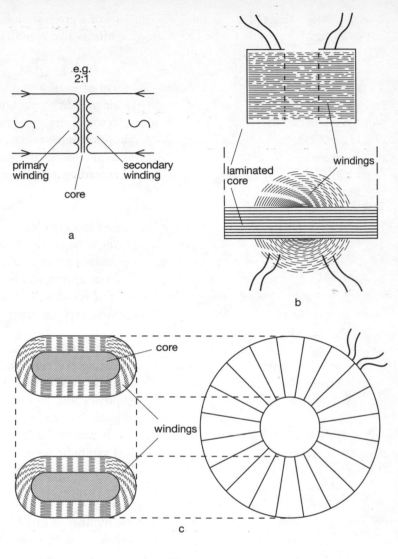

e.g.
2:1

primary
winding

secondary
winding

core

a

laminated
core

windings

b

core

windings

c

Fig. 211

answer to many problems but there are disadvantages too – they tend
to be bulky and heavy, and to generate and pick up external fields unless
well shielded.

Mains transformers
Given an AC mains supply, a transformer is the most efficient way to
derive the supply voltages needed by electronic equipment (now almost

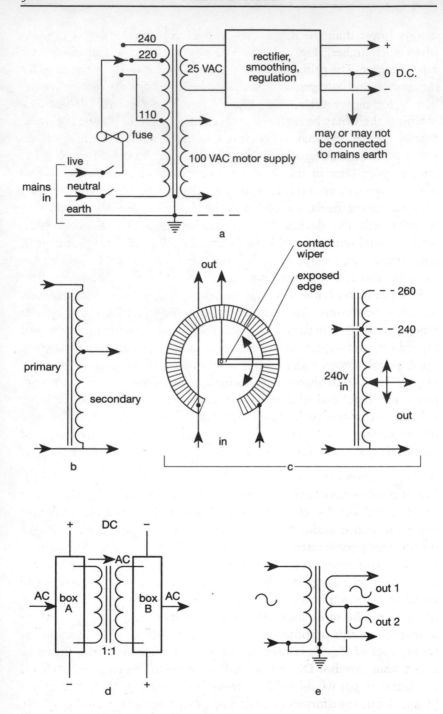

Fig. 212

always lower than the mains, but with earlier valve (tube) equipment often much higher). Fig. 212a shows a possible mains transformer for a tape recorder. The primary has several 'taps' to adjust the turns ratio for different mains voltages, and two secondaries are shown, one delivering 100 V for motor drive, one at 25 V for the electronics. In complex machines there may be several more secondaries. Other points: the transformer isolates the mains from the internal circuitry. Apart from the safety aspect, isolation allows the secondaries to 'float' – an earth reference is given later in the **rectifying**, smoothing and regulating section which supplies clean **direct current** to the electronics. Mains transformers generate strong fields, so they must be carefully placed in relation to sensitive inductive devices (such as playback heads or magnetic pickups), for minimum induced **hum**. Many designers favour ring (toroidal) cores (fig. 211c), a shape which helps to contain the magnetic field within the core, and can be formed in magnetically efficient **ferrite** materials.

When isolation is not required, the mains voltage can be adjusted with an 'auto-transformer' (fig. 212b), consisting of a single coil of wire with tapping point(s). The turns ratio is that of the whole winding to the part tapped off, and as with conventional transformers it can step down or up. A useful version is the continuously variable transformer, or 'variac' (212c). The sketch shows a **potentiometer** arrangement with the input below the 'high' end of the winding, allowing a boost above the input voltage (to compensate for low supply line voltages for example). Motor-driven variacs, used with output detecting circuits, are one type of automatic mains voltage stabilizer.

Audio transformers
Mains transformers have to work at only two frequencies (either 50 or 60 Hz), and can be very efficiently designed. It is another matter to cover the entire audio band with one device because nearly all the transformer's **parameters** are frequency-dependent (**hysteresis** losses in the core, **resonances** caused by the inductances plus their self-**capacitance** etc.). But even though compromise is inevitable, transformers are still useful in many applications. One of these is interfacing low **impedance** (Z) devices like most **microphones** to **amplifier** inputs, i.e. impedance changing. For this purpose a transformer with a turns ratio equal to the square root of Z_{out}/Z_{in} is needed. For example, a transformer to match a 200 **ohm** (symbol Ω) microphone to an input impedance of 10 kΩ (10 k/200 = 50) would need a step-up transformer with a ratio of 1:7 ($\sqrt{49}$). Input transformers handle tiny power levels and can be of subminiature size, but at the output end of valve amplifiers, where many

watts of power are transferred to a low-Z speaker coil, large, robust units are needed. Transistor power amplifiers do not need output transformers because the power stage is already at a very low impedance.

Two further uses (of many) for transformers: 1. Isolating circuits with different DC conditions (compare a similar use for **capacitors**). If isolation is the only requirement a non-transforming 1:1 ratio can be used (fig. 212d). 2. **Phase**-splitting. In cases where a signal is required in both normal and inverted form, if a tap in the centre of a winding is regarded as neutral, the signals from the two half-windings will be in **antiphase**. Fig. 212e shows a set-up for converting from an **unbalanced** to balanced line as used in a **direct box**. For some other uses of transformers see **microphones, ring modulation** and **stereo**.

Transient   A change of short duration in some property of a system, for example a sudden peak in music level or the effect on a circuit of switching on or off. The transient **response** is the behaviour of a circuit or device after a sudden but short-lived change in conditions. See also **filters, time constant** and **tone burst**.

Transistor (TRANSfer resISTOR)   See **amplifiers, field-effect transistor, lattice** and **semiconductor**

Transverse wave   A side-to-side wave motion (in e.g. a string), as opposed to the **longitudinal** (forward and back) motion of, for example, air in a pipe. See **travelling wave**.

Trapezium wave   A **waveform** similar to a **pulse wave** but with sloping sides. It is the simplest shape which can produce an effective musical **envelope**. See **analogue synthesis techniques 4**.

Trautonium   Invented by Friedrich Trautwein (1888–1956), this was one of the first (1930) practical electronic instruments, used by several notable composers including Hindemith and Strauss, and manufactured as a commercial venture. Based on a neon sawtooth **oscillator** (see fig. 147) and subtractive synthesis (see **analogue synthesis techniques 4**). See also **Ondes Martenot, Theremin**, Appleton (1975), Russcol (1972) and Manning (1987).

Travelling wave   As opposed to **standing wave**, a travelling (or progressive) wave consists of a disturbance moving away from a source to surrounding points with the result that energy is transferred with it from one place to another. In the case of sound in air, the energy of the source (say a vibrating diaphragm) pushes and pulls the particles of air touching it, which then excite the next outward layer etc., starting an expanding system in which each particle oscillates elastically with respect to its neighbour. Individual particles move a short distance to and fro along a radius of the total sphere of propagation (rarely achieved because of diffraction, absorption and reflection by obstacles), but their average position does not change. The speed of a wave depends on the medium through which it is travelling. Sound in air at 20°C travels at *c.* 344 metres (1128 feet) per second, and in water and steel (also at 20°) at 1461 and 5000 metres per second respectively.

Treatments Also known as 'effects', these are modifications applied to a signal such as **filtering, modulation, reverberation,** and the devices that perform them (e.g. treatment boxes), as opposed to generators or sources. See **analogue synthesis techniques** 4 onwards and **digital multi-effect unit.**

Tree A hierarchical structure, giving descending levels of control as the 'branches' proliferate. See fig. 213.

Tremolo **Amplitude modulation** at a sub-audio **frequency** applied to musical notes (with the exception of a string 'fingered tremolo' which is **frequency modulation**). In pipe **organs** the 'tremulant' works by varying the wind pressure.

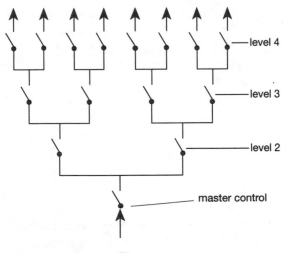

Fig. 213

Triangle wave   A double **ramp waveform** with identical but opposite **linear** slopes, see fig. 9. It contains only odd **harmonics**, with the energy in each diminishing rapidly as the square of the harmonic number, i.e. it has ⅑ of the **fundamental**'s energy in the third harmonic, ¹⁄₂₅ in fifth, ¹⁄₄₉ in seventh, etc. See **analogue synthesis techniques** 4. Compare **pulse** and **square waves**.

Trigger   Signal of a **pulse** or step **waveform** which is used to initiate some action. One type (fig. 214a) resets for each cue, but step type triggers (known also as **gates**) typically initiate different actions at the start and finish of the gate (see fig. 214b, which shows the **envelope** of a **keyboard synthesizer**). See also **analogue synthesis techniques** 4, **flip-flop**, **noise gate** and **one-shot oscillator**.

Trim   1. A fine adjustment, often in conjunction with a coarse one. A 'trimpot' (**potentiometer**) may be a panel control, for example to bring

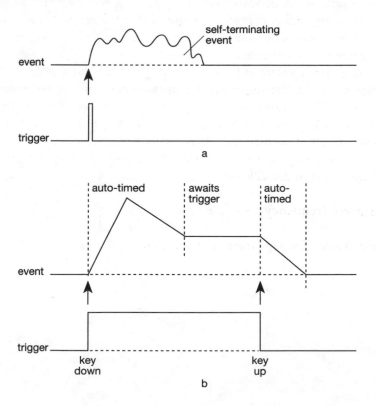

Fig. 214

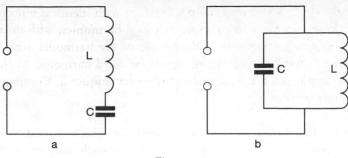

Fig. 215

mixer input levels into line, or an internal screwdriver adjustment. 2. A small length of tape or film removed when making a 'fine cut'.

Triode   See **amplifiers**

Tuned circuit   A network containing **capacitance** (C) and **inductance** (L) whose **impedance** depends on **frequency** and, at a particular value of frequency, exhibits **resonance**. The circuit thus 'picks out' this resonant frequency if a signal containing a range of frequencies is applied to it. The series arrangement of fig. 215a is an acceptor because its impedance becomes very low at its resonant frequency and hence a large current flows in it. The parallel combination (fig. 215b) is a rejector since it has a very high impedance at resonance and hence passes little current at this frequency. Everyday uses of tuned circuits include tuning a radio and the 'bias trap' in tape recorders (see **sound recording techniques**). See also **filters** and **oscillators**.

Turnover frequency   See **filters**

Twin track   See **tape track configurations**

U

Ultrasonics The study and use of sound waves at **frequencies** above the limits of hearing. Standard applications include echo sounding, cleaning electronic components, paint mixing, medical diagnostics, etc., but the principle is now being exploited in live performance electronic music. An example is the EMS Soundbeam, which detects dancers etc. entering its transmission field and converts movement into MIDI data.* See also **sub/-, super/sonic.**

Unbalanced Of signals carried in a two-wire system with one side held at a constant neutral potential (usually **earth**), all amplitude variations taking place on the other ('live') wire. By using a braided copper 'shield' for the neutral wire, with the live wire running centrally inside it (fig. 216a), protection from **interference** is adequate for good signal conditions, but a 'balanced line' (fig. 216b), is superior, particularly when lines are long and levels low (e.g. in **microphone** cables). The two **phase**-opposed signals are insensitive to interference, which arrives in-phase at both wires, and though the figure shows a shield connected to earth, the signal may not be earthed but left 'floating'. If the balance is adequate the shield can be omitted altogether. Balance-to-unbalance and vice versa may be done electronically or by a **transformer** (see fig. 212e).

Undermodulation Too low a signal for the medium in use (such as a radio transmission or tape recording), resulting in a poor **signal-to-noise ratio.** See **overmodulation.**

Unidirectional microphone See **microphones**

Unijunction A type of switching transistor. See **oscillators.**

Unity gain A condition in which **amplifiers** in **active devices** are set

*EMS, Trendeal Vean Barn, Ladock, Truro, Cornwall TR2 4NW, UK.

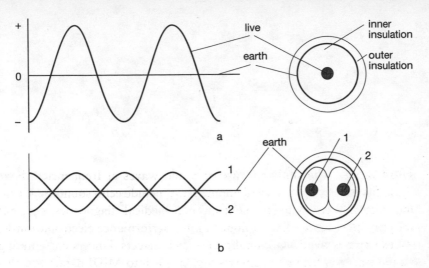

Fig. 216

to make up **insertion loss** but no more than that. It is normal practice with intermediate **treatments** in **patches,** so that units can be added or removed without altering the general levels within the system.

Unix See **operating systems**

V

Variable A quantity whose value may change during the course of a given process or calculation, or from case to case. See **constant, function** and **parameter**.

Variac See **transformers**

VCA, VCF, VCO See **voltage control**

Velocity microphone See **microphones**

Velocity of sound See **travelling wave** and **wavelength**

Very large scale integration (VLSI) See **integrated circuit**

Vibrating reed A type of pitch detector with a group of metal reeds mounted end on to the user so that when sound causes one of them to vibrate the movement can be clearly seen. It is accurate, but only useful for the selected frequencies to which the reeds have been tuned. It can still be a useful device for checking a particular frequency, but in general is now replaced by continuously adjustable electronic **frequency meters**.

Vibrato The **frequency modulation** of a tone at a sub-audio frequency (typically *c.* 3–8 Hz). It is part of the normal playing technique for bowed strings, and used as a special effect in others, particularly those (e.g. trombone) able to produce a glissando. For clavichords, whose direct action permits vibrato by finger pressure variation, the German word 'Bebung' is normally used. Vibrato is more or less regularly **periodic**, but part of its charm as a musical effect is given by changing its speed. Compare **tremolo**.

Video cassette PCM (Pulse Code Modulation) The encoding of sound in such a way that it can be recorded on an unmodified video cassette recorder (VCR), the area normally used for picture modulation being occupied by **pulse code modulated** signals (see also **helical scan**). The first pseudo-video sound processors were for three-quarter-inch U-matic VCRs, but Sony's pioneering PCM-F1 (early 1980s) was the first of a line of processors suitable for domestic Betamax and VHS video formats. The VCR must 'think' it is handling a video signal, so **NTSC** or **PAL/SECAM** protocols must be followed (in fact the screen shows sound modulations in parallel vertical stripes if a recording is played to a TV). In the Electronics Industry Association of Japan (EIAJ) standard which provides a recording format suitable for mastering **compact discs**, **stereo** information is **multiplexed** on to a single track, and a given line scan (fig. 217a) contains three each of left and right signal fourteen bit words, two fourteen bit **error correction** words (known as P and Q words), and one sixteen bit error detection word (CRCC=Cyclic Redundancy Check Code).

To obtain sixteen bit precision, fig. 217b, an option on the Sony machines, the fourteen bit Q word becomes the S word, containing the extra two bits of the six L(eft) and R(ight) words plus two for the P word. This reduces the error safety margin but improves **resolution** and hence sound quality, and the data layout simplifies the playback of unknown tapes because either sixteen or fourteen bit recordings can be played at fourteen bit precision. Fig. 189 (**sound recording techniques**) is a generalized block diagram of the digital record/playback process.

The normal picture sound track (analogue), which is not helically

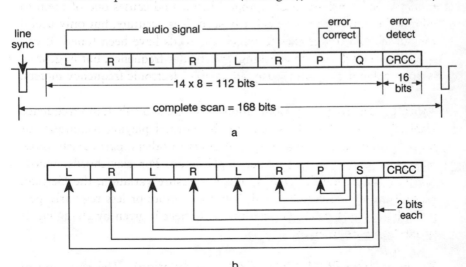

Fig. 217

scanned, is not used in this process, so is still available (though the quality is poor compared with the PCM recording). However, stereo 'hi-fi' video machines, with higher quality sound, can provide quite acceptable **quad** recordings (two PCM helical, two analogue). For detailed descriptions of the various formats, see Watkinson (1988) chapter 8.

VLSI (Very Large Scale Integration)   See **integrated circuit**

Vocoder   (VOice CODER) A device for encoding and re-**synthesizing** speech, developed (originally by H. Dudley in 1936) to reduce speech data for long distance telephone transmission. The principle of the 'channel vocoder' is to split the composite voice **spectrum** by passing the signal through a bank of close-spaced, sharply tuned band pass **filters**. If a matching set of filters is provided at the receiving end, only the value of the **amplitude** detected at each filter need be sent, i.e. very much lower **bandwidth** data than the actual speech **waveform**. This signal is used to control the output level of the corresponding synthesizing filter so that it equals that of the input.

Very simply described, speech consists of vowel sounds of varying pitch (the whole band being shifted between male, female and children's voices), voiced consonants (those with perceptible pitch) and unvoiced consonants (**noise** based). An excitation analysis in the vocoder's transmitter detects whether the current sound is unvoiced or voiced, and if voiced what its pitch is. These two streams of additional data are added to those from the filters, and at the receiver control a voiced/unvoiced switch which selects either a noise generator or a variable frequency pulse generator, and sets the frequency of the generator.

Fig. 218 shows how all the data can be **multiplexed**, i.e. sent serially in a single channel, and today this part of the process and often the whole device is digital. Apart from their application as speech data compressors, various types of vocoder (not necessarily under that name) have been explored as music manipulation devices. For example the voltage controlled vocoder developed by Peter Zinovieff and David Cockerell and made by EMS (London) in the middle 1970s has provision for **patching** any analysing filter to any synthesizing one (giving spectral distortions and inversion), time delay effects like **chorusing**, and complete freedom to change the type of excitation. A digital, computer-controlled version, called the Digital Oscillator Bank (DOB) was in effect a frequency domain synthesizer, because it operated on spectrum rather than waveform.

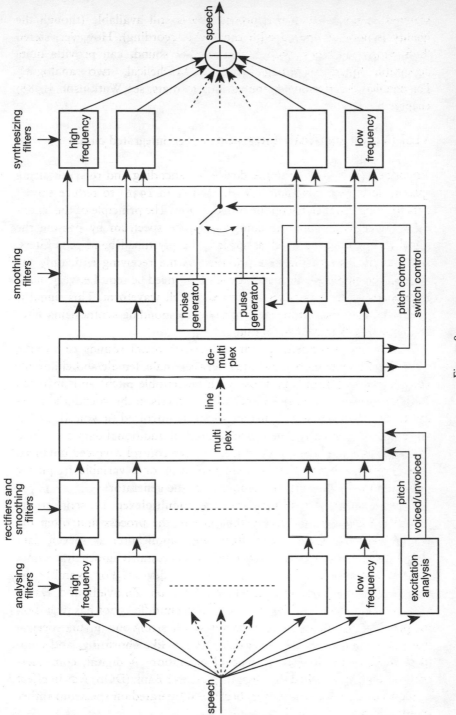

Fig. 218

Another development in the 'filter bank' concept is the **phase** vocoder, in which special filters extract both amplitude and frequency information. For details of this see Dolson (1986). The FOF system described in **digital synthesis techniques** 7 is another variant, in which the separate excitation source and filter are combined as a triggered **oscillator**. For speech work, alternatives to the channel vocoder are devices using formant detection ('peak picking') and linear predictive coding (see **digital synthesis techniques** 5). For a general account of speech synthesis see Witten (1982) and Linggard (1985).

Voice coil   See **loudspeakers**

Voice over   Words recorded to go with a picture image other than that of the speaker, i.e. no 'lip sync' is involved, so such tracks can be **wild**. Voice overs are mostly used for commentary, but also sometimes in dramatic contexts, and with sung as well as spoken material.

Volatile memory   A computer memory that loses its data when it loses its source of power. See **random access memory**.

Volt/age   Named after Count Alessandro Volta (1745–1827), a volt is a unit of electrical **potential** (hence also of potential difference), and electromotive force (EMF). Symbol V, and defined as the potential difference (PD) between two points if one **joule** of energy is expended in moving one **coulomb** of charge between them. See also **Ohm's law, root-mean-square** and **watt**.

Voltage control   (VC) A process whereby the main **parameters** of a device are varied by adjusting a control voltage fed to a special control input which is separate from any audio input there may be. The control input may replace or be in addition to manual control (by moving a knob on the device for example). VC audio modules were pioneered by Robert Moog in the 1960s, and were the basis of the first reasonably compact **synthesizers** (Moog, 1965).

The key VC devices are the VC **amplifier** (VCA), with VC of **gain**, and the VC **oscillator** (VCO), with control of **frequency**. Many others (VC **filters, envelope shapers** etc.) can be derived from these basic units. See **amplifiers, analogue synthesis techniques** 4ff, **filters, mixers and mixing desks** and **oscillators**.

Voltage divider   An arrangement of two or more **resistors** in **series**

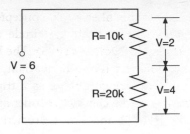

Fig. 219

which split the total voltage across them so that the voltages across the individual components are in the same ratio as their resistances. For example, in fig. 219 the resistors are in a 2:1 ratio so the total voltage is split in the same ratio. **Potentiometers** are variable voltage (**potential**) dividers. See also **ladder** and **parallel**.

Volume The power level of an audio **frequency complex wave** in electrical form, related both to **gain** and (after **transducing** in a **loudspeaker**) to loudness, but not in a very simple fashion because of the non-linear relationship between power (**watts**) and perceived loudness, and the further non-linearity of the human hearing system (see **phon**).

Volume control effect A possible result of increasing only the **level** of a complex sound, particularly a real or well synthesized instrumental timbre. Instead of sounding genuinely 'louder' (i.e. having the **spectral** content expected of a loud sound from that instrument) it just sounds as if someone has 'turned it up', which indeed they have. This effect is one of the **psychoacoustic** problems of electronic composition.

Volume unit (VU) A **logarithmic** programme level unit, such that o VU = +4 dBm (see **decibel**).

Volume unit meter (VUM) A programme level meter calibrated to read **volume units**, with a secondary scale showing **modulation** percentage, and ballistically **damped** so that with a constantly changing audio signal it reads an average or **root-mean-square** (rms) value, i.e. it has a deliberately poor **transient response**, but gives a good idea of general power content. Most cheap VUMs in domestic equipment are not ballistically or electrically correct and cannot be relied on. Many VUMs include a peak-reading **LED** to indicate when peaks exceed the **headroom** region. See also **decibel** and **peak programme meter**.

W

Watt   An **SI unit** of power, symbol W, defined as an energy conversion rate of one **joule** per second. Electrical power is used (energy converted to other forms) when a **current** (I) flows through a **load** with a **voltage** (V) across it. The amount of power used (W) is given by $W = V \times I$. If the load is a **resistor**, and by substitution with **Ohm's law**, which states that $V = IR$ and $I = V/R$, wattage can also be expressed as $W = V \times V/R = V^2/R$, or $W = I \times IR = I^2R$. Hence o dBm (see **decibel**), which is defined as 1 milliwatt (mW) in 600 ohms, can also be expressed as $.001W = V^2/600$. Thus $V^2 = .6$, $V = \sqrt{.6}$ or .775. Acoustic power is also measured in watts, and an indication of the ear's efficiency is that the loud sound of an orchestra of 75 players, output estimated at *c.* 70 watts, would only light a modest bulb. See also **phon**.

Waveform   (or 'waveshape') The appearance of a wave when plotted or displayed on, for example, an **oscilloscope**. The word is used mainly when the waveshape is easily described – **sine, ramp, triangle** etc., and remains fairly constant. If the shape is unstable or confused descriptions like 'noisy', 'rich', **aperiodic** may apply. 'Complex wave', though sometimes used as if it meant confused, strictly applies to any wave with two or more **sinusoids**, and is therefore correct for some quite simple waveforms.

Wavelength   The distance between two equivalent points in successive **cycles** of a wave along the direction of propagation (figs. 220a and b). Wavelength (symbol λ) is given by the velocity (v) of the wave divided by its **frequency** (f), i.e. $\lambda = v/f$. If wave speed is constant (as for example in radio waves) λ and f are always in the same reciprocal relationship. Sound travels at different speeds through different materials, however (see **travelling wave**), and is also recorded on linear media like discs and tapes running at various speeds, so for a given frequency the wavelength varies enormously. In air at 20°C the velocity of sound is 344 metres per second, so 100 Hz has a wavelength of 3.44 m, 10 kHz one of 34.4

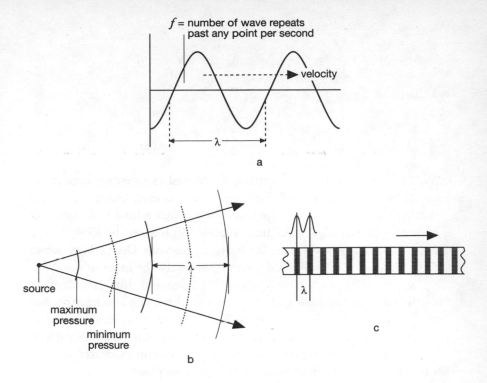

Fig. 220

mm. But recorded on tape running at 19 centimetres per second (fig. 220c) those two frequencies have wavelengths of 1.9 mm and .019 mm respectively, important information when designing, for example, tape heads (see **sound recording techniques**).

Wavetrain   A series of similar waves, particularly a short group such as the Vosim waveform shown in fig. 72 (a four-cycle wavetrain with falling amplitude).

White noise   See **analogue synthesis techniques** 4 and **noise**

Wild track   Sound recorded with no synchronizing arrangements (i.e. without using sprocketed magnetic stock or a **time code**), although intended for use with pictures. Many effects tracks, **voice overs** and dialogue etc. can be recorded wild to rough timings. Music is usually recorded in sync, but in some media (such as animation) may be taken wild, measured and used as the timing basis for the picture. See **synchronization**.

Winding   See **transformers**

Window   The word has many meanings, of which these are a few: 1. A block of samples selected for analysis, also called a 'frame' (see **digital synthesis techniques** 3). 2. A defined area on a computer screen, which may have several windows showing different menus and displays. 3. A dialogue gap in a distributed TV commercial, allowing local variations to be dropped in for transmission prints. 4. A band pass **filter**'s pass range, for example 100–2000 Hz. 5. A type of radar jamming, in which strips of metal foil are dropped from an aircraft, causing large and confusing echoes as they float earthward.

Real windows, e.g. observation and projection windows, are important items in studios, and are usually double glazed, spaced quite widely (to enclose as much 'dead air' as possible), and not parallel (to avoid light reflections and the possibility of sound **standing waves**).

Windshield   See **microphones**

Wireless microphone   See **microphones**

Woodwind instruments   As with 'brass', 'woodwind' describes sound production methods rather than the material of construction for this group of instruments, which may indeed be wood but is frequently metal or plastic, and even ceramic or glass. The families of contemporary woodwinds have evolved over many centuries, and although there are literally thousands of variants, particularly if one includes local and folk instruments, there are only a few basic principles involved. The main distinctions between the woodwind and the other major group of wind instruments, the **brass instruments**, are: 1. Woodwinds generate tone by directing an airstream so as to vibrate the air itself or a 'reed'; in brass instruments the player's lips are themselves the generator. 2. Woodwinds control pitch by uncovering holes to change the effective length of a pierced tube (with a few exceptions such as panpipes – one pipe per note, and the swannee whistle – slide control). All the main brass instruments are airtight systems with no holes. 3. Woodwinds use only two or three **harmonics**, for selecting **registers**, whereas the brass make use of higher numbers in the **harmonic series** as basic pitch controls.

We first consider how the pipe is energized in woodwind instruments, then the pipes themselves.

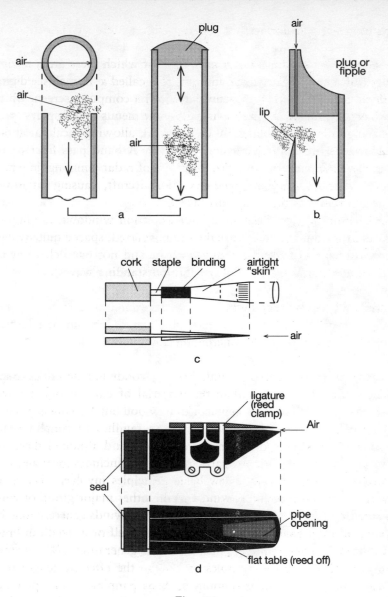

Fig. 221

Generators

The acoustic action of wind instruments is to take a fairly unstable tone source (such as the 'crow' of an oboe reed blown by itself) and bring it into sharp focus by coupling it to a precisely tuned pipe resonator (as opposed to strings, where a precisely tuned source is coupled to a wide band resonator, see **bowed strings**).

There are four main types of generator for woodwind, illustrated in fig. 221. Free air reeds (fig. 221a) use nothing more than holes, either the bore of the pipe itself (e.g. basic pan pipes) or a side hole (e.g. flute) across which the player directs a controlled stream of air. Whistle-type air reeds (fig. 221b) direct the airstream down a thin channel and on to a 'lip' or sharp edge (e.g. recorders). Whistle instruments are easier to sound than simple air holes, but give the player much less control. Double reeds (fig. 221c) were originally a hollow stalk of thick grass flattened at the end. Today two pieces of pared down cane are tied to a metal 'staple' (e.g. oboe, bassoon). The traditional cane is Arundo Donax, for many years supplied to the music trade from Fréjus in the south of France. Most double reeds are 'wet', i.e. the reed is softened by moisture and played directly from the lips. Dry reed instruments (e.g. crumhorn) have a cap over the reed or are indirectly blown (e.g. bagpipe chanter/melody pipe). Single reeds (fig. 221d) are fixed above a firm 'table' upon which they 'beat'. A simple kind is made by splitting a 'tongue' away from the end of a complete cane and plugging the end (e.g. bagpipe drone). The modern, refined single reed instrument (clarinet, saxophone) is the most recent version, dating back only to the early eighteenth century.

The open, free air, instruments work by maintaining a continuous airflow – the larger flutes use up the player's store of air very quickly, and frequent breathing is necessary. Reed instruments need only a small air movement and work largely by pressure – an oboist normally has to get rid of unused air before taking a new breath.

Resonators

The output from the sound source in woodwind instruments is coupled to a **standing wave** system (see fig. 191) in the pipe. The basic open pipe **node** pattern is shown in fig. 26a (brass instruments). The solid and dotted lines show two **antiphase** positions, both of which occur in each cycle, i.e. the **wavelength** is twice the length of the air column. This is the model for the flutes and whistles, which are open to free air at the input end. Open pipes give a complete harmonic series, so when 'overblown' (i.e. when breath pressure and source **frequency** are increased so as to produce higher harmonic modes) the flutes and recorders can all produce a new scale at the **octave** (second harmonic) and, for the highest register, at the double octave (fourth harmonic). The exact shape of the bore, size and spacing of holes etc., is too complex and varied to discuss here, but for centuries was determined by trial and error. In some flutes, for example, a contracting cone (narrower at the free end) was popular for many years. The modern nearly cylindrical concert flute is due to the great Munich instrument maker Theobald Boehm (1794–1881), who revolutionized flute design and whose innovations were soon adopted for the other instruments as well.

Clarinets are also cylindrical except for the short flare or bell, whose shape only affects the lowest notes, when most of the holes are closed – nearly all the sound from woodwind emerges from their sides. In this case the pipe is stopped at one end by the reed and the closed pressure system of the human player, and behaves differently from an open pipe, which as we saw above is a half-wave resonator. Because the closed end must be a point of minimum activity (i.e. a **node**), a stopped cylindrical pipe must have a node at one end and an **antinode** at the other. Fig. 222a shows that its fundamental mode is a quarter-wave, i.e. the clarinet can sound pitches approximately an octave lower than, say, a flute of the same length. Following from this it can be seen that none of the even harmonics are available, and the odd series (3, 5, 7 etc.) accounts also for the 'hollow' **timbre** of the instrument (for a pictorial analysis, see fig. 56). It also means that clarinets do not overblow at the octave but the twelfth, complicating the mechanism because enough holes must be provided to cover an octave plus a fifth of the fundamental ('chalumeau') scale before the overblown ('clarinet') scale can begin. The upper end of the fundamental twelfth is the weakest part of the compass, and the '**break**' where the switch is made to overblown notes is assisted by a 'speaker key' (fig. 222b), which forces the production of the third harmonic antinode and suppresses the fundamental.

Oboes, bassoons and saxophones have conical bores, and their standing wave patterns cannot be represented by the two-dimensional diagrams we have used for the cylinders, because the wave expands as it travels down the tube, giving a spherical rather than a flat wavefront. The practical effect is that conical bores, whether stopped or open, give a complete series (for the fairly complex mathematics see Taylor, 1965, chapter 2, Olson, 1967, chapter 4 or Hutchins, 1978). All these instruments overblow at the octave, therefore, and the oboe and saxophone are fitted with octave keys, acting in the same way as the clarinet's speaker key to assist playing in the upper register.

There are many aspects of woodwind construction and technique that we cannot discuss here – for example the behaviour of the different sizes of instrument in each family, methods of tuning, ingenuities of keywork, the subtle ways in which pitch can be 'lipped' up or down to ensure perfect intonation, the acoustics of 'multiphonics' (playing chords) etc. There is a large body of literature on the playing technique for each

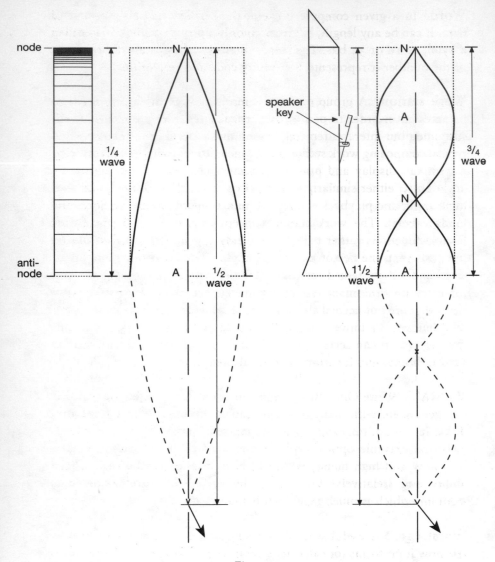

Fig. 222

instrument, and good historical accounts in Sadie (1984). Anthony Baines's *Woodwind Instruments and Their History* is an expert and entertaining survey of the whole subject (1962).

Woofer   See loudspeakers

Word In a given computer system, the smallest addressable unit of data. It can be any length, but is commonly a group of 8 **bits** (also called a **byte**), or 16 or 32 bits. The longer the word, the greater the precision of the number it represents. See **binary code** and **resolution**.

Work station A group of items comprising everything that needs to be accessed in order to perform a particular task. It is usually not self-sustaining but interacts remotely with a much larger central complex. A typical composing work station would include the usual desk accessories, a terminal, display and printer connected to a main computer, music keyboard(s) either similarly connected or stand-alone devices, and analogue input and playback equipment (**mixer, microphone, amplifiers** and **loudspeakers**). The work station concept implies a small package of flexible functions rather than an unwieldy spread of fixed controls, on the basis that one person can only handle so much at one time. Local, small and self-contained computer facilities can be used to prepare work for entry into the main system, optimizing the use of large, expensive items that are not needed all the time or for all jobs, and are uneconomic to duplicate. In university and public access studios, one large **time sharing** system can service many work stations, some of which may be sited in homes etc. far from the central processor.

WORM (Write Once Read Many times) A non-erasable optical disk storage system with many times the capacity of comparably sized **hard disks**. It is used, for example, in the **tapeless studio**. Recording systems based on erasable optical media are now available which provide the reliability and high quality of digital hard disk systems but offer portability and (relatively) lower costs by using a removable recording medium (which is much more robust than tape).

Worst case A useful way of assessing a system or component is to test how it performs (or calculate how it would perform) under the most adverse possible conditions, for example, how much **hum** and **noise** a **mixing desk** produces at maximum level, maximum treble and bass boost, and with all **faders** wide open – a condition never met in ordinary use. The same approach can test software by taking all variables to the extremes that best reveal inefficiencies in the program.

Wow A **periodic** variation in frequency (**frequency modulation**) of a signal (up to *c.* 10 Hz) caused by faulty mechanical parts in turntables, tape transports etc. (a typical source here is a deformed pinch roller).

Wow is especially destructive with recordings of non-**vibrato** instruments like pianos. Higher frequency modulations are called **flutter**. See also **tape recorder design**.

Write/read   Terms used instead of record/play when referring to digital rather than analogue storage media.

WYSIWYG   (What You See Is What You Get) Of computer programs, an expression meaning that what is printed as the computer's final product is the same as the screen image in front of you. A general approach to user-friendly programming, in which menus, graphics etc. are clearly displayed and usable in a non-technical way. Many music programs are of this sort – a **waveform window**, for example, that can be adjusted to size on the screen in the knowledge that exactly the same window will be printed.

X

XLR See **Cannon**

XY plotter A graphics printer so named because it draws under the control of X and Y co-ordinate data. Useful for graphic scores and other musically relevant plots.

Z

Z See **impedance**

Z-axis The axis at right angles to the XY plane, and on flat paper often represented diagonally, giving an isometric three-dimensional plot (see, for example, fig. 56 in **digital synthesis techniques**). In some **oscilloscopes**, a Z input is provided which modulates beam intensity (brightness). With suitable signals this can give the impression that the picture comes forward or retreats from the screen plane.

Zero level See **decibel**

Select Bibliography

Books and articles have been chosen to provide a list of key references; through their own book lists they also open doors to further reading. The abbreviation CMJ is used throughout to refer to Computer Music Journal, published by MIT Press Journals, Cambridge, Mass., USA.

Abbott, Curtis *et al.* 'Machine tongues' I-XI (XI printed as X) CMJ, vol. II no. I (I); vol. II, no. 2 (II); vol. II, no. 3 (III); vol. III, no. I (IV); vol. III, no. 2 (V); vol. III, no. 4 (VI); vol. IV, no. 2 (VII); vol. IV, no. 4 (VIII); vol. VI, no. 3 (IX), vol. VIII, no. I (X), vol. IX, no. 3 (XI printed as X)

Adams, Robert Train *Electronic Music Composition for Beginners* W. C. Brown, Dubuque, Iowa, 1986

Appleton, Jon H. and Ronald C. Perera (eds.) *The Development and Practice of Electronic Music* Prentice-Hall, Englewood Cliffs, NJ, 1975

Babbitt, Milton 'An introduction to the RCA synthesizer' *Journal of Music Theory*, USA, vol. 8, 1964, pp. 251–66

Bacon, Francis, *The New Atlantis* (1622). Many editions and commentaries. Often published with More's *Utopia*

Baines, Anthony *Brass Instruments, Their History and Development* Faber and Faber, London, 1976

—*Woodwind Instruments and Their History* Faber and Faber, London, second edition 1962

Baird, Jock (ed.) *Understanding MIDI* Amsco Publications, London, 1986

Ballou, Glen (ed.) *Handbook for Sound Engineers – The New Audio Cyclopedia* Howard W. Sams, Indianapolis, 1987

Bandt, Ros *Sounds in Space – Wind Chimes and Sound Sculptures* Victorian Arts Council and Council of Adult Education, Melbourne, 1985

Barbeau, L. C. and M. J. Corinthios 'The construction and operation of a high quality audio conversion system' CMJ, vol. VIII, no. 2, 1984

Barnes, William H. *The Contemporary American Organ* J. Fischer, Glen Rock, NJ, seventh edition 1959

Barrière, Jean-Baptiste (artistic director) *IRCAM: Un Portrait* (Record with booklet), IRCAM 0001, IRCAM, Centre Pompidou, Paris, 1983

Beauchamp, James 'Practical sound synthesis using a non-linear processor (waveshaper) and a high-pass filter' CMJ, vol. III, no. 3, 1979

Berlioz, Hector *A Treatise on Modern Instrumentation and Orchestration* trans. Mary Cowden Clarke, Novello, London, 1882. Also enlarged and revised version by Richard Strauss, trans. Theodore Front, Kalmus, New York, 1948. (Originally published in French, 1843)

Blades, James *Percussion Instruments and Their History* Faber and Faber, London, revised edition, 1984

Boom, Michael *Music Through MIDI* Microsoft Press, Richmond, Washington, 1987

Borwick, John (ed.) *Loudspeaker and Headphone Handbook* Butterworth Scientific, London, 1988

Briggs, G. A. *A to Z in Audio* Gernsback Library, New York, 1961 (Originally published by Wharfedale Wireless Works, Idle, UK, 1960)

Brodie, Leo *Starting FORTH* Prentice-Hall, Englewood Cliffs, NJ, 1981

Buck, Percy C. *Acoustics for Musicians* Oxford University Press, 1918

Bunger, Richard *The Well-Prepared Piano* Litoral Arts Press, San Pedro, California, 1981

Busoni, Ferruccio *Sketch for a New Aesthetic of Music* trans. Dr Th. Baker, G. Schirmer, New York, 1911 (Reprinted in *Three Classics in the Aesthetic of Music*, Dover Publications, New York, 1962)

Buxton, William *et al.* 'The use of hierarchy and instance in a data structure for computer music' CMJ, vol. II, no. 4, 1978

Byrd, Donald and Christopher Yavelow 'The Kurzweil 250 digital synthesizer' CMJ, vol. X, no. 1, 1986

Cage, John *Silence* Wesleyan University Press, Middletown, Conn., 1961 (also Marion Boyars, London, 1973)

—*A Year from Monday* Wesleyan University Press, Middletown, Conn., 1967 (also Calder and Boyars, London, 1968)

Cage, John and Lejaren Hiller *HPSCHD for harpsichords and computer-generated sound tapes* Nonesuch Records, New York, H71224–A

Capel, Vivian *Newnes Audio and Hi-Fi Engineer's Pocket Book* Heinemann, London, 1988

—*Public Address Handbook* Keith Dickson Publishing, London, second edition 1981

Carlos, Wendy 'Tuning: at the crossroads' CMJ vol. XI, no. 1, 1987

Cary, Tristram *Narcissus* for flute and tape recorders, first performance by Edward Walker, Queen Elizabeth Hall, London, 1969, score (1970) and record (GAL4007) from Galliard, Great Yarmouth

—*Nonet* Anthology of Australian Music on Disc, CSM: 4(CD), Canberra School of Music, 1989 (GPO Box 804, Canberra, ACT 2601, Australia)

—*Quarts in Pint Pots* Proceedings of the 1984 International Computer Music Conference (ed. William Buxton) Computer Music Association, San Francisco, 1985

—*Sonata for Guitar Alone* Novello, London, 1968

—*345 – A Study in Limited Resources* Galliard, Great Yarmouth, 1970 (score and record – GAL4006)

—*Trios* for VCS3 synthesizer and turntables (2 records and score) Electronic Music Studios, London, 1971

Casabona, Helen and David Frederick *Using MIDI* Alfred Publishing Co., Sherman Oaks, Calif., 1987

Cavaliere, Sergio *et al.* 'Synthesis by phase modulation and its implementation in hardware' CMJ, vol. XII, no. 1, 1988

Chadabe, Joel 'Interactive composing: an overview' CMJ, vol. VIII, no. 1, 1984

Chafe, C. *et al.* 'Toward an intelligent editor of digital audio: recognition of musical constructs' CMJ, vol. VI, no. 1, 1982

Chamberlin, Hal *Musical Applications of Microprocessors* Hayden Book Co, Hasbrouck Heights, NJ, second edition 1985

Chowning, John 'The simulation of moving sound sources' *Journal of the Audio Engineering Society*, vol. XIX, no. 1, 1971, pp. 2–6. Reprinted in CMJ, vol. 1, no. 3, 1977

—'The synthesis of complex audio spectra by means of frequency modulation' *Journal of the Audio Engineering Society*, vol. XXI, no. 7, 1973. Reprinted in CMJ, vol. 1, no. 2, 1977

Chowning, John *et al. Overview* Stanford Center for Computer Research in Music and Acoustics, Stanford University, Calif., 1977

Clifford, Martin *Microphones* Tab Books, Blue Ridge Summit, PA, third edition 1986

Cole, Hugo *Sounds and Signs – Aspects of Musical Notation* Oxford University Press, 1974

Conway, R., D. Gries and E. C. Zimmerman *A Primer on PASCAL* Winthrop Publishers, Cambridge, Mass., 1976

Cope, David *New Music Composition* Schirmer, New York, 1977

Dashow, James 'New approaches to digital sound synthesis and transformation' CMJ, vol. X, no. 4, 1986

Davies, Hugh (Compiler) *International Electronic Music Catalog* MIT Press, Cambridge, Mass., 1967

De Furia, Steve with Joe Scacciaferro *The MIDI Book – Using MIDI and Related Interfaces* Third Earth Productions, Rutherford, NJ, 1986

de Poli, Giovanni 'A tutorial on digital sound synthesis techniques' CMJ, vol. VII, no. 4, 1983

Deutsch, Diana (ed.) *The Psychology of Music* Academic Press, New York, 1982

Dodge, Charles and Thomas A. Jerse *Computer Music* Schirmer, New York, 1985

Dolson, Mark 'The phase Vocoder: a tutorial' CMJ, Vol. X, no. 4, 1986

Douglas, Alan *The Electronic Musical Instrument Manual* Pitman, London, sixth edition 1976

Dunn, David *Music, Language and Environment* Musicworks no. 33 (Journal) Toronto, 1986

—'Speculations: on the evolutionary continuity of music and animal communication behaviour' *Perspectives of New Music*, USA, vol. 22 nos 1–2, 1983–4

Eaton, Manfred L. *Bio-Music* University of Missouri, Orcus Research, Kansas City, 1970

Edmunds, Robert A. *The Prentice-Hall Standard Glossary of Computer Terminology* Prentice-Hall, Englewood Cliffs, NJ, 1985

Eimert, Herbert spoken Introduction (in German) on Deutsche Grammophon disc LPE 17 242 or LP 16132, 1957

Ernst, David *The Evolution of Electronic Music* Schirmer, New York, 1977

Fellgett, P. B. 'Some comparisons of digital and analogue audio recording' *The Radio and Electronic Engineer*, London, vol. LIII, no. 2, 1983

Fletcher, H. and W. A. Munson 'Loudness, its definition, measurement and calculation' *Journal of the Acoustical Society of America*, vol. 5, no. 2, 1933, pp. 82–108

Foster, S. *et al.* 'Toward an intelligent editor of digital audio: signal processing methods' CMJ, vol. VI, no. 1, 1982

Fox, Barry 'Japan has digital recorded tape' *New Scientist* (UK) vol. 110, no. 1505, 1986, pp. 40–43

Gabura, James and Gustav Ciamaga *Computer Control of Sound Apparatus for Electronic Music* Audio Engineering Society Reprint no. 520, New York, 1967

Greenspun, Philip and Charles F. Stromeyer 'Audio analysis IV: compact disk players' CMJ, vol. X, no. 1, 1986

Griffiths, Paul *A Guide to Electronic Music* Thames and Hudson, London, 1979

Grob, Bernard *Basic Electronics* McGraw-Hill, New York, 1987

Harris, C. R. and S. T. Pope (eds.) *Computer Music Association Source Book* Computer Music Association Publications, San Francisco, 1987

Haynes, S. 'The computer as a sound processor: a tutorial' CMJ, vol. VI, no. 1, 1982

Heckman, Harald (ed.) *Elektronische Datenverarbeitung in der Musikwissenschaft* Gustav Bosse Verlag, Regensburg, 1967

Helmholtz, H. von *On the Sensations of Tone as a Physiological Basis for the Theory of Music* Dover, New York, 1954 (facsimile of Alexander Ellis's English edition of 1885. First German edition 1862)

Hiller, Lejaren 'Composing with computers: a progress report' CMJ, vol. v, no. 4, 1981

—*et al. Technical Reports* nos. 8, 9, 13 and 18 University of Illinois School of Music Experimental Music Studios, 1963–8

—and Leonard M. Isaacson *Experimental Music* McGraw-Hill, New York, 1959

Hofstadter, Douglas R. *Gödel, Escher, Bach: An Eternal Golden Braid* Penguin Books, London, 1980

Horn, Delton T. *Digital Electronic Music Synthesizers* Tab Books, Blue Ridge Summit, PA, second edition 1988

Hutchins, Carleen Maley *et al. The Physics of Music* (eight reprints from *Scientific American*) W. H. Freeman, San Francisco, 1978

IRCAM – Centre Georges Pompidou publicity brochure, Imprimerie SEF, Paris, *c.* 1981

Jones, Douglas and Thomas W. Parks 'Generation and combination of grains for music synthesis' CMJ, vol. XII, no. 2, 1988

Kamimoto, Hideo *Complete Guitar Repair* Oak Publications, New York, 1975

Keane, David *Tape Music Composition* Oxford University Press, 1980

Koenig, Gottfried Michael *PROJECT 2. Computer Programme for the Calculation of Musical Structure Variants* (Electronic Music Reports no. 3) Institute of Sonology of Utrecht State University, 1970

Kowalski, M. J. and A. J. Rockmore 'The NYIT digital sound editor' CMJ, vol. VI, no. 1, 1982

Kronland-Martinet, Richard 'The wavelet transform for analysis, synthesis, and processing of speech and music sounds' CMJ, vol. XII, no. 4, 1988

Kufner, A. and J. Kadlec *Fourier Series* trans. G. A. Toombs, pp. 225–8, Iliffe Books, London, 1971

Leipp, Emile *The Violin* University of Toronto Press, 1969

Levinson, Horace C. *Chance, Luck and Statistics* Dover, New York, 1963

Levison, M. and W. A. Sentance *Introduction to Computer Science* Gordon and Breach, New York, 1969

Linggard, R. *Electronic Synthesis of Speech* Cambridge University Press, 1985

Lloyd, Ll. S. and Hugh Boyle *Intervals, Scales and Temperaments* Macdonald, London, 1963 (second enlarged edition 1978)

Loy, Gareth 'The composer seduced into programming' *Perspectives of New Music*, USA, vol. 19, no. 1, 1980–81

—'Musicians make a standard: the MIDI phenomenon' CMJ, vol. IX, no. 4, 1985

Lytel, Allan *ABC's of Boolean Algebra* Foulsham-Sams Technical Books, Slough, 1969

McNabb, Michael 'Dreamsong. The composition' CMJ, vol. V, no. 4, 1981

Manning, Peter *Electronic and Computer Music* Oxford University Press, 1985 (paperback 1987)

Mathews, Max V. *The Technology of Computer Music* MIT Press, Cambridge, Mass., 1969

—*et al. Music from Mathematics* Brunswick Records, London, STA 8523, 1962

—with Curtis Abbott 'The sequential drum' CMJ, vol. IV, no. 4, 1980

—and F. R. Moore *GROOVE – A Program to Compose, Store and Edit Functions of Time* Bell Telephone Laboratories, Murray Hill, NJ (duplicated typescript), 1968

Meyer, Chris and Evan Brooks *A MIDI Time Code System* addendum to the *MIDI 1.0 Detailed Specification* published by International MIDI Association, 5316 W. 57th St., Los Angeles, CA, 90056, USA

Moog, Robert 'Electronic music – its composition and performance' *Electronics World* (USA), 1967

—'Voltage-controlled electronic music modules' *Journal of the Audio Engineering Society*, USA, vol. 13, no. 3, 1965

Moore, F. Richard 'The dysfunctions of MIDI' CMJ, vol. XII, no. 1, 1988

—'The futures of music' *Perspectives of New Music*, USA, vol. 19, no. 1, 1980–81

—'An introduction to the mathematics of digital signal processing (part II)' CMJ, vol. II, no. 2, 1978

—'Table lookup noise for sinusoidal digital oscillators' CMJ, vol. I, no. 2, 1977

Moorer, James A. 'The Lucasfilm audio signal processor' CMJ, vol. VI, no. 3, 1982

—'Signal processing aspects of computer music – a survey' CMJ, vol. I, no. I, 1977

Moorer, J. A. and J. M. Grey 'Lexicon of analysed tones' parts I, II and III, CMJ, vol. I, nos. 2 and 3, 1977, vol. II, no. 2, 1978

Morrison, Philip and Emily *Charles Babbage and his Calculating Engines* Dover Publications, New York, 1961, pp. 248–9

Nisbett, Alec *The Technique of the Sound Studio* Focal Press, London, 1970

—*Use of Microphones* Focal Press, London, second edition 1983

Olson, Harry F. *Music, Physics and Engineering* Dover, New York, 1967

Oram, Daphne *An Individual Note* Galliard, London, 1972

Partch, Harry *Genesis of a Music* University of Wisconsin Press, 1949. Also expanded 2nd ed., Da Capo Press, New York, 1974

Pawera, Norbert *Microphones, Technique and Technology* ARSIS Baedeker and Lang Verlags, 1981

Pierce, J. R. 'The computer as a musical instrument' *Journal of the Audio Engineering Society*, vol. VIII, no. 2, April 1960

Pohlmann, Ken C. *Principles of Digital Audio* Howard W. Sams, Indianapolis, second edition 1989

Principles of Compact Disc Thorn EMI Home Electronics Ltd, Swindon, Ref: PT1165, 1986

Reynolds, Roger *Explorations in Sound/Space Manipulation* La Jolla (UCSD), Reports from the Center for Music Experiment and Related Research, vol. I, no. I, 1977

Rhea, Thomas L. Review (with photographs) of *The Telharmonium* by Reynold Weidenaar CMJ, vol. XII, no. 3, 1988

—Review (with photographs) of *The Art of the Theremin* CMJ, vol. XIII, no. I, 1989

Riddell, Alistair *Towards a Virtual Piano Action* NMA6 (1988), pp. 18–24. NMA Publications, PO Box 185, Brunswick, VIC 3056, Australia

Risset, Jean-Claude *Computer Study of Trumpet Tones* Bell Telephone Laboratories, Murray Hill, NJ, 1966

—*Mutations, Dialogues, Inharmonique, Moments Newtoniens* INA-GRM Records, Paris, AM 564.09, 1978

Roads, Curtis 'Automated granular synthesis of sound' CMJ, vol. II, no. 2, 1978

— (ed.) *Composers and the Computer* The Computer Music and Digital Audio Series, William Kaufman, California, 1985

—'Introduction to granular synthesis' CMJ, vol. XII, no. 2, 1988

— (ed.) 'Symposium on computer music composition' CMJ, vol. X, no. 1, 1986

—'A tutorial on non-linear or waveshaping synthesis' CMJ, vol. III, no. 2, 1979

Roads, Curtis *et al.* 'Artificial intelligence and music' parts 1 and 2 CMJ, vol. IV, nos. 2 and 3, 1980

Rodet, Xavier 'Time-domain formant-wave-function synthesis' CMJ, vol. VIII, no. 3, 1984

—*et al.* 'The CHANT project: from synthesis of the singing voice to synthesis in general' CMJ, vol. VIII, no. 3, 1984

Roederer, Juan G. *Introduction to the Physics and Psychophysics of Music* Springer Verlag, New York, second edition 1979

Rosenboom, David 'The performing brain' CMJ, vol. XIV, no. 1, 1990

Rowntree, John P. and J. F. Brennan *The Classical Organ in Britain* Positif Press, Oxford, 1975

Runstein, Robert E. and David Miles Huber *Modern Recording Techniques* Howard W. Sams, Indianapolis, third edition 1989

Russcol, Herbert *The Liberation of Sound* Prentice-Hall, Englewood Cliffs, NJ, 1972

Sadie, Stanley (ed.) *The New Grove Dictionary of Musical Instruments* (3 vols) Macmillan, London, 1984

Schaeffer, Pierre *A La Recherche d'une Musique Concrète* Editions du Seuil, Paris, 1952

—*Traité des Objets Musicaux* Editions du Seuil, Paris, 1966

Schafer, R. Murray *The Tuning of the World* Alfred A. Knopf, New York, 1977

Schottstaedt, Bill *On 'Leviathan'* Stanford University Department of Music Report no. STAN-M-44, 1988

—'Pla: a composer's idea of a programme' CMJ, vol. VII, no. 1, 1983

Shannon, C. E. and W. Weaver *The Mathematical Theory of Communication* University of Illinois Press, Urbana, 1949

Smith, Julius O. 'Fundamentals of digital filter theory' CMJ, vol. IX, no. 3, 1985

Smith, Leland *SCORE Manual* CCRMA internal document (duplicated typescript) Stanford University, Calif. (version of 1978)

Snell, John 'Design of a digital oscillator which will generate up to 256 low-distortion sine waves in real time' CMJ, vol. I, no. 2, 1977

—'The Lucasfilm real-time console for recording studios and performance of computer music' CMJ, vol. VI, no. 3, 1982

Stevens, S. S. 'The measurement of loudness' *Journal of the Acoustical Society of America* vol. 27, 1955, pp. 815–29

Strange, Allen *Electronic Music: Systems, Techniques and Controls* W. C. Brown, Dubuque, Iowa, second edition 1983

Stockhausen, Karlheinz 'Actualia' *Die Reihe* no. 1, pp. 45–51, Theodore Presser London [etc]:/Universal Edition, Bryn Mawr, PA, 1958 (orig. German ed. 1955)

Sumner, W. L. *The Organ* Macdonald, London, fourth edition 1973

Taylor, C. A. *The Physics of Musical Sounds* English Universities Press, London, 1965

Teitelbaum, Richard *The Digital Piano and The Patch Control Language System* Proceedings of the 1984 International Computer Music Conference (ed. William Buxton), Computer Music Association, San Francisco, 1985

Touretzky, David S. *LISP. A Gentle Introduction to Symbolic Computation* Harper and Row, New York, 1984

Truax, Barry 'Organizational techniques for C:M ratios in frequency modulation' CMJ, vol. I, no. 4, 1977

—'Real-time granular synthesis with a digital signal processing computer' CMJ, vol. XII, no. 2, 1988

Turetsky, Bertram *The Contemporary Contrabass* University of California Press, revised edition 1989

Vilardi, Frank and Steve Tarshis *Electronic Drums* Amsco Publications, New York, 1985

von Foerster, Heinz and James W. Beauchamp (eds.) *Music by Computers* John Wiley and Sons, New York, 1969

von Hornbostel, Erich M. and Curt Sachs 'Systematik der Musikinstrumente' *Zeitschrift für Ethnologie*, XLVI, 1914, English translation in the *Galpin Society Journal*, XIV, 1961

Watkinson, John *The Art of Digital Audio* Focal Press, London, 1988

Weidenaar Reynold (ed.) *Electronic Music Review No. 6* (symposium: tape recording) The Independent Electronic Music Center, Trumansburg, NY, 1968

— *The Telharmonium: A History of the First Music Synthesizer, 1893–1918* Ph.D dissertation, New York University, 1988 (Book publication in preparation)

Wells, Thomas H. *The Technique of Electronic Music* Schirmer, New York, 1981

Witten, Ian H. *Principles of Computer Speech* Academic Press, London, 1982

Wood, Alexander *The Physics of Music* Methuen, London, 1944, 6th ed. (revised by J. M. Bowsher), 1962

Xenakis, Iannis *Formalized Music* Indiana University Press, Bloomington, 1971

—'Musiques formelles' *La Revue Musicale*, editions Richard-Masse, Paris, 1963 (Original version of *Formalized Music*)

Young, E. C. *The New Penguin Dictionary of Electronics* Penguin Books, 1983